A Guide to the Major Trusts

1995/96 Edition

Volume 2
700 Further Trusts

Edited by
Paul Brown
David Casson

A Directory of Social Change publication

A GUIDE TO THE MAJOR TRUSTS
1995/96 Edition
Volume 2

Edited by Paul Brown and David Casson

Copyright © 1995 Directory of Social Change

No part of this book may be reproduced in any form whatsoever without prior permission in writing from the publisher. Permission will normally be given free of charge to non-profit making and charitable organisations.

The Directory of Social Change is a registered charity no. 800517

Published by the Directory of Social Change, 24 Stephenson Way, London NW1 2DP (0171-209 5151), from whom copies may be obtained.

British Library Cataloguing-in-Publication Data
　A catalogue record for this book is
　available from the British Library.

　ISBN 1 873860 64 1

Printed by Unwin Brothers Ltd, Woking

Contents

Introduction	1
How to use this Guide	4
Trusts ranked by grant total	6
Trusts descriptions in alphabetical sequence	27
Subject index	255
Geographical index	274
A list of the trusts in A Guide to the Major Trusts Volume 1	280
Sources of advice on applying to trusts	282
Applying to charitable trusts – how to be successful	289
Index	293

Introduction

Welcome to Volume 2 of *A Guide to the Major Trusts*. This is the second Edition of the second volume and again contains details of a further 700 trusts. Volume 1 (published in January 1995) contains details of the top 300 which collectively give £600 million in grants. This volume covers a total of about £95 million.

Criteria for inclusion

Almost all the trusts in this volume can give at least £45,000 a year from ordinary income; most can give substantially more. Indeed, there are about 55 which by size alone should be in Volume 1. Most of these are included in this volume as they are very restricted in what they can support, either by subject (eg. ITF Seafarers Fund for seafarers), or geographical area (eg. the Beit Trust for three countries in Africa). A few others have resulted from continuing research at the Charity Commission and will appear in Volume 1 next time (eg. the Jones 1986 Charitable Trust and the Methodist Relief & Development Fund).

Like Volume 1, Volume 2 is a national directory. It covers mainly those trusts which can give grants throughout Britain, or at least to a substantial part of it. If we had simply listed the 700 largest trusts outside Volume 1 the resulting Guide would have included many local trusts irrelevant to many fundraisers. We therefore deliberately omitted from this Guide nearly all local trusts giving less than £100,000. There are some notable exceptions such as the Millfield House Foundation and the Wiltshire Community Foundation, included as good examples of local trusts with well-developed policies and clear guidelines for applicants.

Those trusts that can only give – or have a policy of giving – in restricted areas are included in the geographical index. The trusts included which can only give very locally are generally large such as the Norwich Town Close Estate Charity (£281,000 in Norwich) and Sheffield Town Trust (£249,000 in Sheffield). The smaller local trusts included usually cover a larger area such as a county or region.

The layout of the book

The layout of the entries is similar to the established pattern in Volume 1, illustrated on page 5. The main difference is that the entries are generally much shorter, largely because the amounts are less and policies consequently less intricate and wide-ranging. Few have detailed policy statements so the entries tend to reflect our interpretation of a grant-making pattern rather than an illustration of published guidelines. Partly as a consequence of this the editorial comment within the entries is similarly reduced.

Indices

We have again produced a subject and geographical index to all of our top 1,000 trusts. Each is explained more fully in the relevant introduction (see pages 254 and 274). The aim is to reflect our interpretation of each trust's grant-making practice (rather than what each trust could do in principle).

Indices such as these, however, can only be of limited use. They may be a short-cut but you always run the risk either of being too narrow in your focus (and therefore missing out potentially useful trusts) or giving the index a weight and validity it does not possess and sending out too many applications which have little or no chance of success. We recommend that readers also consult at least the ranking table on pages 6 - 26 and, if possible, read all the entries at least once.

Availability of information

The 1992 Charities Act will make annual filing of accounts compulsory and should be in place by the end of 1995. It is interesting, when looking through the Charity Commission files, how many trusts have suddenly supplied copies of the last two years accounts when very few if any accounts had been filed previously. This has meant an increase in the information available on many of the trusts in this Guide.

Introduction

One correspondent stated when responding to correspondence for the previous Edition: "I cannot give any information about this trust, or confirm or amend your entry, until 1994 when the [accounts provisions of the] Charities Act become law". We are pleased to say that we were able to see full accounts to compile an entry for this Edition!

However, the issue of secrecy remains and our position with regard to the necessity of disclosing as an absolute minimum the names of institutions receiving grants and the amount they received is explained in the Introduction to Volume 1.

Unsolicited applications

Applications to grant-making trusts are clearly on the increase. It is not uncommon for trusts in this Guide to have seen a 25-50% increase in the number of applications in the last two years. The responses to this vary. One trust stated: "Since the Foundation has appeared in a number of Guides to Grant Giving Trusts, we have received an enormously increased number of requests. This has enabled us to focus our giving more directly on the principal aims of the Foundation", while another trust stated: "We will not respond to appeals that have been generated by our entry in this Guide".

Similarly: "The trustees have decided NOT to consider ANY further applications for grants unless the organisation is personally known to one of the trustees. This change in policy has been made because of an increase, over recent months, in the number of applications we have been receiving".

This raises the question of what to do when an entry says: "Trusts funds fully allocated; no applications will be considered", or "The trustees only give grants to projects known to them". We would never counsel an indiscriminate mailing of trusts, nor would we recommend that applicants ignore any part of an entry simply because it does not suit their situation. However, in the specific instance of trusts warding off applications with the above wording we accept there is a problem; in some cases it is probably not true that trusts never respond to an unsolicited application. How do you sort out the wheat from the chaff?

When we think it is clear one way or the other if a trust will or will not consider applications we say so. However, more often than not we have refrained from comment because we are not clear either. This leaves the reader none the wiser! If the situation is not clear our advice would be that if a trust **clearly could support your application** apart from the above health warning then send a **short** application with little or no supporting material. The application should recognise that the trust has said it will not respond and should state clearly that **if this is the case the trust should not respond to your application** either (not even with a stamped addressed envelope). Nor should you follow it up with a telephone call or further correspondence. Therefore if the trust's policy is simply to ignore applications you have placed no burden on them to reply to you; if they do sometimes consider applications you have given them enough information to decide whether you will be eligible or not.

We would naturally ask readers to exercise great care when making such applications. Nothing makes our task harder or a grant-making trust's life more frustrating than when our readers send a series of ill-conceived and irrelevant applications to any trust which happens to take their fancy. This kind of indiscriminate mailing leads some trusts to make the above statements when previously they had been willing to consider and reply to relevant applications from any registered charity.

The role of trusts

Much has already been and will continue to be written on the proper role of a grant-making trust, particularly with regard to not funding what should be a statutory responsibility. We will just draw out one interesting comment from a trust in this Guide: "We are appalled by the attitude of the Conservative Government who are expecting Charity to take the place of the taxpayer, and at the same time are preventing local government from raising enough money to do their job properly. Accordingly, we have set our faces against anything that might relieve the Government of its responsibilities, but we are prepared to give grants to organisations in areas which have been financially penalised by government, where they might have hoped for a grant from the rate-capped local authority".

Trust investments

In the light of the decline of certain well-known trusts, it was disturbing to note in the course of our research the large number of trusts with assets wholly in one company. For example, the Cleopatra and Epigoni Trusts, established in 1990 and 1991 respectively, both appear to have all their assets in Nurdin & Peacock plc. It may be that some of these are recently formed trusts and intend to diversify in the near future, but others seem to have made no effort to diversify since the trust was formed a number of years ago. We have warned of the real dangers of such activity; we will continue to do so!

It is also clear that trust income has gone down with lower interest rates and the economic slowdown.

Who's new?

Despite omitting a number of local trusts giving £50,000 to £100,000 from this Edition and the decrease in income of many trusts, nearly all the trusts included have the potential to give at least £45,000 in grants each year. This is up £5,000 from the last Edition. This is due to the appearance of new trusts: some newly founded (eg. the Fawcett Charitable Trust and Judge Charitable Foundation); some "discovered" as a result of the computerisation of the Charity Commission records (eg. the Jones 1986 Charitable Trust and the Leeds Hospital Fund Charitable Trust); at least one by accident (eg. Nesswall Ltd, discovered as the accounts were filed at the Charity Commission with those of another trust we were researching), and a few through provision of information by the trust itself (eg. the Football Association National Sports Centre Trust).

Over 170 trusts are new to these Guides, of which over 50 have never appeared in print before. This includes a wide variety of trusts, from those giving to specific causes (eg. the Irish Youth Foundation (UK) Ltd and the Ove Arup Foundation), to those with more general charitable objects (eg. Burdens Charitable Foundation and the Kobler Trust). There are also a number of

Introduction

trusts that originally had links with a company, but are now independent (eg. the Johnson Group Cleaners Charity and Forte Charitable Trust). Those trusts that maintain strong company links will be covered in *The Major Companies Guide*.

Acknowledgements

We are grateful to the many trust officers, trustees and others who have helped compile this Guide. To name them all would be impossible. We are also indebted once again to the staff of the Liverpool office of the Charity Commission for their diligence and cheerfulness in the face of our barrage of requests for information, particularly Tracey Smith, Bryan Gillings, Cathy Crombie and Lynn Williams.

Although drafts of all the entries were sent to the charities concerned, and any comments noted, the text and any mistakes in it remains ours rather than theirs.

Request for further information

The research for this book was done as fully and as carefully as we were able, but we are sure that there are relevant charities that we have missed and that some of the information is incomplete or will become out-of-date. We regret such imperfections. If any reader comes across omissions or mistakes in this Guide, please let us know so that they can be rectified in the thrice-yearly *Trust Monitor* and in future editions of this Guide. A telephone call to the Research Department of the Directory of Social Change Northern Office (0151-708 0136) is all that is needed.

Thank you and best wishes for your fundraising!

Paul Brown
David Casson

How to use this Guide

The contents

There are entries in alphabetical order describing the work of 700 trusts. Most give over £40,000 a year; almost all can give over £40,000 a year from ordinary income.

The entries are preceded by a listing of the trusts in order of size and are followed by a subject index and geographical index. There is also an alphabetical index at the back of the Guide.

Finding the trusts you need

There are three basic ways of using this Guide:

(a) You can simply read the entries through from A-Z (a rather time-consuming activity).

(b) You can look through the trust ranking table which starts on the opposite page and use the box provided to tick trusts which *might* be relevant to you (starting with the biggest).

(c) You can use the subject or geographical indices starting on pages 255 and 274 respectively. Each has an introduction explaining how to use them.

If you use approaches (b) or (c), once you have identified enough trusts to be going on with, read each entry very carefully before deciding whether to apply. Very often their interest in your field will be limited and specific, and may require an application specifically tailored to their needs - or, indeed, no application at all.

Sending off applications which show that the available information has not been read antagonises trusts and brings charities into disrepute within the trust world. Carefully targeted applications, on the other hand, are welcomed by most trusts and usually have a reasonably high rate of success.

How to use this Guide

A typical trust entry

The Fictitious Trust

£174,000 (1993/94)

Welfare

The Old Barn, Main Street,
New Town ZX48 2QQ
0151-100 0000

Correspondent: Ms A Grant, Appeals Secretary

Trustees: Lord Great; Lady Good; A T Home; T Rust; D Prest.

Beneficial area: UK, with preference for New Town.

Information available: Full accounts are on file at the Charity Commission.

General: The trust supports welfare charities in general with emphasis on disability, homelessness and ethnic minorities. The trustees will support both capital and revenue projects. "Specific projects are preferred to general running costs."

In 1993/94, the trust had assets of £2.1 million and an income of £187,000. Over 200 grants were given totalling £174,000. Grants ranged from £100 to £20,000, with over half given in New Town. The largest grants were to: New Town Disability Group (£20,000), Homelessness UK (£18,000) and Asian Family Support Agency (£15,000). There were 10 grants of £2,000 to £10,000 including those to the Charity Workers Benevolent Society, Children without Families, New Town CAB and Refugee Support Group.

Smaller grants were given to a variety of local charities, local branches of national charities, and a few UK welfare charities.

Exclusions: No support for bodies not having registered charitable status, individuals or religious organisations.

Applications: In writing to the correspondent. Trustees' meetings are held in March and September and applications should be received not later than the end of January and the end of July respectively.

Applications should include a brief description of the project and audited accounts. Unsuccessful applicants will not be informed unless an sae is provided.

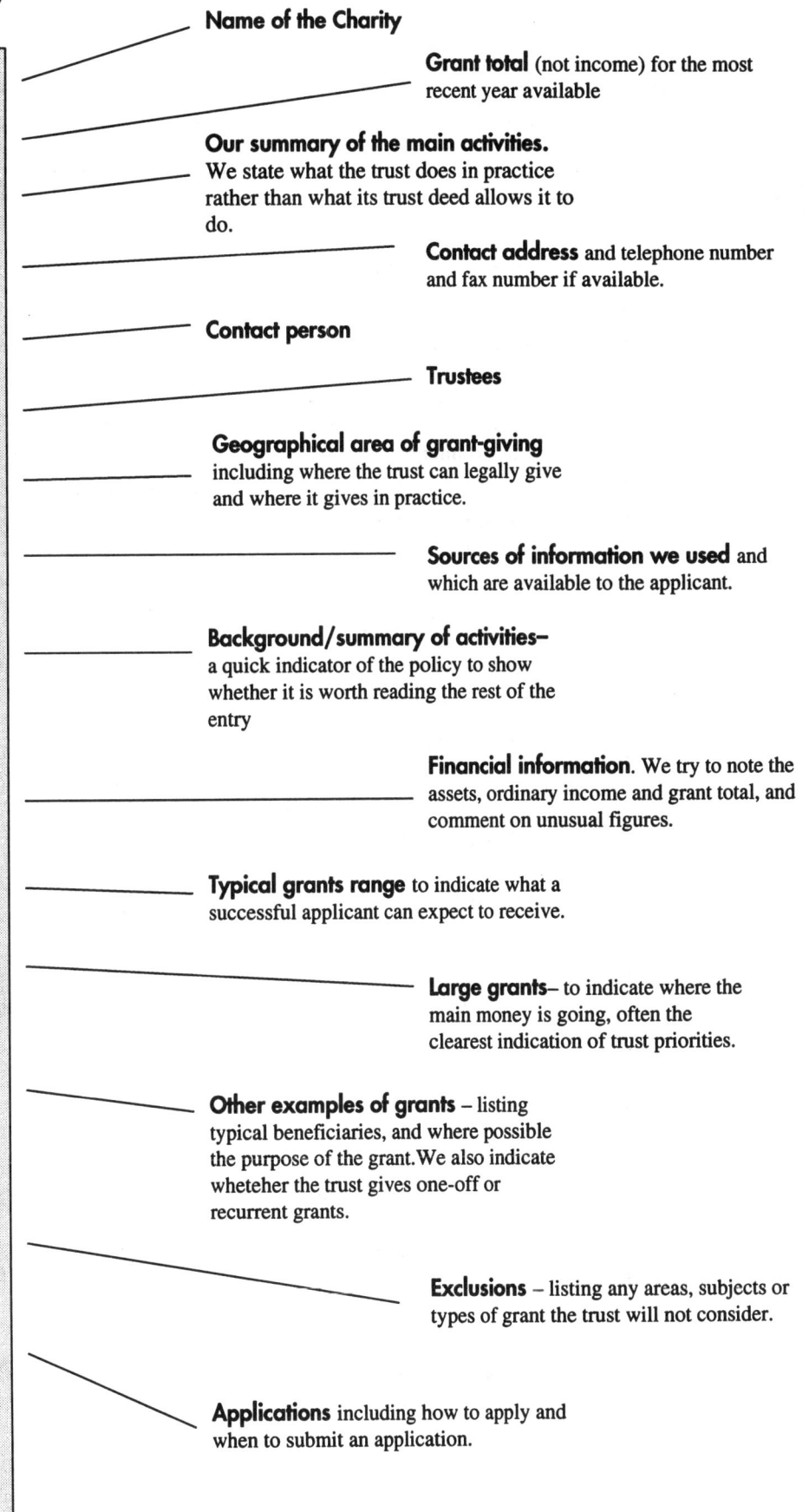

Name of the Charity

Grant total (not income) for the most recent year available

Our summary of the main activities. We state what the trust does in practice rather than what its trust deed allows it to do.

Contact address and telephone number and fax number if available.

Contact person

Trustees

Geographical area of grant-giving including where the trust can legally give and where it gives in practice.

Sources of information we used and which are available to the applicant.

Background/summary of activities – a quick indicator of the policy to show whether it is worth reading the rest of the entry

Financial information. We try to note the assets, ordinary income and grant total, and comment on unusual figures.

Typical grants range to indicate what a successful applicant can expect to receive.

Large grants – to indicate where the main money is going, often the clearest indication of trust priorities.

Other examples of grants – listing typical beneficiaries, and where possible the purpose of the grant. We also indicate wheteher the trust gives one-off or recurrent grants.

Exclusions – listing any areas, subjects or types of grant the trust will not consider.

Applications including how to apply and when to submit an application.

Trusts ranked by grant total

	Grants	Trust	Main grant areas	Page no.
☐	£3,400,000	The ITF Seafarers Trust	Seafarers	Page 138
☐	£1,824,000	The Beit Trust	Work in Zimbabwe, Malawi & Zambia; general	Page 39
☐	£1,300,000	The National Gardens Scheme Charitable Trust	Nursing, gardens, gardening	Page 161
☐	£1,166,000	The Rotary Foundation	Rotary scholarships and exchanges; third world development	Page 203
☐	£1,137,000	Concern Universal	Overseas development	Page 72
☐	£1,000,000	The Pilkington Charities Fund	General	Page 191
☐	£887,000	The Methodist Relief & Development Fund	Overseas aid/development	Page 168
☐	£865,000	The Foundation for Education	Jewish education	Page 99
☐	£788,000	The Leeds Hospital Fund Charitable Trust	Hospitals in Yorkshire, charities in Leeds	Page 154
☐	£775,000	The Ambika Paul Foundation	Children and young people under 25	Page 31
☐	£750,000	The Christmas Cracker Trust	Christian overseas aid and development	Page 64
☐	£700,000	The HSA Charitable Trust	Health care	Page 132
☐	£660,000	The Jones 1986 Charitable Trust	General, especially in Nottinghamshire	Page 142
☐	£660,000	The Welsh Church Funds	General in Wales	Page 242
☐	£562,000	CRUSAID	HIV/AIDS	Page 76
☐	£549,000	Jewish Continuity	Jewish education	Page 141
☐	£500,000	The Ulverscroft Foundation	Sick, especially visually impaired people, ophthalmic research	Page 233
☐	£461,000	The Raymond & Beverley Sackler Foundation	Art, science, medical research	Page 206
☐	£449,000	The Naggar Charitable Trust	Jewish, general	Page 176
☐	£441,000	The Rank Prize Funds	Nutrition, opto-electronics	Page 198
☐	£434,000	The Rudolph Palumbo Charitable Foundation	Education, relief of poverty, conservation, general	Page 186
☐	£411,000	The PPP Medical Trust Ltd	Medical research, care of the elderly and disabled people	Page 192
☐	£382,000	Jewish Child's Day	Jewish children in need or with special needs	Page 140
☐	£379,000	The Moss Charitable Trust	Christian	Page 174
☐	£368,000	Help the Hospices	Hospices	Page 126
☐	£366,000	The Hatter (IMO) Foundation	Jewish, general	Page 124
☐	£354,000	Feed the Minds	Christian literature overseas	Page 95
☐	£345,000	Alexandra Rose Day	Health and welfare	Page 30
☐	£343,000	The United Trusts	General	Page 234
☐	£335,000	The E & F Porjes Charitable Trust	Jewish, general	Page 192
☐	£334,000	The Underwood Trust	General	Page 234
☐	£331,000	The Martin Laing Foundation	General	Page 149

Trusts ranked by grant total

☐	£329,000	The Searle Charitable Trust	Medical, elderly	*Page 213*
☐	£310,000	The Mary Kinross Charitable Trust	Mental health	*Page 147*
☐	£302,000	The Raymond Montague Burton Charitable Trust	Jewish charities, social welfare, education, the arts, especially in Yorkshire	*Page 55*
☐	£286,000	Lewis Family Charitable Trust	Medical research, Jewish charities	*Page 154*
☐	£285,000	The Robert Gavron Charitable Trust	Arts, health and welfare	*Page 104*
☐	£283,000	The Jill Kreitman Foundation	Jewish, disability, children	*Page 148*
☐	£281,000	The Norwich Town Close Estate Charity	Welfare, education in Norwich	*Page 182*
☐	£277,000	Cash for Kids	Children and young people in the West Midlands	*Page 59*
☐	£276,000	The Lister Charitable Trust	Recreation	*Page 156*
☐	£273,000	The Gertner Charitable Trust	Jewish	*Page 105*
☐	£267,000	The Earley Charity	General in Earley and East Reading	*Page 86*
☐	£261,000	The Stanley Kalms Foundation	Jewish education and medical	*Page 144*
☐	£259,000	The Rosemary Bugden Charitable Trust	Arts in Avon	*Page 52*
☐	£254,000	The RVW Trust	Music, especially British, both contemporary and neglected music of the past	*Page 204*
☐	£253,000	The Colchester Catalyst Charity	Health in north east Essex	*Page 68*
☐	£252,000	Saddlers' Company Charitable Fund	General	*Page 206*
☐	£249,000	The Epigoni Trust	Medical, general	*Page 91*
☐	£249,000	The Sheffield Town Trust	General in Sheffield	*Page 214*
☐	£244,000	The Webber Trust	Evangelical Christian, welfare	*Page 241*
☐	£240,000	The Bedford Charity	Education, relief in need and recreation in Bedford and its neighbourhood	*Page 39*
☐	£239,000	Burdens Charitable Foundation	Christian, welfare, general	*Page 53*
☐	£238,000	The Sir Samuel Scott of Yews Trust	Medical research	*Page 211*
☐	£235,000	The National AIDS Trust	HIV/AIDS	*Page 176*
☐	£234,000	The Kobler Trust	Jewish, general	*Page 147*
☐	£231,000	The Laura Ashley Foundation	Education, general	*Page 33*
☐	£223,000	The Alan Sugar Foundation	Jewish, general	*Page 225*
☐	£223,000	The Geoffrey Woods Charitable Foundation	Education, medical and welfare	*Page 250*
☐	£220,000	The Equity Trust Fund	Arts, education and welfare of professional performers	*Page 92*
☐	£218,000	The Iliffe Family Charitable Trust	General	*Page 135*
☐	£216,000	The Thomas Farr Charitable Trust	General, especially in Nottinghamshire	*Page 94*
☐	£214,000	Dr Mortimer and Theresa Sackler Foundation	Arts, hospitals	*Page 205*
☐	£209,000	Spitalfields Market Training Initiative	Education, training in Bethnal Green	*Page 222*
☐	£208,000	The John Porter Charitable Trust	Jewish, education	*Page 192*
☐	£208,000	The Privy Purse Charitable Trust	General	*Page 195*
☐	£203,000	The Puebla Charitable Trust	Education, religion, relief of poverty, general	*Page 195*

Trusts ranked by grant total

☐	£202,000	The W G Edwards Charitable Foundation	Care of elderly	*Page 88*
☐	£201,000	The Children's Research Fund	Child health research	*Page 63*
☐	£200,000	The Divert Trust	Juvenile delinquency and crime prevention	*Page 83*
☐	£200,000	The Football Association Youth Trust	Sports	*Page 98*
☐	£200,000	The Greggs Charitable Trust	General	*Page 115*
☐	£198,000	The Inman Charity	Social welfare, disability, the elderly, hospices	*Page 135*
☐	£197,000	The Miriam K Dean Refugee Trust	Third World development	*Page 81*
☐	£197,000	The Peter Kershaw Trust	Medical research, school fees, general	*Page 146*
☐	£195,000	The Bulldog Trust	Education, Christian	*Page 52*
☐	£195,000	Mrs Waterhouse's Charitable Trust	Health and social welfare	*Page 239*
☐	£195,000	The Harold Hyam Wingate Foundation	Medical aid & disability, medical research, the arts, general	*Page 248*
☐	£194,000	The Radcliffe Trust	Music, crafts, conservation, academic fellowships	*Page 197*
☐	£194,000	The Albert and Florence Smith Memorial Trust	Social welfare	*Page 218*
☐	£193,000	The Sir John Priestman Charity Trust	Social welfare, churches in County Durham	*Page 193*
☐	£191,000	The Homelands Charitable Trust	The New Church, health, social welfare	*Page 129*
☐	£191,000	St James' Trust Settlement	General	*Page 207*
☐	£190,000	The National Catholic Fund	Catholic welfare	*Page 177*
☐	£189,000	The Bernerd Foundation	Arts, Jewish charities, general	*Page 41*
☐	£188,000	The Burden Trust	General	*Page 53*
☐	£188,000	The Hugh & Ruby Sykes Charitable Trust	General, medical, local	*Page 226*
☐	£187,000	The Archbishop of Canterbury's Charitable Trust	Christianity, welfare	*Page 32*
☐	£186,000	Brushmill Ltd	Jewish	*Page 52*
☐	£186,000	The Comino Foundation	Education	*Page 71*
☐	£185,000	Cliff Richard Charitable Trust	Spiritual and social welfare	*Page 201*
☐	£184,000	Entindale Ltd	Jewish, general	*Page 91*
☐	£184,000	The Jean Sainsbury Animal Welfare Trust	Animal welfare	*Page 206*
☐	£183,000	The Emmandjay Charitable Trust	Social welfare, medicine	*Page 90*
☐	£182,000	The Cleopatra Trust	Medical, general	*Page 66*
☐	£181,000	The Frieda Scott Charitable Trust	Lakeland charities	*Page 210*
☐	£180,000	Sir Harold Hood's Charitable Trust	Roman Catholic	*Page 130*
☐	£179,000	The Rose Flatau Charitable Trust	Jewish, social welfare	*Page 97*
☐	£179,000	The Janet Nash Charitable Trust	Medical, general	*Page 176*
☐	£177,000	The Van Neste Foundation	Social welfare, third world	*Page 235*
☐	£176,000	The Christopher Laing Foundation	General	*Page 149*

Trusts ranked by grant total

☐	£175,000	The Platinum Trust	Disability	Page 191
☐	£175,000	The Sarum St Michael Educational Charity	Christian education in Salisbury diocese	Page 209
☐	£175,000	The M J C Stone Charitable Trust	Medicine, education, animals and children	Page 224
☐	£173,000	The Britten-Pears Foundation	Work of Benjamin Britten and Peter Pears, the arts	Page 49
☐	£173,000	The Cecil Rosen Foundation	Not known	Page 203
☐	£173,000	The Tikva Trust	Christian	Page 230
☐	£172,000	The Roald Dahl Foundation	Haematology, neurology (specifically head injury & epilepsy) and literacy	Page 78
☐	£172,000	The Eleanor Rathbone Charitable Trust	General, especially Merseyside	Page 199
☐	£171,000	The Hilda & Samuel Marks Foundation	Jewish	Page 162
☐	£170,000	The W F Southall Trust	Quaker, general	Page 221
☐	£169,000	The Fred & Della Worms Charitable Trust	Jewish, education, arts	Page 251
☐	£168,000	The Charity of Thomas Wade & Others	General in Leeds	Page 237
☐	£167,000	The British Council for Prevention of Blindness	Prevention of blindness	Page 49
☐	£167,000	The Nancie Massey Charitable Trust	Education, medicine, the arts, children and elderly people in Scotland	Page 164
☐	£166,000	The Englefield Charitable Trust	Churches, general	Page 90
☐	£166,000	The A S Hornby Educational Trust	English as a foreign language	Page 130
☐	£165,000	Keswick Foundation Ltd	Social welfare in Hong Kong, China	Page 146
☐	£165,000	The Rayne Trust	Jewish, general	Page 200
☐	£165,000	The Sylvanus Charitable Trust	Animal welfare	Page 226
☐	£164,000	The Ove Arup Foundation	Building education and research	Page 32
☐	£164,000	Melodor Ltd	Jewish, general	Page 168
☐	£163,000	The Lord Austin Trust	Social welfare	Page 36
☐	£163,000	The Chapman Charitable Trust	General	Page 62
☐	£163,000	The Yapp Welfare Trust	Social welfare	Page 253
☐	£162,000	The Finnart House School Trust	Jewish children in need of care	Page 96
☐	£162,000	The Skinners' Company Lady Neville Charity	General	Page 217
☐	£161,000	The P G & N J Boulton Trust	Christian	Page 47
☐	£160,000	The Blair Foundation	Jewish, general	Page 44
☐	£160,000	The Football Association National Sports Centre Trust	Football facilities	Page 98
☐	£160,000	The Wilkinson Charitable Foundation	Scientific research	Page 246
☐	£160,000	Woodlands Green Ltd	Jewish	Page 249
☐	£159,000	The E Alec Colman Charitable Fund	Jewish	Page 70
☐	£159,000	The Charles S French Charitable Trust	Community projects, disability, children and youth	Page 102
☐	£159,000	R W Mann Trustees Limited	Social welfare in the North East	Page 161

● **Trusts ranked by grant total**

❑	£159,000	The Late Barbara May Paul Charitable Trust	Elderly, young people, medical care and research, preservation of buildings	*Page 188*
❑	£159,000	The Ward Blenkinsop Trust	Medicine, social welfare, general	*Page 239*
❑	£158,000	The St Katharine and Shadwell Trust	Education, training, general, in and around Wapping	*Page 207*
❑	£156,000	The Ellinson Foundation	Jewish	*Page 89*
❑	£156,000	The Forte Charitable Trust	Education, disability, Roman Catholic, general	*Page 99*
❑	£156,000	The Hadrian Trust	Social welfare in the North East	*Page 117*
❑	£156,000	The David Shepherd Conservation Foundation	Conservation of endangered mammals	*Page 215*
❑	£155,000	The Francis Coales Charitable Foundation	Historical in Bucks, Beds, Herts and Northants	*Page 67*
❑	£155,000	The Lennox Hannay Charitable Trust	Health, welfare	*Page 120*
❑	£154,000	The Boltons Trust	Social welfare, medicine, education	*Page 46*
❑	£154,000	The C A Redfern Charitable Foundation	General	*Page 200*
❑	£153,000	The A Hubert 1971 Charitable Trust	Jewish	*Page 133*
❑	£153,000	The John Jarrold Trust	Arts, Third World, social welfare, medical research	*Page 139*
❑	£153,000	The Millichope Foundation	General	*Page 170*
❑	£153,000	The Austin & Hope Pilkington Trust	General	*Page 190*
❑	£153,000	The James Weir Foundation	Health, social welfare, heritage, research	*Page 242*
❑	£152,000	The Duke of Cornwall's Benevolent Fund	General in Cornwall	*Page 74*
❑	£152,000	The Roy Fletcher Charitable Trust	General in Shropshire	*Page 98*
❑	£152,000	The Alfred Haines Charitable Trust	Christian, health, welfare	*Page 118*
❑	£152,000	The Locker Foundation	Jewish	*Page 157*
❑	£152,000	The Sir Jack Lyons Charitable Trust	Jewish, arts, education	*Page 160*
❑	£152,000	The Norman Family Charitable Trust	Animal welfare, social welfare and youth in the South West	*Page 181*
❑	£150,000	The Clarkson Jersey Charitable Trust	General	*Page 66*
❑	£150,000	The Man of the People Fund	General	*Page 160*
❑	£150,000	The Scouloudi Foundation	Historical awards, social welfare, environment	*Page 212*
❑	£149,000	The Bornstein Charitable Settlements	Jewish	*Page 47*
❑	£149,000	The Arnold Lee Charitable Trust	Jewish, general	*Page 153*
❑	£149,000	The Catherine Lewis Foundation	Jewish, relief of poverty and sickness, education	*Page 155*
❑	£148,000	The Childs Charitable Trust	Christian missions	*Page 63*
❑	£148,000	The Delves Charitable Trust	Environment, conservation, medical, general	*Page 81*
❑	£147,000	The Bryant Trust	General	*Page 52*
❑	£147,000	The Manny Cussins Foundation	General, with some emphasis on Yorkshire and Jewish projects	*Page 77*
❑	£147,000	The Margaret Davies Charity	Education, health, arts	*Page 80*
❑	£147,000	The Princess of Wales' Charities Trust	Areas in which the Princess of Wales has a particular interest	*Page 194*

Trusts ranked by grant total

☐	£147,000	The South Square Trust	Social welfare, medical, disability, education	Page 221
☐	£146,000	The Acacia Charitable Trust	Jewish, education, medical	Page 28
☐	£146,000	Sue Hammerson's Charitable Trust	Arts, medicine, welfare, Jewish charities	Page 119
☐	£146,000	The Westminster Amalgamated Charity	Welfare in Westminster	Page 244
☐	£145,000	The Cooper Charitable Trust	Medical, disability, Jewish	Page 73
☐	£145,000	The Dorus Trust	General	Page 84
☐	£145,000	The Michael & Ilse Katz Foundation	Jewish, general	Page 144
☐	£145,000	The Ogle Trust	Evangelical Christianity	Page 184
☐	£144,000	British Schools and Universities Foundation (Inc.)	Education	Page 49
☐	£144,000	The Arnold James Burton Charitable Trust	General	Page 54
☐	£144,000	The 10th Duke of Devonshire's Trust	General, especially in Derbyshire	Page 82
☐	£144,000	The Godinton Charitable Trust	General	Page 107
☐	£143,000	The Heritage of London Trust Ltd	Restoration in Greater London	Page 126
☐	£143,000	Hobson Charity Ltd	Social welfare, education	Page 129
☐	£143,000	The Reginald M Phillips Charitable Foundation	General	Page 189
☐	£143,000	The Ruth & Michael Phillips Charitable Trust	General, Jewish	Page 190
☐	£143,000	The Thornton Foundation	General	Page 229
☐	£141,000	The Golden Bottle Trust	General	Page 108
☐	£141,000	The Peter Samuel Charitable Trust	Health and welfare, conservation, Jewish care	Page 209
☐	£140,000	Carlee Ltd	Jewish	Page 58
☐	£140,000	The R J Harris Charitable Settlement	General	Page 122
☐	£140,000	The Lawlor Foundation	Social welfare, education, general, especially in Ireland	Page 151
☐	£140,000	The Lyndhurst Settlement	Social problems, civil liberties, environment, conservation	Page 159
☐	£140,000	The Joseph & Lena Randall Charitable Trust	Jewish, general	Page 198
☐	£140,000	The Vardy Foundation	Education in the North East	Page 236
☐	£140,000	John Watson's Trust	Educational needs of children and young people	Page 240
☐	£139,000	The Lillie Johnson Charitable Trust	General	Page 141
☐	£139,000	The Northmoor Trust	General	Page 181
☐	£138,000	The Robert McAlpine Foundation	General	Page 166
☐	£137,000	Beauland Ltd	Jewish	Page 38
☐	£137,000	The Kathleen Laurence Trust	General	Page 151
☐	£136,000	The Ajahma Charitable Trust	Welfare and, increasingly overseas development	Page 30
☐	£136,000	The George W Cadbury Charitable Trust	Population control, conservation, general	Page 56

Trusts ranked by grant total

☐	£136,000	The D'Oyly Carte Charitable Trust	Arts, environment, medical	Page 77
☐	£136,000	The Rothermere Foundation	Education, general	Page 203
☐	£135,000	The Black Charitable Trusts	Evangelical Christianity, social welfare, young people	Page 43
☐	£135,000	The Cross Trust	Christian work overseas	Page 75
☐	£134,000	The Granada Foundation	Arts and sciences in the North West	Page 111
☐	£134,000	The Joicey Trust	General in Northumberland and Tyne & Wear	Page 142
☐	£133,000	Alglen Ltd	Jewish	Page 30
☐	£133,000	The Church Burgesses Educational Foundation	Religion, education and youth in Sheffield	Page 65
☐	£133,000	The Pyke Charity Trust	Social welfare	Page 195
☐	£133,000	The Walker Trust	Health, education in Shropshire only	Page 238
☐	£132,000	The Batchworth Trust	Medical, social welfare, general	Page 38
☐	£132,000	The Audrey & Stanley Howard Burton 1960 Charitable Trust	Jewish, general in Harrogate	Page 54
☐	£132,000	The Leche Trust	Georgian art, music and architecture	Page 153
☐	£131,000	The Hoover Foundation	Education, health, welfare	Page 130
☐	£131,000	The Idlewild Trust	Preservation, conservation, performing arts	Page 134
☐	£131,000	The Irish Youth Foundation (UK) Ltd	Irish youth	Page 137
☐	£131,000	The Vincent Wildlife Trust	Wildlife, environmental conservation	Page 236
☐	£130,000	The W E Dunn Trust	Medical and social welfare in the Midlands	Page 86
☐	£130,000	The N R Charitable Trust	Christian, general	Page 175
☐	£130,000	The Whitley Animal Protection Trust	Animal care and protection, conservation	Page 246
☐	£129,000	Lord Barnby's Foundation	General	Page 37
☐	£129,000	The Castle Educational Trust	Deprived and disabled children	Page 60
☐	£129,000	May Hearnshaw's Charity	General	Page 125
☐	£129,000	The William Allen Young Charitable Trust	General	Page 254
☐	£128,000	The Dent Charitable Trust	Jewish, general	Page 81
☐	£128,000	The Lord Faringdon First & Second Charitable Trusts	Medical, general	Page 94
☐	£128,000	The Weavers' Company Benevolent Fund	Young people at risk from criminal involvement, young offenders and prisoners' organisations	Page 240
☐	£127,000	The Astor Foundation	Medicine, social welfare	Page 34
☐	£127,000	The Benham Charitable Settlement	Youth, general, especially in Northants	Page 40
☐	£126,000	The Bridge Trust	General in Barnstaple	Page 48
☐	£126,000	Hereward FM CNFM & KLFM Appeal	Disability	Page 126
☐	£126,000	The Albert Hunt Trust	Health, welfare	Page 133
☐	£126,000	The Johnson Group Cleaners Charity	General in Merseyside	Page 141
☐	£125,000	Achiezer Association Ltd	Jewish	Page 29
☐	£125,000	The Chiron Trust	General	Page 63

Trusts ranked by grant total

☐	£125,000	The City Educational Trust Fund	Education	Page 65
☐	£125,000	The Edward Cecil Jones Settlement	General	Page 142
☐	£125,000	The Marsh Christian Trust	General	Page 163
☐	£124,000	The George & Esme Pollitzer Charitable Settlement	Health, social welfare, Jewish welfare	Page 192
☐	£124,000	The Clive Richards Charity Ltd	General	Page 201
☐	£124,000	The Michael Sacher Charitable Trust	Jewish, general	Page 205
☐	£123,000	The Mansfield Cooke Trust	Evangelical Christian missions	Page 72
☐	£123,000	The Enkalon Foundation	Welfare in Northern Ireland	Page 91
☐	£123,000	Entwood Charities Ltd	Jewish	Page 91
☐	£123,000	The Thomas Freke & Lady Norton Charity	Churches, schools, youth and welfare in the beneficial area	Page 102
☐	£123,000	The R T Trust	Health and welfare in Shropshire	Page 196
☐	£122,000	The Barbour Trust	Health and welfare	Page 37
☐	£122,000	The William & Katherine Longman Trust	General	Page 158
☐	£121,000	The Craps Charitable Trust	Jewish, general	Page 75
☐	£121,000	The Harebell Centenary Fund	General, education, medical research, animal welfare	Page 121
☐	£121,000	The E H Smith Charitable Trust	General	Page 218
☐	£120,000	The Greatham Hospital of God	General in the North East	Page 114
☐	£120,000	The Jephcott Charitable Trust	Alleviation of poverty in developing countries, general	Page 140
☐	£120,000	The David Laing Foundation	Not known	Page 149
☐	£119,000	Access 4 Trust	Children, welfare	Page 29
☐	£119,000	The Joseph & Annie Cattle Trust	General in north Humberside	Page 60
☐	£119,000	The Charities Fund	Sick, needy, elderly people	Page 62
☐	£119,000	The Peter Minet Trust	General	Page 171
☐	£119,000	The Victor Mishcon Charitable Trust	Jewish, social welfare	Page 172
☐	£119,000	The Archie Sherman Cardiff Charitable Foundation	Jewish	Page 215
☐	£118,000	Marjorie Coote Animal Charity Fund	Wildlife and animal welfare	Page 73
☐	£118,000	The Lady Eileen Joseph Foundation	General	Page 143
☐	£118,000	Sueberry Ltd	Jewish	Page 225
☐	£117,000	The Bill Butlin Charity Trust	General	Page 55
☐	£117,000	The Charles Littlewood Hill Trust	Health, disability, service, children (including schools)	Page 128
☐	£116,000	The B & P Glasser Charitable Trust	Jewish, social and medical welfare	Page 107
☐	£116,000	The Salamander Charitable Trust	Christian, general	Page 208
☐	£116,000	The Westward Trust	Quaker, general	Page 245
☐	£115,000	The Atlantic Foundation	Education, medical, general	Page 35
☐	£115,000	The Ouseley Trust	Choral services of the Church of England, Church in Wales and Church of Ireland	Page 185

Trusts ranked by grant total

☐	£115,000	The Florence Turner Trust	General	Page 232
☐	£114,000	The Peter Birse Charitable Trust	Health and welfare	Page 42
☐	£114,000	Caritas	Medical, Jewish, general	Page 57
☐	£114,000	The Greater Bristol Foundation	Community projects within about 10 miles of Bristol city centre	Page 112
☐	£114,000	The River Trust	Christian	Page 202
☐	£114,000	The Annie Schiff Charitable Trust	Orthodox Jewish	Page 210
☐	£114,000	The Maurice Wohl Charitable Trust	Jewish	Page 248
☐	£113,000	The Henry & Grete Abrahams Charitable Foundation	Jewish	Page 28
☐	£113,000	The Earl Cadogan's Charity Trust	General	Page 57
☐	£113,000	Macdonald-Buchanan Charitable Trust	General	Page 160
☐	£113,000	The Noel Buxton Trust	Child and family welfare, penal matters, Africa, reconciliation and human rights	Page 180
☐	£112,000	The A H & M A Boulton Trust	Christian	Page 47
☐	£112,000	The Everard & Mina Goodman Charitable Foundation	Jewish, medical/health, general	Page 109
☐	£112,000	The Erich Markus Charitable Foundation	Medical, welfare, general	Page 163
☐	£112,000	The Thornton Trust	Evangelical Christian, education, relief of sickness and poverty	Page 229
☐	£111,000	Michael Bishop Foundation	General	Page 43
☐	£111,000	The J N Derbyshire Trust	Health, social welfare in Nottinghamshire	Page 81
☐	£111,000	The Women Caring Trust	Children and families in Northern Ireland	Page 249
☐	£110,000	The Dinam Charity	International understanding, general	Page 83
☐	£110,000	The Leach Fourteenth Trust	Conservation and disability	Page 153
☐	£110,000	The Milton Keynes Community Trust	General welfare and arts in Milton Keynes	Page 170
☐	£110,000	The Ulting Overseas Trust	Christian	Page 233
☐	£109,000	The Morris Leigh Foundation	Jewish, general	Page 154
☐	£109,000	The I A Ziff Charitable Foundation	Education, Yorkshire, arts, youth, medicine	Page 254
☐	£108,000	The Booth Charities	Elderly people in Salford	Page 46
☐	£108,000	Chownes Foundation	General	Page 64
☐	£107,000	The Alan Evans Memorial Trust	Preservation, conservation	Page 92
☐	£107,000	The Julian Melchett Trust	Social welfare in steel-making areas	Page 167
q	£107,000	The Roughley Charitable Trust	General, with a preference for the West Midlands	Page 204
☐	£107,000	The Jessie Spencer Trust	General	Page 221
☐	£106,000	The Christopher Cadbury Charitable Trust	Nature conservation, general	Page 55
☐	£106,000	The GWR Community Trust	Education, welfare, general	Page 116
☐	£106,000	The Solomon Family Charitable Trust	Education, religion and welfare	Page 220
☐	£106,000	The World in Need	Charities compatible with Christian objects	Page 251

Trusts ranked by grant total

❑	£87,000	The London Law Trust	Children and young people	Page 157
❑	£87,000	The Saints & Sinners Trust	General	Page 208
❑	£87,000	The Williams Family Charitable Trust	Jewish	Page 246
❑	£87,000	The Dame Violet Wills Charitable Trust	Evangelical Christianity	Page 247
❑	£86,000	The Bromley Trust	Human rights, conservation	Page 50
❑	£86,000	The CLA Charitable Trust	Country recreation/education for disabled people	Page 65
❑	£86,000	The Doris Field Charitable Trust	General	Page 96
❑	£86,000	The Edgar E Lawley Foundation	General, medical research, education, elderly people	Page 151
❑	£86,000	The Sandra Charitable Trust	Not known	Page 209
❑	£85,000	Mr Thomas Betton's Charity (Educational)	Church of England or Church in Wales schools	Page 41
❑	£85,000	Lasletts (Hinton) Charity	Church repairs, general in Worcestershire	Page 150
❑	£84,000	Gableholt Limited	Jewish	Page 104
❑	£84,000	The Michael Peacock Charitable Foundation	Elderly, addiction, education	Page 188
❑	£82,000	The A B Charitable Trust	Human dignity	Page 27
❑	£82,000	The Dumbreck Charity	General	Page 85
❑	£82,000	The Grand Order of Water Rats Charities Fund	Arts, medical equipment	Page 111
❑	£82,000	The Mrs C S Heber Percy Charitable Trust	Health, general	Page 125
❑	£82,000	The Willie & Mabel Morris Charitable Trust	Medical, general	Page 173
❑	£82,000	The N Smith Charitable Trust	General	Page 219
❑	£81,000	The Edward & Dorothy Cadbury Charitable Trust	Health, education, arts	Page 56
❑	£81,000	The Vivienne & Samuel Cohen Charitable Trust	Jewish, education, health and welfare	Page 68
❑	£81,000	The Eleanor Hamilton Educational Trust	Education, general	Page 119
❑	£81,000	Localtrent Ltd	Jewish	Page 157
❑	£81,000	The C L Loyd Charitable Trust	General	Page 158
❑	£81,000	The National Hospital Trust	Hospitals	Page 178
❑	£81,000	The Albert Reckitt Charitable Trust	General	Page 200
❑	£81,000	The Stoll Moss Theatres Foundation	Theatre, general	Page 223
❑	£81,000	The John Swire (1989) Charitable Trust	General	Page 226
❑	£80,000	The Bertie Black Foundation	Jewish	Page 43
❑	£80,000	The Dennis Curry Charitable Trust	General	Page 77
❑	£80,000	The Wilfrid Bruce Davis Charitable Trust	Health, especially in Cornwall	Page 80
❑	£80,000	The A M Fenton Trust	General in North and West Yorkshire	Page 95
❑	£80,000	The Frognal Trust	Elderly, children, blind, disabled, medical research, environmental heritage	Page 103

Trusts ranked by grant total

☐	£80,000	The Ireland Fund of Great Britain	Irish organisations	Page 136
☐	£80,000	The Schreib Trust	General	Page 210
☐	£79,000	The Thomas Peter Dibdin Foundation	Christian	Page 82
☐	£79,000	The Elm Trust II	Arts	Page 89
☐	£79,000	Ferguson Benevolent Fund Ltd	Christian, especially Methodist	Page 96
☐	£79,000	The Lawson-Beckman Charitable Trust	Jewish, general	Page 153
☐	£79,000	The Scottish Churches Architectural Heritage Trust	Scottish church buildings	Page 211
☐	£78,000	The Fairway Trust	Education, religion, children's recreation	Page 93
☐	£78,000	The Teresa Rosenbaum Golden Charitable Trust	Jewish, general	Page 203
☐	£78,000	The Swire Charitable Trust	General	Page 226
☐	£78,000	The Vestey Foundation	General	Page 236
☐	£78,000	The Wakefield Trust	General	Page 238
☐	£77,000	The Edwina Mountbatten Trust	Medical	Page 174
☐	£76,000	The Isabel Blackman Foundation	General, especially in the Hastings area	Page 44
☐	£76,000	The Bluston Charitable Settlement	Jewish, general	Page 45
☐	£76,000	Exilarch's Foundation	Jewish	Page 93
☐	£76,000	The Fitton Trust	Social welfare, medical	Page 97
☐	£76,000	The Loftus Charitable Trust	Jewish	Page 157
☐	£76,000	The G M Morrison Charitable Trust	General	Page 174
☐	£75,000	The Armourers & Brasiers Gauntlet Trust	Education in materials science, general	Page 32
☐	£75,000	The Baltic Charitable Fund	General	Page 37
☐	£75,000	The Charles Brotherton Trust	Education & training of young people, medical research, general	Page 51
☐	£75,000	The B G S Cayzer Charitable Trust	General	Page 61
☐	£75,000	The Augustine Courtauld Trust	General	Page 75
☐	£75,000	The J G Graves Charitable Trust	General in the Sheffield area	Page 112
☐	£75,000	The Hospital Saturday Fund Charitable Trust	Medical	Page 131
☐	£75,000	The Patrick Joseph Kennedy Charitable Trust	General	Page 145
☐	£75,000	Watside Charities	Not known	Page 239
☐	£74,000	The Arnopa Trust	Children in need	Page 32
☐	£74,000	The Harry Bottom Charitable Trust	Religion, education, medical, elderly	Page 47
☐	£74,000	The Wilfred & Elsie Elkes Charity Fund	General	Page 88
☐	£74,000	Menuchar Ltd	Jewish	Page 168
☐	£73,000	The Alliance Family Foundation	Jewish, general	Page 31
☐	£73,000	The Billmeir Charitable Trust	Relief of pain or sickness, general in Surrey	Page 42

Trusts ranked by grant total

❏	£73,000	The De Haan Charitable Trust	General	*Page 80*
❏	£73,000	The Hamamelis Trust	Ecological conservation, medical research	*Page 118*
❏	£73,000	The J E Joseph Charitable Fund	Jewish	*Page 143*
❏	£73,000	The Stanley Foundation Ltd	Elderly, medical, education, social welfare	*Page 222*
❏	£73,000	The Peter Stebbings Memorial Trust	Welfare, general	*Page 223*
❏	£72,000	The Ashden Charitable Trust	Green issues, homelessness, third world, community arts, general	*Page 33*
❏	£72,000	The Gibbs Charitable Trusts	Methodist	*Page 106*
❏	£72,000	The Nimrod & Glaven Charitable Settlement	General	*Page 180*
❏	£72,000	Northumberland Village Homes Trust	Children and young people	*Page 182*
❏	£71,000	The Aurelius Charitable Trust	Archaeology, history	*Page 35*
❏	£71,000	The Joels Charitable Trust	Jewish, general	*Page 141*
❏	£71,000	The Orpheus Trust	Music, especially for people with disabilities	*Page 185*
❏	£71,000	The Violet M Richards Charity	Medical research, health and social welfare for the elderly	*Page 201*
❏	£71,000	The Leonard Sainer Charitable Trust	Jewish, arts, welfare	*Page 206*
❏	£70,000	The Norman Collinson Charitable Trust	Social welfare, general, in North Yorkshire	*Page 70*
❏	£70,000	The Holst Foundation	Arts	*Page 129*
❏	£70,000	The Charlotte Marshall Charitable Trust	Roman Catholic, general	*Page 164*
❏	£70,000	The Mount 'A' & Mount 'B' Charitable Trusts	Mainly local projects in Bristol, Jersey and Italy	*Page 174*
❏	£70,000	The Old Possums Practical Trust	Medical, literary history	*Page 185*
❏	£69,000	The Green Foundation	General, social welfare	*Page 114*
❏	£69,000	The Audrey Sacher Charitable Trust	Arts, medical, care	*Page 205*
❏	£69,000	The Leslie Smith Foundation	General	*Page 219*
❏	£68,000	The Beaufort House Trust	Christian, education	*Page 38*
❏	£68,000	The Belvedere Trust	Housing and related community initiatives in south London	*Page 39*
❏	£68,000	The Dr & Mrs A Darlington Charitable Trust	Medical, nature conservation, preservation, elderly people, disability	*Page 79*
❏	£68,000	The Friarsgate Trust	Mainly health and welfare of young and elderly people	*Page 103*
❏	£68,000	The Elizabeth Rathbone Charity	Social welfare, general in Merseyside	*Page 199*
❏	£68,000	Salters' Charities	General	*Page 209*
❏	£67,000	The Jack Goldhill Charitable Trust	Jewish, arts, welfare	*Page 108*
❏	£67,000	The Gresham Charitable Trust	General	*Page 115*
❏	£67,000	The Huntingdon Foundation Limited	Jewish	*Page 134*
❏	£66,000	The Mason Bibby 1981 Trust	Welfare, especially elderly	*Page 41*
❏	£66,000	The Chetwode Samworth Charitable Trust	General	*Page 63*

Trusts ranked by grant total

☐	£66,000	The M A Hawe Settlement	General, especially in Lancashire	Page 124
☐	£66,000	The Millfield House Foundation	Social welfare in Tyne and Wear	Page 169
☐	£66,000	The Mitchell Charitable Trust	Jewish, general in London	Page 172
☐	£66,000	The Esme Mitchell Trust	Arts and culture, general in Northern Ireland	Page 173
☐	£65,000	The Arbib Foundation	Heritage, general	Page 31
☐	£65,000	Benfield Motors Charitable Trust	Christian, poverty, sickness, elderly	Page 40
☐	£65,000	The College Estate Charity	General in Stratford	Page 69
☐	£65,000	The Gwendoline Davies Charity	General	Page 79
☐	£65,000	The Fowler Memorial Trust	General in Essex	Page 100
☐	£65,000	The Gem Charitable Trust	General	Page 104
☐	£65,000	The M B Foundation (also known as Mossad Horav Moshe Aryeh Halevy)	General, educational	Page 160
☐	£65,000	The Stanley Charitable Trust	Jewish religious charities	Page 222
☐	£65,000	The Norman Whiteley Trust	Evangelical Christianity	Page 246
☐	£65,000	The Wiltshire Community Foundation	Community welfare in Wiltshire	Page 247
☐	£64,000	The Emerton Charitable Settlement	Health and welfare	Page 90
☐	£64,000	The L & R Gilley Charitable Trust	General	Page 106
☐	£64,000	The Grahame Charitable Foundation	Jewish	Page 111
☐	£64,000	The P & C Hickinbotham Charitable Trust	Social welfare	Page 127
☐	£64,000	The Ian Karten Charitable Trust	Education	Page 144
☐	£64,000	The Heinz & Anna Kroch Foundation	Medical research and severe poverty or hardship	Page 148
☐	£64,000	The Carole & Geoffrey Lawson Foundation	Jewish, general	Page 152
☐	£64,000	The Arthur James & Constance Paterson Charitable Trust	Medical research, health, welfare of children and elderly people	Page 187
☐	£64,000	The SMB Trust	Christian, general	Page 218
☐	£64,000	The Tramman Trust	General	Page 231
☐	£63,000	The David Brooke Charity	General	Page 51
☐	£63,000	The Beryl Evetts & Robert Luff Animal Welfare Trust	Animal welfare	Page 93
☐	£63,000	The Ironmongers' Quincentenary Fund	Medical research, community work, iron work, crafts	Page 138
☐	£63,000	The Kreditor Charitable Trust	Jewish, welfare, education	Page 148
☐	£63,000	The Jim Marshall Products Charitable Trust	General	Page 164
☐	£63,000	The Leslie Sell Charitable Trust	Scouts and guides	Page 213
☐	£63,000	The Thompson Charitable Trust	Social welfare	Page 228
☐	£62,000	Bill Brown's Charitable Settlement	Health, social welfare	Page 51
☐	£62,000	The Seedfield Trust	Christian, relief of poverty	Page 213
☐	£61,000	The Richard & Frances Harris Charitable Trust	Jewish	Page 122

Trusts ranked by grant total

❏	£61,000	The Hornton Charity	General	Page 131
❏	£61,000	The Hyde Park Place Estate Charity – Civil Trustees	General in Westminster	Page 134
❏	£61,000	INTACH (UK) Trust	Education and Indian culture	Page 136
❏	£61,000	The Dorothy Jacobs Charity	Jewish, medical	Page 139
❏	£61,000	The Leonard Matchan Fund Ltd	Social welfare	Page 165
❏	£61,000	The Mckenna & Co Foundation	General	Page 167
❏	£61,000	The Westcroft Trust	International understanding, overseas aid, Quaker, Shropshire	Page 244
❏	£60,000	The Alan & Rosemary Burrough Charitable Trust	Rowing, disability and ex-service organisations, general	Page 54
❏	£60,000	The Wilfrid & Constance Cave Foundation	Conservation, animal welfare, health and welfare	Page 61
❏	£60,000	The Lance Coates Charitable Trust 1969	General	Page 67
❏	£60,000	The Cumber Family Charitable Trust	Health, housing and social welfare, overseas, Christian, agriculture	Page 76
❏	£60,000	The Kennel Club Charitable Trust	Dogs	Page 146
❏	£60,000	The Laurence Misener Charitable Trust	General, Jewish	Page 172
❏	£60,000	The Stone Foundation	Research into addiction, medical research	Page 224
❏	£60,000	Humphrey Whitbread's First Charitable Trust	Churches, general	Page 245
❏	£59,000	The John & Ruth Howard Charitable Trust	Archaeology, church music, building preservation, general	Page 132
❏	£59,000	The Shuttlewood Clarke Foundation	Health and welfare	Page 216
❏	£58,000	The Lyndhurst Trust	Christian	Page 159
❏	£58,000	The Stevenson Family's Charitable Trust	General	Page 223
❏	£58,000	The Matthews Wrightson Charity Trust	Caring and Christian charities	Page 252
❏	£57,000	Adenfirst Ltd	Jewish	Page 29
❏	£57,000	The Roger & Sarah Bancroft Clark Charitable Trust	General	Page 65
❏	£57,000	The John & Freda Coleman Charitable Trust	Education, training	Page 69
❏	£57,000	The Girling (Cwmbran) Trust	General in Cwmbran	Page 107
❏	£57,000	The D J W Jackson Charitable Trust	Education, disability, general	Page 139
❏	£57,000	The Mole Charitable Trust	Jewish, Manchester, general	Page 173
❏	£57,000	The A R Taylor Charitable Trust	Health, social welfare, independent schools, military charities, general	Page 228
❏	£56,000	The Chris Brasher Trust	Recreation, conservation, general	Page 48
❏	£56,000	The Geoffrey John Kaye Charitable Foundation	Jewish	Page 145
❏	£56,000	The Saint Edmund, King & Martyr Trust	Church of England in London	Page 207
❏	£55,000	The Bowland Charitable Trust	Young people, education, general	Page 48

Trusts ranked by grant total

☐	£55,000	The Carmichael-Montgomery Charitable Trust	Christian	Page 58
☐	£55,000	The Clifton Charitable Trust	General	Page 67
☐	£55,000	The Jill Franklin Trust	Culture/environment, overseas and welfare	Page 100
☐	£55,000	The Norman Franklin Trust	Culture/environment, overseas and welfare	Page 100
☐	£55,000	The Linda Marcus Charitable Trust	General	Page 162
☐	£55,000	The Hon Charles Pearson Charity Trust	General	Page 189
☐	£55,000	The Ripple Effect Foundation	Environment, third world development, deprived young people in the UK	Page 202
☐	£54,000	The Bacta Charitable Trust	Welfare and disaster relief	Page 36
☐	£54,000	Gay & Peter Hartley's Hillards Charitable Trust	Welfare, general	Page 123
☐	£54,000	The McCarthy Foundation	Elderly	Page 166
☐	£54,000	The Anthony & Elizabeth Mellows Charitable Settlement	Arts, heritage, churches, hospitals, hospices, training of young people	Page 168
☐	£54,000	Millhouses Charitable Trust	Christian, overseas, welfare	Page 170
☐	£54,000	The Janatha Stubbs Foundation	General	Page 224
☐	£54,000	The Albert Van Den Bergh Charitable Trust	Jewish, general	Page 235
☐	£53,000	The Charlotte Bonham-Carter Charitable Trust	General, particularly in Hampshire	Page 46
☐	£52,000	The Astor of Hever Trust	General	Page 34
☐	£52,000	The John & Celia Bonham Christie Charitable Trust	General	Page 64
☐	£52,000	The Haymills Charitable Trust	Youth, education, medical	Page 124
☐	£52,000	The Kitty & Daniel Nabarro Charitable Trust	Jewish, health and welfare	Page 175
☐	£52,000	The Susanna Peake Charitable Trust	Disability, general	Page 188
☐	£51,000	Besom Foundation	General	Page 41
☐	£51,000	The J Davies Charities Ltd	Jewish, general	Page 79
☐	£51,000	The General Charity Fund	General	Page 105
☐	£51,000	The Gough Charitable Trust	Youth, Episcopal and Church of England, preservation of the countryside	Page 110
☐	£51,000	The Grove Charitable Trust	Jewish, welfare, general	Page 115
☐	£51,000	The N & P Hartley Memorial Trust	General	Page 123
☐	£51,000	The Jack & Ruth Lunzer Charitable Trust	Jewish education and arts	Page 158
☐	£51,000	The Patients' Aid Association Hospital & Medical Charities Trust	Medical in the Midlands	Page 187
☐	£51,000	The Rainford Trust	Social welfare, general	Page 198
☐	£51,000	The Tory Family Foundation	General in Kent	Page 230
☐	£51,000	The Tower Hill Improvement Trust	General	Page 230
☐	£50,000	The Abrams Charitable Trusts	Probably Jewish charities	Page 28

Trusts ranked by grant total

☐	£50,000	Col-Reno Ltd	Jewish religion & education	*Page 68*
☐	£50,000	The Oliver Ford Charitable Trust	Mental disability, housing	*Page 99*
☐	£50,000	The Sydney & Phyllis Goldberg Memorial Trust	Medical research, welfare, disability	*Page 108*
☐	£50,000	The Gunter Charitable Trust	Medical, welfare, conservation/environment	*Page 116*
☐	£50,000	The Katzauer Charitable Settlement	Jewish	*Page 144*
☐	£50,000	Rachel & Jack Lass Charities Ltd	Children's charities, Jewish	*Page 150*
☐	£50,000	The Sir Edward Lewis Foundation	General	*Page 155*
☐	£50,000	The Marchday Charitable Fund	General	*Page 161*
☐	£50,000	The Shiyich Charitable Trust	Jewish	*Page 216*
☐	£50,000	The Stanley Smith UK Horticultural Trust	Horticulture	*Page 220*
☐	£50,000	The Thames Wharf Charity	General	*Page 228*
☐	£50,000	The Roger Waters 1989 Charity Trust	General	*Page 239*
☐	£49,000	The Thomas Sivewright Catto Charitable Settlement	Medical, overseas aid/development, children and youth, welfare	*Page 60*
☐	£49,000	The Dove-Bowerman Trust	Education	*Page 85*
☐	£49,000	The Gilbert Edgar Trust Fund	General	*Page 87*
☐	£49,000	The Gibbins Trust	General	*Page 105*
☐	£49,000	The Sir Sigmund Sternberg Charitable Foundation	Jewish, Catholic and interfaith causes, general	*Page 223*
☐	£48,000	The Ebenezer Trust	Evangelical Christianity, welfare	*Page 87*
☐	£48,000	The Grace Charitable Trust	Christian	*Page 110*
☐	£48,000	The G D Herbert Charitable Trust	General	*Page 126*
☐	£48,000	The Humanitarian Trust (also known as the Michael Polak Foundation)	Education, health, social welfare	*Page 133*
☐	£48,000	The Jenour Foundation	General	*Page 140*
☐	£48,000	The Robert Kiln Charitable Trust	Archaeology, environmental conservation, musical education	*Page 146*
☐	£48,000	The Raymond Oppenheimer Foundation	General	*Page 185*
☐	£48,000	The Scottish Housing Associations Charitable Trust (SHACT)	Housing associations or housing related projects in Scotland	*Page 212*
☐	£48,000	The Worshipful Company of Shipwrights	Maritime charities, youth and heritage, general	*Page 252*
☐	£47,000	The Bohm Foundation	General	*Page 45*
☐	£47,000	The Walter Guinness Charitable Trust	General	*Page 116*
☐	£47,000	The Higgs Charitable Trust	General	*Page 128*
☐	£47,000	Mrs E G Hornby's Charitable Settlement	General	*Page 131*
☐	£47,000	The Judge Charitable Foundation	General	*Page 143*
☐	£47,000	The Gerald Palmer Trust	General	*Page 186*

● Trusts ranked by grant total

☐	£47,000	The Searchlight Electric Charitable Trust	General	*Page 213*
☐	£46,000	The ATP Charitable Trust	Jewish	*Page 35*
☐	£46,000	The Geoffrey Burton Charitable Trust	General, especially in Suffolk	*Page 54*
☐	£46,000	Ellador Ltd	Jewish	*Page 88*
☐	£46,000	The David Finnie & Alan Emery Charitable Trust	General	*Page 97*
☐	£45,000	The Dyers' Company Charitable Trust	General	*Page 86*
☐	£45,000	The George Elias Charitable Trust	Jewish, general	*Page 88*
☐	£45,000	The Reginald Graham Charitable Trust	Children, medical, education	*Page 110*
☐	£45,000	The C S Kaufman Charitable Trust	Jewish	*Page 144*
☐	£45,000	The Emmanuel Kaye Foundation	Medical research, general	*Page 145*
☐	£45,000	The Mclaren Foundation	General	*Page 167*
☐	£45,000	The Pennycress Trust	General	*Page 189*
☐	£45,000	The Huntly & Margery Sinclair Charitable Trust	Medical, general	*Page 216*
☐	£44,000	The David Cohen Family Charitable Trust	Arts	*Page 68*
☐	£44,000	The Earl Fitzwilliam Charitable Trust	General	*Page 97*
☐	£44,000	The Stanley Grundy Trust	Children and youth, disability	*Page 116*
☐	£44,000	The Hare of Steep Charitable Trust	General	*Page 121*
☐	£43,000	The Combined Charities Trust	General	*Page 71*
☐	£43,000	The A & R Woolf Charitable Trust	General	*Page 250*
☐	£42,000	Airflow Community Ltd	Education, welfare, general	*Page 29*
☐	£42,000	The Daily Prayers Union Trust Ltd	Evangelical Christian	*Page 78*
☐	£42,000	The New Horizons Trust	Elderly people for the benefit of the community	*Page 179*
☐	£42,000	The Newton Settlement	Christian	*Page 179*
☐	£42,000	The Solo Charitable Settlement	Jewish, general	*Page 220*
☐	£42,000	The Sutasoma Trust	Education, general	*Page 225*
☐	£41,000	The Ravensdale Trust	General	*Page 199*
☐	£41,000	The Scarfe Charitable Trust	Research, social welfare, churches	*Page 210*
☐	£40,000	The Chamberlain Foundation	Welgare, general	*Page 62*
☐	£40,000	The Nicholas Coote Charitable Trust	General in Sheffield, Catholic charities nationwide	*Page 74*
☐	£40,000	The GNC Trust	General	*Page 107*
☐	£40,000	The Hesed Trust	Christian	*Page 127*
☐	£40,000	The Frank Parkinson Agricultural Trust	Agriculture	*Page 187*
☐	£40,000	The John Young Charitable Settlement	General	*Page 253*
☐	£39,000	The David Pickford Charitable Foundation	Christian	*Page 190*
☐	£39,000	The Jonathan Towler Foundation	General	*Page 231*

Trusts ranked by grant total

❑	£38,000	Help the Homeless	Homelessness	Page 125
❑	£38,000	The Worshipful Company of Chartered Accountants General Charitable Trust	General	Page 251
❑	£37,000	The Ellis Campbell Charitable Foundation	Youth, education, conservation	Page 57
❑	£37,000	The Vernon N Ely Charitable Trust	Christian, welfare, disability, children and youth, overseas	Page 89
❑	£37,000	The Bernhard Heuberger Charitable Trust	Jewish	Page 127
❑	£37,000	The W L Pratt Charitable Trust	General	Page 193
❑	£36,000	The Elaine Lloyd Charitable Trust	General	Page 156
❑	£36,000	The A M McGreevy No 5 Charitable Settlement	General	Page 166
❑	£36,000	The Charles Skey Charitable Trust	Health and social welfare	Page 217
❑	£35,000	The Everard Foundation	General	Page 93
❑	£35,000	The Willie Nagel Charitable Trust	Jewish, general	Page 175
❑	£35,000	The New Durlston Trust	Christian	Page 178
❑	£34,000	The Loseley Christian Trust	Christian	Page 158
❑	£34,000	The Stella Symons Charitable Trust	General	Page 227
❑	£34,000	The Thompson Family Charitable Trust	General	Page 229
❑	£34,000	The Simon Whitbread Charitable Trust	Medicine, churches, general, Bedfordshire	Page 245
❑	£33,000	The Marchig Animal Welfare Trust	Animal welfare	Page 162
❑	£33,000	The Mayfield Valley Arts Trust	Arts	Page 165
❑	£33,000	The E C Sosnow Charitable Trust	General	Page 220
❑	£32,000	The Homestead Charitable Trust	General	Page 130
❑	£31,000	The Dollond Charitable Trust	General	Page 84
❑	£31,000	The Nazareth Trust Fund	Christian	Page 178
❑	£31,000	The Nigel Vinson Charitable Trust	General	Page 237
❑	£30,000	Sir Alec Black's Charity	Bedding for people who are sick or poor	Page 44
❑	£30,000	The Carlton House Charitable Trust	Jewish, general	Page 58
❑	£30,000	The Countryside Trust	Conservation	Page 74
❑	£30,000	The Maxwell Family Foundation	General	Page 165
❑	£30,000	The Barnett & Sylvia Shine No 1 & No 2 Charitable Trusts	General	Page 216
❑	£29,000	The Beacon Trust	Christian	Page 38
❑	£29,000	The ISA Charity	General	Page 138
❑	£27,000	The Abel Charitable Trust	General	Page 27
❑	£27,000	The Sharon Trust	Christian	Page 214
❑	£25,000	The Altajir Trust	Not known	Page 31
❑	£25,000	The Girdlers' Company Charitable Trust	General	Page 106

Trusts ranked by grant total

☐	£24,000	The Abell Trust	Education, general	Page 28
☐	£23,000	Morrison Charitable Foundation	Jewish	Page 173
☐	£22,000	The Baker Charitable Trust	Jewish	Page 36
☐	£21,000	The Ian Askew Charitable Trust	General	Page 34
☐	£21,000	Datnow Limited	General	Page 79
☐	£21,000	The Old Broad Street Charity Trust	General	Page 184
☐	£21,000	The Stanley Smith General Charitable Trust	General	Page 219
☐	£21,000	The Tufton Charitable Trust (formerly the Wates Charitable Trust)	Christian	Page 232
☐	£20,000	The A S Charitable Trust	Christian	Page 27
☐	£20,000	The DLM Charitable Trust	General	Page 84
☐	£19,000	The Gershon Coren Charitable Foundation	Jewish, general	Page 74
☐	£19,000	The R M Douglas Charitable Trust	General	Page 84
☐	£18,000	The Earl of March's Trust Company	General	Page 161
☐	£18,000	The Harbour Charitable Trust	General	Page 121
☐	£16,000	The Lanvern Foundation	General	Page 158
☐	£16,000	The David Uri Memorial Trust	Jewish, general	Page 235
☐	£14,000	The Viznitz Foundation	Not known	Page 237
☐	£13,000	The Hinrichsen Foundation	Music	Page 128
☐	£11,000	Vendquot Ltd	Jewish education	Page 236
☐	£8,000	The Louis Freedman Charitable Settlement	General	Page 102
☐	£8,000	The Lark Trust	General	Page 150
☐	£5,000	The Hawthorne Charitable Trust	General	Page 124
☐	£4,000	The Freshfield Foundation	Not known	Page 103
☐	£1,500	The Hobart Charitable Trust	Education, religion	Page 129
☐	-	The Dandelion Trust	General	Page 78
☐	-	The Grantham Yorke Trust	Youth organisations, relief-in-need	Page 112
☐	-	The B Hammer Charitable Trust	General	Page 119
☐	-	The Ireland Funds	Reconciliation, arts development, community development	Page 136
☐	-	Newpier Ltd	Jewish, general	Page 179
☐	-	The Charles Peguy Trust	Not known	Page 189
☐	-	Community Trusts		Page 72
☐	-	Lions Clubs International		Page 155
☐	-	The National Association of Rags		Page 176
☐	-	The National Association of Round Tables		Page 177

The A B Charitable Trust

£82,000 (1993/94)

Human dignity

37 Woodsford Square, London W14 8DP

Correspondent: Edmorson Trustee Co Ltd

Trustees: Y J M Bonavero; D Boehm; Mrs A G M-L Bonavero; Edmorson Trustee Co Ltd.

Beneficial area: Worldwide.

Information available: Full accounts are on file at the Charity Commission.

General: The trust was established in 1990 and by April 1991 had received donations of £375,000. Grants in 1990/91 totalled £31,000 and assets decreased accordingly to £344,000. In each of the three years since, the trust has given more in grants than it has received in income (despite receiving further donations as well as interest) and the assets have continued to decrease.

By 1993/94, the assets had decreased to £259,000 and the income had decreased to £31,000 including a £10,000 donation. £82,000 was given in grants, more than in any previous year.

The 21 grants ranged from £2,000 to £7,500 with the largest grant given to MacIntyre Charitable Trust. £5,000 went to each of Action Aid, French Cerebral Palsy Centre, Rathbone Society, RUKBA, Shelter and the YMCA. The other grants all went to health and welfare charities except a single grant to the Parish of St Mary the Virgin, Icomb. 12 of the recipients received a grant the previous year, and five have received a grant in all four years since the trust was formed.

Exclusions: No support for medical research, animal care and any area which should reasonably be funded by Government.

Applications: In writing to the trustees up to a maximum of four A4 pages if appropriate, plus recent detailed audited accounts. The trustees meet on a quarterly basis.

The A S Charitable Trust

£20,000 (1991/92)

Christian

31 Green Street, London W1Y 3FD

Correspondent: R St G Calvocoressi

Trustees: R St G Calvocoressi; C W Brocklebank; Sir Thomas Hare.

Beneficial area: Worldwide.

Information available: Full accounts are on file at the Charity Commission.

General: In 1991/92, the trust had assets of £1.9 million and an income of £120,000. Grants totalled £20,000 leaving £99,000 to be transferred to the capital account. The trust appears to have a regular surplus of income over expenditure. It is unclear if this is to increase the assets base, so more money will be available in future years, if it is saving up for major projects or if it has been unable to find enough suitable applicants.

The trust makes regular donations to Christian International Peace Service (CHIPS) (£17,000 in 1991/92). CHIPS is a registered charity seeking to advance the Christian gospel in areas of unrest. It appears to be the major beneficiary of the trust each year. The correspondent for CHIPS and the A S Charitable Trust is the same and the two trusts appear to be closely connected.

Other grants were made totalling £3,000. The emphasis is on Christian organisations working overseas. The largest grants were to Christian Engineers in Development, a regular beneficiary, (£1,500), Interlock Charitable Trust (£1,150) and the Carr Gomme Society (£250). Four grants were for £100 and one for £25.

Exclusions: Individuals and large charities are not supported.

Applications: In writing to the correspondent.

The Abel Charitable Trust

£27,000 (1993)

General

Balcombe Mill, Mill Lane, Balcombe, Haywards Heath, West Sussex RH17 6QT
01444-811123

Correspondent: Rev D J Abel, Administrator

Trustees: Rev I Smith-Cameron; Rev M Baddeley; Rev A R C Arbuthnot.

Beneficial area: London and south east England.

Information available: The information for this entry was supplied by the trust.

General: In 1993, the trust had assets of £637,000 and an income of £47,000. 18 grants were given totalling £23,000.

The trust is Christian-based and supports welfare causes in London and the South East. It appears to have a particular interest in projects concerned with homelessness. Priority is given to agencies aiming to make the individual more self-sufficient, and to emergent charities, with the trust seeing its role as providing sufficient time "to enable an agency to get off the ground". Support is preferred where charities can use the grant to lever longer-term statutory funding; charities working on the resettlement in the community of those rejected by society, rather than them remaining in institutions and charities whose projects, could be repeated elsewhere.

All suitable applicants are researched and visited. Recipients are visited again after implementation of the grant, in an on-going attempt to measure effectiveness.

The largest grants in 1993, were £3,000 to Cardboard Citizens, a homeless peoples' theatre group and £2,000 each to the Windmill Project run by the Sisters of Notre Dame, Bow Self Help Alcohol Recovery Programme, Elephant Jobs and the Association for Prevention of Addiction. Other grants of £1,000 to £1,600 were given to Croydon College (Chaplaincy Committee), Drug & Alcohol Foundation, Praxis, The Passage Day Centre, Prison Charity Shops, Capital Housing Project, Care-Free, Barking & Dagenham Council – Voluntary Services and Women's Link. There were also two grants of £500 and two of £250.

Exclusions: Only registered charities are supported. No grants for individuals, building appeals, vehicles, research (including medical research), support services for elderly people or large general appeals. The trust does not make loans or pay off mortgages, bank loans or deficits.

Applications: In writing to the correspondent, stating the specific purpose for which help is sought, the status of the organsiation, membership and accounts, a brief description of the work, the amount sought from the trust and how the figure is derived. Trustees consider applications annually in May/June.

The Abell Trust

£24,000 (1991/92)

Education, general

Craigdarroch Cottage, St Fillans, Crieff, Perthshire PH6 2NF
01764-85370

Correspondent: Miss Ann Brocklebank

Trustees: Miss Ann Brocklebank; C W Brocklebank.

Beneficial area: UK.

Information available: Full accounts are on file at the Charity Commission.

General: The correspondent has stated that they do not wish to be included in this Guide, as their funds are always rotated between a set list of organisations. No other organisations can be added to that list, so charities will be wasting their time sending a grant application.

The trust had assets of £762,000 in 1991/92, most of which appear to be from various loans made to the trust. Its income was £54,000; 13 grants totalled £24,000. The two major beneficiaries were the Dorothy Sayer Charitable Trust (£8,000) and Newcastle Polytechnic (£5,000). The trust also supported Exeter University and Westminster College Oxford, welfare charities (including Invalids at Home and Samaritans), National Trust and Ely Cathedral.

The previous year, the trust made grants totalling £340,000 including £250,000 to Lancaster University, £30,000 to Newcastle Polytechnic and £24,000 to the Dorothy Sayer Charitable Trust.

Applications: The correspondent states that the trust "already has commitments that take all its funds and no further applications could be successful".

The Henry & Grete Abrahams Charitable Foundation

£113,000 (1993/94)

Jewish

23 Chelwood House, Gloucester Square, London W2 2SY
0171-727 5382

Correspondent: Mrs G Abrahams

Trustees: Mrs G Abrahams; M H Gluckstein; M R Nathan; D M Maislish.

Beneficial area: Worldwide.

Information available: Full accounts are on file at the Charity Commission.

General: In 1993/94, the trust had assets of £891,000 and an income of £30,000. Grants totalled £113,000 using unspent income from previous years. An exceptional grant of £112,500 was given to Society of Friends of Women Zionists of Great Britain & Ireland. The only other grants were to Nightingale House (£400) and Liberal Jewish Synagogue (£250). All three organisations received grants the previous year.

In 1992/93, grants totalled £160,000 from £41,000 income. Again there was one major grant (£139,000) to Wingate Youth Trust. The Society of Friends of Women Zionists of Great Britain & Ireland received £12,500, with the remaining five grants for £3,000 or less.

Exclusions: No grants to individuals; registered charities only.

Applications: In writing to the correspondent.

The Abrams Charitable Trusts

£50,000 (1992/93)

Probably Jewish charities

130-132 Nantwich Road, Crewe, Cheshire CW2 6AZ
01270-213475

Correspondent: R A Taylor

Trustees: Eric Abrams; Gertrude Abrams; Brian Abrams; Betty Abrams.

Beneficial area: UK, Israel.

Information available: Recent accounts are on file at the Charity Commission, but without details of donations.

General: Two trusts are administered from the address above, the Eric Abrams Charitable Trust and the Brian Abrams Charitable Trust. The trusts operate so closely together that their accounts are practically identical. In 1988/89, the trusts had combined assets of £1,667,000.

In 1992/93, the Brian Abrams Charitable Trust had assets of £861,000. No information about Eric Abrams assets. The trusts had a combined income of £132,000 and appear to have only given grants from the Brian Abrams charity totalling £50,000. Unfortunately there is no grants list on file at the Charity Commission. A significant proportion of the trusts' income each year remains unspent.

There is no recent information available on the sorts of organisations the trusts give to. The only individually listed donations on file relate to 1979, when the same nine grants were made by both trusts, totalling £187,000. These all went to Jewish charities.

Exclusions: No grants to individuals.

Applications: In writing to the correspondent.

The Acacia Charitable Trust

£146,000 (1993/94)

Jewish, education, medical

104 Wigmore Street, London W1H 9DR
0171-486 1884

Correspondent: Mrs Nora Howland, Secretary

Trustees: K D Rubens; Mrs A G Rubens; S A Rubens.

Beneficial area: UK and Israel.

Information available: Full accounts are on file at the charity Commission.

General: In 1993/94, the trust's assets were valued at £1.73 million giving an income of £99,000. 34 grants were made totalling £146,000. About two thirds of the grants were to Jewish organisations.

Four grants were for over £10,000: Jewish Museum (£50,500); University of Reading (£31,000); ORT Trust (£25,000) and CBF World Jewish Relief (£13,000). Eight grants were for £1,000 to £7,500 including those to Duke of Edinburgh's Award (£5,000); Jewish Care (£2,000) and the Royal Photographic Society (£1,000). 13 grants ranged from £100 to £750 with 9 of less than £100. Grants were given to Jewish, medical, education and the arts.

Applications: In writing to the correspondent.

Access 4 Trust

£119,000 (1992/93)

Children, welfare

Bank Buildings, 16A St James's Street, London SW1A 1ER
0171-930 7621

Correspondent: J R F Lulham

Trustees: Miss S M Wates; J R F Lulham.

Beneficial area: Worldwide.

Information available: Full accounts are on file at the Charity Commission.

General: The trustees report for 1993/94 states, "The trust has directed a major part of its resources towards children, and it is intended that this policy will continue." The report goes on to say, "As anticipated, donations paid exceeded net income. The trustees are empowered to realise investments to finance donations and this trend is expected to continue for at least the next few years." In 1992/93, the income was £36,000 and £119,000 was given in grants.

By far the largest grant was £50,000 given to Womankind Worldwide, the first of three annual payments. The remaining £69,000 went mainly to assist deprived children and young people. £10,000 each went to the Thomas Coram Foundation and Barnardo's, and £9,600 to the Post Adoption Centre (which received an exceptional £75,000 in 1991/92).

A further £5,000 went to "various in relief of poverty". The remaining grants ranged from £100 to £3,500, including £3,000 to each of After Adoption, Bawku East Women's Development Association and Parents for Children. Other beneficiaries included Sight Savers (£750); Refugees of Slovenia (£700); Female Prisoners'

Welfare (£500) and the Drug & Alcohol Foundation (£100). The boroughs of Barnet, Tower Hamlets and the City of Westminster all received grants for "relief of poverty".

Applications: In writing to the correspondent.

Achiezer Association Ltd

£125,000 (1992/93)

Jewish

132 Clapton Common, London E5 9AG
0181-800 5465

Correspondent: David Chontow

Trustees: Mrs J A Chontow; D Chontow; S S Chontow; M M Chontow.

Beneficial area: Worldwide.

Information available: Accounts are on file at the Charity Commission, but without a list of grants.

General: In 1992/93, the trust had an income of £278,000 and gave grants totalling £125,000. Most of the income was from covenanted donations and the trust appears to be using some of this to build up its assets, which are currently £236,000.

No information is available on the distribution of grants since 1972, when Jewish organisations were the main beneficiaries. A few small grants were also given to medical and welfare charities.

Applications: The trust states that funds are already committed to existing beneficiaries for the next two years. Unsolicited applications are therefore very unlikely to be successful.

Adenfirst Ltd

£57,000 (1993)

Jewish

99 Grove Green Road, London E11 4EF
0181-556 0192

Correspondent: I M Cymerman, Governor

Trustees: Mrs H F Bondi; I M Cymerman; Mrs R Cymerman.

Beneficial area: Worldwide.

Information available: Full accounts are on file at the Charity Commission.

General: The trust supports Jewish organisations only. In 1993, it gave grants totalling £57,000 from an income of £77,000. 25 grants were for £100 or more, with £543 given in grants of under £100.

£5,000 was given to each of: Agudas Israel of Great Britain Hachnosath Kalloh Fund; Beer Israel Torah Movement; Bnei Emes Institute; Friends of Ponevez Yeshiva; Friends of the Holocaust Memorial Yad Vashem Foundation; Mala Judaica Studies; Russian Immigrant Fund.

The trustees did not wish to appear in this Guide, because they felt that to be included would be to "invite applications at random to which we could not respond".

Applications: In writing to the correspondent.

Airflow Community Ltd

£42,000 (1990/91)

Education, welfare, general

Lancaster Road, High Wycombe, Bucks HP12 3QP
01494-525252

Correspondent: H Beglow, Company Secretary

Trustees: H Cheesewright (Chairman); M Nicholls; M Graham; A N Blond; K R Burroughs; P Downing; L Lewis; P Comley; B Blackburn; W Beglow; I Anderson; G Partis; G Pitcher; S Clews; R Hitchcock.

Information available: Full accounts are on file at the Charity Commission for 1990/91.

General: In 1990/91, the trust had assets of £324,000 and an income of £122,000. It gave 89 grants totalling £42,000. The largest three grants were for £5,000 and were given to: Children in Need, Holmer Green Day Centre and Marlow Age Concern. There were four grants of £1,000 to £1,300 to: Hillcrest Day Centre; High Wycombe Neo-Natal Trust Fund; Oxfam and Save the Children Fund.

Other grants were from £50 to £800, but were generally for £200 to £500. Most were given to medical, welfare, disability, Christian or overseas aid organisations including: ARMS; Asthma Research; Barnardo's; British Heart Foundation; Bucks Age Concern; Church Army; Disabled Youth; Friends of Spastics; Hearing Dogs for the Deaf; Home Farm Trust; Salvation Army; Sibford School; Thames Valley Hospice; Wycombe Women's Aid and World Vision.

According to the Charity Commission the trust had an income of £80,000 in 1993/94.

Applications: In writing to the correspondent.

The Ajahma Charitable Trust

£136,000 (1992/93)

Welfare and, increasingly, overseas development

35 Galveston Road, London SW15 2RZ

Correspondent: Jane Quayle, Administrator

Trustees: Jennifer Sheridan; Elizabeth Simpson; James Sinclair Taylor; Michael Horsman.

Beneficial area: Worldwide.

Information available: Full accounts are on file at the Charity Commission.

General: In 1992/93, the trust had assets of £1.3 million, an income of £116,000 and gave 38 grants totalling £136,000. Five organisations appear to dominate the grants list: Headway (£42,000, also received around £60,000 in the two previous years); International Health Exchange (£20,000); Action on Disability & Development (£34,000); Oxfam (£5,000) and Action Health 2000 (£15,000), all of which received similarly large donations in 1991/92.

Other charities regularly supported, but on a much smaller scale, were mainly national or international in the fields of development and justice. They included Third World First, Population Concern, Apex Trust, Asian Women's Association, Family Rights Group and Prisoners Abroad. A few local charities received a grant, including Cleveland AIDS Support, St Martin in the Field Social Care Unit and Stockport Sharecare.

Exclusions: No support for animal or religious appeals.

Applications: The trustees have recently decided NOT to consider ANY further applications for grants unless the organisation is personally known to one of the trustees. "This change in policy has been made because of an increase, over recent months, in the number of applications we have been receiving." The trustees meet twice a year to consider applications. No application form is available.

Alexandra Rose Day

£345,000 (1992/93)

Health and welfare

1 Castlenau, Barnes, London SW13 9RP
0181-748 4824/5

Correspondent: Mrs Gillian Greenwood, Director

Trustees: HRH Princess Alexandra, President; **The Council:** Lady Grade, Chair; Lady Norton, Deputy Chair; Lord Mayor of London; Robert Sharpe; David Ashton Bostock; Lady Heald; Rex Glenny; Lord King of Wartnaby; Kenneth Barber; Norman Richie; Mrs A Beckman; Captain David Buchan; Hon Mrs Czernin; Hon Mrs Hepburne-Scott; Lord Kenilworth; Mrs Morton Neal; Hon Mrs Patrick Penny; Sir Ian Rankin; Hon Mrs Michael Rawlinson; Mrs Nicholas Stanley; John Talbot; Mrs Anthony Travis.

Beneficial area: UK.

Information available: Annual report and accounts, without details of grants made or of the amounts retained by the participating charities. No information about how much is given to non-participating charities.

General: Alexandra Rose Day is Britain's first Flag Day, founded in 1912 to help organisations caring for people who are sick, elderly or young. Organisations participating in the Alexandra Rose Day collections keep for their own work 80% of what they collect, and may also get further support from the 20% remitted to Alexandra Rose Day. There is also a "trust fund ... set up to provide emergency help to 'people' caring charities facing financial crisis." There is no identifiable information in the annual reports about the scale of this funding or about the recipients. These latter may be restricted in practice to charities participating in the Rose Day collections.

The charity also has other fundraising events. In 1993, the income from these events was broken down as follows: Flag day collections £327,000; donations £40,000; Rose Ball £59,000; raffles £71,000 and other activities £5,000.

In 1993, the trust had assets of £152,000, total income was £502,000. After expenses, the trust had £259,000 available for distribution. Payments and donations to organisations caring for those who are elderly, sick, disabled or young totalled £345,000.

Exclusions: No grants to individuals.

Applications: Applications should be submitted to the above address by 1st October and should be accompanied by the latest annual report and accounts.

Alglen Ltd

£133,000 (1990/91)

Jewish

5 North End Road, London NW11 7RJ
0181-455 6789; Fax: 0181-455 2277

Correspondent: Mrs R Lipschitz, Governor

Beneficial area: Worldwide.

Information available: Accounts are on file at the Charity Commission up to 1990/91, but without a list of grants since 1989/90.

General: The trust supports Jewish organisations only. In 1990/91, it had assets of £551,000 and an income of £184,000, most of which was from interest on cash at the bank (including £485,000 due to a creditor).

Grants totalled £133,000 but no grants list was available for that year.

In 1989/90, 11 grants were given totalling £155,000, including £50,000 each to Merkaz Joseph Trust and Kollel Shomre Hachomoth.

Applications: In writing to the correspondent.

The Alliance Family Foundation

£73,000 (1992/93)

Jewish, general

PO Box 31, Lees Street, Swinton, Manchester M27 7DA
0161-728 5100

Correspondent: Miss J M Ridgway

Trustees: Sir David Alliance; N Alliance; G N Alliance; Mrs S D Esterkin.

Beneficial area: UK, with a possible preference for charities in the Manchester area.

Information available: Accounts are on file at the Charity Commission, but no list of grants is included since that for 1987/88.

General: In 1992/93, the foundation had assets of £1 million, an income of £175,000 and gave grants totalling £73,000. The grant total has reduced over recent years (£97,000 in 1990/1 and £81,000 in 1991/92), it is not known if this is due to a lack of suitable applications or if the trustees are trying to build up the assets to have more money available for distribution in the future. It may be that high legal fees (£37,000 in 1992/93) and bank interest and charges (£30,000 in 1992/93) are part of the problem. The following grant details refer to 1987/88, the latest year for which a list of grants is on file at the Charity Commission.

82 grants were made in 1987/88, all but one to Jewish charities. The exception was an award of £250 to the Institute of Economic Affairs. However, in the previous year the foundation made a grant of £100,000 to CORDA, a national heart charity. In the past there has been a clear interest in charities in the Manchester area.

Applications: In writing to the correspondent.

The Altajir Trust

£25,000 (1992)

Not known

33 Thurloe Place, London SW7 2HQ
0171-581 3522

Correspondent: A C Duncan, Secretary

Trustees: H E Mohammed Mahdi Al Tajir; Peter Tripp; Alan Jones; Dr Roger Williams.

Beneficial area: Worldwide.

Information available: Accounts are on file at the Charity Commission, without a list of grants.

General: The trust is "for the advancement of science, education and research beneficial to the community in Britain or any Arab or Islamic States for needy young people and adults".

It relies on donations each year, having no permanent endowment. Its income steadily increased up to 1991, when it was over £200,000 and grants totalled £73,000. In 1992, income fell to £172,000 and grants totalled only £25,000. No further information is available on where the grants went. Other expenditure includes £100,000 on student fees and maintenance, but no further information is available.

The trustees did not wish to be included in this Guide, they thought the trust was too small; but as the income appears to be between £150,000 and £200,000 it has been included.

Applications: In writing to the correspondent.

The Ambika Paul Foundation

£775,000 (1993/94)

Children and young people under 25

Caparo House, 103 Baker Street, London W1M 2LM
0171-486 1417

Correspondent: S Paul

Trustees: S Paul; Mrs A Paul; Mrs A Punn.

Beneficial area: UK, India.

Information available: Accounts are on file at the Charity Commission, but without a grants list.

General: The trust was set up in 1978 in memory of Mr S Paul's daughter who died in 1968. The trust is funded by the family. It has no paid employees and no renumeration is given for trustees expenses.

In 1992/93, the trust had assets of £895,000 and an income of £171,000, £108,000 from deed of covenant and £63,000 from interest. Grants totalled £66,000 (£50,000 in 1991/92). The trust is building up its assets for major educational projects in the future (the level of donations is expected to increase). Grants will probably be to schools and universities working on engineering, science or arts based projects.

In 1993/94, according to the correspondent, grants totalled £775,000. It is thought the main project supported was the rebuilding of the Children's Zoo within London Zoo. It is not known if some major donations have been or will be received to maintain it's capital base.

Exclusions: The trust does not want to receive any appeals from large or national charities and does not support welfare applications.

Applications: In writing to the correspondent.

The Arbib Foundation

£65,000

Heritage, general

New Farm, Badgemore, Henley-on-Thames, Oxfordshire RG9 4NX
01491-417000

Correspondent: M Arbib, Trustee

Trustees: M Arbib; A H E Arbib; Hon J S Kirkwood.

Beneficial area: UK, preference for the Henley area.

Information available: Full accounts are on file at the Charity Commission.

General: The trust was established "in particular to support the establishment of a museum in the Thames Valley for the education of the general public in the history, geography and ecology of the Thames Valley and the River Thames".

1993/94 was an exceptional year. The trust had an income of £2.85 million including donations of £2.66 milion. Grants totalled £4,051,000 including £4 million to the River & Rowing Museum Foundation. This large grant would have resulted in a large deficit, but the trust also realised profits on investments totalling £1.1 million. It also received a gift of 560,000 Perpetual plc shares during the year.

Other grants, totalling £51,000, included £28,500 to the NSPCC, £5,000 to Help the Hospices, £3,000 to the Water Education Trust and £2,000 to Henley & District Agricultural Association. 28 other grants ranged from £100 to £1,500, mainly to medical and welfare charities. Beneficiaries included the British Wheelchair Sports Foundation (£700), Chemical Dependency Centre Ltd (£400), Open Spaces Society (£500), Racing Welfare Charities (£1,000), Riverside Counselling Services (£1,500) and St Michael's Hospice (£500).

The usual income for the trust is around £60,000 to £70,000. A more representative year for the trust would be 1992/93, when grants totalled £69,000 and the income was £68,000. The main grants went to the Thames Salmon Trust (£20,000), Rowing Museum (£10,000) and the National Autistic Society and Oxfordshire Macmillan Nurse Appeal (both £5,000). A number of grants are recurrent.

Applications: The correspondent stated that applications received as a result of details appearing in a Guide such as this will be ignored.

The Archbishop of Canterbury's Charitable Trust

£187,000 (1993)

Christianity, welfare

Lambeth Palace, London SE1 7JU

Correspondent: The Administrative Secretary

Beneficial area: Worldwide.

Information available: Accounts are on file at the Charity Commission, but without a full list of grants.

General: The previous Archbishop of Canterbury, Robert Runcie, set up this charitable trust in 1983. The main objects are to advance the Christian religion and Christian education, in particular the objects and principles of the Church of England. It also aims to relieve poverty and sickness both within the UK and overseas.

To these ends, the trust gave grants totalling £187,000 in 1993, with most going to unspecified general grants and donations amounting to £171,000. The remainder went to three named charitable funds: The Davidson Bequest Fund (£5,000); Dick & Shiela Stannard Fund (£2,000) and the Taize Pilgrimage Fund (£9,000). The trust states that unfortunately its grant-making abilities can in no way match the need it is being asked to meet. Therefore no new applications can be considered.

Applications: In writing to the correspondent, but note the above.

The Armourers & Brasiers Gauntlet Trust

£75,000 (1993/94)

Education in materials science, general

Armourers Hall, 81 Coleman Street, London EC2R 5BJ
0171-606 1199

Correspondent: The Secretary

Trustees: Rev P E Warburton; E J R Hill; G C Honnywill; M J Paton; C D Thomas.

Beneficial area: UK.

Information available: Full accounts are on file at the Charity Commission.

General: The trust was established by the Worshipful Company of Armourers and Brasiers. Grants to organisations are divided between:

Education in materials science;

Youth organisations;

Armed service charities (most of these are prizes);

Charities working in London (especially the City of London);

Miscellaneous.

In 1993/94, the trust had assets of £1 million and an income of £104,000. Grants totalling £75,000 were given in the categories listed above. Most money (£40,000) is given in education grants. Other grants went to the Sail Training Association, Royal Collection Trust, Motivation Trust and the Lord Mayor's Charity Appeal 1994. Most grants are usually for under £1,000.

Applications: In writing to the correspondent.

The Arnopa Trust

£74,000 (1990)

Children in need

c/o Matlock Bank Ltd, Connaught Place, London W2 2DY
0171-402 5500 ext. 403

Correspondent: B Evans

Beneficial area: UK.

Information available: No accounts are on file since those for 1990, which did not include a list of grants.

General: The trust had assets of £552,000 in 1990 and an income of £72,000. Grants totalled £74,000 to the "care and protection of children in need". No further information about the recipients of grants was available.

Applications: In writing to the correspondent.

The Ove Arup Foundation

£164,000 (1993/94)

Building education and research

13 Fitzroy Street, London W1P 6BQ

Correspondent: K Dawson

Trustees: P Ahm; P Dowson; R Hobbs; J Zunz; B Perry; J Martin; D Michael.

Beneficial area: UK.

Information available: Full accounts are on file at the Charity Commission.

General: The trust was established in 1989 with the principal objective of supporting education in matters associated with the built environment. It also supports building-related academic research. The trustees are appointed by the board of the Ove Arup Partnership.

The trust receives an annual covenanted donation of £240,000. In 1993/94, it received the sixth of a total of seven donations due. This was added to the capital fund which generated an income of £94,000. The assets now stand at £1.64 million.

Six grants were made totalling £164,000, most of which went to the University of Cambridge (£140,000). Four grants were for £4,000 to £10,000, all recurrent from the previous year: Partnership Trust (£9,700); Cranfield Institute of Technology (£5,000); Building Experiences Trust (£5,000) and Loughborough University (£4,000). The only other grant was £600 to Arkwright Scholarships.

In addition to the four recurrent grants mentioned, the only other grants in 1992/93 were to the Construction Industry Council (£2,500) and the Young Designers' Forum (£5,000).

Applications: In writing to the correspondent. Trustees meet quarterly to consider applications.

The Ashden Charitable Trust

£72,000 (1993)

Green issues, homelessness, third world, community arts, general

9 Red Lion Court, London EC4A 3EB
0171-410 0330

Correspondent: Hugh de Quetteville

Trustees: Mrs S Butler-Sloss; R Butler-Sloss; Miss J S Portrait.

Beneficial area: Worldwide.

Information available: Full accounts are on file at the Charity Commission.

General: This is part of the Sainsbury Family Charitable Trusts (*see A Guide to the Major Trusts – Volume 1*). In 1992/93, the trust had assets of £2.2 million and an income of £246,000, of which £150,000 was transferred to the capital account, leaving £96,000 available for distribution. Grants approved totalled £72,000 given to:

- **Green issues** – £32,490
  Between Bristol Energy Centre (BEC), Britain Tanzania Society, Friends of the Earth Trust (Tree of Life Project) and the Groundwork Trust, in Greater Nottingham and Avon.
- **Homelessness** – £19,200
  Between Association for Prevention of Addiction (APA) and Crisis (at Christmas)
- **Third World** – £12,250
  Between Intermediate Technology Development Group (ITDG), Oxfam, University of Northumbria, Newcastle and VetAid.
- **Community arts** – £8,000
  Between New Playwrights Trust (NPT), Wimbledon Theatre (Little Peoples Theatre Company) and two grants to Channel Arts Association, one of which was for the Bridge Youth Theatre.

There was also a cancelled grant of £2,500.

Exclusions: No grants to individuals.

Applications: To the correspondent in writing. "All applications are most carefully considered, but we receive a great many appeals and, unfortunately, the trust cannot make grants to more than a small proportion." The trustees met six times a year to consider grant applications.

The Laura Ashley Foundation

£231,000 to organisations (1993/94)

Education, general

33 King Street, Covent Garden, London WC2E 8JD
0171-497 2503

Correspondent: Mrs Annabel Thompson

Trustees: Sir Bernard Ashley; David Ashley; Lord Hooson; Sir Richard Gaskell.

Beneficial area: UK.

Information available: Full accounts on file at the Charity Commission. The trust publishes a detailed newsletter.

General: The foundation was formed by Bernard and Laura Ashley in 1985. In 1993/94, the trust approved grants to the value of £404,000. 52 grants were given to colleges and other bodies to assist with educational projects throughout the UK totalling £231,000. The remaining £172,000 was awarded to 375 individuals in grants of £80 to £700 to assist with second chance learning in further education. Small funds are also made available to prisoners for courses which are not covered by prison education; most are to help prisoners find work or further training upon their release and which occupies time whilst in prison.

During the year the trust gave grants to: Colleges of art in London, Sussex and Newcastle of between £2,000 and £14,000 for students studying conservation of paper, clocks and ceramics, carvings and works of art; Colleges of Music in London, Manchester and Wales received grants of £12,000 to £17,000 towards fees for students studying particular instruments.

A number of grants of £500 to £2,500 were given to community colleges for basic adult education to help with things such as literacy, dyslexia and English for ethnic minorities, refugees (from Vietnam, Bosnia and Sudan) and Polish students to return to Poland as English teachers. Grants of about £1,000 to £5,000 were given to a number of organisations for unemployed, homeless or disabled people to help them gain new skills for employment or to live independently. Kent Adult Education, Dover received £900 towards tutor costs for French classes for the unemployed, Leonard Cheshire Centre, Newcastle, £4,340 towards a computer tutor for disabled people and MCVS, Liverpool, £5,000 to help with independent living.

Many grants of around £1,000 to £11,000 were given for taster, access and second chance learning courses in Northern Ireland, Scotland and Yorkshire.

Grants of £500 to £1,500 to prisons for materials for mentally ill inmates and towards vocational trianing. A grant of £18,000 was also given to NACRO, a regular beneficiary, towards education and training for ex-offenders.

Youths were supported generally (above) and specifically through projects such as Young People, Cornwall (£6,500) for a youth worker to run courses for 40 young mothers.

Some other interesting grants included: Young Musicians of Mull, £2,000 for travel costs for volunteer music tutors for children on remote islands and Education Extra, Tyneside (£360) towards courses for parents and volunteers to learn after school activities to encourage pupils to stay after school to study, play sport or use homework classes.

Exclusions: No grants are made for running costs, expeditions, conferences, holidays, research, buildings, publications, exhibitions, dance or drama, graduates or undergraduates.

Applications: Send an sae for an information sheet which is now very comprehensive, giving examples of funding, exclusions, dates of trustees meetings and an application form on the reverse side. The foundation only replies to applications it wishes to take further for possible funding.

The Ian Askew Charitable Trust

£21,000 (1993/94)

General

Spectrum House, 20-26 Cursitor Street, London EC4A 1HY
0171-405 2088

Correspondent: Messrs Kidsons Impey

Trustees: J R Rank; Mrs C Pengelley; R A R Askew; R J Wainwright; G B Ackery.

Beneficial area: UK, preference for Sussex, and overseas.

Information available: Full accounts are on file at the Charity Commission.

General: The property owned by the trust includes an SSSI (Site of Special Scientific Interest) and maintenance of this comes out of the trust income. In 1993/94, it had assets of £1.6 million and an income of £74,000.

The trust makes a large number of small grants. In 1993/94, about 150 grants were given totalling £21,000, well over half of which were under £100 and mostly as little as £10. A wide range of charities received support covering medical, welfare, disability, young people, heritage, arts and animal welfare. National and local charities are supported with a preference for Sussex, a few grants also go to overseas charities.

The seven charities which received £1,000 were Glyndebourne Building Appeal, Handicapped Children's Special Needs Trust, Hurstwood Park Neurological Centre, League of Friends Uckfield Hospital, Mental Health Foundation, Princes Trust East Sussex and Ringmer Parochial Church Council.

Applications: In writing to the correspondent.

The Astor Foundation

£127,000 (1993/94)

Medicine, social welfare

5 Northview, Hungerford, Berks
RG17 0DA

Correspondent: Mrs J E Jones, Secretary

Trustees: Sir William Slack; J R Astor; Lord Astor of Hever; Dr H Swanton; R H Astor; C Money-Coutts.

Beneficial area: UK.

Information available: The following information was supplied by the trust.

General: The primary object of the foundation is medical research in its widest sense. Favouring types of research which are being conducted on a broad front in preference to work in too narrow or specialised a field. The foundation are very keen to help give a better quality of life to disabled people. Two examples are Riding for the Disabled and Holidays for the Handicapped. Certain church projects are considered and also some animal appeals.

In 1993/94, the foundation had assets of £2.5 million which generated an income of £121,000. 85 grants totalled £127,000. By far the largest grant was £30,000 to the University College Middlesex School of Medicine (£20,000 to purchase equipment and £10,000 to the Astor Fellowship for postgraduates). Both these are long-term commitments, with similar amounts having been promised for a number of years.

Nine further organisations were promised £1,500 to £20,000 including: Invalids at Home; Help the Hospices; the Samaritans.

The other grants ranged from £1,500 to £3,000. The largest of which were to Help the Hospices, Royal National College for the Blind and the RNLI.

Other beneficiaries included: Animal Health Trust; Astor Theatre, Deal; Changing Faces; Deal Summer Music Festival; Mobility Trust; Peckham Youth Project; Raleigh International; Scottish Wildlife Trust; Jubilee Sailing Trust; Tall Ships Association; World Wide Fund for Nature and Youth Clubs UK.

The priority of the foundation seems to be to support national social welfare and medical charities. Other causes recently supported included the Farming and Wildlife Advisory Group, Tools for Self Reliance and the WWF for Nature. Three cathedral appeals and other local charities were supported, mainly in Kent, but also including Deal Summer Music Festival, Headway Berkshire and Youth Link Northern Ireland.

Although the foundation does not favour tying-up of large amounts in building projects, expenditure on bricks and mortar is not wholly excluded if it should consider this desirable in any particular case.

Exclusions: No grants to individuals and no salaries. Registered charities only. Generally no "bricks and mortar" grants made except in exceptional circumstances.

Applications: There are no deadline dates, applications should be in writing to the correspondent. If the appeal arrives too late for one meeting it will automatically be carried over for consideration for the following. A reply will always be sent irrespective of whether an appeal is successful or not.

The Astor of Hever Trust

£52,000 (1993/94)

General

French Street House, Westerham, Kent
TN16 1PW
01959-562051

Correspondent: Lord Astor of Hever

Trustees: John Jacob; Third Baron Astor of Hever; Irene, Lady Astor of Hever; Hon Philip D P Astor.

Beneficial area: UK, with a preference for Kent and north east Scotland.

Information available: Full accounts are on file at the Charity Commission.

General: The trust gives grants UK-wide and internationally, although it appears to have a preference for Kent. In 1993/94, it had assets of £663,000 and an income of £50,000. Grants totalled £52,000, comprising 21 grants of between £1,000 and £5,000 and 49 grants of between £10 and £500.

£5,000 was given to Ashdown House School Trust and Royal British Legion Industries. The Glydenbourne Appeal and Game Conservancy Trust received £3,000 each. These were two of the largest grants in 1991/92, when they received £7,400 and £5,000 respectively. Other grants of between £2,000 and £3,000 were given to Campaign for Oxford Classics, Canterbury Cathedral Appeal Fund, Commonwealth Press Union, National Asthma Campaign and the Tarland Welfare Trust. Most grants on the list are to well-known national organisations such as RNIB (£50), RNLI (£10), Multiple Sclerosis Society (£50), NSPCC (£400) and two grants to the National Trust (Outridge £1,000 and Scotland £500).

Of the local grants there is a preference for Kent (at least ten of the named areas are in Kent) and the north east of Scotland (at least three grants were given in the Grampian area). About ten grants were given to named churches or cathedrals ranging from £50 to St Paul's Cathedral to £2,250 to Canterbury Cathedral.

Applications: In writing to the correspondent. Applications are not acknowledged.

The Atlantic Foundation

£115,000 (1993/94)

Education, medical, general

7-8 Raleigh Walk, Atlantic Wharf, Cardiff CF1 5LN

Correspondent: Mrs B L Thomas

Trustees: P Thomas; Mrs B L Thomas.

Beneficial area: Worldwide.

Information available: Full accounts are on file at the Charity Commission.

General: In 1993/94, the trust had an income of £115,000 all from covenants. Grants totalled £112,000, categorised by the trust as follows:

- **International appeals and charities** £1,200: £1,000 to Prisoners of Conscience and £200 to Feed the Children.
- **National charities** £15,000: grants were given to the Variety Club of GB and Lord Taverners (£3,500 each); Ivor Novello Statue Appeal, Barry Mind and Harriet Davies Holidays for the Disabled (£1,000 each). Other grants of £100 to £500 were given to 16 other organisations including Children's Hospice, Wales; Weston Spirit; PDSA and Royal National Life Boat Institute.
- **Medical appeals** support £6,000: eight organisations received grants of £250 to £1,000, with most of the money going to Wales-based appeals. The largest was to Aid in Action, others included: Myelin Project; University Hospital Wales; Cystic Fibrosis Trust and Marie Curie.
- **Local authority** support £46,000: restricted to South, West and Mid Glamorgan and Gwent. £37,000 was given for educational support in South Glamorgan. £7,000 was given between the various Social Services.
- **Independent schools and colleges** support increased from £13,000 in 1990/91 to £44,000 in 1993/94. 12 schools were supported, including five which have received regular support recently: Hammond School, Chester (£6,300); Llandovery College (£2,800); Deane Close School, Cheltenham (£2,500); London School of Contemporary Dance (£1,500); Smaller Elmhurst School, Surrey (£850). Other schools to receive large grants were St Cuthberts, Cardiff (£5,000) and London Studio (£1,700). All other grants were for £500 to £1,500 to Cardigan School of Dance, Llandoff Cathedral School, Morley College, Ecole International Theatre and the Laban Centre. Due to such a large portion of the grant total being absorbed by this section, the trustees intend to restrict the amounts of grants given to independent schools and colleges in the future.

There was also a Religious category with one grant of £750 to Albany Road Baptist Church.

Applications: In writing to the correspondent.

The ATP Charitable Trust

£46,000 (1993/94)

Jewish

Heath Cottage, 1 Constable Close, London NW11 6UA
0171-987 5765

Correspondent: M R Bentata, Trustee

Trustees: M R Bentata; J A Bentata; A G A Macfadyen.

Beneficial area: Worldwide.

Information available: Full accounts are on file at the Charity Commission.

General: In 1993/94, the trust had an income of £112,000 including £107,000 from Gift Aid donations. The previous year the income was £170,000 including £160,000 from Gift Aid payments. Grants totalled £46,000 in 1993/94 and £48,000 in 1992/93. The surplus has been used to build up the assets which now stand at £220,000.

15 grants were made in 1993/94, ranging from £350 to £15,500. All but two of the grants were to Jewish organisations with the largest to JPAIME (£15,500), Leo Baeck College (£10,000) and Nightingale House and Youth Aliyah (£5,000 each).

Applications: In writing to the correspondent.

The Aurelius Charitable Trust

£71,000 (1993/94)

Archaeology, history

Kidsons Impey, Spectrum House, 20-26 Curistor Street, London EC4A 1HY
0171-405 2088

Correspondent: P E Haynes

Trustees: W J Wallis; P E Haynes.

Beneficial area: Worldwide.

Information available: Full accounts are on file at the Charity Commission.

General: The assets of the trust have doubled since 1991/92, from £550,000 to £1.1 million in 1993/94. This generated an income of £65,000 and grants totalled £71,000. The trust supports archaeological and historical research. 22 grants were given of which seven were recurrent. Over half the grant total, £30,000 (and £24,000 the previous year) went to the Marc Fitch Fund, concerned with education and research in archaeological and historical studies. £8,000 was given to the British School at Athens (£15,000 in 1992/93).

The other grants ranged from £100 to £5,000. Three universities were supported in each of the last two years: Oxford (£3,000), Leicester (£2,000) and London (£1,000) in 1993/94, Oxford (£4,800), Ioannina (£1,500) and Leeds (£400) in 1992/93. Other beneficiaries included the Council for the Protection of Rural England (£1,000), Huguenot Society (£500), Paper Publications Society (£1,000), Senhouse Museum Trust (£1,500) and the Victorian Society (£4,000).

Applications: In writing to the correspondent.

The Lord Austin Trust

£163,000 (1991)

Social welfare

c/o Martineau Johnson, St Philip's House, St Philip's Place, Birmingham B3 2PP
0121-200 3300

Correspondent: D L Turfrey, Secretary

Trustees: W R Doherty; J M G Fea.

Beneficial area: England, with a special interest in the West Midlands.

Information available: Very brief accounts are on file at the Charity Commission for 1991 and 1988, but the most useful set of recent accounts with a list of grants were for 1985/86.

General: This entry has been compiled from information in the 1991 edition of A Guide to the Major Trusts, since the trust has not replied to correspondence or filed more detailed information with the Charity Commission. The only information updated is the grant total for 1991 of £163,000, taken from the Charity Commission register.

In 1988, the trust held investments with a market value of £1.8 million which generated an income of £126,000.

The trust was established by the will of Lord Austin of Longbridge, the creator of the motor car company of that name, and came into effect following his death in 1941. Although the trustees were given absolute discretion, the following preferences were expressed by Lord Austin in his will as to which institutions should be assisted:

(a) Hospitals and clinics.

(b) Institutions ... where having as their object medical and/or surgical research ...

(c) Institutions having as their object, care, maintenance, education and upbringing of poor children of either sex. In particular.... the claim of Dr Barnardo's Homes and various societies for the relief of waifs and strays.

(d) Institutions having as their object and care of destitute old people.

Following the introduction of the Charities Act 1960, accounts began to be placed on the public file at the Charity Commission. At that time the grants were divided into four categories: children, people, miscellaneous, and research. Many awards were recurrent from year to year and almost all for between £100 and £400, the exceptions being a grant of nearly £1,000 to Barnardo's and £1,000 to the Salvation Army. Many of the organisations being helped then still appear in the 1984/85 lists, though often under updated names. This can be deduced from the lists of grants in the 1985/86 accounts, the most recent on file at the Charity Commission. These are broken down under the following headings:

	Regular	Special
Children and young people:	£16,000	£14,000
Old people:	£9,000	£16,000
Miscellaneous:	£18,000	£16,000

It seems likely that the "regular awards" are in the form of recurrent grants and that the "special awards" represent one-off payments for particular projects.

The regular awards for children and young people, 21 in all, were for £750 each, up from £500 in the previous year. Eleven of the 18 special awards went to the same recipients with additional grants to eight organisations which did not get recurrent awards. The amount of the special awards varied between £500 and £2,000. Although most of the organisations helped are in the West Midlands, grants were also made to North London Rescue Commando, Shaftesbury Homes (a long-standing beneficiary of the trust), and Mansfield House University Settlement. Three organisations are marked as no longer receiving recurrent grants.

The grants for old people were similarly divided with all recurrent grants being for £750. Again, the list includes both West Midlands and national organisations, such as the Alzheimer's Disease Society, which received a "first award" of £1,000.

The miscellaneous heading covers mainly help for sick or disabled people through organisations such as the Midlands Spastic Association, Family Holiday Association and hospices. Two grants, outside the general interest in social welfare, were £2,500 to the Black Country Museum Development Trust and £1,000 to the Avoncroft Museum of Buildings in Bromsgrove.

Exclusions: No grants to individuals.

Applications: In writing with a copy of annual report and accounts, and confirmation of charitable registration.

The Bacta Charitable Trust

£54,000 (1992/93)

Welfare and disaster relief

Bacta House, Regents Wharf, 6 All Saints Street, London N1 9RQ
0171-713 7144

Correspondent: J S White, Clerk to the Trustees

Trustees: Sonia Meaden; Charles Henry; John Bollom; Robert Higgins; Roger Withers, President of Bacta.

Beneficial area: UK.

Information available: The information for this entry was supplied by the trust.

General: The trust only supports charities recommended by Bacta members. Bacta is the Trade Association for the Coin Operated Amusement Industry.

In 1992/93, the trust had an income of £50,000 (from donations) and gave grants totalling £54,000. Major grants were given to the Cancer Relief Macmillan Fund and the Children's Hospice South West. Typically, grants range from £500 to £5,000, but are usually for £2,000. Typical organisations supported by the trust are Mencap, Riding for the Disabled, scout groups and hospitals. Many grants may be recurrent.

Applications: In writing to the correspondent.

The Baker Charitable Trust

£22,000 (1992/93)

Jewish

16 Sheldon Avenue, Highgate, London N6 4JT
0181-340 5970

Correspondent: Dr Harvey Baker

Trustees: Dr A D Baker; Dr H Baker.

Beneficial area: Worldwide.

Information available: Full accounts are on file at the Charity Commission.

General: In 1992/93, the trust had assets of £728,000 and an income of £56,000. Grants totalled £22,000, leaving a surplus of £34,000. The trust appears to be building up its assets, having had a surplus of between £30,000 and £70,000 a year for the last six years.

19 grants were made, all to Jewish causes most of which are regular beneficiaries, including £10,000 to the Jewish Philanthropic Association. Other grants ranged from £100 to £1,500 to regular beneficiaries. The trust states that "grants are restricted to established welfare organisations for the elderly, homeless, the blind, handicapped and deaf. Preference to charities of which the trust has special interest."

Exclusions: No grants to individuals.

Applications: In writing to the correspondent.

The Baltic Charitable Fund

£75,000

General

The Baltic Exchange, 14-20 St Mary Axe, London EC3A 8BH
0171-369 1643

Correspondent: D A Painter

Beneficial area: UK.

Information available: The only accounts on file at the Charity Commission are for 1982/83. The following information was supplied by the trust.

General: In 1994, the trust had an income of £160,000. Grants usually total about £75,000 a year.

The trust gives to a set list of national charities in the fields of education, health, arts, care for the elderly, children in need, churches, life-saving, merchant seafarers' welfare, youth training and armed service charities. There is a preference for appeals connected with seafaring, sailing etc.. £5,000 is also retained for the Lord Mayor's Appeal or a disaster appeal.

Applications: In writing to the correspondent, but note that applications are very unlikely to be successful as the fund supports a set list of charities.

The Barbour Trust

£122,000 (1993/94)

Health and welfare

Saville Chambers, 63 Fowler Street, South Shields, Tyne & Wear NE33 1NS
0191-455 3181

Correspondent: H J Tavroges

Trustees: Mrs Margaret Barbour; Henry Jacob Tavroges; Anthony Glenton.

Beneficial area: Tyneside.

Information available: Full accounts are on file at the Charity Commission.

General: The trust's income comes from shares held in J Barbour & Sons Ltd and £181,000 in a building society account. It is currently accumulating its income, probably to build up a solid asset base. The trust tends to make fairly substantial donations to registered charities appealing for funding for specific projects on Tyneside.

In 1993/94, the trust had an income of £225,000, of which £167,000 was the UK dividend on the company shares. It gave 74 grants totalling £122,000 ranging from £100 to £10,000, predominantly for welfare. The largest were to: Yellow Brick Road (£10,000); South Tyneside Voluntary Project, Minibus (£8,350); Tyne & Wear Foundation (£8,000) and £5,000 each to Barnardo's; Children's Accident and Emergency Service; the Dene Centre; Mental Health Foundation; National Trust for Inner City Project; National Trust; Tyneside Housing Aid Centre and Youth Clubs, Northumbria. Smaller grants were also given to: Body Positive North East, Byker City Farm, Derwentside Women's Aid, Motability NE and South Tyneside Multicultural Project.

Applications: In writing to the correspondent.

Lord Barnby's Foundation

£129,000 (1993/94)

General

c/o Messrs Payne Hicks Beach, 10 New Square, Lincoln's Inn, London WC2A 3QG
0171-242 6041

Correspondent: The Secretary

Trustees: Earl of Westmoreland; Lord Newall; J L Lowther; A O Deas; Sir Michael Farquhar.

Beneficial area: UK.

Information available: Full accounts are on file at the Charity Commission.

General: The foundation holds two funds of varying sizes and relevance to this book – a general fund and an appointed fund (to advance the general interests of the textile industry particularly its scientific and technical aspects). In 1993/94, the general fund had assets of £3 million, an income of £100,000 and gave grants of £129,000. The appointed fund had assets of £124,000 and an income of £5,000, all of which was given to the Textile Institute.

The foundation generally prefers to spread its disbursements broadly over a large number of charitable organisations. In 1993/94, however, the trust gave £30,000 to the Anglo Romanian Education Trust, £15,000 to Rainer Foundation and £10,000 to the Country Trust. Grants of £5,000 each were to: Alone in London; Centrepoint, Soho; St Dunstans and Victim Support, London. 21 grants of £2,000, 11 of £1,000 and 2 for £500 were given to children and youth, medical/disability and services charities such as: Army Benevolent Fund; Barnardo's; British Wheelchairs Sports Foundation; International Spinal Research Trust; NSPCC; SSAFA; Youth Clubs UK and scouts & guides.

Annual grants may still be made to five organisations representing the interests of Polish nationals: the Relief Society for Poles, Polish Institute and Sikorski Museum, Polish Social and Cultural Association Limited, Polish YMCA London Association and the Polish Air Force Association Benevolent Fund.

The rest of the grants included support for large national welfare or heritage organisations.

Exclusions: Registered charities only. No grants to individuals.

Applications: In writing to the correspondent. Applications are usually considered in February, June and October.

The Batchworth Trust

£132,000 (1993/94)

Medical, social welfare, general

33-35 Bellstreet, Reigate, Surrey
RH2 7AW
01737-221311

Correspondent: M Neve, Administrative Executive

Trustees: Lockwell Trustees Ltd.

Beneficial area: Worldwide.

Information available: Full accounts are on file at the Charity Commission.

General: In 1993/94, the trust had assets of £2 million, an income of £153,000 and gave 25 grants totalling £132,000. The main grants were to: Oxfam (£15,000); Prisoners Abroad and Royal Commonwealth Society for the Blind (£10,000 each). 16 grants of £5,000 were made to organisations such as: Bodleian Library; Farm Africa; Heartline Association; Help the Aged; Intermediate Technology and Stepping Stones. A further six grants of £2,500 to £3,000 were also given to organisations such as North London Rescue Commando, PDSA and Spastics Society.

Exclusions: No applications from individuals can be considered.

Applications: In writing to the correspondent.

The Beacon Trust

£29,000 (1993/94)

Christian

2 Tongdean Avenue, Hove, East Sussex
BN3 6TL
01273-552036

Correspondent: G A Stacey

Trustees: Mrs D J Spink; G A Stacey; Miss J M Spink.

Beneficial area: Worldwide.

Information available: Accounts are on file at the Charity Commission, but without a list of grants.

General: The trust's objects are "to advance the Christian faith, relieve poverty and advance education". In 1991/92, the trust had assets of £845,000 generating an income of £84,000. Grants totalled £85,000. The emphasis of the the trust's support is on Christian work overseas, particularly amongst students.

According to the correspondent, the trust had an income of £65,000 in 1993/94, and gave grants totalling only £29,000. We are unsure if the large surplus is due to the trust trying to build up its assets, save for major projects in the future, or if it did not receive enough suitable applications.

Exclusions: Applications from individuals are not considered.

Applications: In writing to the correspondent. The trustees normally meet once a year in December and all applications are generally dealt with at that meeting.

The Beaufort House Trust

£68,000 (1993/94)

Christian, education

Beaufort House, Brunswick Road,
Gloucester GL1 1JZ
01452-528533

Correspondent: John Williscroft, Secretary

Trustees: C Alan McLintock; M R Cornwall-Jones; B V Day.

Beneficial area: UK.

Information available: Full accounts are on file at the Charity Commission.

General: The main aim of the trust "is to promote the Christian religion and to contribute to the funds of charitable institutions". It receives an annual payment (£25,000 in 1992/93 and £65,000 in 1991/92) from Beaufort House Trust Ltd, a company which operates a school fees planning scheme.

In 1992/93, the £25,000 from Beaufort House Trust Ltd was added to the accumulated surplus of £153,000 from previous years. Ten grants were given totalling £65,000. The largest payment was (£35,500) in diocesan educational grants. £16,260 was given for ministry bursary awards and two £4,000 grants to St Albans Cathedral and Kings School Gloucester. There were four grants of £1,000 or £2,000 to St Deiniol's Library, St Williams Foundation, National Waterways Museum, Cathedral and Abbey Church St Albans.

We have also seen the grants list for 1993/94, but not the full accounts. This list showed 11 grants totalling £68,200 which were given to: diocesan educational grants (£36,500); ministry bursary awards (£15,100); Princes Trust Volunteers (£10,000); St Deiniols Library and Headington School (£2,000 each) and St Williams Foundation, York (£1,000). The remaining grants were for £500 or less and were given to: Cheltenham Ladies College; Churchdown School Year Book Fund; Hyde Park Nursery School; North East Ordination Course and Sixteen Choir and Orchestra, Kent.

The trust has stated that it is trying to accumulate a large assets base so it will have more funds available for future projects.

Applications: In writing to the correspondent.

Beauland Ltd

£137,000 (1992/93)

Jewish

4 Cheltenham Crescent, Salford M7 0FE

Correspondent: F Neuman

Trustees: W Neuman; F Neuman; H Neuman; M Friedlander; H Roseman; J Bleir; R Delange; M Neuman; P Neuman; E Neuman; E Henry.

Beneficial area: Worldwide.

Information available: Full accounts are on file at the Charity Commission.

General: In 1992/93, the trust had assets of £805,000 and an income of £170,000. Grants totalled £137,000 all given to Jewish organisations.

The largest grants were to Lakewood Yeshiva (£10,600), Tetz Academy Trust (£10,000), and Merkaz Chinoch Torani and Centre of Jewish Education (both £8,000).

Applications: In writing to the correspondent.

The Bedford Charity (also known as the Harpur Trust)

£240,000 (1993/94)

Education, relief in need and recreation in Bedford and its neighbourhood

101 Harpur Centre, Bedford MK40 1PJ
01234-342424; Fax: 01234-273174

Correspondent: D Wigan, Clerk

Trustees: The Governing Body consists of the Mayor of Bedford and the MP for North Bedfordshire; four university nominations; the nominees of the teaching staff and parents of the trust's four schools; eight co-opted trustees; two representatives from Bedford Borough Council and four from Bedfordshire County Council. The Chairman is Professor C J Constable.

Beneficial area: Bedford and its neighbourhood in Bedfordshire.

Information available: Accounts are on file at the Charity Commission.

General: A new Trust Scheme was sealed in November 1988, giving the objects of:
- Promotion of education
- Relief of the elderly, sick and poor
- Provision of facilities for recreation and leisure for residents of the area of benefit.

The trust owns and administers four independent schools in Bedford with a total pupil roll of 4,300. It also owns or has responsibility for 64 almshouses and flats and distributes grants to a wide range of individuals and institutional projects.

A recent annual report stated "The economic recession persisted throughout the year, hurting the balance sheet, endowment income and parents ability to pay school fees. Interest rates continued to fall during the year, but remained high in real terms. Steps are being taken to limit this exposure in the medium term period."

In 1993/94, the turnover for the main charity was £21 million. The trust has decided to gradually diversify its endowment, well over 90% of which lies in property, bringing £2.8 million rental income and total income of £3.55 million. After estate, centre management and schools' administration costs, £1.89 million was available for distribution. £1.6 million was awarded in Harpur Bursaries towards fees at the trust's four schools.

The charity made 348 grants during the year, 289 of which were to individuals. Of the institutional grants 25 went to recreational projects; 22 for education and 12 on relief. The £240,000 distributed was broken down as follows:

Education: £112,000 for:
Grants to maintained schools for science, technology, music, art, educational visits etc. £13,000;
Further education £24,000;
Post graduate education £24,000;
John Bunyan School – language laboratory equipment £9,000;
Rainbow Special School £10,000;
Development Projects – Disability Arts, Bedford City Council for environmental education and Bedford MENCAP (£5,000 each);
Headway (£12,000);
Others (£14,000).

Relief: £62,000 in grants to:
Youth Action, Bedford (£16,000);
St Mark's Church Hall (£12,000);
Christian Family Care (£10,000);
Others (£24,000).

Recreation: £62,000 in grants to:
Bedford Hockey Club (£20,000);
Duke of Edinburgh Scheme (£6,500);
Bedford Schools Sailing Association (£3,000);
WRVS Children's Holidays (£1,000);
Others (£31,000).

There was also a special grant to Bedford School (£5,000).

Exclusions: No grants to organisations or individuals outside the borough of Bedford.

Applications: In writing to the correspondent.

The Beit Trust

£1,824,000 (1993)

Work in Zimbabwe, Malawi & Zambia; general

5b Chobham Road, Woking, Surrey GU21 1HX
01483-772575

Correspondent: Brigadier C L G Henshaw

Trustees: Sir Alan Munro; Lady Beit; Lord Blake; Sir Cosmo Haskard; R A C Byatt; Prof J G G Ledingham.

Beneficial area: Zimbabwe, Malawi, Zambia.

Information available: Full accounts are on file at the Charity Commission.

General: In 1993, the trust had assets of £53 million and an income of £2 million. Grants totalling £1.8 million were given to hospitals, medical centres, secondary schools, colleges, libraries, animal conservation and specialist trusts. Special grants of over £75,000 were made to Ranfurly Library Service, the Beit Memorial Fellowship for Medical Research and for schemes to provide book packs for schools and medical institutions. Since 1989, the trust has made substantial grants for the conservation and protection of the endangered Black Rhino in conjunction with the World Wide Fund for Nature.

Nearly all grants are given in Zimbabwe, Malawi or Zambia. The 1993 grants categories were as follows:

Zimbabwe	£480,000
Malawi	£256,000
Zambia	£649,000
Rhino Conservation Fund	£256,000
General grants	£196,000

These included:

Book packs for schools	£80,000
Contingency Fund	£34,000
IMPACT Foundation	£5,000
Trust brochure	£2,000

The trust awards ten postgraduate fellowships to students from its beneficial area for PhD or MSc degrees at universities in the UK or Eire. Total annual expenditure on such fellowships is about £360,000.

Applications: In writing to the correspondent.

The Belvedere Trust

£68,000 (1993/94)

Housing and related community initiatives in south London

Rochester House, 2-10 Belvedere Road, London SE19 2HL
0181-768 1990

Correspondent: Kevin Ireland, Director

Trustees: Gillian Davies, Chair; Peter Deakins; Margaret Hall; Elizabeth Hannan; John Howes; Robina Rafferty.

Beneficial area: South London.

Information available: Full accounts are on file at the Charity Commission.

General: In 1993/94, the trust's income was £161,000, most of which was the last Gift Aid donation from Crystal Palace Housing Association. As a result the source of income for the trust has ceased and only limited funds remain available for distribution. Between May 1984 and September 1994, the trust gave over 200 grants totalling over £430,000. The annual grant budget has been between £65,000 and £110,000.

It is unlikely that any funds will be allocated beyond the end of September 1995. This is a great pity because it has been an exemplary grant-maker, providing detailed information in an accessible form.

During 1994 and 1995, the trust has supported a feasibility study and initial development work in relation to the establishment of a community foundation in south east London. It is anticipated that the South East London Community Foundation, encompassing the London boroughs of Greenwich, Lambeth, Lewisham and Southwark, will be established by the middle of 1995. Further information about the foundation will be available from the Director of the Belvedere Trust.

Exclusions: No grants to individuals, general appeals, academic research, or areas outside London.

Applications: The trust may no longer have any funds available for distribution by October 1995. Applicants should in the first instance contact the Director to determine whether or not the trust is able to make any grants, and if the work fits within the trust's grant programmes. An application form will then be sent, as appropriate.

Trustees meet four times a year in March, June, September and December. Completed application forms must be received by specific deadlines in advance of trust meetings, in order to allow time for consultation and visits.

Benfield Motors Charitable Trust

£65,000 (1992/93)

Christian, poverty, sickness, elderly

Newcastle Business Park, Newcastle-upon-Tyne NE4 7YD

Correspondent: Mrs L Squires

Trustees: John Squires; Malcolm Squires; Stephen Squires.

Beneficial area: Worldwide with a preference for the North East.

Information available: Full accounts are on file at the Charity Commission.

General: This trust has been supported by a deed of covenant from Addison Motors of £50,000 a year for four years from 1989. In 1992/93, the trust had an income of £58,000 and gave grants totalling £65,000.

Grants are given mainly to health and welfare and Christian charities, with a range of other charities also supported. Over half the grants were given in the North East. The main grants, of £1,000 to £15,000, were given to: Yellow Brick Road (£15,000); Delavel Road School Minibus and Tyne & Wear Foundation (£10,000 each); RNIB (£5,800); Marie Curie Foundation and Wallsend Health Centre Minibus (£5,000 each).

Grants of £1,000 to £3,000 were given to British Heart Foundation, British Red Cross, Northern Association of Boys Clubs, Save the Children and Tyneside Cyrenians. There were 48 other grants of £600 or less, mostly for £100 or less and included: Belmont Methodist Church; Byker Festival; Help Poland Fund; Riding Mill Drama Club and Tidy Britain Group.

Applications: In writing to the correspondent.

The Benham Charitable Settlement

£127,000 (1993/94)

Youth, general, especially in Northants

Hurstbourne, Portnall Drive, Virginia Water, Surrey GU25 4NR

Correspondent: Mrs M Tittle, Managing Trustee

Trustees: Mrs M M Tittle; Mrs R A Nickols; Edward D D'Alton; Philip Schofield; E N Langley.

Beneficial area: UK, with a special emphasis on Northamptonshire.

Information available: Full accounts are on file at the Charity Commission, together with a narrative report.

General: The settlement was founded in 1964 by the late Cedric Benham and his wife Hilda, both then resident in Northampton, "to benefit charities and for divers' good causes and considerations".

"The trust's policy is to make a substantial number of relatively small grants to registered charities working in many different fields – including charities involved in medical research, disability and handicap, elderly people, children and young people, the disadvantaged, overseas aid, missions to seamen, the welfare of ex-servicemen, wildlife, the environment, education and the arts. The trust also supports the Church of England, and the work of Christian mission throughout the world. Special emphasis is placed upon those churches and charitable organisations within the county of Northamptonshire."

In 1993/94, the settlement had assets at cost value of £1.8 million which generated an income of £137,000. Over 250 grants were made, mostly ranging from £100 to £500. By far the largest (£70,000) once again went to the Northamptonshire Association of Youth Clubs, donations to which have totalled more than £1.5 million to date "specifically for the purchase of a freehold site at King's Park, Northampton, and then to facilitate the financing and construction of an indoor sports arena there. This indoor centre is in strong demand at local, regional and national level and it has established a centre of excellence for sport and the performing arts, attempting to serve these young people who are most in need of such facilities." The trustees plan to give continued support to this project.

Other large grants were given to the Lambeth Fund (£5,000), Holy Trinity, Sunningdale (£2,000) and Northampton Symphony Orchestra (£1,000), all of which have received grants in previous years. £1,000 was also given to London Christian Radio.

Exclusions: No grants to individuals.

Applications: In writing to the correspondent. The trust regrets that it cannot send replies to all applicants, nor will they accept telephone calls. "Applications will be dealt with promptly at any time of year (no application forms necessary), but **no charity will be considered more than once each year** (repeated applications are automatically ignored for twelve months)."

The Bernerd Foundation

£189,000 (1991/92)

Arts, Jewish charities, general

c/o Goodman Derrick, 90 Fetter Lane, London EC4 1EQ
0171-404 0606; Fax: 0171-831 6407

Correspondent: Ian Montrose

Trustees: Ian Montrose; Kenneth Posner; Margaret Fielding.

Beneficial area: UK and overseas.

Information available: Accounts are on file at the Charity Commission up to those for 1991/92.

General: The foundation was established by Elliott Bernerd in 1984. Its 1991/92 accounts show it to be completely reliant on regular donations from the founder (£200,000 in 1989/90 and in 1990/91 and £53,000 in 1991/92) who, unusually, is not one of its trustees. Its assets had fallen into a deficit of £76,000 by April 1992.

In 1991/92, 10 grants totalling £189,000 were given. This contrasted with nearly 30 grants totalling £280,000 given in the previous year. About half the organisations supported each year were specifically Jewish. The major beneficiary recently has been the London Philharmonic Trust (£75,000 in the previous two years). Other large grants were given to the Lubavitch Foundation (£33,430 with £42,000 in the previous year), the Institute of Family Therapy (£30,000) and Help the Aged (£20,000).

The correspondent stated that the foundation's "level of activity is somewhat lower than in previous years, but it is perfectly possible that its activities will increase in current and future years".

Applications: In writing to the correspondent.

Besom Foundation

£51,000 (1993/94)

General

42 Burlington Road, London W4 4BE
0181-742 1779

Correspondent: Mrs H L Odgers

Trustees: James R B Odgers; Fiona J Ruttle, John M E Scott

Beneficial area: Worldwide.

Information available: Full accounts on file at the Charity Commission.

General: The charity was set up in 1987. Its slogan is "Sweep away Suffering – Fund the Future". It stresses that it is a service for donors first and foremost. It therefore seeks to find projects in areas which they have identified. The foundation will only consider requests which are for small items of expenditure which help a group of people to help themselves. Applicant charities should be either very small or just starting up. The foundation prefers projects which are very much at grass roots level.

In 1993/94, the trust had an income of £61,000, of which £60,000 was received in donations. 25 grants were given totalling £51,000, 21 of which were for £1,500 to £4,000 and four were for less than £1,500.

The largest grant in both 1992/93 and 1993/94 was to: Happy Child – for the materials required to build a warehouse on a farm in Belo Horizonte, Brazil to give ex-street children indoor space to learn vocational skills. Other large grants were for a children's home in Poland, Acorns Children's Hospice, Bethany Christian Trust, Child-to-Child, Co-operation for Development, Institute of Urology in Pakistan, Mighty Gully in Jamaica, Northampton Christian Centre Trust Shaftesbury Society and Thomas Street Methodist Church.

In 1992/93, the trust also supported: Addictive Disease Trust – for equipment for a chemical dependency programme at HMP Downview, Surrey, to treat up to 170 addicts. If successful the Home Office will help fund similar programmes in other prisons across the country; Busoga Trust - for a "down the hole" hammer hand drill for building wells in Uganda, to help bring fresh, clean water to all 1.5 million people in Busoga by 1994. The other larger grants were made to: Kerala Balagram; Leeds Methodist Mission; Pot Green Comminty Trust; Prisoners Abroad; Spastics Society; Tropical Health Trust; Wellspring Trust.

Exclusions: No grants for salaries, training or running costs or towards relief work.

Applications: In writing to the correspondent, with as much relevant detail as possible.

Mr Thomas Betton's Charity (Educational)

£85,000 (1993/94)

Church of England or Church in Wales schools

Ironmongers' Hall, Barbican, London EC2Y 8AA
0171-606 2725

Correspondent: The Clerk of the Worshipful Company of Ironmongers

Trustees: Worshipful Company of Ironmongers.

Beneficial area: Greater London, England and Wales.

Information available: Full accounts are on file at the Charity Commission.

General: In 1993/94, the trust had assets of £332,000, an income of £106,000 and gave grants totalling £85,000.

One quarter of the income has to be given to the London Schools Fund. The remaining money appears to be distributed between the England & Wales School Fund, some individual schools and Betton's Charity for Pensions and Relief in need (*see A Guide to Grants for Individuals in Need*).

Applications: In writing to the correspondent.

The Mason Bibby 1981 Trust

£66,000 (1993/94)

Welfare, especially elderly

Rathbone Brothers & Co Ltd, Port of Liverpool Building, Pierhead, Liverpool L3 1NW

Correspondent: Mrs D M Fairclough

Trustees: B A Jones; Dr H M Bibby; K A Allan; J B Bibby; C L Bibby; J P Wood; Mrs D M Fairclough.

Beneficial area: UK, especially Merseyside.

Information available: Full accounts are on file at the Charity Commission.

General: The priority of the trust is to support employees and pensioners in need of J Bibby & Sons plc and associated companies. The trust also supports charities, particularly those concerned with welfare and the elderly, with a preference for Merseyside.

In 1993/94, the trust had assets of £1.33 million and an income of £60,000. Grants totalled £82,000 including £16,000 to pensioners and employees. 48 grants were made to organisations with the largest to Lasers for Life Trust (£10,000), Liverpool Personal Service Society and Age Concern Liverpool (both £5,000), Age Concern Wirral (£3,500) and the Salvation Army (£2,000). Most grants were for £1,000 or £500 including 11 grants to hospices, mostly in Merseyside, but also one in Leeds and one in the Midlands. About 80% of the grants were recurrent.

Applications: In writing to the correspondent.

The Billmeir Charitable Trust

£73,000 (1993/94)

Relief of pain or sickness, general in Surrey

1 Snow Hill, London EC1A 2EN
0171-248 4499

Correspondent: T T Cripps, Accountant

Trustees: B C Whitaker; F C E Telfer; M R Macfadyen.

Beneficial area: UK, with a preference for the Surrey area, specifically Elstead, Tilford, Farnham and Frensham.

Information available: Full accounts are on file at the Charity Commission.

General: Although the trust's main areas of work are the relief of pain or sickness, it also supports general charities in Surrey, especially the Farnham, Frensham, Elstead and Tilford areas.

In 1993/94, the trust's assets had a book value of £679,000 and a market value of £1.7 million. It had a net income of £66,000 and gave 25 grants totalling £72,500.

The two largest grants, of £6,000, were to the United Reform Church and Parochial Church Council of St James, both in Elstead. Most other grants were also to charities in Surrey such as Elstead Community Association (£5,000), Reed School, Cobham (£5,000) and Guildford Laser Appeal (£2,000). Woodlarks Campsite Trust and Woodlarks Workshop both received £3,000. Tilford Parochial Church Council and Tilford Voluntary Trust both received £2,000.

Other grants were given to the RNLI (£5,000), British Home for Incurables and Redgrave Theatre (both £3,000), Arundel Castle Cricket Foundation (£2,000), Old Kilne Museum Trust (£1,500), Campaign for Oxford Trust Fund and National Star Centre for Disabled Youth (both £1,000).

Generally grants range from £1,000 to £5,000, but grants of £500 were given to Farnham District Scouts and the Waverley Singers. 18 of the recipients received a similar size grant the previous year and many have been supported over a number of years.

Applications: In writing to the correspondent.

The Peter Birse Charitable Trust

£114,000 (1993/94)

Health and welfare

Birse Group plc, Humber Road, Barton-on-Humber, South Humberside DN18 5BW
01652-633222

Correspondent: Linda Clark, Secretary to the Chairman

Trustees: Peter Birse; Helen Birse; John Lishman.

Beneficial area: Worldwide.

Information available: Full accounts are on file at the Charity Commission.

General: In 1993/94, the trust had assets of £761,000 (half the assets are held in the Birse Group plc and have a market value of £388,000). The income was £64,000 and donations totalled £114,000. The trust saw a large fall in assets which had risen to about £1.5 million in 1991/92. During that year £1 million was given to the Foundation for Conductive Education, leaving assets at a reduced level.

An interesting note to the accounts states "during the year, due to a legal action brought against the Foundation for Conductive Education by the PETO Institute, Hungary, the capital donation of £1 million made by the trust in 1991/92 was repaid with interest of £118,000. The legal action was settled, also during the year, and the original capital donation and the interest were returned to the Foundation for Conductive Education shortly before the year end".

The main grants in 1993/94 were to: St Lukes Hospice (£60,000); Dove House and St Andrew's Hospice (£10,000 each); St Luke's School (£5,300 for a hydrotherapy pool) and MRI Scanner Appeal and Multiple Sclerosis Society (£2,000 each). There were 20 grants of £1,000 and 11 under £1,000, given to organisations such as: Action Aid; Children's Cancer Fund; Handicapped Children's Action Group; Hull Community Care Scheme; Society for the Autistically Handicapped and the Welsh Centre for Conductive Education.

In 1991/92, the income of the trust was £188,000 and grants totalled £137,000. The Foundation for Conductive Education received a further £50,000 grant from the trust's income account. Other large grants included £10,000 each to the Bangladesh Disaster Appeal, Dove House Hospice, Martin House Hospice and St Andrews Hospice. £5,000 grants went to each of the Kerland Foundation, Neuromuscular Centre and Scunthorpe Health Authority for children's play equipment.

22 of the remaining 30 grants were for £1,000, four for £2,000 and four for £600 or less. Virtually all the grants were to health and welfare charities, mostly national, with a preference for those concerned with children. A few grants were given to local organisations with a preference for Humberside.

Applications: In writing to the correspondent.

Michael Bishop Foundation

£111,000 (1990/91)

General

British Midland, Donington Hall, Castle Donington, Nr Derby DE74 2SB
01332-854000

Correspondent: Mrs R A Mellors, Secretary to the Chairman

Trustees: Grahame N Elliott; John T Wolfe; Peter H T Mimpriss; John S Coulson.

Beneficial area: Worldwide, preference for the Midlands.

Information available: Accounts on file at the Charity Commission, although without the usual grants list and without a narrative report.

General: Sir Michael Bishop of British Midland set up the foundation in 1987 by giving almost £1 million of shares in Airlines of Britain (Holdings) plc, the parent company of British Midland. A further sum was given in 1992. Apparently, it is "his personal foundation" and he gives to "charities he's particularly interested in".

In 1990/91, the foundation had an income of £93,000 and grants totalled £111,000. The majority of the foundation's income has been committed to the the D'Oyly Carte Opera Trust to maintain the active operation of the opera company, of which the foundation is a principal sponsor. In 1992, 20 other organisations were supported, primarily in Birmingham and the Midlands.

Exclusions: Due to the long term commitment to the D'Oyly Carte Opera Trust, the foundation is unable to support new applicants at the present time.

Applications: To the correspondent in writing, but note the above comments.

The Black Charitable Trusts

£135,000 (1992/93)

Evangelical Christianity, social welfare, young people

6 Leopold Road, London SW19 7BD
0181-947 1041

Correspondent: M B Pilcher, Secretary

Trustees: Lady D J Black; A W Black; K R Crabtree; Mrs J D Crabtree.

Beneficial area: UK.

Information available: Accounts are filed at the Charity Commission but since 1983/84 without schedules of donations.

General: There is no up to date information on the policies of these trusts. In the past a brief report preceding the annual accounts stated that the Cyril Black Charitable Trust provides assistance to religious bodies and charities; the Edna Black Charitable Trust provides support for evangelism; the Sydney Black Charitable Trust provides assistance to youth organisations. All the directors are the same and the trusts all share the same administration.

The total income of the three trusts in 1992/93 was £288,000, with grants totalling only £135,000, down from the exceptionally high total of £682,000 in 1990/91.

The Cyril W Black Charitable Trust

In 1992/93, the trust had assets of £1.3 million, and an income of £136,000 which included sundry donations of £56,000, whilst the rest derived from interest from two company holdings – CWB Finance Company Limited of which the trust holds the entire ordinary share capital and Bramham Dealing Company Limited in which it owns a 28% share, plus some bank deposit interest. £54,000 was distributed in donations, but no list of grants was included with the accounts, and therefore it can only be guessed that the trust continues to give mainly for evangelical purposes to both national and local charities.

In 1983/84, the most recent year for which there is any information, the trust gave 250 grants, most for £100 or less. The largest grants were to the Baptist Union of Southern Africa Fundraising Committee (£12,000); Spurgeons College (£7,000); Trinity Trust (£2,000); Church Council on Alcohol and Drugs (£1,500); Care Trust and the Prophetic Ward Ministries (£1,250 each). A number of other evangelical purposes and some small social welfare grants were also made.

The Edna Black Charitable Trust

In 1992/93, the trust had assets of £830,000 and an income of £100,000, just over half of which is a covenanted donation from Leopold Properties Ltd. £55,000 was distributed on "donations and charitable disbursements".

Unfortunately, there is no grants list filed so it is again impossible to see who has benefited from these donations.

The Sydney Black Charitable Trust Ltd

This trust also receives 50% of the profits of Leopold Properties Ltd. In 1992/93, the total income was £52,000 and grants totalled £44,000.

Again, only ancient beneficiaries can be shown. These included Merton and Morden Boys Clubs (£55,000), Wimbledon Parochial Church Council (£2,500) and Holmhurst Lunches Club (£1,000).

Applications: The three trusts operate as one. Applications in writing to the correspondent.

The Bertie Black Foundation

About £80,000 (1992/93)

Jewish

3rd Floor, Beacon House, 15 Christchurch Road, Bournemouth, Dorset BH1 3LP
01202-558484

Correspondent: S J Jones

Trustees: I B Black; D Black; H S Black; I R Broido.

Beneficial area: UK, Israel.

Information available: Full accounts are on file at the Charity Commission.

General: In 1992/93, the trust had assets of £2.1 million and an income of £306,000. The trust has had a regular surplus of income over expenditure and appears to be building up its assets.

Around 90 grants were given only about 10 of which were for over £500. The four main beneficiaries were the Spiro Institute for the Study of Jewish History & Culture (two grants totalling £13,000); Jewish Care (£10,000); Child Resettlement Fund (two grants totalling £7,500) and Association of Jewish Ex-Servicemen and Women (£6,000). Small grants of £10 to £200 were given to non-Jewish organisations.

Applications: In writing to the correspondent.

The Harry & Esther Black Foundation

£103,000 (1993/94)

Jewish

3rd Floor, Beacon House, 15 Christchurch Road, Bournemouth, Dorset BH1 3LB

Correspondent: S J Jones

Trustees: I B Black; S Marks; Mrs H Marks; D L Marks.

Beneficial area: UK.

Information available: Full accounts are on file at the Charity Commission.

General: In 1993/94, the trust had a regular income of £14,000 and a further £123,000 surplus on the sale of property and investments. Grants totalled £103,000 with all 11 grants going to Jewish organisations.

JPAIME was the main beneficiary receiving two grants totalling £80,000. Other large grants went to the Home for Aged Jews (£10,000) and the Hannah Levy House Trust and Manchester Jewish Social Services (both £5,000).

The previous year grants totalled £107,000 from an income of £75,000 which included donations from the H & S Marks Foundation and the B Black Foundation of £25,000 each. JPAIME was again the main beneficiary receiving a total of £100,000.

Applications: In writing to the correspondent.

Sir Alec Black's Charity

£30,000 (1992/93)

Bedding for people who are sick or poor

Messrs R N Store & Co, 17-19 Osborne Street, Grimsby, South Humberside DN31 1HA
01472-348311

Correspondent: Stuart Wilson, Partner

Trustees: G H Taylor; J N Harrison; S Wilson; P A Mounfield.

Beneficial area: UK.

Information available: Full accounts are on file at the Charity Commission.

General: The object of the charity of relevance to this Guide is the "purchase of bed linen and down pillows of the finest quality and their distribution".

In 1992/93, the trust had assets of £640,000 an income of £65,000 and gave grants for the purpose above totalling £30,000 (£51,000 out of an income of £63,000 in 1991/92).

In 1991/92, grants were given in the form of pillowcases (997 pairs), sheets (1,114 pairs) and duvet covers (310). 29 organisations (hospitals, homes and hospices) throughout the UK benefited.

The trust is also able to help sick, poor fishermen of Grimsby.

Applications: In writing to the correspondent. The trustees meet twice yearly in May and November.

The Isabel Blackman Foundation

£76,000 (1993/94)

General, especially in the Hastings area

Stonehenge, 13 Laton Road, Hastings, East Sussex TN34 2ES
01424-431756

Correspondent: A K Vint, Secretary to the Managing Trustees

Trustees: W W Ayling; R A Vint; R T Mennell; D J Jukes; Mrs M Haley.

Beneficial area: UK, but grants are practically all confined to organisations in the Hastings area.

Information available: Full accounts are on file at the Charity Commission.

General: Isabel Blackman was born in Hastings in 1893 and lived there until her death in 1973. Her father had been a successful coal merchant in Hastings and took an active part in the affairs of the area as Councillor, Alderman, five times Mayor and Baron of the Clique Ports. He was always mindful of the needs of those less fortunate than himself. His daughter inherited his wealth and set up the trust in 1966, with several aims:

- Advancing and improving "education and social well-being"
- The relief of sickness and the improvement of health
- The care and comfort of the aged
- Youth organisations
- Furtherance of the Christian religion.

Isabel was more inclined to give help to those who could demonstrate they were in the process of helping themselves, the trustees follow these precepts.

In 1993/94, the trust had a gross income of £199,000, had administration expenses of £18,000 and gave £76,000 in grants. No further information was available for this year.

In 1992/93, it had assets worth £3.1 million. These produced £186,000 of income, £88,000 of which was distributed in grants, £95,000 promises and a further £30,000 in administration costs. The list of promises included: St Michael's Hospice (£50,000); Hastings Volutary Association for the Blind (£10,000); Friends Holy Trinity Church, League of Friends, Pinehill and Mount Denys (£5,000 each); Hastings MIND (£4,000) and £2,000 each to: Brede Methodist Church; Hastings & District Scout Council; Phoenix House Housing Association, Hastings CAB and an individual. All other grants were for £100 to £1,000. Most grants were to Hastings based organisations.

Applications: In writing to the correspondent. The trustees meet bi-monthly to consider applications.

The Blair Foundation

£160,000 (1993/94)

Jewish, general

Smith & Williamson, Onslow Bridge Chambers, Bridge Street, Guildford, Surrey GU1 4RA
01483-302200

Correspondent: Graham Healy

Trustees: Robert Thornton; Jennifer Thornton; Graham Healy; Alan Thornton.

Beneficial area: UK and overseas.

Information available: Full accounts are on file at the Charity Commission.

General: The foundation was set up by Robert Thornton, of Blair House, Ayrshire, in 1989. Although the correspondent appears to want to broaden the trusts' charitable giving from mainly Jewish organisations to general charities, the annual report for 1993/94 states the trusts' aim "continues to be to assist British and Jewish charities in approximately equal shares and in particular to further the case of improved relations between Arab and Jew. The funding of the foundation is due to remain at at least £120,000 per annum including tax refunds".

For the first four years of operation the trust received income from a covenant, this ended in 1993. In 1993/94, the trust had assets of £181,000 of which £153,000 was in the form of Bradford & Bingley shares. The income for the year was £188,000 including a Gift Aid donation of £112,500 net. Grants totalled £160,000.

Grant totals have fluctuated: £289,000 in 1990/91, £164,000 in 1991/92, £205,000 in 1992/93.

30 grants were made ranging from £5 to £50,000. About one third of the grants were to Jewish organisations and five were given to organisations based in Scotland. £95,000 was accounted for by two grants: £50,000 to JPAIME and £45,000 to Hebrew University/Weizman Institute Foundation. A further £15,000 went to British Friends of Shenkar College. All these organisations received similar scale grants in previous years.

Other grants were up to £5,000 including those to Sense (£5,000), Ayrshire Wildlife Series (£2,500), National Trust for Scotland (£2,000), Radio Lollipop and Dailly Football Club (both £1,500), Live Music Now! Wales (£1,000) and the Friends of Peel Castle (£250).

Applications: To the correspondent in writing. The correspondent did not want to be included in this guide: "... I have been inundated with appeals for help, which far exceed the resources available...the costs of administration are now becoming disproportionate to the funds available".

The Neville & Elaine Blond Charitable Trust

£97,000 (1993/94)

Jewish, education, general

c/o H W Fisher & Co, Chartered Accountants, Acre House, 11-15 William Road, London NW1 3ER
0171-388 7000

Correspondent: Jullian Challis, Partner

Trustees: Dame S R Prendergast; Peter Blond; Mrs A E Susman; S N Susman.

Beneficial area: Worldwide.

Information available: Accounts are on file at the Charity Commission, but no list of grants is included for 1993/94.

General: In 1993/94, the trust had an income of £75,000 and grants totalled £97,000. Unfortunately no grants list was available.

There were full and complete accounts for 1992/93 which showed the trust had assets of £2 million and an income of £83,000. It gave 25 grants totalling £78,000. The main grants were to JPAIME (£30,000); CBF World Jewish Relief (£10,000); Battle of Britain Memorial Fund (£6,250) and £5,000 each to WIZO and the Weizman Institute Foundation. All other grants were for £500 to £3,000. The only ones which were not specifically Jewish were Age Concern, Macmillan Nurse Appeal, Royal College of Surgeons and Westminster Children's Society (£1,000 each) and Royal Opera House (£500).

The trust has, over a number of years, built up a surplus of £147,000. It is not known if this money will be used to build up a larger endowment or if it will be distributed to charities at a later date.

Exclusions: Only registered charities are supported.

Applications: In writing to the correspondent.

The Bluston Charitable Settlement

£76,000 (1991/92)

Jewish, general

Flat 8, 40 Chester Square, London SW1W 9HT
0171-935 4499

Correspondent: Edward Langton

Trustees: Edward Langton; Mrs L E Bluston; M D Paisner.

Beneficial area: Mostly UK.

Information available: Full accounts are on file at the Charity Commission up to 1991/92.

General: In 1991/92, the trust had assets of £149,000 and an income of £95,000. 53 organisations received grants totalling £76,000. The three largest were £25,000 to Jewish Care and £5,000 each to the Variety Club of Great Britain and the Jewish Home & Hospital at Tottenham.

£2,000 grants were given to each of the Family Welfare Association, Norwood Child Care, CBF World Jewish Relief and the Friends of Akim.

Applications: In writing to the correspondent. The trustees meet annually in March.

The Bohm Foundation

£47,000 (1993/94)

General

Messrs Bristows, Cooke & Carpmael Solicitors, 10 Lincoln's Inn Fields, London WC2A 3BP
0171-435 5660

Correspondent: D Graham

Trustees: Dorothy Bohm; Charles Green; Louis Bohm.

Beneficial area: Worldwide.

Information available: Full accounts are on file at the Charity Commission for 1993/94.

General: The trust has seen an increase in its income in 1993/94 compared to previous years, arising principally from the receipt of substantial royalty payments under an agreement assigned to the foundation. As a result the trustees have made several grants, but have also retained surplus income in excess of £30,000, in anticipation of further payments in 1994/95.

In 1993/94, the trust had assets of £179,000 and income of £79,000. It gave four grants totalling £47,000. The Photographer's Gallery received most of the grant total, £44,000, to refurbish its premises. The other grants went to Charles Green Foundation (£2,000), Broadlands Pre-school Play Centre (£750) and the Hillel Foundation (£500).

Applications: In writing to the correspondent.

The Boltons Trust

£154,000 (1991/92)

Social welfare, medicine, education

44a New Cavendish Street, London
W1M 7LG
0171-486 4663

Correspondent: Clive Marks

Trustees: Clive Marks; Henry B Levin; Mrs C Albuquerque.

Beneficial area: UK.

Information available: Full accounts are on file at the Charity Commission up to 1991/92.

General: The trust was set up in 1967 by Charlotte Bernstein, and until 1973 it bore her name. Her endowment was 83,000 shares in Granada plc, and these still make up a sizeable proportion of the trust's current £2.4 million assets. It is a "sister trust" to the Lord Ashdown Charitable Trust and Leigh Trust (*see entries in A Guide to the Major Trusts – Volume 1*) with whom it shares the same offices and correspondent.

In 1991/92, the trust had assets of £2.2 million, an income of £120,000 and gave 11 grants worth £154,000. Some recipients have received grants from the trust over a number of years. Several of the organisations reflect the trust's concern with family life. Unusually for a trust in this Guide, few grants are given, but nearly all are very substantial, with the largest to the Global Health Foundation (£75,000). The other beneficiaries were the City University and Jewish Childs Day (£15,000 each); Bayswater Hotel Homeless Project, Friends of Yeshiva Hamvitar and the Jerusalem Foundation (£10,000 each); London College of Music (£6,000); Psychosynthesis Educational Trust (£5,600); Victoria Community Centre (£5,000), Lubavitch Foundation (£2,000) and Community Links (£500).

Applications: The trust is unlikely to support applicants not already known to the trustees. Applications are considered four times a year in February, May, August and November.

The Charlotte Bonham-Carter Charitable Trust

£53,000 (1993/94)

General, particularly in Hampshire

66 Lincoln's Inn Fields, London
WC2A 3LH
0171-242 2022

Correspondent: Sir Matthew Farrer

Trustees: Sir Matthew Farrer; Norman Bonham-Carter; Nicholas Wickham-Irving.

Beneficial area: UK, with emphasis on Hampshire

Information available: Full accounts are on file at the Charity Commission.

General: From the trust's establishment in 1985 until the death of the settlor in 1989, the assets were nominal. However, the execution of her will saw the residue of her estate (around £1 million) wholly placed in the hands of the trust.

Though the trust's objects are general, annual grants to the National Heritage Memorial Fund and the National Trust are both incorporated in the outline. The trustees state that donations are made to "those charities with which Lady Bonham-Carter was particularly associated during her life or had a particular interest in, with an emphasis on Hampshire".

In 1993/94, the trust had assets of £2.3 million and an income of £503,000, of which £400,000 was received from the estate of Dame Charlotte Helen Bonham-Carter. Further funds of about £120,000 are yet to be assigned to the trust. Expenses were only £17,000 and 21 grants were given totalling £53,000.

The main grants were £7,500 to the Royal Academy Trust and £5,000 each to Fitzwilliam Museum, Hampshire County Council, Koestler Award Trust and the Tate Gallery. Other donations were given to general charities working in music, heritage and archaeology. There were nine medium-sized grants of £1,000.

Exclusions: No grants to individuals.

Applications: In writing to the correspondent, but note that the trustees are not anxious to receive unsolicited general applications as these are unlikely to be successful and only increase the cost of administration of the charity.

The Booth Charities

£108,000 (1992/93)

Elderly people in Salford

Midwood Hall, 1 Eccles Old Road,
Salford, Manchester M6 7AE
0161-736 2989

Correspondent: R Spence, Administrator

Trustees: M C Mowat; John R Holt; D C St C Miller; R P Kershaw; W Jones; E Tudor-Evans; J Weston; C W Hunt.

Beneficial area: Salford only.

Information available: Full accounts are on file at the Charity Commission.

General: In 1992/93, the trust had assets of £992,000 and an income of £426,000, of which £300,000 was from Humphrey Booth the Elders Charity and £50,000 from Humphrey Booth the Grandson's Charity. After expenses of £145,000, the trust had £281,000 available for distribution. Grants were given to 23 organisations totalling £108,000 and grants to individuals in Salford totalled £123,000.

The main grants were to Humphrey Booth Clinical Fellowship (£23,000), Manchester YMCA (£21,000), and Kirkdale Holiday Home, Sacred Trinity Centre and Salford Groundwork Trust (£10,000 each). Other large grants were to Humphrey Booth Day Centre (£7,000), Salford Area Health Authority (£5,000), Fairbridge and Ladywell Carers Group (£3,000 each); Age Concern (£2,600) and the Humphrey Booth Club (£2,000). There were also eight grants of £1,000 to £2,000 including those to Humphrey Booth Housing Charity; Salford Children's Holiday Home; Henshaws Society for the Blind and Calderwood Day Centre. The four remaining grants of under £1,000 included Salford Cathedral and Calderdale Parents & Relatives Association.

Applications: In writing to the correspondent. The committee meets once a month.

The Bornstein Charitable Settlements

£149,000 (see below)

Jewish

c/o Morley & Scott, Lynton House, 7-12 Tavistock Square, London WC1H 9LT
0171-387 5868

Correspondent: The Trustees

Trustees: J Bornstein; L Mann.

Beneficial area: UK and Israel.

Information available: Full accounts are on file at the Charity Commission, up to 1988/89.

General: These two trusts (the A Bornstein and M & S Bornstein Charitable Settlements) are administered by the same trustees, from the same address and appear to operate closely together.

In 1987/88, the A Bornstein Charitable Settlement had an income of £223,000 including £154,000 from covenanted donations. 33 grants were made totalling £85,000. Grants, ranging from £35 to £18,000, were all to Jewish organisations, mainly in Israel. The largest were to Ohel Shimon Trust (£18,000), Cosmon (Bels) Ltd and Deedpride Ltd (both £15,000) and Pardes House School (£10,000).

The income of the M & S Bornstein Charitable Settlement was £409,000 in 1988/89. This is a big increase on the previous year, mainly due to dividend income rising from £1,500 to £381,000. £64,000 was given in four grants: Clifton Charities (£50,000), Ohel Shimon (£10,000), Ohel Moishe (£3,500) and Holmleigh Trust (£100).

Applications: In writing to the correspondent.

The Harry Bottom Charitable Trust

£74,000 (1993/94)

Religion, education, medical, elderly

Westons, 55 Queen's Buildings, Queen Street, Sheffield S21 2DX
0114-273 8341

Correspondent: D R Proctor

Trustees: J G Potter; B L Simpkin; G T Edwards; Prof H F Woods.

Beneficial area: UK, with a preference for Yorkshire and Derbyshire.

Information available: Accounts are on file at the Charity Commission, but without a list of grants.

General: In 1993/94, the trust had assets of £1.6 million (£1.5 million in 1992/93), an income of £105,000 (£92,000), administration charges of £17,000 and gave grants totalling £74,000 (£111,000). We were unable to obtain any further information for those years.

The trust states that support is divided roughly equally between religion, education and medical causes. Within these categories grants are given to:

Religion - small local appeals and cathedral appeals.

Education - universities and schools.

Medical - equipment for hospitals and charities concerned with disability.

Grants usually range from £200 to £10,000 although occasional larger grants up to £20,000 have been given.

Exclusions: No grants to individuals.

Applications: In writing to the correspondent.

The A H & M A Boulton Trust

£112,000 (1989)

Christian

11 Radley Road, Wallasey, Merseyside L44 2BU

Correspondent: Mrs G Baird, Secretary

Trustees: Mrs E Boulton; Mrs J R Gopsill; F P Gopsill.

Beneficial area: Worldwide.

Information available: No accounts for the A H & M A Boulton Trust are on file at the Charity Commission since those for 1971. We have not been able to update this information which is taken from the last Edition of this Guide.

General: The trust mainly supports the erection and maintenance of buildings to be used for preaching the Christian gospel, and teaching its doctrines. The trustees are also allowed to support other Christian institutions. In 1989, the trust gave grants totalling £112,000.

Applications: In writing to the correspondent. The trust tends to support a set list of charities and applications are very unlikely to be successful.

The P G & N J Boulton Trust

£161,000 (1992)

Christian

Colin Spurgeon & Co, 7 Thingwall Road, Irby, Wirral, Merseyside L61 3UA
0151-648 5661

Correspondent: B Knight, Accountant

Trustees: Miss N J Boulton; L J Marsh; B J Knight; A L Perry.

Beneficial area: Worldwide.

Information available: No accounts are on file at the Charity Commission since those for 1989, and these did not include a grants list.

We have not been able to update the following information which is taken from the last Edition of this Guide.

General: In 1992, the trust had an income of £182,000 and made grants totalling £161,000.

141 grants were made, mainly to Christian organisations, major national charities and those of special interest to the trustees. Beneficiaries included organisations such as the Save the Children Fund, Age Concern, British Red Cross, Youth with a Mission and the Bible Society.

Exclusions: No grants to individuals.

Applications: In writing to the correspondent. Owing to the number of applications received the trustees cannot acknowledge all of them. Successful applicants will hear within two months.

The Bowland Charitable Trust

£55,000 (1989)

Young people, education, general

T D S House, Lower Phillips Road, Whitebirk Estate, Blackburn BB1 5TH
01254-676921

Correspondent: Mrs Carole Fahy, Trust Administrator

Trustees: H A Cann; R A Cann; D L Walmsley.

Beneficial area: UK, with a preference for north west England.

Information available: Full accounts are on file at the Charity Commission, but we unable to see any since those for 1989.

General: The trust has general charitable purposes but focuses its support on the "promotion of educational character forming activities for young people".

In 1989, the trust had an income of £47,000 mainly from deeds of covenant. Grants totalled £55,000 with the largest to Brantwood (£23,500), Nazareth Chapel (£17,000), Ribble Valley Sports Association (£10,000) and the Cathedral Trust Restoration Fund and Lancashire Outdoor Activities Initiative (both £2,000).

Seven other grants ranged from £25 to £250, with recipients including Lancashire Student Band and Pendle Trust.

Applications: In writing to the correspondent.

The Chris Brasher Trust

£56,000 (1991/92)

Recreation, conservation, general

The Navigator's House, River Lane, Richmond, Surrey TW10 7AG
0181-940 0296

Correspondent: C Brasher, Chairman

Trustees: C W Brasher; S J Brasher; D C Warden; Lord Chorley.

Beneficial area: Worldwide.

Information available: Full accounts are on file at the Charity Commission up to 1991/92.

General: The trust was established in 1988. The latest accounts on file at the Charity Commission included the following information: "The trustees continue to consider providing assistance to a major project for the purchase of an area of wilderness land in Scotland which would involve the application of a substantial part of the trust's funds. The trust's funds have accordingly been carried forward to meet proposed expenditure on these projects, and other possible projects of a similar nature."

In 1991/92, the trust had assets of £779,000 and an income of £138,000 (including £65,000 from donations). 10 grants were given totalling £56,000 of which £30,000 was given to the John Muir Trust. A further £5,500 was for "provision of recreational facilities".

The remaining grants ranged from £50 to £5,000 including those to YHA (£5,000), Sir Edmund Hillary Himalayan Trust (£4,000), Tettenhall Horse Sanctuary (£3,735), New to London (£3,000) and NSPCC (£2,000).

The previous year only three grants were made totalling £53,000. The largest grant was £40,000 for "purchase of property in Wales". The other grants were £12,550 for "provision of recreational facilities" and £167 to Friends of the Lake District.

The trust stated that it has been receiving "thousands" of applications that it has been unable to support. It has been replying to them up to now, but will in future ignore them.

Applications: Applicants are unlikely to receive any reply from the trust, see above.

The Bridge Trust

£126,000 (1994)

General in Barnstaple

7 Bridge Chambers, Barnstaple, Devon EX31 1HB
01271-43995

Correspondent: C J Bartlett, Clerk

Trustees: 16 local trustees, five of whom are councillors.

Beneficial area: Barnstaple and immediate neighbourhood.

Information available: Full accounts are on file at the Charity Commission.

General: In 1994, the trust had assets of £231,000 and an income of £243,000. Grants were given to a wide range of causes, including sport, welfare, elderly and young people, schools, health and medical, and amenities, totalling £126,000. Charities must be within five miles of Barnstaple and most grants are for under £1,000.

Recent support has been given to North Devon Rescue Archaeology, for a wetlands area at Pilton Community College (£500), for the renovation of a salmon fishing boat and for microfilming records at Appledore Maritime Museum.

Exclusions: No support for education.

Applications: In writing to the correspondent. The trustees meet quarterly and make decisions in March.

Harold Bridges' Foundation

£89,000 (1993/94)

General

The Royal Bank of Scotland plc (Trustee Division), 2nd Floor, Guildhall House, Guildhall Street, Preston PR1 3NU
01772-202101

Correspondent: Graham Gell, Manager

Trustees: R N Hardy; J W Greenwood.

Beneficial area: UK, with a preference for the north west of England.

Information available: Full accounts are on file at the Charity Commission.

General: In 1993/94, the trust had assets of £846,000, with a market value of £1.4 million, and an income of £80,000. 64 grants were made totalling £89,000 and ranging from £100 to £10,000.

The largest grants went to the Royal College of Surgeons (£10,000), a regular beneficiary, and to the Road Haulage Benevolent Fund and Airborne Forces Society Fund (both £5,000). Of the remaining grants 47 were for £1,000 and only four were for less.

About 75% of the grants were to local charities in the north west of England including churches, youth organisations, village halls, welfare organisations, a bowling club and the National Trust Lake District Appeal. Most of the grants are recurrent from the previous year.

Virtually all the national charities that receive a grant are regular beneficiaries, including the Army Benevolent Fund, Arthritis & Rheumatism Council, Marine Conservation Society and RNLI. North west charities supported include: Age Concern – Kendal, Barrow & District Society for the Blind, Fleetwood Deep Sea Trawlers, Lancashire Youth Clubs Association, Morecombe Youth Band, Preston Community Transport and St Mary's Hospital Ulverston. The only local charity not in north west England to benefit was the Isle of Scilly Environmental Trust.

Applications: In writing to the correpondent.

The British Council for Prevention of Blindness (also known as SEE: Save Eyes Everywhere)

£167,000 (1993/94)

Prevention of blindness

12 Harcourt Street, London W1H 1DS
0171-724 3716

Correspondent: Jane Skerrett, Executive Officer

Trustees: The Council.

Beneficial area: Worldwide.

Information available: Full accounts are on file at the Charity Commission.

General: The objects of the Council are "to prevent blindness and restore sight in the UK and in the developing world and to assist in the world movement to prevent needless blindness. This is achieved through funding research into various eye diseases in UK hospitals and universities and by funding practical projects abroad such as mobile eye camps to treat cateracts and community based programmes to treat river blindness. Most of the council's income comes from donations [concerts and recordings used to bring in a large income]." In 1993/94, the Council had an income of £205,000. Expenditure totalled £197,000 including £167,000 in grants.

In 1993/94, grants ranging from £3,000 to £28,000 were given to 16 organisations. Nine were for hospitals/institutes of ophthalmology (six were in the UK, the remainder to Nigeria £21,000; Ghana £14,000 and India £3); five to UK universities, an international organisation and third world doctors.

Grants included: £26,000 to the Institute of Ophthalmology for two research projects; £16,000 to the University of Aberdeen, for research into ageing eyes; £10,000 to support two students from Ethiopia and Kenya to spend six months at Moorfields Eye Hospital, London; and £10,000 for research on river blindness in Ghana.

Exclusions: All except projects directly concerned with research into blindness prevention or restoration of sight. "We do NOT deal with the individual welfare of blind people in the UK."

Applications: Application forms are available from the correspondent. Applications are considered in January, June and September.

British Schools and Universities Foundation (Inc.)

£144,000 (1992/93)

Education

6 Windmill Hill, Hampstead,
London NW3 6RU
0171-435 4648

Correspondent: Mrs S Wiltshire

Trustees: The Executive Committee, Suite 1006, 575 Madison Avenue, New York, NY 10022 - 2511, USA.

Beneficial area: UK, Commonwealth, USA.

Information available: Annual report available from the correspondent.

General: The foundation is registered in the USA, but has an honorary secretary in the UK. It was "envisioned by a dedicated group of men in the 1950's led by Thomas E Ward, Snr" and came into being in 1961. Its purposes are threefold:

- Primarily to make donations and loans to schools, colleges, universities and educational, scientific or literary institutions.

- To promote the education of British students at American educational institutions. "There are only a very limited number of awards."

- To promote the education of American students at British institutions. "There are only a very limited number of awards".

The foundation applies two criteria to the selection of institutions within the UK:

1. The applicant institution should be active in seeking financial support for specific projects which are clearly defined and documented. Acceptability should be demonstrated by the efforts of its graduates and others who comprise the institution's constituency.

2. A non-American institution should have a demonstrable record of co-operation with the USA either by acceptance of American students or by collaboration with comparable institutions in the USA.

In 1991, 48 institutions throughout the British Commonwealth (but largely within the UK) received awards from the foundation. Amounts received by each are not broken down, the foundation says these are confidential. The annual report includes a sample of colleges and gives a brief resume of what the funds were used for:

Culford School in Suffolk received an award to help towards the costs of their new recreation centre; the Godolphin and Latymer School in London were helped in their plans to build a new science, art and technology centre; and the University of Newcastle-upon-Tyne won a grant to help improve undergraduate teaching facilities. Most awards detailed were to schools and colleges for capital projects, including libraries, recreation facilities and science and technology centres.

Exclusions: Commercial research, religious appeals, and other projects outside the foundation's charter.

Applications: In writing to the correspondent.

The Britten-Pears Foundation

£173,000 (1992/93)

Work of Benjamin Britten and Peter Pears, the arts

The Red House, Aldeburgh,
Suffolk IP15 5PZ
01372-466655

Correspondent: The Administrator

Trustees: Marion Thorpe, Chair; Dr Donald Mitchell; Dr Colin Matthews; Noel Periton; Hugh Cobbe; Peter Carter; David Drew; Sir John Tooley; Andrew Potter.

Beneficial area: UK, preference for East Anglia.

Information available: Accounts up to 1992/93 on file at the Charity Commission, but without the grants list.

General: The foundation was set up "to promote the musical works and writings of Benjamin Britten and Peter Pears and the principles of musical education established by them." It also aims to promote the arts in general, particularly music. Trustees include musicologists and composers.

The foundation owns and finances the Britten-Pears Library at Aldeburgh which is open to scholars and research students.

In 1992/93, the foundation had assets of £6.5 million, 64% being freehold property, including the library and contents. Its annual income derives from the royalties from the performance worldwide of the works of Benjamin Britten, and is channelled to the foundation through the Britten Estate Ltd by deed of covenant (£646,000 in 1992/93), other income was £147,000 giving a total of £793,000. Expenditure was broken down as:

Grants and donations	£173,000
Britten-Pears Library, for running expenses	£128,000
Red House Complex for running expenses	£23,000
Promotion	£18,000
Administration	£75,000

The foundation does not break down its grant-giving. However it has provided the following details: "Typical grants and donations are: Britten-Pears School for Musical Studies (£95,000); Britten Composition Award (£13,000); Aldeburgh Festival (£11,500); Snape Maltings (£10,000), for new fire exits; Aldeburgh Jubilee Hall Appeal (£5,000); fees for commissioning or recording new works (£4,500) and the Society for the Promotion of New Music (£1,500). Grants of £1,000 were given to: Purcell Centenary Trust, Westminster Cathedral Choir School, Foundation for Young Musicians, Cambridge Boys Choir and Red Cross Yugoslavia Appeal. Numerous smaller donations were made including some for environmental and peace purposes."

Priority is given to supporting activities in the Aldeburgh/East Anglia area. After that commissions and recordings have a high priority followed by specific school musical projects.

Promotional subsidy for performances of rarely-performed or little known works by Benjamin Britten can be sought through the foundation from the Britten Estate Ltd. The estate also gives promotional subsidies for Benjamin Britten and Peter Pears related recordings and publications. In 1992/93, concert, recording and publication promotional subsidy totalled £145,000.

Exclusions: General charitable projects; general support for festivals other than Aldeburgh; individual scholarships, bursaries and course grants other that for Britten-Pears School; purchase or restoration of musical instruments of equipment.

Applications: To the correspondent in writing.

The Bromley Trust

£86,000 (1993/94)

Human rights, conservation

Ashley Manor, King's Somborne, Stockbridge, Hants SO20 6RQ
01794-388241; Fax: 01794-388264

Correspondent: Keith Bromley

Trustees: Keith Bromley; Anna Home; Alan P Humphries; Nicholas Measham; Lady Ann Wood.

Beneficial area: Worldwide.

Information available: Full accounts are on file at the Charity Commission.

General: This trust, in 1989, succeeded the FK & HM Bromley Charitable Trust. The aims and objects of the trust are to make grants to charitable organisations that:

- Combat violations of human rights, and help victims of torture, refugees from oppression and those who have been falsely imprisoned.

- Help those who have suffered severe bodily or mental hurt through no fault of their own, and if need be their dependents; try in some small way to off set man's inhumanity to man.

- Oppose the extinction of the world's fauna and flora and the destruction of the environment for wildlife and for mankind worldwide.

In 1993/94, the trust had assets of £1.6 million and an income of £87,000. Grants were given totalling £86,000.

The trust's objectives are narrow and it hardly ever departs from them. By far the greater part of the income goes to charities that are concerned with human rights; a comparatively small proportion is given to charities concerned with the preservation of the world environment. The main charities supported usually receive their grants in four quarterly payments. One-off grants are occasionally made, but are rare. Grants are only given to registered charities.

The mainstream charities are:

Medical Foundation for the Care of Victims of Torture
Anti-Slavery International
Survival International
Prisoners of Conscience Appeal Fund
Amnesty International (British Section) Charitable Trust
Ockenden Venture
Asylum Aid
Womankind Worldwide
Find Your Feet
Prisoners Abroad
Writers & Scholars Educational Trust
Minority Rights Group
Justice Educational & Research Trust
Childhope UK
International Child Care Trust
Population Concern
Greenpeace Environmental Trust
Birdlife International
Fauna & Flora Preservation Society
Wildfowl & Wetlands Trust

Seven charities received grants totalling between £5,500 and £6,900, two charities received £750. The other grants ranged from nearly £1,200 to almost £5,000. There were also four one-off donations ranging from £250 to £2,000 to FIELD, Manic Depression Fellowship, Diane Fossey Gorilla Fund and Prison Reform Trust.

Exclusions: No grants for individuals.

Applications: In writing to the correspondent, but note above. The trustees meet twice a year; urgent appeals may be dealt with at any time.

The David Brooke Charity

£63,000 (1992/93)

General

Witneys, Upper Basildon, Near Reading, Berks RG8 8NP

Correspondent: D Brooke

Trustees: D Brooke; J R Chamberlain; P M Hutt; N A Brooke.

Beneficial area: UK.

Information available: Full accounts are on file at the Charity Commission.

General: The charity's assets were over £974,000 in 1992/93, generating an income of £56,000. The 34 grants given totalled £63,000 and ranged from £250 to £3,000.

There appears to be a preference for larger, national or brand name charities such as Barnardo's, Children's Society, Fortune Centre, Girl Guides Association, Great Ormond Street Hospital, NSPCC, RNLI, Royal College of Surgeons, RSPB, Salvation Army and the Scout Association.

Other less familiar charities supported included Kennet & Avon Trust, Lord Wandsworth Foundation, Design & Manufacture for Disability and Vandestar Bursary (Sail Training Association). It may be that the trust only supports organisations/people known to the trustees.

Applications: The correspondent stated that all funds are fully committed every year, therefore new applicants are turned down. Sending applications is a waste of time for all concerned.

The Charles Brotherton Trust

£75,000 (1992/93)

Education & training of young people, medical research, general

c/o Simpson Curtis, 41 Park Square, Leeds LS1 2NS
0113-243 3433

Correspondent: The Secretary

Trustees: C Brotherton-Ratcliffe; D R Brotherton; S B Turner; J Riches.

Beneficial area: The cities of Birmingham, Leeds, Liverpool, Wakefield, York and the borough of Bebington.

Information available: Full accounts are on file at the Charity Commission but without a grants list since that for 1990/91.

General: In 1992/93, the trust had an income of £82,000 and grants totalled £75,000. Grants to organisations usually range from £50 to £250 and may be one-off or recurrent.

Grants are given to registered charities in the beneficial areas in the fields of:

- education (including the establishment and maintenance of scholarships and the recreational training and education of young persons);
- medical and surgical research;
- general charitable purposes.

(The scholarships are available to students on scientific courses at the Universities of Leeds, Liverpool, Birmingham and York, but applications for these must be made to the university in question, not to the above correspondent.)

In 1990/91, when the trust had an income of £79,000, it gave grants of £85,000, broken down as follows:

City of Leeds 40% (£34,000), including £13,000 to the University of Leeds, scholarships and the Brotherton Library;

City of Birmingham 20% (£17,000), including £6,100 to the University of Birmingahm;

City of Liverpool 10% (£8,500), including £1,200 to the University of Liverpool;

City of Wakefield 10% (£8,500), including £900 to the University of Leeds;

City of York 10% (£8,500), including £1,800 to the University of York

Borough of Bebington 10% (£8,500), including £2,500 to the University of Liverpool for scholarships.

Most grants are for £100 to £200, the vast majority are recurrent. Beneficiaries include a large number of youth organisations and welfare charities eg. Bebington District Scout Council, East Birmingham Family Service Unit, Friends of the City of Leeds Youth Orchestra, Merseyside Society for the Deaf, Wakefield's Broadcasts to Hospitals Service and York Volunteer Centre.

Exclusions: Grants to registered charities only. No grants to individuals.

Applications: In writing to the correspondent, including a copy of the latest accounts. Applications must be received by the end of December and are considered in January or February.

Bill Brown's Charitable Settlement

£62,000 (1993/94)

Health, social welfare

Payne, Hicks & Beach, 10 New Square, Lincoln's Inn, London WC2A 3QG
0171-465 4300

Correspondent: G S Brown, Trustee and Solicitor

Trustees: Percy W E Brown; Graham S Brown; John E Barnett.

Beneficial area: UK.

Information available: Full accounts are on file at the Charity Commission.

General: In 1993/94, the trust had assets of £945,000 and an income of £81,000. It gave 17 grants totalling £61,500. 12 of the recipients had received a similar grant in the previous year.

The main grants were £10,000 each to Barnardo's and the Salvation Army. £5,000 was given to each of Cancer Relief; Imperial Cancer Research; Leonard Cheshire Foundation; Holy Trinity Church, Roehampton and Mencap. £2,500 was given to Funds for Epilepsy and all other grants were for £1,000 to £2,000.

A wide range of organisations received support including the Alzheimers Disease Society; Friends of the Elderly; Linden Lodge Charitable Trust; National Children's Home; Princess Alice Hospice; Royal Caledonian Schools; Twickenham & District Mental Health Association; Venturers Search & Rescue and WRVS Hasslemere.

The annual income is largely committed to a regular list of charities. Occasional one-off donations are made to other charities.

Exclusions: No grants to individuals; only to registered charities.

Applications: In writing to the correspndent. The trustees meet annually. Applications are acknowledged if a donation is made.

Brushmill Ltd

£186,000 (1991/92)

Jewish

13-17 New Burlington Place, Regent Street, London W1X 2JP
0181-809 2775

Correspondent: Mrs M Getter

Trustees: J Weinberger; Y Getter; Mrs E Weinberger.

Beneficial area: Worldwide.

Information available: Full accounts are on file at the Charity Commission up to 1991/92.

General: In 1991/92, the trust had an income of £158,000, down from £283,000 the previous year. Grants totalled £186,000, a slight rise from £167,000 the previous year.

All the grants were to Jewish organisations, the largest to Bais Rochel (£34,000), Friends of Yeshivas Shaar Hashomaim (£15,000) and Holmleigh Trust (£14,000). According to the Charity Commission, the trust had an income of £183,000 in 1992/93.

Applications: In writing to the correspondent.

The Bryant Trust

£147,000 (1993/94)

General

PO Box 1624, Shirley, Solihull, West Midlands B90 4QZ

Correspondent: J R Clemishaw, Secretary

Beneficial area: Roughly the Birmingham conurbation within about 10 miles of the city centre but only east of the M5/M6 (to include Solihull and Sutton Coldfield).

Information available: Full accounts are on file at the Charity Commission.

General: About 75% of the income is committed to organisations in which the trustees have a special interest. The rest is paid mainly in small grants (£200 to £1,000) to organisations concerned with social welfare, community service and arts, race relations, and disadvantaged people within the beneficial area. Capital projects are usually preferred to core funding.

In 1993/94, the trust had an income of £133,000, mainly from dividends on Bryant Group plc shares, plus £17,000 brought forward from 1992/93. 91 grants totalled £147,000, of which £43,000 was given in small grants to 73 organisations and the remainder to 18 charities in which the trust had a particular concern.

Several of the largest grants in 1993/94 were to regular beneficiaries: the YMCA and Birmingham Settlement (£21,000 each), EMMAUS (£10,000) and Relate (£5,000). Other larger grants were £10,000 each to St James' Church Sutton Coldfield and the Trinity Centre; £7,000 to the Midland Arts Centre; £6,000 to Castle Bromwich Hall Gardens Trust; £5,000 to Birmingham Institute for the Deaf and £3,000 to the Medical Foundation for Victims of Torture.

Exclusions: No grants to non-registered charities, animal welfare or individuals.

Applications: In writing to the correspondent, with a copy of the accounts/budget. Applications should be submitted by mid-March (for the spring meeting) and mid-September (for the autumn meeting).

The Rosemary Bugden Charitable Trust

£259,000 (1992/93)

Arts in Avon

Osborne Clarke, 30 Queen Charlotte Street, Bristol BS99 7QQ
0117-923 0220

Correspondent: J W Sharpe

Trustees: Mrs R A M W Bugden; J W Sharpe; D H Drew.

Beneficial area: UK, with a preference for Avon.

Information available: Full accounts for 1992/93 are on file at the Charity Commission.

General: In 1992/93, the trust had an income of £240,000. It gave grants totalling £259,000 including £237,000 to organisations, most of which are concerned with the arts in Avon. Many of the larger grants appear to be to regular beneficiaries.

Grants totalling £168,000 were made to the Bath City Opera. Other grants included (1991/92 figures in brackets): £37,500 to Bath Georgian Festival (£56,000); £10,000 to Bath Festival Society (£20,000); £5,000 to Kings of Wessex Community School (£5,000); £6,500 to the Great Elm Music Festival (£10,000); £5,000 to Wedmore Opera (which received a smaller grant in 1991/92); £1,000 to the Stroud Festival and £1,200 to Action Aid. Small grants of under £1,000 were made to the Coach House Small Business Centre and the Enuresis Research and Information Centre.

Applications: In writing to the correspondent.

The Bulldog Trust

£195,000 (1993/94)

Education, Christian

Messrs Hoare Trustees, 37 Fleet Street, London EC4P 4DQ
0171-353 4522

Correspondent: Richard Hoare & Messrs Hoare Trustees

Trustees: Richard Hoare; Messrs Hoare Trustees.

Beneficial area: Worldwide.

Information available: Full accounts are on file at the Charity Commission.

General: The trust seeks to give major support to one or two new smaller charities each year, some of which continue to receive support for a number of years. "We always expect to see extra benefits derive from our larger donations such as: matching donations; administrative reorganisation or geared benefits (as with overseas aid). We are also a vehicle for other people's giving. We like to uphold traditional values and encourage leadership qualities."

In 1992/93, the trust had assets of £1 million (£1.2 million market value), and an income of £137,000 (£66,000 from donations and £44,000 from interest and dividends). 27 grants were given totalling £58,000. We were unable to see the accounts for 1993/94, but the grants list shows 60 grants totalling £195,000.

Grants are made mainly to schools, although the largest beneficiary has regularly been the Winchester Cathedral Trust (£20,000), although MERLIN, Medical Emergency Relief International, received two grants totalling £30,000 in 1993/94.

Other large grants went to the Leonara Children's Fund (£20,000), Andover & District Medical Fund (£16,000), Royal Opera House and AMREF (£11,000 each), Prince's Youth Business Trust and Cathedral of Southwell Minster (£10,000), Nilgiri Planters Association (£8,500), Emmaus House (£5,300) and Proms Gala Charity (£5,000).

The schools which received the largest grants were Elstree (£5,300, £7,000 in 1992/93) and Harrow (£4,600). Other schools receiving smaller grants (between £1,000 and £2,500) included Royal Grammar School, Guildford, Reeds School, Francis Holland School and Downe House School.

Other grants of £1,000 to £2,500 were given to organisations such as Tylehurst Trust, Helping Hand Campaign; London Churches Employment Development Trust and St John Opthalmic Hospital Bassir. There were about 40 grants under £1,000 which included those to Bosnia-Hertzegovina Heritage Rescue Foundation; Elgar Birthplace Appeal; Dunkirk Little Ships Restoration Trust; Fortune Centre for Riding Therapy, NSPCC and Tommy Campaign.

Exclusions: No support for individuals or to unsolicited applications.

Applications: In writing to the correspondent, there are no application forms available. Applications received are not acknowledged.

The Burden Trust

£188,000 (1993/94)

General

Little Clandon, West Clandon, Surrey
GU4 7ST
01483-222561

Correspondent: Malcolm Tosh, Honorary Secretary

Trustees: R D Spear, Chair; C A Orton; Dr M G Barker; R E J Bernays; A C Miles; Lady E J White; Prof G M Stirrat; M C Tosh; P R B Barkworth.

Beneficial area: UK and overseas.

Information available: Accounts are on file at the Charity Commission, but without a list of grants.

General: In 1993/94, the trust had net assets with a book value of £2.3 million giving an income of £202,000. After grants of £188,000 and expenses, the trust had a surplus of income over expenditure of £5,000.

The trust supports neurological research, hospitals, retirement homes, schools and training institutions, homes for young people and care of families, and the relief of persons in necessitous circumstances, with an overall adherence to the tenets and principles of the Church of England. No further information available.

Applications: Applications should be made in writing by 31st March each year with project details and the last set of the charity's accounts. All applications sent direct to the trust office are acknowledged, provided a stamped addressed envelope is enclosed. The outcome is acknowledged subsequently only if the application is successful. The trust meets annually in early June.

Burdens Charitable Foundation

£239,000 (1993/94)

Christian, welfare, general

St George's House, 215-219 Chester Road, Manchester M15 4JE
0161-832 4901; Fax: 0161-835 3668

Correspondent: A J Burden

Trustees: A J Burden; R D W Evans; G W Burden; Ms H M Perkins.

Beneficial area: UK, with a preference for deprived areas, chiefly in the North West, Midlands and South West.

Information available: Full accounts are on file at the Charity Commission.

General: In 1993/94, most of the trust's income came from dividends on shares in W T Burden Ltd, amounting to £187,000. The total income for the year was £237,000. There is a separte fund within the trust, the Martin Burton Fund which has as its objects the propagation of Christianity as opposed to social etc work carried out by Christian organisations.

This income is slightly up on the previous year (£221,000), but the grant total has nearly doubled, from £121,000 in 1992/93 to £239,000 in 1993/94. The grants are divided between "Currently annual recurring" grants and "other"; the former are understood to be committed two years in advance.

Currently annual
  recurring   £70,000 (£36,000)
Other   £168,000 (£85,000)

In 1993/94, 15 annual grants were given, a third in Manchester. The largest were to CAB Manchester (£21,000) and Easton Christian Family Centre: Bristol (£9,000). £6,000 was given towards school fees with £5,000 given to FWA Manchester and the Royal Commonwealth Society for the Blind. Other grants included £4,000 towards a pastoral worker at Whalley Range Methodist Church, and £1,000 (final payment) for a youth worker at Sydenham Methodist Church, Belfast. Most beneficiaries were Christian or welfare organisations.

90 other grants were made ranging from £150 to £10,000. The largest grants were to Edinburgh Medical Missionary Society – Nazareth Project (£10,000), Water Aid – Albella Boys Home India (£9,000), Highway Project – Doncaster and St John's Church Keynsham (both £7,500), and Action Partners (£6,000).

Charities in the fields of medicine, welfare and young people as well as Christian causes were supported. Over half the grants were to local organisations especially Manchester, Keynsham and West Midlands. £5,000 was given to each of Bristol Institute for Brain Injured Children, Frail Ambulant Home – Solihull (the general fund and the hardship fund), Grateful Society – Bristol, Christie's Hospital – Manchester, Liverpool School of Tropical Medicine and the Northern Initiative. Beneficiaries of smaller grants included the Braille Chess Association (£2,000), British Red Cross – Solihull (£2,500), CAB Keynsham (£2,500), Markham Junior Band (£250), Rainbow Family Trust – Manchester (£1,000), Salford Urban Mission (£1,000), Talking Newspapers Keynsham (£500) and the Welsh Flood Relief Fund (£1,250).

The accounts include a schedule of grants made since the trust was established in 1977. The main beneficiaries have been CAB Strangeways/Open Door (£96,000 in total), Easton Christian Family Centre (£80,000), Frail Ambulant Home (£44,000) and FWA (£20,000). In addition to a few other regular beneficiaries, a number of organisations have been supported for three or four years.

The correspondent has informed us that "gifts tend to flow geographically to the areas where:
1. The trustees themselves are resident;
2. The company, which is in course developing into a national distributor, has a depot
3. Third world countries, especially Africa; and cover mainly non-popular charities which can find fundraising difficult."

Applications: In writing to the correspondent.

The Alan & Rosemary Burrough Charitable Trust

£60,000 (1991)

Rowing, disability and ex-service organisations, general

Manor Garden, Henley-on-Thames, Oxon RG9 2NH

Correspondent: Alan Burrough

Trustees: Alan Burrough; Bryan Burrough; Christopher Burrough.

Beneficial area: UK.

Information available: Full accounts are on file at the Charity Commission.

General: The correspondent stated "The annual income is mainly committed in advance and unsolicited applications are unlikely to be successful." Unfortunately we have not been able to update the information from the last Edition of this Guide, which is therefore reprinted below.

The trust appeared to have assets of about £700,000 in 1991. The income was £64,000 and grants totalled £60,000. Of the 34 grants given, 11 were recurrent from 1990. Rowing organisations were the major beneficiaries; the Rowing Museum of Henley Foundation received £20,000, Rowing Foundation £12,000 and Thames Rowing Club Charitable Trust £5,000. Other grants ranged from £20 to £5,000, with 21 for £500 or less. Beneficiaries included three masonic charities, schools and colleges, church and cathedral appeals and national health and welfare charities.

Applications: In writing to the correspondent, but note the above.

The Arnold James Burton Charitable Trust

£144,000 (1993/94)

General

Trustee Management Limited, Trust Managers, 27 East Parade, Leeds LS1 5SX
0113-243 6786

Correspondent: Arnold James Burton

Trustees: A J Burton; M T Burton; J J Burton.

Beneficial area: UK.

Information available: Accounts are on file at the Charity Commission.

General: The trust was set up in 1956 by A J Burton, who preferred to support charities concerned with children. In 1991/92, the trust had assets of £2 million, an income of £207,000 and gave grants totalling £201,000. By 1993/94, the assets had risen to £2.5 million, the income had dropped to £183,000 and grants to £144,000.

The correspondent stated "We are already committed to about 200 different charities and do not wish to receive applications from any further organisations."

Exclusions: No support to charities not already known by the trust.

Applications: The trusts funds are already committed.

The Audrey & Stanley Howard Burton 1960 Charitable Trust

£132,000 (1993/94)

Jewish, general in Harrogate

Trustee Management Ltd, 27 East Parade, Leeds LS1 5SX
0113-243 6786

Trustees: Mrs A R Burton; Miss A Burton; P E Morris; Mrs D M Hazan; D J Solomon.

Beneficial area: UK, preference for Yorkshire.

Information available: Accounts are on file at the Charity Commission, without a list of grants for 1993/94. The following information was supplied by the trust.

General: In 1993/94, the trust had assets of £1.13 million and an income of £336,000. Grants totalled £132,000.

The major donations were to Delamere Forest School (£25,000), University of Newcastle (£5,000), Edward Boyle Memorial Trust and Royal College of Psychiatrists (both £2,000), Norwood Child Care and Marie Curie Cancer Care (both £1,000) and Hebrew University of Jerusalem (£500).

Applications: In writing to the correspondent.

The Geoffrey Burton Charitable Trust

£46,000 (1993/94)

General, especially in Suffolk

1 Gainsborough Road, Felixstowe, Suffolk IP11 7HT
01394-285537

Correspondent: E E Maule, Trustee

Trustees: E de B Nash; E E Maule.

Beneficial area: Worldwide, especially Suffolk.

Information available: Full accounts are on file at the Charity Commission, including information on each grant given.

General: In 1993/94, the trust had assets of £494,000 including £410,000 termed "mortgages", which appeared for the first time as a major item in the 1991/92 accounts. The income was £49,000 including £33,000 mortgage interest. Grants totalled £46,000.

26 grants were given ranging from £200 to £15,000. The largest were to Blond McIndoe Centre (£15,000 towards funding for a research registrar) and Christchurch Needham Market (£10,000 to the Restoration Appeal). Most of the grants were given in Suffolk, especially Needham Market, including support for a school, two RSPB appeals and two departments of a hospital. Other beneficiaries included Suffolk Wildlife Trust, Sue Ryder Homes, Woodland Trust and Inland Waterways Association.

Applications: In writing to the correspondent.

The Raymond Montague Burton Charitable Trust

£302,000 (1994/95)

Jewish charities, social welfare, education, the arts, especially in Yorkshire

c/o Trustee Management Ltd, 27 East Parade, Leeds LS1 5SX
0113-243 6786

Correspondent: Raymond M Burton

Trustees: Raymond M Burton; P N Burton; A J Burton.

Beneficial area: England, with a preference for Yorkshire, particularly Leeds, and Humberside; also Israel.

Information available: Accounts on file at the Charity Commission, but without a narrative report.

General: The trust was set up in 1956 by Raymond Burton. The trust is time-limited: the income is distributed for only 50 years after which the capital will go to the decendants of the settlor.

The trustees state that they "do not welcome appeals from new charities which appear to overlap with the work of others already established and supported by us". No funds are given to local charities based outside Yorkshire or Humberside.

In 1992/93, the trust's assets were £2.85 million generating an income of £224,000 from which donations of £197,000 were given. By 1993/94, the assets had risen to £3.4 million, the income had dropped to £220,000 and grants risen to £275,000. Grants rose again in 1994/95 to £302,000.

Nearly 300 grants were given in 1992/93, many of these being very small donations of £100 and less. Most grants were under £1,000, with 37 grants ranging from £1,000 to £9,999. The few grants larger than this are noted below.

The exception to the general rule of modest sized grants was the large donation to the Joint Israel Appeal (JPAIME, now known as JJCT) which received a total of nearly £95,000 in several grants. (The trust has commented that it tends to make one extra large grant each year, with beneficiaries in previous years being the Joint Israel Appeal and Friends of the Jewish Museum.) Following this in scale were Cottages Homes (£12,500); International Spinal Research Trust (ISRT), Leicester University, West London Synagogue, Anchor Housing Trust, British Neurological Research Trust (£10,000 each); Jewish Educational Development Association (£8,500); London School of Economics (£7,000); Friends of the Hebrew University (£7,500); Jewish National Fund (£6,000); Jewish Care, Manor House Trust, the National Trust (£5,000 each); Royal Opera House Trust (£4,000).

The trust itself has stated that while the larger donations often go to Jewsih charities, occasionally in Israel, many smaller grants are made to local Yorkshire or Humberside and especially Leeds groups for general charitable purposes.

Exclusions: Local charities outside Yorkshire and Humberside. "With limited resources the trustees have decided to restrict very closely the support given for individuals."

Applications: In writing to the correspondent at any time. The trustees try to make a decision within a month. Negative decisions are not necessarily communicated.

The Bill Butlin Charity Trust

£117,000 (1993)

General

1 Hanover Square, London W1A 4SR
0171-493 4040

Correspondent: The Secretary

Trustees: R F Butlin; Lady Sheila Butlin; P A Hetherington; R Spooner; T Watts (Snr); T Watts (Jnr); F T Devine.

Beneficial area: UK.

Information available: Full accounts are on file at the Charity Commission.

General: This trust was established by Sir William E Butlin in 1963, it has a preference for organisations working with children, especially those who are disabled, and elderly people. The trust has a list of regular beneficiaries, to which only a few charities may be added each year.

In 1993, the trust had assets of £1.6 million and an income of £124,000. Grants were given to 17 organisations and totalled £117,000. The majority of the grant total was given in two grants: Drive for Youth (£50,000) and United Response (£25,000). The other grants were to: Canadian Veterans Association of the UK (£10,000); BACTA and St Barnabas (£5,000 each); Duke of Edinburgh Awards – Devon (£4,000); Stars Organisation for Spastics (£3,750); Cup of Kindness (£2,500); Grand Order of Water Rats and Saint & Sinners Club of London (£2,000 each); Bud Flanagan Leukaemia Fund (£1,750); Royal London Society for the Blind (£1,250) and five grants of £1,000 to Chailey Heritage Appeal Fund, Entertainment Artistes Benevolent Association, Leeds European Refuge Trust (ALERT), London Business School Anniversary Trust and the Queen Elizabeth Foundation.

Exclusions: Appeals from individuals are not normally considered.

Applications: In writing to the correspondent.

The Christopher Cadbury Charitable Trust

£106,000 (1993/94)

Nature conservation, general

New Guild House, 45 Great Charles Street, Queensway, Birmingham B3 2LX
0121-212 2222

Correspondent: Roger Harriman, Trust Administrator

Trustees: J C Cadbury; Roger V J Cadbury; Dr C James Cadbury; Mrs V B Reekie; Dr T N D Peet; P H G Cadbury; Mrs C V E Benfield.

Beneficial area: UK, with a strong preference towards the Midlands.

Information available: Regular annual accounts are on file at the Charity Commission.

General: In 1993/94, the trust had assets of £226,000 (market value £1.1 million) and an income of £78,000. Over 100 grants were given totalling £106,000, 26 of which were for £1,000 or more. Recurring annual commitments, subject to annual review, total almost £31,000.

About half of the trust's money is given in a few large grants to conservation projects. In 1993/94, these included: Royal Society for Nature Conservation (five grants totalling £31,000); Cornwall Trust for Nature Conservation (£11,000); Kent Trust for Nature (£5,000) and Norfolk Naturalists Trust (nearly £4,000).

Other large grants were given to Playthings Past Museum Trust, which is a museum of children's toys and dolls (£10,000) and Croft Trust (£5,000) towards adult education. 27 grants were for £500 to £2,000 and included those to the International Planned Parenthood Federation (£2,000); Almeida Theatre Company (£750) and Medical Aid Palestinians (£500).

69 grants were for £250 or less and were given to a wide range of organisations including Action for Blind People and Anti-Slavery International (£250 each); Girl Guides (£16 nationally and three local groups received £100 to £600); Red Cross, Yugoslavia (£100); Falklands Conservation and Howard League (£50 each) and the British Dragonfly Society (£6).

Applications: No unsolicited applications are considered by the trustees. There are annual schedules of grants on file at the Charity Commission which suggest that the trust's funds are not so much committed in advance but that the trustees, with their own strong areas of interest, neither wish to disappoint nor to be troubled by outside applications.

The Edward & Dorothy Cadbury Charitable Trust

£81,000 (1993/94)

Health, education, arts

Elmfield, College Walk, Selly Oak, Birmingham B29 6LE
0121-472 1838

Correspondent: Mrs M Walton, Secretary

Trustees: Philippa S Ward; Mrs P A Gillett; Dr C M Elliott.

Beneficial area: Preference for the West Midlands.

Information available: Full accounts are on file at the Charity Commission.

General: The trust supports registered charities only, with a special preference for West Midlands appeals and the fields of health, education and the arts. The size of grant varies but most are within the range of £50 to £500. On-going funding commitments are rarely considered.

In 1991/92, it received about 700 appeals about 300 of which were successful. In 1992/93, the trust stated "Once again there was a large increase in the number of appeals for funding received, all of which are seen by the trustees. The total reached 901... Grants were made to 407.

In 1993/94, the trust had assets of £513,000 and an income of £81,000. Grants totalled £81,000, but we have been unable to obtain a grants list.

In 1992/93, when grants totalled £96,000, the largest grants were £10,000 to Leighton Park School, £3,000 to Bromsgrove Festival, and £2,000 each to Bromsgrove Bereavement Council and Centre for Black & White Christian Partnership. £1,000 was given to each of: Acorns Hospice, Birmingham Botanical Gardens, Queen Elizabeth Hospital, Retreat – York, Society of Friends – Malvern, St Francis Church – Bournville and Worcester Cathedral Choir Tour Fund. About half of the above are regular beneficiaries.

All other grants were between £50 and £500 and given to a variety of local and national organisations, predominantly in the West Midlands.

Exclusions: No grants to individuals.

Applications: To the correspondent in writing, clearly giving relevant information concerning the project's aims and its benefits. Up-to-date accounts and annual reports where available would be helpful.

The George W Cadbury Charitable Trust

£136,000 (1993/94)

Population control, conservation, general

New Guild House, 45 Great Charles Street, Queensway, Birmingham B3 2LX
0121-212 2222

Correspondent: Roger Harriman, Trust Administrator

Trustees: G W Cadbury; Mrs C A Woodroffe; Mrs L E Boal; P C Boal; Miss J C Boal; N B Woodroffe; Miss J L Woodroffe.

Beneficial area: Worldwide.

Information available: Full accounts are on file at the Charity Commission.

General: In 1993/94, the trust had assets of £1.7 million (market value £3.3 million) generating an income of £137,000, all of which was given in 41 grants. Grants were given in the following geographical areas:

UK – £53,000 (some of which has been used in other geographical areas by worldwide operating trusts);
USA – £38,000;
Canada – £45,000.

The trustees expect the available income for 1995 to be about £130,000. They will consider adding the unspent income from previous years (£125,000) and distributing the total (£255,000) during the year. Recurring commitments will account for about £30,000.

The vast majority of grants both by number and value were for population control, followed by conservation. Here is a small sample: Conservation Council of Ontario (£34,000); Maternity Alliance Educational & Research Trust (£15,000); Belfast Brook Advisory Centre (£10,000); Planned Parenthood Federation of Canada (£5,164) and Brook Advisory Centres (£5,000). Many of the above are regular beneficiaries.

The only grants given for the trust's other main area of interest (conservation) were to the Gloucester Adventure (£33,000); World Wide Fund for Nature (£7,000) and PDSA (£100).

Other grants exceeding £1,000 were: Action on Smoking and Health (£2,000); British Pregnancy Advisory Service (£1,500); Christian Aid (£2,000); Health Services Research Centre at the University of North Carolina (£1,345); Institute of Child Health (£4,000); New York State Council of Churches (£3,400); Oakville Trafalgar Memorial Hospital Charitable Corporation (£2,600); Planned Parenthood of Toronto Barbara Cadbury Library (£2,600). There were a further 26 donations of £1,000 or less, many of which are supported on a regular basis.

Exclusions: No unsolicited applications will be considered by the trustees.

Applications: In writing to the correspondent. However it should be noted that trustees' current commitments are such that no unsolicited applications can be considered at present.

The Earl Cadogan's Charity Trust

£113,000 (1992/93)

General

The Cadogan Office, 18 Cadogan Gardens, London SW3 2RP
0171-730 4567

Correspondent: Miss J Castle

Trustees: The Earl Cadogan; The Countess Cadogan; Viscount Chelsea.

Beneficial area: UK.

Information available: Full accounts are on file at the Charity Commission.

General: Cadogan is one of the few landowners who gives large sums to charity. He inherited a large portion of Chelsea, and Earl Cadogan's Charity owns 837,500 shares in his private company, Chelsea Land.

In 1992/93, the trust had an income of £104,000 and gave grants totalling £113,000. The main grants were £36,000 to the Salvation Army (over the previous two years they had been given over £100,000); £6,000 to Action for Disability, Kensington & Chelsea, and £4,000 to Westminster & Chelsea District Nursing Trust.

£3,000 each was given to the British Heart Foundation, British Red Cross, Game Conservancy Trust, Help the Hospices, Kensington & Chelsea Community Transport Ltd and the Royal Wiltshire Yeomanry Benevolent Fund. Grants of £2,000 were made to each of the Cancer Relief Macmillan Fund, Marie Curie Cancer Care, East Chelsea Community Contact and Shaftesbury Homes & Arethusa. There were 32 grants of £1,000 and 2 of £500 to a wide range of mainly national organisations in the fields of youth, animal welfare, religious, welfare and medical.

Applications: In writing to the correspondent, who states: "Please note that contributions are given to a regular list of charities".

The Ellis Campbell Charitable Foundation

£37,000 (1993)

Youth, education, conservation

Craven House, West Street, Farnham, Surrey GU9 7ES
01252-722333

Correspondent: Graham Gardner Donald, Secretary

Trustees: Michael D C C Campbell; Mrs Linda F Campbell; Doris Campbell; Jamie L C Campbell; Alexandra J Campbell; Trevor M Aldridge.

Beneficial area: UK, with a preference for Perthshire and Hampshire.

Information available: Full accounts are on file at the Charity Commission.

General: "The foundation was established in 1989 by Michael Campbell, chairman of the Ellis Campbell Group of companies, and other members of his family who are also shareholders. Various companies within the group have covenanted £200,000 a year for four years to establish an endowment of £1 million. ...."

"Special emphasis is placed upon donations towards youth, education, and conservation (historical, architectural, and constructional heritage including modes of transport) in Hampshire and Perthshire." In the 1993 accounts, the chairman stated: "Since appearing in a number of Guides, we have received an enormously increased number of requests. This has enabled us to focus our giving more directly on the principal aims of the foundation although the "other" category is still supported."

In 1993, the trust had assets of £837,000 and an income of £78,000. Grants were given to 21 organisations totalling £37,000. Grants are given in the categories: youth; education; conservation, and other.

Three grants totalling £11,900 were to heritage projects in Hampshire, including £10,000 to Winchester Cathedral. £500 was given between Music in Blair Atholl and Perthshire Preservation, also towards heritage. 16 grants totalling £25,000 were given mainly to national or Surrey based organisations. 11 of these were in the "other" category, Surrey Scouts received £12,500 in the youth category and two grants were given towards education

including £5,000 to the Prince's Youth Business Trust.

Exclusions: No grants to individuals unless known by a trustee.

Applications: In writing to the correspondent. "Applicants should observe the areas of special interest and should not necessarily expect to receive an acknowledgement."

Caritas

£114,000 (1991/92)

Medical, Jewish, general

c/o Saffery Champness, Fairfax House, Fulwood Place, Gray's Inn, London WC1V 6UB

Correspondent: The Secretary

Trustees: Lord Rothschild; Lady Rothschild; M E Hatch.

Beneficial area: UK and Israel.

Information available: Full accounts are on file at the Charity Commission.

General: Caritas (charity in Latin) was set up in 1953 and now has assets of over £14 million. In 1991/92, these generated an income of £953,000. Although the income has been relatively constant (usually around £1.8 million), grants seem to fluctuate widely: £114,000 in 1991/92; £136,000 in 1990/91; £52,000 in 1989/90; £380,000 in 1988/89.

In recent years, grants have been substantially less than the available income. During 1991/92, £2.5 million was carried forward as a surplus, perhaps to be distributed in future years. "Grants are made entirely at the discretion of the trustees and surplus income is carried forward against likely [but unspecified] substantial commitments in the future."

In 1991/92, the trust made 56 grants, 25 of them for £1,000 or more. The largest grants were to the National Gallery (£37,000) and Glyndebourne Products Ltd (£15,000). It continues to support the hospital medical schools of Guys and St Thomas' (£8,000 each). Other large grants were to Dulwich Picture Gallery (£6,000) and the Jerusalem Foundation and Ashmolean Museum (£5,000 each).

There were 18 grants of £1,000 to £4,000 to Jewish, elderly, welfare, education and arts organisations including: Bucks Age

Concern; Glyndebourne Arts; Jerusalem Botanical Gardens Group; Research into Ageing; Save Britain's Heritage; Save Venice; Shelter; Waddesdon C of E Secondary School; World Movement Fund.

Applications: In writing to the correspondent. Applicants must include an sae.

Carlee Ltd

£140,000 (1990/91)

Jewish

6 Grangecourt Road, London N16 5EJ

Correspondent: Secretary

Trustees: H Grunhut; Mrs P Grunhut.

Beneficial area: Worldwide.

Information available: Accounts are on file at the Charity Commission up to 1990/91, but without a list of grants.

General: In 1990/91, the trust had assets of £808,000 and an income of £189,000 including £164,000 from deeds of covenant. Grants totalled £140,000 but unfortunately no information was available on the beneficiaries. The trust supports Jewish causes.

Applications: In writing to the correspondent.

The Carlton House Charitable Trust

£30,000 (1992/93)

Jewish, general

Craven House, 121 Kingsway, London WC2B 6PA
0171-242 5283

Correspondent: Stewart S Cohen, Trustee

Trustees: Stewart S Cohen; Peoul C Cohen; Fiora A Stein.

Beneficial area: Worldwide.

Information available: Full accounts are on file at the Charity Commission.

General: In 1992/93, the trust had assets of £364,000 and an income of £62,000 including £17,000 from a Gift Aid payment. Grants totalled £30,000 with the surplus of income over expenditure being used to build up the trusts assets.

41 grants were given in 1992/93, with the largest to Bnai Brith Charities Fund (£17,000 in two grants). About two thirds of the beneficiaries were Jewish organisations, the next largest grants being to the Western Marble Arch Synagogue (£2,700 in 11 grants) and Bnai Brith Hillel Foundation (£1,000).

The largest grant to a non-Jewish organisation was £3,000 to the Worshipful Company of Insurers. No other grants were over £600. Beneficiaries included the Army Benevolent Fund, Barnardo's, Drug & Alcohol Foundation and World Wide Fund for Nature UK, all of which received £50.

Applications: In writing to the correspondent.

The Carmichael-Montgomery Charitable Trust

£55,000 (1991/92)

Christian

3 Bear Close, Henley-in-Arden, Warwick B95 5HS
01564-793561

Correspondent: Mrs N Johnson

Trustees: Mrs B Baker; D J Carmichael; Miss B Exley; K Forrest; Mrs N Johnson; Revd M G Hanson; P Maskell; Mrs S Nicholson

Beneficial area: UK.

Information available: Full accounts are on file at the Charity Commission.

General: In 1991/92, the trust had assets of £485,000 and an income of £59,000. Grants totalled £55,000. 21 grants totalling about £10,000 were to individuals. The remaining £45,000 was given to 25 organisations.

Grants ranged from £100 to £5,000. Support is given chiefly to United Reformed Churches or ecumenical projects, usually with a URC constituent. Grants for capital expenditure have preference over running costs.

In 1991/92, other recipients included the Leicester University Chaplaincy, North of England Institute for Christian Education, Iona Community, Leicester Centre for Disability and Arts (this is not typical of the organisations supported), Windermere Centre and the Peartree Craft Centre (Derby). Only a few of the grants were recurrent.

Exclusions: Grants are not made for medical aid.

Applications: In writing to the correspondent. Consideration is given to individuals known to the trustees. Unsuccessful applications will not be acknowledged.

The Carnegie Dunfermline Trust

£103,000 (1992)

Social, recreational or cultural facilities in Dunfermline.

Abbey Park House, Abbey Park Place, Dunfermline, Fife KY12 7PB
01383-723638

Correspondent: William C Runciman, Secretary

Trustees: There are 16 life trustees, a further six appointed by Dunfermline District Council and three by Fife Regional Council.

Beneficial area: Dunfermline and its immediate environs. Applicants must be based in, or have a strong connection with, this area.

Information available: The trust publishes an annual report and guidance notes for applicants.

General: The trust was founded in August 1903. In Mr Carnegie's original instructions to the Gentlemen of the Commission, he said the endowment was "all to be used in attempts to bring into the monotonous lives of the toiling masses of Dunfermline more of sweetness and light ... some elevating conditions of life ... that the child of my native town, looking back in after years, however far from home it may have roamed, will feel simply by virtue of being such life has been made happier and better. If this be the fruit of your labours you will have succeeded; if not, you will have failed ... I have said your work is experimental ... If you can prove that good can be done you open new field to the rich which I am certain they are to be more and more anxious to find for their surplus wealth ... Remember you are pioneers, and do not be afraid of making mistakes; those who never make mistakes never make anything. Try many things freely, but discard just as freely ... As conditions of life change rapidly, you will not be restricted as to your plans or the scope of your activities."

Favoured applications

1. Schemes which are new and enterprising – ideas which will put Dunfermline or a Dunfermline club ahead of other comparable communities or clubs.
2. Schemes where people are helping others as well as themselves.
3. Schemes which result in attainment of an exceptionally high standard of accomplishment or excellence.
4. Schemes which would benefit young people so that in later life they feel they had an extra "something" simply because they came from Dunfermline.

Types of trust assistance available

1. **Loans** for major capital schemes, usually repayable over maximum of 5-7 years; usually interest-bearing (variable rate).
2. **Grants** usually only to organisations which are accepted by the Inland Revenue as having charitable status.
3. **Provision of equipment** – the trust will sometimes buy equipment and give it out on long loan.
4. **Sponsorship** eg. guarantee and grant-aid for training/coaching courses, sponsorship of courses arranged in Dunfermline by local groups.
5. **Guarantees** against loss on certain functions or events.

The most recent major project of the trust has been to assist the setting up a Heritage Centre for Dunfermline. In 1991, the trust paid the final £25,000 of its £200,000 cash commitment (it also conveyed free of charge the Abbot House building, conservatively valued at £220,000). A further £20,000 was offered in late 1990 towards the cost of appointing a director. £40,000 was transferred to a special fund for a major project in either the year 2000 or 2003 (the trust's centenary). It also gave the first half of its £20,000 allocation for an art feature at the new Dunfermline District Hospital.

The trust spent £12,000 on arts projects (plus a further £25,000 on grants, guarantees and payments on the trust's own arts schemes) and £58,000 on community projects. Of the latter, £34,000 was given in grants and equipment to local primary and secondary schools for new craft, design and technology equipment, a minibus, videos and outdoor equipment. Other grants given included training courses for sportsmen and sportswomen and help with special fundraising activities for sports clubs, and general social welfare grants to groups such as Abbeyfield Holiday Association (to take a group on holiday), Dunfermline Women's Aid (for equipment and toys), and Fairhaven Ministries (towards the cost of incorporation).

The trust owns and manages properties, three of which were sold in 1991 for £237,000. This has now been added to the trust's endowment. The trust's overall income in 1991 was £300,000.

Exclusions: No grants for:

1. Individuals (except in very special cases).
2. Closed clubs (ie. groups not open to the general public to join - this does not exclude minority groups catering for specialised interests).
3. Political organisations or causes, commercial enterprises, religious or sectarian bodies, or military or warlike pursuits.
4. Organisations which simply want help with maintenance and running costs; the trustees think these should be met out of subscription income. Exceptions might be made in special cases or for new bodies.
5. Projects which have already been started.

Applications: By letter at any time. "It is sometimes difficult for the trust to steer the correct course between helping a deserving group and sapping its initiative." Applicants are always expected to have applied to all relevant statutory bodies "and to show members' willingness to commit existing reserves or to embark on special fundraising activities".

Applications should be submitted by 31st May, 30th September or 31st January, and are considered three times a year.

Cash for Kids
(formerly BRMB— Birmingham Walkathon)

£277,000 (1991/92)

Children and young people in the West Midlands

96.4 FM BRMB/XTRA am, Radio House, Aston Road North, Aston, Birmingham B6 4BX
0121-359 4481; Fax: 0121-359 1117

Correspondent: Robert Ramsay, Head of Community Affairs

Trustees: David Bagley; John Buckingham; Richard Eyre; Peter Languard; Mike Owen; Richard Park; Dr Barry Roseman.

Beneficial area: West Midlands only (50 mile radius of Birmingham).

Information available: Accounts were on file at the Charity Commission up to 1991/92.

General: The charity aims to help disadvantaged children and young people (under the age of 18) living within Birmingham and the West Midlands area. It is keen to support a wide range of activities and projects for the relief of poverty or deprivation, both mental and physical or for the general welfare of children.

In 1991/92, the trust had an income of £170,000 and gave grants totalling £277,000. The vast majority of this (£200,000) was given to Telethon, and the Lions & Round Table Group received £20,000. Other grants were broken down as follows:

Fixtures & Fittings – £12,600 between four beneficiaries including Cannock Child Helpline and Stirchley Old Peoples Home.

Equipment – £20,000 between 15 beneficiaries including Mencap Saturday Playscheme (£6,000), Tamworth ATC (£4,500) and Jewish Youth Centre (£3,000).

Transport – £8,000 all to St Coles Hospice.

Local Groups (direct) – £13,000 between 10 grants of £400 to £4,000. The largest of which was to the Scout Association. Others included Children in Cities, Turning Point and Queen Alexandra College for the Blind.

Local schools – £3,000 between three schools.

Trustees will consider requests for help with salaries on the understanding that any grant given will be for one year only. The applicant must show evidence of future funding for the post.

Money may only be distributed to registered charities. If you are not registered, you may still apply but must have obtained permission from a registered charity willing to accept any money on your behalf.

Please do not telephone the trust, unless you have a specific enquiry.

Exclusions: No grants to organisations outside the West Midlands. No grants to individuals, for research, trips abroad, medical treatment, unspecified expenditure, deficit funding or repayment of loans, for distribution to other organisations or for administration costs.

Applications: On a form available from the correspondent. Applications must be received between 1st March and 1st July. Enclose an sae for receipt of application. Applicants will be informed by letter as to the outcome of their application.

The Castle Educational Trust

£129,000 (1992/93)

Deprived and disabled children

Baylis House, Stoke Poges Lane, Slough, Berks SL1 3PB
01753-558458

Correspondent: K H Holmes, Managing Trustee

Beneficial area: UK with a preference for Humberside.

Information available: Full accounts are on file at the Charity Commission.

General: In 1992/93, the trust had assets of £641,000 and an income of £149,000. Grants are made from the surplus generated by a school fees planning operation, offered by the trust through the Royal Insurance Group. Most grants are to national charities helping with the education of deprived and disabled children, such as Barnardo's and the Save the Children Fund.

In 1992/93, grants totalled £129,000 and were broken down into the following categories:

Local societies & activities – 59 grants of £50 to £5,000 totalling £69,000. The largest of these grants were to Age Concern - East Riding, Lord Mayor's Charity Appeal Fund and Godfrey Robinson Home for the Disabled (£5,000 each). Other beneficiaries included the Fish Trades Youth Club (£2,000), Mobility Trust and Hull Faith in the City Homeless Fund (£1,000 each) and Do Something Different Club (£500).

National societies – 16 grants of £100 to £5,000 totalling £26,000. Beneficiaries included Sequel (£5,000), Salvation Army (£2,500) and the British Sports Association for the Disabled (£2,000).

Churches and missions – 7 grants of £700 to £8,000 totalling £16,000. These included Trafalgar Street Church (£8,000), Royal National Mission to Deep Sea Fishermen (£1,000) and Youth for Christ in Hull (£700).

Sponsoring & assisting local people with disabilities and for training. Six organisations received grants for a number of people: the Community Resource Team for People with Physical Disabilities (£5,000), Dyslexia Institute (£4,500), Disability Rights Advisory Service (£3,200), Humberside Probation Service (£1,000), and Sailors Families Society and CAB (£500 each).

Applications: In writing to the correspondent. Grants to individuals can only be considered if the application is made through/by a child welfare agency.

The Joseph & Annie Cattle Trust

£119,000 (1993/94)

General in north Humberside

Western, 12 Packman Lane, Kirkella, Hull HU10 7TL
01482-653250

Correspondent: R Waudby

Trustees: J A Collier; M T Gyte; R Waudby.

Beneficial area: UK with a preference for north Humberside.

Information available: Full accounts are on file at the Charity Commission.

General: In 1993/94, the trust gave grants totalling £119,000. Grants are given to the following areas:

- Churches and missions. Recipients included Hull Livelink, Trafalgar Street Church (Hull) and the Royal National Mission to Deep Sea Fishermen.
- Local societies and activities. Grants ranged from £90 to £5,000 to Humberside charities. Many receive regular support such as Age Concern (Hull), Hull Fish Trades Boys Club, North Humberside Association for Mental Health, PHAB and Dove House Hospice.
- National charities. Grants of £1,000 were given to organisations such as the Royal Commonwealth Society for the Blind, Institute for the Deaf and Blind and Paul O'Gorman Foundation. Other beneficiaries include St John's Ambulance Brigade and the Camphill Village Trust.
- Individuals. Grants are given to local individuals, usually ranging from £100 to £1,000 and totalling about £7,000.

Some regular benefciaries receive grants twice yearly, including Hull & East Riding Charitable Trust (£1,500); Martin House Hospice Huddersfield and St Leonards Hospice (both £1,000 twice a year); St Matthews Church and the Sailors Families Society (both £500 twice a year).

Applications: In writing to the correspondent.

The Thomas Sivewright Catto Charitable Settlement

£49,000 (1992/93)

Medical, overseas aid/development, children and youth, welfare

23 Great Winchester Street, London EC2P 2AX

Correspondent: Miss Ann Uwins

Trustees: Hon Isabel Catto; Hon Mrs Ruth Bennett; Lord Catto.

Beneficial area: Worldwide.

Information available: Full accounts are on file at the Charity Commission.

General: In 1992/93, the trust had assets of £356,000 and an income of £71,000, consisting of £10,666 from a donation and £60,000 from investments. Grants totalled £49,000.

42 grants were given, the largest being £14,000 to Westminster Abbey Trust, £10,000 to London Cancer Trust, £5,000 to Minchampton Centre for the Elderly and £2,000 to the NSPCC Trading Co Ltd. Seven grants of £1,000 were given to Care International; Elgin Museum; Multiple Sclerosis Society; Margaret Pyke Trust; St Wilfrids Hospice; YMCA; YWCA of Great Britain. Most remaining grants were for £250 to £500 (although there were some very small grants) given to a wide range of causes including animal welfare, Christian, homelessness, sickness, children and overseas.

Applications: In writing to the correspondent.

The Wilfrid & Constance Cave Foundation

£60,000 (1993/94)

Conservation, animal welfare, health and welfare

c/o New Lodge Farm, Drift Road, Winkfield, Windsor SL4 4QQ
01344-890351

Correspondent: W C Varney

Trustees: Mrs T Jones; Mrs J Pickin; Rev P Buckler; F Jones.

Beneficial area: UK, with a preference for Wiltshire.

Information available: Full accounts are on file at the Charity Commission.

General: In 1993/94, the trust had assets of £1.3 million and an income of £124,000. Grants totalled £60,000 leaving a surplus, after expenses, of £47,000. There have been slightly larger surpluses in previous years.

There is a preference for the west of England especially Wiltshire. 32 grants were given, the largest being £10,000 to Clwyd Special Riding School and £6,000 to Chiltern Nursery Training College.

£5,000 grants went to Nuneaton & North Warwickshire Equestrian Centre, All Saints Church, Long Ashton and the Peto Institute (for an individual).

There were 20 other grants of £1,000 to £3,000 to organisations working in the fields of medical, welfare, education, religion, animal welfare and the environment. There were also seven smaller grants of £120 to £850. Charities supported included Berkshire Trust for Conservation Volunteers, Cotswold Canal Trust, Countryside Workshops and the National Federation of City Farms.

Applications: In writing to the correspondent.

The B G S Cayzer Charitable Trust

£75,000 (1992/93)

General

Cayzer House, 1 Thomas More Street, London E1 9AR
0171-481 4343 ext. 274

Correspondent: Jeff Tottman

Trustees: Peter N Buckley; Peter R Davies.

Beneficial area: UK.

Information available: Accounts are on file at the Charity Commission, but without a grants list for 1992/93.

General: The trust was set up in 1982 by the beneficiaries of the Will of the late Bernard Cayzer, a former director of Caledonia Investments. The trust owns 200,000 cumulative preferred ordinary shares in the Cayzer Trust Company and nearly 33,000 shares in Caledonia Investments.

In 1992/93, these shares and donations generated an income of £152,000. Grants totalled £75,000, leaving a surplus for the year of £76,000. The trust is currently accumulating its income and formulating a policy to fund a few major projects.

In 1991/92, when the charity had an income of £64,000, it gave 25 grants of £50 to £2,500 totalling only £14,000. The largest of these grants were: Glyndebourne Festival Society (£2,500) and Save the Children Fund (£2,400). There were four grants of £1,000 to: Friends of the Royal Botanical Gardens; St Paul's, Knightsbridge; John Younger Trust and the Bulldog Trust. Other grants were given to church, medical, disability, children, welfare and conservation/environment organisations.

Exclusions: Unsolicited appeals will not be supported.

Applications: The trust tends to support only people/projects known to the Cayzer family or the trustees.

The Amelia Chadwick Trust

£105,000 (1993/94)

General

Layton & Co, Victoria House, 20 Hoghton Street, Southport PR9 0NX
01704-547117

Correspondent: J R M McGibbon, Partner

Trustees: J R McGibbon; Mrs M Bibby; J C H Bibby.

Beneficial area: UK, especially Merseyside.

Information available: Full accounts are on file at the Charity Commission.

General: In 1993/94, the trust had assets of £995,000 and an income of £87,000. Grants totalled £105,000 and are listed in the accounts in date order through the year.

Of the 95 grants given, 27 were to the Merseyside Development Foundation totalling £32,000, with the largest single grant being £19,000. Other major beneficiaries were St Helens Women's Aid (£10,000), Women's Education Training Trust, Liverpool Early Years Centre and Adullam Homes Mersey Appeal (£5,000 each). There is a preference for Merseyside, with a wide range of charities supported. Other beneficiaries included All Saints Church Thornton Hough (£500), Garston Adventure Playground, Liverpool Gingerbread Trust and Merseyside Association for the Disabled (all £1,000), and Merseyside Youth Orchestra (£200).

Many of the recipients appear to receive an annual grant, particularly the non-Merseyside charities which included Amnesty International (£750), CPRE (£200), Oxfam (£1,000) and Oxford Dyslexic Association (£750).

Applications: In writing to the correspondent.

The Chamberlain Foundation

£40,000 to organisations (1992/93)

Welgare, general

Devon House, The Green, Winchmore Hill, London N21 1SA
0181-882 9366

Correspondent: Ms C Elmer, Secretary

Trustees: Mrs G M Chamberlain; G R Chamberlain; A G Chamberlain; Mrs S J Kent; Mrs C M Lester; Mrs L A Churcher; Mrs M J Spears.

Beneficial area: UK.

Information available: Full accounts are on file at the Charity Commission.

General: In 1992/93, the trust had assets of £1.2 million and an income of £210,000 (£261,000 in 1991/92). It made grants totalling £131,000 (£103,000 in 1991/92) leaving a surplus of £64,000 (£143,000 in 1991/92).

Grants to organisations totalled just over £40,000. The largest were to the Respite Care Trust (£20,000); Good Neighbours Scheme in Eastern Enfield (£4,000); Seven Rivers Cheshire Home (£3,750); Winged Fellowship (£3,000). Other grants of £500 upwards were given to organisations such as Action Research, St Matthews Children Fund UK (Ethiopia), Worshipful Company of Tin Plate Workers and Bishop Stopford School.

Grants were also given to individuals, in need £62,000; for education £10,000 (including £1,000 to three schools); and around £20,000 to other individuals.

Applications: In writing to the correspondent.

The Chapman Charitable Trust

£163,000 (1994)

General

Messrs Crouch Chapman, 62 Wilson Street, London EC2A 2BU
0171-782 0007

Correspondent: Roger S Chapman

Trustees: Roger S Chapman; W John Chapman; Richard J Chapman; Bruce D Chapman.

Beneficial area: UK.

Information available: Full accounts are on file at the Charity Commission.

General: In 1994, the trust had assets of £3.6 million and an income of £146,000. After very low expenses of £3,500, the trust made 102 grants (ranging from £250 to £25,000) totalling £163,000. The largest grants were to the Field Studies Council (£25,000) and the Aldeburgh Foundation (£20,000). The following all received grants of £10,000: Methodist Homes for the Aged, National Children's Home, Queen Alexandra Hospital Home and St Bridgets Cheshire Home. All the above groups received similarly large grants in previous years. There were two grants for £5,000, to the Leysian Mission and the National Trust for Scotland, and a £2,500 grant for the Fitzwilliam Museum. There were four grants of £2,000, 35 grants of £1,000, 42 of £500 and seven of £250.

The above grants are broken down in the trust's report into the following general categories:

	Local £ (no)	National £ (no)	Total £ (no)
Cultural and recreational	8,250 (11)	23,500 (5)	31,750 (16)
Education and research	2,000 (1)	28,000 (5)	30,000 (6)
Health	22,500 (8)	7,500 (9)	30,000 (17)
Social services	18,500 (17)	43,500 (36)	62,000 (53)
Environment and heritage	1,500 (3)	1,500 (2)	3,000 (5)
Religion	6,500 (5)	- -	6,500 (5)
Total	59,250 (45)	104,000 (57)	163,250 (102)

Most grants were given to national charities especially in the fields of health, welfare and disabilty, with a few grants to local charities including Cambridge and District Spastics Society, Girls Brigade Sheffield and Gwynedd Hospice at Home. The local grants do not appear to be tied to any particular part of the country.

Exclusions: No grants to individuals.

Applications: In writing at any time. The trustees currently meet twice a year at the end of September and March. They receive a great many applications and regret that they cannot acknowledge receipt of them. The absence of any communication for six months thus means that an application must have been unsuccessful.

The Charities Fund

£119,000 (1993)

Sick, needy, elderly people

c/o Sovereign Health Care, PO Box 86, 26 Manningham Lane, Bradford BD1 3DN
01274-729472

Correspondent: Gerard Clarkson, Secretary

Trustees: E Bentham; G McGowan.

Beneficial area: West Yorkshire.

Information available: Accounts are on file at the Charity Commission, but without a list of grants.

General: The trust has been set up for:

- The provision of amenities for hospital patients
- General charitable organisations
- Relief and assistance to those who are sick, needy or elderly

In 1993, the fund had an income of £258,000. This included a donation of £187,500 from Sovereign Health Care, which is the registered trading name of the Hospital Fund of Bradford, and £62,500 from reclaimed tax. This is a non-profit making provident and mutual benefit company, providing health care insurance.

The fund makes grants to charities for the relief of needy, sick and elderly people. In 1993, grants totalled £119,000 (£92,000 in 1992) made up as follows (1992 figures in brackets):

Associations and institutions	£93,000	(£70,000)
Hospitals	£15,000	(£7,500)
Hospices	£4,500	(£2,000)
Nurses' training grants	£8,000	(£12,000)

There was no further information as to the associations supported.

Applications: In writing to the correspondent.

The Chetwode Samworth Charitable Trust

£66,000 (1992/93)

General

Samworth Brothers, Fields Farm, Cropwell Butler, Notts NG12 3AP
0115-933 5221

Correspondent: J G Ellis, Secretary

Trustees: Malcolm R Allen; John C Samworth.

Beneficial area: Preference for Leicestershire and Northamptonshire.

Information available: Full accounts are on file at the Charity Commission.

General: In 1992/93, the trust had assets of £1.2 million, generating an income of £66,000. The trust's grant-making rose consistently from £29,000 in 1985/86 to £82,000 in 1988/89; since then the grant total has decreased, and was £66,000 in 1992/93. Preference is given to appeals from Leicestershire and Northamptonshire, together with national medical charities.

Nearly 40 grants were made ranging from £5 to £25,000. The largest went to the Sports Aid Foundation and the Prince's Trust (£25,000 each). The British Field Sports Society received the largest grant in 1991/92 (£15,000). Other large grants were given to: St Gorran PCC (£2,260), Cottesmore Hunt Charitable Trust (£1,500) and three grants of £1,000 each to the Worshipful Company of Butchers; Exeter 92 British Transport Games and 75th Anniversary Appeal Fund. All other grants were for £5 to £500 and were given to welfare, medical and religious organisations.

Applications: In writing to the correspondent.

The Children's Research Fund

£201,000 (1993)

Child health research

6 Castle Street, Liverpool L2 0NA
0151-236 2844

Correspondent: H Greenwood, Chairman

Trustees: The Council.

Beneficial area: UK.

Information available: Full accounts are on file at the Charity Commission.

General: The trust supports research into children's diseases and child health problems at institutes and university departments of child health.

Grants in 1993 totalled £201,000, up from £170,000 in the previous year. The major beneficiary in each year was the Institute of Child Health at the University of Leicester, with the two grants of £90,000 each probably being part of an on-going project over a number of years. Similarly, grants of £35,000 in each year went to Children's Research International. The other beneficiaries in 1993 were the Department of Paediatric Surgery at Alder Hey Hospital in Liverpool (£13,000), Child Health Research Foundation (£10,000) and the Disabilities Study Unit (£3,000). Although the trust excludes capital projects (see below), a final award of £40,000 is recorded in the accounts as being to a Lecture Theatre and Library at the University of Southampton.

Exclusions: No grants for capital projects.

Applications: Applicants from child health research units and university departments are invited to send in an initial outline of their proposal; if this is acceptable they will then be sent an application form. Applications are considered in March and November.

The Childs Charitable Trust

£148,000 (1990/91)

Christian missions

2 & 4 Saffrons Road, Eastbourne, East Sussex BN21 1DQ
01323-417944

Correspondent: D Martin

Trustees: D N Martin; Hettie V Childs; R H Williams.

Beneficial area: Worldwide.

Information available: Full accounts are on file at the Charity Commission for 1990/91.

General: The objects of the trust are the furtherance of the Gospel of God, education and the relief of poverty. Regarding the principal object, the furtherance of the Gospel of God; the trustees are "actively involved in supporting and encouraging all Christian persons and societies to achieve this goal". There is a preference for large scale projects in the UK and abroad.

In 1990/91, the trust had assets of £5.4 million and an income of £424,000. Grants totalled £148,000 with other expenditure of £43,000, including £28,000 for repairs and maintenance. The trust has a regular surplus of income over expenditure. This is being used to build up the assets base to support large projects in the future.

Grants were made under the following headings:

- **Religion** – 15 grants totalling £124,000. Beneficiaries included Martin Charitable Trust (£19,000); Counties Evangelical Work (£12,000); Evangelical Missionary Alliance and the Scripture Gift Mission (£10,000 each). Grants of around £1,000 went to the Gideons, Philipines Church and the Slavic Gospel Association. 55 miscellaneous grants of under £1,000 totalled £7,400.

- **Relief of Poverty** – £11,000 in total including £9,000 to Medical Missionary News. Voluntary Workers for Overseas Projects received £400 and 15 miscellaneous grants of under £300 totalled £1,300.

- **Education** – £13,000 including Evangelical Press (£3,000); Family Foundation Trust (£2,000); Sarnia Evangelical Trust, Blanchard (£1,250); Feba Radio (£1,000) and 49 miscellaneous grants of under £500 totalling £6,000.

Applications: In writing to the correspondent.

The Chiron Trust

£125,000 (1992/93)

General

Farrer & Co, 66 Lincoln's Inn Fields, London WC2A 3LH
0171-242 2022

Trustees: D M Tinson; C J Tinson; I R Marks.

Beneficial area: Worldwide.

Information available: Accounts are on file at the Charity Commission, but without a list of grants.

General: In 1992/93, the trust had assets of £1.5 million and an income of £118,000. Grants totalled £125,000, but unfortunately no grants list was available. The only other accounts on file at the Charity Commission were those for 1988.

Applications: In writing to the correspondent.

Chownes Foundation

£108,000 (1993/94)

General

The Courtyard, Beeding Court, Steyning, West Sussex BN44 3TW
01903-816699

Correspondent: R A Brooker

Trustees: Charles Stonor; Joan Stonor; the Abbot of Worth.

Beneficial area: UK.

Information available: Full accounts are on file at the Charity Commission.

General: The foundation has wide interests and its objects include making grants to social non-political causes with explicit reference to Amnesty International, the relief of poverty and the advancement of education.

For 1993/94, the foundation had assets of only £69,000 (down from £238,000 in 1989/90) and an income of £134,000 (£170,000 in 1989/90), most of which was Gift Aid donations from sponsors.

55 grants were made totalling £108,000 (48 grants totalling £115,000 in 1989/90), the largest of which was to Amnesty International (£5,000). There were 20 grants of £2,000 to £3,000, of which 17 were to individuals for the education of the young and relief of poverty for the elderly. The other three were to the Howard League for Penal Reform, Friends of the Samaritans and St Annes Convent. Other beneficiaries included St Paul's Church, Haywards Heath (£1,500); Burnside Social Club & Spinal Injuries Association (£1,000 each) and £3,500 for a foundation in Peru.

Applications: In writing to the correspondent.

The John & Celia Bonham Christie Charitable Trust

£52,000 (1993/94)

General

PO Box 6, Bath BA1 2YH

Trustees: Mrs J R Bonham Christie; R Bonham Christie; Mrs Roger Kerr; P R Fitzgerald; N R Brown.

Beneficial area: UK.

Information available: Full accounts are on file at the Charity Commission.

General: In 1993/94, the trust had assets of £890,000 and an income of £42,000. It made about 120 grants totalling £52,000, only 20 of which were to new beneficiaries. These included University of Edinbugh TASK Appeal (£800), Insitute of Psychiatry (£500) and Transport for the Disabled (£300).

Grants are generally small, the largest in 1993/94, were £5,000 to the Psychiatry Research Trust (Triumph over Phobia) and £1,000 to Somerset Council on Alcoholism. Other grants of £600 or more included those to the Industrial Therapy Centre, North Somerset; London Chest Hospital Appeal; National Osteoporosis Society; Pembury Hospital; Royal Academy of Music; Sick Children's Trust; Toc H, Bangor; Tuberous Sclerosis Association. The vast majority of grants appear to be recurrent over three to five years.

The other grants were given to a wide range of local and national organisations, with some preference for the Avon district. Beneficiaries included Avon Riding for the Disabled, Bath Bach Choir, Battersea Churches Housing Trust, BLISS, Brecon Disabled Club, Imperial Cancer Research Fund, Lincoln Toy Library, London Chest Hospital, Manchester Leukas Aid, Midland Sports Centre Trust, MIND (Tower Hamlets), National Council of YMCA – Ireland, Scottish Council for Spastics, Shropshire & Mid Wales Hospice, Sussex and Birmingham Universities, Toc-H (Aylesbury).

Applications: In writing to the correspondent. The trustees regret that the income is fully allocated for the foreseeable future. Only a small number of new applications are supported each year.

The Christmas Cracker Trust

£750,000 (1992/93)

Christian overseas aid and development

87 Blackfriars Road, London SE1
0171-928 9422

Correspondent: G J Mungeam, Secretary

Trustees: Ram Gidoomal; Rev Steve Chalke; Dr Raju Abraham; Lt Col Brian Phillips; David Roberts; Philip Warland.

Beneficial area: Worldwide.

Information available: Full accounts are on file at the Charity Commission.

General: The trust raises money through projects run throughout the UK (and more recently overseas) by groups of young people, to provide resources for developing countries. In 1989 and 1990, youth groups were encouraged to set up and run "Eat Less – Pay More" restaurants. In 1991 and 1992, "Tune In – Pay Out" radio stations were set up.

In 1992/93, for the first time there were two main projects. "Radio Cracker" involved 83 local special event radio stations and raised over £650,000 for overseas development. "The Alternative Christmas" held in the summer, involved young people being given £1 and having 48 hours to use that £1 to raise as much as possible. Over £100,000 was raised in total for rapid relief.

The £650,000 was distributed to 32 countries in response to bids made against set criteria. About 80% was distributed to established UK relief and development agencies, the rest to smaller local organisations and individuals.

The geographical distribution was as follows:

Central & South America	17%
Eastern & Central Europe	7%
South & South East Asia	37%
Africa & the Middle East	39%

The causes benefiting were as follows:

Relief	£125,000
Disadvantaged, disabled	£119,000
Medical care, community health	£214,000
Cottage industry, education, training	£142,000

The £100,000 for rapid relief went to Bosnia, Africa and India.

Applications: There is an application form that should be completed. The trustees usually meet at the begining of each calendar year, but final decisions are not taken, nor the money distributed, before 31st July.

The Church Burgesses Educational Foundation

£133,000 (1991)

Religion, education and youth in Sheffield

c/o Dibb Lupton Broomhead & Prior, Fountain Precinct, Balm Green, Sheffield
S1 1RZ
0114-272 0202

Correspondent: Mrs Conley

Beneficial area: Sheffield.

Information available: Accounts are on file at the Charity Commission up to 1991.

General: In 1991, the trust had an income of £128,000 and gave grants totalling about £133,000 under the five following schemes:

Scheme A, 23 grants to church schools totalling £17,700. This money was for tables and chairs, books, calculators, computers, playground equipment, alarms, etc..

Scheme B, 30 special grants totalling £23,700. Grants ranged from £100 to £5,000 for religion or youth.

Scheme C, 23 grants to individuals for education totalling £23,400. Grants ranged from £200 to £4,000, many recurrent.

Scheme D, 14 grants to individuals for education, ranging from £155 to £500 and totalling £5,400.

Scheme E, 9 grants to youth organisations ranging from £1,000 to £5,000 and totalling £30,000.

The trust also made two loans of £150 and £7,500.

Applications: In writing to the correspondent.

The City Educational Trust Fund

£125,000 (1993/94)

Education

Corporation of London, PO Box 270, Guildhall, London EC2P 2EJ
0171-332 1405

Correspondent: Town Clerk

Trustees: Corporation of London.

Beneficial area: Generally organisations within London.

Information available: Accounts are on file at the Charity Commission, but without a list of grants.

General: Grants generally range between £1,000 and £28,000 and are awarded to a variety of educational groups and institutions in London, primarily City University. Other preferences include: science, technology, business management and commerce, biology, ecology and the cultural arts, by the promotion of research, study, teaching and training in such subjects.

In 1993/94, the trust had assets of £2.7 million and an income of £115,000. It gave grants of between £1,000 and £28,000 totalling £125,000. The main beneficiaries were City University (£94,500 in total); St Paul's Cathedral Choir (£20,000) and the Juliette Alvin Music Therapy Fund (£3,000). In 1991/92, recipients included Alleyn's School (£7,500), Young Person's Concert Foundation (£5,000) and the Community Language Centre (£500).

Applications: In writing to the correspondent.

The CLA Charitable Trust

£86,000 (1993)

Country recreation/education for disabled people

16 Belgrave Square, London SW1X 8PQ
0171-235 0511

Correspondent: Colonel A F Mackain-Bremner

Trustees: C J Balfour; Peter Giffard; M A Gregory; G D Inge-Innes-Lillingston.

Beneficial area: UK.

Information available: Annual report and summary of accounts available from the trust. (No full accounts on file at the Charity Commission since those for 1980/81).

General: The main object of the trust is: "The relief of persons who are mentally or physically handicapped by the making of grants or loans to landowners for the provision of facilities for recreation and leisure time occupation for such persons...". This is a collecting rather than an endowed trust, working through the Country Landowners Association with which it is closely linked.

Projects supported in the past include: provision of flat-bottomed boats suitable for wheelchairs; laying of hard paths and suitable lavatories for disabled people; special bird hides – including a wheelchair lift to give access to a bird hide in a tree; Braille trails, and greenhouses for an horticultural project for mentally disabled people.

Although no up-to-date accounts were on file at the Charity Commission, the trust gave its grant total as £86,000 in 1993.

Applications: In writing to the correspondent.

The Roger & Sarah Bancroft Clark Charitable Trust

£57,000 (see below)

General

40 High Street, Street, Somerset
BA16 0YA

Correspondent: Mrs B L Gunson

Trustees: Eleanor C Robertson; Mary P Lovell; Stephen Clark; S Caroline Gould.

Beneficial area: UK and overseas.

Information available: Full accounts are on file at the Charity Comission.

General: The objects of the trust are general charitable purposes with particular reference to:

1. The Religious Society of Friends and associated bodies;

2. Charities connected with Somerset;
3. Individuals for education.

The trust has two separate funds, unfortunately we have only been able to update the information on one. In 1993, the RBC Charitable Trust had assets of £259,000, an income of £37,000 and gave grants totalling £16,000. The main grants were: University of Edinburgh (£10,000) and the Architectural Heritage Society of Scotland and Edinburgh Monthly Meeting (£1,500 each). Other grants ranged from £5 to £400.

In 1991, the SBC Fund had assets of about £1 million and an income of £97,000. Grants totalled £72,000. 140 grants to organisations totalled £41,000, ranging from £50 to £1,500, but mostly under £500. The largest grants were to Oxfam (Oxford) and Quaker Peace and Service (both £1,500). £1,000 grants were given to the Dance Scholarship Trust, Quaker Social Responsibility Higher Education Awards, Retreat Benevolent Fund (York), Rook Lane Chapel (Frome), Sibford School, Sibford School Music Centre Appeal, Society for the Protection of Ancient Buildings and the University of Stirling, South Africa Scholarship Trust. Smaller grants were given to a range of mostly local organisations throughout the UK, including grants to a number of churches. In addition £31,000 was given to individuals for educational purposes.

According to the Charity Commission, the trust had an income of £82,000 in 1993.

Applications: In writing to the correspondent. There is no application form and telephone calls are not accepted. Trustees meet about three times a year. Applications will be acknowledged if sae is enclosed.

The Clarkson Jersey Charitable Trust

£150,000 (1991)

General

Les Tisserands, Rue des Landes, St Peter, Jersey, Channel Islands

Correspondent: Mrs C A Weaver

Trustees: Mrs D M Clarkson; M Unwin; Mrs C Hunter Blair.

Beneficial area: UK, with a preference for Jersey.

Information available: The trust is registered in the Channel Islands. We have been unable to confirm the information on this trust.

General: We have been unable to up date this entry and no reply was received from the correspondent to our requests for information. The entry therefore repeats that from the previous Edition of this Guide.

In 1991, the trust had an income of £250,000 and made grants totalling £150,000. Grants are one-off payments for specific projects and tangible items rather than administration or running costs. Grants are usually for £1,000 or over.

Applications: In writing to the correspondent. Trustees meet quarterly.

The Cleopatra Trust

£182,000 (1993)

Medical, general

Charities Aid Foundation, Foundation House, Coach & Horses Passage, The Pantiles, Tunbridge Wells, TH2 5TZ
01892-512244

Correspondent: Trust Manager

Trustees: Charles Peacock; Bettine Bond; Clare Peacock.

Beneficial area: Worldwide.

Information available: Full accounts are on file at the Charity Commission.

General: The trust was established in 1991 and holds 1.5 million shares in Nurdin & Peacock plc, as does the Epigoni Trust for which there is a separate entry in this Guide. The two trusts also share two trustees and an interest in medical charities. In 1993, its total assets were £2.88 million generating an income of £128,000. Grants totalled £182,000.

20 grants were made ranging from £2,500 to £19,000, mostly to medical charities. The largest were to Orbis International (£19,000), VSO and Cancer Research Campaign (both £15,000), and British Association of United Cancer Patients & Families & Friends (£12,500).

Eight organisations received £10,000 including Aspire, Centrepoint Soho, Primary Immunodeficiency Association and Society for Horticultural Therapy.

Non-medical organisations which received support included Actionaid (£8,000), Charities Aid Foundation (£2,500), Canine Partners for Independence (£5,000) and the Marine Conservation Society (£5,000).

Applications: In writing to the correspondent.

The Cleveland Community Foundation

£96,000 (1993/94)

General in Cleveland and neighbourhood

Cleveland Business Centre, Watson Street, Middlesbrough, Cleveland TS1 2RQ
01642-245284

Correspondent: Sylvia Noddings, Director

Trustees: Sir Ron Norman; Jack Ord; John Bloom; Robert Sale; Pate Sole; J Kirton; A Kitching; M Stewart; D Peart; S Still; Bernard Storey; H Thornton; Kath Taylor.

Beneficial area: Cleveland and neighbourhood.

Information available: Full accounts are on file at the Charity Commission.

General: In 1993/94, the trust completed the CAF/Mott Challenge and established an endowment fund of over £2 million. It will receive an extra £666,000 from the Challenge.

Grants ranging from £100 to £5,000 were given to 69 organisations totalling £96,000. The main areas of support appear to be community groups, health/disability and youth organisations. Grants of £5,000 were given to Burbank Community Centre; Cleveland Carousel; Menro House and West View Advice & Resource Centre. Grants of over £4,000 went to: Hartlepool Challenge for Youth; Shelter and Ayresome Asian Ladies Group. There were 15 grants of £2,000 to £3,740 and ten grants of £1,000 to £2,000 to groups such as: Big Ears Appeal; Cleveland Youth Association; Eastern Ravens (Plus+) Project; Jam Pot Project, Hartlepool and Riding for the Disabled.

Smaller grants of £150 upwards were given to a range of organisations including a number of credit unions, Southside Christian Broadcasting, Grangetown Special Olympics Group and Cruse Bereavement Care, Guisborough.

Exclusions: No support for individuals, sponsored events, major national fundraising appeals, holidays or social outings.

Applications: On a form available from the correspondent. Applications are considered in February, June and October and should be submitted by the 1st of the previous month.

The Clifton Charitable Trust

£55,000 (1993)

General

15 Pembroke Road, Bristol BS8 3BG
0117-946 4000

Correspondent: Alfred Hill, Partner

Trustees: Avon Executer and Trustee Company.

Beneficial area: UK and overseas, preference for the South West.

Information available: Full accounts are on file at the Charity Commission.

General: In 1993, the trust had assets of £835,000, an income of £53,000 and gave 101 grants totalling £55,000. The largest were to the Greater Bristol Trust (£11,000), Save the Children Fund (£10,000) and Bras Manuel Aleixo (£9,400 for the relief of poverty in Mozambique).

Four other grants were over £1,000: Clifton Scientific (£1,200), NSPCC (£5,100), Sarawingin Gram Vikas Kendra – Palamau District Aid Organisation, India (£2,000) and St George's Music Trust (£2,500). Most of the other grants were under £500. A range of causes were supported including medicine, welfare, arts, environment/conservation and Christian.

Beneficiaries included Bristol Cathedral Trust (£330), CLIC (£600), City of Bristol Choir (£50), Evangelical Alliance (£25), Greenbelt (£155), Prisoners Abroad (£100), RSPCA (£100), UNICEF (£200) and Wells Cathedral School (£50).

Also included under the registered heading of the Clifton Charitable Trust is the Craig Fund, which generated an income of over £38,000, having assets of £663,000. Set up in 1988 through a will, it makes annual donations to both Barnardo's and the Salvation Army (specifically for its rescue work), both of whom received nearly £12,000 during the year.

Applications: In writing to the correspondent.

The Francis Coales Charitable Foundation

£155,000 (1992)

Historical in Bucks, Beds, Herts and Northants

The Mount, Parsonage Hill, Somerton, Somerset TA11 7PF
01458-272545

Correspondent: J Coales

Beneficial area: UK, especially Beds, Bucks, Herts and Northants.

Information available: Full accounts are on file at the Charity Commission.

General: The trust was established nearly 20 years ago following the winding up of the Francis Coale & Son corn merchant's business. It mainly provides grants and loans for:

- The repair and restoration of any ecclesiastical or other buildings built before 1875 which are open to the public, including their contents;
- Archaeological and other research into antiquarian sites, buildings or items (including the cost of books, theses and lectures);
- The purchase and stocking of public libraries to provide a supply of books relating to historical buildings and objects.

The trustees give priority to buildings in Buckinghamshire, Bedfordshire, Hertfordshire and Northamptonshire, where most of the merchant's business was carried out. Buildings in other counties are only considered in exceptional cases, although grants are made for monuments in churches irrespective of location.

Most of the grants in 1992 were in the range of £1,000 to £5,000. However, there was also a donation of £6,750 for an architectural student's scholarship. £5,000 grants were made towards work undertaken on: Windsor Castle's Aerary; the chantry tomb at Kingston-on-Soar; the tower and spire at Brixworth Northamptonshire; Lathbury in Buckinghamshire; monuments at Great Hampden in Buckinghamshire, and the Poyntz Monument at North Ockendon in Essex.

In 1992, the trust had assets of nearly £1.2 million and an income of £126,000. The report for the year states that the trust received 135 enquiries, 98 completed application forms, and paid 85 grants.

Applications: In writing to the correspondent for an application form.

The Lance Coates Charitable Trust 1969

£60,000 (1992/93)

General

Springhill Centre, Cuddlington, Aylesbury, Bucks HP18 0AE
01296-747157

Correspondent: Hugh L Coates

Trustees: H L T Coates, E P Serjeant, S M Coates.

Beneficial area: UK.

Information available: Full accounts are on file at the Charity Commission.

General: In 1992/93, the trust had assets of £757,000 and an income of £46,000.

Grants totalled £60,000 given to three organisations, all of which are regularly supported. The beneficiaries were Springhill Cancer Rehabilitation Centre (£25,000 and £35,000 in 1991/92), Springhill Cancer Pace (£20,000 and £32,000 in 1991/92) and the Country Trust (£15,000 and £25,000 in 1991/92).

In 1991/92, the only other grants were to Whitchurch PCC (£350) and Owermoigne (£250).

Applications: In writing to the correspondent.

The David Cohen Family Charitable Trust

£44,000 (1993)

Arts

33a Elsworthy Road, London NW3 3BT
0171-586 3192

Correspondent: Duncan Haldane

Trustees: Dr David Cohen; Veronica Cohen; Imogen Cohen; Olivia Cohen.

Beneficial area: UK.

Information available: Full records are on file at the Charity Commission accompanied by an annual report giving an account of the trust's artistic choices.

General: In 1993, the trust had assets of £975,000 and an income of £60,000. It gave 25 grants totalling £44,000. The largest was £15,000 to the Arts Council for the David Cohen British Literature Prize. From 1991 to 1996, the trust is sponsoring the award (to be made biennially by the Arts Council) to honour a British author for his/her work as a whole (not for a particular publication). The total cost to the trust will be £90,000 (six payments of £15,000).

Other large grants included: £5,000 to the Poetry Society; £3,000 to Out of Joint; £2,500 to Fitzwilliam Museum Trust and £2,225 to the Glyndebourne Festival Opera. All other grants were for £25 to £2,000 and were given to a number of theatres and arts organisations. Payments of £1,000 each have continued to be given to Almeida Theatre, Camden Arts Centre and National Art Collections Fund.

Exclusions: Grants to registered charities only; no grants to individuals.

Applications: No response is made to applications unless it is decided to make a grant. There are no application forms. Applicants should state the purpose for which a donation is required briefly outlining related work and the financial circumstances. Trustees normally meet three times a year.

The Vivienne & Samuel Cohen Charitable Trust (also known as the Charitable Trust of 1965)

£81,000 (1991/92)

Jewish, education, health, welfare

8 Linnell Drive, London NW11 7LT
0181-455 4781

Correspondent: Prof S I Cohen

Trustees: Dr V Cohen; Prof S I Cohen; M Y Ben-Gershon; Elizabeth Hacohen; D H J Cohen; J S Lauffer.

Beneficial area: UK and Israel.

Information available: Accounts are on file at the Charity Commission.

General: In 1990/91, the trust had assets of £800,000 and an income of £43,000. In 1991/92, assets were £323,000 and the income £44,000. It is not clear why the assets have decreased.

Nearly 120 grants totalled £81,000 in 1991/92. Most were under £500 and about 10% were to non-Jewish organisations eg. London Hospital Medical College, Aidis Trust, Royal Academy and National Trust. The largest grants were given to British Friends of Ariel (£10,000) and £5,000 each to Yeshivath, British Friends of Ezrath Nashim Hospital and Karim Schools.

Exclusions: No grants to individuals.

Applications: In writing to the correspondent.

Col-Reno Ltd

£50,000 (1991/92)

Jewish religion & education

15 Shirehall Gardens, Hendon, London NW4 2QT
0181-202 7013

Correspondent: M H Stern

Trustees: M H Stern; A E Stern; Mrs C Stern.

Beneficial area: UK, Israel.

Information available: Full accounts are on file at the Charity Commission.

General: In 1992/93, the trust had assets of £167,000 and an income of £58,000. It gave 10 grants totalling £50,000 all to Jewish organisations. The largest were to SOFOT (£19,000), Agudas Yisroel of California (£16,000) and JSSM (£7,000).

According to the Charity Commission, the trust had an income of £55,000 in 1994.

Applications: In writing to the correspondent.

The Colchester Catalyst Charity

£253,000 (1993/94)

Health in north east Essex

15 High Street, West Mersea, Essex CO5 8QA

Correspondent: P Fitt

Trustees: Directors: R D Hart, President; C F Pertwee, Chairman; A C Blaxill; R W Whybrow; Dr R W Griffin; A H Frost; A R W Tomkins; P W E Fitt.

Beneficial area: North east Essex.

Information available: Full accounts are on file at the Charity Commission.

General: The trust was set up with the aim of improving the health care within the community of north east Essex. It was set up in 1989 with assets of £5 million.

The policy of the trust is to "provide support where it will benefit the greatest number of people, principally by direct contributions to organisations for specific and well defined projects including grants for therapeutic aids, equipment and buildings for medical or nursing care."

The charity recognises the need of specialised equipment for some disabled people. Where it is established that such equipment is not available from statutory organisations a contribution may be made to the cost involved."

In appropriate cases a grant or loan may be offered for full or part-time funding of a project or equipment. It is developing a more pro-active approach to its support, rather than just responding to appeals.

The trust has now completed five years of grant-making, and seen its grant total increase each year. This is set to increase further with the increase of £1.4 million in its funds in three years time, following the sale of an old hospital. In the time it has been operating the trust has distributed over £1 million and processed over 600 applications. Grants have ranged from £50 to £25,000 to meet a range of needs including special equipment for children and helping organisations focusing on physical and learning disabilities, family support, drug addiction, accident and emergency and terminal care.

Research instigated by the charity showed a need for day centres throughout its beneficial area and it is keen to help those charities who wish to buy their own centre or bring others together where there is the possibility of doing something jointly.

This Day Care Committee produced the results of a survey which pointed to a particular need for:

- More respite care
- More sheltered work experience and preparation for people with disabilities leaving school
- Increased integration of people with similar disabilities
- Taking advantage of scope for sharing facilities, advice and experience
- More drop-in centres for social contact, information and refreshment.

During 1993/94, the trust received 117 applications for grants (8 more than the previous year). 46 grants were made, 35 refused and there are 36 still awaiting decision. The cost of grants approved was £253,000.

The summary of costs of sanctioned grants by category during the year was as follows:

Category	Amount	%
Mental disability	£75,000	(29.7%)
Physically disability	£82,000	(32.3%)
Medical	£11,000	(4.3%)
Special individual needs	£30,000	(11.9%)
Family support	£10,000	(3.8%)
Terminal illness	£12,500	(4.9%)
Drugs, alcohol & HIV advice	£25,000	(9.9%)
Accident/emergency	£1,000	(0.4%)
Information/services	£7,000	(2.8%)

Grants ranged from £68 to Colchester Stroke Club (to fund security straps for a minibus) to £25,500 to Colchester Community Transport Scheme (to fund a new minibus for disabled people). Other beneficiaries included Open Road - an organisation giving care and support to people who use drugs and alcohol and advice on HIV/AIDS (£25,000 towards larger premises), Colchester MIND (£2,400 towards special furniture, fittings and equipment), Hamilton Lodge (£20,000 to help provide day care services), Huntington's Disease Association (£910 towards a computer for administration) and Colchester Phoenix Swimming Club (£180 towards water polo equipment).

Exclusions: No support for general funding, staff or running costs. Retrospective funding is not considered.

Applications: In writing to the correspondent.

The John & Freda Coleman Charitable Trust

£57,000 (1992/93)

Education, training

Messrs Lawrence Jones Solicitors, Sea Containers House, 20 Upper Ground, Blackfriars Bridge, London SE1 9LH
0171-620 1311

Correspondent: P B Spark

Trustees: P B Spark; J P Coleman; Mrs F M K Coleman; L P Fernandez; A J Coleman; P H Coleman; B R Coleman.

Beneficial area: UK, with a preference for Surrey and Hampshire.

Information available: Full accounts, including a trustees report, are on file at the Charity Commission.

General: This trust has nearly doubled its level of grant giving from the previous year. Part of its support is to a wide range of charities, but the major support is currently directed to "the Practical Alternative". This is the title given by the trust to "an alternative to an essentially academic education, to encourage and further the aspirations of young people with practical talents to develop manual skills and relevant technical knowledge to fit them for satisfying careers, and useful employment. The aim is to develop the self confidence for individuals to succeed within established organisations or on their own account and to impress upon them, the importance of service to the community, honesty, good manners and self discipline."

In 1992/93, the trust had assets of £722,000, an income of £48,000 and gave ten grants totalling £57,000. "General" charitable donations were given for distribution through the Charities Aid Foundation (£5,000) and to the National Back Pain Association (£250). All other grants were towards Educational Practical Training and were given to: Standing Conference on Schools, Science & Technology (£17,500) and University of Surrey SATRO (£7,500) both received similarly large donations in 1991/92; St David's School (£6,000); St Loyes College (£5,000); Hampshire Technology Centre and Barnardo's (£2,500 each) and Information Technology (£500).

In 1991/92, the trust gave grants totalling £101,000, of which £88,500 was to "the Practical Alternative". The trust's support for the YEC's network has been extended from Surrey into Hampshire and the newly promoted national scheme. 12 grants were made in this field of which four were recurrent from the previous year.

Applications: In writing to the correspondent.

The College Estate Charity

£65,000 (1991)

General in Stratford

Stratford-upon-Avon Town Council, 14 Rother Street, Stratford-upon-Avon CV37 6LU
01789-269332

Correspondent: Philip Lathom, Town Clerk

Trustees: The Town Council.

Beneficial area: The town of Stratford-upon-Avon.

Information available: Full accounts are on file at the Charity Commission up to 1991.

General: This large trust is for the benefit of the people of the town of Stratford-upon-Avon. In 1991, it had fixed assets, including properties let for income, of just over £2 million. Income, mainly from rents, totalled £350,000.

Expenditure was just under £243,000 including maintanance of the town's two public halls and the cemetery. Charitable expenditure totalled £65,000. This included the provision of bus passes, grants to local schools and organisations, contributions to footpath maintenance and repairs, Christmas lighting and trees, and contributions to the Shakespeare Birthday

Celebrations. Some of these payments would appear rather to blur the distiction between statutory and non-statutory responsibilities.

According to the Charity Commission, the trust had an income of £607,000 in 1993, but unfortunately we were unable to obtain any further up-to-date information.

Exclusions: Very few grants are made to individuals and no education grants are made to individuals.

Applications: Applications are considered once a year only, at the end of May or early June and must be on the official application form.

The Norman Collinson Charitable Trust

£70,000 to organisations (1993)

Social welfare, general, in North Yorkshire

13 Sandstock Road, Stockton Lane, York
YO3 0HB
01904-422759

Correspondent: Dennis Holman, Secretary

Trustees: K Denham; F E Dennis; D C Fotherington; D B Holman; J M Saville.

Beneficial area: Generally York and district.

Information available: Full accounts are on file at the Charity Commission.

General: The trust was founded in 1979 by F Norman Collinson who provided most of the trust's capital. It generally restricts its support to York and district, but does make grants to several national charities. It principally helps young, elderly, infirm and disabled people, and individuals or organisations concerned with such people.

In 1993, the trust had assets of £1.23 million and an income of £89,000. 573 applications were received and grants were made to 386 totalling £106,000. This was made up of 104 grants to local charities/organisations amounting to £59,000; 48 grants to national charities/organisations amounting to £11,000; 234 grants to individuals amounting to £33,000.

In addition, the trust owns 14 electric powered wheelchairs which it loans out, free of charge, to disabled people for as long as they can use them. The cost of repairs and renewal of these was £3,000.

Grants made in York and district went to a wide range of organisations including York Community Council, Age Concern York, Victim Support Group, Disabled in York and local scout and youth organisations. The grants to individuals are made through the social services department, Victim Support, Citizen's Advice Bureau, Age Concern, etc..

Grants to non-York organisations are mostly annual donations to the same national organisations including missions/churches, medical charities and charities concerned with children, disabled and elderly people.

Exclusions: No grants for the repair or maintenance of buildings unless such work would be of direct benefit to people meeting the trust's criteria.

Applications: In writing to the correspondent. Applications from individuals should be through recognised agencies. Applications from organisations should give details of their officers, recent accounts and/or budget and information on how any grant would be used. Trustees usually meet on the second Tuesday of each month.

The E Alec Colman Charitable Fund Ltd

£159,000 (1992/93)

Jewish

c/o E Alec Colman & Co, Colman House,
121 Livery Street, Birmingham B3 1RS
0121-212 2551

Correspondent: Alan N Carless, Secretary

Trustees: Directors: Mrs E A Colman; S H Colman; M Harris.

Beneficial area: UK and overseas; mainly Israel.

Information available: Accounts are on file at the Charity Commission.

General: This charitable company was set up in 1963 by Mr E A Colman who died in 1991. In 1992 it had assets of £832,000 mostly held as cash in the bank. In 1992/93, half its income of £427,000 was generated from the sale of investments. An annual covenant of £133,333 was also received, but has now stopped. Donations fell to £159,000 from £260,000 in 1991/92, but a useful surplus of £267,000 was held over so total grant-aid may be expected to rise.

The foundation gives two outstanding grants each year to Friends of Bar-Ilan University (£101,000 with £171,000 in the previous year) and the Lubavitch Foundation (£50,000 and the same in the previous year). Other grants were given to United Synagogue (£2,500) and the Jewish Philanthropic Association for Israel and the Middle East (£2,500 with £22,000 in the previous year).

Applications: In writing to the correspondent.

The Sir Jeremiah Colman Gift Trust

£96,000 (1992)

General

Malshanger, Basingstoke, Hants
RG23 7EY

Correspondent: Sir Michael Colman

Trustees: Sir Michael Colman; Lady Judith Colman; Oliver J Colman; Cynthia Colman; Jeremiah M Colman.

Beneficial area: UK, preference for Hampshire especially Basingstoke.

Information available: Full accounts are on file at the Charity Commission.

General: The trust was set up in 1920 by a deed of indenture between Jeremiah Colman and Jeremiah Colman the Younger which made over to the trust £36,000 of investments in five companies (one of which was the London Brighton and South Coast Railway Company). The trust now has over £1.3 million of assets, generating £97,000 of income. 1991 saw a steep rise in annual service fees from Kleinwort Benson, moving from £3,000 in the previous year to £7,000 and in 1992, to just over £6,000.

The first of the trust's purposes is to make donations to any friends or relatives "who may through no fault of their own be in indigent circumstances or in need of pecuniary assistance". Another is to make grants to "past, present or future employees of any club, institution or company of which Sir Jeremiah Colman may be or may have been President, Director or member".

Other objects are the maintenance of churches and their ministers, the promotion of education and recreation.

Grants are not broken down by category, and there is no narrative report, making it almost impossible to decipher any trends in the five pages of donations. Almost all of these are recurrent, and most organisations are receiving the same amounts as they have over recent years. Most awards are for under £1,000, with an emphasis on Hampshire, particularly Basingstoke. National grants generally seem to go to the bigger, well-known charities.

Grants totalled £96,000 and are broken down into

Annual grants – nearly 200 grants totalling £54,000;
Extra grants totalling £5,000;
Special grants totalling £37,000.

Annual grants ranged from £50 to £2,500, but were generally for £200 to £700. Only nine grants were for £1,000 or more including those to Age Concern (nationally and Basingstoke and Deane) and Arthritis Care. Ten beneficiaries were based in Basingstoke such as the Boys Club and the Samaritans. Other groups supported included: British Sporting Arts; Careforce; Children's Country Holidays Fund; Clergy Retirement Houses Fund; Dyslexia Institute; Family Welfare Association; KIDS; NSPCC; National Art Collections Fund; National Trust; Salvation Army.

The "special" grants, are often larger and usually from £500 for four years to £5,000 for five years. In 1991/92, these included ten grants totalling £19,000 to organisations such as the Industrial Christian Fellowship, Royal Botanical Gardens Kew, Jodrell Laboratory Research and Salisbury Cathedral Spire Trust. 30 smaller grants totalled £25 to £2,500 to the likes of Airborne Initiative, Game Conservancy Trust, Solent Christian Trust, Stoneham Housing Association, Tibetan Education Trust and Winged Fellowship Trust.

Extra grants generally range from £100 to £750 but can be from £25 to £1,500. Recipients included the Lambeth Fund, Partnership for Church Revival (£1,500); Bulldog Trust (£750); Surrey Care Trust – Romanian Children's Hospital (£500).

Other interests supported are children, sports, people with disabilities and preservation.

Applications: "The funds of the trust are fully committed and any unsolicited applications are most unlikely to be successful."

The Combined Charities Trust

£43,000 (1991/92)

General

Barclays Bank Trust Co Ltd, Trust Management Office, Octagon House, Gadbrook Park, Northwich, Cheshire CW9 7RE
01606-40123

Correspondent: Barclays Bank Trust Co Ltd

Trustees: Barclays Bank Trust Co Ltd; Mrs Irene J Evans; Ms Rosalind H Ashley.

Beneficial area: UK.

Information available: Full accounts are on file at the Charity Commission.

General: In 1991/92, the trust had assets of £502,000, and an income of £43,000 all of which was given in grants. Grants were given to: Frame Appeal and Bucks Age Concern (£5,000 each); Save the Children, Shelter, Co-workers for Mother Teresa and Riding for the Disabled (£4,000 each); Royal Society for Nature Conservation (£3,000) and Redwings Horse Sanctuary (£2,000).

Donations can also be given to individuals.

Applications: In writing to the correspondent.

The Comino Foundation

£186,000 (1993/94)

Education

29 Hollow Way Lane, Amersham, Bucks HP6 6DJ
01494-722595

Correspondent: A C Roberts, Administrator

Trustees: Norman P Bailey; Anna Comino-Jones; J A C Darbyshire; Dr W Eric Duckworth; Professor John Tomlinson.

Beneficial area: UK.

Information available: Full accounts are on file at the Charity Commission.

General: Established by Demetrius Comino in 1971, the size of the trust was greatly increased when his daughter Anna gave shares in Dexion Comino International Ltd to the trust in 1971. The company itself was subsequently taken over by an American business. In 1993/94, the trust had assets of £4.9 million, generating only £290,000 of income. After £72,000 of expenses and £92,000 of consultancy fees and expenses, grants totalled £186,000. Grants approved but not yet given, to projects which have the trustees continuing support, totalled £312,000.

The objects of the foundation as stated in the trust deed are primarily "the promotion, advancement and development of education and knowledge in management, organisation, and administration", although in the accounts these objects have become more specific: aiming to promote an awareness of the importance of commerce and industry "in producing the basic goods, services and resources on which the well-being and quality of life of all of us depend", and "to promote a clearer understanding of the basic processes involved in getting results, and thus improve people's power and will to create opportunities and achieve their purposes".

"The foundation pursues these purposes in two ways: directly, through the work of its Education and Industry Fellows Dr E B Bates and Kenneth Adams respectively; and indirectly by financial support of other bodies with similar purposes, usually in the difficult early stages of projects."

The 11 grants given by the trust were to the Foundation for Manufacturing & Industry (£50,000); Dudley Education Services (£30,000); King Alfred's College, Winchester (GRASP Approach) (£28,000); Liverpool University (£25,000); University of Warwick (£17,000); Hallam University and North West Educational Management Centre (£15,000 each). The remaining four grants were for £250 to £3,000 to the General Teaching Council, Foundation for Science and Technology, Parish of Leeds City and Stoke Poge's First School.

Exclusions: No grants to individuals or general appeals.

Applications: In writing to the correspondent.

Community Trusts

General: The definition of a community trust (or foundation) is an "active fundraising and grant-making organisation committed to building permanent endowment and working within defined geographic areas".

In 1991, the movement established its own umbrella organisation known as the Association of Community Trusts and Foundations (ACTAF) which aims to support the work of community trusts and foundations in the UK. There are currently 15 full members and 19 associate members of ACTAF.

Full members 1993/94 with grant total and endowment in brackets

Berkshire Community Trust	£24,700	(£480,600)
Greater Bristol Trust *see separate entry*	£114,400	(£1,934,900)
Calderdale Community Foundation	£31,600	(£417,000)
Cleveland Community Foundation *see separate entry*	£96,100	(£1,390,800)
Dacorum Community Trust	£8,600	(£50,000)
Hertfordshire Community Trust	£44,700	(£367,400)
Isle of Dogs Community Trust	£24,500	(£684,700)
Community Trust for Greater Manchester	£22,000	(£31,700)
Milton Keynes Community Trust *see separate entry*	£82,300	(£1,724,200)
Northern Ireland Voluntary Trust *see Volume 1*	£478,200	(£4,310,000)
South East Wales Community Trust	£6,800	(£184,300)
South Yorkshire Community Foundation	£72,300	(£395,600)
Stevenage Community Trust	£23,000	(£100,000)
Tyne & Wear Foundation *see Volume 1*	£544,200	(£4,664,400)
Wiltshire Community Foundation *see separate entry*	£65,300	(£168,000)

In 1993/94, the grants given by these trusts totalled £1.64 million, an increase of almost £0.33 million on the previous year. The total endowment now stands at almost £17 million an increase of nearly £4 million in each of the last three years. Six of the above trusts are sufficiently large to have separate entries in this Guide or in Volume 1.

Associate members:
 AIM Foundation
 Birmingham Community Foundation
 Caledonian Foundation
 Colchester & Tendring Community Trust
 County Durham Foundation
 Ealing Community Foundation
 Foundation for Community Leadership Development
 Gloucestershire Community Foundation
 Harlow Community Foundation
 Harrow Community Trust
 Heart of England Community Foundation
 Highland Community Foundation
 Nottinghamshire Coalfield Community Trust
 Redbridge Community Trust
 St Katherine & Shadwell Trust – *see A Guide to the Major Trusts Volume 1*
 South East London Foundation
 Southern Derbyshire Community Foundation
 South West London Community Foundation
 Telford & Wrekin Community Trust

Further information on Community Trusts and Foundations including contact addresses, please contact: Kalpana Joshi, Information Officer, ACTAF, High Holborn House, 52-54 High Holborn, London WC1V 6RL (0171-831 0033).

Concern Universal

£1,137,000 (1992/93)

Overseas development

14 Manor Road, Chatham, Kent ME4 6AN
01634-813942; Fax: 01634-402942

Correspondent: Alo Donnelly, Executive Director

Trustees: Don McLeish (Chair); Friedenstern Howard; Rachel Shirley; Josephine Hughes; Finbarr O'Donavan; Colm Lennon; Bishop Donald Arden; Joan McGee; Fr Tiziano Laurenti.

Beneficial area: Overseas, especially Africa and South America.

Information available: Full accounts are on file at the Charity Commission.

General: The charity's main activities relate to raising funds to relieve suffering and to promote development in the third world.

In 1992/93, the trust had assets of £550,000 and an income of £1.5 million. The vast majority of income (£1.4 million) was from donations received (mainly from European Community £547,000; UN High Commission for Refugees £157,000; ODA £117,000 and Caritas, Netherlands £110,000. Other donations came from organisations around the world). Only £32,000 was from investment income.

Grants were given to 62 organisations in 15 different countries in Africa, Asia and South America. By far the largest portion of grants were distributed to Malawi, mainly for water, medical/health, educational and women's projects. These appear to be the charity's main areas of concern elsewhere.

Applications: In writing to the correspondent. Applications can be submitted at any time. Projects must receive the approval of the appropriate local, regional and national authorities. They must also be evaluated by the Concern Universal projects committee.

The Mansfield Cooke Trust

£123,000 (1993/94)

Evangelical Christian missions

PO Box 201, West Malling, Kent ME19 5RS

Correspondent: Nigel A M Cooke

Trustees: N A M Cooke; B O Chilver.

Beneficial area: Worldwide.

Information available: Full accounts are on file at the Charity Commission.

General: Nearly all grants are for some form of evangelical work – missions, youthwork, Scripture etc.. Grants are given locally, nationally and overseas. In 1993/94, the trust had assets of £420,000 and an income of £71,000. The trust had been steadily increasing its assets but in recent years it has been giving more in grants than it has received in income. During the year, 35 grants were made totalling £123,000.

Almost half the grant total went to five organisations: Worthing Tabernacle

(£28,000); International Christian Films (£13,500); TEAR Fund (£7,000) and Dayspring Trust and Operation Mobilisation (£6,000 each). There were four grants of £5,000 to Latin Link, Haggai Institute, Timothy Trust and Action Partners. There were only five grants under £1,000. About half the grants are recurrent from the previous year.

Applications: The correspondent states that the trust is "established for specific purposes related to the personal contacts of the trustees" and that "funds are fully committed and that applicants should not waste their time or ours by writing". There would therefore seem little point in applying to this trust unless you have personal contact with a trustee.

The Cooper Charitable Trust

£145,000 (1993/94)

Medical, disability, Jewish

Messrs Denton Hall, 5 Chancery Lane, Cliffords Inn, London EC4A 1BU
0171-320 6463

Correspondent: Miss J S Portrait, Head of Department or Terry Miles, Solicitor

Trustees: H C Cooper; Mrs S Roter; Miss J S Portrait; Miss T Cooper.

Beneficial area: UK.

Information available: Full accounts are on file at the Charity Commission.

General: The trust was originally endowed with shares in Lee Cooper plc, which was taken over by Vivat Holdings plc. These shares were sold in 1990/91 and the assets of the trust are now invested in government stocks.

The trust appears to give major support to one project/organisation each year and give a number of smaller grants to mainly medical causes. In 1993/94, £100,000 out of a grant total of £145,000 was given to the Brain Research Trust, in 1992/93, £50,000 was given to Brunel University and in 1991/92, £130,000 was given to Royal Brompton National Hospital.

29 other grants were given in 1993/94, about 16 of which were recurrent from the previous year. Support was given to medical and disability charities with five grants to Jewish organisations (10 the year before).

£6,000 went to Jewish Care and £5,000 to the Marie Curie Cancer Memorial Foundation. The other grants ranged from £500 to £2,000 with beneficiaries including North London Hospice (£2,000), Neurological Research Trust (£1,500), and Design & Manufacture for Disability, Leukaemia Research Fund, Norwood Child Care, Riding for the Disabled Association and Royal School for Deaf Children (all £1,000).

Applications: In writing to the correspondent.

The Marjorie Coote Animal Charity Fund

£118,000 (1993/94)

Wildlife and animal welfare

Barn Cottage, Lindrick Common, Worksop, Notts S81 8BA

Correspondent: J H Neill

Trustees: J H Neill; Mrs J P Holah; N H N Coote.

Beneficial area: Worldwide.

Information available: Full accounts are on file at the Charity Commission.

General: The trust was established for the benefit of five named charities working for the benefit of animals. Other charitable organisations caring for horses, dogs or other animals or birds are also supported. The trustees are currently concentrating their resources on animal health and research and on the protection of species, while continuing to apply a proportion of the income to general animal welfare including animal sanctuaries.

In 1993/94, the trust had assets of £2 million, an income of £114,000 and gave 22 grants totalling £118,000. Beneficiaries included: Animal Health Trust and Longford Trust for Animal Welfare (£25,000 each); Oxfordshire Animal Sanctuary Society (£14,000); British Horse Society, Friends of Conservation, Guide Dogs for the Blind, World Wildlife Fund and FRAME (£5,000 each).

In 1991/92, grants were given to: University of Liverpool Veterinary School (£25,000); British Horse Society (£14,000 for research and £5,000 for welfare); Oxfordshire Animal Sanctuary Society (£14,000); Greek Animal Welfare Fund (£2,000); People's Trust for Endangered Species (£1,500) and Wildlife and Wetlands Trust (£2,000).

Applications: In writing to the correspondent. Applications should reach the correspondent during September.

The Marjorie Coote Old People's Charity

£104,000 (1992)

Elderly

Barn Cottage, Lindrick Common, Worksop, Notts S81 8BA

Correspondent: J H Neill

Trustees: J H Neill; Mrs J A Lee; Mrs C A M Neill.

Beneficial area: South Yorkshire.

Information available: Full accounts are on file at the Charity Commission.

General: The trust is for the benefit of old people of small means who were born in, or have lived for not less than 20 years in, the area of jurisdiction of the Company of Cutlers in Hallamshire, this being substantially the same as South Yorkshire. The trust concentrates its support on established charitable organisations and is particularly keen to support new initiatives.

In 1993/94, the trust had assets of £1.4 million (£2 million at market value), an income of £108,000 and grants totalled £104,000. The five main grants were to Age Concern, Sheffield (£30,000); University of Sheffield (£25,000); Sheffield Dial-a-Ride Club (£21,000); Weston Park Hospital (£15,000) and Voluntary Action, Sheffield (£12,000). Age Concern and Voluntary Action regularly receive large grants from the trust; both received the same grant the previous year.

Applications: In writing to the correspondent. Applications should reach the correspondent during May.

The Nicholas Coote Charitable Trust

£40,000 (1993/94)

General in Sheffield, Catholic charities nationwide

Barn Cottage, Lindrick Common, Worksop, Notts S81 8BA

Correspondent: J H Neill

Trustees: N H N Coote; J H Neill; Mrs P J Coote.

Beneficial area: UK and Sheffield.

Information available: Full accounts are on file at the Charity Commission.

General: The trustees apply the income in approximately equal parts between charities for the benefit of people in Sheffield and charities nationwide connected with the Catholic religion.

In 1993/94, the trust had an income of £42,000 down from £124,000 in 1992/93, when a donation of £118,000 was received from NHNC Investments Ltd. 16 grants were given and totalled £40,000 in 1993/94. The largest grants were to the South Yorkshire Foundation (£10,000), Catholic AIDS Link (£6,000), Voluntary Action Sheffield (£5,000) and Sons of Divine Providence (£3,000).

Applications: In writing, to reach the correspondent during June.

The Gershon Coren Charitable Foundation

£19,000 (1992/93)

Jewish, general

263 Upper Street, Islington, London N1 2UJ
0171-226 4848

Correspondent: G Coren

Trustees: G Coren: Mrs M Coren.

Beneficial area: UK.

Information available: Full accounts are on file at the Charity Commission.

General: In 1992/93, the trust had assets of £624,000, an income of £50,000 and grants totalled £19,000. The surplus £31,000 was transferred to the assets. The trust has a regular surplus and appears to be building up its assets so it will have more money available for distribution in the future.

Of the 119 grants made, all but seven were for under £500 and 69 were for under £100. The largest grants were given to: Society of Friends of Jewish Refugees (£5,000); GRET and Yesodah Hatoral School (£2,000 each); Central British Fund for World Jewish Relief (£825) and three grants for £500 each to University College, London, London Museum of Jewish Life and Gordon Boys Messenger Corps.

The accounts indicate a strong preference for Jewish and Middle East organisations, but the trust states that it will consider "all worthy and approved charity organisations". In fact, about two thirds of the smaller grants were to non-Jewish organisations, mainly medical and welfare causes, national and a few local, including four in Wales. Recipients included Anglesey Mencap Society; Greenpeace; Nottinghamshire Royal Society for the Blind; Prince & Princess of Wales Hospice and Shelter.

Applications: In writing to the correspondent.

The Duke of Cornwall's Benevolent Fund

£152,000 (1992/93)

General in Cornwall

10 Buckingham Gate, London SW1E 6LA
0171-834 7346

Correspondent: FAO Angela Wise

Trustees: The Earl Cairns; J N C James.

Beneficial area: South west England.

Information available: Accounts are on file at the Charity Commission.

General: The fund receives donations from the Duke of Cornwall (Prince Charles) based on amounts received by the Duke as Bona Vacantia (the causal profits of estates of deceased intestates dying domiciled in Cornwall without kin) after allowing for costs and ex-gratia payments made by the Duke in relation to claims on any estate.

Priority is given to charitable organisations in the south-west of England, in areas in which the Duchy has landed interests. The fund's objectives are the advancement of education, the advancement of religion, the advancement of the arts, the preservation for the benefit of the public of lands and buildings and relief-in-need.

In 1992/93, the trust received a donation of £25,000 from Prince Charles. The trust had assets of £1.65 million (market value) and an income of £81,000. Grants were broken down as follows:

Annual subscriptions – £18,000, including three of over £500 to Business in the Community and Thames Salmon Trust (£2,500 each) and St Mary's PCC (£1,000).

Donations – £134,000. 43 grants of £500 or more totalling £130,000, and £4,000 in smaller grants. The largest grants were to St Anta & All Saints Church (£25,000); Hale Clinic and Marlebone Health Centre (£15,000 each); St Luke's Hospice, Devon Wildlife Trust and Prince of Wales Hospice (£10,000 each).

About half the grants were to a range of beneficiaries in the south west including Bath Abbey Trust (£3,000); Dorchester Rifle and Pistol Club (£1,000); Avon Rural Initiatives Fund, Cornish Language Board and Stonesfield Community Trust (£500 each). Eight churches also received grants.

According to the Charity Commission, the trust had an income of £142,000 in 1993/94.

Applications: In writing to the correspondent. Applicants should give as much detail as possible, especially information of what amount of money has been raised to date, what the target is and how it will be achieved.

The Countryside Trust

£30,000 (1993/94)

Conservation

John Dower House, Crescent Place, Cheltenham, Gloucestershire GL50 3RA
01242-521381; Fax: 01242-584270

Correspondent: Mrs Lynne Garner, Secretary

Trustees: Sir John Johnson; Michael Dower; John L Evans.

Beneficial area: England.

Information available: The trust publishes a leaflet, available from the correspondent.

General: The trust's objects are "to promote the conservation, preservation and restoration of the natural beauty of the countryside of England for public benefit". In practice, the trustees offer seed corn grants to community or voluntary organisations concerned with the care of the local countryside of England. The grants are for the specific purpose of financing fundraising appeals where the money raised will benefit practical conservation projects of local (rather than national) significance.

Possible recipients are a county wildlife trust, local amenity group or local branch of a national charity. Possible projects include fundraising for securing the protection of ancient woodland, restoring an historic countryside landmark or creating a new wildlife habitat. Priority will be given to projects offering public access and providing conservation education. Grants are up to a maximun of £5,000, but usually range from £100 to £3,500.

In 1993/94, the trust had assets of £586,000 and an income of £75,000, £50,000 of which was from legacies. It gave 31 grants totalling £30,000. Of the 14 grants of £1,000 or more, eight were to local wildlife trusts: Devon (three grants totalling £3,000); Durham (£1,500); Gloucestershire (£1,200); Lancashire (£1,000); Northants (£2,000); Cornwall (£1,250); Northumberland (£1,175); Suffolk (£1,250).

The other grants of £1,000 to £2,300 were given to organisations such as the Urban Wildlife Trust, Whirlow Hall Farm, Windmill Hill City Farm and World Memorial Fund. The smaller grants (under £1,000) were to support similar organisations involved with conservation, ecology and the environment. Grants have been made to help raise funds for local projects and increase membership.

Since the trust was set up in 1990/91 it has given 105 grants totalling about £125,000.

Exclusions: Funds would not normally be used to support the costs of staff posts.

Applications: On a (simple) standard application form together with a map and supporting material as appropriate. Applications are considered in February and August; deadlines are the end of January and the end of July respectively. Applicants are expected to show how a grant would be used to raise considerably more funds.

The Augustine Courtauld Trust

£75,000 (1991/92)

General

Messrs Birkett Westhorp & Long, Red House, Halstead, Essex CO9 2DZ
01787-475252

Correspondent: Richard Long, Clerk

Trustees: Lord Bishop of Chelmsford; Rev A C C Courtauld; Lord Braybrook; Col N A C Croft; J Courtauld.

Beneficial area: UK, with a preference for Essex.

Information available: Full accounts are on file at the Charity Commission, up to 1991/92.

General: In 1991/92, the trust had assets of £800,000 and an income of £79,000. About 75 grants were given totalling £75,000. The largest grants were to the Friends of Essex Churches (£7,500), Gino Watkins Memorial Fund (£6,000), Bishop of Chelmsford's Appeal for East London & Essex Churches Urban Fund (£5,000), and the Essex Association of Boys' Clubs (£4,000). The Lord Lieutenant's Discretionary Fund, Bishop of Chelmsford's Discretionary Fund, Christian Aid and the Essex Heritage Trust all received £3,000. Other grants ranged from £250 to £2,000 and were given mainly to Essex charities or Essex branches of national charities. A range of causes were supported including the environment, Christian, youth, medical, disability and welfare.

Exclusions: No grants to individuals.

Applications: In writing to the correspondent.

The Craps Charitable Trust

£121,000 (1993/94)

Jewish, general

c/o Robson Rhodes, Bryanston Court, Selden Hill, Hemel Hempstead, Herts HP2 4TN
01442-60200

Correspondent: C E Shanbury

Trustees: C E Shanbury; C S Dent; J P M Dent.

Beneficial area: UK, Israel.

Information available: Full accounts are on file at the Charity Commission.

General: In 1993/94, the trust had assets of £1.1 million and an income of £78,000. 17 grants were given totalling £121,000, mainly to Jewish organisations. The largest were £30,000 to JPAIME, £22,000 to Jewish Care and £20,000 to Friends of the Federation of Women Zionists. Most grants were recurrent.

There were five grants to non-Jewish organisations: £3,000 to Friends of the Earth, £1,000 each to Greenpeace Environment Trust, Amnesty International and Motor Neurone Disease Association, and £500 to the Campaign for Oxford Trust Fund.

Applications: The trust states that "no further applications for funds can be considered".

The Cross Trust

£135,000 (1993/94)

Christian work overseas

Bourbon Court, Nightingale Corner, Little Chalfont, Bucks HP7 9QS
01494-765428: Fax; 01494-763911

Correspondent: D J Stephenson

Beneficial area: UK, overseas.

Information available: Full accounts are on file at the Charity Commission.

General: The funds of the charity are directed to charities and individuals carrying out Christian work overseas and in the UK. However, the funds are fully committed for the foreseeable future. In 1993/94, grants totalled £135,000. No further information was available for this year.

In 1991/92, the trust had an income of £97,000 from covenants and Gift Aid. 15 grants were made totalling £94,000. In 1990/91, the major beneficiaries were Campus Crusade for Christ - Eastern Europe and Soviet Union (£22,000) and Lugoj Baptist Church in Romania (£10,000). Neither of these had received grants previously, but both received further grants of about £5,000 in 1991/92.

Most other grants were for between £1,000 and £8,000 including those to the Rock Foundation; expenses for Missions in India & Australia; support of Iraqi Christian Ministry and an Iraqi Christian student at the Cornhill Training College for Theological Studies. Four grants of about £1,000 were given to charities in the areas of disability, ordination, Asian students and a church pastor. The smallest grants were for £500 or less, given towards aid work, the church, pastoral aid and sundries.

Most other grants were to past beneficiaries, including the Motivation Educational Trust for the Disabled and Navigators.

Applications: In writing to the correspondent.

CRUSAID

£562,000 (1992/93)

HIV/AIDS

Livingstone House, Carteret Street, London SW1H 9DH
0171-976 8100; Fax: 0171-976 8200

Correspondent: Jane Young, Secretary (Projects Committee)

Trustees: Lord Eatwell, Chairman; Lady Cameron; Mark Chataway; Andrew Stone; David Charlton; Jeff Solender; Andrew Stone; Colin Tweedy; Robert Venables; Pamela Lady Harlech; Susan Perl; Liz Airey; Derek Granger; Geoffrey Henning.

Beneficial area: UK.

Information available: Full accounts on file at the Charity Commission.

General: "CRUSAID is a national charity focusing on the needs of men, women and children affected by HIV and AIDS. Since its launch in 1986 it has raised over £6 million... its efforts as a fundraiser have not only paid for the largest Hardship Fund in Britain [HIV/AIDS related], but have also sustained an enormous number of small support groups all over the country, each playing a vital role which would be impossible without the support of CRUSAID. Indeed there's hardly a significant [HIV/AIDS related] capital project anywhere in the country that has not received some funding from CRUSAID.

"This year it has become clear that over the next five years CRUSAID faces even greater challenges. The pressures on the public purse are leading to ever greater demands being placed on the voluntary sector. At the same time the number of people needing CRUSAID's help continues to rise."

In 1992/93, the trust had assets of £130,000, an income of £1.2 million (of which about £900,000 was from gifts and donations and £200,000 from its trading subsidiary). Grants totalled £562,000 (almost £1.5 million in the previous 15 months) and were used for:

Education and care:
38 organisations received grants towards projects to develop knowledge and understanding throughout all sectors of the community in England and Scotland. Projects included drama and "theatre-in-education" to help young people understand the issues, and projects aimed at Asian, Turkish, Iranian and Arabic communities and also people who are deaf.

Living with AIDS:
20 organisations providing day care centres, counselling centres and respite care received grants including: ACASIA; Immune Development Trust; Mansfield Settlement; Middlesex Hospital; Mildmay Mission Hospice and the Red Admiral Project.

The CRUSAID Centre:
This will be the first AIDS treatment centre in the UK. It will provide a new fast route to ways of helping people with AIDS live longer and have a better quality of life. The centre will run alongside an existing clinical treatment unit at Chelsea & Westminster Hospital. North West Regional Health Authority has agreed to match £ for £ the £1 million CRUSAID has pledged to raise towards the hospital.

Individual Hardship Fund:
Over £200,000 was given in grants mainly in response to social workers' applications on behalf of their clients. Seven grants were also given to organisations.

Applications: To the correspondent in writing, with CRUSAID's application form and including a copy of the most recent audited accounts. Trustees meet monthly.

The Cumber Family Charitable Trust

£60,000 (1993/94)

Health, housing and social welfare, overseas, Christian, agriculture

Manor Farm, Marcham, Abingdon, Oxon OX13 6NZ
01865-391327

Correspondent: Mrs M J Cumber

Trustees: Miss M Cumber; A R Davey; W Cumber; Mrs S Cumber; Mrs M J Cumber.

Beneficial area: Worldwide with a preference for Berkshire and Oxfordshire.

Information available: Full accounts are on file at the Charity Commission.

General: In 1993/94, the trust had an income of £84,000 and made grants totalling £60,000 to 55 projects. A number of small grants were made to local organisations. Larger grants went to national and overseas projects.

Grants of £1,500 to £3,000 were given to 14 organisations including the Leprosy Mission; Methodist Homes for the Aged; Oxfordshire Macmillan Nurse Appeal; Queen Elizabeth's Foundation for the Disabled; Refugee Council; Romanian Development Trust; Marie Stopes International; URC Rural Consultants, Stoneleigh; YMCA Development Trust.

There were 17 grants of £500 to £1,000 mainly to local projects working in the homelessness, disability and welfare fields. Overseas projects supported included a project in Thailand to help prostitutes; Prisoners of Conscience - refugees in former Yugoslavia; Churches Commission on Overseas Students Hardship Fund, and to the Mission Aviation Fellowship for a Chorley family in Tanzania.

Over 20 grants of up to £500 went mainly to local organisations working in similar areas to those above. Two individuals were also supported with a specialist publication and a tropical medicine course.

Exclusions: No grants for animal welfare or individuals without local connections. Local appeals outside Berkshire and Oxfordshire are not usually supported.

Applications: In writing to the correspondent. Applications are considered in February and September.

The Dennis Curry Charitable Trust

£80,000 (1993/94)

General

Messrs Alliotts, 5th Floor, 9 Kingsway, London WC2B 6XF
0171-240 9971

Correspondent: N J Armstrong

Trustees: M Curry; Mrs A S Curry; Mrs M Curry Jones; Mrs P Edmond.

Beneficial area: UK.

Information available: Full accounts are on file at the Charity Commission.

General: The trust has general charitable objects with special interest in the environment and education; occasional support is given to churches and cathedrals.

The assets of the trust have been steadily rising and in 1993/94 had reached £2.5 million, but were only producing an income of £109,000. Eight grants were given totalling £80,000. The previous year, grants totalled £30,000 with a surplus of £95,000.

The four trustees receive an equal share of the distributable income. It is thought they distribute it as they see fit. Grants in 1993/94, were given to Techniquest (£30,000); Open University (£12,500); Postgraduate Medical Studies (£11,000); National Children's Orchestra (£10,000); Council for National Parks (£10,750); Raleigh International (£5,000); Cambridge University & Explorers Club (£500) and Red R Disaster Fund (£300). The Council for National Parks and Raleigh International also received grants the previous year.

Applications: In writing to the correspondent.

The Manny Cussins Foundation

£147,000 (1992/93)

General, with some emphasis on Yorkshire and Jewish projects

Stone Acre, Harrogate Road, Leeds LS17 8EP
0113-268 3222

Correspondent: Arnold Reuben

Trustees: A Cussins; A Cussins; J Cussins; A Reuben; Mrs A Reuben.

Beneficial area: UK, with some emphasis on Yorkshire.

Information available: Full accounts are on file at the Charity Commission.

General: In 1992/93, the trust had assets of £502,000 and an income of £71,000. It gave 31 grants totalling £147,000, using unspent accumulated income from previous years.

15 of the recipients were supported in the previous year and 16 were new grants. Of the recurrent grants Angels International Appeal for Polish Children received £7,500 (£13,000 in 1991/92); Leeds Jewish Welfare Board, £4,000 (£2,150 in 1991/92) and Manny Cussins House, £2,500 (£3,500 in 1991/92). The largest new grants included: St James Hospital "Jimmy's Diabetes Fund" (£100,000); United Hebrew Congregation (£16,000); Central British Fund for World Jewish Relief (£2,500). The other grants were to specifically Jewish organisations except for those to: British Red Cross (£1,000); British Heart Foundation (£500); Lifescan Appeal and Handicapped Children's Fund (£100 each).

Exclusions: Personal applications for the benefit of individuals.

Applications: THE CORRESPONDENT STATES THAT **APPLICATIONS ARE NOT SOUGHT.**

The D'Oyly Carte Charitable Trust

£136,000 (1991/92)

Arts, environment, medical

1 Savoy Hill, London WC2R 0BP
0171-836 1533

Correspondent: Mrs J Thorne

Trustees: J Elliott, Chairman; Mrs J Sibley; J McCracken; Sir Martyn Beckett; Mrs F Radcliffe; Sir John Batten.

Beneficial area: UK.

Information available: Full accounts are on file at the Charity Commission.

General: The trust was established in 1972 by the late Dame Bridget D'Oyly Carte.

The trust has assets of £6.5 million (mostly in Savoy Hotel plc shares) generating an income of only £139,000. The income is used to support general charitable causes mainly connected with the arts, the environment and medical/welfare. Certain charities in which Dame Bridget took a special interest in her lifetime continue to be supported on a regular basis. Other charities receive one-off grants. In 1991/92 grants were allocated as follows:

Arts: 45 grants were made totalling £52,000. Most were for £1,000 or less; larger grants of £5,000 were awarded to the Actors' Charitable Trust, London Library, Crafts Council and the Theatre Museum. Other grants were distributed to a wide variety of applicants including Live Music Now!, British School at Rome, Blackheath Concert Halls, Early English Opera Society, Koestler Award Trust, Judy Segal Trust, York Theatre Royal, Framework Children's Theatre and the London Opera Festival. In addition, £20,000 was distributed to training establishments in the form of D'Oyly Carte Scholarships.

Environment: 10 grants totalling £18,000. This included grants of £5,000 to the Council for the Protection of Rural England and the Royal Botanic Gardens, Kew. The balance was divided between a variety of causes, including the Farming and Wildlife Advisory Trust, National Trust and the Portsmouth Cathedral Development Trust.

Medical/welfare: 29 grants totalling £46,000. The Breakthrough Trust for the Deaf received £6,000 and grants of £5,000 went to Help the Hospices and the National AIDS Trust. Most grants were in the range of £500 to £3,000 and included the British Home and Hospital for Incurables, Chalfont Centre for Epilepsy, Land and City Families Trust, Network for the Handicapped, Macmillan Fund for Cancer Relief and the Starlight Foundation.

Exclusions: Individuals seeking financial assistance with further education and training are no longer supported.

Applications: In writing to the correspondent who has written: "It should be noted, however, that the resources of the trust are directed to specific charities from year to year, and the trustees are therefore restricted in considering new applications". The trustees meet twice a year, in June and December. Applications should arrive at least one month before these meetings.

Dahl/Daily/Dandelion

The Roald Dahl Foundation

£172,000 (1992/93)

Haematology, neurology (specifically head injury & epilepsy) and literacy

92 High Street, Great Missenden, Bucks HP16 0AN
01494-890465

Correspondent: Amanda Conquy

Trustees: Felicity Dahl, Chairman; Quentin Blake; Ernest Cole; Martin Goodwin.

Beneficial area: UK.

Information available: Full accounts are on file at the Charity Commission.

General: In 1994/95, grants will be given in three areas which were of great personal interest and significance to Roald Dahl: literacy, haematology and neurology. Within these areas there is a wide range of grants.

Neurology and haematology
Support for children and young people up to the age of 25 and their families who suffer from blood disorders which are not cancer related, from epilepsy and head injury. Specifically grants are for:

- Pump-prime funding of specialist paediatric nursing and other care, especially where there is an emphasis on community care, for a maximum of two years. Information about the source of permanent funding after the two years is required;
- Assistance to residential and day care centres for children and young people who come into the above medical categories. Such grants would normally be awarded on a project basis.
- Small items of medical equipment that will allow the patient to be cared for in the home, with community care/ hospital back-up.
- Individual grants of £50 - £500 for specified needs to the children in the above categories from families that are suffering financial hardship. Applications should be addressed to the Hardship Grant Secretary at the above address.

Literacy
The foundation is actively involved in promoting literacy throughout the UK, through Readathon. In addition during the next few years the main areas of grant making will be:

- After-school clubs for children and their families who would like to improve their literacy skills.
- Centres which offer or wish to initiate literacy programmes for young people (16-25) as part of their normal activities.
- Computer/technological assistance for reading for people who are partially sighted, blind or have a head injury.

Grants to organisations for whom funds are not readily available can range form £1,000 to £25,000. Preference for small or new organisations.

In 1993/94, the trust committed £272,000 in several main grants, some of which will be spent over two years.

Exclusions: No grants will be made to non-charities or to fund research or for general appeals from large, well-established charities or national appeals for building projects. No support for core funding, projects outside the UK or for school or higher education fees.

Applications: On an application form, available from the correspondent and submitted with a covering letter. The trustees usually meet in May and October. Applications should be received by the 1st February or 1st September at the latest. When writing from a hospital regarding a new post or small items of equipment, the application must be signed by the relevant consultant or head of department. The trustees endeavour to visit as many applicants as possible, but may just telephone for more information. No further correspondence will be entered into with unsuccessful applications.

The Daily Prayers Union Trust Ltd

£42,000 (1993/94)

Evangelical Christian

10 Belitha Villas, London N1 1PD
0171-607 7359

Correspondent: Sir Timothy Hoare, Trustee

Trustees: Bishop T Dudley-Smith; R J Knight; Rev I D Neill; Rev G C Grinham; Canon J Tiller; Lt Col Bartholomew; Canon A Neech; Sir T Hoare; Rev J Eddison; Rev J Fletcher; Mrs E Bridger; Mrs A Thompson.

Beneficial area: UK.

Information available: Accounts are on file at the Charity Commission, but without a list of grants.

General: In 1992/93, the trust had an income of £74,000 including £68,500 from the Estate of Sir Edgar Plummer. "Charitable disbursements" totalled £60,000 with £22,000 committed for the following year. This includes £7,000 "grants to societies" and £35,000 "special grants". According to the Charity Commission, the trust had an income of £74,000 in 1993/94.

There is no information on the beneficiaries of the trust but it supports evangelical Christian causes.

Applications: The trusts supports causes already known to the trustees, unsolicited applications are unlikely to be successful.

The Dandelion Trust

Not known

General

41 The Limehouse Cut, 46 Morris Road, London E14 6NQ
0171-538 5633

Correspondent: Mrs J Bowman

Beneficial area: UK.

Information available: We were unable to see this file at the Charity Commission.

General: The trust has been set up for: (a) relief of poverty; (b) relief of sickness; (c) education of children; (d) promotion of agricultural, industrial, commercial or scientific techniques; (e) promotion of artistic, musical, theatrical and literary pursuits; (f) furtherance of religious and charitable work; (g) protection and preservation of natural features and buildings; (h) promotion of good community relations.

According to the Charity Commission, the trust had an income of £50,000 in 1992.

Applications: In writing to the correspondent.

The Dr & Mrs A Darlington Charitable Trust

£68,000 (1994)

Medical, nature conservation, preservation, elderly people, disability

Ford Simey Daw Roberts, 8 Cathedral Close, Exeter EX1 1EW
01392-74126

Correspondent: V A Donson

Trustees: Lloyds Bank plc; V A Donson.

Beneficial area: Preference for south west England, in particular Sidmouth and East Devon.

Information available: Full accounts are on file at the Charity Commission.

General: In 1994, the assets of the trust brought in an income of £89,000 (£77,000 in 1993). 33 grants totalled £68,000.

The largest grant was to Hospiscare, Exeter (£18,750), which also received £19,000 in 1991. DIRECT received £11,250 and Healthy Heart £2,500. There were five grants of £2,000 to Hospital Radio Exeter, Iris Fund, Royal Devon & Exeter Hospital, Stallcombe House and the Stroke Association. A grant of £1,500 was made to Devon Wildlife Trust and the three smallest grants of £500 went to Women's Voluntary Service, St Julias Hospice and Devon Rural Skills Trust.

The remaining 21 grants were for £1,000 and were given to a wide range of organisations involved mainly in medical/disability or welfare including Church Action on Disability, Crossroads, Diabetes Foundation, Motor Neurone Disease Association, RNID and the Salvation Army. A number of beneficiaries had educational/religious links such as Friends of Mill Water School (Honiton), Salcombe Regis PCC - Church Clock Appeal, Bicton College of Agriculture, Winged Fellowship and St Loyes College.

Exclusions: Applications from individuals, including students, are most unlikely to be successful.

Applications: In writing to the correspondent. The trustees regret that they cannot send replies to unsuccessful applicants. The trustees meet quarterly in March, June, September and December.

Datnow Limited

£21,000 (1993/94)

General

16 Notting Hill Gate, London W11 3JE

Correspondent: E L Datnow

Trustees: Mrs E M Datnow; E L Datnow; J A Datnow; A D Datnow.

Beneficial area: UK.

Information available: No full accounts are on file at the Charity Commission.

General: The trust has general objects, but in practice appears to have a very strong preference for Jewish related causes. In 1992/93, the trust had assets of £544,000 and an income of £69,000.

In the last edition of this Guide the trust stated: "In 1993, the trust expects to give grants totalling about £60,000 to £70,000, mainly to medical research". In actual fact about 80 grants were given totalling only £21,000. The vast majority of grants were to Jewish organisations or well-known national charities. The largest grants were to the Joint Israel Appeal (£4,100), Birthright, National Society for Epilepsy and SAGE Jewish Old Age Home (£2,000 each), and GRET and the Institute of Economic Affairs (£1,000 each).

Applications: In writing to the correspondent, but replies will not be sent to unsuccessful applicants.

The Gwendoline Davies Charity

£65,000 (1993/94)

General

Perthybu Offices, Sarn, Newtown, Powys SY16 4EP
01686-670404

Correspondent: Mrs S Hamer

Trustees: Hon I E E Davies; R D Davies; Hon J H Davies; Dr J A Davies; T A Owen.

Beneficial area: UK, especially Wales.

Information available: Accounts are on file at the Charity Commission, but without a list of grants.

General: The trust was set up in 1934. In 1993/94, it had assets of £1.37 million and an income of £75,000. After expenses of only £4,000, the trust gave £65,000 in grants.

Unfortunately no grants list is available since that for 1975, when there was a clear preference for Welsh organisations, especially those involved in music, education, welfare, Christian, heritage, young people, disability and animals.

Applications: In writing to the correspondent.

The J Davies Charities Ltd

£51,000 (1992/93)

Jewish, general

22 Hillcrest Avenue, Edgware, Middlesex HA8 8PA
0181-951 5466

Correspondent: M Rabin, Auditor

Trustees: F Davies; M Kayne; G Munitz; S L Ohrenstein; P J Rabin.

Beneficial area: Worldwide.

Information available: Full accounts are on file at the Charity Commission.

General: The grant total of this trust has been steadily rising in recent years. In 1992/93, its assets were £319,000 and the income £52,000. 71 grants were made totalling £51,000, with 57 under £1,000.

The largest grants were to the Lubavitch Foundation (£8,300), Educational Institute Oholei Torah (£4,000), and Lubavitch of Edgware and Tzivos Hashem (both £2,000). About three quarters of the grants were to Jewish organisations.

Other beneficiaries were mainly well-known medical or welfare charities with a few less well-known and local causes, all of which received under £1,000. Examples include Brent Crossroads, British Diabetic Association, British Tay Sachs Foundation, Cancer Relief Macmillan Fund, Help the Aged, Metropolitan Hospital Sunday Fund and Save the Children Fund. Most are regular beneficiaries.

Applications: In writing to the correspondent.

• Margaret Davies/Davis/De Haan

The Margaret Davies Charity

Over £147,000 (1993)

Education, health, arts

Perthybu Offices, Sarn, Newtown, Powys SY16 4EP
01686-670404

Correspondent: Mrs S Hamer

Trustees: Hon I E E Davies; Dr E Davies; Hon J H Davies; Dr J A Davies; R D Davies.

Beneficial area: UK, with a preference for Wales.

Information available: Full accounts are on file at the Charity Commission.

General: This trust's assets have risen quite considerably from £1 million in 1976 to over £4 million in 1992. The two ladies who founded the trust used to live at the Gregynog, a building in the country, which is now being used by the main University of Wales for seminars, council meetings etc..

Grants range from £100 up to £300,000 given over 5 years for the refurbishment of the National Museum of Cardiff (this exceptionally large grant may be due to a trustee's personal interest). The other main recurrent grants have been given to the University of Wales. Regular support has also been given to hospitals (for scanners), hospices, and the Temple of Peace, Cardiff.

Grants totalled over £137,000 in 1993 and according to the Charity Commission, the trust had an income of £288,000 in 1994.

Exclusions: No grants to individuals.

Applications: In writing to the correspondent.

The Wilfrid Bruce Davis Charitable Trust

£80,000 (1993/94)

Health, especially in Cornwall

La Feock Grange, Feock, Truro, Cornwall TR3 6RG
01872-862795

Correspondent: W B Davis

Trustees: W B Davis; Mrs D F Davis; Mrs D S Dickens; A J Robotham.

Beneficial area: In practice Cornwall.

Information available: Full accounts are on file at the Charity Commission. A full history of the development, activities and achievements of the trust was published with the accounts for the year ended 5th April 1993. A copy of this is available from the correspondent on request.

General: The trust was set-up in 1967, the objects being "such charities as the settlor in his lifetime and the trustees after his death shall determine". The trust presently concentrates on "improving the quality of life for those who are physically disadvantaged and their carers". The geographical area covered is almost exclusively Cornwall.

In 1993/94, the trust had assets of £706,000 and an income of £48,000. 24 grants were made totalling £80,000, of which 13 were recurrent from the previous year. During the year two large commitments were entered into:

(1) The trust bought Beach Cottage, on Porthmeor Beach, St Ives for holidays for cancer patients and their carers. The trust already has a cottage there, which in 1992/93 was used for holidays for 22 families. All bookings are through the Cancer Relief Macmillan Fund in London with patients being referred by Macmillan nurses throughout the country.

(2) £25,000 has been pledged to the National Network of St Julia's Hospital Capital Appeal, spread over three years. This is in addition to the £10,000 annual grant received from the trust.

Grants are made both to local charities in Cornwall and local branches of national charities. The largest grant was £30,000 to the Royal Cornwall Hospital Trust. Regularly among the largest grants are the Macmillan Fund (£12,000 in 1993/94, £11,000 in 1992/93) and St Julia's Hospice (£15,000 in 1993/94, £10,000 in 1992/93).

Other large grants included those to Marie Curie Cancer Care (£4,500), Bruce Davis Training Fund and Cornwall County Association for the Blind (£3,000 each) and the British Kidney Patient Association (£2,700). There were six grants of about £1,000 to Derby Toc H Children's Camp, Distressed Gentlefolks Association, Inkerman Housing Association, Laura Gregory Appeal, Pathway and St Petrocs.

All other grants were for up to £500 and were given mainly to medical and disability charities and those concerned with children and young people. In 1992/93, large grants were to Children's Hospice South West and Cornwall Friends Mobility Centre (£5,000 each), Pathway (£4,600) and Physiotherapy at Home (PatH) Fund (£10,000). The trust also gives some small (under £50), unnamed grants. In 1993/94, these totalled £69 and in 1992/93, 11 totalled £384.

Applications: No replies are made to unsolicited applications. Mr Davis has stated that his budget for many years to come is fully committed and that he receives hundreds of applications, none of which he can satisfy.

The De Haan Charitable Trust

£73,000 (1993/94)

General

The Saga Building, Middelburg Square, Folkestone, Kent CT20 1AZ
01303-711401

Correspondent: P C De Haan

Trustees: P C De Haan; R M De Haan; Mrs M De Haan.

Beneficial area: UK.

Information available: Ful accounts are on file at the Charity Commission.

General: In 1993/94, the trust had assets of £1.8 million, mainly in shares in Saga Leisure Ltd given to the trust by S de Haan. These generated an income of £134,000. 48 grants were given totalling £73,000, mainly to health, welfare and disability organisations. The policy of the trustees is to support organisations which help elderly and very young people who cannot help themselves.

The largest grants were given to Holiday Care Scheme (£20,000), Sidney De Haan Charity (£16,500) and Research into Ageing (£10,000). These three charities are all regular beneficiaries of the trust. The Sidney De Haan Charity in turn gave two grants: £15,000 to the Coach House Project, Somerset County Council and £378 to the Folkestone branch of the Pensioners Association.

Nine other grants made by the trust ranged from £1,000 to £2,000, with the remaining

36 for £100 to £500. Both national and local charities were supported, with some preference for Kent.

Beneficiaries included Children's Hospice South West (£2,600), Tenterden District Age Concern Centre (£2,000), Heart of Kent Hospice (£1,500), Lymphoma Research Trust (£500), Electronic Aids for the Blind (£200) and Kent Learning Club (£100). Six local Age Concern groups received grants.

Applications: In writing to the correspondent.

The Miriam K Dean Refugee Trust Fund

£197,000 (1993)

Third World development

c/o Amery-Parkes & Co, 12a London Street, Basingstoke RG21 7BG
01256-56262

Correspondent: B Tims

Trustees: Trevor Dorey; Val Dorey; Hugh Capon; Jill Budd; Gina Livermore.

Beneficial area: Mainly Tanzania and India (including Tibetan refugees).

Information available: Full accounts are on file at the Charity Commission.

General: In 1993, the trust had assets of £207,000 generating £8,000 income. A further £87,000 was received in donations. Grants for the year totalled £197,000. A letter on file at the Charity Commission dated September 1992 stated that someone had left the trust an unspecified sum in a will and the deceased person's solicitor was trying to contact the trust. It is not known whether this legacy was substantial.

Grants are given to individuals and institutions working with:

The poor in Tanzania (£68,000 in 1993, £7,000 in 1992)

Tibetan refugees (£75,000 in 1993 and £38,000 in 1992)

People with leprosy and other disadvantaged groups:

In South India (£29,000 in both the last two years)

Zimbabwe (£24,000 in 1993)

Elsewhere (£2,000 in 1992 and £3,000 in 1992).

Exclusions: Grants are not made to UK residents or to finance individual journeys to third world projects.

Applications: In writing to the correspondent.

The Delves Charitable Trust

£148,000 (1993/94)

Environment, conservation, medical, general

New Guild House, 45 Great Charles Street, Queensway, Birmingham B3 2LX
0121-212 2222

Correspondent: Roger Harriman

Trustees: Mary Breeze; John Breeze; George Breeze; Dr Charles Breeze; Elizabeth Breeze; Roger Harriman.

Beneficial area: UK.

Information available: Full accounts are on file at the Charity Commission.

General: In 1993/94, trust had assets of £1.8 million, with a market value of £4.1 million and an income of £163,000. It gave £148,000 in grants. "The present recurring annual commitments for grants subject to annual review total £139,000. It has been the trustees' policy to commit the bulk of the annual funds available in this way and to fund one-off donations largely from previously unspent income."

Annual donations during the year totalled £139,000, the largest of which was £19,000 to the British Heart Foundation. Other grants ranged from £1,000 to £8,000 to environment and conservation and medical and welfare causes eg. CPRE, Crisis, Foundation for the Study of Infant Deaths, National Trust, Save the Children Fund and Survival International. Of the eight one-off grants SEQUAL (endowment fund) received £5,000 and Selly Oak Nursery School £1,000. The other grants were for £250 to £500 and were to similar beneficiaries as the annual grants.

Applications: "The funds of the trust are currently fully committed and no unsolicited requests can therefore be considered by the trustees."

The Dent Charitable Trust

£128,000 (1993/94)

Jewish, general

c/o Robson Rhodes, Bryanston Court, Selden Hill, Hemel Hempstead, Herts HP2 4TN
01442-60200

Correspondent: C E Shanbury

Trustees: C E Shanbury; C S Dent; J P M Dent.

Beneficial area: Worldwide.

Information available: Full accounts are on file at the Charity Commission.

General: In 1993/94, the trust had assets of £1.2 million and an income of £78,000. 38 grants were given totalling £128,000.

13 grants were for £1,000 or more and many were repeated from the previous year. The largest grants were to British Technion Society (£40,000); Friends of the Hebrew University (£34,000) and the Jerusalem Foundation (£12,000). The largest non-Jewish grants were given to the Save the Children Fund and MIND (£4,000 each), both of whom received grants in previous years. The trust also gave many grants of £25 to £500 to small, local, medical, educational and theatrical organisations.

Applications: The trust states that "no further applications for funds can be considered".

The J N Derbyshire Trust

£111,000 (1993/94)

Health, social welfare in Nottinghamshire

Foxhall Lodge, Gregory Boulevard, Nottingham NG7 6LH
0115-962 6578

Correspondent: P R Moore, Secretary

Trustees: Mrs A L Carver; Mrs E Cathery; S J Christophers; R F Holloway; P R Moore; Mrs L Whittle.

Beneficial area: Nottingham and Nottinghamshire.

Derbyshire/Devonshire/Dibdin

Information available: Accounts are on file at the Charity Commission, without a list of grants.

General: The objects of the trust are "the general promotion of health, the development of physical improvement, the advancement of education and the relief of poverty, distress and sickness".

In 1993/94, the trust had assets of £2.8 million, an income of £124,000 and gave grants totalling £111,000 and were categorised as follows:

Old age	£4,500	(3)
Physical health and handicap, deafness, dumbness and blindness	£37,000	(25)
General medical and ambulance	£1,500	(1)
Protection and welfare of children	£25,000	(21)
Youth organisations	£12,000	(14)
Relief of poverty	£19,000	(14)
Miscellaneous	£12,000	(12)

The largest grants were: £10,500 to Distressed Gentlefolk's Aid Association and £5,000 each to Newark and District Hospice, Queen of Hearts Cardiac Theatre Appeal, Children's Hospice Appeal and Just for the Day Appeal. Grants are made to Nottinghamshire charities and local (Nottingham) branches of national charities.

Exclusions: No grants directly to individuals.

Applications: Applications can be made at any time, but trustees usually only meet to consider them twice a year in March and September. The trust does not have its own application forms. Details of the project are required. A reply is only given to unsuccessful applicants if they enclose an sae.

The 10th Duke of Devonshire's Trust (1949)

£144,000 (1992/93)

General, especially in Derbyshire

Messrs Currey & Co, Solicitors,
21 Buckingham Gate, London SW1E 6LS
0171-828 4091

Correspondent: Theresa Skelton, Trustee Manager

Trustees: Marquess of Hartington; R G Beckett; N W Smith.

Beneficial area: UK, with a preference for Derbyshire.

Information available: Full accounts are on file at the Charity Commission.

General: The trust gives grants to a range of national charities and to local charities with a preference for Derbyshire.

In 1992/93, the trust had assets of £6.7 million. This is a substantial increase from £4.7 million in 1991/92, due to a gift from the Duke of £667,000 and unrealised capital gains of £1.5 million. The trust had an income of £257,000 down from £309,000 the previous year. Grants totalled £144,000 (£120,000 in 1991/92).

The Chatsworth House Trust is consistently the largest recipient, usually receiving £60,000 to £80,000 and exceptionally £1,260,000 in 1990/91 out of a grant total of £1,318,000. Other grants made by the trust total about £60,000 a year. Presumably the surplus is accumulated for the benefit of the Chatsworth House Trust in exceptional years.

In 1992/93, 73 other grants were made and split into three lists. The first list appears to be small annual grants, of £50 or £100, to 15 Derbyshire charities totalling about £1,000.

The second list contained 16 grants totalling £36,000 including Yorkshire Children's Hospital (£10,000); Governors of Pilsley C of E School (£8,000); Ian Gow Memorial Fund (£5,000) and Manchester Cathedral Development Trust (£2,500). Other grants of £500 to £1,500 went to organisations such as Baslow Sports Field; Keighley Sea Cadets Corps; LGI Life Scan Appeal and Pornography and Violence Research Trust. At least a third of grants were given in Yorkshire.

The third and largest list included 42 grants totalling £105,000, including the Chatsworth House grant. The only other grants of £1,000 or more included those to the RNLI, Eastbourne (£25,000); Keighley Cadet Corp (£5,000); Eastbourne War Memorial Housing (£4,000) and £1,000 each to Horticultural Therapy and Royal School for the Deaf - Derby and Trent College. The remaining grants were for £500 or less, to national organisations and local organisations with a preference for Derbyshire. These included Derby Community Arts, Genesis Project, National Schizophrenia Fellowship, RSPCA and Sheffield Conservation Volunteers.

Applications: In writing to the correspondent.

The Thomas Peter Dibdin Foundation

£79,000 (1991/92)

Christian

Grange & Wintringham, St Mary's Chambers, Grimsby DN31 1LD
01472-350631

Correspondent: T J Carson, Trustee

Trustees: T J Carson; T P Dibdin.

Beneficial area: UK.

Information available: Full accounts are on file at the Charity Commission for 1991/92.

General: In 1991/92, the trust had assets of almost £1 million and an income of £353,000 (up from £131,000 in 1990/91). This included £90,000 from Gift Aid donations, £129,000 from rent and £133,000 dividend from Immingham Industrial Estates Ltd. Loan interest of £50,000 was paid to the TSB and only four grants were given totalling £79,000.

The beneficiaries were the Christian Centre (Humberside Ltd) (£62,000 and £20,000 in 1990/91); Don Summers Evangelistic Association (£11,000 and £10,500 in 1990/91); Christian Broadcasting Council of GB (£4,800 and £4,100 in 1990/91) and Rock Youth Centre (£1,500 and £4,100 in 1990/91). The two main beneficiaries are the same each year.

In 1990/91, six other grants were given to three churches, two other Christian organisations and £1,100 to Electronic Aids for the Blind.

According to the Charity Commission, the trust had an income of £165,000 in 1992/93.

Applications: In writing to the correspondent.

The Dinam Charity

£110,000 (1992/93)

International understanding, general

Southampton Place, London WC1A 2EA
0171-405 4374

Correspondent: J H Davies, Secretary to the Trustees

Trustees: Mrs M M Noble; Mrs G R J Cormack; E D G Davies; J H Davies; J S Tyres.

Beneficial area: Worldwide.

Information available: Accounts are on file at the Charity Commission, but without a full list of grants since 1988/89.

General: In 1992/93, the trust had assets of £2.5 million and an income of £133,000. Grants totalled £110,000. This included £88,000 to the David Davies Memorial Institute - a regular beneficiary - and £22,000 for general charitable donations.

The most recent full list of grants on file at the Charity Commission is for 1988/89, when the grant total was £131,000. As usual the largest grant was to the David Davies Memorial Institute (£70,000) and another regular beneficiary, the Welsh Centre for International Affairs, received £25,000. Other large grants were £6,500 to Christian Aid and £2,500 to the Caldecott Community.

A further 58 grants were made ranging from £50 to £1,500. About 20% of grants were for overseas aid/development including £500 to WaterAid and £1,000 to the Oxfam Nicaraguan Hurricane Disaster Appeal. A further 20% went to organisations in Wales including the Montgomery County Music Festival (£500) and Blaenau Ffestiniog Memorial Hospital (£1,000). Other beneficiaries included national and local charities, especially those concerned with animal welfare, children and youth.

Exclusions: Grants are only given to registered charities. No grants to individuals.

Applications: Applications can be made at any time. Unsuccessful applicants will not be notified unless an sae is enclosed with the application.

The Divert Trust
(formerly the Intermediate Treatment Fund)

About £200,000

Juvenile delinquency and crime prevention

33 King Street, London WC2 8JD
0171-379 6171; Fax: 0171-240 2082

Correspondent: The Director

Trustees: Lord Elton; Simon Rodway; Ms V Stern; B A Thompson; M O Hawker; Col A Pagan; Lord Henderson; Mike Milan; C Weston-Evans; Mrs Weitzmann.

Beneficial area: England and Wales.

Information available: Full details of the work of the fund are available from the address above.

General: Divert is a new trust, which has taken over from the Intermediate Treatment Fund (ITF). It aims to help ordinary people be more effective in fighting youth crime. It offers a variety of services designed to foster good relations between local voluntary groups and statutory agencies.

"Community groups (such as small charities, tenants' groups, neighbourhood centres, church groups and youth clubs) know the problems of young people in their area. They are often best placed to come up with the solutions. They can identify very quickly what is missing in a community that is influencing children to offend. The strength of voluntary groups in providing preventative and diversionary schemes is that they are not part of the justice system but can act as an independent advisor, mentor and friend.

"Divert supports organisations working on youth projects (especially on crime prevention). Currently the main scheme giving grants is 'Communities and Football'. Grants are given out of an annual grant from the Football Trust. Only football projects are supported, for young people (10 to 25 years) of either sex, regardless of race, colour or religion. Grants can be towards: the costs of setting up teams or leagues, including affiliation fees and costs of match officials and kit and equipment."

At the time of going to print, the trust was developing other grant-giving schemes to support voluntary organisations. For the latest details of these, contact the correspondent at the address above.

The trust also runs tailor-made courses for organisations and publishes research and information useful to organisations working with young people. They are also able to put people in contact with projects (working to reduce youth crime) throughout the country with a proven track record in developing these services, so that others can benefit from their experience.

Applications: All applications must be made on a form available from the correspondent. However the fund welcomes enquiries at any stage of the project's development and staff will be happy to visit or correspond with applicants considering an application.

All applications must be accompanied by a letter of support from a senior officer in one of the statutory services (an officer in the Intermediate Treatment/Juvenile Justice section of the social services department would be the most appropriate person). This should indicate the degree of local authority involvement and the way in which the proposed project relates to local needs and other available provision.

All applicants must submit full audited accounts for the last full year of the project (unless the project is a new one), a budget for the current/next year, and suppliers' estimates for the cost of any equipment to be purchased with the fund's grant.

Applications which satisfy the criteria are, after investigation, considered by the committee in April, July, October, and January of each year. As most projects are visited by fund staff, applications should be submitted when ready, without consideration of committee dates.

Following investigation all grant decisions are made by the Committee. The fund has established a grants monitoring procedure which applies when a grant is made. To achieve full accountability and the transfer of experience the fund requests receipts, details of expenditure and an analysis of project development following an award. Officers of the fund are pleased to provide advice and support to ensure the successful achievement of its grant monitoring procedures.

The DLM Charitable Trust

£20,000 (1993/94)

General

Messrs Cloke & Co, Warnford Court, Throgmorton Street, London EC2N 2AT
0171-638 8992

Correspondent: J A Cloke

Trustees: Dr E A de la Mare; J A Cloke; Mrs P Sawyer.

Beneficial area: UK, especially the Oxford area.

Information available: Full accounts are on file at the Charity Commission.

General: The trust was established in 1990, after R D A de la Mare left 25% of the residue of his estate for charitable purposes. In 1990/91, the assets of the trust were £959,000 and a further £204,000 was added to the investment funds. In its first year of grant giving, £3,000 was given to six organisations, including £1,000 each to Driving for the Disabled and Oxford Preservation Trust Magdalen Bridge Appeal.

By 1993/94, the trust's assets were worth over £2 million and the income was £75,000. Grants had risen to £20,000. 22 organisations received grants ranging from £50 each to Bosnia Aid Committee, Oxford and NSPCC, Appleton up to £5,000 each to Oxford City Football Club Trust and the Rainbow Club. MacIntyre Homes received £2,000 and £1,000 was given to each of Oxford Diabetes Centre Campaign, Cothill House School and Handicapped Children's Trust. All other grants were for £250 or £500 and went to a range of what appear to be mainly national charities, such as National Playbus Association, National Playing Fields Association, British Wireless for the Blind Fund and the Neuromuscular Centre.

The five grants given in 1992/93 totalling £7,300 were not supported in 1993/94. There is a preference for the Oxford area and for charities supported by the late Mr de la Mare. Current projects include nearly £20,000 a year towards supporting a city centre chaplaincy for Oxford.

Applications: In writing to the correspondent.

The Dollond Charitable Trust

£31,000 (1992/93)

General

122 Edgwarebury Lane, Edgware, Middlesex HA8 8NB
0181-958 9903

Correspondent: A L Dollond

Trustees: A L Dollond; A Dolland; Dr I Dolland.

Beneficial area: UK, with a preference for Middlesex.

Information available: Full accounts are on file at the Charity Commission.

General: The trust tends to support people/projects known to the trustees or the Dolland family.

In 1992/93, the trust had assets of £1.9 million, an income of £140,000, but only gave grants totalling £31,000. 13 grants totalled £30,000 and 21 grants of under £100 each, totalled £1,000. The largest grants were to Jerusalem College of Technology (£26,500) and Boystown, Jerusalem (£1,200). The remaining grants, of £100 to £500, were to Jewish organisations such as the Lubovitch Foundation, Norwood Childcare and Yeshiva for Chozrim.

Applications: Unsolicited applications are not welcomed.

The Dorus Trust

£145,000 (1993)

General

Foundation House, Coach & Horses Passage, The Pantiles, Tunbridge Wells, Kent TN2 5TZ
01892-512244

Correspondent: R H Berwick

Trustees: Charles Peacock; Bettine Bond; Michael Bond.

Beneficial area: Worldwide.

Information available: Full accounts are on file at the Charity Commission for 1993.

General: The trust was registered in 1990 and has since increased in size considerably. In 1993, the trust had assets of £2.9 million (£2.5 million in 1990) and an income of £123,000 (£38,000 in 1990). Grants totalled £145,000.

Fourteen grants were given ranging from £2,500 to £30,000. The largest were to Sight Savers (£30,000); Children's Society (£20,000); VSO, British Diabetic Association and Multiple Sclerosis Society (£15,000 each), and £10,000 each to Quest Cancer Test and the Breakthrough Trust.

The remaining grants were given to the Rio Mazan Project (£2,500); Arthritis & Rheumatism Council, Marine Conservation Society and Lupus UK (£5,000 each); Simon Community (£6,500); National Association for the Family (£7,000) and Sane (£9,000).

Applications: The trust states that all funds are fully committed and no unsolicited applications will be considered.

The R M Douglas Charitable Trust

£19,000 (1992/93)

General

Dunstall Hall, Barton-under-Needwood, Nr Burton-on-Trent DE13 8BE
01283-712471

Correspondent: Sir Robert Douglas OBE

Trustees: Sir Robert Douglas OBE; J R T Douglas OBE; F W Calder.

Beneficial area: UK, preference for Staffordshire.

Information available: Accounts are on file at the Charity Commission, but without a list of grants for 1992/93.

General: The trust was set up for relief of poverty (including provision of pensions) especially for present and past employees (and their families) of Robert M Douglas (Contractors) Ltd, and for general charitable purposes especially in the parish of St Mary, Dunstall.

In 1992/93, it had assets of £846,000 including £505,000 in ordinary shares in Tilbury Douglas plc. The income from these assets rose markedly from £22,000 in 1991/92 to £70,000 in 1992/93. This increase in income had no effect on the grant total which was £30,000 in both years, including £8,000 to individuals in

1991/92 and £11,000 in 1992/93. No further information on the grants was available for 1992/93.

In 1991/92, 126 grants were made to organisations totalling £22,000. The largest were to St Mary's Church, Dunstall and Burton Graduate Medical Centre (both £5,000), Lichfield Cathedral (£1,500) and St Giles Hospice and St James' Church Restoration Appeal (both £1,000). The remaining grants were mostly for £50 or less to a wide range of national and local causes.

Applications: In writing to the correspondent.

The Dove-Bowerman Trust

£49,000 (1993/94)

Education

Bracken Cottage, Chearsley Road, Long Crendon, Buckinghamshire HP18 9BT
01844-201034

Correspondent: Miss A Dudley-Smith, Secretary

Trustees: Christine Canti; Kathleen Overton; David Marques; Christina Alderson; William P W Barnes; Margaret Anderson; Gillian Fletcher-Watson; Caroline Davis; Peter Wolton.

Beneficial area: UK.

Information available: Full accounts are on file at the Charity Commission for 1993/94.

General: In 1993/94, the trust had assets of £1 million (market value) and an income of £48,000. It gave nine grants totalling £49,000 to: Wass Bursary Fund (£20,000); Wycombe Abbey School (£12,500); Neville Rolfe Awards (£7,000); Ware College (£4,000); Coleg Elidyr Foundation, St Loyes College and UGS Settlement, Peckham (£1,700 each). The smallest grants of £300 or under were to Camphill Community and Thomas Coram Foundation. All recipients received a similar grant the previous year.

Applications: The trust appears to have a list of causes it supports; unsolicited applications are unlikely to be successful.

The Dumbreck Charity

£82,000 (1993/94)

General (see below)

Messrs Price Waterhouse & Co, Cornwall Court, 19 Cornwall Street, Birmingham B3 2DT
0121-200 3000

Correspondent: The Trust Department

Trustees: A C S Hordern; H B Carslake; Miss B Y Mellor.

Beneficial area: Worldwide, especially the Midlands.

Information available: Full accounts are on file at the Charity Commission.

General: In 1991/92, the trust had assets of £1.1 million (including £59,000 in investments given during the year by one of the trustees) generating an income of £68,000. Grants totalled £72,000. By 1993/94, assets were £1.2 million and the income £84,000. It gave grants totalling £77,000. Most grants were for either £500 or £750, except for nine grants of between £1,000 and £3,000. The grants list is divided into the following categories:

Animal welfare/conservation

International – £3,000 was distributed between five organisations: World Wide Fund for Nature; Friends of Conservation; Horses and Ponies Protection League; Rare Breeds Survival Trust and the International League for the Protection of Horses.

National - £8,250 between 10 organisations: the largest grant was £3,000 to Brooke Hospital for Animals, Cairo. Other beneficiaries included: Blue Cross Animal Hospital, Donkey Sanctuary; Hedgehog Sanctuary, Aylesbury; Wildfowl Trust, and two horse charities.

Local - £5,500 between five local projects in the Midlands area.

Children's Welfare

National - £4,500 was shared between five national charities including the Save the Children Fund (£3,000), NSPCC (£1,000) and Farms for Inner City Children (£500).

Local - £2,500 between four local (Midlands) branches of national charities.

Care of Elderly and Physically/Mentally Disabled People

National - 12 charities, mainly well-known national organisations, received £7,500.

Local - 15 Midlands organisations received £10,000 between them, the largest of which was £1,500 to Warwickshire Association for the Blind.

Medical

National - 14 grants totalling £9,000 including £2,000 to the Cancer Relief Macmillan Fund.

Local - £5,500 to seven Midlands projects, the largest being £1,500 to St Mary's Hospice, Birmingham.

Miscellaneous

Grants totalling £1,750 were shared between Intermediate Technology Development Ltd, Oxfam and the Salvation Army for overseas projects.

National - Seven grants totalling £4,250 to organisations such as British Field Sports Association, Hunt Servants' Benefit Society, the Farming and Wildlife Trust and some better known organisations such as RNLI, SSAFA, Shaftesbury Society Housing Association and the Leonard Cheshire Foundation.

Local - Seven local grants totalling £4,500, consisted of three for museum developments, two for mayor's funds, one towards the Midland Canal and one to Relate.

Extraordinary - Four of the largest grants were given in this section to: Birmingham Children's Hospital - ICU Appeal; Himbleton Church and Warwick Old People's Friendship Centre (all of whom received £1,000) and West Midlands Ambulance Service (£2,000). Other beneficiaries in this category included Birmingham Repertory Theatre, British Sports Association for the Disabled, Oxfam Indian Earthquake Appeal and Prisoners of Conscience Appeal Fund.

The first four categories are effectively annual subscription lists. The recipient organisations hardly vary at all; the amounts given to them can. The only category where there is scope for new grants is the Extraordinary category in Miscellaneous. Some of the extraordinary grants become regular grants the following year onwards.

Most grants are £500 or £750. Local grants are generally given in the Midlands, especially the West Midlands.

Applications: In writing to the correspondent. The trustees meet annually. Unsuccessful applications will not be acknowledged.

The W E Dunn Trust

£130,000 (1993/94)

Medical and social welfare in the Midlands

Coopers & Lybrand, 43 Temple Row, Birmingham B2 5JT
0121-200 4000

Correspondent: D J Corney

Trustees: C E Corney; D J Corney; D F Perkins.

Beneficial area: The Midlands.

Information available: Full accounts are on file at the Charity Commission.

General: The general policy of the trust is to benefit people who are sick or in adversity and live in the Midlands, particularly Wolverhampton, Wednesbury, North Staffordshire and surrounding areas. Support is given to local charities, occasionally national charities, and to individuals in need through social service departments. Occasionally students from the Midlands who have special difficulties are assisted. There is a preference for people who are either old or very young.

In 1992/93, the trust had assets of £996,000 and an income of £133,000. Grants totalled £158,000 (£130,000 in 1993/94), including £27,000 to individuals.

Grants to 59 organisations totalled £131,000. The largest grants were to Compton Hospice (£30,000), William E Dunn Unit of Cardiology, Keele (£25,000), St Basil's Centre (£8,000), West Midlands Macmillan Appeal (£6,000) and three grants of £5,000 to Valley Home Association, Gas Hall Development and the Institute of Orthopaedics.

There were 24 grants of between £1,000 and £2,500, mainly to medical and education appeals such as Baby Lifeline, Horder Centre for Arthritics, Spastics Society, Royal Merchant Navy School and Royal Wolverhampton School. Grants were also given to St James Community Support & Advice Centre and to Wolverhampton scout groups.

Of the 27 grants of £500, many were for educational purposes, community projects and national organisations' appeals such as Castle Vale Home Start, Church Army, St Bedes Community Project, Staffordshire University and YMCA, West Bromwich.

One grant of £800 was given to the Salvation Army. Only 15 grants were recurrent.

Exclusions: No grants to settle or reduce debts already incurred.

Applications: In writing to the correspondent. Grants to individuals are considered every week; grants to organisations, every three or four months. At present the trustees have decided to concentrate their resources on one main objective and are not making large grants to organisations for the next two years.

The Dyers' Company Charitable Trust

£45,000 (1989/90)

General

Dyers Hall, Dowgate Hill, London EC4R 2ST
0171-236 7197

Correspondent: The Clerk

Beneficial area: UK.

Information available: Full accounts are on file at the Charity Commission.

General: The correspondent has asked not to be included in this Guide as the requests for assistance have escalated to several hundred a year, virtually all of which are refused. We maintain our policy of including all relevant grant-making trusts, but unfortunately we have not been able to update the information.

In 1989/90, the trust had assets of £847,000 and an income of £81,000. Grants totalled £45,000 leaving a surplus of £36,000. Grants were given in the following categories:

Education and the craft: Eight grants totalling £24,000. £16,000 was given to Norwich School for assisted places and £1,000 to Hyde Park Nursery School Trust (both regular grants). Others were to advance the study of textiles (including £5,000 to a PhD student at the Scottish College of Textiles).

Health & welfare: 19 grants totalling £7,000, ranging from £100 to £800. Recipients included the Aidis Trust, BACUP, Connection, Herts Care Trust, St Christopher's Hospice and West London Family Service Unit. Some are recurrent.

The church: Three grants totalling £1,700, the main award being an annual one.

The services: Five grants totalling £8,000, ranging from £5,000 to the Airborne Forces Security Fund to £25 to a local scout group.

Other appeals: 10 grants ranging from £50 to £1,000 and totalling £4,000. Recipients included Chelsea Physic Garden, London Wildlife Trust, Outward Bound Association (Merseyside) and the Swan Sanctuary, Egham.

Applications: The trust does not welcome unsolicited applications.

The Earley Charity

£267,000 (1992)

General in Earley and east Reading

The Liberty of Earley House, Strand Way, Earley, Reading, Berks RG6 4EA
01734-755663

Correspondent: L G Norton, Clerk

Trustees: R F Ames; D A Chilvers; Mrs M Eastwell; R Hadfield; Dr D G Jenkins; C A Nichols; I M Robertson; D C Sutton.

Beneficial area: The civil parish of Earley, the eastern and south eastern part of Reading borough and the immediate surrounding area.

Information available: Full accounts are on file at the Charity Commission.

General: During 1994, substantial grants were made to local organisations, generally for £3,000 to £7,000. The major grant, of £19,000, was towards a reading room (the Earley Charity Room) in Reading Museum.

Other local organisations receiving grants of £5,000 or more were the Association for the Blind (for an extension to their works), Council for Racial Equality, Victim Support and CRUSE Bereavement Care (in each case for help with staff costs), and the Churches Drop-in Centre (for building costs).

Other beneficiaries included: Caresham Hall Trustees (building work); Earley Bus; Earley Mobile Information Centre; Friends of Reading Samaritans; Orlando Fund (holiday costs for children in a local hospital cancer ward); Reading Festival Chorus (contribution towards the costs of a VE Day concert); Reading International

Support Centre (photcopier for community group's use); Reading Mentally Handicapped Society (towards the purchase of vehicles).

Exclusions: No national or international appeals are considered. Educational grants are limited to vocational training.

Applications: On the form available from the charity.

The Ebenezer Trust

£48,000 (1992/93)

Evangelical Christianity, welfare

31 Middleton Road, Shenfield, Brentwood, Essex CM15 8DJ
0171-936 3000

Correspondent: N T Davey

Trustees: N T Davey; R M Davey.

Beneficial area: Worldwide.

Information available: Full accounts are on file at the Charity Commission.

General: Most of this trust's income is from covenants and Gift Aid and totalled £60,000 in 1992/93. Grants totalled £48,000 of which £16,000 was given to Brentwood Baptist Church and £4,500 to Olive Tree Christian Fellowship. 46 other grants were given ranging from £25 to £3,500 but mostly under £500.

Most grants go to evangelical Christian causes with a few smaller grants to UK welfare charities. Most appear to be recurrent. Beneficiaries included TEAR Fund (£3,500), Bible Society (£500), CARE Trust (£400), Gideons International (£1,300), London City Mission (£1,200), RNLI (£100), and the Salvation Army (£300).

Applications: The trust states that they "are most unlikely to consider unsolicited requests for grants".

The Ecological Foundation

£89,000 (1992/93)

Environment/conservation

Lower Bosneives, Withiel, Bodmin, Cornwall PL30 5NQ
01208-831236; Fax: 01208-831083

Correspondent: J Faull, Director

Trustees: The Marquis of Londonderry; Sir James Goldsmith; John Aspinall; R Hanbury-Tenison.

Beneficial area: Worldwide.

Information available: Full accounts are on file at the Charity Commission.

General: The foundation mainly funds its own projects and reports. In 1992/93, charitable expenditure was £89,000 of which £34,000 was termed "public outreach".

The largest grants were to Genetic Diversity in British Agriculture (£11,000), Ecoropa (£10,000) and the Danish People Movement (£16,000). Other beneficiaries included Safe Alliance (£6,500 and an exceptional £65,000 in 1990/91), Survival International (£4,000) and Gaia for a conference and the proceedings (£4,000).

None of the these received a grant the previous year when the main beneficiaries were Environmentally Concerned (£28,000) 1992, UNCED (£16,000 and £41,000 in 1990/91) and World Uranium (£10,000).

In addition to the two grants give in 1990/91 mentioned above, £28,000 was also given to Environmentally Concerned Shareholders.

Applications: In writing to the correspondent.

The Gilbert & Eileen Edgar Foundation

£104,000 (1994)

Medical research, arts, general

c/o Chantrey Vellacott, 23-25 Castle Street, Reading RG1 7SB
01734-595432

Correspondent: Mrs Avril Hallam

Trustees: A E Gentilli; J G Matthews; Mrs M R Lloyd Johnes, Trustee Emeritus.

Beneficial area: UK (and some international appeals).

Information available: Full accounts are on file at the Charity Commission.

General: The settlor expressed the desire that preference be given to the following objects:

a) The promotion of medical, surgical science in all forms;

b) Helping people who are young, old or needy;

c) Raising artistic taste of the public in relation to and promoting the fine arts;

d) The promotion of academic education;

e) The promotion of religion;

f) The promotion of facilities for recreation or other leisure time occupation.

In 1994, the trust had assets of £1.2 million and an income of £79,000. After accountancy charges of £8,800, the trust gave about 218 grants, mainly of £250 to £500, totalling £104,000. Grants were given to a wide range of organisations, especially those concerned with children, medical, welfare or disability. Most grants were recurrent. In 1993, the largest grants were to British Southern Slav Society (£5,000 in both 1993 and 1992), Iris Fund (£2,500 in 1993 and £3,000 in 1992) and Royal National Theatre (£2,500 in both 1993 and 1992).

25 grants of £1,000 to £1,500 included those to the Brain Research Trust, Concern Worldwide, Help the Hospices, Mental Health Foundation, Research into Ageing, Shakespeare Globe Trust and Toynbee Hall.

Applications: To the correspondent in writing. There are no application forms.

The Gilbert Edgar Trust Fund

£49,000 (1992/93)

General

Huttons Farm, Hambledon, Henley-on-Thames, Oxon RG9 6NE

Correspondent: S C E Gentilli

Trustees: Mrs G R Sinclair-Hogg; S C E Gentilli; A E Gentilli; Dr R E B Solomons.

Beneficial area: UK.

Information available: Full accounts are on file at the Charity Commission.

General: In 1992/93, the trust had assets of £738,000 generating an income of £44,000. Grants totalled £49,000 and are awarded to a long list of beneficiaries which are virtually the same each year. 109 grants were given ranging from £20 to £1,000; 83 were for £400. There were 20 new beneficiaries during the year, replacing 24 of the previous recipients. The trust supports mainly national charities in the fields of health, welfare, disability and children and youth. A few local charities are also supported. There were nine grants of £1,000 including British Red Cross, Centrepoint Soho, Foundation for Conductive Education, NSPCC, Oxfam and the YMCA.

Applications: In writing to the correspondent.

The W G Edwards Charitable Foundation

£202,000 (1992/93)

Care of elderly

Wedge Property Co Ltd, 123a Station Road, Oxted, Surrey RH8 0QE
01883-714412

Correspondent: S K Phillips

Trustees: Margaret E Offley Edwards; Wendy D Savage; S K Phillips.

Beneficial area: UK.

Information available: Full accounts are on file at the Charity Commission.

General: In 1992/93, the trust had assets of £3.2 million, an income of only £147,000. It gave only four grants totalling £202,000. The main beneficiaries were Hospice at Home (£100,000), Shropshire Rural Housing Association (£60,000) and Age Concern, Tower Hamlets (£41,000). There was also a grant of £1,000 to Oxted & District Link Association.

It appears that the trust regularly only makes a few large donations. In 1990/91, the trust had assets of £3.1 million, an income of £114,000 and gave grants totalling £190,000. These grants were to Bridge Care, Bath (£92,000) and Age Concern groups in Sevenoaks (£75,000) and Tower Hamlets (£23,000).

Applications: In writing to the correspondent.

The George Elias Charitable Trust

£45,000 (1992/93)

Jewish, general

Elitex House, Moss Lane, Hale, Altrincham, Cheshire WA15 8AD
0161-928 7171

Correspondent: N G Denton

Beneficial area: UK and Israel.

Information available: Full accounts are on file at the Charity Commission.

General: The trust was founded in 1977, and the original trustees were all members of the Elias family. By 1992/93, the trust had accumulated assets valued in the accounts at £380,000, including various investments, land and buildings listed at cost, and shares in two private companies, G H Elias Ltd and I C Shaw & Co.

The trust's income was nearly £88,000 in 1992/93, in part deriving from the proceeds of investments, but also including a deed of covenant of £40,000. Donations totalling £45,000 were made in the year, down from £65,000 in 1991/92. Grants went mainly to Jewish causes, with the larger gifts including Asos Chesed (£10,000); JPAIME (£7,500); Machon Levi Yitschok, Jewish National Fund Charitable Trust and Horev School in Jerusalem (£5,000 each).

Smaller donations went mainly to Jewish causes, including very even-handed gifts of around £400 each to both the Labour and Conservative Friends of Israel. Some donations went to more general charitable causes. These included: Childline (£750), Manchester Charitable Trust (£200) and the North West Industrial Council (£100).

Applications: In writing to the correspondent.

The Wilfred & Elsie Elkes Charity Fund

£74,000 (1992/93)

General

Trustee & Taxation Office, Royal Bank of Scotland plc, PO Box 356, 45 Mosley Street, Manchester M60 2BE
0161-236 8585

Correspondent: The Trust Officer

Trustees: Royal Bank of Scotland plc.

Beneficial area: UK, with a preference for Staffordshire and especially Uttoxeter.

Information available: Full accounts are on file at the Charity Commission.

General: In 1992/93, the trust's income was £103,000; it gave over 50 grants totalling £74,000. The Trust Manager stated that the surplus arose because "the trustees had not approved sufficient grants to utilise all of the available income ... any surplus ... is carried forward to the following year".

The trust deed makes specific reference to animal welfare, individuals in need and small charities based in Uttoxeter. Of the 52 grants, the largest were to the Hearing Research Trust (£8,000), Staffordshire University (£5,000), Doctor Charles Bamford Memorial Homes of Rest (£5,000) and Uttoxeter BASICS Appeal (£4,000).

There were 30 grants of between £1,000 and £3,000, to national and local organisations involved in mainly health/disability (such as National Deaf Children's Society and British Red Cross) or for young people (such as National Association of Boys' Clubs and Denstone Expeditions Trust) generally towards expeditions/outward bound type projects. There were a small number of grants to animal causes such as International Fund for Animal Welfare and Cheadle & District Animal Welfare Society.

The smaller grants of £500 to £750 were given to a wide range of organisations including British Agencies for Adoption and Fostering, Children in Need, GAP Activity Projects Ltd and Peter Pan Playgroup.

Applications: In writing to the correspondent.

Ellador Ltd

£46,000 (1992/93)

Jewish

20 Ashtead Road, London E5
0171-242 3580

Correspondent: J Schreiber

Trustees: J Schreiber; S Schreiber; Mrs H Schreiber; Mrs R Schreiber.

Beneficial area: Worldwide.

Information available: Full accounts are on file at the Charity Commission.

General: In 1992/93, the trust had an income of £64,000, all of which was from donations, Gift Aid or covenants. 58 grants totalled £46,000 all to Jewish organisations.

Applications: In writing to the correspondent.

The Ellinson Foundation

£156,000 (1993/94)

Jewish

15 Gresham Gardens, Golders Green, London NW11 8NX
0191-281 8191 (Accountants to the trust)

Correspondent: Messrs Robson, Laidler & Co

Trustees: C O Ellinson; Mrs E Ellinson; A Ellinson; A Z Ellinson.

Beneficial area: Worldwide.

Information available: Full accounts are on file at the Charity Commission.

General: The income of the trust consists of rents received from properties and covenanted receipts from its subsidiary company, Ozer Properties Ltd. In 1993/94, the trust had an income of £202,000, down on the previous year, as there was no donation from Ozer. It gave £156,000 in 105 grants, over half of which were recurrent. 23 grants were for £1,000 or over; most of the rest were for under £500.

The trust supports hospitals, education and homelessness in the UK and overseas, usually with a Jewish teaching aspect. The trust regularly supports organisations such as boarding schools for boys and girls teaching the Torah. All grants were to Jewish organisations, the largest to the Friends of United Institution of Arad (£30,000) and Emuno Education Centre (£20,000).

Applications: In writing to the correspondent.

The Elm Trust II

£79,000 (1991/92)

Arts

Personal Financial Management, 12 Hans Road, London SW3 1RT
0171-584 4277

Correspondent: P D Green

Trustees: R E Downhill; P D Green; Mrs C M Hawley.

Beneficial area: UK.

Information available: Full accounts are on file at the Charity Commission up to 1991/92.

General: In 1991/92, the trust had an income of £72,000 and gave £79,000, all to the National Portrait Gallery.

The previous year it gave two grants totalling £19,000 from an income of £87,000. The National Portrait Gallery received £10,500 and the Victoria & Albert Museum £8,500.

Applications: In writing to the correspondent.

The Elmgrant Trust

£100,000 (1993/94)

Education, arts, social sciences

The Elmhirst Centre, Dartington Hall, Totnes, Devon TQ9 6EL
01803-863160

Correspondent: Mrs M B Nicholson, Secretary

Trustees: Maurice Ash; Michael Young; Claire Ash Wheeler; Sophie Young.

Beneficial area: UK, with a preference for Devon and Cornwall (occasional overseas grants).

Information available: Full accounts are on file at the Charity Commission.

General: In 1993/94, the trust had assets of just over £2 million and an income of £131,000. Grants are generally around £250 to £2,000 and totalled £100,000. Grants were broken down as follows:

Education and educational research: £44,000 in 74 grants ranging from £50 to £5,000. The largest were awarded to the Small School, Hartland (£5,000); Iron Mill Centre (£2,350); Poughill C of E School Trust (£2,000) and Bicton College of Agriculture and the College of Homeopathy (£1,350 each).

Arts and arts research: £23,000 in 22 grants, the largest of which was £3,750 to Beaford Arts Centre and £2,500 each to Dartington International Summer School and the Institute of Community Studies (for the Open College of the Arts).

Social sciences & scientific research: £16,000 in 18 grants. The largest were to Elmhirst Institute of Community Studies, Bengal (£4,000) and the Association for Neighbourhood Councils (£2,000).

Pensions & compassionate grants: £5,000, all to individuals.

Donations: £11,450 in 20 grants generally of £200 to £2,500. The largest were to the Cambodia Trust (£2,500), Totnes Natural Health Centre (£1,150) and £1,000 each to SCOPE and the Self Healing Association.

Grants are also given to individuals wanting to make a change of direction in their lives, but only to individuals in Devon and Cornwall, aged 30 and over.

Exclusions: Postgraduate study and expedition/travel grants are not considered.

Applications: In writing to the correspondent. Meetings are held in March, June, September and December. Applications for "change of direction" awards should be made in response to an annual local advertisement in the spring.

The Vernon N Ely Charitable Trust

£37,000 (1993/94)

Christian, welfare, disability, children and youth, overseas

16 St George's Road, Wimbledon, London SW19 4DP
0181-946 9191

Correspondent: Mrs E M Collins, Secretary

Trustees: J S Moyle; D P Howorth; M S Main.

Beneficial area: Worldwide.

Information available: Full accounts are on file at the Charity Commission for 1993/94.

General: In 1993/94, the trust had assets of £1.2 million, an income of only £48,000 and gave 66 grants totalling £37,000. There were eight grants of £1,000 to £3,800 to: Cottage Homes (£3,800); London Playing Fields (£3,500); Methodist Church, Epsom (£2,500); Oxfam and Christian Aid (£2,000 each); Christchurch United Reform Church (£1,250); Save the Children and British Red Cross (£1,000 each).

There were 14 grants of £500 to welfare, disability, Christian, children, medical and community organisations including: Lest We Forget; Merton Associations for (a) the Blind and (b) the Disabled; Methodist Church East End Mission and Wimbledon Cheshire Homes. The remaining grants were for £75 to £350 and included the Association of Combined Youth Clubs; BLISS; Cancer Relief; London City Mission; RSPCA, Wimbledon; Salvation Army; Ursuline Convent High School and Streatham Youth Centre.

Applications: In writing to the correspondent.

The Emerton Charitable Settlement

£64,000 (1993/94)

Health and welfare

2 New Square, Lincoln's Inn,
London WC2A 3RZ
0171-404 5941

Correspondent: Messrs Dawson & Co (Ref AFN)

Trustees: A F Niekirk; D G Richards.

Beneficial area: UK.

Information available: Full accounts are on file at the Charity Commission.

General: The trust was established in 1971 by Maud Emerton and Vera Bishop Emerton. In 1993/94, it had assets of £1.45 million and an income of £64,000 (down from £68,000 in 1992/93 and £98,000 in 1990/91). It gave 29 grants of between £1,000 and £6,000, all of which were decided at a meeting in November. The largest grants were to SENSE (£6,000), a regular large beneficiary, and the Royal School for the Blind, Leatherhead and Malcolm Sargent Cancer Fund (£5,000 each).

£4,000 was given to each of Missions to Seamen, Harnhill Centre for Christian Healing, Children's Society and Bob Champion Cancer Fund, with £3,000 to both the RNLI and NSPCC. Six grants of £2,000 were given, including two to disability organisations, the Disabled Living Foundation and British Sports Association for the Disabled. There were also 14 grants of £1,000 mainly to sickness/disability, elderly people and benevolent organisations.

Exclusions: No support for religious or international charities.

Applications: In writing to the correspondent.

The Emmandjay Charitable Trust

£183,000 (1993/94)

Social welfare, medicine

PO Box 31, Bradford, West Yorkshire BD1 5NH

Correspondent: The Administrator

Trustees: John A Clegg; Mrs Sylvia Clegg; Mrs S L Worthington; Mrs E A Riddell.

Beneficial area: UK, with a special interest in West Yorkshire.

Information available: Full accounts are on file at the Charity Commission.

General: The trust was established in 1962 by Frederick Moore, his wife Elsie, their daughter and son-in-law, Sylvia and John Clegg "as a token of gratitude for the happiness given to them by their late daughter and grand-daughter". It is a time charity; all remaining capital will be distributed to the descendants of the family in 50 years from 1962, or 21 years from the death of the last survivor of the descendants of George V, whichever is the sooner.

The trust gives "most particularly to help disadvantaged people but many different projects are supported - caring for the disabled, physically and mentally handicapped and terminally ill, work with young people, medical research. The trust likes projects which reach a lot of people. The trustees are keen that grants are actually spent."

In 1993/94, the assets of the trust were £3.5 million (almost double the £1.8 million in 1990/91), generating an income of £177,000 (down from £213,000 in 1990/91). Grants totalled £183,000.

Over 300 donations were made, mainly for a few hundred pounds. Only 14 were for £1,000 or more. The larger grants were given to West Yorkshire Youth Association (£20,000); Age Concern (£25,000); DATA (£5,500) and Research into Ageing (£3,000). All appear to have received similarly large donations in recent years. The trust also made grants to BIME (£34,000); Cancer Support Centre (£11,000); ASBAH (£6,000); National Heart Research (£5,000); Camphill Village Trust (£5,000) and the Airdale Drug & Alcohol Project (£2,000). In the past, the trust has made grants of £100 to several more radical, and "unpopular" organisations.

Exclusions: "The trust does not pay debts, does not make grants to individual students, and does not respond to circulars."

Applications: In writing to the correspondent.

The Englefield Charitable Trust

£166,000 (1993/94)

Churches, general

Englefield Estate Office, Theale, Reading RG7 5DU
01734-302504

Correspondent: Sir William Benyon

Trustees: William R Benyon; James Shelley; Mrs Elizabeth Benyon; Richard H R Benyon.

Beneficial area: UK with preference for the Berkshire area.

Information available: Full accounts are on file at the Charity Commission.

General: Most trusts in this book give lots of grants. There seems no particular reason for this. Why shouldn't trustees just support one carefully selected organisation or project at a time, and do it properly before moving on to another? The Englefield trust tends towards this. Though it has a fairly regular programme of small grants, many of them around Englefield in Berkshire, most of its recent expenditure went in one £500,000 grant for the new interdenominational Christian church in Milton Keynes. In 1992/93, the grant total fell away again because the trust was preparing itself for another big scheme in the field of social housing development.

In 1993/94, the trust had assets of £5.2 million, an income of £303,000 and gave £166,000 in grants. £55,000 was given for Housing for the Elderly (in the two previous years it gave £62,000 and £60,000). Other Charitable Donations totalled £131,000 (£179,000 and £633,000 in the two proceeding years).

Some substantial grants in 1991/92 included: £58,000 to St Mary's Church, Mortimer and £10,000 each to the Berkshire Care Trust and St. Peters Church, Islington, in London. There were six other grants of £5,000 or more, most of them local, to Theale Green School, Breast Cancer Trustees (sic), Englefield Parish Church Fabric Fund, the Lambeth Fund, Mortimer Parish Council, and the National Trust Sutton House appeal. The rest of the 43 grants were for £1,000 or less, and were to very varied recipients, from the Transplant Games Association (£200) to the Hydrotherapy Pool in Nairn, Scotland (£500), via the Royal Botanic Gardens in Kew (£1,000).

Applications: In writing to the correspondent. Trustees meet in June and December.

The Enkalon Foundation

£123,000 (1992/93)

Welfare in Northern Ireland

25 Randalstown Road, Antrim, Northern Ireland BT41 4LJ
018494-63535

Correspondent: J W Wallace, Secretary

Trustees: R L Schierbeek; J A Freeman; D H Templeton.

Beneficial area: Northern Ireland.

Information available: The trust is registered in Northern Ireland. The information for this entry was supplied by the trust.

General: In 1992/93, the trust had assets of £1 million and an income of £85,000. Grants are given mainly for starter finance and can be up to £6,000. Grants are given to cross-community groups, self-help groups and groups helping unemployed or disadvantaged people.

Exclusions: No grants to individuals unless ex-employees. No grants are given outside Northern Ireland or for travel outside Northern Ireland.

Applications: In writing to the correspondent. Trustees meet four times a year. Applications should provide the following information:

- Description of the organisation and a copy of the constitution and rules.
- Proposed budget and details of the project.
- Audited accounts (if available) or statement of accounts for the most recent completed financial year and a copy of the latest annual report.
- Details of charitable status.
- Other sources of finance for the organisation at present and for the proposed project.
- Experience and/or qualifications of staff and committee members.
- A list of officers and committee members.
- Contact address and telephone number.

Entindale Ltd

£184,000 (1992/93)

Jewish, general

14 Mayfield Gardens, London NW4 2QA
0181-458 9266

Correspondent: B L Bridgeman

Trustees: D Toledano; Mrs B A B Sethill; Mrs Bridgeman; S J Goldberg.

Beneficial area: UK.

Information available: Full accounts are on file at the Charity Commission.

General: The trust was set up mainly to advance the Orthodox Jewish faith. In 1992/93, the trust had assets of £1.76 million and an income of £496,000, £398,000 of which was rent received and £92,000 a covenant from its subsidiary company Rodsham Properties Ltd. Expenses totalled £171,000, including £122,000 bank interest and bank charges.

All 47 grants, totalling £184,000, were given to Jewish organisations. There were six grants of £10,000 to £26,000 including those to Acheizer, Beis Shammai School and Tevini Ltd. The grants list was a typical Jewish grants list supporting all the regular Jewish organisations.

Applications: In writing to The Trustee of Entindale Ltd, Equity House, 86 West Green Road, London N15 5NS.

Entwood Charities Ltd

£123,000 (1989/90)

Jewish

23 Overlea Road, Springfield Park, London E5 9BG
0181-557 9557

Correspondent: H Feldman, Director

Trustees: D Feldman.

Beneficial area: Worldwide.

Information available: Accounts are on file at the Charity Commission up to 1989/90, but without a list of grants.

General: Unfortunately the Charity Commission file contained no up-to-date information on this trust. In 1989/90, the trust received a donation of £124,000 and £123,000 was given in grants.

No grants list is included in the accounts at the Charity Comission since that for 1985/86, when grants totalled £58,000 all given to Jewish organisations.

Applications: In writing to the correspondent.

The Epigoni Trust

£249,000 (1993)

Medical, general

Charities Aid Foundation, Foundation House, Coach & Horses Passage, The Pantiles, Tunbridge Wells TH2 5TZ
01892-512244

Correspondent: Trust Manager

Trustees: Charles Peacock; Bettine Bond; Michael Bond.

Beneficial area: Worldwide.

Information available: Full accounts are on file at the Charity Commission.

General: The trust was established in 1990 and holds 1.5 million shares in Nurdin & Peacock plc worth £2.52 million in 1993. Its income in the three years it has been operating has risen steadily from £111,000 to £128,000 in 1993, while the grant total has fluctuated: £90,000 in 1991; £6,000 in 1992; £249,000 in 1993.

29 grants were given in 1993, ranging from £2,000 to £17,000. The largest were to Orbis International (£17,000), VSO (15,400), National Eye Research Centre (£12,500) and Hodgkins Disease Association (£12,000). £11,000 each went to Richmond Fellowship for Community Mental Health and Reynaud's Association Trust.

Nine organisations received £10,000 including Carers National Association, Intermediate Technology Development Group, Cottage & Rural Enterprises Ltd, Centrepoint Soho and the Barnabas Trust, in addition to other medical charities such as British Sjogrens Syndrome Association.

Smaller grants went to a range of organisations including Afdam National, Arthritis Care, Charities Aid Foundation, Handicapped Adventure Playground Association, Marine Conservation Society and the Rio Mazan Project.

In the previous year only two grants were made, to the Kerland Foundation and Royal Commonwealth Society for the Blind.

Applications: In writing to the correspondent.

The Equity Trust Fund

£220,000 (1993/94)

Arts, education and welfare of professional performers

Suite 222, Africa House, 64 Kingsway, London WC2B 6AH
0171-404 6041

Correspondent: Carla Hanreck, Secretary

Trustees: Harvey Ashby; Colin Baker; John Barron; Derek Bond; Nigel Davenport; Barbara Hyslop; Milton Johns; John Johnson; Norman Mitchell; Peter Plouviez; Gillian Raine; Hugh Manning; Ian McGarry; Jeffrey Wickham; Frank Williams; Graham Hamilton; Jean Ainslie; Frederick Pyne; Harry Landis; Louise Mahoney; Annie Bright.

Beneficial area: UK.

Information available: Accounts are on file at the Charity Commission, but without a list of grants.

General: This is a relatively new trust, established in 1989. As of 31st March 1992, it had assets of £5.2 million; by 1993/94, the assets were valued at £6 million and generated an income of over £850,000. Grants and donations were given totalling £221,500. The fund helps those who make their living from the various aspects of the world of professional entertainment and performance. This includes those from back stage, as well as performers.

The fund supports individuals in need with educational grants (*see A Guide to Grants for Indivduals in Need and The Educational Grants Directory.*)

It also has a small provision to help theatres with essential capital costs. Revenue or project costs (including tour and production costs) are excluded. It has also given interest-free loans to organisations.

In 1993/94, it gave 10 theatre loans totalling £82,000 (£132,000 in 1991/92 and £66,000 in 1990/91). The largest loan was £30,000 to the Theatre Royal - Margate (£100,000 in 1991/92 and £50,000 in 1990). The remaining loans were between £2,600 and £12,500 to the Electric Theatre, Good Company, Merseyside Young People's Theatre, Hey Hey Theatre, Compass Theatre, First Bite Productions, Collar and Tie and the Pit Prop Theatre. Mull Little Theatre was the only new beneficiary.

Grants were broken down as follows:

	1993/94	1991/92	1990/91
Theatres	£83,500	£127,000	£109,000
Education	£84,000	£100,000	£95,000
Welfare & benevolent	£54,000	£34,000	£40,000

Organisations supported include: Artsline (£2,000) for an information service to disabled people; British Performing Arts Medicine Trust (£12,500) for equipment to treat voice and throat problems and the two nursing/retirement homes for the profession (£9,000 each). Support has also been given to "Other bodies" such as: The Actors Acre, an acre of land for the burial/scattering of ashes of anyone associated with the performing arts.

Grants and loans from the Theatres Fund were given to 14 theatres and totalled nearly £100,000. Grants ranged from £880 to £45,000 with large grants to: Theatre Royal - Margate (£45,000 towards building work); Shakespeare's Globe Theatre, Southwark (the second £15,000 payment of £30,000 towards seating bays); Watermill Theatre (£6,500 to significantly increase the seating capacity). There were five grants of £5,000 given towards new touring boxes, a building programme, building dressing rooms and two emergency loans. Other smaller grants were towards lighting, to help raise funds and for building work.

Small grants were also given to the Actors Performing Studio, towards setting up pilot workshops and the Actors' Centre towards purchasing a building in Covent Garden.

Applications: In writing to the correspondent enclosing an A5 sae. Details should be presented on no more than four sides of A4 paper, including a brief history of the organisation, its current funders, what the money is needed for, and a concise breakdown of costs relevant to the application.

The Alan Evans Memorial Trust

£107,000 (1993/94)

Preservation, conservation

Coutts & Co, Trustee Dept, 440 Strand, London WC2R 0QS
0171-753 1000

Correspondent: The Trust Manager

Trustees: Coutts & Co; John W Halfhead.

Beneficial area: UK.

Information available: Full accounts are on file at the Charity Commission.

General: The trust gave 82 grants totalling £107,000 in 1993/94, ranging between £500 and £15,000. The largest group of beneficiaries were the various county wildlife trusts, church and cathedral preservation charities and rural charities both local and national (such as the Wildfowl & Wetlands Trust).

The largest grants were given to the National Trust Prior Park Appeal (£15,000); Winchester Cathedral – Silkstede Chapel (£4,000); St Tiggywinkles Wildlife Hospital and Craswall Grandmontine Society (both £3,000); and £2,500 each to the RSPB, Shared Earth Trust, Home-Start UK, Dyfed

Wildlife Trust and Kent Trust for Nature Preservation (to buy land). There were eight grants of £2,000, seven of £1,500 and 25 of £1,000. Most of the smaller grants of £750 and £500 were given to churches.

Exclusions: No grants to individuals or for management or running expenses. Grants to registered charities only. Any appeal falling outside the trust criteria will not be acknowledged.

Applications: In writing to the correspondent. Trustees normally meet three times a year.

The Everard Foundation

About £35,000 (1992/93)

General

Castle Acres, Narborough, Leicester LE9 5BY
0116-281 4100

Correspondent: R A S Everard

Trustees: R A S Everard; Mrs S A Richards; N W Smith.

Beneficial area: East Midlands, with a particular emphasis on Leicestershire.

Information available: Full accounts are on file at the Charity Commission.

General: In 1992/93, the trust had assets of £475,000 (with a book value of £372,000). It had an income of £62,000 and gave 36 grants totalling about £35,000. The largest grants were to the Rainbow Appeal (£20,000), Nuffield Hospital (£3,000) and £1,000 each to Apex Leicester Project Ltd, Household Cavalry Central Charitable Fund and Noseley Chapel Trust.

Most grants were for £50 to £600 and mainly to Leicestershire or national organisations such as the Born Free Foundation, Contact, Leicester Help the Aged, Leicester Wild Fowl Association, Save the Children and the Sports Aid Foundation. Grants are generally not recurrent.

Applications: In writing to the correspondent.

The Beryl Evetts & Robert Luff Animal Welfare Trust

£63,000 (1992/93)

Animal welfare

294 Earls Court Road, Kensington, London SW5 9BB
0171-373 7003

Correspondent: R C W Luff

Trustees: R C W Luff; Sir R Johnson; B Nicholson; R P J Price; M Tomlinson; Mrs J Tomlinson.

Beneficial area: UK

Information available: Full accounts are on file at the Charity Commission.

General: The trust appears to make substantial commitments to a few organisations over several years, whether to build up capital funds or to establish fellowships. As a result, in 1992/93, there were few organisations who received funding for the first time and the largest grant was a donation of £26,000, which was the fourth instalment towards the Royal Veterinary College's Beryl Evetts and Robert Luff Fellowship.

In 1992/93, the trust had assets of £1.2 million, an income of £83,000 and gave grants totalling £63,000.

The Animal Health Trust received £25,000 as the second donation towards the establishment of a Small Animals Orthopaedic Unit, as well as £10,000 as the eighth instalment for the Beryl Evetts Memorial Fund (now standing at £40,000). Other beneficiaries included the National Equine and Smaller Animals League, which received a £1,000 donation to its capital fund and £250 to the RSPCA's Windsor & Staines branch. Other grants included Brooke Hospital for Animals (£400) and £250 each to PDSA and National Canine Defence League. In the past beneficiaries have included the Cats Protection League and the Humane Research Trust.

Applications: The correspondent has stated that this is a private foundation. "No applications thank you."

Exilarch's Foundation

£76,000 (1992)

Jewish

20 Queen's Gate Terrace, London SW7 5PF
0171-589 4448

Correspondent: N E Dangoor, Trustee

Trustees: D A Dangoor; M J Dangoor; R D Dangoor; E B Dangoor.

Beneficial area: UK.

Information available: Accounts are on file at the Charity Commission for 1992, but without a grants list.

General: In 1992, the trust had assets of £1.5 million and an income of £114,000. Grants totalled £76,000, mainly to Jewish organisations in the UK. The main non-Jewish organisations supported were Age Concern, Action Research, Huntingdon's Disease Association, MENCAP and the Anthony Nolan Fund (£1,000 each).

Applications: In writing to the correspondent.

The Fairway Trust

£78,000 (1991/92)

Education, religion, children's recreation

MacFarlane & Co, 2nd Floor Cunard Building, Water Street, Liverpool L3 1DS
0151-236 6161

Correspondent: F J Sweeney, Secretary

Trustees: Lord Grantchester; Mrs Janet Grimstone.

Beneficial area: Worldwide.

Information available: Full accounts for 1991/92 are on file at the Charity Commission.

General: The trust supports:

Universities, colleges and schools in the UK and abroad;

Religious purposes (including the promotion of religion and supporting the clergy);

Clubs and recreational facilities for children and young people;

Preservation and maintenance of buildings of particular interest.

Scholarships, grants and loans are also given to postgraduates and undergraduates.

The correspondent regularly asks us not to include them in this Guide as they are being inundated with requests for help that they are unable to support. We maintain our policy of including all relevant grant-making trusts, but would ask all potential applicants to ensure they meet the trust's criteria before applying.

In 1991/92, the trust had assets of only £24,000 and an income of £78,000, of which £20,000 was in donations from Lady Grantchester and £55,000 from the Moores Family Charity Foundation. It gave 60 grants totalling £73,000, 17 of which were for £1,000 to £12,000.

The largest grants were to Young Enterprise (£12,000); Family Education Trust (£11,000); Merseyside Improved Houses (£10,000); British Sailors Society (£7,000); Lucy Cavendish College (£6,000). The 12 grants of £1,000 to £2,000 included: Ex-Services Mental Welfare Society; Northern Ireland Association of Boys Clubs; Park of Friendship, Malta; Prayer Book Society; Voluntary Services, Belfast; Welsh National Opera; YMCA, Liverpool.

There appears to be a preference for Liverpool and north west England, though organisations in the south east, Northern Ireland and Scotland are also supported.

Exclusions: No grants to individuals.

Applications: In writing to the correspondent.

The Lord Faringdon First & Second Charitable Trusts

£128,000 (1991/92)

Medical, general

Alliance House, 12 Caxton Street, London SW1H 0QY
0171-222 1391

Correspondent: Bernard French, Trust Manager

Trustees: L Parsons; H Trotter.

Beneficial area: UK.

Information available: Full accounts are on file at the Charity Commission for 1991/92.

General: The first and second charitable trusts have separate accounts, but appear to have similar interests. In 1991/92, the trusts had assets of over £2 million and a joint income of £135,000. The combined grant total has increased significantly over the last year, from £57,000 to £128,000. Both trusts tend to give a relatively small number of large grants.

12 grants were given by the first trust totalling £80,000, and 10 by the second trust totalling £48,000. Grants ranged from £5,000 to £15,000.

Beneficiaries of the first trust included The Faringdon Collection Trust (for the benefit of Buscot Farm), a regular beneficiary, which received £15,000 (having received £25,000 from the other trust the previous year). Eight of the other beneficiaries have already been promised the same grant in 1992/93, including the Princess Royal Trust for Carers (£15,000), British Federation of Young Choirs and Prader Willi Syndrome Association (both £5,000), Mary Hare School (£2,500) and the Women Caring Trust (£2,000). Two hospital appeals also received grants.

The Queen Elizabeth Training College was the major beneficiary of the second trust, receiving two grants totalling £15,000. (The college also received a grant from the first trust.) Other recipients included St Luke's Hospice for the Clergy (£10,000) and the Royal Choral Society, RAFT and National Art Collections Fund (all £5,000).

Applications: In writing to the correspondent.

The Thomas Farr Charitable Trust

£216,000 (1992)

General, especially in Nottinghamshire

Kleinwort Benson Trustees Ltd,
PO Box 191, 10 Fenchurch Street,
London EC3M 3LB
0171-956 5093

Correspondent: Chris Gilbert, Charities Manager

Trustees: B H Farr; E M Astley-Arlington; P K Farr; Kleinwort Benson Trustees Ltd.

Beneficial area: UK, especially Nottinghamshire.

Information available: Accounts are on file at the Charity Commission.

General: According to the Charity Commission, the trust had an income of £122,000 in 1994. In 1992, the trust had an income of £150,000 and gave grants totalling £216,000.

Applications: In writing to the correspondent.

The Fawcett Charitable Trust

About £100,000

Rehabilitation of physically disabled, selected local causes

Blake Lapthorn, 8 Landport Terrace, Portsmouth PO1 2QW
01705-822291

Correspondent: S G Campbell

Trustees: Derek Fawcett; Frances Fawcett; David Russell.

Beneficial area: UK, with a preference for Hampshire and West Sussex.

Information available: Full accounts are on file at the Charity Commission.

General: The trust was set up in 1991 by Derek and Frances Fawcett with an endowment of 17,461 shares in their company, Nautech Ltd, with a value of £1.6 million. In its first year it had a large income of £573,000 but "this includes a dividend from the sale of the business and will not be repeated in future years. Estimated gross income for normal years will be about £150,000". No donations were made in its first year of operation.

The correspondent states that grants are made to all kinds of charities, but there is a preference for local organisations. So far, donations have been given to Portsmouth Cathedral, the local grammar school, SENSE and Children in Need. There is a current commitment to the Royal Yachting Association Seamanship Foundation.

In 1992/93, the trust's assets at market value were £1.4 million and it had an income of £125,000. Only nine grants were given totalling £55,000. In 1993/94, nine grants were again given totalling £65,750. These grants were to Portsmouth Hospice (£40,000); Africa on a Knife Edge

(£10,000); RYA Seamanship Foundation (£4,000); Pioneer Centre and Winged Fellowship (£1,500 each); Inspire Foundation (£1,000), Disability Aid Fund (£500) and Friends of Radiotherapy (£250). An individual also received £4,000.

Applications: To the correspondent in writing.

Feed the Minds

£354,000 (1993/94)

Christian literature overseas

Robertson House, Leas Road, Guildford GU1 4QW
01483 577877; Fax: 01483-301387

Correspondent: Dr Alwyn Marriage, Director

Trustees: Chairman of Executive Committee: John Clark.

Beneficial area: The developing world and Eastern Europe.

Information available: Full accounts on file with the Charity Commission for 1993/94 with a detailed breakdown of grants. Policy, guidelines and application forms are available from the head office.

General: In 1993/94, the trust's report and accounts stated that "1994, is the 30th birthday of Feed the Minds. During the last three decades we have supported Christian Literature projects in over 100 countries around the world. We have been committed to programmes concerned with long-term growth and development, so as to bring greatest benefit to the poorer sections of the community.

"Thousands have learned to read and write; publishing companies have been enabled, through training and funding, to publish good Christian books; radio programmes have taught about agriculture, health and development; magazines and newspapers have touched the lives of their readers; bookshops have opened and bookvans travelled to remote areas; children, theological students and adults have all benefited from theological literature at different levels.

"This year money was raised for 48 projects, ranging from a radio and cassette studio working in war-torn areas of Sudan, theological education in India, publishing houses and programmes and the training of the future leaders of the Eastern European Church. As well as funding, the ministry of Feed the Minds includes encouraging, advising and evaluating overseas projects, and in January the Director visited partners in southern Africa. New emphases to our African programme have occurred as a result of the visit."

In 1993/94, the trust had assets of £153,000, an income of £340,000 and gave grants totalling £354,000. The income was broken down as:

Churches, individuals and trusts	£179,000
Legacies	£24,000
Membership fees	£15,000
Contributions from member bodies	£88,000
Government agencies	£30,000
Bank interest	£5,000

Grants and related expenses were broken down as:

Africa	£74,000
Asia	£95,000
South East Asia & Pacific	£16,000
Central & South America	£30,000
Eurolit	£14,000
Worldwide	£7,000
Overseas training, consultation and advice	£2,000
USCL: UK book grants	£14,000
Grants expenses	£38,000

Below is a taster of grants given during the year. Under the headings:

Publishing and Book Distribution. The trust gave £6,000 to the Reformed Church in Budapest, Hungary. This was part of a three-year commitment to help produce secondary school RE books. The six books for 14-18 year olds will be for school and church youth education and also help Hungarian-speaking believers in Romania, Karpato-Ukraine, Slovakia and the former Yugoslavia;

Libraries and Theological Education by Extension included £1,000 to Seminario Teologico Batista do Ceara, Brazil for a library grant for this new seminary, situated in the poorest region of Brazil, which needs basic books such as Bible Commentaries and Dictionaries, mainly in Portuguese and Spanish;

Worldwide £4,000 to Theological Book Service for a service which collects second-hand specialist books and offers them, free of charge, to 500 libraries and colleges in 63 countries. The grant covers the annual cost of postage and of twice-yearly production of the catalogue;

Special Interest included £5,000 towards a radio station for the Sudan Council of Churches providing Christian programmes and information about health and nutrition. The studio also assists the government and other rural development and relief agencies;

Development included £5,000 to Bolivia for Radio Esperanza, which is a community radio serving a mountainous area where over half the population are illiterate. The station encourages grassroots communication by developing local studios;

Education by using videos in rural areas to create awareness of current issues.

Exclusions: Grants are given only to Christian organisations and not to individuals or private enterprises.

Applications: To the correspondent in writing. Applications need to be made up to 18 months before funds are required.

The A M Fenton Trust

£80,000 (1993)

General in North and West Yorkshire

14 Beech Grove, Harrogate, North Yorks HG2 0EX
01423-504442

Correspondent: J L Fenton

Trustees: J L Fenton; C M Fenton.

Beneficial area: North and West Yorkshire.

Information available: Full accounts are on file at the Charity Commission.

General: The trust was created by Alexander Miller Fenton in 1975. After his death in 1977, the residue of his estate was transfered to the trust.

By 1993, the trust had assets of £696,000 and an income of £87,000. It gave 40 grants of between £30 and £20,000, totalling £80,000. Many of these were recurrent from previous years.

The largest recurrent grants were given to Yorkshire County Cricket Club Charity Youth Trust (£20,000 a similar amount has been donated for a number of years),

Hipperholme Grammar School (£10,000) and the Dewsbury and District League of Friendship for Disabled People (£5,000). Other large grants included those to Whitcliffe Mount School (£15,000), CAB Harrogate (£3,000), Tweed Foundation and Kenmore Cheshire Home (£2,000 each), Yorkshire Association for the Disabled (£1,500) and Variety Club of Great Britain (£1,000).

All other grants were for £30 to £650 to organisations such as AID Group, Accrington, Bath Institute of Medical Engineering Ltd, Batley & Dewsbury Amateur Boxing & Fitness Club and Victim Support, Harrogate. Over half the grants are usually to local organisations in West and North Yorkshire. A few grants were given to large national, medical and welfare organisations and also to the RNLI, Game Conservancy Council and Newcastle Children's Adventure Group.

A small number of grants of £1,000 to £5,000 were given for individuals for educational purposes and £250 was given for a wheelchair.

Applications: In writing to the correspondent.

Ferguson Benevolent Fund Ltd

£79,000 (1992/93)

Christian, especially Methodist

Rawfell, Great Langdale, Ambleside, Cumbria LA22 9JS
01539-437217

Correspondent: Ms S C Ferguson, Secretary

Trustees: Mrs E Higginbottom, Chairman; Ms S C Ferguson, Secretary; Mrs M W Ferguson ; Mrs C M A Metcalfe; P A L Holt; Mrs P M Dobson.

Beneficial area: UK.

Information available: Accounts are on file at the Charity Commission for 1992/93, but without a list of grants.

General: The trust has a preference for projects related to the Methodist church. In 1992/93, the trust had assets of £618,000, an income of £110,000, of which £65,000 was from the sale of investments. Grants totalled £79,000. No further information available.

According to the Charity Commission, the trust had an income of £62,000 in 1994.

Applications: In writing to the correspondent.

The Doris Field Charitable Trust

£86,000 (1992/93)

General

Ref KCK, Cole & Cole, Solicitors, Buxton Court, 3 West Way, Oxford OX2 0SZ

Correspondent: Mrs K Knight

Trustees: E E Church; N A Harper; W G S Crouch.

Beneficial area: UK, with a preference for Oxfordshire.

Information available: Full accounts are on file at the Charity Commission.

General: Doris Field died in 1988, but she left provisions in her will to leave the whole of her estate to charity. As a result the executors established the Doris Field Charitable Trust in 1990, to receive the proceeds of her estate.

In 1992/93, the trust held total funds valued at over £3 million, comprising of a considerable portfolio of shares worth £1.3 million, farms, land and residential property in and around Oxford with a book value of almost £1million and nearly £750,000 in cash. During the year, these various assets generated an income of £152,000, of which £86,000 was given in charitable donations.

The donations made by the trust over recent years show a general preference for charities in the Oxfordshire area, although charities from all over England and Wales have been supported. Larger grants have included funding for a children's day care ward at Oxford's John Radcliffe Hospital and a ward at a hospice in the same town, as well as the costs of ambulances for the British Red Cross and Multiple Sclerosis Society. Ongoing funding for major projects includes the restoration of the bells and bell tower of Lundy Church on Lundy Island and the construction of a pastoral centre in Headington.

The larger donations in 1992/93, included Omerod School (£35,000); Restore (£15,000); Frank Wise Special School, Banbury (£5,000 for a hydrotherapy lift); Nuffield Orthotics Appeal (£3,000); Pathway Sheltered Workshop and Gipsy Lane Community Hall (£2,500 each). A variety of smaller grants of between £250 and £2,000 were made for purposes such as children's play groups, scout groups, family centres and individuals with specific needs resulting from a disability.

Applications: On a form available from the correspondent.

The Finnart House School Trust

£162,000 (1993/94)

Jewish children in need of care

707 High Road, North Finchley, London N12 7ER
0181-445 1670

Correspondent: Peter Shaw, Clerk

Trustees: David Barr; Robert Cohen; Jane Grabiner; Hilary Norton; Dr Louis Marks; David Fobel; Lilian Hochhauser; Jane Leaver; Harry Cohen.

Beneficial area: Worldwide.

Information available: Annual accounts and a brief statement of policy are available from the trust.

General: In 1993/94, the trust had assets of £2.9 million and an income of £185,000. After expenses of £25,000, 30 grants were given to almost exclusively Jewish organisations totalling £162,000.

The largest grants were to Delamere Forest School Extension Project (£20,000); Redbridge Jewish Youth Community Centre (£15,000 and £10,000 in 1992/93); Leeds Jewish Welfare Board and Chabad, Chernobyl Children (£10,000 each). There were 16 grants of £5,000 to £7,500; eight grants of £1,000 to £4,000 and two for under £1,000. All grants were to Jewish organisations working with children, welfare, education and disability across England and Scotland, in Chernobyl and Israel.

Applications: There is an application form, which needs to be submitted together with a copy of the latest annual report and accounts.

The David Finnie & Alan Emery Charitable Trust

£46,000 (1993/94)

General

8 Baker Street, London W1M 1DA
0171-486 5888

Correspondent: BDO Stoy Hayward

Trustees: J A C Buck; Mrs N R Barnes; R J Emery.

Beneficial area: UK.

Information available: Full accounts are on file at the Charity Commission.

General: In 1993/94, the trust had assets of £837,000 and an income of £60,000. Grants were given to 40 organisations totalling £46,000. A further £7,000 was given to individuals. The vast majority of grants appear to have been recurrent over recent years.

Grants to organisations ranged from £500 to £5,000. The largest were given to Muskelsvind Fonden Physiotherapy Project (£5,000); St Joseph's Hospice (£2,500) and four grants of £2,000 to the Birmingham Settlement, British Diabetic Association, Help the Aged and the Samaritans.

Support is mainly for national organisations working in the fields of medical and health and welfare, together with a number of benevolent funds which are regular beneficiaries (including the Chartered Accountants Benevolent Fund and the ECBA Bowlers Benevolent Fund). A few local organisations are also supported such as Greater London Fund for the Blind, Thamesdown Association of Youth Clubs, Welsh Association of Youth Clubs and Southend Holiday Home for the Disabled.

Applications: In writing to the correspondent. Trustees usually meet in June or the summer each year to consider applications. Replies will be sent to applicants who include an sae.

The Fitton Trust

£76,000 (1992/93)

Social welfare, medical

PO Box 649, London SW3 4LA
0171-236 4232

Correspondent: The Secretary

Trustees: Dr R P A Rivers; D M Lumsden; D V Brand.

Beneficial area: UK.

Information available: Accounts are on file at the Charity Commission, but without a list of grants.

General: In 1992/93, the trust had assets of £1.2 million generating an income of £92,000. The trust has high expenses of £20,000, £13,000 of which were for legal charges. Grants dropped from £96,000 in 1991/92, to £76,000 in 1992/93. The trust supports social welfare and medical charities; no further details as to individual beneficiaries is available.

Exclusions: No grants to individuals.

Applications: In writing to the correspondent. The trust states: "no application considered unless accompanied by fully audited accounts. No replies will be sent to unsolicited applications whether from individuals, charities or other bodies."

The Earl Fitzwilliam Charitable Trust

£44,000 (1992/93)

General

Estate Office, Milton Park, Peterborough PE6 7AH
01733-267740

Correspondent: J M S Thompson

Trustees: Hon Lady Hastings; J M S Thompson.

Beneficial area: UK.

Information available: Full accounts are on file at the Charity Commission.

General: The trust was established by the Rt Hon Earl Fitzwilliam in 1975 with £10,000 and land valued (for stamp duty) at £450,000. Further land was added in 1980, valued at £513,000.

In 1992/93, the trust had assets of about £1.5 million and an income of £158,000. Grants totalled £44,000, leaving a surplus of £99,000. It has been the policy of the trustees to increase the level of their charitable donations at the same time ensuring the gradual growth of the trust's capital reserves.

During 1992/93, over 70 grants were made, the largest of which were to the Trustees of Christ the Sower Trust (£15,000); Camvet (£5,000); St Kyneburgha Castor PCC Tower Appeal and St James Braithwell PCC (£3,000 each); St Mary's Priory Church, Malton and Peterborough Macmillan Nurse Appeal (£2,000 each). There were six recipients of £1,000 including the Game Conservancy Trust, Royal Garden Appeal, Rural Youth Trust Appeal and St Williams Community Appeal.

Over 30 grants were between £100 and £1,000 mainly to welfare, religious and medical organisations. There were also 29 small grants of £2.50 to £80, some of which are recurrent. Many grants are given to churches or church related appeals with a preference for the east of England, especially Yorkshire. Other favoured causes are animal welfare and local communities especially in rural areas.

Applications: In writing to the correspondent.

The Rose Flatau Charitable Trust

£179,000 (1994)

Jewish, social welfare

5 Knott Park House, Wrens Hill, Oxshott, Leatherhead KT22 0HW
01372-843082

Correspondent: M E G Prince

Trustees: M E G Prince; A E Woolf; N L Woolf.

Beneficial area: UK.

Information available: Full accounts are on file at the Charity Commission.

General: In 1994, the trust had assets of £914,000 and an income of £107,000. Almost 50 grants totalling £180,000 were made, with about a third in value and number to Jewish organisations. Over 10 grants were given to medical or disability charities.

The largest grants were to: Nightingale House (£25,000); Victoria Community (£20,000); Ravenswood Foundation and Cancer Research Campaign (£15,000 each) and Education Trust and Jewish Care (£10,000 each). Other beneficiaries included Crisis, Friends of Cobham Hospital and New Horizon Youth Centre (£5,000 each) and Childline and Talking Newspapers Association of the UK (£1,000 each). About half of the grants were for £1,000 or less.

Applications: The trust states: "No further applications can be accepted as the income available is fully committed." No application forms are available. No set dates for trustees meetings.

The Roy Fletcher Charitable Trust

£152,000 (1992/93)

General in Shropshire

95 Mount Pleasant Road, Shrewsbury, Shropshire SY1 3EL
01743-236622

Correspondent: The Secretary

Trustees: Mrs R A Coles; Mrs G M Mathias; Mrs E J Fletcher; Cooper; D N Fletcher.

Beneficial area: Shrewsbury and Shropshire.

Information available: Full accounts are on file at the Charity Commission with a grants list including brief details of what each grant was for.

General: The trust states its main areas of work as "youth and elderly, educationally disadvantaged, and mentally and physically handicapped".

The capital fund, as at 5th April 1992, was worth £580,000. The trust has sold a property it owned and has inherited the Harrington Estate, worth £1.1 million, on the death of the founder G R Fletcher. The Harrington Estate was not included in the 1992 accounts.

In 1992/93, the trustees placed the assets in the hands of outside professionals to manage. Administration expenses increased from £2,000 in 1990/91, to £49,000 in 1991/92 (£11,000 in salaries, £13,000 estate management, £7,000 legal & professional, £3,000 forestry maintenance, £4,000 property repairs and £3,000 river maintenance), but the trustees state they are content with the level of donations at the end of the year.

In 1992/93, the trust had assets of £626,000, an income of £246,000 and gave 130 grants totalling £152,000. 29 grants were of £1,000 to £35,000, with the main areas supported being children and youth, medical/disability, education and welfare. The trust also supports arts organisations.

Grants were given to: Oswestry College, for a lift (£35,000); Ludlow & District Community Association and Africa in Crisis (£10,000 each); Arthritis Research Centre, Bridgnorths Footbridge, Lyneal Trust to purchase a cottage for holidays for disabled people, Mencap Support Services and Meeting Point House, Telford towards extensions (£5,000 each); Relate towards rent for premises (£4,000) and Sandpits Playgroup towards play equipment and a building.

Grants of £2,000 were given to: Community College; Oswestry Youth Exchange; Shropshire Hills Appeal towards employing a worker, 2nd Chance towards the Mascall Centre, a regular beneficiary and Youth Service, for a reprint of Wide World Directory. Other grants to organisations were generally for £500 to £1,500.

By far the largest number of grants are to individuals for expeditions and education and are generally for £150 to £300. Shropshire students have been supported through Operation Raleigh and BSEJ to go on expeditions to all parts of the world, from Costa Rica to Thailand.

Exclusions: The trust is unlikely to fund projects eligible for statutory funding.

Applications: In writing to the correspondent.

The Football Association National Sports Centre Trust

£160,000 (1993)

Football facilities

9 Wyllyotts Place, Potters Bar, Herts EN6 2JD
01707-651840

Correspondent: The Director

Trustees: Chairman of the Football Association (FA) (currently Sir Bert Millichip), and a committee appointed by the executive committee of the FA, currently: W T Annable; A W Brett; A D McMullen; T Myatt.

Beneficial area: UK.

General: The main activity of the trust is the preservation and protection of the physical and mental health of the community; the provision of facilities for recreation and other leisure time occupations for members of the public in the interests of social welfare.

In 1993, the trust had assets of £2 million. It receives a regular donation from the FA Charity Shield (£35,000 in 1993). The assets of the trust generated over £100,000, to which the Football Association added a £37,500 donation under the Gift Aid scheme. Over £160,000 was given in grants.

Hard surface play area (HPSA) schemes at clubs, schools and community centres were the main beneficiaries, receiving £128,000 in total. A major new scheme was launched in partnership with the Football Trust whereby grants of up to £5,000 are made to grassroots football clubs to improve their facilities. Nearly £24,000 has been given within the first few months, and this is expected to increase substantially in the coming year.

Applications: On a form available from the correspondent (which also gives details of eligible clubs/organisations).

The Football Association Youth Trust

Over £200,000 (1993/94)

Sports

16 Lancaster Gate, London W2 3LW
0171-262 4542

Correspondent: Mark Day, Chief Accountant

Trustees: Chairman of the Football Association (FA) (currently Sir Bert Millichip), and a committee appointed by the executive committee of the FA, currently: W T Annable; A W Brett; A D McMullen; T Myatt.

Beneficial area: UK.

Information available: Accounts are on file at the Charity Commission, but without a grants list.

General: The trust was set up by the Football Association in 1972 for the "furtherance of education of schools and universities encouraging football or other sports to ensure that due attention is given to the physical education and character development of pupils".

The trust makes grants towards equipment, lectures, training colleges and playing fields. The trust also assists in providing facilities for physical recreation in the interests of social welfare in the UK. Beneficiaries must be under 21 or in full-time education.

In 1993/94, the trust had assets of £1.2 million. It receives a regular donation from the Football Association Charity Shield (a match held at Wembley before the beginning of the football season between the Premiership winners and the winners of the FA Cup). In 1993, this donation amounted to £50,000. The assets of the trust generated £88,000 of income, to which the Football Association added a £37,500 donation under the Gift Aid scheme.

A range of projects were supported and the grant total exceeded £200,000 for the first time. The major beneficiaries were again the County Associations, schools (especially the English Schools Football Association) and universities. Nearly £47,000 was given in small grants to clubs and schools.

Applications: All applications should be made to the chairman of the trust in writing. Grants are made throughout the year. There are no application forms, but a copy of the most recent accounts should be sent.

The Oliver Ford Charitable Trust

£50,000 (1993/94)

Mental disability, housing

Messrs Macfarlanes, 10 Norwich Street, London EC4A 1BD
0171-831 9222

Correspondent: Matthew Pintus

Trustees: Derek Hayes; Lady Wakeham; Valerie Profumo; George Levy; Johnathan Norton.

Beneficial area: UK.

Information available: Full accounts are on file at the Charity Commission.

General: The founder of this trust, Oliver Ford, died in 1992. In 1993/94, the trust received £40,000 from his estate, taking the assets to almost £2 million.

Only nine grants were made during the year totalling £50,000, but they were all for fairly substantial amounts. The grants were to: MacIntyre Charitable Trust (£10,000); Break (two grants totalling £10,000); St Martin's Urban Project (£6,000) and Fitzwilliam Museum (£4,000). All remaining grants were for £5,000 and were given to Solden Hill House, Camphill Village Trust; E Fitzroy Homes and the Ravenswood Foundation.

Applications: In writing to the correspondent.

The Forte Charitable Trust

£156,000 (1993/94)

Education, disability, Roman Catholic, general

166 High Holborn, London WC1V 6TT
0171-836 7744

Correspondent: George Proctor

Trustees: Hon R J V Forte; Hon Mrs Pilizzi di Sorrentino CBE; G F L Fletcher.

Beneficial area: Worldwide.

Information available: Full accounts are on file at the Charity Commission.

General: The trust was established in 1982 by R J V Forte. In 1993/94, the trust had assets of £1.6 million, mostly invested in Forte shares. The value of these has decreased, though it still holds 500,000 ordinary shares, and the trust does appear to be diversifying its investments. 41 donations were made totalling £155,500, but no further information was available on the grants made in this year.

In 1992/93, the income of the trust was £161,000 including £66,000 dividends from Forte plc, £35,000 interest on investments and £60,000 rental income. Grants totalled only £11,000 leaving a surplus for the year of £144,000. The four grants made were to the British House & Hospital for Incurables (£5,000), Charles Peguy Centre (£2,500), Childline (£2,000) and Don Monti Research Foundation (£1,000).

In 1991/92, grants totalled £100,000 from an income of £121,000. 12 grants were made with the largest to Westminster Cathedral Choir School Fund and Westminster Roman Catholic Diocese Trust (both £15,000) and St Gregory's Charitable Trust (£12,500). £10,000 was given to each of Downside Settlement, Jewish National Fund, Mayor of Guildford's Christmas & Local Distress Fund and the Tablet Trust. £5,000 went to English College Rome Trust, Duke of Edinburgh Award and the Royal Watercolour Society.

Applications: In writing to the correspondent.

The Foundation for Education

£865,000 (1993)

Jewish education

Jewish Welfare Board, Balfour House, 741 High Road, Finchley, London N12 0BQ
0181-446 1477; Fax: 0181-458 3282

Correspondent: M Garfield

Trustees: Sir Trevor Chinn; M Levy.

Beneficial area: UK.

Information available: Full accounts are on file at the Charity Commission.

General: In 1993, the foundation's income was £856,000 mainly from donations and Gift Aid, and grants totalled £865,000. Only seven grants were given, all to Jewish educational organisations and all of which received support the previous year. These were: Zionist Federation Educational Trust (£324,000); Jewish Educational Development Trust (£251,000); United Synagogue (£239,000); National Jewish Chaplaincy Board (£27,000); Friends of the Union of Jewish Students (£10,000); Hillel Foundation (£9,000) and the Association of Jewish Sixth Formers (£5,000).

In 1992, grants were also given to the Union of Jewish Students, British Israel Arts Foundation and the Hamilton Trust, and in previous years support has also been given to Jewish youth organisations.

Applications: In writing to the correspondent.

The Fowler Memorial Trust

£65,000 (1991/92)

General in Essex

Messrs Tolhurst Fisher, Trafalgar House, Nelson Street, Southend-on-Sea, Essex SS1 1EF
01702-352511

Correspondent: J E Tolhurst

Trustees: J E Tolhurst; W J Tolhurst; P J Tolhurst.

Beneficial area: Essex.

Information available: Full accounts are on file at the Charity Commission.

General: In 1991/92, the trust had an income of £132,000, mainly from rents. 27 grants were given totalling £65,000. The trust supports both local charities and local branches of national charities in Essex.

The largest grants went to the Kingsdown School Parents Association (£15,000), St James with St Lukes Development Appeal (£10,000), NSPCC (£7,500), Diocese of Brentwood (£5,500 for a new organ) and Hawkwell Baptist Church (£5,000). Most of the other grants were for £500 or £1,000. Beneficiaries ranged from the British Legion Leigh-on-Sea to the Salesian Convent to the Basildon District Camping Club.

In 1992/93, it received £150,000 from the Albert & Florence Smith Memorial Trust (*see separate entry*). According to the Charity Commission, the trust had a total income of £426,000 in 1992/93.

Applications: In writing to the correspondent.

The Jill Franklin Trust

£55,000 (1993/94)

Culture/environment, overseas and welfare

78 Lawn Road, London NW3 2XB
0171-722 4543

Correspondent: N Franklin

Trustees: Andrew Franklin; Norman Franklin; Sally Franklin; Sam Franklin; Tom Franklin.

Beneficial area: Worldwide.

Information available: Full accounts are on file at the Charity Commission.

General: In 1993/94, the trust had assets of £571,000, an income of £58,000 and gave grants totalling £55,000. 22 grants were for £249 or less; 17 for £250 to £499; 14 for £500 to £999; 15 for £1,000 to £1,999 and one for £11,840.

The policy of the trust concerning those categories it supports, the division of funds and recipient projects within the different categories is the same as for the Norman Franklin Trust (*see separate entry*).

- **Culture and the environment** (7%, £3,650). The largest grant was to the British Architecture Library (£1,000) towards overcoming archive storage problems.
- **Overseas relief and development** (35%, £19,400). The largest grants were to: Munongo School, Masvingo, Zimbabwe (£11,840) to build a classroom; St Georges College, Romania Appeal (£2,000) for the Ceziani orphanage and three grants of £1,000 to: Medical Aid for Iraq; Africa Now, towards work in Gambia and Cheshire Homes (Malawi), the last of three payments.
- **Relief**, subdivided into:
Welfare (26%, £14,600). The largest grants were £1,000 each to: Twig Lane Workshop, towards training; Camberwell Circle Project, towards a furniture scheme and British Deaf Association, towards an Asian Deaf Leader Project and Derry Well Women (£700).
Disability (27%, £14,700). The largest grants were: Rathbone Society, Manchester (£1,500) the fourth payment towards the cost of an information officer; Elfrieda Rathbone, Camden (£1,000), the last of three payments towards a Bengali speaking advocacy worker; Praxis Mental Health (£875), towards furnishing a flat for schizophrenics in West Belfast and St Omers (£600) for holidays for children with disabilities.
Prisoners (5%, £2,500). The largest of which were £1,000 each to Stonham Housing Trust and Prisoners of Conscience Appeal Fund, towards the Bosnia appeal.

Other smaller grants (generally of £100 to £500) included those to the Acquired Aphasia Trust; Action on Dysphasic Adults; Age Concern; Bradford City Farm Assn Ltd; Bristol Women's Workshop; British Red Cross; Cancer Relief Macmillan Fund (two grants totalling £1,000); Cut Back; Hampstead Old Peoples Housing Trust; Link Romania; Liverpool One Parent Family Trust; Samaritans, Worcester; SOS Sahel; Village Aid Project.

Exclusions: Grants are not given where statutory funding is available; for restoration; to heritage schemes; animals; students; building appeals; religious organisations or endowment funds.

Applications: Annual reports and accounts as well as a budget are essential if the request is to be taken seriously. "The trustees tend to look more favourably on an appeal which is simply and economically prepared; glossy, 'prestige' and mailsorted brochures are likely to find their way into the recycling bin." No acknowledgement is usually given to unsolicited applications, except where a sae is enclosed. An application to this trust is also considered by the Norman Franklin Trust. Separate applications to both trusts are binned. Telephone applications are not accepted, but enquiries may be made.

The Norman Franklin Trust

£55,000 (1993/94)

Culture/environment, overseas, welfare (see below)

78 Lawn Road, London NW3 2XB
0171-722 4543

Correspondent: N Franklin

Trustees: Norman Franklin; Thomas Franklin; Samuel Franklin.

Beneficial area: Worldwide.

Information available: Full accounts are on file at the Charity Commission.

General: In the trusts' annual report and accounts, the trustees state "We are appalled by the attitude of the Conservative Government who are hoping that charity will take the place of the taxpayer, and at the same time are preventing local government from raising enough money to do their job properly. Accordingly, we have set our faces against anything that might relieve government of its responsibilities, and we will not consider applications that arise from underfunding or price-cutting in the 'contract culture'." The trust may be prepared to give grants to organisations in areas which might have been financially penalised by government, where they might have hoped for a grant from the rate-capped local authority.

"The trustees current concerns are for: advice for those with a disability or problem, and for their carers (parents etc); holidays for respite care (in the UK only); access and mobility for the disabled (but not cars); training for those with a disability etc... Overseas, our interests are in special projects with low overheads, that will actually deliver (particularly in the Commonwealth)."

In 1993/94, the trust had assets of £550,000, an income of £48,000 and gave grants totalling £55,000. 93 grants were under £500; 34 between £500 to £999; 13 for £1,000 to £1,999 and one for £7,200. Grants were given for the following:

- **Culture and the environment** (2%, £850). Church restoration of medieval and Victorian churches of architectural importance (half a page in Pevsner is the normal criterion). No church halls or conversion of part of a church to social needs. Access to the countryside, but not car parking. Restoration of ancient buildings.
- **Overseas relief and development** (10%, £5,000). Support for special projects with low overheads, both in the Third World (particularly in the Commonwealth). The two largest grants in this category were both for £1,000 to Oxfam for two separate programmes.
- **Relief**, subdivided into:
  Welfare (23%, £12,300), including the continuing grant to Camden Bereavement Service of £7,200. Other beneficiaries included Faithfull Foundation, for work with abusers/ees, CARA and Merseyside CVS towards the Shomobility project (£1,000 each) and Newham Play Association (£705). Local charities such as Age Concern (Knaresborough), Luton Day Centre for the Homeless and Thurrock Women's Refuge Association were also supported.
  Relief of distress: The largest grants were to Alzheimer's Disease Society (£1,000) for respite care or counselling carers and Terence Higgins Trust (2 grants of £1,000) for legal advice and benefit work.
  Disability (18%, £10,034): access to buildings, counselling and information, holidays (in the UK only), particularly when carers get respite, training, groups, but not medical research or therapy. The largest grants were Camphill Village Trust (£1,000), SWOP (£1,000) for protective clothing and Heathrow Gymnastics Club (£550) towards a climbing frame for people with disabilities.
  Prisoners (11%, £6,100): grants for the education of prisoners (including books and fares), who should apply themselves, with the endorsement of the prison education officer or governor. Grants are not provided for welfare, nor for prisoners who have been discharged. There were 32 grants given to 20 prisons totalling just under £6,000 the largest of which were HMP Blantyre House and HMP Durham (£1,000 each).

Prison welfare and reform - (9%, £4,750) grants are also given to organisations working with and on behalf of prisoners whether serving their sentence or discharged. The largest grants were £1,000 each to New Bridge and NACRO. Grants may be given jointly with another charity, but a grant can often be given to cover the whole cost.

"Grants tend to be given to organisations in more impoverished districts, eg. Camden rather than Wandsworth, Liverpool rather than Knutsford, Middlesbrough rather than York, but can be given to any organisation, whether registered as a charity or not anywhere in the British Isles or overseas."

Other grants given during the year were generally for around £50 to £500 and included those to the Apex Charitable Trust; Asian Welfare Foundation; Boys Clubs of Northern Ireland; Derbyshire Centre for Integrated Living; Disabled Living Foundation; Downtown Women's Centre; Dubrovnik Gymnasium; Friends of Khasdobir; Garston Adventure Playground; Gingerbread Advice Centre, Scunthorpe; Mobilty Trust; Prison Reform Trust; Rochdale Petrus Community; Sandwell Rape Crisis Centre; Send a Cow; Sheffield Advice Centres Group; Theatre in Prisons Project; Wells in India and Welsh Association of Youth Clubs.

Exclusions: Grants are not given where statutory funding is available; for restoration; to heritage schemes; animals; students; building appeals; religious organisations or endowment funds, individuals.

Applications: Annual reports and accounts, as well as a budget are essential if the request is to be taken seriously. "The trustees tend to look more favourably on an appeal which is simply and economically prepared; glossy, 'prestige' and mailsorted brochures are likely to find their way into the recycling bin."

No acknowledgement is usually given to unsolicited applications, except where a sae is enclosed. Applications to this trust will also be considered by the Jill Franklin Trust. If separate applications are sent to both trusts, both will be binned. Telephone applications are not accepted.

The Gordon Fraser Charitable Trust

£87,000 (1993/94)

General, but see below

Holmhurst, Westerton Drive, Bridge of Allan, Stirling FK9 4QL

Correspondent: Mrs M A Moss

Trustees: Mrs M A Moss; W F T Anderson.

Beneficial area: UK.

Information available: Full accounts are on file at the Charity Commission.

General: The trustees have absolute discretion as to the charities to be assisted. Currently the trustees are particularly interested in help for children/young people in need, the environment and the visual arts. The trust states that "applications from or for Scotland will receive favourable consideration, but not to the exclusion of applications from elsewhere."

In 1993/94, the trust had assets of £2 million and an income of £89,000. It gave 174 grants totalling £87,000. The largest were to the Aberlour Child Care Trust (£10,000 and £13,500 in 1992), Braendam Family House (£8,000), Hunterian Art Gallery (£4,000), Royal Botanic Garden Edinburgh (£5,000 and £10,000 in 1992).

There were 17 grants of between £1,000 and £3,750 to a wide range of organisations including the British Red Cross, Buildings of Scotland Trust, Crisis, Girl Guides Association (Scotland), London Children's Flower Society, Romanian Orphanage Trust and the Scottish Youth Theatre, many of which have received a number of grants over recent years. The remaining grants were for under £1,000.

Exclusions: No grants for organisations which are not registered charities, or to individuals.

Applications: In writing to the correspondent. Applications are considered in January, April, July and October. Grants towards national or international emergencies can be considered at any time. All applicants are acknowledged; an sae would therefore be appreciated.

The Louis Freedman Charitable Settlement

£8,000 (1993/94)

General

25 Chargate Close, Burwood Park, Walton-on-Thames, Surrey KT12 5DW

Correspondent: T B Hughes

Trustees: Mrs V Freedman; T B Hughes.

Beneficial area: UK.

Information available: Full accounts are on file at the Charity Commission.

General: The trust has been building up its assets which have risen to over £1 million. In 1993/94, grants totalled only £8,000 from an income of £88,000. The rest, as in previous years was transferred "to enable substantial endowments and charitable donations to be made in the future".

20 grants were made, with the largest to Hoxton Health Group (£4,000). The rest ranged from £10 to £660 given to a range of charities including medical, welfare and animal welfare causes. Grants tend to be given to organisations that the trustees have a personal knowledge of.

Exclusions: No grants to individuals. Only registered charities are considered for support.

Applications: There is no application form. Applications should be in writing to the correspondent. Applications will not be acknowledged.

The Thomas Freke & Lady Norton Charity

£123,000 (1993/94)

Churches, schools, youth and welfare in the beneficial area

22 Queens Road, Hannington, Swindon, Wilts SN6 7RS
01793-765058

Correspondent: S J Whiteman

Trustees: Mrs M G Hussey-Freke; Mrs V J Davies; R G Higgins; Dr K T Scholes; J M E Scott.

Beneficial area: Parishes of Hannington, Inglesham, Highworth, Stanton Fitzwarren, Blunsdon St Leonards and Castle Eaton.

Information available: Full accounts are on file at the Charity Commission.

General: The assets of the charity in 1993/94 were £2.3 million. It had an income of £150,000 and gave grants totalling £123,000 to organisations within the beneficial area. If income cannot be spent, it may be given for any charitable purpose in the borough of Thamesdown. During the year £17,000 was given in Christmas gifts to individual pensioners. The trust also paid £2,800 for school bus fares.

The correspondent stated "Many applications are being received from organisations outside the beneficial area, unfortunately we are unable to support ANY of these."

Exclusions: No grants are given for ordinary running expenses. No applications from outside the beneficial area can be considered.

Applications: In writing to the correspondent for help with capital projects such as buildings or equipment, or with emergency or unforeseen expenditure. Clear outline details of the project or circumstances are required, together with a reliable estimate of the cost and a statement of the funds in hand or anticipated from other sources. The trustees meet at least four times a year at irregular intervals.

The Charles S French Charitable Trust

£159,000 (1993/94)

Community projects, disability, children and youth

169 High Road, Loughton, Essex
IG10 4LF
0181-502 3575

Correspondent: R L Thomas

Trustees: W F Noble; R L Thomas; D B Shepherd.

Beneficial area: UK, with a particular preference for north east London and south west Essex.

Information available: Accounts are on file at the Charity Commission, without a list of grants.

General: The trust has a policy of concentrating grants in north east London and south west Sussex and specifically for children and the local community. In 1993/94, the trust had assets of £2.6 million, an income of £162,000 and gave grants totalling £159,000, categorised as follows:

Community projects	24%
Projects for disabled people	23%
Children and youth	18%
Elderly	8%
Education	4%
Art and music	3%

Exclusions: Registered charities only.

Applications: In writing to the correspondent, including a copy of the latest accounts.

The Freshfield Foundation

£4,000 (1991/92)

Not known

2nd Floor, Macfarlane & Co, Cunard Building, Water Street, Liverpool L3 1DS
0151-236 6161

Correspondent: A T R Macfarlane

Trustees: P A Moores; A Moores; Mrs E J Potter.

Beneficial area: UK.

Information available: Full accounts are on file at the Charity Commission for 1991/92.

General: The trust was established in 1991 and the only accounts available at the Charity Commission were those for 1991/92. The trust had received donations giving it assets of £1.7 million, which generated an income of £117,000. Only one grant of £4,000 was given in the year, to Bronte Neighbourhood Organisation. Presumably the grant total will increase to something over £100,000 in future years.

Applications: In writing to the correspondent.

The Friarsgate Trust

£68,000 (1992/93)

Mainly health and welfare of young and elderly people

Messrs Thomas Eggar & Son, 5 East Pallant, Chichester, West Sussex PO19 1TS
01243-786111

Correspondent: G N M Scoular

Trustees: R F Oates; H R Whittle; G N M Scoular.

Beneficial area: UK, with a strong preference for East and West Sussex, especially Chichester.

Information available: Full accounts for recent years are on file at the Charity Commission.

General: The trust was set up by the late C P B Shippam for/to:

a) Academic and general education of orphans (infant and adult) and children whose parents are poor.

b) Mental, moral, physical, technical and social education of children and young people under 21.

c) Equip and maintain for forms of education camping grounds, holiday camps, playing fields, club rooms and other accommodation and facilities.

d) Relief and care of important persons suffering from disease or disability affecting their body or mind.

e) Relief of persons over 60 years old by the provision of maintenance, food clothing and housing for those in need of care and attention.

f) Charitable institutions, purposes and projects anyway connected to the above.

In 1992/93, the trust had assets of £1 million and an income of £70,000. £68,000 was given in 32 grants of £1,000 to £10,000 (24 of which were for £1,000 to £1,500) and 18 of £200 to £625.

The largest grants were given to Chichester Eventide Housing Association (£10,000) and St Richard's Diabetes Care Appeal (£3,000). £2,600 was given to each of: Arthritis & Rheumatism Council; Children's Family Trust; Friends of Chichester Hospital, Institute of Opthalmology and St Christopher's Fellowship. £2,080 was given to Chichester Marriage Guidance Council and Chichester & District Scout Council (two grants of £1,225). There were also 19 grants of £1,310 to organisations including the Church of England Children's Society; Highgate Group; Sea Cadets Navy League; YMCA. West Sussex VSO received £625.

Applications: In writing to the correspondent.

The Frognal Trust

£80,000 (1993/94)

Elderly, children, blind, disabled, medical research, environmental heritage

c/o Charities Aid Foundation, Coach & Horses Passage, The Pantilles, Tonbridge Wells, Kent TN2 5TZ
01892-512244

Correspondent: The Grants Administrator

Trustees: Mrs P Blake-Roberts; J P Van Montagu; P Fraser.

Beneficial area: UK.

Information available: Full accounts are on file at the Charity Commission.

General: In 1993/94, the trust gave grants totalling £80,000, unfortunately no grants list was available for this year.

The accounts on file at the Charity Commission for 1992/93, showed the trust gave 28 grants totalling £47,000. Nine grants of £2,222 were given to: the Brendon Care Foundation; Children's Hospice for the Eastern Region; Cystic Fibrosis Research Trust; Hampstead Old Peoples Housing Trust; National Listening Library; Richmond-upon-Thames Churches Housing Trust; Royal London School for the Blind; Society for the Study of Inborn Errors of Metabolism; Woodland Trust. Grants of £1,000 to £2,000 were given to ten organisations including: Aidis Trust; Childline; Fifth Trust; Leeds Colony Holidays. Seven smaller grants of £500 to £861 included those to Dark Horse Venture; Disability Aid Fund; London Federation of Boys Clubs; Sequal; University of Birmingham.

Exclusions: The trust does not support charities concerned with animal welfare, religious organisations or charities for the benefit of people outside the UK. No grants are given for educational or research trips.

Applications: In writing to the correspondent.

The Patrick Frost Foundation

£100,000 (1992/93)

General

c/o Trowers & Hamlins, 6 New Square, Lincoln's Inn, London WC2A 3RP

Correspondent: Mrs H Frost

Trustees: Mrs Helena Frost; Donald Jones; Luke Valner; John Chedzoy.

Beneficial area: Worldwide.

Information available: Full accounts are on file at the Charity Commission.

General: In 1992/93, the trust had assets of £866,000 and an income of £51,000. This was only the trusts second year of operation and the grant total rose from £15,000 in 1991/92, to £100,000.

The trust is unusual compared to most trusts in this Guide in that it gives a relatively small number of large grants. In 1992/93, it gave 15 grants, all for £5,000 or £10,000, mainly to welfare or disability charities. The trustees tend to try to help charities that rely on a considerable amount of self help and voluntary effort.

£10,000 was given to Acorn Christian Healing Trust, Drug & Alcohol Foundation, Family Holiday Association, Littlehampton Family Makers Project and the National Library for the Handicapped Child. Beneficiaries of £5,000 included Action for Blind People, Intermediate Technology, Samaritans and To Romania with Aid.

The previous year £10,000 was given to Pine Ridge Dog Sanctuary and £5,000 to London Children's Flower Society.

Applications: In writing to the correspondent, accompanied by the last set of audited accounts.

Gableholt Limited

£84,000 (1991/92)

Jewish

4 Queensway, Hendon, London NW4 2TN
0181-202 1881

Correspondent: Solomon Noe

Trustees: S Noe; Mrs E Noe; C Lerner.

Beneficial area: UK.

Information available: Accounts are on file at the Charity Commission up to 1991/92, but without a list of grants.

General: In 1991/92, the trust had assets of £1.7 million, an income of £201,000 and gave grants totalling £84,000. Unfortunately we have been unable to obtain any more up-to-date information on the trust. The information below is taken from the last edition of this Guide.

Set up as a limited company in 1978, the trust grants practically all its donations to Jewish institutions, particularly those working in accordance with the orthodox Jewish faith. The company's grant total does not truly reflect its wealth, whether it be the income of £201,000 or its assets of over £1.5 million. Most of this has been achieved because of the company's large property holdings, though the last set of accounts shows a move into listed investments.

Some examples of the thirty-two beneficiaries include: the Rachel Charitable Trust (£34,000); Friends of Harim Establishment (£10,000); Gur Trust (£10,000) and Torah Venchased Le'Ezra Vasad (£10,000). At the other end of the scale there were many smaller donations, including the Mengrah Grammar School (£100); Afula Society (£40); Child Resettlement (£22) and Friends of the Sick (£10).

This last set of accounts saw a dramatic drop in grant total, from £270,000 in 1990/91, though as there seems no apparent financial reason behind this perhaps next year will see a return to the previous levels of funding.

Applications: This trust strongly requested not to be included in Trust Monitor, arguing that "in the Governors' view, true charitable giving should always be coupled with virtual anonymity and for this reason they are most reluctant to be a party to any publicity." Along with suggesting that the listed beneficiaries might also want to remain unidentified, they also state that the nature of the giving (to orthodox Jewish organisations) means the information is unlikely to be of much interest to anyone else. Potential applicants would be strongly advised to take heed of these comments.

The Robert Gavron Charitable Trust

£285,000 (1993/94)

Arts, health and welfare

44 Eagle Street, London WC1R 4AP
0171-400 4200

Correspondent: R Gavron

Trustees: Robert Gavron; Charles Corman; Katherine Gavron.

Beneficial area: UK.

Information available: Full accounts are on file at the Charity Commission.

General: In 1993/94, the trust had assets of £5.24 million and an income of £292,000, more than double the previous year. Grants totalled £285,000.

The largest grants went to: Open College of the Arts, a regular beneficiary (£40,000 and over £60,000 over the three previous years); Institute of Community Studies (£17,000); Adventure Unlimited, Francis Holland (C of E school for girls), Friends of Covent Garden and Tel Aviv University Trust (£10,000 each). Grants were mainly to arts and health/medical charities including London Choral Society, Opera Factory, Rambert Dance Company, Royal Court Theatre, Fight for Sight, Leukemia Research Fund and Raynaulds Scleroderma Association.

Other beneficiaries included the Capital Housing Project and Rathbone Society (£500 each); Prison Reform Trust and the Noise Abatement Society (£25). About a third of the beneficiaries received grants the previous year, a number of which appear to receive regular grants.

Applications: In writing only to the correspondent.

The Gem Charitable Trust

£65,000 (1993/94)

General

Messrs Farrer & Co, 66 Lincoln's Inn Fields, London WC2A 3LH
0171-242 2022

Trustees: N J Marks; I R Marks; C F Woodhouse.

Beneficial area: Worldwide.

Information available: Full accounts are on file at the charity Commission.

General: In 1993/94, the trust had an income of £40,000 and gave grants totalling £65,000. Most of this (£38,000) went to the C Foundation. The remaining three grants went to regular beneficiaries of the trust: the New Economics Foundation (£19,000), Dartington Hall Trust (£5,000) and WYSE (£2,500).

The previous year, grants again totalled £65,000, but the income was £100,000. The largest grant (£50,000) went to Mansfield Max Neef via the Gaia Foundation. The three regular beneficiaries mentioned above received £5,000, £5,000 and £2,500 respectively. One other grant was given, to Aston Tirrold & Upthorpe PCC (£2,000).

Applications: In writing to the correspondent.

The General Charity Fund

£51,000 (1993/94)

General

Coopers & Lybrand, Richmond House, 1 Rumford Place, Liverpool L3 9QS
0151-227 4242

Correspondent: Alan Bentley

Trustees: Dr L H A Pilkington; A P Pilkington; D D Mason; Hon Mrs J M Jones.

Beneficial area: UK, with a preference for Merseyside.

Information available: Full accounts are on file at the Charity Commission.

General: The fund is one of the Estate of the Late Colonel W W Pilkington Will Trusts. In 1993/94, the trust had assets of £636,000, an income of £45,000 and gave grants totalling £51,000. 84 organisations benefitted of which 44 received two grants and three received three grants. Only four grants were for £1,000 or more, two to St Helens Hospice (£3,000 and £1,000), while Clonter Opera For All and the Royal School for the Blind both received two grants of £1,000 and £500. The remaining grants were for £100 to £650.

Youth and welfare organisations received most support. Over half the organisations supported were in Merseyside, with beneficiaries including Edgehill Boys Club, Liverpool Rape Crisis, Liverpool Stroke Club, St Helens Groundwork, WRVS St Helens, Wirral Girls Guides and five local URC churches. National beneficiaries included the British Epilepsy Association, Intermediate Technology, MENCAP, RNLI and Youth Clubs UK. Most beneficiaries also received grants the previous year.

Applications: In writing to the correspondent. Grants were distributed in July 1993, February and June 1994.

The Gertner Charitable Trust

£273,000 (1991/92)

Jewish

Fordgate House, 1 Allsop Place, London NW1 5LF
0171-224 1234

Correspondent: Mrs M Gertner

Trustees: Mrs M Gertner; M Gertner; S Bentley.

Beneficial area: Unrestricted.

Information available: The only accounts on file at the Charity Commission were those for 1987/88 and 1991/92.

General: In 1987/88, the income of the trust was £54,000, most of which was from a single donation. All grants went to Jewish organisations or individuals. Eleven grants were for over £1,000, but most of the 70 grants listed were between £100 and £200, with a further £8,000 in grants of under £100.

In 1991/92, the income was £210,000, mostly from donations and grants totalled £273,000. The grants list goes on for 23 pages showing 1,100 grants, most for under £100. The largest were to Chesed Charity Trust (£19,000) and Zemach Zedek (£11,700). There were no further grants over £5,500. Many grants appear to be to individuals.

Applications: In writing to the correspondent.

The Gibbins Trust

£49,000 (1993/94)

General

c/o Thomas Eggar Verrall Bowles, 5 East Pallant, Chichester, West Sussex PO19 1TS
01243-786111

Correspondent: R F Ash

Trustees: R S Archer; R F Ash; P M Archer.

Beneficial area: UK, with local grants being given in Sussex.

Information available: Guidance notes for applicants reprinted below. Full accounts are on file at the Charity Commission.

General: In 1993/94, the trust had assets of £781,000 with an income of £45,000. Almost 120 grants were given totalling £49,000. In exceptional years the trust gives larger grants out of capital. The trust generally gives three types of grant, all to registered charities:

- Support for about 60 charities, mostly small to medium-sized, with regular grants once or twice a year. This list is viewed by the trustees as flexible, with some charities leaving and joining the group from time to time.
- Small grants, usually in the range £250 to £500, on the basis of one-off donations to special appeals or to support new funds in the area.
- The trust occasionally makes more substantial grants, generally to funds on its regular list, for special appeals.

The trust mainly supports charities active in the relief of hardship and disability with a particular interest in the young and the very old. Occasionally grants are made for medical research. Support is given to a number of funds that provide holidays for disabled people. Most grants are to national organisations; of the local grants, almost all are given to Sussex-based charities.

It appears that in 1993/94, about half the grants were to organisations working in the sickness and disability fields (with many of these to support older people). Welfare and youth organisations were the next largest area. The trust makes payments in June and December with the larger grants usually given in December.

There were three grants of £1,000 to Horder Centre for Arthritics, Sussex Housing Association for the Aged and the Lord Mayor's Treloar Trust (the latter two also received £950 each in December).

Other beneficiaries, many of which received two grants included Age Concern East and West Sussex (£1,250 each in total); Carr-Gomm Society (£1,175 in total); Chichester Cathedral Trust (£1,750 in total); Counsel and Care for the Elderly (£1,150), and West Sussex Association for the Blind (£1,050).

Recipients of smaller grants included 9th Bexhill Scout Group; Brighton Unemployed Centre; CHICKs - Camping Holidays for Inner City Kids; National Association of Swimming Clubs for the Handicapped; Toy Libraries Association and Incorporated Homes for Ladies with Limited Income.

Exclusions: No grants are given to individuals and only very rarely to charities for animal welfare or for the preservation of buildings or other heritage appeals.

Applications: In writing to the correspondent. Generally applications will not be acknowledged. Trustees meet twice a year, normally in May and November.

The Gibbs Charitable Trusts

£72,000 (1993/94)

Methodist

1 Portland place, Marine Parade, Penarth CF64 3DY
01222-706304

Correspondent: Dr John M Gibbs

Trustees: Mrs S M N Gibbs; J M Gibbs; J N Gibbs; A G Gibbs; W M Gibbs; J Gibbs; S E Gibbs.

Beneficial area: UK.

Information available: Full accounts are on file at the Charity Commission.

General: The three main categories supported by the trust are:
1) Work undertaken by Methodist churches and organisations;
2) Other Christian causes, especially of an ecumenical nature, and
3) Wider charitable aims, especially in creative arts.

In 1993/94, the trust had assets of £1.1 million and an income of £65,000. The trustees do not claim any expenses that they incur in the administration of the trust, either for secretarial work or travel. 30 grants were given totalling £72,000, divided as follows:

- **Methodist churches, circuits and districts:** £27,000 (£9,000 in 1992/93). Seven grants were given, the largest being £10,000 to South Wales District Fund and £9,000 to Trinity Methodist Church, Penarth. Other grants of £500 to £3,000 went to churches throughout England and Wales.
- **Methodist divisions and organisations:** £11,000 (£20,000 in 1992/93). Three grants were given to the Overseas Division (£6,000); Division of Education and Youth (£4,000) and Division of Ministries (£1,000).
- **Methodist colleges and schools:** £16,250 (£1,600 in 1992/93). Four grants to: Charles Wesley Heritage Centre (£10,000); Urban Technology Unit (£5,000); Westminster College (£1,000) and Queens College, Taunton (£250).
- **Other Christian groups:** £5,000 (£7,000 in 1992/93) in grants to: Riding Lights Christian Arts Centre (£2,000); Christian Education Movement (£700); Genesis Arts Trust (£250) and Fund for World Mission (£75).
- **Other organisations:** £12,488 (£14,300 in 1992/93). Llangynida New Village Hall and National Museum, Wales received £5,000 each, Farnham Maltings £1,288, Bosnia Students Fund £700 and Carmel Woods Campaign £500.

Applications: In writing to the correspondent. The trustees meet three times a year, at Christmas, Easter and in August.

The L & R Gilley Charitable Trust

£64,000 (1992/93)

General

c/o Shakespeares, 4 Pritchatts Road, Birmingham B15 2QT
0121-454 9316

Correspondent: Miss C M Tempest, Secretary to the Trustees

Trustees: John Richard Bettinson; Richard Anthony Bettinson; Yvonne Garfield-Smith.

Beneficial area: UK, with a preference for Torbay and South Devon.

Information available: Full accounts are on file at the Charity Commission

General: The trust was set up to give grants to the League of Friends of Torbay Hospital, Imperial Cancer Research Fund, Royal National Lifeboat Institute, Royal National Institute for the Blind and Rowcroft House Foundation. However, it also gives grants to other organisations concerned with the care of the terminally ill, and elderly people.

In 1992/93, the trust had assets of £815,000 and an income of £64,000, all of which was given in grants. 12 recipients received a grant the previous year. Half the grants were for local Devon & Cornwall charities, including the Devon & Cornwall Cavitoon Appeal (£10,000), Torbay Hospital League of Friends (£5,000) and Torbay Blind Persons Club (£3,000). There were two grants of £5,000, to Birmingham Heartlands Hospital and Midlands Spastics Association. Other grants were to national medical charities such as the Motor Neurone Disease Association, RNIB, Cancer Research Campaign and £7,000 was given to Victim Support Scheme.

Applications: In writing to the correspondent.

The Girdlers' Company Charitable Trust

£25,000 (1993/94)

General

Girdlers' Hall, Basinghall Avenue, London EC2V 5DD
0171-638 0488

Correspondent: The Clerk

Trustees: The Girdlers' Company.

Beneficial area: UK.

Information available: Accounts are on file at the Charity Commission, but without a list of grants.

General: In 1993/94, the trust had assets of £550,000 and an income of £114,000, including £75,000 in covenanted and Gift Aid donations from the Girdlers' Company. The trust is currently giving one grant of £25,000 a year to fund a research fellowship at an Oxford College.

This trust will eventually take over from the Geoffrey Woods Charitable Trust, and for the time being the objective is to build up the capital.

Applications: In writing to the correspondent.

The Girling (Cwmbran) Trust

£57,000 (1993)

General in Cwmbran

c/o Grange Works, Cwmbran, Gwent NP44 3XU
01633-834000

Correspondent: Ken Maddox

Trustees: K L Maddox; A Rippon; B E Smith.

Beneficial area: Cwmbran.

Information available: Full accounts are on file at the Charity Commission.

General: The trust holds assets of about £860,000 and in 1993 had an income of £54,000. It operates specifically in the urban area of Cwmbran in Gwent, Wales. Grants are to provide social amenities in the area, the advancement of education and the relief of poverty and sickness.

In 1993, about 60 grants were given totalling £57,000, about £20,000 of which was given to individuals with special needs.

The largest grants to organisations went to Torfean Community Enterprises (£9,000), Citizen's Advice Bureau (£2,773), Torphab (£2,100) and £2,000 each to Congress Theatre Countdown and Royal Gwent Hospital Cardiology. Grants of around £1,000 were given to ten organisations: four concerned with sickness and disability; three schools (two of which were to Coed Eva); two hospitals and one church.

The smaller grants, mostly between £100 and £500, were given to a wide variety of groups including: Cwmbran Amateur Swimming Club; Cwmbran Rugby FC; Fairwater Playgroup; Llanyravon AFC; Lleisiau Gwent Choir; Salvation Army; St Dial's Youth Club and Torfaen Accordian Band.

Applications: In writing to the correspondent. Trustees usually meet every two months, starting at the end of February.

The B & P Glasser Charitable Trust

£116,000 (1991/92)

Jewish, social and medical welfare

Stafford, Young, Jones & Co, The Old Rectory, 29 Martin Lane, London EC4R 0AU
0171-623 3501

Correspondent: B Christer, Partner

Trustees: Benjamin Glasser; Harry Glasser; John C Belfrage; James D H Cullingham.

Beneficial area: UK.

Information available: Full accounts are on file at the Charity Commission up to 1988 and for 1991/92.

General: In 1991/92, the trust had assets of £1 million, an income of £105,000 and gave 25 grants totalling £116,000. The largest were to Jewish Care (£60,000) and Nightingale House (£10,000). There were five grants of £5,000 to: British Heart Foundation; Jewish Blind & Physically Handicapped Society; Norwood Children's Home; RNIB and Wendover Abbeyfield Society. The remaining grants were given to either Jewish causes or large national charities such as Guide Dogs for the Blind, Imperial Cancer Research Fund, RNLI and the Samaritans. Four grants were for £2,000 to £2,500, 12 of £1,000 and two for £500. It appears that most grants are recurrent.

Applications: In writing to the correspondent.

The GNC Trust

£40,000 (1993)

General

c/o Messrs Price Waterhouse & Co, Cornwall Court, Cornwall Street, Birmingham B3 2DT
0121-200 3000

Correspondent: The Secretary

Trustees: R N Cadbury; G T E Cadbury; Mrs J E B Yelloly.

Beneficial area: Preference for Avon, Cornwall, Hampshire and the Midlands.

Information available: Full accounts are on file at the Charity Commission.

General: In 1993, the trust had assets of £696,000 generating an income of £56,000. The trust consists of two funds; the Main Fund, which gave grants totalling £31,500 and the Mrs J E B Yelloly's Fund, which gave grants totalling £8,500. Grants from the two funds were listed together in the accounts.

The grants list for 1993 shows the trust gave about 80 grants to a wide range of organisations. Most grants appeared to be in the areas of medical, religious, children and youth, seafaring and womens' groups. Most other areas were also supported including the elderly, animal welfare, buildings/heritage/conservation and homelessness and welfare.

There were eleven grants of £1,000 to £5,000 including: Society of Friends (£5,000, £6,000 in 1990); Special Trustees of the Former UBH Fund (£3,000); NSF and Endeavour Training Trust (£2,500 each); Joy to the World and Womenslink (£2,000 each); Bath Institute of Medical Engineering (£1,500). About half of the grants were for £500 to £750 and 30 grants were for under £500. Some of the smaller recipients have received large grants in the past including the Downs Light Railway Trust (£750 and £9,000 in 1990) and St Richard's Hospice (£50 and £5,000 in 1990).

Applications: In writing to the correspondent.

The Godinton Charitable Trust

£144,000 (1992/93)

General

Godinton Park, Ashford, Kent TN23 3BW

Correspondent: A W Green

Trustees: W G Plumtree; J D Lee-Pemberton; M F Jennings; M V Hingston Caplat.

Beneficial area: UK.

Information available: Full accounts are on file at the Charity Commission.

General: The trust's assets rose from £590,000 in 1991/92, to £1.9 million in 1992/93. The income rose from £261,000 to £288,000. In 1992/93, only half the income (£144,000) was distributed in over 400 grants (£268,000 was distributed the previous year). Grants were generally for either £100, £250 or £500, though there were 15 grants of between £1,000 and £5,000.

The largest grant, £5,000, was given to Glyndebourne Opera and £2,000 was given to each of: Blond McIndoe; Centre for Medical Research; Charities Aid Foundation; Leonard Cheshire Foundation, English National Opera; Home Farm Trust; Royal Commonwealth Society for the Blind; Spastics Society.

Incorporated Liverpool School of Tropical Medicine received £1,500 and £1,000 was given to Sail Training Association, Operation Raleigh, East Kent Pilgrims Trust and welfare, arts and medical organisations. Smaller grants are given to the full range of charitable organisations in the UK. Many individuals are also supported.

Applications: In writing to the correspondent. The trust meets approximately twelve times a year.

The Sydney & Phyllis Goldberg Memorial Trust

£50,000 (1992/93)

Medical research, welfare, disability

Coulthards Mackenzie, Five Kings House, 1 Queen Street Place, London EC4R 1QS
0171-236 7892

Correspondent: H Vowles, Trustee

Trustees: H Vowles; C J Pexton.

Beneficial area: UK.

Information available: Full accounts are on file at the Charity Commission.

General: In 1992/93, the trust had assets of £749,000 and an income of £54,000. A further £20,000 tax repayment was received after the year end. Grants totalled £50,000, with a further £17,000 distributed after the year end.

12 grants were given, eight for £5,000 including those to the Ty Olwen Trust (a hospice in Swansea), Sue Ryder Foundation – Akron Trust (to provide accommodation for young people in Wales with drug/alcohol problems), RNLI, Royal Hospital & Home in Putney (for rehabilitation of people with severe disabilities), and the Isaac Goldberg Charity Trust (for distribution to other charities with which Sydney Goldberg would have wished to be associated). The other three grants of £5,000 went towards medical research including the Marrow Environment Foundation and the Association of Stammerers.

Other grants, of £2,000 or £3,000, went to the Disability Law Service, Dystonia Society and Single Homeless Project. Eight of the beneficiaries also received a grant the previous year.

Applications: In writing to the correspondent.

The Golden Bottle Trust

£141,000 (1994)

General

C Hoare & Co, 37 Fleet Street, London EC4P 4DQ
0171-353 4522

Correspondent: Secretariat

Trustees: A S Hoare; H C Hoare; D J Hoare; R Q Hoare; M R Hoare; A M Hoare.

Beneficial area: UK.

Information available: Full accounts are on file at the Charity Commission.

General: In 1993/94, the trust had assets of £725,000 and an income of £241,000, including £200,000 from C Hoare & Co under deed of covenant and Gift Aid. The trust gave 177 grants totalling £141,000 (199 grants totalling £149,000 in 1991/92). 22 grants were for £1,000 and 20 were for over £1,000. The main beneficiaries, each receiving £10,000 were the Bulldog Trust, British Records Association, MERLIN and the National Trust.

Other grants were given to a wide range of organisations working in the areas of arts, disability, medical, welfare, conservation etc. including: Trinity Hospice (£2,000); Aidis Trust (£1,500); British Brain & Spine Foundation; Floating Point Science Theatre; National Manuscripts Conservation Trust; Puppet Centre Trust and Wiltshire Wildlife Trust (£1,000 each); Electronic Aids for the Blind (£800); Handel Society and Save the Rhino (both £250).

Exclusions: No grants for individuals or organisations that are not registered charities.

Applications: In writing to the correspondent, who stated "Trustees meet on a monthly basis, but the funds are already largely committed and, therefore, applications from sources not already known to the trustees are unlikely to be successful."

The Jack Goldhill Charitable Trust

£67,000 (1993)

Jewish, arts, welfare

85 Kensington Heights, Campden Hill Road, London W8 7BD

Correspondent: Jack Goldhill

Trustees: G Goldhill; J A Goldhill.

Beneficial area: UK.

Information available: Full accounts are on file at the Charity Commission.

General: In 1993, the trust had assets of £418,000, including property, which generated an income of £70,000.

77 grants were given totalling £67,000, with about one third of the grant total and many of the larger grants to Jewish organisations. Other larger grants went to arts organisations.

The largest grants went to Jewish Care (£22,000), Royal Academy Trust (£10,000), Royal Academy of Arts, Royal London Hospital Special Trustees and London Philharmonic Society (£3,000 each) and the Foundation for Education and JPAIME (both £2,500).

The remaining grants ranged from £50 to £2,000, with most for £100. Health, welfare and arts organisations were all supported with many of the grants being recurrent. Recipients of smaller grants included BACUP (£1,000), Glyndebourne Festival Arts Trust (£500), NSPCC (£260), Mencap and Shelter (both £100).

Applications: The trustees have a restricted list of charities to whom they are committed, and no new applications can be considered at the present time.

The Good Neighbours Trust

£96,000 (1994)

Mentally and physically disabled people

16 Westway, Nailsea, Bristol BS19 1EE

Correspondent: P S Broderick, Secretary

Trustees: Kenneth G Long, Chairman; G V Arter; R J Laver; R T Sheppard.

Beneficial area: UK and Bristol, Somerset and Gloucestershire.

Information available: The trust produces guidance notes for applicants (quoted in full below under "exclusions" and "applications") and files accounts with the Charity Commission.

General: In 1994, the trust had assets of £1.67 million, an income of £82,000 and gave grants totalling £96,000. These were broken down as into:

Local – over 30 grants of £100 to £4,000 totalling £21,000

National – over 130 grants of £100 to £5,000 totalling £75,000.

There is a preference for organisations working with people with disabilities.

The main local grants were: South Meade Hospital and Computers for Life (£4,000 each); Scope South West Region (£3,100); Churchtown Outdoor Activity Centre, Cornwall (£1,750). There were a further seven grants of £1,000.

The main national grants were: Help the Hospices (£5,000) and RNIB Scotland (£3,000) both received similarly large grants in the previous year. Other beneficiaries included Canine Partners for Independence (£2,500) and Birmingham Royal Institute for the Blind (£1,825). A further 21 grants were for £1,000.

Exclusions: The following are excluded:

- Overseas projects, including those projects formulated and designed in this country for overseas application.
- General community projects other than those wholly or predominantly on behalf of the mentally and physically handicapped.
- Individuals.
- General educational projects (other than those wholly or predominantly on behalf of the mentally and physically handicapped). Religious and ethnic projects (excluding those made by religious and ethnic organisations with the aim of relieving the suffering of and benefiting such persons as are defined above and always provided that such persons are in no way deprived from benefiting from a project by reason of their religious beliefs and/or ethnic origins).
- Projects for the unemployed and related training schemes, excluding those projects which are wholly for the benefit of such persons as are defined above. Projects on behalf of offenders and ex-offenders. Projects pertaining to or arising from the abuse of drugs and/or alcohol.
- Wildlife and conservation schemes, except for those projects directly benefiting such persons as are defined above (for example, a nature trail, including aids, designed for use by the blind).
- General restoration and preservation of buildings, purely for historical and/or architectural purposes.
- On-going grants.

Applications: The trust does not issue official forms of application – appeals should be in letter form, addressed to the Secretary and may be made at any time. The following notes should be carefully considered by those contemplating making an appeal to the trust for financial aid:

Appeals will be considered only when made by bodies registered as charities and/or recognised as such by the Charity Commissioners. An appeal must be accompanied by a copy of the latest available audited accounts (normally for the previous financial year) or, in the case of newly registered charities, by a copy of provisional accounts showing a projection of estimated income and expenditure for the current financial year.

Appeals will be considered principally in respect of specific projects on behalf of the mentally and physically handicapped of all ages.

The project for which an appeal is being made must be shown to be both feasible and viable. Where applicable, the starting date of the project should be given, together with the anticipated date of completion.

The estimated cost of the project should be included in the appeal, together with the appeal's target-figure (usually, but not always, the latter is the same as the project's cost). Details of funds already raised (if any) and fund-raising schemes in respect of the specific project should also be given. A "shopping list", where appropriate, may be included with the appeal.

Where applicable, due consideration will be given to evidence of voluntary and self-help (both in practical and fund-raising terms), and to the number of people expected to benefit from the project.

The Everard & Mina Goodman Charitable Foundation

£112,000 (1993/94)

Jewish, medical/health, general

5 Bryanston Court, George Street, London W1H 7HA
0171-486 4684

Correspondent: Everard N Goodman

Trustees: Everard N Goodman; Mina Goodman; M P Goodman.

Beneficial area: UK, Israel.

Information available: Full accounts are on file at the Charity Commission for 1993/94.

General: The trust was set up in 1962 by Everard and Mina Goodman for general charitable purposes. The income is derived principally from Goodman family donations. In 1988, it had an income of only £26,000 and yet paid out £156,000 in grants. £129,000 was paid out of capital, leaving only £274,000. By 1993/94, the assets had dropped to £130,000 and income was only £25,000 but grants totalled £112,000.

The vast majority of grants are to Jewish organisations, although the correspondent has contacted us to say it is not a Jewish foundation. The trustees define their policy as "A preference for medical/health, also the needs of children and youth, rehabilitation and training, the relief of poverty, the advancement of education and the advancement of religion."

In 1993/94, the trust gave 42 grants, 10 of which were for between £1,000 and £11,500 and 27 grants were for less than £500. There was also one exceptional grant of £63,000 to Rebecca Seif Hospital Sfat Neo-Natal Department. Other main beneficiaries were Jewish Care (£11,500); Office of Chief Rabbi's Womens Group (£10,000) and Friends of the English Opera and Board of Deputies of British Jews (£5,000 each). The smaller grants included: WIZO (£420); Academy of Concerts Society (£100); Association for Research into Stammering Children (£300), Bulgarian Orphanage Appeal (£60) and Care for Children (£55).

Exclusions: No grants to individuals.

Applications: To the correspondent in writing.

The Gough Charitable Trust

£51,000 (1992)

Youth, Episcopal and Church of England, preservation of the countryside

Thames Valley Area Office, The Clock House, 22-26 Ock Street, Abingdon, Oxon OX14 5SW

Correspondent: Mrs E Ostorn-King (Ref: TT/98625/EOK)

Trustees: Lloyds Bank plc; N de L Harvie.

Beneficial area: Preference for Scotland.

Information available: Full accounts are on file at the Charity Commission for 1992.

General: In 1993/94, the trust had an income of only £33,000. This was made up of: £20,000 generated by £333,000 invested in a Guernsey Fixed Term Deposit Account; £8,500 from shares, £4,000 from an Income Tax repayment and just over £400 in other income. A balance of £67,000 was carried over from the previous year.

Only 12 grants were given totalling less than £4,000. Three grants of £1,000 were given to: Downside Settlement; Scottish Scenic Trust and Childline. ISCA received £500, Trinity Hospice £100 and the other grants ranged from £10 to £50. In each month between £1,200 and £1,600 was deposited in the Guernsey Deposit Account and the trust still carried forward £79,000 to the next year. It is not known why the trust is accumulating its income in this way.

In 1992, the trust had assets of about £140,000 and an income of £64,000. Grants totalled £51,000 and were given to 22 organisations working in a wide variety of fields. Beneficiaries included the National Trust for Scotland (£10,000); National Army Museum (£7,000) and £5,000 each to Trinity Hospice, Calcutta Tercentenary Trust and the International Scientific Support Trust. The Highland Hospice received £3,000. Seven grants were paid to regular beneficiaries, mainly service and insurance benevolent funds.

Exclusions: No support for non-registered charities and individuals including students.

Applications: In writing to the correspondent at any time. No application forms are available, no acknowledgements are sent. Applications are considered quarterly.

The Grace Charitable Trust

£48,000 (1991)

Christian

Rhualt House, Rhualt, St Asaph, Clwyd LL17 0TG
01745-583141

Correspondent: Mrs G Payne

Beneficial area: UK.

Information available: Full accounts are on file at the Charity Commission up to 1990/91.

General: In 1991, the trust had assets of £118,000 and an income of £96,000. Grants totalling £48,000 were given to 41, mainly Christian, charities. The largest grants were: £11,000 to Children in Need; £5,000 to Gideons International; £4,000 to Pocket Testament League; £3,000 to Eurovangelism; £2,000 to Echoes of Service, £1,500 to European Christian Mission and £1,200 to Gospel Literature Outreach. Seven grants of £1,000 were given. The only grants to non-Christian organisations were to Children in Need (see above), Mencap (£200) and the NSPCC (£500).

According to the Charity Commission the trust had an income of £117,000 in 1994.

Applications: The trust states: "applications for grants or donations are not considered".

The Reginald Graham Charitable Trust

£45,000 (1991/92)

Children, medical, education

c/o Messrs Bircham & Co, 1 Dean Farrar Street, London SW1H 0DY
0171-222 8044

Correspondent: Michael David Wood, Trustee

Trustees: Reginald Graham; Mrs Melanie Jane Boyd; Michael David Wood; James William Dolman.

Beneficial area: UK.

Information available: Until the 1992 Charities Act the most recent accounts on file at the Charity Commission were those for 1975/76. There are now accounts for 1991/92. According to the trust, accounts are also on file for 1992/93 and 1993/94.

General: In 1991/92, the trust had assets of £271,000 (property in Southampton) and an income of £86,000, including £45,000 property income and £37,000 from covenants. 74 grants were given totalling £45,000. In the previous year the trust had an income of £376,000, of which £333,333 was in covenants, it gave £346,000 in grants. The trust supports "health, child and institutional educational causes".

In 1991/92, grants ranged from £2 to £14,000, 27 of which received a grant in 1990/91. The main beneficiaries were: Pembroke College (£14,000), Airbourne Memorial Fund & Victory Club (£5,000) and Bournemouth Reform Synagogue (£2,500). There were seven grants of £1,000 to £2,000 to organisations such as: Birthright; English Chamber Orchestra & Music Society; NSPCC and Winchester Cathedral. Of the other grants, 28 were for £50 or less and 35 were for £50 to £550. Health, welfare, arts, environment and animal welfare charities all received a number of grants including Action on Addiction, Childline, CPRE, English National Opera, Help the Aged, Royal Academy Trust and Survival International.

Applications: In writing to the correspondent.

The Grahame Charitable Foundation

£64,000 (1993)

Jewish

5 Spencer Walk, Hampstead High Street, London NW3 1QZ
0171-794 5281

Correspondent: H P Organ

Trustees: Gitte Grahame; Jeffrey Greenwood.

Beneficial area: UK.

Information available: Full accounts are on file at the Charity Commission.

General: In 1993, the trust had assets of £158,000 (£260,000 in 1990 and £178,000 in 1991) and an income of £48,000 (£155,000 in 1990 and £48,000 in 1991). 88 grants were given totalling £64,000 (£177,000 in 1990 and £125,000 in 1991).

Only four grants were given to non-Jewish organisations, all for £100 or less to Greenpeace, Chartered Accountants Benevolent Society, Cancer Relief Macmillan Fund and the Spastics Society. The largest grants were to the Child Resettlement Fund (£10,000) and Jewish Care (£6,500). There were 14 grants for £1,000 or more and most of the rest were under £500.

Applications: In writing to the correspondent.

The Granada Foundation

£134,000 (1993/94)

Arts and sciences in the North West

Granada Television Centre, Manchester M60 9EA
0161-832 7211; Fax: 0161-827 2145

Correspondent: Kathy Arundale, Administrator

Trustees: Advisory Council: Sir Robert Scott, Chairman; Prof T M Husband; Prof Denis McCaldin; Prof F F Ridley; Margaret Kenyon; Alexander Bernstein (trustee); Colin Hubbard (trustee); Kathy Arundale.

Beneficial area: The North West of England.

Information available: Terms of reference and guidelines for applicants are available from the trust. Full accounts are on file at the Charity Commission for 1992/93.

General: The Granada Foundation was established in 1965 as the Northern Arts and Sciences Foundation to encourage the study and appreciation of fine arts and science and to promote education. Since then it has given a total of £1.6 million in grants.

"The Foundation wishes to encourage and promote the following: the study, practice and appreciation of the fine arts including drawing, architecture and landscape architecture, sculpture, literature, music, opera, drama, ballet, cinema, and the methods and means of their dissemination." There is a clear preference for organisations working in the Granada Television transmission area (the North West of England).

"From time to time the Advisory Council may take an initiative by offering, for instance, a specialist prize, a residency or even a university chair. In general, however, the Council looks for imaginative proposals from organisations (preferably with charity status) which will in some way make the North West in particular a more attractive place in which to live and work. There is a clear preference for new projects and the Foundation will not provide salaries (except residencies) nor take on long-term revenue funding. Although the Foundation will support festivals and other annual events, it is on the understanding that such support should not be automatically renewable."

In 1993/94, the trust had assets of £1.4 million generating an income of £112,000. The main grants for the year were Manchester – City of Drama "year of Drama" (£50,000, the first of two payments) and Walker Art Gallery – Liverpool (£25,000, the second of two payments) towards refurbishment. Neither of these are typical amounts. More typical are: The Granada Power Game – an annual competitive science engineering project for schools received £14,000, divided between: prizes, materials, hire of hall and equipment, administration, and travel, refreshment etc.; Red Star Brouhaha – Liverpool (£10,000) towards a young peoples theatre festival; Buxton Opera Festival (£6,000) towards a festival; Green Room Theatre – Manchester (£5,000) to developing new studios and rehearsal rooms and Octagon Theatre Trust, Bolton (£3,000) to refurbish and instal a new hearing system.

Of the 17 other grants ranging from £500 to £2,000, most were given to projects in Manchester, three were in Merseyside and one each in the Lake District and Chester for summer festivals. The smaller grants were given towards projects such as: signed performances for deaf people; performances and workshops for children with special needs; a festival of Chinese New Year and a painting exhibition for UK based African painters.

Exclusions: No grants will be given for general appeals, individuals (including courses of study), expeditions, overseas travel or youth clubs/community associations.

Applications: Write for an application form, giving an outline of the project. Detailed information can be added when the formal application is submitted. Details of the next trustees meeting will be given when an application form is sent (trustees meet three to four times a year at irregular intervals). All letters are acknowledged, whether possible successful applicants or immediate rejections.

The Grand Order of Water Rats Charities Fund

£82,000 (1993)

Arts, medical equipment

328 Gray's Inn Road, London WC1X 8BZ
0171-278 3248

Correspondent: John Adrian, Secretary to the Trustees

Trustees: David Berglas; Wyn Calvin; Declan Cluskey; Roy Hudd; Bert Weedon.

Beneficial area: UK.

Information available: Full accounts are on file at the Charity Commission.

General: The Grand Order of Water Rats was established in 1889 to assist needy members of the Music Hall Profession and their dependants. Now the scope of the trust deed also covers members of the Variety and Light Entertainment

Profession. The Charities Fund also supplies medical equipment to certain hospitals and institutions. Due to the "very specific nature of the GOWR funds the trustees have asked not to be included in grant directories". However we maintain our policy of giving information of all trusts we know of with the ability to give over £40,000 a year.

The trust deed has a wonderful range of celebrity signatures, and the chairman of the trustees (Paul Daniels for 1995) "is to be known as King Rat". The fund aims primarily to assist light entertainers, or charities that support them. (There is a separate category in the accounts for fruit and flowers). It is mainly funded by donations, and had only £541,000 in assets in 1991. In that year, income was £136,000. Awards fluctuate with the level of donations and have been as follows: 1988: £82,000; 1989: £161,000; 1990: £67,000; 1991: £113,000.

By 1993, the assets had dropped to £493,000, but the income had risen to £151,000, £122,000 of which was in miscellaneous receipts including donations received. £54,000 was given to individuals for weekly allowances, grants and Christmas gifts. Grants to organisations totalled £82,000, of which £3,000 was for fruit and flowers. 22 grants were for £600 to £12,500 and totalled £61,000.

The Entertainment Artistes' Benevolent Fund is the main regular beneficiary. In 1993, it received £12,500 towards Brinsworth House and £8,500 for various needs. This fund was set up by the Rats, runs a home in Twickenham and also receives the proceeds from the Royal Variety Performance. Other large grants were given to: Relate (£9,500); Servite Ltd (£4,600); Bud Flanagan Leukaemia Fund and RTF (£3,000 each); GOLR Butlins Trust (two grants totalling £4,500). Other grants of £600 to £2,000 were given to organisations such as: Disabled Living Foundation; Multiple Sclerosis Therapy Centre; Roborough Hospital; Rotary Club, Bromley; Salvation Army and Theatre Royal (for a wheelchair lift). There were also various donations of under £500 totalling £18,000.

Exclusions: No grants to students.

Applications: To the correspondent in writing.

The Grantham Yorke Trust

Not known

See below

Martineau Johnson, St Philip's House, St Philip's Place, Birmingham B3 2PP
0121-200 3300

Correspondent: D L Turfrey

Beneficial area: West Midlands, in particular the Birmingham area.

Information available: No recent accounts are on file at the Charity Commission.

General: Very little is known about the grant-making of the trust. It gives grants for education and relief in need to individuals and also appears to give grants to youth organisations. The most recent year for which accounts are on file at the Charity Commission is 1974/75, when it had assets of £648,700 generating an income of £64,200. The income for 1990, the only figure on file at the Charity Commission, was £194,000. We were unable to obtain any further information on this trust, either from the Charity Commission or the correspondent.

Applications: In writing to the correspondent.

The J G Graves Charitable Trust

£75,000 (1993)

General in the Sheffield area

Knowle House, 4 Norfolk Park Road, Sheffield S2 3QE
0114-276 7991

Correspondent: R H M Plews, Secretary

Trustees: G F Young; R S Sanderson; Mrs A H Tonge; T H Reed; R T Graves; Mrs D E Hoyland; S Hamilton; D S Lee; Mrs A C Womack; G W Bridge; P Price.

Beneficial area: Mainly Sheffield.

Information available: Full accounts are on file at the Charity Commission.

General: The trust's objects are "the provision of parks and open spaces, libraries and art galleries; advancement of education and science; the general benefit of the sick and poor; other charitable objects". Grants are concentrated in the Sheffield area and are for capital rather than for running costs.

In 1993, the trust had assets of £1.7 million, an income of £110,000 and gave grants totalling £75,000. Grants usually total £70,000 to £80,000. Surpluses are used to support occasional major projects. In 1993, the main grant was £20,500 to Church Army. Sheffield YWCA received £2,500; Trinity Day Care Trust £2,000; Sheffield Family Service Unit £1,500 and Ecclesfield Chapelgreen Youth Project £1,500. Most grants were for Sheffield or Yorkshire-based organisations; only a small percentage of grants were recurrent.

Exclusions: Grants are generally not made to or for the benefit of individuals.

Applications: In writing to the correspondent. Applications should reach the secretary by 31st March, 30th June, 30th September or 31st December. Applications should indicate whether the applicant is a registered charity, include audited accounts and include a statement giving such up-to-date information as is available with regard to the income and any commitments the organisation has.

The Greater Bristol Foundation

£114,000 (1993/94)

Community projects within about 10 miles of Bristol city centre

PO Box 383, Bank of England Chambers, Wine Street, Bristol BS99 5JG
0117-921 1311

Correspondent: Penny Johnstone, Director, or Alice Berrisford, Grants Officer

Trustees: Peter Durie, Chairman; Sir John Wills; Christopher Curling; David Norton; Anthony Brown; Douglas Claisse; Stella Clarke; Marrion Jackson; David Kenworthy; Phil Gregory; Lady Merrison; Hugh Pye; Jay Tidmarsh; Dereth Wood; Bishop Barry Rogerson.

Beneficial area: Greater Bristol, within ten miles of Bristol Bridge.

Information available: Very full reports and accounts are available from the foundation.

General: This is a fundraising as well as a grant-making charity, seeking to build up an endowment which will be available to meet the charitable needs of Bristol. It is also an agent in managing and distributing specific funds on behalf of other donors. Emphasis is on communities that are at a special disadvantage through lack of opportunities, specific discrimination or poverty. The foundation would like to:

- Strengthen community involvement and action at local level through voluntary organisations, and to be particularly accessible to small neighbourhood groups.
- Support new and existing projects that provide services or opportunities for communities and will contribute to enhancing the quality of life for local residents. The organisations do not have to be based in those commuities.

In 1993/94, the foundation had assets of over £2 million and an income of £211,000, of which £116,000 came from donations. After core expenditure of £99,000 (£16,000 internal administration, £27,000 fund development, £30,000 grants programme and £26,000 initiatives in the community) the trust gave £114,000 in grants.

The four main priority areas are:

Housing and homelessness

Programmes addressing problems faced by people with no home or whose housing is inappropriate, particularly young people, women and those who are at risk on the streets and who may have additional problems. "Homelessness in Bristol has not diminished this year and the trust has sought to address this issue in a number of different ways." Priority will be given to those projects that fall outside immediate statutory provision.

In 1993/94, some of the main grants in this category were: £4,000 to Bristol Methodist Centre to fund a volunteer co-ordinator for a day centre for homeless people; £3,000 to Cold Weather Project, to fund transport costs in an emergency shelter during the winter; £2,000 to ARA towards life skills training for recoverers of addiction, and £1,800 to the Space Trust towards a volunteer co-ordinator providing support and advice to families living in bed and breakfast accommodation.

Isolation

Projects which are focused on isolation amongst older people, young single parents, people being cared for in the community after leaving institutional care, carers themselves and those whom through language barriers, limited access to training and employment opportunities, feel a sense of isolation. Projects relating to Alzheimer's Disease and HIV/AIDS will be welcome.

The grants in this category ranged from £250 to £2,500. Some of the main grants were: Citizen's Advice Bureau (£2,500) towards the costs of the Debt Advisory Service; Bristol Home Start (£1,500) for a training programme for new volunteers to befriend families with young children experiencing difficulties; Bristol Playbus/ Asian Women's Project (£500) towards the mobile community resource service; Inkworks (£2,000) towards a nursery in the community arts centre.

Disability

Programmes which address the issue of access for disabled people, whether through practical modification of buildings, availability of training or access to the full range of social and cultural activities enjoyed by non-disabled people. Projects involving people with learning difficulties will be included in this category. Evidence that disabled people are consulted and involved in the planning of projects, if not actually on management committees, should be provided.

The number of grants given in this category has nearly trebled to 14 in 1993/94. Grants ranged from £500 to £2,500 including £2,000 to Bristol Mencap towards summer playschemes for children with disabilities; £1,000 towards office costs to identify job opportunities for disabled people and £1,000 to Greenhill House Cheshire Home towards a computer for residents to produce a newsletter and other communications.

Young people

The emphasis is on projects working with young people between the ages of 12 and 25, looking at particular needs and working in full consultation with them. Programmes with young people on the management committee will be especially welcome. Preference for projects that motivate, encourage self-esteem and enable young people to play a full and significant part in shaping and being in control of their future. It is hoped that many such projects would include an element of service to the community as well as self-help. Projects involving younger children will be considered, but will not be given priority.

The foundation states: "There is an increasing awareness of the problems facing young people today and a concern from many quarters that provision for this group has diminished". In 1993/94, grants ranged from £480 to £5,000 and were given to 18 groups including: Bedminster Down Girls Club (£2,000) towards the conversion of a small hall for use as a young women's centre; Broad Plains House Youth Club (£800) towards a football coach for a girls team at a youth club; Southmead Weightlifters (£500) towards equipment for this women's group and Youth Holiday Project/Avon & Somerset Constabulary (£1,500) towards the costs of taking young people on an outward bound course in North Wales.

Initiatives relating to community arts and links with Europe have not been included as separate categories. However it is assumed that all of the above categories could include projects of this nature.

Lesser concerns are: one-off events; exhibitions; publications; holiday projects; major capital projects; umbrella organisations; vehicles.

The foundation states it is "always ready to consider exceptionally interesting proposals in any area of work. A strong case would have to be made, amply supported by relevant experts in the field concerned."

Donor Advised

These are grants made on the request of donors who hold funds within the trust and are given to a wide range of organisations including scout groups, Asian women's groups, a photography project, swimming club, nursery projects and a unit for schoolgirl mothers. Small grants of £100 to £500 were given to 15 organisations.

Exclusions: Grants will not normally be given to general appeals, individuals, general overseas travel, fee-paying schools, direct replacement of public funds, promotion of religious causes, medical research and equipment, organisations without a permanent presence in Bristol, or sports without an identifiable charitable element.

Applications: On the form available from the Grants Office, whom potential applicants are advised to speak to informally in the first instance and who will supply detailed guidelines. Applications are considered four times a year in January, April, July and October, but there is a small grants budget for amounts of up to £500 which can be considered between such meetings. All applicants are encouraged to talk to the Director or the Grants Officer before making a formal application. It is likely that the Director or Grants Officer will visit your organisation to discuss your work in more detail before you make a written application. The whole procedure of applying and being awarded a grant usually takes several months.

The Greatham Hospital of God

£120,000 (1993/94)

General in the North East

Estate Office, Greatham Hospital, Hartlepool, Cleveland TS25 2HS
01429-870247; Fax: 01429-871469

Correspondent: G Leggatt-Chidgey

Trustees: Rev D C Couling; D de Guise Walford; Ven P Elliott; Ven G G Gibson; George R Bull; A A Kennedy; N D Abram; Mrs J Foreman; Dr H Welsh; R N Spark; P M T Jackson.

Beneficial area: Cleveland, Co Durham, Northumberland and Tyne and Wear.

Information available: Full accounts are on file at the Charity Commission.

General: The main object of the charity is to provide almshouse accommodation, with grant-making only a secondary purpose. In 1993/94, grants totalled £120,000 of which £29,000 were grants to individuals; these grants are made via the Dioceses of Durham and Newcastle and Social Services departments throughout the region with which the charity has established arrangements. No other applications from or for individuals can be considered. In 1993/94, 28 other grants were given ranging from £200 to £35,000.

All the grants went to organisations in the North East with the emphasis on accommodation related projects and those aimed at the relief of poverty, elderly people and community development including credit unions and employment advice centres. The charity has also provided funding to a number of women's refuges in recent years.

The largest grant, £35,000, was to Butterwick Hospice, which has been a regular beneficiary. However the trustees have recently reconsidered their support for the hospice movement and it is unlikely, due to the level of demand from "less popular" applicants that hospices will be funded in future. Other grants went to: Durham Rural Community Council (£7,500) for community development in East Durham; Benwell Christian Project (£5,000); Friendly Seniors, Middlesbrough (£3,500); Hartlepool Alzheimer's Trust, Hartlepool Women's Aid and Wearside Disablement Centre Trust (£3,000 each); Funding Information North East (a regular beneficiary £2,000). It is thought that about half the grants are for core funding, the others for specific projects.

Exclusions: No grants to organisations or individuals outside the North East. No grants to individuals other than via agencies with which the charity has arrangements. No grants for capital building projects, the acquisition or the repair of buildings. Preference is given to smaller, less popular projects.

Applications: In writing to the correspondent who is willing in the first instance to discuss possible applications on the phone. The grants committee meets in January, April, July and October. All applications should include:
- A clear description of the work for which funding is sought.
- A copy of the latest audited accounts and budget for the year in question.
- Any other information relevant to the application.

The Green Foundation

£69,000 (1993/94)

General, social welfare

Powerbreaker plc, South Road, Templefields, Harlow, Essex CM20 2BG
01279-434561

Correspondent: D R Green

Trustees: Mrs Toby Green; Mrs Kate Birk; H Richard Green; David R Green.

Beneficial area: UK.

Information available: Full accounts are on file at the Charity Commission.

General: The trust was established in 1990 and receives all its income from covenants, Gift Aid and donations. In 1993/94, the trust received no income, it was due after the year end, but still gave grants of £69,000. The income for the previous year was £64,000 and grants totalled £59,000.

51 grants were given with 17 recurrent from the previous year. Over half the grants, and most of the grant total, went to Jewish organisations. The largest awards were to the Foundation for Education (£20,000), Jewish Care (£21,000) and Ravenswood Foundation (£9,000) all regularly among the largest recipients. The largest non-Jewish donation was £4,000 to Spina Bifida & Hydrocephalus Sheltered Workshop.

Most other grants were for £25 to £1,000 with non-Jewish organisations supported including the Masonic Trust for Boys & Girls, NSPCC, North London Hospice, Save the Children Fund and the Samaritans.

Applications: In writing to the correspondent. Applications will not be acknowledged.

The Barry Green Memorial Fund

£105,000 (1992/93)

Animal welfare

Claro Chambers, Horsefair, Boroughbridge, York YO5 9LD

Correspondent: Clerk to the Trustees

Trustees: Richard Fitzgerald-Hart; Mark Fitzgerald-Hart.

Beneficial area: UK with a preference for Yorkshire and Lancashire.

Information available: Accounts are on file at the Charity Commission without a grants list.

General: The trust has recently been formed in accordance with the will of the late Mrs E M Green. It will support animal welfare charities concerned with the rescue, maintenance and benefit of cruelly treated animals.

The trustees report states "payments were made to numerous small charities working within the specified objects of the fund. However, larger payments were made to some larger charities. The trustees continue to seek out smaller charities working at 'grass roots level'. In some cases these have been found to be desperately short of funds while many of the larger ones seem to be well endowed and have substantial reserves despite the general economic recession. The trustees are always willing to consider urgent appeals from small charities working within the objects of the fund which would otherwise have to wind up."

In 1992/93, it had assets of £1.5 million and an income of £106,000 which had dropped from £149,000 in 1991/92. Grants totalled £105,000. Unfortunately no further information was available on the size or beneficiaries of grants.

Applications: In writing to the correspondent.

The Greggs Charitable Trust

£200,000 (1992)

General

Messrs Wilkinson Maughan, Sun Alliance House, 35 Mosley Street, Newcastle-upon-Tyne NE1 1XX

Correspondent: N Calvert

Beneficial area: UK, with a preference for north east England

Information available: Full accounts are on file at the Charity Commission for 1992.

General: In 1992, the trust had assets of £262,000 and an income of £217,000. This included £30,000 from Greggs plc and £173,000 from members of the Greggs family. Grants totalled £200,000. Local causes supported would usually be in the north east of England.

Donations were categorised as follows (1991 figures in brackets):

Arts: 17 grants of £50 to £1,000 totalling £7,300 (£2,750). The largest were: Horse and Bamboo Theatre (£1,000); Northgate Arts Project (£500) and Aldwick Music Festival (£300).

Environment: 6 grants totalling £10,000 (£6,000) including: Greenpeace (£4,000); Northumberland Wildlife Fund and WWF (£2,000 each), others ranged from £250 to £1,000.

Special needs: 29 grants of £100 to £1,500 totalling £16,500 (£6,000). Beneficiaries included: Forest & Gardens Northumbria (£1,500); Blyth Valley Disabled Forum (£1,000); Mental Health Foundation (£500); Friends of the Young Deaf (£250). Grants were also given to individuals.

Medical: 19 grants of £100 to £7,000 totalling £20,500 (£2,850). The main grants were: Children's Foundation (£7,000); Breathe North Appeal and Marie Curie Cancer Appeal (£2,000 each). The other grants were given to a range of national and local organisations.

Elderly: 6 grants totalling £5,500 (£1,850) including £2,000 each to Age Concern, Newcastle and Bakers' Benevolent Society (Greggs plc is a bakers).

Social: 26 grants totalling £40,700 (£10,250), most of which (£23,000) was given to the Tyne & Wear Foundation. The remaining grants were for £100 to £1,500 to a wide range of organisations including: Catholic Care NE (£1,000); Jesmond Swimming Pool Appeal (£1,500); PDSA (£1,500) and Turning Point (£500).

Youth and children: 34 grants totalling £8,000 (£8,900). The largest grant was to Newcastle Compact (£2,000). Other grants ranged from £50 to £500 and were given to scout and guide groups, youth clubs and other youth organisations. Individuals were also supported.

The accounts also included the following geographical breakdown:

Gosforth	£20,700	(£3,400)
Rutherglen	£14,000	(£2,250)
Thurston	£10,500	(£2,500)
Manchester	£15,000	(£2,000)
Braggs	£13,500	(£2,500)
Treforest	£8,750	(£2,000)
Jesmond	£8,500	(£3,500)

Applications: In writing to the correspondent.

The Gresham Charitable Trust

£67,000 (1992/93)

General

Brebner, Allen & Trapp, Chartered Accountants, The Quadrangle, 180 Wardour Street, London W1V 4LB
0171-734 2244

Correspondent: Mrs Woodhams, Personnel Officer

Trustees: R Taylor; P Jay.

Beneficial area: UK.

Information available: Full accounts are on file at the Charity Commission.

General: In 1992/93, the trust had assets (at market value) of £770,000 and an income of £63,000. The trust gave £2,400 each to 28, mainly national organisations, 26 of which had received a grant the previous year. Most recipients appear to receive support for more than two years.

Organisations supported in 1992/93 included: Age Concern; Barnardo's; RNIB; RNID; NSPCC; Spastics Society and three Methodist Church organisations: Little Chalfont; Overseas Division; and Homes for the Aged. Chiltern Hills Charitable Trust, Radio Cracker and the Royal College of Pathologists were last years new recipients. The two new beneficiaries this year were Methodist Church – West London Mission and the Samaritans.

Applications: In writing to the correspondent.

The Grove Charitable Trust

£51,000 (1992)

Jewish, welfare, general

40 Highfield Gardens, London NW11 9HB
0171-609 4181

Correspondent: A Bodner, Trustee

Trustees: A L Bodner; R R Bodner; J Pearlman; B Bodner; M Bodner.

Beneficial area: UK.

Information available: Full accounts are on file at the Charity Commission for 1992.

General: In 1992, the trust had assets of £348,000 and an income of £61,000 from rent received. After expenses of £4,000 the trust gave 31 grants totalling £51,000. The main grants were: Pardes House School (three grants to different addresses in London totalling £18,500); Friends of Laniado Hospital (£16,350) and Service to the Aged (£4,000). All grants were to Jewish organisations, most were in London except for two in Gateshead, five in Israel and one in Manchester. There are also grants to the Edgeware Foundation (£500) and Marie Curie Cancer Care (£100).

Applications: In writing to the correspondent.

The Stanley Grundy Trust

£44,000 (1992/93)

Children and youth, disability

Russell House, 46 Uxbridge Road,
Hampton Hill, Middlesex TW12 3AD
0181-979 7897

Correspondent: L Allum

Trustees: C Southgate; C Ide; L W Allum; Mrs S C Greenhill.

Beneficial area: UK.

Information available: Full accounts are on file at the Charity Commission for 1992/93.

General: In 1992/93, the trust had assets of £311,000 in investments, mainly in Grundy Group Ltd. It had an income of £64,000 including £50,000 from donations. Of 123 applications supported, the trust gave 54 grants broken down as follows:

Organisations:
  National   £5,800   32
  Local   £5,900   22
Support for young people:
  Medical electives £5,200   48
  Operation Raleigh etc. £1,300 13
NBPA grant: branches (4), lunches (3)
  Total   £26,000

The National Back Pain Association received £25,000, with all other grants for £600 or less. Most were for about £100 and were given to a range of charities including youth organisations, medical and welfare charities. The Twickenham Blue Watch received a grant to compete in the 2nd World Fire Fighters Games, Las Vegas.

Applications: In writing to the correspondent.

The Walter Guinness Charitable Trust

£47,000 (1993/94)

General

Biddesden House, Andover,
Hants SP11 9DN
01264-790237

Correspondent: The Secretary

Trustees: Elisabeth, Lady Moyne; F B Guinness; Mrs R Mulji.

Beneficial area: Worldwide, with a preference for Wiltshire and Hampshire.

Information available: Full accounts are on file at the Charity Commission.

General: The trust was set up in 1961, in memory of the settlers' father Walter Edward First Lord Moyne.

In 1993/94, the trust had assets of £1.3 million and an income of £117,000. Almost 100 grants were given totalling only £47,000, we are unsure if the surplus of income over expenditure is due to the trust saving up for the future or if it did not receive enough suitable applications.

The grants were mainly to charities that the trust has supported regularly over the years. 20 grants were for £1,000 to £5,000, the largest of which were to: NSPCC (for Ashdown Centre, Tidworth); International Social Service (UK); Oxford Medical Students Elective; Project Trust; Wiltshire & Berks Canal Amenities Group; Franco-British Parliamentary Relations Committee. The 14 grants of £1,000 were given to education, welfare, medical, overseas and children and youth causes. The trust also supports other causes such as Christian, animal welfare and environmental projects, usually with smaller grants of around £100 to £500.

The trust states, "We are unlikely to be able to support anything unless there is a personal connection, a local connection or unless the organisation has previously been supported by our trust."

Exclusions: No grants to individuals.

Applications: In writing to the corespondent, but most of the funds are committed to existing beneficiaries. "It is not possible for us to reply to an appeal unless the reply is a positive one."

The Gunter Charitable Trust

£50,000 to organisations (1991/92)

Medical, welfare, conservation/ environment

4 John Carpenter Street, London
EC4Y 0NH
0171-615 8000

Correspondent: Bill Gibbs, Partner

Trustees: J de C E Findlay; H R D Bilson.

Beneficial area: UK.

Information available: Full accounts are on file at the Charity Commission up to 1991/92.

General: In 1991/92, the trust had assets of £1 million and an income of £67,000. The trustees gave grants totalling £61,000, of which £11,000 was between seven students. 65 organisations received grants of £100 to £7,000 totalling £50,000. The largest grants were to Friends of Dr Pearey Lal Charity Hospital (£7,000); Save the Children Fund (£3,550); Queen Mary & Westfield College (£3,200); VSO Leeds local group (£3,000 plus £2,500 for the same group for Malawi). A further eight grants of £1,000 to £2,500 were given to charities such as: Friends of the Elderly; Oxfam and St Columba's Hospice.

All other grants were for under £1,000 and were mainly to UK charities, with a few to local organisations. At least six grants were given in Scotland. Medical, welfare and environment/conservation causes are all supported, with other beneficiaries in 1991/92 including the Anglo-Italian Society for the Protection of Animals; Childline; Crossroads, Glasgow; Hampshire & Isle of Wight's Naturalist Trust; Riding for the Disabled; SENSE; Scottish Wildlife Trust and the Sue Ryder Foundation.

Applications: In writing to the correspondent.

The GWR Community Trust

£106,000 (1992/93)

Education, welfare, general

PO Box 2000, Swindon, Wilts SN4 7EX
01793-440300

Correspondent: Jo Wellington, Administrator

Trustees: Richard MacDonnel, Chair; Sir John Cripps; Tom Turvey; Simon Cooper; Rev Francis Ballinger; Fraser Townend; Bill Martin; Marion Michaux; Bill Sims; David Durbin; Elaine Waddington; Shaun Hodgetts; Steve Orchard.

Beneficial area: GWR Radio's transmission area (ie. Bristol, Swindon and Bath and their surrounding areas).

Information available: Full accounts are on file at the Charity Commission.

General: GWR Radio set up the community trust in 1985 to administer funds raised by the station's annual Christmas charity auction appeal. This takes the form of a weekend-long on-air auction broadcast across GWR's entire transmission area (ie. Bristol, Bath and Swindon).

The principal objects of the trust are "to foster and promote the advancement of education and the relief of poverty and sickness". The trustees aim to achieve this by furthering the work of existing charitable organisations and other voluntary groups and, where necessary, supporting the establishment of new ones. They wish especially to encourage new ideas and initiatives within local communities. The chief guidelines applied are as follows:

1. Consideration will be given to the extent to which a project will foster a sense of community.
2. Preference will be given to local community groups over county and regional organisations. It is not the intention of the trustees to assist national organisations through local branches unless the branch has a large degree of autonomy in the expenditure of money to meet local needs.
3. Preference will be given to specific projects rather than to contributions to recurring expenses of general administration and maintenance.
4. Grants will normally be between £50 and £500, but grants of up to £1,000 may be given in special cases.
5. The trustees see merit in projects involving shared resources, and may earmark special funds for suitable schemes.

In 1992/93, the trust had assets of £46,000 and an income of £144,000 including £102,000 from the Christmas auction and £34,000 from Swindon walkathons. Grants totalled £106,000 and are categorised in the annual report by area of benefit.

Most of the money goes to the Bristol, North Wiltshire and Thamesdown areas. The other areas are counties, districts and towns including Avon, Berkshire, Gloucestershire, Somerset, Wiltshire and Oxfordshire. Five individual grants are listed (presumably the larger ones): NSPCC, Swindon (£32,000); Scrapstore (£1,000); Anchor Society (£500); Russ Conway Cancer Fund (£410) and Bristol Initiative (£250).

Applications: Application forms are available on receipt of an sae. Local charities and community groups are invited to apply for a grant by 31st January each year. Some form of financial statement is obligatory.

The Hadrian Trust

£156,000 (1993/94)

Social welfare in the North East

36 Rectory Road, Gosforth, Newcastle-upon-Tyne NE3 1XP
0191-285 9553

Correspondent: John Parker

Trustees: Richard Harbottle; Brian J Gillespie; John B Parker.

Beneficial area: Northumberland, Tyne and Wear, Durham.

Information available: Full accounts are on file at the Charity Commission.

General: The trust was established by Kathleen Armstrong in 1976 and is important for its support of social welfare organisations in the oft-neglected North East of England.

Most grants go towards the running costs of social welfare organisations in the area of benefit. The trust will support organisations which it feels are less likely to get grants from other trusts and will make grants to organisations which are not registered charities but which are doing charitable work. Grants to individuals are only made in exceptional circumstances and almost invariably through a social worker or probation officer.

Applications for capital and revenue projects are treated equally. Repeat applications are considered. Crisis applications can be dealt with outside the quarterly meetings. As only the object need be charitable, the grant will often be made through a CVS or Probation Service. National appeals are not likely to be considered, and almost without exception grants are limited to projects within the area of benefit. The trustees will consider applications from former statutory projects.

In the year to September 1994, donations were distributed amongst the following categories:

Churches	20 grants	£12,500
Social services	64	£80,300
Youth	16	£8,750
Women	9	£5,250
Environment	7	£11,000
Arts	6	£9,500
Elderly & disabled	11	£11,750
Individuals	-	£7,400
Schools & education	2	£3,000
Ethnic minorities	4	£2,250

Most of the 162 grants made during the year were for either £500 or £1,000, although there was one of £10,000 to the Tyne and Wear Foundation, completing a five year commitment towards their start-up costs.

Grants of £5,000 were given to: Beamish Open Air Museum; Northern Sinfonia Development Appeal; Leonard Cheshire (local branch) Red Feather Appeal and the Marie Curie Foundation for Conrad House Hospice.

Grants are wide ranging eg. at one quarterly meeting grants were given to: The Three C's South Shields (camping holidays for deprived children); Them Wifies (training weekend for women's group); Action on Disability (towards purchasing a van for assessing disabled drivers).

Grants are made to individuals via various organisations – social services, relief agencies, disability aid funds, citizens advice bureaux and probation services amongst others.

Exclusions: General appeals from large national organisations and smaller bodies working outside the beneficial area.

Applications: In writing to the correspondent setting out details of the project and the proposed funding. Applications are considered at meetings usually held in October, January, March and July each year, or as otherwise required.

The Alfred Haines Charitable Trust

£152,000 (1993/94)

Christian, health, welfare

c/o Bloomer Heaven, 33 Lionel Street, Birmingham B3 1AB

Correspondent: The Trustees (Ref. DSC)

Trustees: W I Jollie; A L Gilmour.

Beneficial area: Worldwide, with a preference for the West Midlands.

Information available: Accounts are on file at the Charity Commission for 1993/94.

General: In 1994, the trust had assets of £1.6 million, an income of £143,000 and made 138 grants totalling £152,000 (90 grants totalling £105,000 in 1992/93). A significant number of these were to Christian organisations working in the social field. Grants are broken down as follows:

Health, welfare and rehabilitation	34 grants	£38,500
Clubs, centres and local associations	26	£32,750
Housing and homelessness	18	£22,250
Youth work and young people	21	£20,250
Training	15	£16,750
Holidays (especially disadvantaged/disabled)	14	£11,300
Humanitarian aid (including some overseas)	9	£9,500

One other grant was given for £1,000.

Exclusions: No support for individuals, animal charities, church buildings, hospitals and research projects. The trust prefers to support specific projects rather than general running costs.

Applications: The trustees have asked us to have applicants quote reference "DSC", presumably this is to monitor both the number and quality of applications generated by this Guide. Trustees meet bi-monthly to consider written applications for grants. Replies are only sent where further information is required. No telephone calls or correspondence will be entered into for any proposed or declined applications.

Hallam FM – Help a Hallam Child Appeal (Money Mountain Trust)

£88,000 (1994)

Children in South Yorkshire and North Midlands

900 Herries Road, Sheffield S6 1RH
0114-285 3333

Correspondent: Lisa Roseby

Trustees: Bill MacDonald; Tony Parsons; Andrew Darwin; Surriya Falconber; Steve King; Lisa Roseby.

Beneficial area: South Yorkshire and North Midlands.

Information available: The accounts on file at the Charity Commission do not contain a grants list. Most of the information for this entry was supplied by the trust.

General: The trust started in the mid-seventies and has since raised about £500,000. The station has produced a leaflet containing the names of over 70 wide-ranging children and youth charities and organisations in South Yorkshire and the North Midlands that they have supported. The trust also supports individual children and young people, be they ill, disabled or in need of anything from a vital piece of equipment to a toy.

The trust raises money all year round with the climax being an auction day in October. 1993/94 was another record breaking year with the final total raised being £92,000. This included a cheque for £45,000 from McDonalds, through the sale of more than 30,000 badges in their "Big Smile" campaign, and fundraising by staff. Other companies supported the "Three Peaks Challenge", while further money was raised through sponsored walks, raffles, lorry pulls etc..

The correspondent states that no money is retained for administration, wages, overheads, bank charges or for any other reason. Every penny raised for the appeal goes directly to the recipient charities. The number of applicants supported continues to rise. The appeal gave grants totalling £88,000 mainly to organisations working with children. The main grant was the final contribution towards Rygate's Gait Analysis equipment which had been installed previously. This equipment helps children suffering with walking and mobility difficulties, allowing specialists to consider more precise treatments than were previously possible.

Applications: In writing to the correspondent, for consideration at quarterly meetings.

The Hamamelis Trust

£73,000 (1992/93)

Ecological conservation, medical research

c/o Penningtons, Highfield, Brighton Road, Godalming GU7 1NS
01483- 423003

Correspondent: Mrs F Collins, Secretary

Trustees: Michael Fellingham; C I Slocock; Dr Leslie Martin; Duncan Stewart.

Beneficial area: UK but with a special interest in the Godalming and Surrey areas.

Information available: Accounts are on file at the Charity Commission but without a list of grants.

General: The trust was set up in 1980 by John Ashley Slocock and enhanced on his death in 1986. Although the trust is a general trust, the trustees have followed the Settlor's known interests in medical research and conservation of the countryside. The trustees therefore commit about half of the income to medical research and the purchase of equipment and the other half to conservation projects. Grants are for specific projects and usually in units of £5,000 or £10,000.

In 1992/93, the trust had assets of £1.6 million and an income of £91,000. The 14 grants totalled £73,000. In 1991/92, the trust gave 33 grants of £500 to £10,000, these included High Blood Pressure Foundation (£10,000); Surrey FWAG (£5,700) and ten grants of £5,000 including Bath Institute for Rheumatic Diseases; Dorset Respite & Hospice; Guildford Laser Appeal; Sail Training Association; Somerset Trust for Nature Conservation; Youthscan and Scottish Wildlife Trust.

A number of grants are recurrent.

Exclusions: Projects outside the UK.

Applications: To the correspondent. All applicants are asked to include a short synopsis of the application along with any published material and references. Unsuccessful appeals will not be replied to. The trustees usually meet twice a year.

Medical applications are assessed by Dr Leslie Martin, one of the trustees, who is medically qualified.

The Eleanor Hamilton Educational Trust

£81,000 (1993)

Education, general

43 Lancaster Close, St Petersburgh Place, London W2 4JZ
0171-229 0589; Fax 0171-229 5964

Correspondent: Mrs A Khadr, Secretary

Trustees: Lady Hamilton; Mrs J Nyiri; R D Orr; E S Higgins; Q Miskin; E Ribchester; William Brandon.

Beneficial area: UK.

Information available: Full accounts are on file at the Charity Commission.

General: Both national and local charities are supported in a wide range of fields, with most grants going to welfare and medical causes, especially those concerned with children, but with support also for groups concerned with women, wildlife and homelessness.

In 1993, the trust had an income of £88,000 and expenditure of £107,000. About half the grant total is given to individual children for education (but paid direct to the schools) and the rest to other charities.

In 1993, educational grants totalled £41,000 and other charitable grants £40,000. 81 grants were given to organisations, the larger grants being: £5,000 each to Disabled Living Foundation and Possum Trust; £2,000 to Wytham Hall; £1,250 to Winged Fellowship Trust.

Recipients of £1,000 grants included British Agencies for Adoption and Fostering, Centre for Studies in Integrated Education, Contact a Family, Downs Syndrome Association, North London Rescue Commando, London Connection and the Royal Association in Aid of Deaf People. The remaining grants were for £650 or less.

Applications: In writing to the correspondent.

The B Hammer Charitable Trust

Not known

General

47 Highfield Avenue, London NW11 9EU
0181-458 7327; Fax: 0181-458 0551

Correspondent: B Hammer

Trustees: B Hammer.

Beneficial area: Worldwide.

Information available: The trust was registered in 1975. No accounts are on file at the Charity Commission since then.

General: According to the Charity Commission database, the trust had an income of £100,000 in 1991. We have not been able to obtain any further or more up-to-date information.

Applications: In writing to the correspondent.

Sue Hammerson's Charitable Trust

£146,000 (1993/94)

Arts, medicine, welfare, Jewish charities

H W Fisher & Co, Acre House, 11/15 William Road, London NW1 3ER
0171-388 7000

Correspondent: A J Bernstein

Trustees: Sir Gavin Lightman; Richard Mordant; Sydney Mason; Patricia Beecham.

Beneficial area: UK.

Information available: Full accounts are on file at the Charity Commission.

General: The Trust Deed states that after 100 years from the settlement date (1957) or a "specified date", whichever was the earlier, all the capital should be divided between the grandchildren of the settlor. The "specified date" was "the twentieth anniversary of the date of the death of the last to die of all the descendants now living of his late Majesty King George V".

After considering the needs of the Lewis W Hammerson Memorial Home, there is a preference for the advancement of medical learning and research and for the relief of sickness and poverty.

In 1993/94, the trust's assets rose from £5 million to £5.4 million (principally held in Hammerson plc), but gross income dropped from £351,000 to £204,000. Grants totalling £146,000 were given, of which £120,000 was for the Lewis W Hammerson Memorial Home (£224,000 and £50,000 in the previous two years). Only £26,000 was available for other charities. These included some regular beneficiaries: Royal National Theatre £2,500; Royal Opera House £1,500; New Shakespeare Co Ltd and English National Opera (£1,000 each). The remaining funds were distributed in small grants.

A more typical year may be 1991/92, when larger grants were given to the above organisations, with grants also to the Sue and Lew Hammerson Charitable Trust (£11,500), Whittington Hospital Academic Trust Endocrine Research Fund and North London Hospice (£10,000 each). Medical, welfare and arts organisations, many Jewish, were supported and have been on a regular basis.

Exclusions: Grants are made to registered charities only.

Applications: In writing to the correspondent. The trustees stated that funds are heavily committed for the foreseeable future and do not wish to encourage further applications.

The Handicapped Children's Aid Committee

£103,000 (1992)

Equipment for disabled children

28 Beechwood Avenue, Finchley, London N3 3AX
0171-935 5737

Correspondent: P Maurice, Treasurer

Trustees: M Harris, Chairman.

Beneficial area: UK.

Information available: Sporadic accounts are on file at the Charity Commission, the most recent being those for 1992, which did not include a list of donations.

General: The committee was set up in 1961 "to assist organisations concerned with handicapped or under-privileged children". Incorporated into the charity's letterhead is a quote from Abraham Lincoln: "man never stands so tall as when he stoops to help a child".

In 1992, the trust had assets of £476,000 and an income of £201,000. This included £102,000 from legacies and donations, £60,000 from fundraising events and £36,000 income generated by the assets. Grants were given totalling £103,000. No further information is available on the grants given.

Applications: In writing to the correspondent.

The Lennox Hannay Charitable Trust

£155,000 (1991/92)

Health, welfare

Finsbury Dials, 20 Finsbury Street, London EC2Y 9AQ
0171-638 5858

Correspondent: Robert Fleming Trustee Company Ltd

Trustees: Robert Fleming Trustee Company Ltd; Walter L Hannay; Caroline F Wilmot-Sitwell.

Beneficial area: UK.

Information available: Full accounts are on file at the Charity Commission.

General: The trustees did not wish the trust to appear in this Guide, but we maintain our policy of including all relevant grant-makiing trusts.

The trust was established in 1988. In the first four years of operation its grant-giving increased from £83,000 to £155,000. In 1991/92, the trust had assets of £343,000 and an income of £137,000.

56 grants were given ranging from £350 to £16,000, most being for £1,000 or more. The largest went to the Royal Commonwealth Society for the Blind (£16,000); British Deaf Association (£12,000); Sue Ryder Foundation (£10,000), and the Army Benevolent Fund (£7,000). £6,000 grants went to the Royal London Society for the Blind (one of three London charities concerned with blind people to receive a grant), Ex-services Mental Welfare for the Blind, National Society for Cancer Relief, Guide Dogs for the Blind Association and SSAFA. Most of the other grants went to health and welfare charities, the exceptions being the RNLI, St Lawrence Church (Bourton-on-the-Hill) and four animal/wildlife charities including the British Horse Society and Gloucestershire Wildlife Appeal.

49 of the 56 grants were recurrent from the previous year, when grants totalled £104,000. In general, the larger grants went to the same charities in both years.

According to the Charity Commission, the trust had an income of £175,000 in 1994.

Applications: In writing to the correspondent.

The James Hannington Memorial Trust

£94,000 (1991)

Evangelical Christianity

28-29 Oldsteam, Brighton, Sussex BN1 1GF
01273-570030

Correspondent: J A Head, Chairman of the Trustees

Trustees: John A Head, Chairman; Gareth A Stacey; Patrick L Cowley; Rev Alex Ross; John E Puttock; Brian Hogbin.

Beneficial area: Worldwide.

Information available: Full accounts are on file at the Charity Commission.

General: "The trust was formed to receive and distribute the giving of the members of Bishop Hannington Memorial Church, Hove to spreading the Good News of the Lord Jesus Christ outside the parish of the church. Around 97% of the trust's income is designated on receipt from the donors for the support of missionaries, Christian workers and missionary and Christian societies either linked with the Memorial Church or personally supported by those church members. The remaining 3% of the trust's income is used to meet its modest administrative expenses and to make small contributions towards the expenses of church members under training to serve the Lord Jesus outside the parish."

In 1993, the trust had an income of £82,000. It gave 39 grants of £200 to £7,000 to Christian societies and workers totalling £94,000; most had received a grant the previous year.

The main beneficiaries were: Open Doors with Brother Andrew (£7,000); Operation Mobilization and Mid Africa Ministry (£6,600 each); UFM Worldwide and TEAR Fund (£4,500 each). There were 16 grants of £1,000 to £4,000 including the Bible Society, Brighton & Hove Town Mission, Hove YMCA, Open Air Campaigners, Romanian Christians, South American Missionary Society and Youth with a Mission.

Smaller grants of £200 to £700 were given to organisations such as: Aged Pilgrims, Church's Ministry Among the Jews, Intercontinental Church Society, Kisiizi Hospital (Uganda) and Navigators.

Applications: In writing to the correspondent.

The Hanover Charitable Trust

£100,000 (1992)

Jewish, general

Midland Bank Trust Co, 47 London Road, Enfield EN2 6BX
0181-364 6000

Correspondent: S Rhodes

Trustees: Mrs B Klug; Mrs P Sumeray; Midland Bank Trust Co.

Beneficial area: Worldwide.

Information available: Full accounts are on file at the Charity Commission.

General: In 1992, the trust had an income of £60,000 and gave grants totalling £100,000, with a further £30,000 transferred to the CB Trust.

33 grants were made, with 26 to Jewish organisations. The largest was £40,000 to JPAIME, with other large grants to the Friends of the Zionist Educational Trust (two grants of £7,500), Carmel College (two grants of £2,500) and Bournemouth Jewish Blind Aid Society (£4,000).

Non-Jewish recipients of grants were the American Diabetes Association (£2,000), British Sports Association for the Disabled (£1,250), RNIB (£1,000) and Marie Curie Cancer Care (£100).

Applications: In writing to the correspondent.

The Harbour Charitable Trust

£18,000 (1988)

General

Addison Beyer Green & Co, 233-237 Old Marylebone Road, London NW1 5QT
0171-724 6060

Correspondent: Mrs B Green

Trustees: B B Green; Z S Blackman; J F Avery Jones.

Beneficial area: UK.

Information available: We were unable to see this file at the Charity Commission.

General: In 1988, the trust had assets of £660,000 and an income of £50,000. Grants only totalled £18,000.

By 1993, the income had risen to £234,000, but no further information was available on the amount given in grants, or the beneficiaries.

Applications: In writing to the correspondent.

The Harbour Foundation

£93,000 (1993/94)

Jewish, general

8-10 Half Moon Court, Bartholomew Close, London EC1A 7HE
0171-935 8188

Correspondent: S Green, Secretary

Trustees: S R Harbour; A C Humphries; S Green; M D Posen; G M Harbour.

Beneficial area: Worldwide.

Information available: Accounts are on file at the Charity Commission, but with no grants list.

General: The trust was set up to relieve poverty, suffering and distress among Jewish refugees, homeless and displaced people throughout the world. It can also give grants for the advancement of education. Major national charities such as the RSPCA, NSPCC and Help the Aged have also received grants of between £200 and £500.

In 1993/94, the trust had an income of £1.6 million, of which £1.4 million was received under deed of covenant. This is not likely to be repeated. Grants were given totalling £93,000 and the surplus of £1.5 million was added to the assets which now stands at £3.9 million. Unfortunately there is no grants list so we have been unable to find out how many grants were given, what they were for or what type of organisation is supported.

Applications: In writing to the correspondent.

The Hare of Steep Charitable Trust

£44,000 (1993/94)

General

Island Millstone, Steep, Petersfield, Hampshire GU32 1AE
01730-263264

Correspondent: Mrs M E Jackson, Secretary

Trustees: P L F Baillon; R J de C Glover; V R Jackson; A H Marshall.

Beneficial area: UK.

Information available: Full accounts are on file at the Charity Commission.

General: In 1993/94, the trust had assets of £831,000 and an income of only £34,000. This is a fall in income from £49,000 the previous year. The trustees state that this is for two reasons: firstly "on recommendation of our financial advisers we reduced our substantial holding in Scottish & Newcastle Brewery and reinvested proceeds, much of the new income from which was not received until 1994/95"; secondly the tax rebate for the year was not received until 1994/95.

Grants in 1993/94 totalled £44,000, mainly to medical and welfare charities. Only three grants were over £1,500: £3,000 to Petersfield Hospital; £2,000 to REHAB; £1,750 to the Army Benevolent Fund. 45 other grants ranged from £250 to £1,500 including support for a number of service/ex-service charities.

Among those receiving smaller grants were Barnardo's (£750), Hampshire Association for the Care of the Blind (£1,000), Hampshire & Isle of Wight Association of Boys Clubs (£250), Multiple Sclerosis Society (£1,000), SSAFA (£1,000) and WRNS Benevolent Fund (£750). "There is a preference for local charities in the south, particularly Hampshire. The trustees already support as many charities as they could wish and would certainly not welcome any appeals from others."

Applications: In writing to the correspondent, but note the trustees' comment above.

The Harebell Centenary Fund

£121,000 (1992/93)

General, education, medical research, animal welfare

20 Blackfriars Lane, London EC4V 6HD
0171-248 4282

Correspondent: Ms P J Chapman

Trustees: J M Denker; M I Goodbody; F M Reed.

Beneficial area: UK.

Information available: Full accounts are on file at the Charity Commission.

General: This is a relatively new trust. Its general objectives are governed by interests in: "providing scholarships and bursaries for young people in need of help to further their studies; neurological research; and the relief of sickness and suffering animals". The correspondent has updated this to: "concentrate on making donations to registered charities which do not receive widespread public support and to keep administration expenses to a minimum. For this reason the trustees have decided to suport only registered charities and not individuals. The trustees are unlikely to make donations to charities from whom they receive unsolicited materials, preferring to make donations to charities whose work they have come across through their own research. Furthermore, in keeping with their policy of restraining administrative expenses, the decision has been taken not to reply to any unsolicited requests for donations."

In 1993/94, the trust had assets of £1.29 million, an income of £73,000 and gave grants totalling £55,000.

All the requests received during the year were considered in November 1993, using information obtained by Rowe & Maw "to establish the size of the various charities, the percentage of annual income of these charities which was put towards charitable causes rather than administration expenses and the use to which any donations received would be put."

During the year the trust departed from its previous practice and made a smaller number of large donations, rather than a large number of smaller donations. There were 12 grants, six of £7,500 given to: Cancer Relief Macmillan Fund, Canine Partners for Independence, Elizabethan Foundation for deaf children, Haemophilia Society, Princess Alice Hospice and REMAP for technical equipment for disabled people. Other grants included animal welfare and medical causes such as the Cats Protection League and Sussex Wildlife Trust (£1,000 each) and Motor Neurone Disease Association (£1,500).

Applications: In writing to the correspondent. Unsolicited applications will no longer be replied to.

The Harris Charity

£96,000 (1993/94)

Young people in Lancashire

Richard House, 9 Winckley Square, Preston PR1 3HP
01772-821021

Correspondent: P R Metcalf, Secretary

Trustees: W S Huck, Chairman; E C Dickson, Vice-chairman; E J Booth; J Cotterall; T W S Croft; S R Fisher; S Huck; Mrs S Jackson; Mrs C Marshall; Mrs A Scott; S B R Smith; Mrs R Jolly.

Beneficial area: Lancashire, with a preference for the Preston district.

Information available: Full accounts, including the purpose of the grants as well as the beneficiaries, and a report are on file at the Charity Commission.

General: The charity, originally known as the Harris orphanage, was established in 1985 following the sale of the Harris orphanage premises. The proceeds, together with previously held investments, "resulted in a substantial endowment which has been invested for the future benefit of young people under 25 resident in the county of Lancashire, with preference given to borough of Preston".

In 1993/94, the trust had assets of £1.9 million and an income of £115,000. Grants totalled £96,000. Over 120 grants were given to organisations for all types of young people's needs. Grants ranged from just under £100 to £5,000. Examples of grants given are: £5,000 to Derion House Trust for a building project and £4,000 each to Lonsdale District Scout Council for disabled toilet facilities; Lancashire Youth Clubs Association for training resources and sports equipment; a residential course organised by young people, and the Boys' Brigade NW District for showers and drainage to a new sports barn. £3,500 was given to Euxton Villa Football Club to improve facilities.

There were seven grants of £3,000: four to schools towards new minibuses; one each to a cricket club, a tennis club and Guys Farm Activity Centre of the Girl Guides Association towards the construction of first aid rooms, toilets and rest rooms with access for disabled people. Other beneficiaries include playgroups, church groups, youth centres and charities working with disabled young people. Most grants were for less than £1,000.

In addition, a number of grants were given to individuals in respect of the Harris Charity Young Musician of the Guild Competition, in association with National Westminster Bank.

Applications: Application forms can be obtained from the correspondent. Appeals received before 31st March are considered by July each year. Appeals received before 30th September are considered by the following January.

The R J Harris Charitable Settlement

£140,000 (1992/93)

General

Messrs Thrings & Long, Midland Bridge, Bath BA1 2HQ
01225-448494

Correspondent: J J Thring, Secretary

Trustees: H M Newton-Clare, Chairman; T C M Stock; J L Rogers.

Beneficial area: UK, with a preference for west Wiltshire, Avon, north Somerset, and south Gloucestershire.

Information available: Full and detailed accounts are on file at the Charity Commission for 1992/93.

General: The Trust Deed of 1969 directs the trustees to use the income for 40 years for charitable purposes as they see fit. In 1992/93, the trust had assets of £696,000 (valued at £990,000), which had risen from £264,000 (valued at £956,000) the previous year. The income was £80,000 and grants totalled £139,000.

90 grants of £250 to £5,200 were given. The trust appears to support mainly south west-based organisations, particularly in the Avon and Wiltshire area. Unusually, very few grants are given to large, well-known national charities. Grants were categorised by the trust as follows:

Medical and mental health: £58,800 (42.2%)
These included: National Eye Research Centre (five grants of £5,000); Bath Institute for Rheumatic Diseases (four grants of £5,200); Royal National Hospital for Rheumatic Diseases (two grants of £5,000) and Home Farm Trust (£1,000).

The arts: £8,000 (5.7%)
The only grants in this category were to: Bristol Old Vic (£2,000); Bristol Old Vic School (£2,000) and Theatre Royal Bath (£4,000).

Education: £16,000 (11.5%)
Most of these grants were to individuals, the largest part being taken up by four grants to an individual (or individuals) at Sherborne School totalling over £12,000. Ashton Street Adult Training Centre received £250.

Youth organisations and projects: £5,400 (3.9%)
There were ten grants given in this category, three of which were for cub/scout groups in Avon. Other grants were to a Boys' Club, a playgroup, two trusts, two individuals and Fairbridge, Avon. Grants were for between £250 and £1,000.

Social welfare and disabled people: £40,000 (28.9%)
By far the largest number of grants (41) were given in this category ranging from £250 to £5,000. These included: Research Institute for Care of the Elderly (three payments totalling £14,500); West Wiltshire Enterprise (£2,000); Disabled Drivers Association (£500); Bath Churches Housing Association (£500).

Nature conservation, archaeology, building restoration and environment in general: £11,500 (8.3%)
Seven grants ranging from £200 to £5,000. Beneficiaries were Bath Abbey Trust (£5,000); Wiltshire Trust for Conservation

(£3,500); Wiltshire Farming & Wildlife Advisory Group (£2,500 in three grants); World Pheasant Association (£200) and Mells Group of Parishes (£300).

Applications: In writing to the correspondent. Trustees meet three times each year.

The Richard & Frances Harris Charitable Trust

£61,000 (1992/93)

Jewish

Walsh Lawson, 54-62 Regent Street, Piccadilly, London W1R 5PJ
0171-393 9393; Fax: 0171-393 9303

Correspondent: David Walsh

Trustees: Richard M Harris; Frances Harris; David Walsh.

Beneficial area: UK, Israel.

Information available: Full accounts are on file at the Charity Commission.

General: In 1992/93, the trust had an income of £60,000, including £47,000 in covenants and Gift Aid payments. It gave ten grants totalling £61,000. The largest grants were given to Jewish Care (£30,500), JPAIME (£15,000) and Jerusalem Foundation (£10,000). The ten remaining grants, of between £100 and £2,500, were to Jewish organisations and Abbeyfield West London Society.

Applications: The trust states that it "receives so many applications from charities which are known to the trustees that it is extremely unlikely that applications from other charities will produce any donations".

The N & P Hartley Memorial Trust

£51,000 (1992/93)

General

Kennel Farm, Knayton, Near Thirsk, North Yorkshire YO7 4BS

Correspondent: Mrs V Procter, Secretary

Trustees: Edmund Cook; Virginia Procter; John Thompson.

Beneficial area: UK, with an interest in Yorkshire.

Information available: Full accounts are on file at the Charity Commission.

General: In 1992/93, the trust had assets of £868,000, an income of £66,000 and gave 32 grants totalling £51,000. The trustees' report states that emphasis is placed on "children, the elderly and the handicapped."

"In view of the recent substantial number of applications being made as a result of publication of the trust details in several charity journals, the trustees have decided that no applications are to be invited from the general public or other charities and notice is served that they will not be acknowledged or responded to."

"The trustees concentrate on charities in the West Riding of Yorkshire through contacts and channels which are already established and which utilise all of the available funding."

The accounts include a "schedule of disbursements" which covers the last five years. In the past, £10,000 or more has been given to East Cheshire Hospice, Holly Bank Appeal, Crisis, Pontefract Family Care and the Children's Society.

In 1992/93, 32 grants were given, of which 17 had not received any grants in the previous five years. Only one, East Cheshire Hospice, has received a grant every year from 1989, though this was down from £10,000 in previous years to £2,000. Another four organisations have received grants for the last three years: Beverley Croft Hostel (£500); MOVE (£1,000); Kirkwood Hospice (£6,000) and Neuromuscular Centre (£2,000). Other large grants in the year included those to Botton Village (£7,500) and Crossroads Care Scheme (£5,500). Beneficiaries of smaller grants included: Crisis; Care & Repair, Leeds; Mencap, Huddersfield; Oxfam (3 grants, 1 specifically for Uganda, one for India and one for the head office), and Wakefield HIV Centre.

Grants are given for a wide range of charitable purposes with a possible preference for health and social welfare. Grants were given to national organisations and local projects in Yorkshire. They are generally not recurrent, although East Cheshire Hospice has received £41,500 over the last four years, and Kirkwood Hospice £18,000.

Applications: The trust states: "the trustees select the beneficiary charities through a number of existing contacts and we have more than sufficient applications through these contacts". There would, therefore, appear to be little point in applying to the trust, unless there is a personal contact with a trustee.

Gay & Peter Hartley's Hillards Charitable Trust

£54,000 (1993)

Welfare, general

400 Shadwell Lane, Leeds LS17 8AW
0113-266 1424

Correspondent: Mrs Gay Hartley

Trustees: P A H Hartley; S R H Hartley; Mrs R C Hartley; Miss S J H Hartley; A C H Hartley; Miss A E H Hartley.

Beneficial area: Areas served by a Hillard's store, mainly the North of England, especially Yorkshire.

Information available: Full accounts are on file at the Charity Commission.

General: Up to December 1993, the trust had assets of £1 million and gave grants totalling £54,000. The trust distributes its income once a year. Its main priority is to support organisations (especially registered charities) in areas which were served by Hillards stores, supporting poor, needy and sick people. Churches, community centres and schools are also supported. National charities are not usually supported.

In 1992, the trust gave grants to: Christ Church, Ilkley towards a new community centre (£10,000); Leeds Methodist Mission towards building a charities/community centre (£5,000); Camphill Village Trust, a regular beneficiary (£1,000); Salvation Army, Leeds (£1,200); Victim Support, Leeds (£1,000).

Applications: In writing to the correspondent. No application forms are available. Applications should be received before 1st November for consideration in December. Applicants will no longer be acknowledged, as the trust receives an overwhelming number, but will be informed if they have not been successful. Grants will be paid out the following year.

The Hatter (IMO) Foundation

£366,000 (1992/93)

Jewish, general

Messrs BDO Stoy Hayward, 8 Baker Street, London W1M 1DA

Correspondent: J S Newman

Trustees: Maurice Hatter; Norman Freeman; Harold Connick; Jeremy Newman; Richard Hatter.

Beneficial area: Worldwide.

Information available: Full accounts are on file at the Charity Commission.

General: The trust was established in 1987. In its first two years of operation, it received income of £452,000 and £495,000, mostly from covenants. Grants only totalled £2,500 and £7,600 respectively, allowing the trust to build up its assets. In 1989/90, the assets were already about £1.5 million and the income was £636,700 (including £137,000 from investments). Grants totalled £114,000. By 1992/93, the assets had reached £3.4 million and the income was £1.2 million, of which £1 million was from donations and £200,000 from interest. The trust gave 13 grants totalling £366,000, almost all of which was given to Jewish organisations.

The largest grants in 1992/93 were: Haifa University (£161,000) for the Maurice Hatter Fund for Maritime Studies; Special Trust for UCH (£120,000); JPAIME (£33,333); Lubavitch Foundation (£25,000); Prince's Youth Business Trust (£15,000); Lewis Family Charitable Trust (£5,000) and Rambam Research Fund (£3,500). The remaining grants were for £100 to £1,000 and were nearly all to Jewish organisations.

Applications: Unsolicited applications will not be considered.

The M A Hawe Settlement

£66,000 (1992/93)

General, especially in Lancashire

94 Park View Road, Lytham St Annes, Lancashire FY8 4JF
01253-796888

Correspondent: M A Hawe

Trustees: M A Hawe; Mrs G Hawe; Marc G Hawe.

Beneficial area: UK, with preference for Lancashire

Information available: Full accounts are on file at the Charity Commission.

General: The trust has assets of over £4.5 million generating an income of £447,000 in 1992/93. Grants totalled £66,000. The trustees' report states that forthcoming priorities have meant expenditure of £244,000 on a property bought from Lancashire County Council. The trust intends to convert the building to a short-stay hostel for young homeless people.

The range of grants, both in size and destination, was extremely varied, although a number of beneficiaries have received a grant in each of the five years of the trust's operation. A high proportion of the grants have also gone to Lancashire-based organisations. Grants ranged from £5 up to £11,500 given for the welfare of retired Roman Catholic priests in the Lancaster diocese.

£11,000 each went to Fylde Coast Women's Refuge and to buy an incubator for use in the former Yugoslavia. Grants of £5,000 went to Derian House, the Reverend Father Yeend and the Holy Cross Church and Soup Kitchen. Childline received £4,500 with a further £13,500 promised. Other beneficiaries included Peartree School and the Ringway Tutorial Centre (both £2,000); Vincent House (£1,500); Autistic Resource Centre and Streetlife Trust (both £1,000). Grants of under £1,000 went to Barnardo's, Fylde & Wyre Dyslexia Association, Macmillan Nurse Appeal, Manchester's Booth Hall Childen's Hospital and Veteran Car Club's Charity Appeal.

Applications: In writing to the correspondent.

The Hawthorne Charitable Trust

£5,000 (1993/94)

General

c/o Messrs Baker Tilly, 2 Bloomsbury Street, London WC1B 3ST
0171-413 5100

Correspondent: Roger Clark

Trustees: Mrs A S C Berington; R J Clark.

Beneficial area: UK.

Information available: Full accounts are on file at the Charity Commission.

General: The trust was registered in 1964. In 1993/94, the trust had assets of £2.8 million and an income of £82,000. Donations totalled only £5,000 (£259,000 in 1991/92 and £46,000 in 1992/93).

The trust had accumulated income of £114,000 by 1993/94. This was distributed in 1994/95.

In 1993/94, the grants were given to World Society for the Protection of Animals (£3,000); Society of Friends of Little Malvern Priory (£1,000), and Headway Worcester Trust Ltd and Museums & Galleries Commission (£500 each).

Exclusions: No grants to individuals.

Applications: In writing to the correspondent.

The Haymills Charitable Trust

£52,000 (1993)

Youth, education, medical

Empire House, Hanger Green, Ealing, London W5 3BD
0181-997 5602

Correspondent: I W Ferres, Secretary to the Trustees

Trustees: G A Cox; E F C Drake; A M H Jackson; K C Perryman; J A Sharpe; J L Wosner; I W Ferres.

Beneficial area: UK.

Information available: Full accounts are on file at the Charity Commission.

General: The trust was set up by the late Dudley Cox and Geoffrey A Cox. In 1984, it changed its name from Haymills Charitable Trust to the Dudley Cox Charitable Trust and then, in 1991, changed it back again to the Haymills Charitable Trust.

In 1992/93, the trust had assets of £672,000 and an income of £78,000. It gave grants totalling £52,000 in the following categories:

Youth and welfare organisations: 25 grants totalling £25,000, £2,600 of which was given to six individuals. The largest grants were to: Raleigh Trust (£3,400, including sponsoring an individual); Inter Action - HMS President and Middlesex Association of Boys' Clubs (£3,000); Aldeburgh Foundation (£2,600) and £2,000 each to Project Trust and Young Enterprise Scheme. £1,500 was also given to the Salvation Army, a regular beneficiary. There were five grants of £1,000 to: the Building Industry Youth Trust; Police Foundation; St Loyle's College for Training the Disabled; Royal Anniversary Trust and Lord Mayor Treloar College.

Educational establishments: Eight grants totalling £17,600. The largest were to: Merchant Taylors' Company (two grants totalling £5,000); Thames Valley University (£3,000 towards the Haymills Chair of Accountancy) and Heathfield School (£1,000 towards an individuals fees). £7,000 was given in general grants and towards a learning and resource centre. Four grants are annual payments.

Medical bodies and hospitals: Four grants totalling £7,000. £2,000 went to each of: Ealing Hospital League of Friends, Central Middlesex Hospital League of Friends and the Royal College of Physicians. Mount Vernon Post Graduate Medical Centre received £1,000.

The trust also gives grants to present and past employees of the Haymills Group of companies.

Applications: In writing to the correspondent, though applications are not necessarily acknowledged.

May Hearnshaw's Charity

£129,000 (1991/92)

General

The Law Partnership, City Plaza,
Sheffield S1 2GU
0114-270 0999

Correspondent: David Law

Trustees: David Law; Jack Rowan.

Beneficial area: UK.

Information available: Accounts are on file at the Charity Commission.

General: This trust was set up by the will of the late May Hearnshaw who died in 1988. During the administration of the estate, grants were given totalling £244,000 largely to national and local charities specified during the settlor's lifetime.

The trust has assets of about £1.5 million, and the income is expected to be in the region of £75,000 a year. In 1991/92, grants totalled £129,000 to charities benefiting wholly, or mainly, people living in the UK.

Exclusions: No grants to individuals.

Applications: Unsolicited applications are counter-productive. "The trustees make their selections from Charity Choice and similar publications and do not want to receive a volume of paper work. Verbal applications are not considered."

The Mrs C S Heber Percy Charitable Trust

£82,000 (1993/94)

Health, general

c/o Kleinwort Benson Trustees Ltd,
PO Box 191, 10 Fenchurch Street,
London EC3M 3LB
0171-956 6600

Correspondent: The Secretary

Beneficial area: Worldwide.

Information available: Full accounts are on file at the Charity Commission.

General: In 1993/94, the trust had assets of £1.3 million and an income of £54,000 (£188,000 in 1990/91 including £105,000 in donations, partly from the Sir Cyril Kleinwort Charitable Settlement). The trust appears to have a preference for medical, elderly and overseas causes.

29 grants were given totalling £82,000, including £50,000 to International Health and Bio Medicine. This organisation appears to have received around £50,000 in a number of recent years. Large grants were also given to the Life Education Centre (£15,000), BRACE (£5,000), Sue Ryder Homes - Leckhampton Court (three payments totalling £4,000) and Foundation for the Study of Infant Deaths (£1,500). £1,000 was given to both the Museum for Hunting Trust and St Peter's Church - Upper Slaughter. Other beneficiaries included: Cotswold Canal Trust; Friends of the Elderly; Hunt Servants Benevolent Society; Medjugarje Appeal; VSO.

Exclusions: Individuals are not supported.

Applications: To the correspondent in writing.

Help the Homeless

£38,000 (1993/94)

Homelessness

Yeoman House, 168-172 Old Street,
London EC1V 9BP
0171-336 7774

Correspondent: Ms V Knibbs, Secretary

Trustees: Archbishop of Canterbury, President; Sir Robert Mark and Rev Austen Williams, Vice Presidents; F J Bergin; E G Jones; L A Bains; H J Stearn; B H Woods; T S Cookson.

Beneficial area: UK.

Information available: Full accounts are on file at the Charity Commission.

General: In 1993/94, the trust had assets of £432,000 and an income of £75,000. After expenses of £10,000, it gave five grants totalling £38,000 and had a surplus of £26,000. The main grant was once again given to National Association for Voluntary Hostels (£35,000). Other beneficiaries were Front Housing Advice & Referral Agency and Tower Hamlets Mission (£1,000 each), Homeless Action (£800) and Spear Ltd (£402).

In 1992/93, 14 grants were given totalling £68,000, nearly all of which was given to National Association for Voluntary Hostels (£55,000, and £79,000 in 1991/92, £26,000 in 1990/91 and £96,000 in 1989/90). Third House Trust and Stockton Churches received £2,000 each and six charities received around £1,000 each including Spear Ltd, Keyhouse Project, Haven Night Shelter, Rugby Mayday Trust and Vincent House. Other grants were for up to £500 to mainly local women's groups and churches.

The majority of grants are given in the London area, where homelessness is particularly acute/visible. Grants are given only for capital expenditure.

Applications: In writing to the correspondent.

Help the Hospices

£368,000 (1993/94)

Hospices

34-44 Britannia Street, London WC1 9JG
0171-278 5668

Correspondent: Terry Taylor, Chief Executive

Trustees: Rt Hon Lord Hayhoe, President; Sir Robert Evans and Martin Lewis, Vice Presidents; Duchess of Norfolk, Chairman; Michael Bayley; Philip Byam-Cook; Ronald Griffin; Dr Peter Griffiths; Dr Andrew Hoy; Dr George Mitchell; Mrs Hilary McNair; Prof Peter Quilliam OBE; Mrs Angela Walton; Prof Eric Wilkes OBE.

Beneficial area: Worldwide.

Information available: Accounts are on file at the Charity Commission.

General: The trust's activities include:

(a) Grants to local hospices (NHS or voluntary) and Home Care Teams. Priority is given to funding equipment for assisting patient care, including syringe drivers, special beds, bathroom equipment etc.. Help is also given to initiate new and improved hospice services, such as physiotherapy, use of creative arts, better medical cover and facilities for the care of AIDS patients and those with other life-threatening or terminal illnesses. Particular help is given to hospices which have been established recently.

(b) Training for hospice staff and education of the public. This includes medical fellowships to train doctors in the techniques of pain and symptom control, basic courses for nurses and tutors, and special courses on management, counselling and bereavement.

(c) Research funding following satisfactory refereeing and publication.

(d) Advisory services to hospices.

In 1993/94, the trust had assets of £1.14 million and an income of £798,000. Grants totalled £368,000 with a further £288,000 spent on education and training.

Exclusions: No grants for major capital costs.

Applications: On a form available from the correspondent, Brendan O'Mahoney. The grants committee meets every six weeks, and applications should be received four weeks beforehand.

The G D Herbert Charitable Trust

£48,000 (1993/94)

General

Tweedie & Prideaux Solicitors, 5 Lincoln's Inn Fields, London WC2A 3BT

Correspondent: J J H Burden, Trustee

Trustees: M E Beaumont; J J H Burden.

Beneficial area: Worldwide.

Information available: Full accounts are on file at the Charity Commission.

General: In 1993/94, the trust had assets of £1.2 million and an income of £47,000. 29 grants were made totalling £48,000.

Most of the grants were for £1,500. The only larger grants were to the National Trust (£3,000) and Oxfam and Save the Children Fund (both £2,800 – these are the final intended donations after a number of years support). Recipients of £1,500 included the Abbeyfield Society, Aged in Distress, National Association of Boys' Clubs, NSPCC, PDSA, Professional Classes Aid Council, Rainer Foundation, Royal College Surgeons of England, Shelter, St Christopher's Hospice and the Woodland Trust.

Applications: In writing to the correspondent. No applications are invited other than from those charities currently supported by the trust.

The Hereward FM CNFM & KLFM Appeal (previously known as the Hereward Radio Appeal)

£126,000 (1992/93)

Disability

PO Box 225, Queensgate Centre, Peterborough PE1 1XJ
01733-460460

Correspondent: Jane Piercey, Appeals Co-ordinator

Trustees: H W Giltrap, Chairman; S Francis; R W Bird; D Ball; I Stockwell.

Beneficial area: Peterborough area (Hereward Radio franchise area).

Information available: The information for this entry was supplied by the trust.

General: The trust has a year long appeal, with the main fundraising drive being from autumn until Christmas. Grants are given to organisations working with disabled people in the Peterborough area, namely the region covered by Hereward Radio Station.

In 1992/93, the trust had assets of only £17,000, but an income of £139,000. The Christmas auction raised £63,000 and the Thomas Cook Fun Run raised £24,000. It had expenses of £55,000 but gave grants totalling £126,000. According to Charity Trends 1993, the appeal is the sixth largest in the broadcasting category behind national appeals such as Children in Need, Comic Relief, Blue Peter and Capital Radio's Help a London Child.

During the year, six minibuses were presented to local charities including: Heltwate Special School, Bretton; St Peter's Resource Centre, Eye and Fenland, and Mind, Peterborough. These were presented by Sir Jimmy Saville, Kris Akabusi and Roger Black. A heating system (£4,300) was provided at Castle Project Workshop, Cambridge, for people who are mentally ill, and equipment for a resource room (£1,800) at Camsight at Oakington, near Cambridge. £19,000 was given in three grants for the East of England Show outing and £7,500 to Milton Children's Hospice.

Applications: In writing to the correspondent.

The Heritage of London Trust Ltd

£143,000 (1993/94)

Restoration in Greater London

23 Saville Row, London W1X 1AB
0171-973 3809

Correspondent: Sir John Lambert, Director

Trustees: Board of Management: William Bell, Chairman; Sir Hugh Cubitt; Sophie Andreae; Ronald Barden; Ashley Barker; Alistair Buchanan; Bridget Cherry; Robert Chitham; Baroness Gardner of Parkes; Norman Howard; Michael Medlicott;

Gordon Passmore; Ronald Peet; James Pilditch; Sir Angus Stirling; Robert Vigars; Sir William Whitfield; Lady Gibson; Sir Robin Dent.

Beneficial area: Greater London.

Information available: Full accounts are on file at the Charity Commission.

General: The principal activity of the charity is to support the conservation and restoration of buildings of architectural and historical interest in Greater London.

Following the demise of the GLC, the trust lost its main public sector support. This has been partly replaced by assistance from the London Boroughs Grants Scheme. It receives technical support from English Heritage. The trust seeks to obtain partners to match their own contribution wherever possible.

In 1993/94, grants ranged from £500 to £10,000. The largest was to St Pancras Chambers (£10,000). About half the grants were offered to churches. Other beneficiaries included Salisbury House, Edmonton; Caledonian Market Clock, Islington and the Ragged School Museum, Bow.

In 1992/93, the trust had assets of £303,000 and an income of £129,000, £14,000 of which was a grant from London Borough Grants Scheme and £115,000 from donations. £25,000 was spent on consultancy fees. Grants were given totalling £24,000, the largest of which were: St Andrew's, Enfield (£5,000); Theatre Royal, Stratford East and Croydon Fund, St Marks, S Norwood (£4,000 each); and Chelsea Riverside Benches (£3,000). Other grants were for £1,000 to £2,000 and included: Guys Hospital Statue; HOLT Operations and Richmond Socy River God Fund.

A further £64,000 was approved but not yet distributed. The provision for grants approved but not yet given date back to 1985/86. These grants include a number for churches, such as £5,000 each for Trinity Church, Brixton and St John's Church, Waterloo Road.

Applications: In writing to the correspondent, after which a site visit may be made. Board meetings are held three times a year.

The Hesed Trust

£40,000 (1992/93)

Christian

14 Chiltern Avenue, Cosby, Leicestershire LE9 1UF
0116-286 2990

Correspondent: G Rawlings, Secretary

Trustees: G Rawlings; B Shutt; R J Aubrey.

Beneficial area: Worldwide.

Information available: Accounts are on file at the Charity Commission, but without a list of grants.

General: In 1992/93, the trust had an income of £77,000. Expenditure included £40,000 under the heading "gifts to other charities" but no further information was available.

Applications: In writing to the correspondent.

The Bernhard Heuberger Charitable Trust

£37,000 (1992/93)

Jewish

45 Cranbourne Gardens, London NW11 0HU
0181-807 5555

Correspondent: B Hueberger, Secretary

Trustees: B Heuberger; D H Heuberger; S N Heuberger.

Beneficial area: Worldwide.

Information available: Accounts are on file at the Charity Commission.

General: The trust was established in 1986. In 1992/93, it had assets of £2.8 million and an income of £197,000. Expenses totalled £39,000 and grants £37,000, leaving a surplus for the year of £120,000. The trust appears regularly to have a large surplus. It is not known if this is to build up assets, if it is saving for any major projects or if it simply did not receive enough suitable applications.

All grants were given to Jewish organisations, most of which were based in the UK. It is not known how many, if any, were recurrent. We were unable to obtain any further information on the grants made.

Applications: In writing to the correspondent.

The P & C Hickinbotham Charitable Trust

£64,000 (1992/93)

Social welfare

69 Main Street, Bushby, Leicester LE7 9PL

Correspondent: Mrs C R Hickinbotham

Trustees: Mrs C R Hickinbotham; P F J Hickinbotham; R P Hickinbotham.

Beneficial area: UK, with a preference for Leicestershire and the East Midlands.

Information available: Full accounts are on file at the Charity Commission.

General: In 1992/93, the trust had assets of £682,000 and an income of £50,000. Grants totalled £64,000 and were mainly given in Leicestershire and the East Midlands.

The trust gives occasional, one-off larger grants usually between £5,000 and £20,000. In 1992/93, there was an exceptional grant of £50,000 to Age Concern Leicester (a regular recipient; in the previous three years they have received £10,000, £49,000 and £5,000). Other grants included: Richard Attenborough Centre for Disabled and the Arts (£5,000) and Society of Friends (15 grants of £100 to £250 totalling around £3,000 to local groups from London to Glasgow). There were three grants of £1,000 to two Quaker and one local project. All other grants were for up to £500.

Grants are generally not recurrent and are largely to social welfare organisations, and also to some churches and Quaker meetings. They are mainly under £500. The trust also gives some smaller grants to a variety of registered charities.

Exclusions: No grants to individuals applying for bursary type assistance.

Applications: In writing to the correspondent, giving a brief outline of the purpose of the grant. Replies will not be sent to unsuccessful applicants.

The Higgs Charitable Trust

£47,000 (1994)

General

Messrs Moger & Sparrow, 24 Queen Square, Bath BA1 2HY
01225-444882

Correspondent: J M Gaynor

Trustees: J M Gaynor; T W Higgs; Mrs L Humphris.

Beneficial area: UK, and local in Avon.

Information available: Full accounts are on file at the Charity Commission.

General: Since the trust was set up, it has distributed £686,000 mainly to national charities and charities in the Avon area. In 1994, the trust had assets of £640,000 and an income of £46,000. About 88 grants were given totalling £46,500.

£25,000 was given to TWJ Foundation (an annual beneficiary), £2,000 each to the Jobson Foundation and Skinners Company and £1,000 to the Rwanda Emergency Appeal. £800 was given to BCVS Homes and £500 each to Avon Weirs Trust, British Red Cross, Edinburgh Gynaecological Cancer Fund, Linton Lock Supporters Club, PDSA, River Wye Restoration Fund, Severn Navigation Restoration Trust, Whale & Dolphin Conservation Society and an individual.

The remaining grants of £100 to £300 were mainly to medical, welfare, wildlife and children-related organisations such as Army Benevolent Fund, Barnardo's, CRUSE, Great Ormond Street Hospital, Leukaemia Research Fund, Pellipar Festival, Salvation Army and the Woodlands Trust. Most grants were recurrent from the previous year and went to national or Avon-based organisations, with a preference for health and social welfare. The trust usually appears to give more grants of £500 or over than in this year.

Applications: In writing to the correspondent, not less than two months before the annual general meeting in November.

The Charles Littlewood Hill Trust

£117,000 (1994)

Health, disability, service, children (including schools)

Eversheds, 14 Fletcher Gate, Nottingham NG1 2FX
0115-936 6000

Correspondent: Mrs Rees, Secretary

Trustees: W D Crane; J A L Barratt; C W L Barratt; W F Whysall.

Beneficial area: UK, with an interest in Norfolk and Nottingham.

Information available: Accounts are on file at the Charity Commission, but without a list of grants

General: In 1994, grants totalled £117,000. No further information is available for this year. In 1993, the trust had an income of £120,000 and gave grants totalling £170,000.

Recently there has been no grants list, but the list for 1990 shows that the trust gave 54 grants of between £500 and £10,000. The largest was £10,000 to the Norfolk Child Care Centre. Grants of £5,000 each went to Claremont School, Nottingham, St John's Ambulance and St Mary's Trust; £3,000 to the Winged Fellowship Trust; and £2,500 each to the Children's Haven Appeal, Norwich & Norfolk Far East POW's Association and the Royal Norfolk Military Heritage Appeal.

The trust also gave 32 grants for £1,000, and 13 for £500. Grants are given to local and national charities in the fields of health and disability, service and children and there may be a slight preference for charities in the Norfolk and Nottingham areas.

Applications: In writing to the correspondent including the latest set of audited accounts. Unsuccessful applications will not be acknowledged.

The Hinrichsen Foundation

£13,000 (1992/93)

Music

10-12 Baches Street, London N1 6DN
01372-375138

Correspondent: The Secretary

Trustees: Mrs C E Hinrichsen; P Strang; K Potter; Prof A Whittall; M Davies; P Standford; I Horsbrugh; S Walsh.

Beneficial area: UK.

Information available: Full accounts are on file at the Charity Commission.

General: In 1992/93, the trustees report stated: "The Hinrichsen Foundation is a charity devoted to the promotion of music. Although the objects of the trust are widely drawn, the trustees have decided for the time being to concentrate on assisting in the 'written' areas of music, that is, assisting contemporary composition and its performance and musical research."

During the year, the trust had assets of £29,000 and an income of £69,000, including £60,000 from dividends from Peters Edition. Grants totalled only £13,000, but the trust did have commitments to pay a further £43,000 within one year. A further £38,000 was given in respect of grants approved in the previous year. Grants were also given to individuals.

Grants to organisations were given to national and local groups throughout the UK. All grants (given or approved) were for music theatres, festivals, ensembles and orchestras. The largest was to Huddersfield Contemporary Music Festival, a regular beneficiary (£6,000). All other grants were for £500 to £2,500 and included: Music Projects, London and Rainbow Over Bath 93/94 (£2,500 each); Sonic Arts Network (£2,000); Contemporary Music Ensemble of Wales (£1,500); Little Missenden Festival (£750) and Milton Keynes Chorale and Lowry Piano Trio (£500 each).

Applications: In writing to the correspondent.

The Hobart Charitable Trust

£1,500 (1992/93)

Education, religion

140 Trustee Company, 36 Broadway, London SW1H 0BH
0171-973 8044

Correspondent: C H Rawlings, Company Secretary

Trustees: Rt Hon Viscount Camrose; Rt Hon Viscountess Camrose; Rt Hon Baron Hartwell.

Beneficial area: UK.

Information available: Accounts are on file at the Charity Commission, but without a list of grants.

General: The trust was established in 1989. In the four years of its operation up to 1992/93 its assets rose to £318,000, while its income rose from £44,000 to £115,000. This includes a "distribution of income from discretionary settlement" which was £42,000 in 1990/91 and £95,000 in the last two years.

The grant total was only £1,500 in 1992/93, having been £8,900, £16,300 and £6,500 in the previous three years respectively. No information was available on the beneficiaries. Presumably as the assets continue to rise, the trust will start to spend more of its income in grants.

Applications: In writing to the correspondent.

Hobson Charity Ltd

£143,000 (1992/93)

Social welfare, education

21 Bryanston Street, Marble Arch, London W1H 7AB
0171-499 7050

Correspondent: A E Broomfield

Trustees: R F Hobson; P M Hobson; Sir Donald Gosling.

Beneficial area: UK.

Information available: Full accounts are on file at the Charity Commission.

General: In 1990/91, the trust had assets of only £89,000, but had an income of £139,000, of which £135,000 was received as a donation. In 1992/93, the trust had an income of £364,000, of which £360,000 was received as a donation. Grants were given totalling £143,000, leaving a surplus of £217,000 to add to the assets, now £302,000.

Of the grants given, 13 were for £3,000 to £33,000 and three had received a grant the year before: Barnet Mayor's Appeal for Leukemia Children (£20,000 and £10,000 in 1991/92); Childline (£25,000 in both years), and English National Opera (£12,500 and £25,000 in 1991/92).

The other grants included: £33,000 to Salisbury Cathedral Spire Trust; £10,000 each to Providence Row Charity, Save the Children Fund and Chigwell Police Show; £5,000 to Royal Free Hospital School of Medicine and Max Jaffa Scholarship Fund, and £3,000 to each of Sea Cadet Corps, Astrid Trust, Gosport/Fareham Rescue Service and the Royal Submarine Museum.

Applications: In writing to the correspondent.

The Holst Foundation

£70,000 (1989/90)

Arts

Messrs Forsythe Kerman, 79 New Cavendish Street, London W1M 8AQ
0171-637 8566

Correspondent: Peter Carter, Secretary

Trustees: Ken Haswell; Dr Colin Matthews; Noel Periton; Rosamund Strode; Bryan Northcott; Prof Arnold Whittall; Peter Carter.

Beneficial area: UK.

Information available: Accounts up to 1989/90 are on file at the Charity Commission.

General: The trust has two objects: firstly, to promote public appreciation of the musical works of Gustav and Imogen Holst and secondly, to encourage the study and practice of the arts.

In practice the trust tends to be pro-active. Funds are available almost exclusively for the performance of music by living composers. An annual awards scheme is offered to performing groups who wish to commission new work. The trust has historical links with Aldeburgh in Suffolk and is a major funder of new music at the annual Aldeburgh Festival.

In 1989/90, about 75 grants were given totalling about £70,000. Recipients included the Almeida Festival and the Huddersfield Festival (both about £2,500). £12,000 was given under the annual awards scheme for four commissions.

Exclusions: No support for the recordings or works of Holst that are already well supported.

Applications: In writing to the correspondent.

The Homelands Charitable Trust

£191,000 (1992/93 - but see below)

The New Church, health, social welfare

c/o Alliotts, Ingersoll House, 9 Kingsway, London WC2B 6XF
0171-240 9971

Correspondent: Mrs Taylor, Secretary

Trustees: D G Ballard; L D Casbolt.

Beneficial area: UK.

Information available: Full accounts are on file at the Charity Commission.

General: This trust is unusual in that both the capital and income, although administered as one, are allocated to individual settlors (which makes it complicated to tot up which organisations got what). The settlors were four members of the Curry family and the original endowment was in the form of shares in the Curry company. H F Curry and the Rev Clifford Curry are now deceased but four funds are maintained. Two original settlors, Misses Elizabeth and Freda Curry, each have their own allocation, whilst two further parts are distributed by the Rev C Curry Junior and the trustees as a whole.

The trust's objectives are "to support a wide range of general charitable causes, together with special emphasis towards contributions to the general conference of the New Church, medical research and the care and protection of children".

In 1992/93, the trust had assets of £1.6 million and an income of £119,000.

£132,000 was allocated in charitable donations from its general unrestricted fund and £59,000 was gifted to Southampton General Hospital from its Hospital Fund.

Annually the trust continues its New Church commitments to the General Conference of the New Church and the Bournemouth Society of the New Church. These received £29,000 and £33,000 respectively in 1992/93 whilst the New Church College received £15,400.

Other larger grants, apart from £8,000 to the Broadfield Memorial Trust were given mainly to well-known national organisations: RNLI (£5,700); NSPCC (£5,550); Action Research (£5,200); Oxford Committee for Famine Relief (£5,000).

Applications: In writing to the correspondent.

The Homestead Charitable Trust

£32,000 (1992/93)

General

B M Birnberg & Co, 103 Borough High Street, London SE1 1NN
0171-403 3166

Correspondent: B N Birnberg

Beneficial area: UK.

Information available: Full accounts are on file at the Charity Commission.

General: Most of this trust's income comes from dividends from Park Lane Hotel plc. In 1992/93, it received £32,000 in dividends (out of a total income of £47,000). Grants totalled £32,000 (£38,000 the previous year).

12 grants were given to organisations with the Breast Cancer Research Trust receiving £10,000. Three grants of £5,000 went to Guide Dogs for the Blind, Co-workers of Mother Theresa and the Society of St Peter the Apostle.

Other grants went to a range of charities including the Dog Rescue & Welfare Society (£500), Anthony Nolan Bone Marrow Trust (£100), Turner Exhibition Fund (£2,000), two Church of England church schools and three churches including one Roman Catholic.

Three beneficiaries also received a grant the previous year, with all the remaining grants in 1991/92 to health or welfare causes.

Applications: In writing to the correspondent.

Sir Harold Hood's Charitable Trust

£180,000 (1992/93)

Roman Catholic

31 Avenue Road, St John's Wood, London NW8 6BS
0171-722 9088

Correspondent: Sir Harold Hood

Trustees: Sir Harold J Hood; Lady Ferelith R Hood; Kevin P Ney; Mrs Margaret Gresslin.

Beneficial area: Worldwide.

Information available: Full accounts are on file at the Charity Commission.

General: In 1992/93, Sir Harold Hood added investments to the trust with a market value of £133,000, and cash of £24,000, bringing the value of assets to £758,000. There was also a profit on the sale of investments of £50,000.

£56,000 was given in 17 grants out of an ordinary income of £50,000 (see below). A further £124,000 was given out of capital, but there were no details about this.

The largest of the 17 grants were to the Royal Naval Ecclesiastical Fund for the Sisters Rowner (£6,000) and Montford House and Catholic Council for Polish Welfare (£5,000 each). £4,000 was given to each of Little Sisters of the Poor, Lambeth; Poor Sisters of Nazareth, Hammersmith; Catholic Housing Aid Society; Holy Cross Hospital, Haslemere and Handicapped Children's Pilgrimage Trust. There were two grants of £3,000 and seven of £2,000 for church buildings, homelessness, hospices and leprosy/sickness. All grants were to Catholic organisations.

Exclusions: No grants for individuals.

Applications: In writing to the correspondent. Applications are considered in late November.

The Hoover Foundation

£131,000 (1991/92)

Education, health, welfare

Pentrebach, Methyr Tydfil, Mid-Glamorgan CF48 4TU
01685-721222

Correspondent: Mrs Marion Heaffey

Trustees: D M Metcalfe; D Thomas; C Knight.

Beneficial area: National, but with a special interest in the South Wales and Glasgow areas.

Information available: Accounts, but without details of donations made, are on file at the Charity Commission.

General: The trust is "primarily committed to supporting children and locally based charitable works in and around the immediate areas of our employee locations".

In 1991/92, the trust had assets of £2 million generating an income of £150,000 (about the same for 1993/94). Grants totalled £131,000 and are categorised as follows in the accounts (1992/93 figures in brackets):

Education	£81,000	(£70,000)
Medical and welfare	£56,000	(£18,000)
Youth organisations	£8,000	(£8,000)
Other activities	£4,000	(£18,000)

Exclusions: Few grants for individuals.

Applications: In writing to the correspondent.

The A S Hornby Educational Trust

£166,000 (1993/94)

English as a foreign language

8 Singers Close, Henley-on-Thames, Oxon RG9 1HD
01491-575177

Correspondent: D M Neale

Trustees: D M Neale; P C Collier.

Beneficial area: Worldwide.

Information available: Full accounts are on file at the Charity Comission.

General: The trust was set up for the advancement of the English language, its teaching and learning as a foreign language, and especially to provide scholarships and grants to enable foreign teachers to come to the UK to study teaching English as a foreign language.

The overall finances of the trust have remained stable owing to a strong asset base which includes investments worth over £2.56 million at market value. In 1993/94, it had an income of £299,000 including £161,000 royalties mainly from Oxford University Press. After rather high expenses of £31,000, mainly due to investment and scholarship management fees, grants totalled £166,000, of which £105,000 went to the British Council (£75,000 for scholarships, £25,000 for summer schools and £5,000 for a general purpose fund). The British Council is regularly the main beneficiary, with other regular grants going to: the English Speaking Union (£2,000) towards summer school bursaries; International Association for Teachers of English as a Foreign Language (£1,600) and VSO (£7,500 towards training volunteers in English-language teaching).

The only other grants were for £12,000 to £12,500 to universities for studentships, at Leeds, Lancaster, Reading and University College London.

Applications: All grants are made through existing contacts. No funds are available for other applications.

Mrs E G Hornby's Charitable Settlement

£47,000 (1993/94)

General

Kleinwort Benson Trustees Ltd,
PO Box 191, 10 Fenchurch Street,
London EC3M 3LB
0171-956 6600

Correspondent: Christopher Gilbert, Secretary

Trustees: N J M Lonsdale;
Mrs P M W Smith-Maxwell.

Beneficial area: UK.

Information available: Full accounts are on file at the Charity Commission.

General: As at 31st January 1994, the trust had assets of £524,000. In 1993/94, the trust had an income of £54,000 and gave grants totalling £47,000.

58 grants were given, ranging from £200 to £2,000. Many grants appear to be given to the same groups each year, especially the larger ones: Friends of the Elderly and Gentlefolk's Help and St Richard's Hospice (£2,000 each); Queen Elizabeth's Foundation for the Disabled (£1,750); Countryside Foundation – Campaign for Hunting and Irish Draught Horse Society (£1,500 each) and the Institute for the Study of Drug Dependence (£1,200). 15 grants of £1,000 were given; three to animal welfare charities (including Battersea Dogs Home); four to sickness/disability charities, and the rest to a wide range of causes concerned with prison reform; children; a hospice; service organisations and rape counselling.

Exclusions: Individuals are not supported.

Applications: In writing to the correspondent. The trustees meet annually in March but applications are considered throughout the year.

The Hornton Charity

£61,000 (1993/94)

General

Messrs Price Waterhouse & Co,
Cornwall Court, 19 Cornwall Street,
Birmingham B3 2DT
0121-200 3000

Correspondent: B Taylor

Trustees: A C S Hordern; A R Collins;
S M Wall; S W B Landale.

Beneficial area: Preference for the Midlands.

Information available: Full accounts are on file at the Charity Commission.

General: In 1993/94, the charity had assets of £769,000 and an income of just over £43,000. Grants totalled £61,000 and were mainly to national or Midlands charities. There may be a preference for arts organisations and medical charities. Churches and disability charities also receive some support.

The largest grants were given to: Macmillan Cancer Fund (£12,500); CCHA Extra Care and Evans Cottage Homes (£2,500 each); New English Orchestra (£2,000) and Queen Alexandra College (£1,800). Previous recipients of large grants include the University of Birmingham, St Mary's Hospice and the Children's Hospice.

Exclusions: No grants to individuals.

Applications: In writing to the correspondent.

The Hospital Saturday Fund Charitable Trust

£75,000 (1993/94)

Medical

24 Upper Ground, London SE1 9PQ
0171-928 6662

Correspondent: K R Bradley, Administrator

Trustees: L Fellman, Chairman; A Tierney, Vice Chair; K R Bradley; K Fleming Roberts; H Palma; Mrs P Shaw;
E W Smith.

Beneficial area: UK.

Information available: Accounts are on file at the Charity Commission.

General: The trust was formed in 1987 to take over the discretionary grant-making activities of the Hospital Saturday Fund, thereby maintaining the aims and ideals of the founders of the fund.

The trust aims to support a wide variety of hospitals, hospices and medically associated charities for care and research. It also gives grants to individuals whose health problem has entailed financial hardship or towards the cost of a special piece of equipment because of disability or to make life easier.

In 1993/94, the trust had an income of £82,000 (£68,000 of which was in donations and gifts, mainly from the Hospital Saturday Fund). Grants to "charities, hospitals and hospices" totalled £75,000 and to individuals £12,000. No further information was available as to beneficiaries or the size of grants. Reserves were used to maintain this level of giving.

In 1994/95, the trust is maintaining its 1993/94 level of giving and using more reserves. It anticipates a reduction in donations for 1995/96.

Grants, by number, in 1991/92 were categorised as follows:

National organisations		25	
National but for specific areas		9	
South & London:	hospitals 21	other	18
England Mid & West & Wales:	hospitals 3	other	4
England North:	hospitals 6	other	2
Scotland:	hospitals 7	other	10
Isle of man		1	
N Ireland		2	
Ireland:	hospitals 6	other	1
Overseas		2	

and 2 further grants were also given.

All grants were for £500 except for eight for £750, one for £300 and one for £200.

Applications: Hospitals, hospices and medically-related charities are invited to write detailed letters or to send a brochure with an accompanying letter. There is a form for individuals to complete available from the personal assistant to the trust administrator.

The John & Ruth Howard Charitable Trust

£59,000 (1993/94)

Archaeology, church music, building preservation, general

93 High Road, Willesden Green,
London NW10 2TB
0181-459 1125

Correspondent: Alec S Atchison, Chairman

Trustees: Alec S Atchison; John H Hillier; Nina Feldman; Richard Hobson.

Beneficial area: England, and Greater London for general grants.

Information available: Accounts are on file at the Charity Commission but without a list of grants.

General: The trust was set up in 1991 with a £127,000 endowment and received a further £350,000 over the following year from the estates of J H Howard and Mrs R M Howard. The aim of the trust is to spread its support equally across four specified areas: archaeology; church music; preservation and protection of public buildings, and general charitable causes. Grants can only be given to organisations in England and general grants are restricted to Greater London.

Grants are not usually evenly spread across the four specified areas in any one year. Sometimes considerable sums may be promised on condition that further sums are raised by the recipient, or that work is completed to a point where the publication of results can be guaranteed.

In 1993/94, grants were given totalling £59,000 (£70,000 in 1992/93) split between:

	1993/94	1992/93
Archaeology	£33,000	£19,000
Buildings	£9,000	£31,000
Choral	£3,500	£6,500
General	£14,000	£14,000

The correspondent stated that "with the exception of choir school and church music, grants have been made in all areas leaving only relatively small sums available". The trust had apparently had difficulty finding suitable applicants for the church music section, but now supports choir scholars at Lichfield, Gloucester, Exeter, Lincoln and Cambridge. It is thought that £33,000 has been earmarked for choral projects.

Exclusions: No grants to large appeals.

Applications: In writing to the correspondent.

The HSA Charitable Trust

£700,000 (1993/94)

Health care

Hambleden House, Andover,
Hants SP10 1LQ
01264-353211

Correspondent: The Secretary

Trustees: P S Howard; I D Adam; J A Elliott; P Benner; R Crawford; Mrs C G Lemon.

Beneficial area: UK.

Information available: Leaflet and accounts available from the trust.

General: "The Hospital Saving Association was founded in 1922 when there was no national Service in existence. It provided essential peace of mind for those who were sick or injured but would have been otherwise unable to pay for their hospital treatment. The HSA Charitable Trust was first established in 1972 as part of the Golden Jubilee Celebrations of the Association itself. Each year the Charitable Trust makes donations to contributors with special needs, to health care oriented charities, to the 'free funds' of hospitals and to finance nursing scholarship awards.

"Although the trust is committed to providing financial help to a wide range of deserving causes, it is particularly concerned to support those charities and charitable organisations that are likely to benefit a substantial number of HSA contributors.

"The principle for distribution of funds is that all charities with medical research, aftercare and welfare aims and ambitions are considered. Each year the HSA Charitable Trust is covenanted a large donation from the HSA."

The chairman of the trust, Phillip Howard, explains "The donations are always made to charities associated with health care. It's very difficult to decide which of the many thousands of these we will support but we tend to be more sympathetic towards smaller and lesser known organisations - particularly those that might benefit HSA members. In addition, we do make substantial donations to the larger charities from time to time."

In 1993/94, the Hospital Saving Association covenanted £500,000 to the trust. In 1992/93, the Association covenanted £480,000 to the trust together with a special Gift Aid donation of £500,000. In 1993/94, grants were as follows:

Donations to Free Funds of hospitals	£97,000
HSA Scholarship Awards	£100,000
Grants to institutions and individuals	£479,000
Grants to hospices	£24,000

Applications: In writing to the correspondent, including a copy of the most recent audited accounts. Trustees meet four times a year.

The A Hubert 1971 Charitable Trust

£153,000 (1993)

Jewish

c/o Messrs Porter Matthews & Marsden, Oak Mount, 6 East Park Road, Blackburn BB1 8BW
01254-679131

Correspondent: Collin Willis, Secretary

Trustees: W I Hubert; T Murphy.

Beneficial area: Worldwide, particularly Israel.

Information available: Full accounts are on file at the Charity Commission.

General: This trust was set up in 1971 with £100 by Arthur Hubert. In 1993, it had total assets worth over £190,000 and an income of £88,000. After expenses of £19,000, the trust had £70,000 available for distribution. 37 grants were given ranging from £100 to £50,000 and totalling £153,000. Some grants were for under £500, but most were for £500 to £1,000. All the grants were to Jewish organisations, mainly in Israel, 22 of which had been supported in the previous year. Some small grants are given to Jewish organisations in England.

12 grants were for over £1,000, with the largest to Sde Chemed Children's Village (£50,000), College of Judea & Samaria (£40,000) and Gateshead Girls Seminary (£25,000). There were five grants of £2,000 to £6,500 and the remaining grants were all for under £2,000.

Applications: In writing to the correspondent.

The W I Hubert 1974 Charitable Trust

£93,000 (1991/92)

Jewish

c/o Messrs Porter Matthews & Marsden, Oak Mount, 6 East Park Road, Blackburn BB1 8BW
01254-679131

Correspondent: Collin Willis, Secretary

Trustees: W I Hubert; T Murphy.

Beneficial area: UK, Israel.

Information available: Full accounts are on file at the Charity Commission.

General: The trust was set up in 1973 by Walter Isaac Hubert. In 1991/92, it had assets of £989,000 and an income of £127,000, all from investments. It gave 41 grants totalling £93,000, all to Jewish organisations except for the Children's Day Nurseries and Children's Town (£4,000) and British Association for Cancer Research (£2,600).

All other grants ranged from £39 to £15,000 and were specifically Jewish. The largest were: Ezrat Nashim Hospital (£15,000); Bnei David (£10,000); Bet Shammai Grammar School (£8,500) and Poor People in Jerusalem (£8,000). There were also four grants of £5,000.

Applications: In writing to the correspondent.

The Humanitarian Trust (also known as the Michael Polak Foundation)

£48,000 (1993)

Education, health, social welfare

64 Aberdare Gardens, London NW6 3QD

Correspondent: Mrs M Myers, Secretary

Trustees: Sir Isaiah Berlin; M Jacques Gunsbourg; Lord Rothschild.

Beneficial area: Worldwide, mainly Israel.

Information available: Full accounts are on file at the Charity Commission.

General: The trust was founded in 1946. In the early years donations were made overwhelmingly to educational causes in Israel. Nowadays the trust is giving to a wider range of causes, still mainly Jewish, but some smaller grants are given to British organisations. In 1992/93, the trust had assets of £1.5 million and an income of only £64,000. Grants totalled £48,000 and are divided into three headings:

- **Academic and educational:** 36 grants were given. By far the largest grant is usually to the Friends of the Hebrew University of Jerusalem (2 grants of £10,000). £3,000 was given to Technion and £2,000 to ORT. Small grants of around £200 were given to universities and colleges throughout England, including Liverpool, York, Leeds, Oxford, Cambridge and Warwick.
- **Medical and charitable:** 10 grants were given totalling £6,000, the largest being: Shaare Zedek Medical Centre (£1,500); Magden David Adam and Jewish Care (£1,000 each).
- **Social service:** 9 grants totalling £7,300. This heading is usually almost entirely devoted to the Jerusalem Foundation (£5,000 in 1992/93). Other grants were of £100 to £600 to CBF World Jewish Relief, Russian Immigrant Aid Fund, Motability, Talking Newspapers for the Blind, Samaritans and Jewish Children's Holiday Fund.

Exclusions: Awards are not given for travel or the arts (such as theatre, dance, music etc.) but for academic purposes only. They are intended only as supplementary assistance and are to be held concurrently with other awards. One-off grants to individuals only up to a maximum of £200.

Applications: In writing to the correspondent for consideration in September and February each year.

The Albert Hunt Trust

£126,000 (1993/94)

Health, welfare

Messrs Coutts & Co, Trustee Department, 440 Strand, London WC2R 0QS

Correspondent: R J Collis, Trust Manager

Trustees: Miss M K Coyle; G Grusin; Miss F I Reakes.

Beneficial area: UK.

Information available: Full accounts are on file at the Charity Commission.

General: In 1993/94, the trust had assets of £2.8 million (an increase from £1.6 million in 1991/92) and an income of £162,000 (down from £181,000 in 1991/92). 54 grants were given totalling £126,000.

The trust has a list of charities which it regularly supports. Grants go mainly to large national charities (including service charities) concerned with health and welfare. Typical beneficiaries include Shelter, Leukaemia Research Fund, Friends of the Elderly, YMCA, Catholic Services for Prisoners and the Simon Community.

Applications: The correspondent stated that no unsolicited correspondence will be acknowledged.

The Huntingdon Foundation Limited

£67,000 (1992/93)

Jewish

Forframe House, 35-37 Brent Street, London NW4 2EF
0181-202 2282

Correspondent: Mrs S Perl, Secretary

Trustees: B Perl; S Perl; Mrs S Perl.

Beneficial area: Worldwide.

Information available: Full accounts are on file at the Charity Commission.

General: In 1992/93, the trust had assets of £4.3 million and an income of £1 million, half of which was received in gifts and donations. Grants made during the year totalled £67,000 and a further £200,000 was allocated for distibution in the following year.

Almost 200 grants were given, all to Jewish organisations and generally ranging from as little as £10 to £1,000, though more commonly £200 to £300. The largest grants were to Parsha Ltd (£14,000); Yeshiva Gedolah of Seagate (£10,000); Finchley Road Synagogue (£4,000); Ariel, Israel and Yeshivat Hamvitar (£3,000 each).

Applications: Grants appear to be given in March, June, September and December.

The P Y N & B Hyams Trust

£91,000 (1992/93)

Jewish, general

Hyams Organisation, Regent House, 235-241 Regent Street, London W1R 8J
0171-734 3147

Correspondent: N Hyams

Trustees: N Hyams; Mrs M Hyams; D Levy.

Beneficial area: Worldwide.

Information available: Full accounts are on file at the Charity Commission.

General: In 1993, the trust had assets of £1.1 million and an income of £80,000 (£98,000 in 1992). 65 grants were given totalling £91,000 (£142,000 in 1992) and mainly to Jewish organisations. The largest grants were to: British Ort (£19,000); Ben Gurion University Foundation (£16,000) and JPAIME (£5,000). A further 15 grants of £1,000 or more were given to Jewish organisations.

Most grants were for £500 or less, with 17 under £100. Some of the non-Jewish beneficiaries included: Royal Academy of Arts (£250); Architectural Foundation (£200); RNLI (£130) and Metropolitan Hospital Saturday Fund (£25). Many of the grants appear to be recurrent.

Applications: In writing to the correspondent.

The Hyde Park Place Estate Charity – Civil Trustees

£61,000 to organisations (1990/91)

General in Westminster

St George's Vestry, 2a Mill Street, London W1R 9LB
0171-629 0874

Correspondent: Miss E Crichton, Clerk

Beneficial area: Westminster.

Information available: Full accounts are on file at the Charity Commission up to 1990/91.

General: In 1990/91, the trust had an income of £143,000 and gave grants totalling £116,000. This included £16,000 in personal grants made through agencies and £38,000 in educational grants.

31 grants were given to organisations, totalling £61,000. A range of local charities in Westminster were supported, including Childlink, Disabled Living Foundation, House of St Barnabas in Soho, Thomas Coram Foundation, Westminster Play Association and the Women's Therapy Centre, all of which received £5,000. Other grants were £200 or above.

Applications: In writing to the correspondent.

The Idlewild Trust

£131,000 (1993)

Preservation, conservation, performing arts

54-56 Knatchbull Road, London SE5 9QY
0171-274 2266

Correspondent: Ms Lyn Roberts, Administrator

Trustees: Dr G W Beard, Chairman; Mrs Peter B Minet; H J Parratt; Mrs F L Morrison-Jones; Mrs A C Grellier; Lady Judith Goodison; M H Davenport.

Beneficial area: UK.

Information available: Full accounts and annual report are on file at the Charity Commission.

General: In 1993, the trust had assets of almost £1.9 million and an income of £174,000. Grants ranging from £500 to £6,000 and totalling £131,000 were given to 49 organisations involved mainly in classical arts activities such as: Central School of Ballet (£6,000); Royal Northern College of Music (£5,600); Yehudi Menuhin School Ltd (£5,000); Purcell School (£3,000); Amadeus Scholarship Fund (£2,000); Slade School of Fine Art (£1,000, with a further £1,000 to follow in 1994); Association of British Orchestras Trust (£1,000).

Other beneficiaries included: Croydon Alternatives Theatre Company (£5,000); Cathedral Camps (£1,500); Scottish Sculpture Workshop (£1,000); Berkshire, Buckinghamshire & Oxfordshire Naturalists' Trust Ltd and Durham Wildlife Trust (both £500).

Exclusions: Grants to registered charities only. No grants are made to individuals. The trust will not give to:
- Repetitive nationwide appeals by large charities for large sums of money;
- Appeals where all, or most of, the beneficiaries reside outside the UK;
- Appeals in respect of church or school buildings where the buildings have no distinctive and outstanding merit,

except where the school provides very specialised training;
- Parochial appeals. In this context, parochial means that all, or most of, the beneficiaries reside within the applicant's immediate locality;
- Appeals from organisations whose sole or main purpose is to make grants out of the funds which they collect;
- Appeals received from an organisation within 12 months of a previous grant;
- Research grants, deficit funding or endowment funding.

Applications: In writing to the correspondent, including the last audited accounts. There is no formal application form. Meetings are usually held in April, August and December. Only successful applications will be acknowledged unless an sae is enclosed.

The Iliffe Family Charitable Trust

£218,000 (1994)

General

Barn Close, Yattendon, Newbury, Berks RG18 0UY
01635-201255

Correspondent: J R Antipoff

Trustees: N G E Petter; J R Antipoff; R P R Iliffe.

Beneficial area: Worldwide.

Information available: Full accounts are on file at the Charity Commission.

General: The trust appears consistently to have an income of around £200,000. In 1994, it had assets of £1.2 million which gave a very good income of £277,000. Almost 70 grants were given totalling £218,000, of which over 40 were for only £50 to £600.

The largest 25 grants ranged from £1,000 to over £60,000 and were distributed as follows: National Trust, Basildon (£61,000); Bradfield Foundation and Coventry Cathedral (£20,000 each); Game Conservancy Trust (£12,500). There were four grants of £10,000 to: CCHA Extra Care; Enterprise Sailing; West Midlands Macmillan Nurses and Castle Bromwich Hall Garden.

17 grants of between £1,000 and £5,000 were given to a wide range of organisations including: Birmingham Hippodrome; Campaign for Oxford; Countryside Foundation; Frilsham Church Appeal; Green Island Holiday Trust; Rural Berks Community Care Trust and Study Cot Death.

The smaller grants were given to national and local organisations working in the areas of: welfare, including a number of benevolent funds; children; animals, and medical, including hospitals. Organisations supported included: British Heart Foundation; Lord Leycester Hospital; Newspaper Press Fund; Operation Raleigh; Reading YMCA; RNLI, RSPCA and Spastics Society.

Applications: In writing to the correspondent. Only successful applications will be acknowledged.

The Inland Waterways Association

£100,000

Inland waterways

114 Regents Park Road,
London NW1 8UQ
0171-586 2510/2556

Correspondent: Mrs Francis Hart, Chief Executive

Trustees: The Council of the Association.

Beneficial area: UK.

Information available: Accounts are available from the association.

General: The IWA was founded in 1946 for the retention, conservation, restoration and development of the inland waterways for the fullest possible commercial and recreational use. Grants or loans are made to Canal Trusts and Societies for developing their work.

In 1993, the asociation had assets of over £580,000 and an income of £508,000, almost £200,000 of which was from subscriptions, £88,000 from donations and £68,000 from Aston Appeal grants. There was also £39,000 categorised as coming from grants received. Expenditure totalled £536,000, including administration (£113,000), "Waterways" and regional magazines (£42,000), and membership support and campaign costs (£358,000).

Presumably the latter includes £26,000 given in grants to local clubs and organisations using the canals throughout the country. Grants to the north of England and Wales appear to be under represented during the year.

Applications: In writing to the correspondent.

The Inman Charity

£198,000 (1993)

Social welfare, disability, the elderly, hospices

10 New Square, Lincoln's Inn,
London WC2A 3QG
0171-242 6041

Correspondent: Messrs Payne Hicks Beach (fao. Alan Walker)

Beneficial area: UK.

Information available: This charity files half-yearly accounts at the Charity Commission. Between 1991 and 1993, full information covering one complete year has not been filed.

General: In 1993, the trust had assets of £3 million and an income of £200,000. £198,000 was given in grants. The correspondent sent full details of the grants made for the year. This list showed 50 grants ranging between £1,000 and £10,000, with the sole grant of £10,000 to Uppingham School for the Victor Inman Bursary Fund. This grant stands outside its main areas for support – disability and hospices.

Seven hospices received support totalling £36,000. Five organisations working with the elderly, including Alzheimer's Disease Society (£6,000), received £22,000.

Grants were given to many organisations working with disabled people, from the older "establishment" organisations – such as RNIB, RNID, and RADAR – to Opportunities which works to improve employment prospects of disabled people (£3,000 each). A particular interest in holidays and access for disabled people was shown by grants to the Winged Fellowship Trust which arranges holidays and respite care for disabled people (£6,000), National Trust (Access for all

Appeal) (£3,000), Care Holidays for Older People with Disabilities (£1,000) and the Cystic Fibrosis Holiday Fund for Children (£3,000). Other social welfare beneficiaries included the Salvation Army, Samaritans and Royal British Legion.

Exclusions: "Applications from individuals rejected."

Applications: In writing only to the correspondent. Trustees meet half-yearly in March and September.

INTACH (UK) Trust

£61,000 (1991)

Education and Indian culture

10 Barley Mow Passage, London W4 4PH
0181-994 6477

Correspondent: Dr Philip Whitbourn, Secretary

Trustees: Martand Singh, Chair; Sir B M Feilden; Sir J Thomson; R W Skelton; Cyrus Guzder; Dr D W MacDowell.

Beneficial area: UK and India.

Information available: Full accounts are on file at the Charity Commission.

General: INTACH stands for the Indian National Trust for Art and Cultural Heritage, and its money is derived from the will of Charles William Wallace, who died in 1916. His estate was divided between the British Treasury and the Treasury of India, which has subsequently become India, Bangladesh, Burma and Pakistan. In addition to the INTACH trust, the governments of India and Britain set up educational funds. Details of the Charles Wallace India Trust for Indian students can be found in *The Educational Grants Directory*. There are also smaller trusts for the other countries.

The INTACH (UK) Trust was set up in 1987 with £1.2 million. It aims to promote the education of the inhabitants of India and the UK through the preservation of the art, cultural and natural heritage of India. This primarily takes the form of support for conservation projects in India and funding for British students and scholars to study and travel in the country.

In 1991, the trust had assets of £1.4 million generating an income of £120,000. Grants totalled £83,000, of which £43,000 went towards documentation of Indian art objects in the UK, £18,000 to INTACH Conservation, and £22,000 went to 12 individuals to visit India in connection with projects relating to the trust's aims.

Applications: In writing to the correspondent.

The Ireland Fund of Great Britain

About £80,000 annually

Irish organisations

8-10 Greyfriars Road, Reading, Berkshire RG1 1QE
01734-569111; Fax: 01734-505519

Correspondent: Mrs Jacqueline Dutton, Executive Secretary

Trustees: Josephine Hart; Brian Hayes; Kevin Pakenham; Dr Anthony O'Reilly; John Riordan; Gavin O'Reilly.

Beneficial area: Ireland and Great Britain.

Information available: Full accounts are on file at the Charity Commission.

General: The fund was set up in the late 1980's. Its objects are to "alleviate the problems in Ireland, to improve British-Irish friendship and to help the less fortunate Irish in England". Half the money raised by the Ireland Fund of Great Britain is allocated in Ireland, both North and South, and decisions about its disbursement are made by the Central Advisory Committee of the parent body – The Ireland Funds in Dublin. The other half is allocated within the British mainland to organisations of the Irish community, or those working with them.

In 1993, the three established fundraising events raised £67,000 (from the Midsummer Night's Ball), £18,000 (from the Greyhound Dinner) and £22,000 (from the golf tournament). A Young Ireland Christmas Ball raised £3,000, Kempton Park Dinner £35,000 and a City Luncheon £27,000. The amount raised through functions increased by £60,000, but income dropped from £221,000 to £176,000, because the £104,000 donation from K Club Golf Tournament in Ireland in 1992 was not repeated.

The fund has a policy of retaining funds for the years when fundraising is less successful. It is currently carrying forward £110,000.

The trust gave 25 grants totalling £75,000. The largest grants were: Safe Start Foundation (£6,000); Corrymeela Community and Haven House (£5,000 each); three grants of £4,000 to Camus Craft, Southill House and Greater Blanchardstown Development Group; British Irish Association (£3,500) and Women's Information Centre (£3,000). Other beneficiaries included the Irish Welfare Information Centre and Irish Comminty Care, Merseyside (£2,000 each); Conference of Irish Historians (£700) and Irish Studies Dept (£500).

Applications: In writing to the correspondent.

The Ireland Funds

Not known

Reconciliation, arts development, community development

20-22 College Green, Dublin 2
010 3531-679 2743

Correspondent: Michelle Lynch, Executive Director

Beneficial area: Ireland.

Information available: The following information was supplied by the funds.

General: The Ireland Funds comprise seven independent trust funds and foundations. The separate funds are in America, Canada, Gt Britain, Australia, France, Germany and New Zealand. The purpose of the funds is to raise money internationally for the promotion of peace, culture and charity in Ireland. Since its inception, $50 million has been raised for worthy projects. Each fund is a registered charity in the country in which it operates and grants are made in Ireland only to bodies pursuing similar charitable objectives. The funds are non-denominational and non-political serving all of Ireland, North and South.

The funds have responded to need in Ireland on a broad front, and have assisted numerous projects across a wide range of activity. In order to maximise impact, the Ireland Funds have decided, from 1993 to 1995 inclusive, to target their resources on supporting programmes which are specifically designed to help people develop positive responses to conflict in Northern Ireland, unemployment, inner city disadvantage and rural depopulation.

In particular the funds are interested in stimulating local leadership, fostering self-help, promoting women's contribution in society, encouraging young people's creativity and generally promoting renewal, rejuvenation and regeneration.

The Programme areas supported from 1993 to 1995, for which applications had to be received by October 1994, were:
Reconciliation
Arts development
Community development/leadership/enterprise.

When a project is multi-stranded it will be at the discretion of the Advisory Council to decide the Programme area to which it belongs.

The trust has information sheets specifically tailored to the particular Programme areas it is supporting.

Exclusions: Grants are not given for: general appeals; purchase of buildings or land; capital costs for equipment, computers, lighting, costumes, etc.; major construction or repairs to buildings; other grant-making trusts; individuals; purchase of vehicles; sports clubs; debt repayment; tuition or student expenses; travel or transport costs; choirs or bands; commercial trading businesses; projects not based in Ireland; replacement of statutory funding; medical research or health related programmes; general administration of national or provincial organisations; uniformed organisations (unless in an interface area).

Applications: If your project meets the stated criteria, an application form is available on request. All applications are centrally processed through the Dublin office of the Ireland Funds.

Applicants should only apply to the programme relating to their project; please check the closing dates for each programme area. There will be stringent application of the guidelines and exclusions criteria. Groups must have charitable status and submit copies of their constitution and audited accounts. Projects supported must make regular reports of progress, monitoring, and provide promotional material and publicity.

"Notification of outcome will be by letter. In the meantime we would ask you not to contact the office, due to our small staff number. Lobbying will disqualify."

The Irish Youth Foundation (UK) Ltd

£131,000 (1992/93)

Irish young people

Pembroke House, Pembroke Street, Oxford OX1 1BL
01865-791990

Correspondent: Dallas Brett, Trustees Solicitor

Trustees: M Clancy; P Devlin; D Downes; J Dunne; F Gormley; F Hucker; K Hynes; P Kelly; N Kelly; Rev J Kiely; D Murray; S McGinley; Lord Mountcharles; J O'Neill; N O'Neill; N Smurfit.

Beneficial area: UK and Ireland.

Information available: Full accounts are on file at the Charity Commission.

General: The trust raises funds and gives grants for projects benefiting young Irish people, especially those that are disadvantaged and are in need. It was established in 1989 and since then has given grants totalling £284,000. The trust has produced comprehensive guidelines from which the following information is taken.

"The foundation supports a wide range of projects concerned with enhancing the personal and social development of young Irish people. These can be of a preventative nature ie. aimed at preventing problems arising in the first instance, or can respond to particular problems facing young Irish people."

In particular the foundation grant aids programmes and projects:

1. Attempting to resolve the accommodation problems of young Irish immigrants.
2. Tackling the problem of unemployment among young Irish people.
3. Benefiting disadvantaged young Irish people.
4. Tackling drug and alcohol abuse among young Irish people.
5. Aiming to reduce young Irish people's involvement with crime and violence.
6. Alleviating the plight of young Irish people who are homeless.
7. Of a preventative nature aimed at harnessing the boundless energies of young Irish people in a constructive and creative manner.
8. Developing facilities and amenities for young Irish people.
9. Providing equipment for use by young Irish people.
10. Action research aimed at developing more effective means of resolving the problems of Irish young people in Britain today.
11. Contributing to the development of young Irish people in Britain so as to enhance their prospects of making a mature and positive contribution to their society.

"The foundation is concerned with supplementing state aid. We are not in the business of substituting it. We are not in the business of replacing funding lost as a result of cutbacks in statutory support. However, we may consider offering interim support, provided that you are taking steps to resolve your long-term funding situation by exploring new sources and examining the impact of these changes on your services and structures.

"We give priority to small organisations working directly with young Irish people at community level, which do not have the ability to fund raise for themselves. Larger or national organisations will only be eligible for funding if they can demonstrate that the project to be funded either breaks new ground in the given field and/or will significantly benefit small community based projects benefiting young Irish people.

"The foundation considers requests for:

1. Programmes development grants, ie. grants to enhance existing programmes or to develop new ones.
2. Seeding grants, ie. grants to help start up projects, especially ones of an innovatory nature. While salaries are not funded, in certain circumstances contributions towards salary costs may be considered.
3. Grants to upgrade premises/equipment.
4. Small grants.

"In general no more than one grant will be given to any one organisation in one year. However, in certain special circumstances commitment to a particular project may extend beyond one year, subject to continuous review."

In 1992/93, the trust had an income of £151,000 with £80,000 from activities/events and £45,000 from covenanted donations. Grants totalled £131,000 and were categorised by the trust as follows:

Programme/
  development: £84,000 (21 grants)
Premises/equipment: £26,000 (6 grants)
Small grants: £21,000 (22 grants)

The comprehensive accounts give information on each beneficiary including the reason for the grant. The largest grants in the programme/development category were £9,750 to Centrepoint Soho to fund a six-month pilot project to establish a referral system and secure appropriate supportive accommodation, and £7,000 to Safe Start Foundation for an Employment & Training Co-ordinator. Other grants ranged from £2,000 to £6,000 to organisations such as Brent Irish Advisory Service, Irish Families Project, Kilburn Irish Youth Project and Sheffield Gypsy & Traveller Support Group. Grants were given for the development of information and other services, towards training projects, emergency accommodation, outreach workers and running costs.

In the premises/equipment category £8,000 was given to the Irish Commission for Prisoners Overseas to upgrade and develop their services through a computer system and secretarial help, and £6,000 to the Irish Support & Advice Centre. Three of the other grants were towards provision of accommodation.

In the small grants category, £3,000 was given to the Greater Manchester Games Movement – towards the 1993 Anglo Irish Games (travel and accommodation costs). The rest of the grants were for £1,500 or less with organisations supported including Cara Irish Homeless Project, Gagile Theatre Company, Irish Gay Helpline and the New Horizon Youth Centre. Grants were given towards a day centre, youth projects, training projects, bereavement counselling, homeless projects, Irish music, dance and theatre schemes and Irish language projects.

Exclusions: The foundation generally does not support: projects which cater for people under 12 years or over 21 years of age; grants to individuals; general appeals; work in the arts, museums, or of an environmental nature; grants for academic research; educational bursaries; to substitute state support, alleviate deficits already incurred; services run by statutory/public authorities; major capital appeals.

Applications: In writing to the correspondent, requesting an application form. The application period is short, in 1994 from October 17th to November 4th. Applications are considered in November and all applicants notified in January. Applications are assessed on the following requirements: need; continuity; track record/evaluation; disadvantaged young people; innovativeness; funding sources; budgetary control.

The Ironmongers' Quincentenary Fund

£63,000 (1992/93)

Medical research, community work, iron work, crafts

Ironmongers Hall, Barbican,
London EC2Y 8AA
0171-606 2725

Correspondent: J A Oliver, Clerk

Beneficial area: UK.

Information available: Accounts are on file at the Charity Commission, but without a list of grants.

General: The trust supports medical research, community work, iron work, research connected to ferrous metallurgy, and crafts.

In 1992/93, the fund had assets of £543,000 and an income of £130,000, including £50,000 from Gift Aid, £39,000 from covenants and £32,000 from dividends. Grants totalled £63,000. In the last few years the fund has received large Gift Aid payments, but has only slightly increased its level of grant-giving. Excess income over expenditure in the year was £60,000. It is not known whether the trust is building up its assets, or if there is another purpose for accumulating income.

Applications: In writing to the correspondent.

The ISA Charity

£29,000 (1992)

General

29-35 Rathbone Street, London W1P 1AG
0171-636 4301

Correspondent: Stephen Dabbs, Financial Controller

Trustees: R Paice; Mrs M Paice; P A Lintatt.

Beneficial area: UK.

Information available: Accounts are on file at the Charity Commission, but without a list of grants.

General: In 1992, the trust had assets of £559,000 and an income of £61,000 (£140,000 in 1991). The trust gave grants totalling only £29,000 (£25,000 in 1991), after expenses of only £250. There was a surplus of £28,000 (£115,000 in 1991). This regular surplus presumably will help to increase its assets base and future payments.

Applications: For the time being, all funds have been allocated for several years ahead and no further applications can be considered.

The ITF Seafarers Trust

£3,400,000 (1992)

Seafarers

133-135 Great Suffolk Street,
London SE1 1PD
0171-403 2733

Correspondent: Mark Dickinson, General Secretary

Trustees: James Douglas Hunter; David Cockroft; John Fay; William Morris; James Knapp; Margaret Fitzgerald; Knud Mols Sorenson; John Connolly.

Beneficial area: Worldwide.

Information available: Full accounts are on file at the Charity Commission for 1992.

General: In 1992, the trust had assets of £38.5 million and an income of £7.2 million, of which £3.2 million was received in covenants from the International Transport Workers Federation (this will continue until 1995). Grants totalling £3.4 million were given to 96 seafaring organisations.

These were broken down as follows:

12 grants of £126 to £5,000, totalling £36,000;

13 grants of £5,001 to £10,000, totalling £88,000;

37 grants of £10,001 to £15,000, totalling £330,000;

14 grants of £15,001 to £20,000, totalling £239,000;

10 grants of £20,001 to £35,000, totalling £266,000;

7 grants of £35,001 to £50,000, totalling £212,000;

13 grants of £50,001 to £950,000, totalling £1.8 million.

No further information is available concerning the beneficiaries. In 1993, the trust had an income of £7.4 million.

Applications: In writing to the correspondent. Applications must be supported by an ITF affiliated Seafarer's or Docker's Trade Union.

The D J W Jackson Charitable Trust

£57,000 (1992/93)

Education, disability, general

3 Adams Road, Cambridge CB3 9AD
01223-464800

Correspondent: S Jackson

Trustees: Sean D Jackson; David J W Jackson; Suzanne Jackson.

Beneficial area: UK.

Information available: Full accounts are on file at the Charity Commission.

General: The trust takes its name from that of its founder, David Jackson, who created it in 1978. The main aims of the trust are to support the education of young people, to help children with disabilities or dyslexia, and to assist people in need.

In 1992/93, the trust gave £57,000 in grants, most of which (£40,000) was to Open Doors. The East African School of Theology received £160. The remaining £17,000 was paid to CAF, probably to distribute to other charities. In previous years, donations have been made primarily through CAF and totalled £27,000 in 1991/92 and £61,000 in 1990/91.

Applications: The correspondent stated that the trust has a list of charities it regularly supports. It is therefore unlikely that any other applications will be supported.

The Dorothy Jacobs Charity

£61,000 (1993)

Jewish, medical

Messrs Arthur C Heyward & Co, Avon House, 360-366 Oxford Street, London W1N 0LE
0171-629 7826

Correspondent: R H Moss

Trustees: R H Moss; A M Alexander.

Beneficial area: UK.

Information available: Full accounts are on file at the Charity Commission.

General: In 1993, the trust had assets of £530,000 and an income of £37,000. 16 grants were given totalling almost £61,000. 15 grants were for £4,000 and one for £500. Four were to hospitals, four to Jewish charities and five to medical charities including British Red Cross Society, Leukemia Research Fund, BBC Children in Need, Oxfam and the Spastics Society. In the previous year only two grants were given: £25,000 to the Ravenswood Foundation and £3,000 to the Ben Uri Art Gallery.

Applications: In writing to the correspondent.

The Ruth & Lionel Jacobson Trust (Second Fund) No 2

£89,000 (1993/94)

General

High Wray, 35 Montagu Avenue, Newcastle-upon-Tyne NE3 4JH

Correspondent: Mrs I R Jacobson

Trustees: Irene Ruth Jacobson; Malcolm Jacobson.

Beneficial area: UK, with a preference for the North East.

Information available: Full accounts are on file at the Charity Commission.

General: The trust supports national charities and organisations based in the North East. In 1992/93, the trust had assets of £741,000 and an income of £59,000. Grants were given totalling £89,000. Of the 154 grants given, only nine were for £1,000 or more with one outstanding donation of £25,000 to the Jewish Philanthropic Association. About 30 grants were to Jewish organisations.

The largest were to: WIZO Charitable Fund (£15,000); Children & Youth Aliyah and Speech, Language & Hearing Centre (£5,000 each); Ravenswood Centre (£1,750); Society of Friends of the Torah (£1,500) and £1,000 each to Northumbria Leonard Cheshire Centre, Peoples' Theatre Art Group and the Dene Centre. All other grants were for under £1,000 and most were for under £500.

Over 40 grants were given to North East organisations and beneficiaries included the Borough of Sunderland Council for the Disabled; Cleveland Arts; Forest and Gardens, Northumbria; Motability North East; North Shields Sea Cadets and Victim Support, Durham.

The remaining grants were given to a wide range of national charities, particularly medical and health related organisations, including Action for Disability, Child Abuse Listening Service, Meningitis Research, PDSA, Shelter, Prisoners of Conscience Appeal and UNICEF.

Exclusions: No grants for individuals. Grants only to registered charities.

Applications: In writing to the correspondent.

The John Jarrold Trust

£153,000 (1993/94)

Arts, third world, social welfare, medical research

Messrs Jarrold & Sons, Whitefriars, Norwich NR3 1SH
01603-660211

Correspondent: G Bloxsom, Secretary

Trustees: Members of the Jarrold family: R E Jarrold; A C Jarrold; P J Jarrold; Mrs D J Jarrold; Mrs J Jarrold; Mrs A G Jarrold; Mrs W A L Jarrold.

Beneficial area: Worldwide, with a preference for East Anglia.

Information available: Full accounts are on file at the Charity Commission.

General: In 1992/93, the trust had an income of £174,000, of which £168,000 was in dividends from shares in Jarrold & Sons Ltd. About 220 grants were given (about 30 to individuals for expeditions such as Operation Raleigh). There is a clear preference for charities in Norwich and East Anglia.

About a third of grants were for £1,000 or more and included: Action Aid-Africa; Concern Worldwide; Dawson First School Playgroup; Iris Fund; MSS; NCH; Norfolk History Fair; Romanian Orphanages Trust; Warehouse Artists Studios Ltd. The trust supports a wide range of organisations including churches, medical, arts, environment/conservation, welfare and overseas aid.

Exclusions: Educational purposes that should be supported by the state will not be helped by the trust.

Applications: In writing to the correspondent.

The Jenour Foundation

£48,000 (1992/93)

General

Fitzalan Court, Newport Road,
Cardiff CF2 1TS
01222-481111

Correspondent: Karen Griffin

Trustees: P J Phillips; G R Camfield.

Beneficial area: UK, with an interest in Wales.

Information available: Full accounts are on file at the Charity Commission.

General: In 1992/93, the trust had assets of £728,000, an income of £56,000 and gave 30 grants totalling £48,000. The main grants were: Red Cross International and Provincial Grand Lodge of Monmouth (£5,000 each); Wales Council for the Blind and Cancer Research (£3,000 each) and Cancer Research Wales (£2,500). There were four grants of £500 to Parish of Llanisham & Lisvane Church, Physiotherapy Training Board, Samaritans and Welsh St Donats Art. All other grants were for £1,000 to £2,000 to organisations such as NSPCC; Prince of Wales Committee; RNLI – Welsh District; Welsh National Opera and Welsh Wildlife Fund.

Applications: In writing to the correspondent.

The Jephcott Charitable Trust

£120,000 (1993/94)

Alleviation of poverty in developing countries, general

Old Ford Farm, Wilmington, Honiton, Devon EX14 9JU

Correspondent: Mrs Meg Harris, Secretary

Trustees: N W Jephcott, Chairman; C J Stephenson; Ms P Davis; Judge A North; Mrs A Morgan.

Beneficial area: UK, developing countries overseas.

Information available: Full accounts are on file at the Charity Commission.

General: The trust usually supports smaller national and international projects, or part of a project (that is under £500,000). Currently one of the areas of interest is the improvement of the quality of life of the poor and developing countries. Grants are usually for a specific project or part of a project. Core funding and/or salaries are rarely considered. "Pump-priming" donations are offered - usually small grants to new organisations and areas of work for short periods of time. Monitoring of how the grant is spent is usually required.

In 1994, the assets had risen to over £2.7 million. It gave 13 grants totalling £120,000, the largest of which were: Antarctic Environment Project (£25,000); Harvest Help Lakeshore Project (£16,000); Farm Africa and Friends of ADESA (£15,000). Smaller grants included Water Air Ethiopia and St Vincents in Pinner (£5,000 each) and Horticultural Therapy and Kilifi Childrens' Hospital (£2,500 each).

Exclusions: No grants to individuals, including students, or for medical research. No response to general appeals from large, national organisations nor from organisations concerning themselves with poverty and education in the UK. Core funding and/or salaries are rarely considered.

Applications: Guidelines are available on request. Applications should be in writing at any time to the correspondent. Trustees meet twice a year.

Jewish Child's Day

£382,000 (1993/94)

Jewish children in need or with special needs

5th Floor, 707 High Road, North Finchley,
London N12 0BT
0181-446 8804; Fax: 0181-446 7370

Correspondent: P Shaw, Executive Director

Trustees: The National Council.

Beneficial area: Worldwide.

Information available: Accounts are on file at the Charity Commission but without a narrative report or schedule of grants.

General: The trust's grants are given to projects benefiting Jewish children in the UK or overseas. It disburses funds raised itself through appeals. In 1993/94, the trust had assets of £106,000 and had an income of £468,000 made up of: contributions from children (£11,000); contributions from provincial groups (£12,000); Chanuka Appeal (£55,500); Pesach Appeal (£28,000); New Year Appeal (£41,000); legacies (£61,000); covenants (£20,000); other donations (£263,000) and bank deposit interest (£4,500).

The direct costs incurred in raising that money totalled £28,000. After staff expenses (£50,000), office expenses (£14,000) and professional charges (£13,000) the trust broke down its grants as follows:

Israel	£113,500
Great Britain	£17,000
Children and Youth Aliyah	£20,000
Chernobyl	£228,000
Elswhere	£4,000

Similar sized grants were given to the same categories over the previous two years. Unfortunately these grants are not broken down any further.

It is understood that grants generally range up to £3,000 and are usually given for specific equipment for, or projects by, organisations working with Jewish children.

Applications: There is an application form which needs to be submitted together with a copy of the latest annual report and accounts.

Jewish Continuity
(amalgamated with the Jewish Educational Development Trust)

£549,000 (1992)

Jewish education

201 Haverstock Hill, London NW3 4QG
0171-431 7761

Correspondent: M Mail, Operations Manager

Trustees: M L Phillips; S Kalms; H Knobil; P L Levy; R Metzger; A Millet; C Morris; M Paisner; B Rix; Sir H Solomon; C Stein; M Teacher; F Worms.

Beneficial area: UK.

Information available: Full accounts are on file at the Charity Commission.

General: This entry is for the former Jewish Educational Development Trust, which in 1992 had an income of £1.39 million. This comes from donations, many made by other trusts in this guide. Grants totalled £549,000 including £312,000 to Immanuel College. The other larger grants were made to the Institute of Jewish Education (£80,000), Centre for Education (£40,000) and Redbridge School (£27,000). Other recipients included the Association of Jewish Sixth Formers, Manchester Grammar School and the Massoret Institute. Many are regular beneficiaries.

This new trust was launched in September 1993. It is thought that its aims are similar to above, but it may also support individuals.

Applications: In writing to the correspondent.

The Joels Charitable Trusts

£71,000 (1993/94)

Jewish, general

Messrs M S Zatman & Co, Refuge House, 9/10 River Front, Enfield EN1 3SZ
0181-367 3030

Correspondent: The Trustees

Trustees: N Joels; H Joels. In addition, Myriam Joels and Jessica Joels are also trustees of the Norman Joels Charitable Trust; Valerie Joels and Nicholas Joels are trustees of the Harold Joels Charitable Trust.

Beneficial area: Worldwide.

Information available: Full accounts are on file at the Charity Commission.

General: There are three trusts which are all administered from the same office, have members of the Joels family as trustees, have most of their assets still in Marks & Spencer plc and support mainly Jewish causes.

Harold Joels Charitable Trust
This trust gave 40 grants totalling £23,000 from an income of £26,000 in 1993/94. The largest grant was to the University College School Charitable Trust (£7,500). The other five grants of £1,000 or more all went to Jewish organisations including Congregation Kneses Tifereth Israel, CBF World Jewish Relief and Jewish Care. Over half the grants were for under £100 and about one third, mainly smaller grants, were to non-Jewish charities, mainly national medical and welfare causes, including Marie Curie Cancer Care, MSS, Samaritans, RNIB and Friends of the Tate Gallery.

Norman Joels Charitable Trust
This trust gave 75 grants totalling £16,000 from an income of £31,000 in 1993/94. The largest grant was to JPAIME (£7,500). The other two grants of £1,000 or more went to Children & Youth Aliyah and the New London Synagogue. The remaining grants were for £100 or less and about one third, mainly smaller grants, were to non-Jewish charities, mainly national medical and arts organisations, including Action Research, Age Concern, Friends of Covent Garden, MENCAP and the National Art Collections Fund.

Jacob & Lena Joels Charitable Trust
In 1992/93 and 1991/92, the trust gave a single large grant: £32,000 to Moriah School in 1992/93 and £20,000 to the New London Synagogue in 1991/92. Before this, the trust gave a number of grants each year distributed in a similar manner to the trusts above.

Applications: In writing to the correspondent.

The Johnson Group Cleaners Charity

£126,000 (1993/94)

General in Merseyside

c/o Johnson Group Management Services Ltd, Mildmay Road, Bootle, Merseyside L20 5EW

Correspondent: Miss Angela Smith, Director of Trustee Company

Trustees: Johnson Group Cleaners Trustee Co (No 1) Ltd.

Beneficial area: Merseyside.

Information available: Accounts are on file at the Charity Commission, but without a list of grants.

General: The trust was created in January 1990, evolving from a previous company-linked trust first created in 1914. By 1992/93, the trust had assets with a market value of £1.68 million with an income of £103,000. Grants totalled £126,000.

Grants are restricted to the Merseyside area, although the trusts states that the limited resources available are fully committed for the forseeable future.

Applications: Unsolicited applications are not supported.

The Lillie Johnson Charitable Trust

£139,000 (1992/93)

General

136 Hagley Road, Edgbaston, Birmingham B16 9PN

Correspondent: John Desmond, Secretary

Trustees: Arthur Riley; Peter Adams.

Beneficial area: UK, with a preference for the West Midlands.

Information available: Full accounts are on file at the Charity Commission.

General: In 1988/89 the trust received £1.6 million from the estate of Miss L C Johnson. In 1992/93, the trust had assets of £1.9 million and an income of £146,000. It gave 74 grants totalling £139,000, ranging from around £100 to £12,200. Grants have risen steadily from £36,000 in 1989/90.

Large grants were given to a number of charities in the West Midlands (about a quarter of the grants are given to West Midlands organisations) including Albrighton Moat Project (£8,000) and Birmingham Youth Theatre (£7,200). Other large grants included: Turning Point (£12,200), RNIB (£11,000) and Sense (£10,000). There were 42 other grants of £1,000 to £6,000 and the remaining grants were for under £1,000.

Recipients of smaller grants included Alexander Hospital, Birmingham Dogs Home, Heart of England Association, National Toy Libraries, Motor Neurone Disease Association, Rathbone Society and Woodgate Valley Urban Farm.

Applications: In writing to the correspondent.

The Joicey Trust

£134,000 (1993/94)

General in Northumberland and Tyne & Wear

c/o Dickinson Dees, Cross House, Westgate Road, Newcastle-upon-Tyne NE99 1SB
0191-261 1911

Correspondent: N A Furness, Appeals Secretary

Trustees: Lord Joicey; Lady Joicey; R H Dickinson; Hon A H Joicey; Elizabeth Lady Joicey.

Beneficial area: The county of Northumberland and the part of the old metropolitan county of Tyne & Wear lying north of the River Tyne.

Information available: Full accounts are on file at the Charity Commission.

General: The trustees will support both capital and revenue projects. Specific projects are likely to be preferred to funding general running costs. Where support is given in respect of start-up finance, it will be on the basis that the project can become viable without the trust's assistance over a relatively short period. National appeals are only supported where there is specific evidence of activity within the beneficial area.

In 1992/93, the trust had assets of £1.1 million and an income of £145,000. Over 210 grants were given totalling £143,000. Grants ranged from £100 to £5,000. The largest grants were to: Ford Church (£5,000), Newcastle Diocesan Repairs (£4,000) and Marie Curie Cancer Care, Conrad House (£3,000). There were 12 grants of £2,000 such as: Tyne & Wear Foundation; Abbeyfield, Newcastle-Upon-Tyne; Northern Counties School for the Deaf; St James' Church, Morpeth and the British Horse Society. Other grants were given to a variety of local charities and to local branches of national charities, based in the beneficial area.

Exclusions: No support for: bodies not having registered charitable status; personal applications; individuals; groups that do not have an identifiable project within the beneficial area.

Applications: There is no application form and applications should be made in writing to the correspondent. Trustees' meetings are held in January and July and applications should be received not later than the end of November and the end of May respectively.

Applications should include a brief description of the project, together with a copy of the previous year's audited accounts and, where possible, a copy of the current year's projected income and expenditure. In the case of large projects, an indication of how the major sources of funding are likely to be secured should be included. Unsuccessful applicants will not be informed unless an sae is provided.

The Jones 1986 Charitable Trust

£660,000 (1991/92)

General, especially in Nottinghamshire

Evershed Wells & Hind, 14 Fletcher Gate, Nottingham NG1 2FX
0115-936 6000

Correspondent: Mrs Chris Rees, Secretary

Trustees: J O Knight; R B Stringfellow.

Beneficial area: UK, especially Nottinghamshire.

Information available: Full accounts are on file at the Charity Commission.

General: This trust receives most of its income each year from four family settlements (£457,000 in 1991/92). This together with the income tax recoverable, interest on investments and other donations gave a total income of £797,000. The assets of the trust stand at £1.1 million.

The grant total has varied markedly in the last three years: 1992/93: £660,000; 1991/92: £433,000; 1990/91: £752,000. (Half the income was unspent in 1991/92.)

The £660,000 was given in only 33 grants. The largest were given to Nottingham University for Nottingham Health Authority (£166,000); Jessop Educational Charity (Hollygirt School £100,000); Portland Training College (£50,000); Nottinghamshire Wildlife Trust (£43,000); Riding for the Disabled Association (Highland Group £40,000); New Appeals Organisation for the City and County of Nottingham (£34,000), and St John Ambulance Brigade (£30,000).

Most grants were to medical or welfare charities and appear to go to regular beneficiaries in Nottinghamshire. There also appears to be an interest in horses with support for Redwings Horse Sanctuary (£20,000), Donkey Sanctuary (£10,000) and the Isle of Man Home of Rest for Old Horses (£5,000).

Of the other grants 12 were for £10,000 to £25,000 and 13 for £500 to £7,000. Beneficiaries included Ruddington Framework Knitters Museum (£25,000); Nottingham Old People's Welfare Housing Society Ltd (£20,000); Ear Foundation (£12,000); Intermediate Technology (£10,000); Samaritans Nottingham Branch (£5,500), and Long Eaton & District Friendly Invalid & Handicapped Group (£2,000).

Exclusions: No grants to individuals.

Applications: The trustees prefer to identify their own target charities and do not acknowledge applications.

The Edward Cecil Jones Settlement

£125,000 (1992)

General

Messrs Tolhurst & Fisher, 4th Floor, Liverpool Victoria House, New London Road, Chelmsford, Essex CN2 0PP
01245-495111

Correspondent: The Trustees

Trustees: J E Tolhurst; J S Cue; W J Tolhurst.

Beneficial area: UK or local to Essex.

Information available: Full accounts are on file at the Charity Commission up to 1992.

General: Although the trust has general charitable objects, in practice it tends to support church buildings, Christian poverty action groups and children (including uniformed organisations such as scout groups).

In 1992, the trust had assets of £406,000, an income of £218,000 and gave grants totalling £125,000. Grants are usually about £400 or £500, although an exceptional grant of £80,000 was given to the Fowler Memorial Trust (which shares the same correspondent and two trustees - see separate entry). Other recipients of larger grants were St Theresa Parish Church (£15,000); St Cedds Church and Avenue Baptist Church (£10,000 each) and the Raleigh Trust (£5,000). The smaller, more typical grants (about £500) were given to organisations such as Family Care, Belvue Baptist Church, Friends of St Nicholas School and scout groups.

Exclusions: The trustees have stated that they will not fund things they believe are the responsibility of social services or the state. Recently they have turned down a request from Great Ormond Street Hospital for funding towards a parent accommodation block, and a request to refurbish a house to help a patient leaving a psychiatric hospital as the trustees believed this to be the responsibility of social services. The trustees stated that charitable trusts cannot afford to take on the traditional role of the state.

Applications: In writing to the correspondent.

The J E Joseph Charitable Fund

£73,000 (1993/94)

Jewish

Royex House, 5 Aldermanbury Square, London EC2V 2HD
0171-457 3000

Correspondent: Timothy M Simon, Secretary

Beneficial area: UK, with a preference for London and Manchester; the Near and Far East, Israel and Palestine.

Information available: Full accounts are available at the Charity Commission for 1993/94.

General: The trust was set up for the benefit of Jewish communities for the relief of poverty; relief of suffering of poor Jews; advancement of education and the Jewish religion; other purposes beneficial to Jewish communities. Grants are only given to or through Jewish organisations.

In 1993/94, the trust had assets of £2 million and an income of £82,000. Grants totalled £73,000 and were broken down as follows:

Home organisations (general): 20 grants of £500 to £5,500 totalling £38,000

Home organisations (schools): six grants of £1,000 to £2,500 totalling £10,000

Far East organisations: five grants of £200 to £2,500 totalling £4,000

Israel student scheme: seven grants of £500 to £6,000 totalling £19,000

Individuals and sundry: five grants of £440 to £1,000 totalling £2,000

All grants were to Jewish organisations, the largest of which were: Jacob Benjamin Elias Synagogue (two grants totalling £9,100); Spanish & Portuguese Jews Congregation (£5,000) and National Jewish Chaplaincy Board (£3,500).

Exclusions: No grants to individuals.

Applications: In writing to the correspondent.

The Lady Eileen Joseph Foundation

£118,000 (1992/93)

General

Stoy Hayward, 8 Baker Street, London W1M 1DA
0171-486 5888

Correspondent: A A Davis

Trustees: Lady Joseph; A A Davis; Mrs J Sawdy.

Beneficial area: UK.

Information available: Full accounts are on file at the Charity Commission.

General: The trust was registered in 1987. The accounts for 1992/93 show the trust had assets of £766,000 and an income of £159,000, about half of which was from donations. 18 grants were given totalling £118,000, £100,000 of which was to Help the Hospices. The other main grants were GRET and Open University (£5,000 each). The remaining grants were for £50 to £1,400 and included Action on Addiction (£200); Living Image Appeal (£450); National Aids Trust (£1,000); Royal Opera House Trust (£1,400); Spinal Injuries Association (£1,000), and the Weizmann Institute Foundation (£1,000).

Applications: In writing to the correspondent.

The Judge Charitable Foundation

£47,000 (1992/93)

General

Grange Farm, Elmbridge, Droitwich, Worcestershire WR9 0DA
01527-861204

Correspondent: P R Judge, Trustee

Trustees: Paul R Judge; A M Judge.

Beneficial area: UK, with a preference for Worcestershire.

Information available: Full accounts are on file at the Charity Commission.

General: This trust was established in 1992. In early April 1992 and 1993, it received substantial donations from Paul Judge totalling £4.1 million. By April 1993, its assets were £5.23 million.

Grants in 1992/93 totalled £47,000. Three grants were given: £30,000 to Worcester Cathedral Trust; £10,000 to the Prince's Trust, and £7,000 to Worcestershire Nature Conservation Trust Ltd.

The trustees' report states: "The main cash resources of the charity were maintained in bank deposits to meet future commitments of the trustees to fund a major part of the development of the new Institute of Management Studies at the University of Cambridge".

Applications: In writing to the correspondent.

The Stanley Kalms Foundation (formerly the Kalms Family Charitable Trust)

£261,000 (1993/94)

Jewish education and medical

29 Farm Street, London W1X 7RD
0171-499 3494

Correspondent: Miss O Morgan

Trustees: Stanley Kalms; Pamela Kalms; Richard Kalms; Stephen Kalms; Paul Kalms.

Beneficial area: Worldwide.

Information available: Accounts are on file at the Charity Commission, but without a list of grants.

General: The foundation was set up in 1989 with £2.8 million when all capital and income of the former Kalms Family Charitable Trust was transferred to it. "The main objectives of the foundation are the encouragement of orthodox Jewish education in the UK and Israel and to be particularly involved in the granting of scholarships, fellowships and research grants. Other activities include support for the arts and medicine and other programmes both secular and religious."

In 1993/94, the trust had assets of £1.93 million and an income of £94,000 (down from £192,000 the previous year owing to a fall in investment income). Grants totalled £261,000 and have for the past few years been considerably higher than the income, with the trust spending capital. In 1992/93, grants totalled £604,000 and the income only £192,000; in 1991/92 grants totalled £566,000 and the income £210,000.

No grants list was available for 1993/94 or 1992/93.

In 1991/92, grants totalled £556,000, broken down as follows (1990/91 figures in brackets):

Annual donations	£355,700	(£323,000)
Other donations	£149,000	(£186,000)
Fellowship grants	£56,000	(£36,000)
Research grants	£5,000	(£11,000)

The vast majority of recipients were Jewish charities, particularly those concerned with education, including the Jewish Educational Development Trust (£200,000, the fourth of five grants). £68,000 was given to the Traditional Alternatives Foundation (established by Stanley and Pamela Kalms in 1990), which receives a regular grant. The number of years over which a grant is given varies, the Pelech Charitable Trust receiving the seventh of eight payments of £36,000. All the other annual grants were to Jewish organisations. Of the 15 annual donations listed in 1991/92, seven were due to receive their final payment in 1992/93, and a further three in 1993/94.

"Other donations" included two major grants: £29,000 to Jerusalem College and £25,000 to Jews College. The only award of over £500 to a non-Jewish charity seems to be the £1,500 to the Royal Opera House Trust.

Applications: In writing to the correspondent, but note that most of the trust's funds are committed to projects supported for a number of years.

The Ian Karten Charitable Trust

£64,000 to organisations (1993/94)

Education

The Mill House, Newark Lane, Ripley, Surrey GU23 6DP

Correspondent: I H Karten

Trustees: I H Karten; Mrs M Karten; T M Simon.

Beneficial area: Mainly UK.

Information available: Accounts are on file at the Charity Commission, but without a list of grants.

General: In 1993/94, this trust had assets of £5.8 million and an income fund of £250,000. Grants to charities totalled £64,000 and £178,000 was given in scholarships and bursaries to 200 students.

The grants to charities include many to Jewish organisations. For information on the grants to individuals see *The Educational Grants Directory*.

Applications: In writing to the correspondent. It is understood that the trustees prefer to take their own direct initiatives in support of charities.

The Michael & Ilse Katz Foundation

£145,000 (1990/91)

Jewish, general

New Garden House, 78 Hatton Garden, London EC1N 8JA
0171-831 7393

Correspondent: A D Foreman, Trustees' Accountant

Trustees: Norris Gilbert; Osman Azis.

Beneficial area: Worldwide.

Information available: Full accounts are on file at the Charity Commission up to 1990/91.

General: In 1990/91, the trust had assets of £1.15 million and an income of £82,000. Grants totalled £145,000, with over half that total going to one organisation, the Federation of Jewish Relief Organisations, which received five grants during the year totalling £81,000.

Over 60 grants were given, with just under half to Jewish organisations. Other large grants went to Glyndebourne Productions Ltd (£20,000) with a further £2,500 to the Glyndebourne Festival Society, Group Relations Educational Trust (£7,000) and the Western Orchestral Society (£6,000).

A further 11 grants were for £1,000 or more, all to Jewish organisations. The remaining grants ranged from £50 upwards, with most for a few hundred pounds. Most grants to non-Jewish beneficiaries were to medical or welfare charities including Age Concern, British Retinitis Pigmentosa Society, Ex-Services Mental Welfare Society, MIND, Northern Ballet Theatre and the Samaritans.

Applications: In writing to the correspondent.

The Katzauer Charitable Settlement

£50,000 (1992/93)

Jewish

Devonshire House, 1 Devonshire Street, London W1N 2DR
0171-637 2841

Correspondent: P M Emanuel

Trustees: A Katzauer; P M Emanuel; G C Smith.

Beneficial area: UK and Israel.

Information available: Full accounts are on file at the Charity Commission.

General: In 1992/93, the trust had assets of £500,000 and an income of £74,000. Grants were given totalling £50,000. The previous year's grants totalled £32,000 from an income of £76,000. All grants are to Jewish organisations, mainly in Israel.

The largest included those to: Meir Hospital Infar Saba (£16,000); Tzeirei Agudat Chabad (£4,500); Kollel Ra'aniana (£3,700), and Children of Chernobyl (£500). Other grants of £150 or less totalled £4,000.

Applications: In writing to the correspondent.

The C S Kaufman Charitable Trust

£45,000 (1992/93)

Jewish

162 Whitehall Road, Gateshead, Tyne & Wear NE8 1TP
0191-477 3929

Correspondent: C S Kaufman

Trustees: I I Kaufman; J Kaufman.

Beneficial area: UK and overseas.

Information available: Full accounts are on file at the Charity Commission.

General: In 1992/93, the trust had assets of £178,000 and an income of £53,000 (from rents). 23 grants were given ranging from £50 to £30,000, and totalling £45,000.

All the beneficiaries were Jewish organisations. The largest grants went to the Telz Academy Trust (£30,000), Society of Frinds of the Torah (£4,900), Jewish Teachers Training College Gateshead (£2,800) and Gateshead Jewish Primary School (£2,600).

Applications: In writing to the correspondent.

The Emmanuel Kaye Foundation

£45,000 (1993/94)

Medical research, general

Messrs Gouldens, 22 Tudor Street, London EC4Y 0JJ
0171-583 7777

Correspondent: D P H Burgess

Trustees: Sir Emmanuel Kaye; Lady Kaye; John Scriven; Michael Cutler.

Beneficial area: UK and overseas.

Information available: Full accounts are on file at the Charity Commission.

General: The founder's personal interest was medical research and he funded research at two London teaching hospitals. The trust will probably follow that lead.

In the four years up to 1990, the trust's income consisted of a £10,000 donation, with grants being given up to this figure. Since then the trust has regularly received a donation taking its annual income to well over £100,000. It appears that the trust is building up its assets, with a consistent surplus of income over expenditure. By 1993/94, assets had increased to £646,000 which is held as cash at the bank, possibly for future large projects.

In 1993/94, the trust had an income of £147,000 including a further donation of £65,000. Grants totalled only £45,000. 16 of the 40 grants made were of £1,000 or more, with the largest to St Michael's Hospice (£10,000), Thames Salmon Trust (£3,750), BTCV and Summer Fields School (both £3,000), Holocaust Educational Trust (£2,500) and the Psionic Medical Society and Save the Children Fund (both £2,000).

Smaller grants were given to a range of causes, especially medical charities. Beneficiaries included the Adam Smith Research Institute, Basingstoke Churches Housing Group, Glyndebourne Festival, Horder Centre for Arthritis, Natural Medicines Society, Population Concern and Relate. About a quarter of the grants were to Jewish organisations.

Applications: In writing to the correspondent.

The Geoffrey John Kaye Charitable Foundation

£56,000 (1992/93)

Jewish

Messrs Philips Eli & Gross, 54 Welbeck Street, London W1M 7HE
0171-935 1339

Correspondent: R J Freebody

Trustees: G J Kaye; S Rose.

Beneficial area: UK and overseas.

Information available: Full accounts are on file at the Charity Commission.

General: In 1992/93, the trust had assets of £738,000 and an income of £44,000. 10 grants totalled £56,000. All but one were given to Jewish organisations, seven of which were recurrent from previous years.

Grants of £6,000 to £15,000 went made to the Austen Trust, JPAIME, Lubavitch Foundation, Nightingale House and Tova Trust. The three "new" beneficiaries were Jewish Care (£1,000), Friends of Yeshiva Gedola Lubavitch (£500) and Variety Club Children's Charity (£250).

Applications: In writing to the correspondent.

The Patrick Joseph Kennedy Charitable Trust

£75,000 (1993/94)

General

Touche Ross & Company, 74 Mosley Street, Manchester M60 2AT
0161-228 3456

Correspondent: Brown Street Nominees Ltd

Trustees: Patrick J Kennedy; John T Kennedy; Brown Street Nominees Ltd.

Beneficial area: UK.

Information available: Full accounts are on file at the Charity Commission.

General: This general trust was set up in 1973 by Patrick Joseph Kennedy and has substantial holdings in Kennedy Construction Group Ltd and Kennedy Civil

Engineering. Kennedy Construction also set up a deed of covenant for £10,000 a year starting in 1990.

In 1993/94, the income of £158,000 included £152,000 in Gift Aid payments and £6,000 from investments.

51 grants were given totalling £75,000. The trust has generally followed a consistent pattern in both size of payment and nature of beneficiaries. Most but not all grants were, as previously, to Catholic church affiliated groups receiving funding for educational, medical and parish/diocese work, the largest being the Brian Robson Scanner Appeal which received a grant of £5,000, and the Columban Fathers which received a grant of £3,000.

The Rainbow Family Trust exceptionally received a donation of £25,000. The average grant was about £1,000.

Applications: In writing to the correspondent.

The Kennel Club Charitable Trust

£60,000 (1993/94)

Dogs

1-5 Clarges Street, Piccadilly, London W1Y 8AB
0171-493 6651

Correspondent: J A MacDougall

Trustees: J A MacDougall; M J R Stockman; R J Clifford.

Beneficial area: UK.

Information available: Full accounts are on file at the Charity Commission.

General: The trust funds organisations dedicated to helping disadvantaged dogs and disadvantaged humans aided by dogs. In 1993/94, the trust had assets of £360,000 and an income of £33,000 (down from £84,000 the previous year mainly due to a fall in donations received from £58,000 to £12,000). Grants totalled £60,000.

It is currently funding two major projects: £25,000 was given to the Animal Health Trust – the first of three grants in support of an epidemiological study of the incidence of canine disease, and £20,000 was given to the Royal Free Medical School for work on distinguishing between breeds of dogs using DNA research. A further £2,500 was given to the Royal College of Veterinary Surgeons Trust Fund for bursaries for nurses.

Smaller grants were given to: UK charities concerned with welfare of dogs such as PDSA (£4,000) and Blue Cross Kennels (£1,500); local charities concerned with welfare of dogs, including "sanctuaries" and "rescue" organisations; UK charities concerned with dogs aiding humans, including Hearing Dogs for the Deaf and Dogs for the Disabled (both £1,500).

Applications: In writing to the correspondent. The trustees meet three times a year.

The Peter Kershaw Trust

£197,000 (1993/94)

Medical research, school fees, general

KPMG, St James' Square, Manchester M2 6DS
0161-838 4000

Correspondent: H W E Thompson, Secretary

Trustees: P Kershaw; H F Kershaw; B B Pugh; M L Rushbrooke; R Kershaw.

Beneficial area: Manchester and the surrounding district.

Information available: Full accounts are on file at the Charity Commission.

General: The principal activities of the trust continue to be funding medical research projects, making grants to medical institutions and to schools for bursaries. In addition, it funds joint operations for up to six patients per year.

In 1993/94, the trust had assets of £704,000 and an income of £238,000. Grants totalled £197,000 distributed as follows:

School fee grants	£25,000
Medical research	£26,000
Joint operations	£11,000
Medical institutions	£90,000
Other donations	£45,000

The largest grants were given to Booth Hall Children's Hospital (£69,000), David Lewis Appeal Fund (£21,000), Family Welfare Association (£19,000), Withington Girls' School (£17,000), and East Cheshire Hospice and Lifeshare (both £10,000).

Exclusions: No grants to individuals or to organisations outside the beneficial area.

Applications: In writing to the correspondent.

Keswick Foundation Ltd

£165,000 (1990)

Social welfare in Hong Kong, China

c/o Frere Chomley Bischoff, 4 John Carpenter Street, London EC4Y 0NH
0171-615 8000

Trustees: J J Brown; Lady Cater; Prof N Chow; Mrs C P Courtauld; Mrs M K Jencks; S Keswick; Mrs E Keswick; R C Kwok; F Lee; W Turnbull; S Yung; Mrs C Weatherall; Mrs V Morrison; Ms M Yung; Mrs E Wong.

Beneficial area: Hong Kong, China.

Information available: We were unable to see the Charity Commission file for this trust.

General: Set up in 1979, the foundation concentrates on funding pilot projects for social welfare services in Hong Kong.

By 1990, it had built up assets of about £5 million, consisting mainly of 2.7 million shares in Jardine Matheson Holdings. These provided most of the £237,000 income for the year. Grants of £165,000 were made, although the beneficiaries were not specified.

According to the Charity Commission database, the foundation had an income of £525,000 in 1992, but no further information was available.

Applications: Should be made by social welfare organisations with an attached Funding Application Form duly completed.

The Robert Kiln Charitable Trust

£48,000 (1993/94)

Archaeology, environmental conservation, musical education

15a Bull Plain, Hertford SG14 1DX

Correspondent: Mrs Margaret Archer

Trustees: Mrs S F Chappell; S W J Kiln; Mrs B Kiln; Dr N P Akers; Mrs J E Akers.

Beneficial area: UK, with a special interest in Hertfordshire and Bedfordshire.

Information available: Full accounts are on file at the Charity Commission.

General: The trust was formed in 1970 by Robert Kiln, a Lloyd's underwriter, and the five present trustees are all members of his family. It's income comes from dividends on the shares it holds in Lloyds and investments in UK equities and unit trusts.

The trust supports organisations concerned with archaeology, environmental conservation and musical education. Grants are usually one-off or instalments for particular projects. Salaries are not considered. Grants generally range from £100 to £1,000. The trust supports a wide range of causes, local, national and international, with a preference for Hertfordshire and Bedfordshire-based organisations, some of which appear to be regular beneficiaries.

In 1993/94, the trust had assets of £335,000 and an ordinary income of £56,000. It gave 57 grants totalling £48,000. 24 were for £1,000 or more, with the remainder ranging from £75 to £750. The largest grant was £5,000 to Hertford Museum. Other grants of £1,000 to £2,000 were mostly to organisations within the trust's main areas of support including East Sussex Archaeological Museums Project, Hatfield Philharmonia Orchestra, Hertford Symphony Orchestra, Institute of Archaeology, Intermediate Technology and Ware Priory Appeal.

Other groups receiving grants of £1,000 or more included Bath Institute of Medical Engineering, Insulin Dependent Diabetic Trust, Parent Network and Hertford branch of Save the Children. Smaller grants went to a range of organisations including Avoncroft Museum Development Trust, CPRE, 1st Hertford Scout Group, Link Romania, Royston Home Start and Talking Newspaper for the Blind - Hertford branch.

Exclusions: Applications from individuals, churches, schools or artistic projects (eg. theatre groups) will not be considered. The trust will no longer acknowledge receipt of applications.

Applications: In writing to the correspondent, setting out as much information as seems relevant and, if possible, costings and details of any other support. Two distribution meetings are held a year, usually in Jan/Feb and July/August.

The Mary Kinross Charitable Trust

£310,000 (1993/94)

Mental health

36 Grove Avenue, Moseley, Birmingham B13 9RY

Correspondent: Fiona Adams, Secretary

Trustees: Fiona Adams; H Jon Foulds; Robert McDougall; Elizabeth Shields; John Walker-Haworth; Peter Wreford.

Beneficial area: Mainly England.

Information available: Full reports and accounts are on file at the Charity Commission.

General: The trust has a clear policy following the wishes of the founder "to use the trust income to support a few carefully researched projects, rather than to make many small grants. At least one trustee takes responsibility for ensuring close involvement of the trust with organisations to which major grants are made. The trust no longer has a policy of supporting projects for the elderly."

In 1993/94, the trust had assets of £2.8 million generating an income of £311,000. The report accompanying the accounts states: "Several organisations are due to receive instalments of sizeable, continuing grants. The payment to the London Suzuki Group forecast in last year's report will be made in 1994/95. Planning for the extension to the Warstock Community Centre has continued throughout the year, and the majority of the expenditure is likely in 1994/95. No new major projects can be considered until 1997 at the earliest. Future expenditure is likely to be concentrated in the mental health field".

The trust made 16 grants during the year, giving details of the eight largest. These included £164,000 to the National Schizophrenia Fellowship - the second payment of a grant over 3/4 years towards the core funding of the London and South East Region Office, and £50,000 towards Schizophrenia Research at the Royal Free Hospital (this was the fourth grant made to the project and the research work carried out is outlined in the report of the trust).

Other large grants included £25,000 to the Birmingham Rathbone Society, the third of three grants for core office costs; £19,000 to HARP (Helping with Alcohol and Related Problems), towards salary costs at a project in Birmingham, a continuing interest of the trust; £14,500 to Warstock & Billesley Detached Youthwork Project, an on-going commitment towards salary costs.

The remaining eight grants of up to £1,000 are either continuing payments to organisations in which the trust takes a special interest, or one-off small grants to meet a particular need. Beneficiaries included Alzheimer's Disease Society, City of London Migraine Clinic, Penumbra and the CARE Fund. In addition, trustees continue to give time to two projects, Student Homes Ltd and the Bendrigg Trust, initiated but no longer funded by the trust.

Exclusions: No grants to individuals.

Applications: By letter to the correspondent. However, the trust states (and its grant-making seems to confirm) that it hardly ever responds to unsolicited appeals. Trustees meet quarterly.

The Kobler Trust

£234,000 (1992/93)

Jewish, general

Stoy Hayward, 8 Baker Street, London W1M 1DA
0171-486 5888

Correspondent: Alfred A Davis

Trustees: Alfred A Davis; A Xuereb; A H Stone.

Beneficial area: UK.

Information available: Full accounts are on file at the Charity Commission.

General: Fred Kobler set up the trust in 1963 with an endowment of 250,000 shares in Grand Metropolitan Hotels Ltd. It shares the same correspondent as the Adint Trust (see *A Guide to the Major Trusts Vol. 1*).

In the last two years the grant total of the trust has risen to over £200,000, its level of about four years ago, after falling to £69,000 in 1990/91. In 1992/93, the trust had assets of £2.8 million and an income of £220,000.

18 grants were given totalling £234,000 and ranging from £1,000 to £102,000. By far the largest grant was to Imperial College of £102,000. Other grants over £10,000 went to Crusaid (£27,000), Beit Issie Shapiro (£20,000), Bud Flanagan Leukaemia Fund & Variety Club Golfing

Society (£17,500) and Tel Aviv University Trust (£12,000). Adventures in Motion Pictures, British Olim Society and Royal Academy of Music each received £10,000.

The remaining grants were to Jewish, welfare and arts organisations including Barnardo's (£2,000), British ORT (£3,000), Family Welfare Association (£2,000), Leeds Community Foundation (£1,500) and Mount View Theatre School Ltd (£2,000).

Exclusions: Grants are given to individuals only in exceptional circumstances.

Applications: In writing to the correspondent.

The Kreditor Charitable Trust

£63,000 (1992/93)

Jewish, welfare, education

Gerald Kreditor & Co, Chartered Accountants, Tudor House, Llanvanor Road, London NW2 2AQ
0181-209 1535

Correspondent: G Kreditor

Trustees: Gerald Kreditor; Merle Kreditor.

Beneficial area: UK.

Information available: Accounts are on file at the Charity Commission for 1992/93.

General: This trust was set up in 1985, but there is only one set of accounts (for 1992/93) on file at the Charity Commission. Those accounts reveal that although it only has assets of £8,000, its income through "collections and donations" totalled over £63,000.

Numerous donations were made during the year, mainly to Jewish organisations working in education and social and medical welfare. Beneficiaries were scattered across London and the north east of England. The vast majority of grants were for less than £100. A notable exception was Fordeve Ltd (two grants totalling £20,000) which is another charitable trust for which Gerald Kreditor is also the named correspondent.

Other recipients included: London Academy of Jewish Studies; Jerusalem Ladies Society; NW London Talmudical College; Ravenswood; Academy for Rabbinical Research; British Friends of Israel War Disabled; Kosher Meals on Wheels; Jewish Marriage Council and Jewish Care. Non-Jewish organisations supported included: RNID; UNICEF UK and British Diabetic Association.

Applications: In writing to the correspondent.

The Jill Kreitman Foundation

£283,000 (1993/94)

Jewish, disability, children

Citroen Wells (Chartered Accountants), 1 Devonshire Street, London W1N 2DR
0171-637 2841

Correspondent: Eric Charles, Trustee

Trustees: Mrs Jill Luck-Hille; P M Luck-Hille; Eric Charles.

Beneficial area: UK and Israel.

Information available: Full accounts are on file at the Charity Commission.

General: The foundation was established for general charitable purposes in 1975 by Jill Kreitman (now Mrs Luck-Hille), daughter of Hyman and Irene Kreitman (see entry for the Kreitman Foundation in *A Guide to the Major Trusts Vol. 1*). All three of the Kreitman Foundations share Eric Charles as trustee and correspondent, but each seem to have different priorities.

In 1993/94, assets were £2.6 million. Like its brother foundation the Neil Kreitman, this makes donations to few organisations but in large amounts. The grant total fluctuates widely from year to year (the income figure is given in brackets):

1990/91	£171,000 (£256,000)
1991/92	£240,000 (£192,000)
1992/93	£111,000 (£191,000)
1993/94	£283,000 (£174,000)

In 1993/94, 12 organisations received funding, four of which were on the grants list for the previous year. The largest award went to the King Alfred School Appeal Fund which received £209,000 and has been a regular beneficiary. The British Disabled Water Ski Association received £38,000 and has also received large grants in previous years. The other regular beneficiaries, Norwood Child Care and Childhope UK both received £1,000. Other larger grants went to Birthright (£13,000), Lord's Taverners (£7,500) and Marylebone Foundation (£5,000). The remaining grants went to two Jewish organisations and three hospital appeals which each received under £500.

Exclusions: No grants to individuals.

Applications: To the correspondent in writing. The trustees seem to have a list of regular beneficiaries and it may be unlikely that any new applications will be successful.

The Heinz & Anna Kroch Foundation

£64,000 to organisations (1993/94)

Medical research and severe poverty or hardship

PO Box 17, Worsley, Manchester M28 2TL
0161-793 4201

Correspondent: Mrs H Astle

Trustees: Mrs Ann Carol Kroch-Rhodes; Benjamin Rhodes; Henry Justus Kroch; Christopher Richardson; Peter English.

Beneficial area: UK.

Information available: Accounts are on file at the Charity Commission, but without a list of grants.

General: In 1993/94, the trust had assets of £2 million and an income of £406,000. The increase in income from £110,000 in 1992/93 is due to the sale of one half of the trust's half share in Possum Controls. This high level is a one-off, and income in the future is likely to be in the region of £150,000. Total expenditure in 1993/94 was £167,000, of which £64,000 was given to organisations.

The foundation gives grants to new and existing medical research projects.

It also gives to individuals suffering severe financial hardship (applications must be made through welfare agencies – see *A Guide to Grants for Individuals in Need*).

Exclusions: Students of any kind, churches or holidays. Funds for refurbishing hospitals and newly created care homes are not supported.

Applications: Appeals are considered on a regular basis. Applications normally receive a reply.

The Christopher Laing Foundation

£176,000 (1992/93)

General

c/o Ernst & Young, 400 Capability Green, Luton LU1 3LU
01582-400700

Correspondent: The Secretary

Trustees: Donald Stradling; Peter Jackson; Christopher Laing.

Beneficial area: UK.

Information available: Full accounts are on file at the Charity Commission.

General: This trust had assets of £2.2 milion in 1993. Its income from investments is reducing. In 1992/93, it gave 15 grants ranging between £1,000 and £60,000, the largest disbursement being the £60,000 to the Charities Aid Foundation, presumably to handle the adminstration of smaller grants.

The named grants give an "eclectic" impression. The larger grants were made to the Chartered Institute of Building reflecting the family business interests (£40,000); the Sports Council Trust (£25,000); Save the Children (£15,000); Simona Trust Romania (£7,500). Other grants were given to the Undetected Tumour Survey, London Suzuki Group and the Letchworth Centre for Homeopathy and Complementary Medicine.

Exclusions: Donations to registered charities only.

Applications: In writing to the correspondent.

The David Laing Foundation

£120,000 (1992/93)

Not known

The Studio, Mackerye End, Harpenden AL5 5DR

Correspondent: The Trustees

Trustees: David Eric Laing; John Stuart Lewis; Richard Francis Barlow; Frances Mary Laing.

Beneficial area: Worldwide.

Information available: Accounts are on file at the Charity Commission, without a list of grants, up to 1990/91 only.

General: We have not been able to update the information for this trust. This entry repeats that in the previous edition.

In 1991/92, the trust had assets of £2.2 million and an income of £280,000. Grants totalled £375,000, dropping to £120,000 in 1992/93 after a decrease in the assets following a £540,0000 donation from the capital account to MacIntyre in 1992.

No further information is available on the grant distribution.

Applications: In writing to the correspondent.

The Martin Laing Foundation

£331,000 (1993/94)

General

c/o Ernst & Young, 400 Capability Green, Luton LU1 3LU
01582-400700

Correspondent: The Secretary

Trustees: John Martin Laing; Donald Stradling; Brian O Chilver; Edward Charles Laing.

Beneficial area: UK.

Information available: Full accounts are on file at the Charity Commission.

General: This trust, in common with the David and Christopher Laing Charitable Trusts, had a large increase in its assets in 1990/91 following the sale of investments.

In 1993/94, the trust had assets of £2.3 million and an income of £172,000. Grants totalled £331,000 distributed as follows (figures in brackets are for 1992/93):

Charities Aid Foundation	£200,000	(£240,000)
Princess Helena College	£50,000	(£75,000)
World Wide Fund for Nature	£34,000	(£45,000)
Young Enterprise	£7,500	–
Hertfordshire Heritage	£10,000	–
City of London Sinfonia	£26,000	–
Prince of Wales – Business in the Environment Programme	£3,333	(£10,000)

In 1992/93, grants totalled £390,000 from an income of £241,000. The only beneficiary not listed above was Cranfield Institute of Technology which received £20,000.

The excess of grants given over income for the last two years is more than accounted for by the surplus of income over expenditure carried forward from the previous two years.

Applications: In writing to the correspondent. The trust states that, "annually, they [the trustees] consider an ever increasing amount of applications for assistance and accordingly have requested that the entry for the foundation be excluded". We maintain our policy of including all relevant grant-making trusts, but potential applicants should note that the trust appears to make a small number of large mostly recurrent grants.

The Langdale Trust

£100,000 (1993)

Social welfare, general

c/o Lee Crowder & Co, 24 Harborne Road, Edgbaston, Birmingham B15 3AD
0121-456 4477

Correspondent: M J Woodward

Trustees: T R Wilson; Mrs T Elvin; M J Woodward.

Beneficial area: Worldwide, but with a special interest in Birmingham.

Information available: Full accounts are on file at the Charity Commission.

General: In 1993, the trust had an income of £100,000 all of which was given in grants. 39 grants were made of which 30 were recurrent from the previous year.

The largest grants went to Christian Aid (£6,000) and the Bible Society and Oxfam (both £5,000). Grants of £4,000 each went to Help the Aged, Leprosy Mission and Save the Children. 10 grants were for £3,000, 19 for £2,000 and 4 for £1,000. Over half the grants went to national charities such as AIDS Care Education & Training, Barnardo's and the Mental Health Foundation. Most were in the fields of social welfare and health.

Other grants went to local charities in Birmingham (eg. Birmingham Association of Youth Clubs, Samaritans Birmingham and Balsall Heath Church Centre URC), Christian organisations and overseas relief and welfare organisations.

Applications: In writing to the correspondent.

The Lanvern Foundation

£16,000 (1993)

General

PO Box 7017, Hook, Hampshire RG29 1UL
0171-395 2168

Correspondent: J C G Stancliffe

Trustees: J C G Stancliffe; R A Stancliffe; A H Isaacs.

Beneficial area: UK.

Information available: Full accounts are on file at the Charity Commission.

General: The trustees report for 1993 stated that the trust supports charities working primarily in the fields of education and health, with particular emphasis on children. The foundation is still building up its assets.

In 1993, it had an income of £49,000 and grants totalled £16,000. The previous year, grants totalled £7,000 from an income of £155,000.

Five grants were given in 1993: £5,000 to both Joy to the World and the Treloar Trust; £2,500 to both I CAN and St Michael's Hospice, and £1,000 to the Friends of St Mary's Church, Greywell.

Applications: In writing to the correspondent.

The Lark Trust

£8,000 (1993/94)

General

Narrow Quay House, Prince Street, Bristol BS1 4AH
0117-927 6567

Correspondent: Burges Salmon

Trustees: I G Tute; G W Tute.

Beneficial area: UK.

Information available: Full accounts are on file at the Charity Commission.

General: The trust was established in 1988, since when its assets have risen steadily, owing to very little of the annual income being given in grants. In 1992/93, the trust had an income of £110,000, including a £75,000 donation; grants totalled only £13,000. In 1993/94, it had an income of £250,000 including a £150,000 donation. Grants totalled only £8,000. The assets of the trust now stand at £683,000.

The £8,000 was distributed between 16 charities, with £2,000 each given to the Society of Friends and Avon Counselling & Psychotherapy Service. Barnardo's received £1,000 and the remaining grants ranged from £50 to £500 including those to Artspace, Friends of the Earth, Help the Aged, Oxfam and the Salvation Army. A number of the grants were recurrent.

Applications: In writing to the correspondent.

Lasletts (Hinton) Charity

£85,000 (1992)

Church repairs, general in Worcestershire

3-5 Sansome Place, Worcester WR1 1UQ
01905-726600

Correspondent: H E Wagstaffe

Beneficial area: Mainly the city and county of Worcester.

Information available: Accounts are on file at the Charity Commission but without a list of grants.

General: This trust is mainly for church repairs and general charitable causes in Worcestershire. In 1992, the trust had assets of £2.4 million and an income of £139,000. Property expenses totalled £76,000. Grants and church repairs totalled £85,000. No further information is available.

Applications: In writing to the correspondent.

Rachel & Jack Lass Charities Ltd

£50,000 (1991/92)

Children's charities, Jewish

Cohen Arnold & Co, 13-17 New Burlington Place, Regent Street, London NW1X 2JP

Correspondent: B A Abrahams

Trustees: The Directors.

Beneficial area: UK.

Information available: Full accounts are on file at the Charity Commission.

General: In 1991/92, the trust had an income of £149,000 all from Covenants and Gift Aid donations. Grants totalled £50,000. The trust states that it prefers to support children's charities.

68 grants were given of which 56 were for £250 or less. The largest grants were given to Yeshiva Horomo and Friends of Harinin Establishment (both £10,000), Yesodey Hatorah (£7,500) and Shaare Zedek Medical Centre (£5,000).

The largest grant to a non-Jewish organisation was £550 to St John's Ambulance, with smaller grants to Alzheimers Disease Society, British Sports Association for the Disabled, Motability and SENSE.

Exclusions: No grants to students.

Applications: In writing to the correspondent.

The R & D Lauffer Charitable Foundation

£90,000 (1993/94)

Jewish, general

15 Wilwood Road, London NW11 6UL

Correspondent: R R Lauffer

Trustees: R R Lauffer; J S Lauffer; G L Lauffer.

Beneficial area: Worldwide.

Information available: Full accounts are on file at the Charity Commission.

General: In 1993/94, the foundation had assets of £365,000 and an income of

£84,000. The trustees gave grants to about 150 organisations totalling £90,000.

16 grants were for £1,000 or more, all to Jewish organisations including British Friends of OHR Somayach (£14,500), CBF World Jewish Relief (£4,000), Hillel House (£5,000) and JPAIME (£7,500).

Most of the remaining grants were under £500 with about one third to non-Jewish organisations including BTCV, Crisis, Friends of English National Opera, Hearing Research Trust, Samaritans and SENSE.

Exclusions: No support for individuals.

Applications: In writing to the correspondent.

The Kathleen Laurence Trust

£137,000 (1992/93)

General

Coutts & Co, 440 Strand, London WC2R 0QS
0171-753 1000

Correspondent: Manager, Trustee Department

Trustees: Coutts & Co.

Beneficial area: UK.

Information available: Full accounts are on file at the Charity Commission.

General: In 1992/93, the trust had an income of £117,000 and gave grants totalling £137,000. 36 grants were made ranging from £1,000 to £10,000.

The largest were to Cot Death Research & Support and the Mental Health Foundation £10,000 (each). 16 grants of £5,000 were all to medical or welfare causes including the AIDIS Trust, Contact a Family, DEBRA, Hodgkin's Disease Association, NSPCC and Wessex Cancer Trust.

Most of the other grants were also to medical and welfare causes with other beneficiaries being Greater Manchester Play Resources Unit (£1,000), Live Music Now! (£2,500) and Playdays (£2,500). About one third of grants were recurrent from the previous year.

The previous year 43 grants were made totalling £137,000, again predominantly to health and welfare causes. £10,000 was given to both Downside & Worth Boys' Club and the Field Lane Foundation.

Applications: In writing to the correspondent. Trustees meet quarterly.

The Edgar E Lawley Foundation

£86,000 (1992/93)

General, medical research, education, elderly people

c/o Lawley House, Sloane Court East, London SW3 4TO
0171-730 0929

Correspondent: J N Richardson

Trustees: Mrs M D Heath; J N Richardson; Miss E Jacobs; J H Cooke; Mrs G V H Hilton.

Beneficial area: UK.

Information available: Full accounts are on file at the Charity Commission.

General: The trust's objects are general charitable purposes with "particular reference to medicine, to necessitous elderly persons, and to educational purposes with reference to the arts, commerce and industry".

In 1992/93, the trust had assets of £725,000 and an income of £145,000. About 140 grants were made totalling £86,000.

The vast majority of the grants were for £500. The only two over £1,000 went to Epsom Health Care Trust – Air Beds Appeal (£5,000) and Bournemouth Old People's Welfare Housing (£1,500). Grants of £1,000 were given to Birmingham Children's Hospital, British Digestive Foundation, British Lung Foundation, British Wheelchair Sports Foundation, Fight for Sight, Jewish Care, London Clinic - Diamond Jubilee Fund, Marie Curie Memorial Foundation, Ronald McDonald House, Police Dependant's Trust, Royal Hospital & Home for Incurables, Springhill Cancer Centre & Hospice, St Martin's Dorking roof appeal, and St Richard's Hospice Foundation.

Smaller grants went to a wide range of national and local charities such as Birmingham Dogs Home, Dorking & District Age Concern, Lichfield Stroke Club, Oxfordshire Cheshire Home, Radio Lollipop, Royal Ballet Benevolent Fund and Samaritans.

Applications: In writing to the correspondent.

The Lawlor Foundation

£140,000 (1993/94)

Social welfare, education, general, especially in Ireland

117 High Street, Epping, Essex CM16 4BD
01992-561121; Fax: 01992-578727

Correspondent: Mrs Carley Brown

Trustees: Edward Lawlor; Virginia Lawlor; Stephen Morris; Kelly Lawlor; Martin Spiro; Frank Baker.

Beneficial area: In effect Ireland, London and the home counties.

Information available: A comprehensive annual report and accounts on file at the Charity Commission.

General: This trust has produced an exemplary report of its activities with commentary on its policy and financial capability, an analysis of its grant-aid and a brief description of each project supported. The trustees have a "particular interest in promoting cooperation and mutual understanding between the peoples of Ireland, North and South. Currently, the emphasis is on education, and the principal beneficiaries include a number of Northern Irish educational establishments and individual students, British-based organisations which support Irish immigrants, and vulnerable young people."

Grants are made on a one-off or recurring basis and can include core funding and salaries. A substantial proportion of the foundation's income is committed on a long-term basis, which restricts disposable income. This is because education, the area of support which is of particular interest to the trustees, has no logical "cut-off" point to stop funding and other funders would be unlikely to step in should support from the trust cease. Block grants to educational establishments and to individual students will become the main focus of grant-making for the forseeable future. Although the trust cannot yet support women's projects in general to the extent the trustees would wish, grants to girls' schools and "second chance" education for women will remain a priority.

The trust also notes that financial constraints of the past few years have meant that the maximum grant is now reduced with grants ranging from £250 to £10,000 to organisations and from £100 to

£1,500 to individuals. The maximum length of support is normally three years, but schools are invited to re-apply at the end of this period.

The trust had assets of £2.2 million in 1993/94 which generated a net income of £167,000. Grants totalled £140,000.

Grants were allocated as follows:

Geographical

	No. of grants	Total
Britain	11	£42,670
Northern Ireland	16	£75,600
Republic of Ireland	3	£10,700
Other	16	£11,030

Category

Education	27	£72,080
Social Welfare	12	£39,755
Women's Interest	4	£15,000
Peace & Reconciliation	3	£13,500

The larger grants in 1993/94 were annual grants of £10,000 each to Johnston House, to support the organisation's treatment of and research into adolescent breakdown, and to St Louise's College, Belfast, to help disadvantaged ex-pupils at UK and Irish universities and to support school projects and individual pupils, at the Principal's discretion. In total almost £61,000 went to five schools in Northern Ireland and one in the Republic, to Jesus College Cambridge to assist students from Northern Ireland, and to individual Irish students.

The social welfare programme included grants to Belfast Home Start (£2,500 towards administrative costs), Stepping Stone Project, Belfast (£1,000 to buy a computer system for a community centre for young people) and Youth in Need, Republic of Ireland (£1,000, the first of four grants towards the cost of helping unemployed and homeless Irish people in Britain return to Ireland).

The Women programme included support for Sydenham House, Belfast (£2,500) and Youth Action Northern Ireland (£5,000 towards the salary of a support worker for women and girls). The Peace and Reconciliation programme included the Civil Liberties Trust for a research project based at the Department of Law (£7,500, 2nd of 2).

Exclusions: No grants are made in response to general appeals from large national organisations or from organisations outside the geographical areas of Ireland, London and the Home Counties. Grants are not normally made to the arts, medicine, the environment, expeditions, children's projects or international causes.

Applications: By letter to the correspondent at any time, with a description of the project and a copy of latest accounts. The report notes that preliminary telephone enquiries are welcomed. Applications will only be acknowledged if they relate to the trustees' general interests. The trustees normally meet in March, June, September and December.

The Mrs F B Lawrence 1976 Charitable Settlement

£88,000 (1992/93)

General

c/o Haynes Hicks Beach, 10 New Square, London WC2A 3QG
0171-465 4300

Trustees: M Tooth; G S Brown; D A G Sarre.

Beneficial area: Worldwide.

Information available: Full accounts are on file at the Charity Commission.

General: The accounts on file at the Charity Commission for this trust cover six month periods. The assets in 1993 were £1.25 million, which generated an income of £49,000 in the six month period to June 1993, down from £60,000 in the previous six month period.

Grants totalled £88,000 over the year. Three beneficiaries are named in the trust deed, the RAF Benevolent Fund, RNLI and Stock Exchange Benevolent Fund. Two of these received a grant in the last year.

In the half-year ending June 1993, 23 grants were given ranging from £1,000 to £3,500. A wide range of charities were supported, with larger grants going to Guildhall School of Music & Drama (£3,500), West Sussex Macmillan Fund (£3,000), Carr-Gomm Society and Royal Star & Garter Home (both £2,500). Other benficiaries included the Architectural Association, Simon Community, Stepney Children's Trust and the World Memorial Fund for Disaster Relief (all £2,000), and Friedrich's Ataxia Group, Leaving Home Project, Tradescant Trust - Museum of Garden History and Wildlife Aid (all £1,000).

Applications: In writing to the correspondent.

The Carole & Geoffrey Lawson Foundation

£64,000 (1993/94)

Jewish, general

Stilemans, Munstead, Godalming, Surrey GU8 4AB
01483-420757

Correspondent: G C H Lawson

Beneficial area: UK.

Information available: Full accounts are on file at the Charity Commission.

General: In 1993/94, the trust had an income of £57,000 and gave nine grants totalling £64,000.

Five grants went to Jewish organisations: £10,000 was given to each of JPAIME, Jewish Care and Nightingale House; £5,000 to both of Friends of Alyn and London Museum of Jewish Life.

The other four grants went to four very different causes: Holy Cross Hospital (£10,000); St Botolph's Crypt Centre (£5,000); Cranleigh CAB Appeal (£5,000); Royal Opera House Trust (£4,000).

The trustees report states: "During the year the trustees have continued negotiations for the funding of a major project in the health research field in London. The negotiations have not yet reached a fruitful conclusion, but the trustees anticipate that they will in due course and are retaining the major resources of the foundation for this objective."

Exclusions: No grants to local charities or individuals.

Applications: The correspondent stated: "we are already inundated with requests that we cannot support, so charities will be wasting their time writing to us".

The Lawson-Beckman Charitable Trust

£79,000 (1993/94)

Jewish, general

c/o Hacker Young, St Alphage House, 2 Fore Street, London EC2Y 5DH
0171-216 4600

Correspondent: M A Lawson

Trustees: M A Lawson; J N Beckman.

Beneficial area: UK.

Information available: Full accounts are on file at the Charity Commission.

General: Grants from the trust are allocated two years in advance. In 1993/94, the trust had assets of £1 million and an income of £104,000. 46 grants were given totalling £79,000. Grants range from £250 to £20,000, but are usually about £1,000. The trust mainly supports Jewish causes, with the larger grants going to Nightingale House (£19,300), Jewish Care (£18,000), British Ort (£5,700), Jewish Educational & Development Trust and the Tel Aviv Foundation (both £5,000). All of these receive regular support.

Most other grants were for £500 or less and many are recurrent. Non-Jewish beneficiaries included a number of medical and health-related charities (eg. Cancer Research Campaign, Multiple Sclerosis Society and British Dyslexia Institute) and the Royal Opera House which received £2,900.

Applications: In writing to the correspondent, but note that grants are allocated two years in advance.

The Leach Fourteenth Trust

£110,000 (1993/94)

Conservation and disability

19 Church End, Haddenham, Bucks HP17 8AE

Correspondent: Mrs M B Watson

Trustees: W J Henderson; M A Hayes; Mrs J M M Nash; Mrs M B Watson.

Beneficial area: UK.

Information available: No accounts are on file at the Charity Commission, since those for 1977. The following information was supplied by the trust.

General: Although the trust's objectives are general, the trustees are following the interest of the founder, which was to support mainly conservation (ecological). In 1993/94, the trust had assets of £1.8 million and an income of £70,000. Grants totalled £110,000.

About 20 charities (about one third of grants) receive regular payments. The trustees prefer to give large grants for specific projects rather than small awards towards general funding. The trust has bought some cliffs, supported a nature reserve, and a hostel for homeless people. Grants are usually £500 to £5,000, but can be as large as £50,000.

Exclusions: Only registered charities are supported.

Applications: In writing to the correspondent. Only successful appeals can expect a reply.

The Leche Trust

£132,000 (1992/93)

Georgian art, music and architecture

84 Cicada Road, London SW18 2NZ
0181-870 6233

Correspondent: Louisa Lawson, Secretary

Trustees: Gillian Wagner, Chair; Jeremy Benson; Primrose Arnander; John Porteous; Diana Hanbury; Peter K Thornton; Sir John Riddell.

Information available: Accounts are on file at the Charity Commission (without a schedule of grants).

General: Founded and endowed by the late Mr Angus Acworth CBE in 1950 the trust had assets in 1992/93 of £3.4 million. The income was £188,000 and grants totalled £142,000.

The trust sent the following details from its annual report for the year ending July 1993.

Grants are normally made in the following categories:

1. Preservation of buildings and their contents, primarily of the Georgian period;
2. Repair and conservation of church furniture, including such items as bells or monuments, but not for structural repairs to the fabric – preference is given to objects of the Georgian period;
3. Assistance to the arts and for conservation, including museums;
4. Assistance to organisations concerned with music and drama;
5. Assistance to students from overseas during the last six months of their doctoral postgraduate studies in the UK.

Applicants should note the changes in these categories since the last edition of the Guide. Unfortunately no further details of grants, or amounts given in each category of interest, are available.

Exclusions: No grants are made for religious bodies; overseas missions; schools and school buildings; social welfare; animals; medicine; expeditions.

Applications: In writing to the secretary; trustees meet three times a year.

The Arnold Lee Charitable Trust

£149,000 (1992/93)

Jewish, general

47 Orchard Court, Portman Square, London W1H 9PD
0171-486 8918

Correspondent: A Lee

Trustees: A Lee; H Lee; A L Lee.

Beneficial area: UK.

Information available: Full accounts are on file at the Charity Commission.

General: "The policy of the trustees is to distribute income to established charities of high repute for educational, health and religious purposes."

In 1992/93, the trust had assets of £1.4 million and an income of £125,000. Grants ranged from £40 to £35,000 and totalled £149,000. The largest grant was £35,000 given to JPAIME. Other large grants also went to Jewish organisations including £15,000 each to the Jewish Educational Development Trust and Lubavitch Foundation, and £10,000 to Project SEED Europe.

Only a few small grants were given to non-Jewish organisations including the Institute of Contemporary Arts (£200), Mental After Care Association (£200), Royal Marsden Cancer Appeal (£500) and Tate Gallery Foundation (£100).

Applications: In writing to the correspondent.

The Leeds Hospital Fund Charitable Trust

£788,000 (1994)

Hospitals in Yorkshire, charities in Leeds

41 St Pauls Street, Leeds LS1 2JL
0133-245 0813

Correspondent: M A Finch

Trustees: V Barker; C Bell; K Brook; Mrs P J Dobson; T Hardy.

Beneficial area: Yorkshire.

Information available: Full accounts are on file at the Charity Commission.

General: The fund was formed in 1887 in the Leeds area to help finance local voluntary hospitals. It continued to do so until the establishment of the NHS in 1948. In that year, a new "contributory benefit scheme" was drawn up offering financial help to contributors and a convalescent service to help in recuperation.

In 1887, contributory income was £1,883; in 1994, £14,040,000. The fund supports two trusts, the Convalescent Homes Charity and the Charitable Trust.

In 1994, the assets of the fund totalled £14.9 million, contributory income was £14 million and investment and other income was about £750,000. Benefits paid to contributors came to £12.3 million and other expenditure about £1.1 million. £723,000 was covenanted to Leeds Hospital Fund Charitable Trust, leaving a surplus of £600,000.

The charitable trust in 1994, had assets of £487,000 and an income of £723,000. Donations totalling £788,000 (£607,000 in 1993) consisted of (1993 figures in brackets):

Hospitals	£432,000	(£387,000)
Other	£71,000	(£92,000)
Christmas gifts for hospital patients	£20,000	(£17,000)
Convalescent Homes Charity	£265,000	(£50,000)

Other expenditure amounted to £12,000 giving a total expenditure of £800,000 and therefore a deficit of £79,000.

The £432,000 given to hospitals and hospices was made up of 26 grants ranging from £1,000 to £75,000. Seven were to hospices; the rest to hospitals. St James's Trust received a total of £135,000 in two grants, both for medical equipment, and LGI Trust received a total of £91,000 in four grants for equipment. The other grants were mainly for £10,000, usually towards equipment for hospitals and towards running costs for hospices.

28 grants were made under "Other donations", ranging from £100 to £5,000, with half for £1,000. £5,000 was given to the Salvation Army, and £3,000 each to the Arthritis & Rheumatism Society and Breast Cancer Care. Most grants were medically related and usually for very general purposes such as to help with running costs or as a donation to an appeal. Beneficiaries included the Belle Isle Elderly Winter Aid, Disabled Housing Trust, Leeds & Bradford Association for Spina Bifida and Leeds Childrens Holiday Camp. Sport-related causes, especially for disabled people, also received a number of grants in 1994, including Leeds Blind Sports & Special Club, Leeds Cricket & Football Relay Association, Northern Sports for the Handicapped and White Rose Cricket Club.

Applications: The trustees meet in February, July and November to consider applications.

The Morris Leigh Foundation

£109,000 (1992/93)

Jewish, general

Bouverie House, 154 Fleet Street, London EC4A 2DQ
0171-353 0299

Correspondent: M D Paisner

Trustees: M Leigh; Sir Geoffrey Leigh; A A Davis; Mrs M Leigh; Mrs E C Greenbury; M D Paisner.

Beneficial area: Worldwide.

Information available: Full accounts are on file at the Charity Commission.

General: In 1992/93, the trust had assets of £678,000 and an income of £71,000. Grants totalled £109,000. About half the grants, including most of the larger ones went to Jewish organisations, with the others to health, welfare and arts causes, mainly the larger well-known UK charities.

61 grants were given with 16 for £1,000 or more and the rest mainly for £500 or less. The largest were to Council for a Beautiful Israel (£29,000), Chief Rabbinate Charitable Trust (£12,500) and British Ort (£10,000). Others included Action on Addiction (£100), British Friends of the Art Museums (£5,900), Help the Hospices (£250), London Philharmonic Orchestra (£3,000), RNIB (£450) and Royal Northern College of Music (£2,500).

Applications: In writing to the correspondent.

The Lewis Family Charitable Trust

£286,000 (1991/92)

Medical research, Jewish charities

Chelsea House, West Gate, London, W5 1DR
0181-998 8822

Correspondent: David Lewis

Trustees: David Lewis; Bernard Lewis.

Beneficial area: UK and overseas.

Information available: Accounts on file at the Charity Commission for the years 1975/76, 1987/88 and 1991/92.

General: "The trust's main areas of interest and support are:

(a) The Birth Defects Foundation
(b) The Lewis National Rehabilitation Institute
(c) Jewish communal charities
(d) Gene therapy for cancer."

Four Lewis brothers established the trust in 1969 – Bernard, David, Geoffrey and Godfrey – in an agreement with Lewis Trusts plc, which granted a seven year endowment to the trust of £2,000 a year. In 1991/92, the trust's assets were £3.4 million, and £442,000 of income was generated largely from rents and the interest on cash in the bank.

Only 39 donations were made totalling £286,000. Large grants went to the two daughter charities, the Birth Defects Foundation (£40,000) and the Lewis National Prosthetic Institute (75,000). Other large grants were given to St George's Hospital Medical School (£54,000), the Medical Aid Committee for Israel (£34,000), JPAIME (£25,000) and Jewish Care (£20,000).

Of the other grants, four were for £5,000 to £8,000, seven for £1,000 and 22 for £750 or less. About three quarters of the grants were to Jewish organisations, with the rest to mainly medical causes and hospital appeals such as Cancer Research Campaign, Great Ormond Street Hospital, Leukaemia Research Fund and the Mental Health Foundation.

Exclusions: No grants to individuals.

Applications: To the correspondent in writing. The trust once stated that it did not want to be included in this guide which, however, seeks to be comprehensive.ABBGrants are normally made only once a year. The trust states: "grants are not made on the basis of applications received".

The Catherine Lewis Foundation (formerly The David Lewis Charitable Foundation Ltd)

£149,000 (1992/93)

Jewish, relief of poverty and sickness, education

76 Gloucester Place, London W1H 4DQ
0171-487 3401

Correspondent: J N Davis

Trustees: D J Lewis; Mrs H Lewis; H S Lewis; Miss N R Lewis.

Beneficial area: Worldwide.

Information available: Full accounts are on file at the Charity Commission.

General: This trust requested removal from this Guide, but our policy remains to include all relevant grant-making trusts. In 1992/93, the trust had assets of £160,000. Ordinary income for the year was £63,000 including £28,000 from donations and £34,000 net proceeds from a memorial concert. Grants totalled £149,000. The trust has been spending capital for a few years and its assets have been decreasing.

The largest grants were £75,000 to the Tel Aviv Foundation and £49,000 to the Royal Post Graduate Medical School; both also received large grants in 1991/92. Eight other grants were for £1,000 or more, and 30 were for less than £1,000, most being under £500.

Over three quarters of the grants were to Jewish organisations. The grants to non-Jewish organisations were mainly for health and social welfare. Recipients included the British Red Cross (£200), Cancer Relief Macmillan Fund (£1,000), North London Hospice Group (£100) and University College London (£3,750).

Applications: In writing to the correspondent.

The Sir Edward Lewis Foundation

£50,000 (1992/93)

General

Moors Farm, Flanchford Road, Reigate Heath, Surrey RH2 8AB
01737-243973

Correspondent: R A Lewis

Trustees: R A Lewis; K W Dent.

Beneficial area: UK and overseas, with a preference for Surrey.

Information available: Full accounts are on file at the Charity Commission.

General: In 1992/93, the trust had assets of £1.4 million and an income of £98,000. 73 grants were given totalling £50,000. Although the trust had a surplus this year, the previous year it gave grants totalling £263,000 from an income of £99,000.

In 1992/93, only four grants were over £1,500: £2,500 to St Bartholomew's Church, Leigh; £2,000 to both St Catherine's Hospice and Heatherly Cheshire Home; £1,500 to St John's Ambulance Brigade.

The trust supports mainly national charities in the fields of health, welfare and disability. Many receive regular grants of £500 or £1,000. Other beneficiaries included the Institute of Economic Affairs, PDSA, Surrey Opera and Weald & Downland Open Air Museum.

In 1991/92, exceptionally large grants were given to East Surrey Hospital "CT Scanner Appeal" (£176,000), University College and Middlesex School of Medicine (£30,000) and Rugby 2000 (£10,000).

Exclusions: Grants are only given to charities, projects or people known to the trustees.

Applications: In writing to the correspondent. The trustees meet every six months.

Lions Clubs International

General: The International Association of Lions Clubs was started in the USA in 1917 and is the largest service club in the world. It now has around 1.4 million members in about 170 countries and provinces. Recently 37 Lions Clubs have been formed in eight Eastern European countries. There are 891 Lions Clubs in the UK and Ireland, with over 21,300 members. Membership is by invitation; each club is totally autonomous.

A typical Lions Club usually consists of between 20 and 40 members from all walks of life and background with a common aim to help those less fortunate than themselves. Most clubs meet once a month to discuss community service, fundraising and social activities; many also hold a monthly dinner meeting. A Board of Directors administers the club and presents projects for consideration to the members. Most members are usually a part of a committee involved in assessing community service projects, raising or allocating funds, giving a helping hand or special projects. Generally most of the club activities concentrate on the needs of their local community.

Lions In The Community

The Lions raise money to provide:

  Outings and holidays for elderly or handicapped people and deprived young people;

  Equipment for hospitals and hospices;

  Minibuses, office equipment, furnishings etc. for voluntary community organisations;

  Eye Camps in India, Water Wells in Africa etc.;

  Help with emergency disaster relief anywhere in the world;

Sponsorship for international youth camps and youth exchange visits.

There are many other projects that the Lions help to run or organise such as swimming galas for disabled people, a national youth football competition and the distribution of food parcels at Christmas.

The amount raised for charities can vary considerably from one club to another. A small club might raise between £10,000 and £12,000 a year, while the larger clubs might regularly raise upwards of £100,000. If there was a major charity project or fundraising appeal, such as a new hospice opening, several clubs may join together to support the cause, but that would be additional to the work already being done by the clubs.

All Lions clubs are run completely autonomously. They decide which causes/charities to support and how to support them. Most Lions clubs are inundated with requests for help and so many applications will be turned down. Charities seeking to raise funds with the Lions' help are prefered to charities wanting the Lions to fundraise for them. Projects must be beneficial to the community.

The name and address of your local Lions Club can be obtained from: Peter Jay, General Secretary, 257 Alcester Road South, Kings Heath, Birmingham B14 6BT (0121-441 4544), or the local telephone book (under "Lions International").

The Lister Charitable Trust

£276,000 (1993/94)

Recreation

Windyridge, The Close, Totteridge, London N20 8PT
0181-446 7281

Correspondent: A C Southon

Trustees: A C Southon; Mrs J Douglas-Withers; B J C Hall; N A V Lister; I R D Andrews.

Beneficial area: UK.

Information available: Full accounts are on file at the Charity Commission.

General: This trust was set up in 1981 by Noel Lister, and by the mid-eighties had been endowed with 75,000 shares in MFI with a cost value of £101,000. This holding was cashed in when MFI was bought by ASDA in 1985.

The trust funds the UK Sailing Centre and Cowes Leisure Management College on the Isle of Wight to help youth development, as well as other recreational facilities.

In 1993/94, the trust had assets of £4.8 million and an income of £380,000. The only grants were given to the UK Sailing Centre totalling £276,000.

Exclusions: No support for individuals.

Applications: In writing to the correspondent.

The Liverpool & Merseyside Charitable Fund

£98,000 (1992/93)

General in Liverpool and neighbourhood

14 Castle Street, Liverpool L2 0NJ
0151-236 7728; Fax: 0151-258 1153

Correspondent: Edward Murphy, Chief Executive

Trustees: The Executive of Liverpool Council of Social Service.

Beneficial area: Liverpool and neighbourhood, ie. Merseyside, West Lancashire and Halton.

Information available: Accounts up to 1991/92 are on file at the Charity Commission, but do not include a list of grants.

General: Grants are made in support of the following programmes:

- **Autonomy** – work which will have the effect of increasing user control of social welfare services or a stronger voice for users of services.
- **Equity** – work which confronts discrimination against particularly black people, disabled people and women, both directly and by promoting organisations of such people and positive images of them.
- **Economy** – support for projects in the economic development/urban regeneration field.
- **Efficiency** – work which either generates new income for local voluntary organisations, or which assists organisations to improve the use made of existing income.
- **Policy** – work which directly supports policy priorities in the council's field and communication services.
- **Emergency** – on very rare occasions, grants are made to sustain strategically significant voluntary organisations threatened with closure by decisions of statutory agencies.
- **Accountability** – support efforts by charities to make their activities better known to, and more readily scrutinised by, the communities they are established to serve.

In 1992/93, the fund had an income of £194,000 and gave grants totalling £98,000. Up to half the grant may be applied to Liverpool Council for Voluntary Service for its own purposes. Grants may be up to £3,000 and, exceptionally, recurrent grants for up to three years may be considered. In 1992/93, 80 grants of over £500 were made as well as a few smaller ones.

Exclusions: No grants for building work, to buy mini-buses, for trips/camps/outings (except where there is a clear educational purpose) or morris dancers(!). Generally no grants will be given to replace statutory funding; however the cost of replacing such schemes with schemes staffed with volunteers may be funded. Applications which are eligible for local authority small grants/community chest funds will not normally be supported.

Applications: In writing to the correspondent. Applications are considered four times a year in March, June, September and December. This may mean that applications are not responded to for 16 weeks. To avoid lengthy delays, applications should be submitted by the end of February, May, August and November.

The Elaine Lloyd Charitable Trust

£36,000 (1992)

General

Messrs G Hakim, Tunsgate Square, 98-110 High Street, Guildford, Surrey GU1 3HE
01483-304147

Correspondent: J S Gordon

Trustees: E M Lloyd; A S Lloyd; J S Gordon.

Beneficial area: UK. There may be a preference for the south of England and Newport, Wales.

Information available: Full accounts are on file at the Charity Commission up to 1991/92.

General: No more recent information was available on this trust. This entry repeats the information from the last edition.

In 1992, this trust and the Mr Angus Lloyd Charitable Settlement were amalgamated and will probably be known as the E M Lloyd Charitable Trust.

Information from the accounts of the Elaine Lloyd Charitable Trust follow, with the Angus Lloyd information in brackets. In 1992, the trust had assets of £585,000 (£191,000), an income of £52,000 (£18,000) and gave grants totalling £36,000 (£34,000).

Grants tend to be about £200 to £500, and occasionally £1,000. Many are recurrent, with some paid quarterly. Typical beneficiaries include Oxfam, Christian Aid, Barnardo's, parish churches, and organisations working with blind people.

Applications: In writing to the correspondent.

Localtrent Ltd

£81,000 (1993/94)

Jewish

44 Waterpark Road, Salford, Manchester M7 4ET
0161-720 6188

Correspondent: M Weiss, Secretary

Trustees: Mrs M Weiss; B Weiss; J L Weiss; P Weiss; S Feldman.

Beneficial area: UK.

Information available: Full accounts are on file at the Charity Commission.

General: In 1993/94, the trust had assets of £191,000 and an income of £68,000. 55 grants were made totalling £81,000.

All the grants were to Jewish organisations except one of £50 to Manchester Charitable Trust. The largest were to Chasday Yoel Charitable Trust (£26,000), Beis Minchas Yitzchak (£12,000), and Yeshiva of Nitra and Telz Academy Trust (both £5,000).

Applications: In writing to the correspondent.

The Locker Foundation

£152,000 (1992/93)

Jewish

9 Neville Drive, London N2 0RE
0181-455 9280

Correspondent: I Carter

Trustees: I Carter; M Carter; Mrs E Friedman.

Beneficial area: UK and overseas.

Information available: Full accounts are on file at the Charity Commission.

General: In 1993/94, the trust had assets of £1.1 million and an income of £81,000. Grants totalled £65,000 down from £152,000 the previous year and £248,000 in 1991/92.

Six grants were made, all to Jewish causes: Jewish National Fund Trust (£30,000), Friends of the Torah (£28,000), Jewish Care (£4,000), Ravenswood Homes (£2,000), Jewish Children's Holiday Fund (£1,000) and Jewish Women's Week 1993 (£100).

Applications: In writing to the correspondent.

The Loftus Charitable Trust

£76,000 (1992/93)

Jewish

48 George Street, London W1H 5PG
0171-486 2969

Correspondent: A Loftus

Trustees: R I Loftus; A L Loftus; A D Loftus.

Beneficial area: UK and overseas.

Information available: Accounts for 1990/91 and 1992/93 are on file at the Charity Commission, but without a list of grants.

General: In 1992/93, the trust had assets of £818,000 and an income of £76,000. Grants (probably all to Jewish organisations) totalled £76,000. No further information is available.

Applications: In writing to the correspondent.

The London Law Trust

£87,000 (1993/94)

Children and young people

203 Temple Chambers, Temple Avenue, London EC4Y 0DB

Correspondent: G D Ogilvie, Secretary

Trustees: Prof A R Mellows; Sir Jeffrey Darell; R A Pellant.

Beneficial area: UK.

Information available: Full accounts, including comprehensive narrative reports and a list of beneficiaries, are on file at the Charity Commission.

General: The trustees have continued their policy of supporting charities for:

- The prevention, alleviation, and reduction of the causes of illness and disability in children and young people.
- The encouragement and development in young people of the qualities of leadership, responsibility and service.

In many cases the trustees pay greater attention to seedcorn or small research projects and to new ventures. During the year under review they have employed a grant-advisor particularly with a view to appraising applications for grants in these categories.

In 1993/94, the trust had assets of £2.7 million and an income of £119,000. Grants totalled £87,000, divided into the following categories:

- Charities which prevent and cure illness and disability in children and young people: £26,500 in 12 grants, including £5,000 to Sheffield Limb Equality Service. Other grants were for £1,000 or £2,500, with beneficiaries including Aberdeen Paediatric Research, Birth Defects Foundation, Chronic Granulomatous Disease Research Trust and the Restoration of Appearance and Function Trust.
- Charities which alleviate or reduce the causes or likelihood of illness and disability in children and young people: £32,000 in 23 grants of £500 to £5,000.

Beneficiaries included the Association of Stammerers, Bobath Cymru, Brittle Bone Society, Ellenor Foundation, Horticultural Therapy and United Kingdom Sports Aid Foundation.

- Charities which encourage and develop in young people the qualities of leadership and service to the community: £28,500 in 17 grants of £500 to £2,500, including the Adventure Farm, Discovery Camps Trust, Rugby 2000, Weston Spirit and Youth Link NI.

Exclusions: No grants for individuals.

Applications: Applicants should make an initial aproach in writing, which will be followed up if appropriate. Applications should be submitted by 1st September each year. The trustees meet in November.

The William & Katherine Longman Trust

£122,000 (1992/93)

General

Charles Russell, Hale Court, Lincoln's Inn, London WC2A 3UL
0171-242 1031

Correspondent: W P Harriman

Trustees: W P Harriman; J B Talbot; A C O Bell.

Beneficial area: UK.

Information available: The trust was registered in 1988. The only accounts on file at the Charity Commission are those for 1989. The following information was supplied by the trust.

General: In 1992, the trust had assets of £2.4 million. 34 grants were given in 1992/93 totalling £122,000. The largest grants included £5,000 each to Alexandra Rose Day, Earls Court Project, FRAME, Helen Arkell Dyslexia Centre, Prison Fellowship and the Royal National Orthopaedic Hospital Trust.

Exclusions: No grants to individuals.

Applications: The trustees believe in taking a pro-active approach in deciding which charities to support and it is their policy not to respond to unsolicited appeals.

The Loseley Christian Trust

£34,000 (1993/94)

Christian

Loseley Park, Guildford, Surrey GU3 1HS
01483-304440

Correspondent: The Secretary

Trustees: Major J R More-Molyneux; R Shelbourne; M G More-Molyneux; Mrs S More-Molyneux; Rev Pat Ashe; Miss N Cheriton-Sutton.

Beneficial area: Worldwide.

Information available: Full accounts are on file at the Charity Commission.

General: In 1993/94, the trust had assets of £1.17 million generating an income of £65,000. Grants totalled only £34,000 leaving a surplus of £15,000. There was also a surplus the previous year of £29,000 with grants totalling £27,000 from an income of £67,000. It is not known if the trust is still building up its assets or accumulating funds for a specific project in the future.

All 61 grants given in 1993/94 were to Christian organisations, both in the UK and overseas. They ranged from £25 to £5,000, though most were for £500 or less. Beneficiaries included Acorn Christian Healing Trust (£3,000), Leprosy Mission (£400), Missions to Seamen (£300), Salvation Army (£1,000), Shaftesbury Society (£1,000), World Vision (£200) and Youth Link Northern Ireland (£200).

Exclusions: No grants to individuals.

Applications: In writing to the correspondent.

The C L Loyd Charitable Trust

£81,000 (1992/93)

General

Lockinge, Wantage, Oxon OX12 8QL
01235-833265

Correspondent: C L Loyd

Trustees: C L Loyd; T C Loyd.

Beneficial area: UK, with a preference for Berkshire and Oxfordshire.

Information available: Full accounts are on file at the Charity Commission.

General: The trust supports a wide range of local charities in Berkshire and Oxfordshire, together with UK health and welfare charities. A few UK animal welfare charities also receive support.

In 1992/93, the trust had assets of £610,000 with an income of £121,000. 107 grants totalled £81,000. Only seven organisations received £1,000 or more. The remaining grants were all under £1,000 and most were under £100.

The main beneficiaries were the Village Housing Charitable Trust (£45,000 in two grants); Lockinge Church (£14,500 in two grants); Country Buildings Protection Trust (£9,500 in five grants); Ardington Church (£1,200). £1,000 was given to each of Ardington and Lockinge British Legion, Cambridge Foundation and Friends of Wantage Hospital.

Applications: In writing to the correspondent.

The Jack & Ruth Lunzer Charitable Trust

£51,000 (1993/94)

Jewish education and arts

7 Turner Drive, London NW11 6TX
0171-242 5303

Correspondent: J Lunzer, Trustee

Beneficial area: UK.

Information available: Full accounts are on file at the Charity Commission.

General: In 1993/94, the trust had assets of £188,000, an income of £46,000 and gave 42 grants totalling £51,000, almost all to Jewish organisations.

There were six grants of £5,000 to: the Lubavitch Foundation; Services to the Aged; Jewish Educational Development Trust; Independent Jewish Day School and Yesodey Hatorah Schools. Other large grants were made to GGBM Ladies Guild (£2,500), Huntingdon Foundation and British Library Endowment Fund (£2,000 each).

There were seven grants of around £1,000 including those to GGBH Congregation; KKL Executor & Trustee Co Ltd;

University College, London; Royal College of Music; Gateshead Talmudical College Building Fund and NW London Jewish Day School. Nine grants were for around £500 including Sion College, Corporation of London, African Medical Research Foundation and Medical Aid Foundation.

There were 17 grants of £50 to £250. Those that were not specifically Jewish were to the University of Cambridge, University of London Library and Feed the Children.

Applications: In writing to the correspondent.

The Lyndhurst Settlement

£140,000 (1994/95)

Social problems, civil liberties, environment, conservation

c/o Bowker Orford & Co, 15-19 Cavendish Place, London W1M 0DD

Correspondent: Michael Isaacs

Trustees: Michael Isaacs; Peter Schofield; Anthony Skyrme.

Beneficial area: Usually UK, but local or foreign applications are considered if there is a strong civil liberty component.

Information available: Full accounts are on file at the Charity Commission.

General: The policy of the Lyndhurst Settlement is to encourage research into social problems with a specific emphasis on safeguarding civil liberties, maintaining the rights of minorities and protecting the environment which the trustees regard as an important civil liberty. The trustees prefer to support charities (both innovatory and long-established) that seek to prevent, as well as ameliorate, hardship.

Some recipients are regular beneficiaries. They include not only civil liberty, immigration and penal reform organisations, but a number of birth control advisory centres, environmental and conservation groups, AIDS groups and homeless organisations. In 1994/95, 61 grants were made totalling £140,000. They ranged from £1,000 to £6,000. Requests are considered throughout the year and about 1,000 are received.

While supporting the larger environmental organisations such as Friends of the Earth and BTCV (£2,000 each), the settlement tries to encourage smaller local groups such as Stepping Stones Farm (£2,000), Community Gardening Projects Scotland and North Pennines Heritage Trust (£1,000 each).

It is the view of the trustees that an essential element in the protection of the environment is the limitation of population growth. Grants were given to the Birth Control Trust and Brook Advisory Centre (£6,000 each), Marie Stopes International (£5,000), Population Concern (£4,000) and Family Planning Association (£3,000).

The settlement was one of the first trusts to be concerned with the civil rights of prisoners. A grant was given to Prisoners Abroad (£4,000).

Minority groups, both here and abroad, are a continuing concern. Grants included Immigrants Aid Trust (£6,000), Tibet Foundation, Survival International and Northern Refugee Centre (£3,000 each), and Refugee Support Centre (£2,000).

The settlement does not generally give grants to medical charities, but was prompt to respond to the social needs of people with AIDS and people who are HIV positive. Grants were given to Terrence Higgins Trust, Positively Irish Action on AIDS and Crusaid (£2,000 each).

Over the past few years the settlement has been concerned with the threat to our national heritage. Beneficiaries included SAVE Britain's Heritage, Ironbridge Gorge Development Trust and Black Country Museum (£2,000 each).

Exclusions: Grants are only given to registered charities. Grants are not given to individuals. The trustees do not normally support medical or religious charities.

Applications: Requests for grants should include a brief description of the aims and objects of the charity, and must be in writing and not by telephone. Unsuccessful requests will not be acknowledged unless a pre-paid self-addressed envelope is provided.

The Lyndhurst Trust

£58,000 (1992/93)

Christian

The Mill House, Crathorne, Yarm, Cleveland TS15 0BD

Correspondent: W P Hinton

Trustees: W P Hinton; J A L Hinton; Dr W J Hinton.

Beneficial area: UK and overseas.

Information available: Full accounts are on file at the Charity Commission.

General: The objects of the trust are "the advancement, promotion and support of the Christian religion in any part of the world". In practice the trust supports specific charities on a regular basis. The trust states: "There is little scope for supporting additional appeals of which we already receive a large quantity".

In 1992/93, the trust had assets of £1.4 milion and an income of £59,000. Grants totalled £58,000.

The trust's grants were divided geographically as follows:

Third World	£28,700
European	£11,200
North East England	£5,500
Other UK	£13,100

No list of grants was available for 1992/93, but more information was available for the previous year. In 1991/92, the distribution was categorised slightly differently:

Third World £33,000: all the beneficiaries also received a grant the previous year, including Africa Inland Mission, Bible Society, Haggai Institute, Operation Mobilisation and Tear Fund.

Europe and the Rest of the World £16,300: 12 organisations were supported, two of which had not received support the previous year, both in the Middle East, one of which continued to receive support in 1992/93.

North East England: 20 grants were given, all recurrent, mostly to churches.

UK: 20 grants, three to new beneficiaries, the Don Summers Evangelistic Association Nicky Cruz Crusade (£4,500), Evangelistic Christian Literature (£50) and the Courage Trust (£500). In 1992/93, 24 grants were given, four to new beneficiaries.

Exclusions: No support for individuals or buildings.

Applications: In writing to the correspondent, enclosing an sae if a reply is required. Requests are considered quarterly.

The Sir Jack Lyons Charitable Trust

£152,000 (1991)

Jewish, arts, education

Sagar Croudson, Elizabeth House, Queen Street, Leeds LS1 2TW
0113-243 5402

Correspondent: M J Friedman

Trustees: Sir Jack Lyons; Lady Lyons; M J Friedman; J E Lyons.

Beneficial area: UK and overseas.

Information available: See below.

General: According to the Charity Commission database, the trust had an income of £89,000 in 1993/94, no further information was available for this year.

The trust gave grants totalling £152,000 in 1991. No information was available on the grant distribution for this year and the following is taken from the 1991 Edition of *A Guide to the Major Trusts*.

In 1988/89, the trust had assets of £838,000 generating a disposable income of £81,600. It gave 80 grants, most of which were quite small. 37 grants were between £100 and £1,000, 27 were under £100, and only four grants were over £10,000.

The largest grant was given to the National Osteoporosis Society (£20,000) which had not been supported before. Other major grants were to the Ben Gurion University Foundation (£15,200) and Friends of the Hebrew University of Jerusalem (£10,400); both organisations were supported in previous years. The fourth major grant was to the Foundation for Education.

The trust shows a particular interest in Jewish charities and also a consistent interest in the arts, particularly music. The Royal Academy of Music Foundation received £5,000 and the Heslington Foundation for Music and Associated Arts received £4,600.

The trust also supports in a smaller way major organisations working in aspects of social welfare, disadvantage and disability such as St John's Ambulance, NSPCC and Help the Hospices.

Exclusions: No grants to individuals.

Applications: In writing to the correspondent. The trust did not wish to have an entry in this guide and stated that "In the light of increased pressure for funds, unsolicited appeals are less welcome and would waste much time and money for applicants who were looking for funds which were not available".

The M B Foundation
(also known as Mossad Horav Moshe Aryeh Halevy)

£65,000 (1991)

General, educational

Clark & Terry Ltd, Newhaven Business Park, Barton Lane, Eccles, Manchester M30 0HH
0161-787 7898

Correspondent: S B Bamberger

Trustees: Rabbi W Kaufman; Rabbi M Bamberger; S B Bamberger.

Beneficial area: Worldwide.

Information available: No accounts are on file at the Charity Commission since those for 1983.

General: In 1991, the trust gave grants totalling £65,000. We have not been able to obtain any further information on this trust, other than that it supports general and educational causes.

Applications: In writing to the correspondent, although the trust states that its funds are already over-committed.

The Macdonald-Buchanan Charitable Trust

£113,000 (1993)

General

c/o Kleinwort Benson Trustees Ltd, PO Box 191, 10 Fenchurch Street, London EC3M 3LB
0171-956 6600

Correspondent: The Secretary

Trustees: Capt John Macdonald-Buchanan; Alexander Macdonald-Buchanan; Mrs R W Humphreys; Mrs C R Philipson.

Beneficial area: UK.

Information available: Full accounts are on file at the Charity Commission.

General: The Hon Catherine Macdonald-Buchanan set up this trust in 1952 for general charitable purposes and endowed it with 40,000 shares in the then Distillers Company. The trust now has substantially more assets, spread over a wide range of investments with a value of £2.2 million in 1993. These produced an income of £113,000 out of which £20,000 went on administration expenses and £113,000 in donations.

In 1993, about 130 donations were made, mostly for a few hundred pounds. Only sixteen were for amounts of £1,000 or above. The King Edward VII Hospital for Officers received £15,500, whilst two organisations received £10,000: Saranda Charitable Trust and the Orrin Charitable Trust, both of which appear to be regular beneficiaries. Other beneficiaries of £1,000 or more included the Church of the Holy Sepulchre Restoration Trust, Coronary Care Unit Addenbrooks, Game Conservancy Trust, Help the Aged, National Art Collections Fund and Victim Support.

Most grants are to health and welfare charities including service/ex-service organisations, with an interest also in conservation and horse riding shown by grants to the Donkey Sanctuary, Injured Jockeys Club, International League for the Protection of Horses, Jockey Club Charitable Trust and WWF UK.

The accounts also list two supplementary grant schedules under "Captain John Macdonald Buchanan Account" and "Mrs Mary Cynthia Anne Philipson Account". It appears that these trustees have discretion to give a certain amount each year.

Exclusions: No grants to individuals.

Applications: In writing to the correspondent.

The Man of the People Fund

£150,000 (1994)

General

1 Canada Square, London E14 5AD
0171-293 3842

Correspondent: John Smith, Administrator

Trustees: The Editor, Chairman, Finance Director and Company Secretary of *The People* newspaper.

Beneficial area: UK.

Information available: No complete accounts are on file at the Charity Commission since those for 1983/84.

General: The fund raises money by organising an annual appeal to the readers of *The People* newspaper. The trust supports organisations concerned with disabled and underprivileged children, elderly people in need, research into killer diseases and local support and self-help groups.

In 1994, the appeal raised about £150,000. The fund tends to give a large number of small grants.

Exclusions: No grants to individuals or to charities applying on behalf of an individual.

Applications: In writing to the correspondent. Only registered charities should apply, enclosing supporting literature. Applications will only be acknowledged if accompanied by an sae. Applications can be made at any time, but grants are only given in the March of each year.

R W Mann Trustees Limited

£159,000 (1993/94)

Social welfare in the North East

56 Leazes Park Road, Newcastle-upon-Tyne NE1 4PG
0191-284 2158; Fax: 0191-285 8617

Correspondent: John Hamilton

Trustees: Directors: Mrs Judy Hamilton, Chairman; Guy Javens; Mrs Monica Heath.

Beneficial area: UK, but grants are practically all confined to organisations in Tyne & Wear, with a preference for north Tyneside.

Information available: Full accounts are on file at the Charity Commission.

General: Set up 1959 by R W Mann with an endowment in Victor products (the founder died in 1991), the trust is keen that family control should be kept to continue its giving in the North East. In 1993/94, the trust had assets of £2 million and an income of £196,000. Grants totalled £159,000.

186 grants were made, the vast majority being for £500 or less to broadly welfare organisations in North Tyneside. The largest grants went to Newcastle CVS (£6,800), Northern Counties School for the Deaf (£6,500), Stepping Stones (£6,000), Barnardo's (£5,700) and Barnardo's Whitley Bay Project (£5,000). Other recipients of £1,000 or more included Anchor Housing Trust, BTCV, Child Abuse Listening Line, Derwentside College, Live Theatre Co Ltd, Meadow Well Community Resource Centre, North Tyneside Education Business Partnership and Toc H.

Exclusions: "No grants to individuals, except in the form of particular educational scholarships through an agency."

Applications: In writing to the correspondent, with an sae.

The Earl of March's Trust Company Ltd

£18,000 (1993/94)

General

Goodwood House, Chichester,
West Sussex PO18 0PY
01243-774107

Correspondent: Duke of Richmond

Trustees: Duke of Richmond; Duchess of Richmond; Sir Peter Hordern; Mrs C M Ward.

Beneficial area: Worldwide.

Information available: Full accounts are on file at the Charity Commission.

General: In 1993/94, the trust had assets of £226,000, an income of £51,000 and gave grants totalling £17,000. After expenses, the surplus for the year was £31,000.

Of the 42 grants given, the largest was to Lancing College Development Fund (£2,000). Six grants of £1,000 were given to: Christian Aid; Shaftesbury Society; Lavant Parish Church; Aldingborne Trust; Chichester Celebrations Ltd and Chichester Cathedral Trust.

Other grants generally of around £100 to £700 were given to a range of organisations including: Sussex Association of Boys' Clubs; Loman's Trust; Zambia Society; African Medical Research; Boxgrove Parish Church; Bulgarian Orthodox Church; Samaritans; CORAT; Tiptree Youth Centre; Kickstart; Greek Animal Welfare Trust; Riding for the Disabled Association; CARE and King Edward VII Hospital. Only ten grants were recurrent from 1992/93.

Applications: Grants are only made to charities known personally to the trustees.

The Marchday Charitable Fund

£50,000 (1993)

General

43 Portland Place, London W1N 3AG
0171-636 8623

Correspondent: Mrs R Leigh

Trustees: David Goldstein; Alan Kleiner; Lyndsey Kleiner; Dudley Leigh; Rose Leigh; Maureen Quinn.

Beneficial area: Preference for south east England.

Information available: Accounts are on file at the Charity Commission but without a list of grants for 1993.

General: In 1992/93, the trust had an income of £51,000 including covenanted donations of £50,000. Grants totalled £50,000 but no grants list was available. This was surprising following the 1992 accounts which not only list every beneficiary but give the precise purpose of each grant.

14 grants were made in 1992 totalling £53,000. Grants ranged from £1,000 to £7,000 given to a range of organisations.

The trustees wish to assist small charities where a grant will support a particular project or make a difference to the continuation of the charity. There is a preference for charities in the South East. The trust also prefers to commit itself to three years' support rather than give a one-off grant. The trustees like to have continual involvement with supported charities.

Beneficiaries included Centrepoint Soho (£7,000 towards the salary of a resettlement worker), British Wheelchair Foundation (£6,500 towards the annual paraplegic games), Medical Foundation for the Victims of Torture (£6,000 for a volunteer supervisor), St Francis Hospice (£5,000 for general running costs), Neti Neti Theatre (£5,000 for a schools' video)

Coral Atkins Homes (£4,500 for the resurfacing of a kids games area), London Wildlife Trust (£4,400 for a Watch Officer), Anne Frank Educational Trust (£3,000 to cover printing costs) and DEBRA (£3,000 for continued research support).

Other beneficiaries included Wycombe Women's Aid, St Martin in the Fields Care Centre, Live Music Now, Huntercombe Creative Writing Journal ad HYOMI, with grants given for diverse purposes including art workshops for the homeless, training for female refugees and fees for an ex-inmate of HYOMI to attend the Guildhall School of Music.

Exclusions: The trust prefers not to support local organisations outside the South East.

Applications: In writing to the correspondent.

The Marchig Animal Welfare Trust

£33,000 (1992)

Animal welfare

Case Postale 14, 1223 Cologny, Geneva, Switzerland
010 4122-349 6800

Correspondent: Mrs Jeanne Marchig, Chairman

Trustees: Jeanne Marchig; Clive Hollands; Trevor H Scott.

Beneficial area: Worldwide.

Information available: The information for this entry was supplied by the trust. Accounts up to 1992 are on file at the Charity Commission, but without a list of grants.

General: The trust was created in 1989 by Madame Jeanne Marchig of Geneva out of her concern for nature and animals and in memory of her late husband, the Italian painter Giannino Marchig. The trust is registered in Great Britain.

The purpose of the trust is to protect animals generally and to promote and encourage practical work in preventing cruelty to animals. The relief of suffering is considered very important by the trustees. Two types of support are given:

Welfare awards: for outstanding work in the following two categories:

- The development of alternative methods to the use of animals in experimental work, and the practical implementation of such alternatives in scientific or manufacturing procedures;

- Practical work in the field of animal welfare by a society or individual anywhere in the world.

The awards are worth Swiss Francs 20,000 and Swiss Francs 40,000 (about £9,000 and £18,000).

Welfare grants: given to organisations and individuals for positive contributions which meet the objectives of the trust as outlined above. Since it was founded the trust has supported a wide variety of projects including poster campaigns, mobile clinics, scientific research, anti-poaching programmes, as well as helping experts to attend important international meetings and funding special projects in a variety of sanctuaries and refuges.

In 1992, the trust had assets of £348,000 and an income of £108,000. Grants totalled £33,000.

Exclusions: Only animal welfare causes are supported. Applications from students going on expeditions, study trips etc. do not qualify for a grant and will not be considered.

Applications: In writing to the correspondent.

The Linda Marcus Charitable Trust

£55,000 (1992/93)

General

Personal Financial Management,
12 Hans Road, London SW3 1RT
0171-584 4277

Correspondent: J J Bates, Secretary

Trustees: Sir Leslie Porter; Dame Shirley Porter; Mrs Linda Marcus.

Beneficial area: Worldwide.

Information available: Full accounts are on file at the Charity Commission.

General: For the last edition of this guide the correspondent stated: "I cannot give any information about the trust, or confirm or amend your entry, until 1994 when the Charities Act becomes law". We are now pleased to report that the trust has produced admirably clear accounts for 1991/92 and 1992/93.

In 1992/93, the assets of the trust were £3.4 million and the income was £138,000. Grants totalled £55,000 leaving a surplus for the year of £77,000. 13 organisations received grants with six awards to the International Scholarship Foundation Charitable Trust totalling £13,000. Other large grants went to the Family Therapy Advancement Charitable Trust (£20,000), Tel Aviv University (£10,000, with the British Friends of the University receiving two grants totalling £3,700), and the Israel Commonwealth Association (£5,000).

The remaining seven grants were for £1,000 or less, with beneficiaries including the City of Westminster Charitable Fund, Shakespeare Globe Trust, Cancer Relief Macmillan Fund and Shapira House for Mental Health. About half the grants were recurrent from the previous year.

Applications: In writing to the correspondent.

The Hilda & Samuel Marks Foundation

£171,000 (1993/94)

Jewish

1 Wootton Gardens, Bournemouth, Dorset BH1 1PW
01202-558484

Correspondent: S J Jones

Trustees: S Marks; Mrs H Marks; D L Marks; Mrs R D Selby.

Beneficial area: UK.

Information available: Full accounts are on file at the Charity Commission.

General: In 1993/94, the trust had assets of £2.7 million and an income of £154,000. Over 70 grants were given totalling £171,000.

The largest grants went to Bournemouth Hebrew Congregation and the Child Resettlement Fund, both of which received three grants totalling £55,000. The next largest grants were given to Norwood Child Care (£10,000) and Jewish Marriage Council (£7,000).

19 grants were for £1,000 to £5,000 with all the other grants for £25 or more. The only non-Jewish organisation to receive a grant was the Imperial Cancer Research Fund (£50).

Applications: In writing to the correspondent.

The Erich Markus Charitable Foundation

£112,000 (1993/94)

Medical, welfare, general

Paynes Hicks Beach, 10 New Square, Lincoln's Inn, London WC2A 3QG
0171-242 6041

Correspondent: A Walker, Trust Manager

Trustees: Erich Markus Charity Trustees Ltd.

Beneficial area: UK.

Information available: Full accounts are on file at the Charity commission.

General: In 1993/94, the trust had assets of £1.4 million. Accounts are filed every six months. In the first six months of 1994, the trust had an income of £55,000 and made grants totalling £51,000. 24 grants were made ranging from £300 to £3,000. Most beneficiaries were medical and welfare causes including three Jewish charities and three hospices. Recipients of £3,000 included DGAA, Iris Fund, North London Hospice, NSPCC, Ravenswood Foundation and SSAFA. A grant of £300 was made to Battersea Dogs Home.

In the previous six months the income was £57,000 and grants totalled £61,000. 23 grants were made, with six charities receiving a grant in both six month periods. £5,000 was given to each of the Royal Star & Garter Home and Westminster Society "Erich Markus House".

The other beneficiaries were again medical and welfare causes, with grants also made to the National Trust (£3,000) and Redwings Horse Sanctuary and Wiltshire Trust for Nature Conservation (both £300).

Applications: In writing to the correspondent.

The Marsh Christian Trust

£125,000

General

Granville House, 132-135 Sloane Street, London SW1X 9AX
0171-730 2626; Fax: 0171-823 5225

Correspondent: The Secretary

Trustees: B P Marsh; M Litchfield; A B Marsh; R J C Marsh; N C S Marsh.

Beneficial area: UK.

Information available: Full accounts are on file at the Charity Commission.

General: The trust was established in 1981, with an initial sum of £75,000. Since then, additions to the endowment have increased the size of the trust's funds to over £1.9 million. Grants totalling about £125,000 are given annually.

Only registered charities experienced in their field are supported. The trust prefers to give long-term core funding to appropriate work, subject to yearly re-submission and review. Single projects and sponsorship proposals are therefore not supported. Grants range from £100 to £5,000.

The causes supported are categorised within seven areas of work, with the proportion of funds allocated to these areas together with brief details about 1992/93 grants as follows:

- **Social welfare 30%:** Many small donations go to charities helping people with physical and mental disabilities. CRUSAID receives a grant from the trust, and all other appeals concerned with AIDS are passed on to that charity (this policy is under constant review). Charities working with the young, elderly, homeless, alcoholics and drug abusers are also supported, especially those that have a Christian emphasis to their work.
- **Environmental causes/animal welfare 20%:** Both UK and overseas organisations concerned with nature conservation and the well-being of wildlife are supported, including the Wildlife Information Network.
- **Healthcare and medical research 15%:** Most of the money goes to hospices and other organisations working with terminally ill people. General hospitals are not supported because "it is the responsibility of the local and national community to maintain these".
- **Education and training 12.5%:** Regular grants are given to the Slade School of Fine Art and the English Speaking Union. The trust also supports Young Enterprise and the Oxford Evangelical Research Centre and funds various specific awards, three through the Zoological Society of London and two through the Authors' Club. Grants are not given to ordinary schools or universities.
- **Arts and heritage 12.5%:** Grants are given to a number of museums and galleries, including the National Portrait Gallery, V & A Museum, Natural History Museum and the British Museum. The Royal College of Music is also supported. No support for individual church buildings or cathedrals.
- **Overseas appeals 7.5%:** Organisations supported include Oxfam, VSO, Christian Aid and the Commonwealth Society for the Blind.
- **Miscellaneous 2.5%:** Beneficiaries have included the Council for Arms Control and Population Concern. In both cases, in addition to grants, assistance in fundraising was given by seconding a trust staff member for a period of some months. Highgate Cemetery and Prisoners Abroad also received support.

In 1992/93, the trust gave 254 grants, just under half of which were recurrent from the previous year.

Exclusions: No grants to individuals.

Applications: In writing to the correspondent, including a copy of the most recent accounts. The trustees currently receive about 550 applications every year. Decisions are made at fortnightly trustee meetings. The trustees attempt to visit each recipient charity at least once every three years to review the work done, learn of future plans and renew acquaintance with those responsible for the charity concerned.

The Charlotte Marshall Charitable Trust

£70,000 (1992/93)

Roman Catholic, general

Ponswood, Hastings, East Sussex
TN34 1YS
01424-446262

Correspondent: S M Lennard

Trustees: S M Lennard; K F Menzies; A M Cirket; C C Cirket.

Beneficial area: UK.

Information available: Accounts are on file at the Charity Commission, but without a list of grants.

General: The trust divides its income between educational, religious and other charitable purposes for Roman Catholics in the UK, and general purposes. Two thirds of the income is allocated to the former and one third to the latter.

In 1992/93, the trust had an income of £73,000 and gave £70,000 in grants. No further information is available.

Applications: In writing to the correspondent.

The Jim Marshall Products Charitable Trust

£63,000 (1993)

General

Simpson Wreford & Co, Accountants,
62 Beresford Road, London SE18 6BG
0181-854 9552

Trustees: J C Marshall; M Hill; K W J Saunders; G T Leaver.

Beneficial area: UK.

Information available: Accounts are on file at the Charity Commission, but without a list of grants.

General: The trust was established in 1989 by Jim Marshall (Products) Ltd, now Marshall Amplification plc. In 1993, it had an income of £108,000, nearly all of which was a covenanted payment from the company. Grants totalled £63,000 "mainly to organisations for the benefit of children, young people, families and the sick and disabled". No list of grants was available.

Applications: In writing to the correspondent.

John Martin's Charity

£90,000 to organisations (1993/94)

Religious activity, relief-in-need and education in Evesham

16 Queen's Road, Evesham,
Worcs WR11 4JP
01386-765440

Correspondent: David J Harries, Clerk

Trustees: Rev J Bomyer; Rev L L Burn; J F Icke; Mrs M Tosswill; M J Davey; A W Bennett; Mrs J Turner; J G Robbins; Rev R N Armitage; J H Smith; R G Gould; N J Lamb; C C Scorse; R G Emson.

Beneficial area: Evesham.

Information available: Full accounts are on file at the Charity Commission.

General: In 1993/94, the trust had assets of £4.9 million and an income of £345,000. Grants to individuals and organisations totalled £291,000, of which £90,000 was given to organisations.

The accounts categorises the grants made as follows:

- **Relief-in-need:** £82,000. Grants were given to 771 individuals. For further information see *A Guide to Grants for Individuals in Need 1994/95*.
- **Donations to organisations:** £25,000. Grants were given to organisations including Age Concern, Evesham Community Hospital, Garage Art Group, Made Court, Mind, Newspaper for the Blind and Vale of Evesham Volunteer Centre. Major contributions included part funding the proposed stroke rehabilitation unit at Evesham Hospital.
- **Education grants:** Schools £17,000 and students £142,000 (for further information see *The Educational Grants Directory 1994/95*). Grants to schools are for items not usually funded by the local education authority eg. computers, additional books for libraries and equipment for special needs education.
- **Religious activity:** £48,000 in grants to the churches of St Andrew, All Saints and St Peter, two of which have major building projects.

Exclusions: No grants for the payment of rates or taxes.

Applications: On a form available from the correspondent on written request. The trustees normally meet on the second and fourth Thursday in each month, with one meeting in June and December. The trust can make urgent grants in exceptional circumstances.

The Nancie Massey Charitable Trust

£167,000 (1992/93)

Education, medicine, the arts, children and elderly people in Scotland

3 Albyn Place, Edinburgh EH2 4NQ
0131-225 7515

Correspondent: J G Morton

Trustees: J G Morton; C A Crole; E K Cameron.

Beneficial area: Scotland, particularly Edinburgh and Leith.

Information available: The trust is registered in Scotland.

General: The trust was established in 1989 to help organisations supporting elderly people, children, medical research, education and the arts. Assistance is primarily given to projects established in the Edinburgh and Leith areas. In 1992/93, the trust gave grants totalling £167,000 from an income of £177,000, but no information is available on the grants.

In 1991/92, the trust had assets of £2.5 million and an income of £219,000. 50 grants totalled £189,000. The largest grants were to the University of Edinburgh MRI Unit (£25,000), National Gallery of Scotland (£15,000) and the Scottish National Portrait Gallery (£12,500). Grants of £10,000 went to the Royal Lyceum Theatre, Royal Infirmary of Edinburgh, Scottish International Disaster Relief Agency, Edinburgh International Festival,

Scottish Wildlife Trust, Buildings of Scotland Trust and the Edinburgh Festival.

Other grants ranged from £100 to £5,000 to Scottish charities, local charities in Scotland and local (Scottish) branches of UK charities. About 25% of beneficiaries also received support in 1990/91.

Exclusions: Grants are not given to individuals.

Applications: In writing to the correspondent setting out in detail why the application is being made, how the donation will be spent and the overall cost of the project. Applications will be acknowledged, confirming whether they will be considered further.

The Leonard Matchan Fund Ltd

£61,000 (1992/93)

Social welfare

One Bridewell Street, Bristol BS1 2AA

Correspondent: Miss J E M Sutherland, Secretary

Trustees: Miss B A Thompson; Miss S D Groves; Miss J E M Sutherland; K H Thompson; P A Rosenthal.

Beneficial area: UK.

Information available: Full accounts are on file at the Charity Commission.

General: In 1992/93, the trust had assets of £622,000 and an income of £62,000. Grants totalled £61,000.

21 grants were made, ranging from £1,000 and £6,000. About half of these grants were recurrent from the previous year. Larger grants were to Trinity Hospice (£6,000) and St John Ambulance & Rescue Service – Guernsey (£5,000); both received smaller grants the previous year. Four charities received £3,000 in both years: Centrepoint Soho, Children's Society, St Mungo Community Trust and Willow Trust.

New beneficiaries in 1992/93 included Cancer Relief Macmillan Fund, Guernsey Motor Neurone Association, Martha Trust and RNID (all £3,000). There appears to be some preference for the Channel Islands with grants to the Jersey Christmas Appeal and RAF Association Jersey, in addition to those mentioned above. The previous year grants also went to Age Concern Jersey, Channel Islands Air Search and WRVS Day Centre Guernsey.

Applications: In writing to the correspondent, c/o 16 The Towers, Lower Mortlake Road, Richmond, Surrey TW9 2JR.

The Maxwell Family Foundation

£30,000 (1992/93)

General

181 Whiteladies Road, Clifton, Bristol BS8 2RY
0117-970 6570

Correspondent: E M Maxwell, Trustee

Trustees: E M Maxwell; P M Maxwell; R P Spicer.

Beneficial area: UK.

Information available: Full accounts are on file at the Charity Commission.

General: This trust requested to be omitted from the last Edition of this Guide. However, we maintain our policy of including all relevant trusts. This appears to have resulted in the trust rejecting all requests that are generated by our publications.

It was established to "help alleviate suffering, sponsor medical research and support religious charities and worthy causes".

In 1992/93, the trust had assets of £1.3 million and an income of £239,000. 28 grants totalled £30,000 leaving a surplus of income over expenditure of £209,000. The income is being accumulated for one or two specific projects, limiting the amount available to other causes.

The largest grant was £10,000 to the One in Twelve Appeal. The only other grants of £1,000 or more were to regular beneficiaries: RAF Benevolent Fund (£6,500), Robert Owen Foundation (£1,500) and the Royal National Institute for the Deaf (£1,000). Other grants ranged from £100 to £750 to national charities in the fields of welfare, disability, conservation, education and animals.

Applications: We do not know if the trust responds to unsolicited appeals, but it does not support appeals that have been generated by its entry in this Guide.

The Mayfield Valley Arts Trust

£33,000 (1992/93)

Arts

Kershaw Tudor Solicitors, Hutton Buildings, 146 West Street, Sheffield S1
01904-645738; Fax 01742-756933

Correspondent: Delma Tomlin, Administrative Director

Trustees: A Thornton; R J Thornton; Priscilla Thornton; D Whelton.

Beneficial area: Unrestricted, but with a special interest in Sheffield and South Yorkshire.

Information available: Full accounts are on file at the Charity Commission.

General: The trust supports the arts, particularly music, by promoting concerts, educating young musicians and supporting musicians in need, including the purchase of musical instruments.

In 1992/93, the trust had assets of £1.7 million and an income of £95,000. £16,000 was spent on administration and £33,000 was given in four grants (£64,000 in 1991/92). This left a surplus of £46,000 (£19,000 in 1991/92) although provision was also made in the 1992/93 budget for £18,000 to Sheffield Chamber Music Festival and £1,500 for the Crucible Studio Theatre.

The four grants given were to York Early Music Festival 1992 (£5,000), Lindsay String Quartet (£4,500), Live Music Now! (£2,000) and Sheffield Chamber Music Festival (£22,000 in total).

The trust also purchased a cello and bow (cost £8,300) for use by exceptional young music students.

Exclusions: "No unsolicited applications are considered by the trustees."

Applications: In writing to the correspondent, but note the above.

The Robert McAlpine Foundation

£138,000 (1986/87)

General

40 Bernard Street, London WC1N 1LG

Correspondent: Graham Prain

Trustees: David McAlpine; M H D McAlpine; Kenneth McAlpine; Cullum McAlpine; Adrian N R McAlpine.

Beneficial area: UK and the Commonwealth.

Information available: Full accounts are on file at the Charity Commission for the years up to 1975/76 with the usual details of donations. Accounts are also available for 1983/84 and 1986/87 but the details of grants are no longer included.

General: We have not been able to update the information for this entry from that in the 1991 edition of *A Guide to the Major Trusts*.

In 1986/87, the trust had assets of £2.2 million and an income of £188,000. Grants totalled £138,000, but we have not been able to obtain any information concerning their distribution.

The most recent list of grants on file at the Charity Commission is that for 1975/76 when the trust gave a total of £55,000 to 28 organisations. Both national and local charities received support, mainly in the field of social welfare. It is not known if the current policy of the trust is the same.

Exclusions: The trust does not like to fund overheads.

Applications: In writing to the correspondent.

The McCarthy Foundation

£54,000 (1993/94)

Elderly

Homelife House, 26 Oxford Road, Bournemouth BH8 8EZ
01202-315064

Correspondent: The Company Secretary

Trustees: Sir Marcus Fox; Prof Michael Hall; Jane Kerr; Mark Cato; Peter Girling; Simon Metcalf; Dean Tufts; Nigel Bannister; David Walden.

Beneficial area: UK.

Information available: Full accounts are on file at the Charity Commission.

General: The foundation has recently changed its name from the John McCarthy Foundation "in order to avoid confusion with John McCarthy who was previously a hostage in Beirut".

The trust aims: "To help older people in need on low incomes and particularly older victims of violence and crime". Particular emphasis has been given to projects in inner-city areas. The trust runs two grant schemes:

Small grant scheme: To help individuals and organisations in immediate need. Grants are usually under £1,000.

Large projects scheme: With particular interest in schemes which are innovative and which could be replicated in other areas. The trustees like to initiate such schemes themselves. Major projects have included setting up and running a sheltered home in Liverpool for 12 elderly victims of crime and running home security projects in Bristol, Plymouth and Eastbourne. New schemes are now set up in Nottingham and Leeds. The Nottingham scheme – set up in 1993 – was initiated through the Nottinghamshire Constabulary with an initial grant of £15,000 from the foundation. It involves a mobile workshop which calls round to all elderly victims and carries out necessary security repairs.

In 1993/94, five grants to major projects totalled £31,000. £10,000 was given to Care & Repair/Victim Support/Age Concern (Leeds Project), a further £8,000 for the Nottingham project, £5,000 each to Victim Support Bristol and Care & Repair Bristol and £3,000 to Care & Repair/Victim Support Eastbourne. The major home security projects funded by the trust usually involve two or three charities working together. This would seem to be a very good way of getting larger projects up and running, though very few examples of charities working in this way have come to light in the research for this Guide.

£23,000 was given in small grants from £200 to £5,000 including grants to Age Concern groups, Care and Repair groups, Victim Support organisations and other groups working with elderly people throughout England, plus two grants in Wales and one in Northern Ireland, as well as support for individual victims of crime.

Applications: Applications should include a clear indication of what is proposed, together with budgeted costs; other funding being used; the position if the foundation was unable to make a grant; the likely cost of the total scheme together with the maximum amount being requested from the foundation. A form is available from the foundation. Up-to-date accounts should be submitted with any application. The trustees meet about four times a year.

The A M McGreevy No 5 Charitable Settlement

£36,000 (1993/94)

General

15 Pembroke Road, Clifton, Bristol BS8 3BG
0117-946 4000

Correspondent: KPMG

Trustees: Avon Executor & Trustee Co; Anthony M McGreevy; David Johnstone; Charles Sommerville; Miss Elise McGreevy.

Beneficial area: UK, with a preference for Avon.

Information available: Full accounts are on file at the Charity Commission.

General: In 1993/94, the trust had assets of £1.5 million and an income of £60,000. Grants totalled only £36,000 leaving a surplus for the year of £24,000. No further information was available on the grants given in this year. The trust has had a large surplus in each of the previous few years resulting in its assets steadily increasing.

In 1992/93, grants totalled £54,000. The Greater Bristol Trust received £48,000, a regular beneficiary, though not usually of such a large grant. Other grants were given to the British Antique Dealers Association, Furniture History Society, Greenhill House Cheshire Home, Edward James Foundation, Timsbury Parish Council and Wansdyke Enterprise Agency, some of which are regular beneficiaries. The trust has a preference for charities in Avon.

In 1991/92, 14 grants were given ranging from £15 to £12,000. The largest grant again went to the Greater Bristol Trust

(£12,000), with the NSPCC and SS Great Britain Project each receiving £5,000. The only other grants over £500 were £4,700 to the Edward James Foundation and £1,250 to the Friends of Bristol Art Gallery Pocock Appeal.

Applications: No applications required as funds are already committed.

The Mckenna & Co Foundation

£61,000 (1993/94)

General

Mckenna & Co, Mitre House, 160 Aldersgate Street, London EC1A 4DD
0171-606 9000

Correspondent: C B Powell-Smith

Trustees: C B Powell-Smith; Mrs C F Woolf; R S Derry-Evans.

Beneficial area: UK.

Information available: Full accounts are on file at the Charity Commission.

General: In 1993/94, the foundation had an income of £50,000 of which £34,000 comprised donations received. £30,000 of this amount was from McKenna & Co.

57 grants were made totalling £61,000. The largest was £18,000 to the City Solicitors' Educational Trust. Other grants ranged from £100 to £5,000 and included both national and local charities including the National Asthma Campaign, Macmillan Nurse Appeal, Aldeburgh Foundation and Save the Children Fund.

Exclusions: No grants to organisations that are not registered charities.

Applications: In writing to the correspondent.

The Mclaren Foundation

£45,000 (1989)

General

Clouds Estate Office, East Knoyle, Salisbury, Wilts SP3 6BG

Correspondent: Col S E Scammell

Trustees: H Arbuthnott; Mrs F S Maclaren Webster.

Beneficial area: UK.

Information available: We were unable to obtain the file for this trust at the Charity Commission.

General: In 1989, the trust had assets of £1.3 million and an income of £66,000. Grants totalled £45,000 and were given to a range of causes.

In 1994, the income was £60,000 according to the Charity Commission database, but we have been unable to obtain information as to how much of this was distributed in grants or which causes were supported.

The trust did not wish to appear in this Guide and has not amended or updated the above information. However, we maintain our policy of publishing information on all relevant grant-making trusts.

The trust requested us to state: "full up-to-date details of the foundation and its grants are available in the Directory of Grant Making Trusts". This can be found on page 790 of the latest edition of the Charities Aid Foundation (CAF) book.

In brief, CAF states the objects as being: "Animal welfare, war-disabled, regimental charities, distressed widows and pensioners of the professional income group, preservation of the national landscape, general charitable purposes".

The rest of the entry appears to deal with exclusions, basically saying that no grants are made to students for degree studies or to individuals for expeditions including Operation Raleigh. These exclusions are expressed in the strongest possible terms.

Applications: In writing to the correspondent. The CAF book includes the statement: "Charities or appeals that are able to state in their application that they do not employ professional fund-raisers or pay senior staff at commercial rates will be given priority for any funds available".

The Julian Melchett Trust

£107,000 (1992/93)

Social welfare in steel-making areas

9 Albert Embankment, London SE1 7SN
0171-735 7654

Correspondent: R Reeves, Secretary

Trustees: P J K Ferguson, Chairman; Keith Brookman; Paul Monk; Richard Reeves.

Beneficial area: Present and former steel-making areas.

Information available: Full accounts with an annual report are on file at the Charity Commission.

General: The trust was established by the British Steel Corporation to "benefit the communities in the areas in which the steel industry operates". The trust supports a wide range of projects and aims to encourage community development and self-help initiatives, stimulate voluntary service and promote partnerships between statutory and voluntary bodies engaged in community care. It supports projects which improve the quality of life by providing recreational opportunities and enhancing the environment.

In 1992/93, the trust had an income of £118,000, including £100,000 from British Steel plc and £10,000 from United Engineering Steels Ltd. It gave 183 grants totalling £107,000 divided geographically as follows:

Scotland	£10,750 (10%)
North East England	£31,960 (29%)
Rotherham	£10,600 (10%)
West Midlands	£10,650 (10%)
Northants	£7,500 (7%)
Wales	£30,900 (28%)
Others	£6,500 (6%)

The geographical split was very similar in 1991/92.

The largest grants went to Teesside Hospice Care Foundation (£8,000), Rotherham Scanner Appeal (£6,000) and Ropner Convalescent Home (£3,000). Other beneficiaries of £1,000 or more included Blantyre Crossroads Care Attendant Scheme, Eleanor Hodson Home for the Elderly, Mayor of Workington's Charity Appeal, Motherwell District Disability Forum, Partially Blind Society, 2nd Scunthorpe Sea Scout Group and the Welsh Initiative for Conductive Education. Most grants are for £250 to £500 and go to amenities and projects to benefit socially deprived groups.

Applications: In writing to the correspondent.

The Anthony & Elizabeth Mellows Charitable Settlement

£54,000 (1993/94)

Arts, heritage, churches, hospitals, hospices, training of young people

22 Devereux Court, Temple Bar, London WC2R 3JJ

Correspondent: Prof A R Mellows

Trustees: Prof A R Mellows; Mrs E A Mellows.

Beneficial area: UK.

Information available: Full accounts are on file at the Charity Commission.

General: In 1993/94, the trust had assets of £479,000 and an income of £28,000. Grants totalled £54,000. The trust supports four main areas as outlined in the trustees' report:

Arts and national heritage: Grants are only given to national institutions. In 1993/94, two grants were given totalling £16,000. One was given to the Royal Academy Trust (£5,000) for its gallery refurbishment programme, and a further grant was given to the Royal Opera House Trust (£11,000).

Church of England churches: Recommendations must come from the Council for the Care of Churches, unless there are exceptional circumstances. A grant of £1,000 was given for the conservation of a thirteenth century polychromed reredos at Holy Innocents Church, Adisham, Kent. A number of offers of other grants were made for conservation work in churches recommended by the Council. A further grant of £6,000 was made to the Lambeth Fund.

Hospitals and hospices: Six grants were given totalling £19,000. Beneficiaries included Dorset Respite and Hospice Trust, with further grants to Help the Hospices, the Order of St John and St John Ophthalmic Hospital.

Training and development of children and young people: A grant of £10,000 was given to the Duke of Edinburgh's Award for continuance of projects in Manchester and Northern Ireland, and £750 was given to the Friends of the Hebrew University, Jerusalem.

In addition to the above, £1,200 was given in 20 minor grants of £500 or less.

Applications: Only accepted from national bodies with whom the trustees are in contact.

Melodor Ltd

£164,000 (1991/92)

Jewish, general

6 Brantwood Road, Salford, Manchester M7
0161-792 8000

Correspondent: Henry Neuman, Administrator

Trustees: H Weiss; M Weiss; P Weiss; S Weiss; J L Weiss; H Weiss; R Sofer; W Neuman; F Neuman; H Neuman; M Neuman; E Neuman; M Friedlander; E Zimet.

Beneficial area: UK and overseas.

Information available: Accounts are on file at the Charity Commission but without a list of grants.

General: In 1991/92, the trust had an income of £177,000 including £157,000 net income from properties. Grants totalled £164,000, but unfortunately no further information was available on the grants made.

Applications: In writing to the correspondent.

Menuchar Ltd

£74,000 (1993/94)

Jewish

Flack Stetson, Mattey House, 128-136 High Street, Edgware, Middlesex HA8 7EL
0181-952 1986

Correspondent: The Secretary

Trustees: M Bude; A E Bude; N Bude; R Bude.

Beneficial area: UK.

Information available: Full accounts are on file at the Charity Commission.

General: In 1993/94, the trust had assets of £440,000 and an income of £128,000 (£101,000 of which was a Gift Aid payment from Silvase Ltd, a subsidiary trading company dealing in properties). 31 grants totalled £74,000.

All the grants were to Jewish organisations, the largest being £18,000 to Friends of Harim Establishments, and £10,000 to both the Woodstock Sinclair Trust and Friends of Seret Wiznitz. Over half the remaining grants were under £500. Grants were generally one-off.

Applications: In writing to the correspondent.

The Methodist Relief & Development Fund

£887,000 (1992)

Overseas aid/development

Methodist Church, 1 Central Buildings, Westminster, London SW1H 9NH
0171-222 8010

Correspondent: The Secretary

Beneficial area: Worldwide.

Information available: Full accounts are on file at the Charity Commission.

General: This is the main fund of the Methodist Church contributing to overseas aid and development. Much of its support overseas is given through other agencies particularly CICARWS (Commission on Inter Church Aid, Refugee & World Service, World Council of Churches). It also supports organisations in the UK in the categories detailed below.

In 1992, total income was £1.2 million, most of which is from gifts. Grants totalled £887,000, and are categorised in the accounts by country.

The largest grants outside the UK were: £110,000 to the Red Cross - emergency relief, Somalia; £32,000 to the Tigray Transport & Agricultural Consortium, Ethiopia; £26,000 for drought relief via CICARWS, Mozambique; £24,000 to Agroforestry Programme of Methodist and other churches, West Africa; £20,000 to the Christian Relief & Development Association, Ethiopia.

While a number of grants were to specifically Methodist organisations, many did not appear to be, with beneficiaries of smaller grants including: Health Unlimited – China (£7,500); Belize Enterprise for Sustained Technology (£5,000); Inter-Church Emergency Fund for Ireland (£4,000); Tools for Self Reliance (£5,000) and the International Service for Human Rights (£960).

Grants in the UK are given in two categories:

- **Education for peace, human rights and development.**
  21 grants were given in this category totalling £63,000. The largest was £23,500 to the World Development Movement: Action for World Development Fund. Other larger grants were given to the Grassroots Programme (£7,500), UK Support Committee of the Relief Society of Tigray (£6,200), One World Week (£4,900), Philippine Resource Network (£3,350) and Eltsa for economic justice in South Africa (£3,000). Beneficiaries of smaller grants included the Churches Human Rights Forum (£500), EIRIS (£1,500), International Broadcasting Trust (£500) and the New Economics Foundation (£2,000).

- **Relief & development projects.**
  Two organisations received support totalling £40,000: the Methodist Church: Fund for Multi Racial Projects (£33,000) and the Churches Commission on Overseas Students Hardship Fund (£6,200).

Applications: In writing to the correspondent.

The Millfield House Foundation

£66,000 (1993/94)

Social welfare in Tyne and Wear

66 Elmfield Road, Gosforth, Newcastle-upon-Tyne NE3 4BD

Correspondent: The Secretary

Trustees: W Grigor McClelland; Diana A McClelland; Rosemary Chubb; Jenifer McClelland; Stephen McClelland.

Beneficial area: The county of Tyne and Wear.

Information available: Guidance notes for applicants are available from the foundation, and printed in full below. Full accounts are on file at the Charity Commission.

General: The trustees are particularly interested in projects having the following characteristics:

1. Located in areas of particular need in Tyne and Wear, indicated, for example, by poor physical surroundings, high rates of unemployment, and lack of satisfactory community facilities.

2. From voluntary bodies with a record of achievement in the sort of work proposed, or from people who are proposing new but well thought out ways of meeting needs.

3. With some prospect of continuing, once help from the foundation has come to an end; or, where the work is experimental or innovatory, with definite plans to make the results known to relevant bodies.

4. Seeking not simply to alleviate the symptoms of deprivation but to tackle its causes, as might occur, for example, through new skills and knowledge being acquired, demonstrating new possibilities and approaches, or encouraging self-help and self-development.

The trust aims to determine the effectiveness of its grants but states in the trustees' report: "In many cases it is difficult to evaluate effectiveness because the Foundation's grants are able only slightly to supplement inadequate statutory provision or to provide minor alleviation of the consequences of deteriorating social conditions".

The objectives for each field of grant-making are set out below, although not every field is significantly supported each year.

Housing: Bodies offering a service of information and advice to individuals and groups, using their experience for public education and the development of policy proposals. Special emphasis on the single homeless and on young people, eg. those coming out of care or otherwise at risk.

Children and the family: Attempts to minimise the adverse effects on children of family break-up. Social facilities and support for good parenting. Support for independent living, including help for carers and volunteer visitors, and neighbourhood activities.

Youth: Provision of information, advice and support for school leavers and those particularly at risk. Special reference to attempts to help those for whom conventional provision is inappropriate.

Employment and community development: Facilities and support to help certain housing estates and other deprived communities to undertake community activities and realise their own potential, eg. through community projects on the edge of commercial viability. Help for those without the prospect of paid employment to find meaningful activity.

Health and the elderly: Promotion of healthy living, support for carers, provision of information and advice.

Research and publication: The provision of information likely to help improve the quality of life in Tyne and Wear.

Strengthening services to the voluntary sector: Provision of common services which will assist voluntary bodies to become more effective.

Small grants: A block grant is made to Tyne & Wear Foundation to be allocated by them in grants not exceeding £2,000 in accordance with Millfield House guidelines.

In 1993/94, the trust had assets of £1.86 million generating an income of £92,000. £66,000 was given in grants in the following categories:

Housing and homelessness	£15,000
Children and the family	£3,000
Young people	£6,000
Health and the elderly	£6,300
Employment and community development	£18,350
Support for the voluntary sector	£17,000

22 grants were given ranging up to £10,000. A total of £14,000 was given to the Tyne and Wear Foundation (£4,000 for running costs and £10,000 for its small grants programme); £6,000 to Teamwork Services, and £5,000 each to Sunderland MIND and Tyneside Housing Aid Centre. Other beneficiaries included Stepping Stones (£10,000); A Dad's Place (£3,000); Byker & Hebburn Advice Centres (£3,000 and £2,500); Hebburn Junior Football Institute (£2,000).

Exclusions: Generally the foundation does not:

- Give grants unrelated to the needs of people in Tyne and Wear.
- Support large well-established national charities, or respond to general appeals.
- Support work in the arts, medicine, conservation, or travel/adventure

projects, or provide educational bursaries, or make grants for individuals in difficulty.
- Give grants for buildings or for purely academic research.
- Give grants to make up deficits already incurred, to replace withdrawn or expired statutory funding, or to provide social care where this should properly be the responsibility of statutory agencies.

Applications: In the first instance, applications should be made in writing to the correspondent. Where there is some prospect that the trustees may be interested, there is likely to be an opportunity to provide additional details by telephone or personally – on site, if that is appropriate. The trustees meet twice a year (normally in May and November), and cannot therefore normally deal with substantial applications on a basis of urgency. There is, however, limited discretion to make some small grants between meetings. Once a grant has been made the foundation will wish to receive in due course a report on the progress of the project. Applications should include:

1. A general description of the project and its objectives.
2. A budget showing how total expenditure will be made up and what other sources have promised support or are being approached.
3. Accounts for any previous history of the project or for the sponsoring body.
4. If appropriate, the names of other people who know about the project and the applicant, to whom the foundation could refer.
5. If appropriate, how the progress of the project is to be assessed and made known to others.

The Millhouses Charitable Trust

£54,000 (1992/93)

Christian, overseas, welfare

79 Beverly Road, Hull HU3 1XR

Correspondent: J S Harcus

Trustees: Mrs J S Harcus; Dr A W Harcus.

Beneficial area: UK.

Information available: Full accounts are on file at the Charity Commission.

General: Grants are given mainly to national, well-known charities in the fields of social welfare and overseas aid, almost always with a Christian emphasis. Generally, the trust only supports charities/organisations with which the trustees have a personal knowledge of/contact with.

In 1991, the trust had assets of £373,000 in the form of cash, after paying £46,600 in 31 grants. In 1992/93, the trust had an income of £62,000 and gave 29 grants totalling £54,000. The largest awards were: Yorkshire Baptist Association (£12,600); Baptist Union, NSPCC and Christian Aid (£5,000 each); Northern Baptist College (£3,000); British Red Cross (£1,500) and Save the Children (£1,100).

The remaining grants were for £100 to £500 to organisations such as: Samaritans; Oxfam; Bible Society; Leprosy Mission and Children of the Andes. Over half the recipients had received a grant the previous year. The trust has a clear preference for Baptist charities.

Applications: The correspondent states that: "the trust receives about 500 applications a year and does not respond to unsolicited applications".

The Millichope Foundation

£153,000 (1993/94)

General

c/o SUMIT Ventures Ltd, Edmund House, 12 Newhall Street, Birmingham B3 3EJ
0121-236 1222

Correspondent: Mrs Linda Collins

Trustees: M L Ingall; L C N Bury; S A Bury; Mrs B Marshall.

Beneficial area: UK, especially Birmingham and Shropshire.

Information available: Full accounts are on file at the Charity Commission.

General: In 1993/94, the foundation's assets were £1.7 million and the income was £144,000. Grants totalled £153,000.

About 175 donations ranging from £50 to £10,000 were made to a wide range of organisations (but generally from £500 to £1,000). The largest grants were to the City of Birmingham Touring Opera (£10,000), Lady Willingdon Hospital (£10,000 in two grants), Zoological Society of London and Worcester Nature Conservation (both £7,000), and the National Trust and Corvedale School (both £5,000).

Recipients of £1,000 to £2,000 included Birmingham Settlement, League of Friends of Birmingham Children's Hospital, Coventry Boys' Club, Samaritans, Cut Boat Folk Ltd, Save the Children Fund, Welsh National Opera, Whizz Kids, Shropshire Regimental Museum Appeal, Indian Earthquake Trust, Little Sisters of the Poor and South Birmingham Health Authority.

Exclusions: No grants to individuals.

Applications: In writing to the correspondent. Only registered charities may apply and should include an sae.

The Milton Keynes Community Trust Ltd

110,000 (1993/94)

General welfare and arts in Milton Keynes

Acorn House, 381 Midsummer Boulevard, Central Milton Keynes MK9 3HP
01908-690276; Fax: 01908-233635

Correspondent: Maggie Tideswell, Grants Administrator

Trustees: Jim Barnes; Richard Bentley; Robert de Grey; Rob Gifford; Bob Hill; Brian Hocken; Simon Ingram; Andrew Jones; Bob King; Juliet Murray; Stephen Norrish; Ken Taylor; Sir Peter Thompson; Lady Elspeth Tudor-Price; Dr Tony Walton.

Beneficial area: The borough of Milton Keynes.

Information available: Accounts are on file at the Charity Commission, but without a list of grants. General leaflets, information sheets and application forms will be sent to potential applicants on request. A full policy document is held for reference at Acorn House. The trust also publishes an Annual Review and a quarterly newsletter.

General: The trust was established in 1987 to raise an endowment fund, which as at 31st March 1994 stood at £1.7 million. The trust primarily raises money through members (mainly local companies) who make annual donations.

On 1st January 1994, MK Foundation merged with the Milton Keynes Community Trust, becoming the Arts Fund of the trust.

General Fund

The general fund gives three types of grants: *Short-term grants* for one-off expenditure up to £4,000; a small number of *Development Funding awards* typically for sums of £6,000 to £20,000 a year over a maximum term of three years; and grants given to *local umbrella groups* to distribute as small grants to groups in their particular field of interest.

Currently grants are primarily for the purchase of equipment, towards small building projects, and to fund fixed-term projects and one-off training courses. The trust will also consider grants for revenue costs through Development Funding.

In 1993/94, the trust made grants totalling £85,000 from the General Fund. Beneficiaries included Bletchley Sea Rangers (£2,500 to buy a double sculling boat); National Schizophrenia Fellowship – Milton Keynes branch (£1,500 for computer equipment, workstation, typewriter and display boards); Milton Keynes Hospital Radio Service (£750 towards an Outside Broadcast Unit); New Bradwell Community Group (£4,000 for installation of new heating system); Milton Keynes Arts Association (£4,000 towards lighting and sound equipment); Only Olney Playscheme (£220 to buy play equipment) and Milton Keynes Rural Youth Team (£205 towards costs of activity day for disabled young people).

Arts Fund

The fund aims to help and encourage the artistic and cultural life of Milton Keynes and surrounding districts. It supports projects, events and activities which are of high quality, are innovative and imaginative. Grants are for a minimum of £1,000 and may be awarded to individuals as well as organisations. The trustees currently have set grant-giving priorities as follows: the support, where appropriate, of existing arts organisations in Milton Keynes for projects of citywide significance; the identification of innovative arts projects from any source which could have citywide impact and significance; the encouragement of arts provision for young people; the commissioning of new works.

The Arts Fund awarded grants totalling £25,000 in 1993/94. 11 grants were made including £7,500 to the Milton Keynes Arts Association for disbursement as small grants under £1,000 to grass-roots community arts projects within the borough.

Other beneficiaries included Milton Keynes International Festival of Folk Art (£2,000 to help with the development of a long-term administrative structure and financial base for the festival); Heart of England Opera (£2,000 towards the design costs of a production of Rossini's "Cinderella" in Stantonbury Campus Theatre); Milton Keynes Craft Guild (£1,000 towards the cost of appointing a Craft Development Officer), and the Silbury Group of Artists (£2,000 towards setting up an administrative base at the Group's new base at Westbury Farm in Milton Keynes).

Exclusions: General Fund: The trust will not normally give grants to individuals, animal charities or those applying for grants for equipment that would become the responsibility of a statutory authority; replace statutory funding; support those applying for ongoing costs such as salaries and rents (except in exceptional circumstances or through Development Funding); fund political, campaigning or narrowly religious activities; cover costs already incurred.

Arts Fund: The same exclusions apply as to the General Fund, although in some circumstances it will fund individual artists. It will not normally give grants to proposals focused on the following: equipment (including musical instruments); travel expenses; commercial publications; conferences or seminars; university or similar research; formal education or training.

Applications: Applications for General Fund grants are made using an application form obtainable from the trust. Application forms for grants from an umbrella body can be obtained direct from the relevant umbrella group (address details from the trust office). Application forms for Arts Fund grants can be obtained through the Arts Fund Consultant, Maggie Nevitt, on 01908-563349. Applicants are encouraged to discuss their application with the grants administrator or arts consultant before submitting a form.

General Fund short-term grants meetings are held quarterly, with the deadlines for submissions being the first Friday in February, May, August and November. Development Funding applications are considered once a year; submissions should be made by mid-October. Arts Fund applications are considered three times a year, the deadlines being 15th January, 15th May and 15th September.

The Peter Minet Trust

£119,000 (1993/94)

General

54-56 Knatchbull Road, London SE5 9QY
0171-274 2266

Correspondent: Ms Lyn Roberts

Trustees: Mrs Peter B Minet, President; J C B South, Chairman; N McGregor-Wood; H J Parratt; Mrs R L C Rowan; Mrs S P Dunn; Ms P Jones.

Beneficial area: UK, but mainly the London boroughs of Lambeth and Southwark.

Information available: Full accounts are on file at the Charity Commission.

General: In the mid sixties, the Minet family sold much of their property to local councils for housing. Part of the proceeds were used by Peter Minet to set up the trust in 1969. Peter Minet himself died in 1988. This trust is administered from the same address and with the same secretary as the Idlewild Trust (*see separate entry*) which makes grants mainly for the performing arts, preservation and conservation. The trusts also have one trustee in common.

The trust gives priority to registered charities in the London boroughs of Lambeth and Southwark, particularly those working with young people, sick, disabled and disadvantaged people, the elderly, the arts and the environment. Occasional support is given to capital projects by national charities working in the same fields of interest. Grants are normally not recurrent.

The trust has all its investments in equities (some very shrewdly invested – one has grown by over 850% since purchase) and gilts. These produced an income of £129,000 in 1993/94, almost all of which was distributed after expenses had been paid.

90 grants were given, with more than two thirds of these for amounts under £2,000. 17 were approved by the Playschemes Committee. The largest grants were £5,000 each to Christ Church, Gipsy Hill (towards

a community hall) and the London & Quadrant Housing Trust (for the Camberwell Foyer project).

Exclusions: Grants to registered charities only. No grants are made to individuals. It will not give to:
- Repetitive nationwide appeals by large charities for large sums of money.
- Appeals where all, or most of, the beneficiaries reside outside the UK.
- Appeals in respect of church or school buildings (other than those within the trust's immediate locality) where the buildings have no distinctive and outstanding merit, except where the school provides very specialised training.
- Local appeals outside the trust's immediate locality (ie. all, or most of, the beneficiaries must live within the applicant's and the trust's immediate locality.
- Appeals from organisations whose sole, or main, purpose is to make grants out of the funds which they collect.
- Appeals in respect of holiday schemes or summer playschemes except where the applicant is well known to the trust, or has received support in the past, or is concerned with the trust's immediate locality.
- Appeals received from organisations within three years of the date of a letter from the trust telling them that the trust cannot provide annual support.
- Appeals received from an organisation within 12 months of a previous grant.
- Research grants or deficit funding.

Applications: In writing, including audited accounts. Meetings are usually held in January, April, July and October. Unsuccessful applicants will not be acknowledged unless a stamped addressed envelope is enclosed.

The Laurence Misener Charitable Trust

£60,000 (1993/94)

General, Jewish

Sovereign House, 212-224 Shaftesbury Avenue, London WC2H 8HQ
0171-240 5821

Correspondent: Messrs Bourner Bullock

Trustees: J E Cama; P M Tarsh.

Beneficial area: UK.

Information available: Full accounts are on file at the Charity Commission.

General: In 1993/94, the trust had assets with a market value of £1,489,000 and an income of £58,000. 28 grants were made totalling £60,000. They ranged from £1,300 to £5,000 with the largest to the Richard Dimbleby Cancer Fund (£5,000 and a second grant of £4,200).

Six of the grants were to Jewish organisations including £4,200 to both Nightingale House and Jewish Association for the Physically Handicapped and £4,100 to Jewish Care. The other grants were to UK medical and welfare causes including Age Concern (£1,300), Iris Fund (£1,400), Living Again Trust (£2,100), Pestalozzi Children's Village Trust (£1,300) and the RNLI (£1,300).

Applications: In writing to the correspondent.

The Victor Mishcon Charitable Trust

£119,000 (1993/94)

Jewish, social welfare

Mishcon De Reya, 21 Southampton Row, London WC1B 5HA
0171-413 5100

Correspondent: The Secretary

Trustees: Lord Mishcon; Lady Mishcon; P A Cohen.

Beneficial area: UK.

Information available: Full accounts are on file at the Charity Commission.

General: In 1993/94, the trust had assets of £926,000 generating an income of £94,000. Grants totalled £119,000 using unspent income from previous years.

11 grants were for £1,000 or more, with by far the largest being £41,000 to University College London, which received £60,000 the previous year. Another London College - Birkbeck - received £5,000 (and £5,000 the previous year). The other nine larger grants were all made to Jewish organisations including JPAIME (£27,000), Home for Aged Jews (£1,800) and Institute of Jewish Affairs (£1,300).

Over 130 grants were given in total, most for under £500 and 37 under £100. About one third were to Jewish organisations, with others mainly to health, medical and welfare causes. Probably fewer than half the grants were recurrent.

Beneficiaries included Accommodation for Recovery from Addiction Ltd, Barnardo's, Bromley Victims Support, Medical Aid for Palestinians, Prisoners Abroad, Research into Ageing and the Royal Academy Trust.

Applications: In writing to the correspondent.

The Mitchell Charitable Trust

£66,000 (1993/94)

Jewish, general in London

24 Rochester Road, London NW1 9JJ
0171-284 1761

Correspondent: Ashley Mitchell

Trustees: Ashley Mitchell; Parry Mitchell; Elizabeth Mitchell; Hannah Lowy.

Beneficial area: Mainly London.

Information available: Full accounts are on file at the Charity Commission.

General: In 1993/94, the trust had assets of £1 million and an income of £51,000. 27 grants were given, ranging from £50 to £21,000, and totalling £66,000 (a surplus of income was carried forward from the previous year). The largest grants all went to Jewish organisations including Jewish Care (£21,000 and the same the previous year), Norwood Child Care (£10,000), CBF World Jewish Relief (£9,000) and Ravenswood Hospital (£4,000).

Other recipients of grants of £1,000 or over included St Pancras Welfare Trust, Kosher Meals on Wheels, Crisis, Camden Family Service Unit and the LSE Foundation. Most of the smaller grants went to local welfare charities in London, exceptions being Inverclyde Child Support Volunteers and Redwings Horse Sanctuary.

Exclusions: No grants to individuals, or for research, education, overseas appeals or non-Jewish religious appeals.

Applications: In writing to the correspondent.

The Esme Mitchell Trust

£66,000 (1993/94)

Arts and culture, general in Northern Ireland

PO Box 800, Donegall Square West, Belfast BT2 7EB

Correspondent: The Northern Bank Executor & Trustee Co Ltd

Trustees: P J Rankin; Cmdr D J Maxwell; R P Blakiston-Houston.

Beneficial area: Mainly Northern Ireland.

Information available: The trust is registered in Northern Ireland.

General: The objects of the trust are general charitable purposes in Ireland as a whole, but principally in Northern Ireland. It has a particular interest in culture and the arts.

The trust has, on occasion, given grants over a period of two or three years, but in general does not become involved in commitments of a long-term nature. No further information is available.

Exclusions: It is most unlikely that applications from individuals wishing to undertake voluntary service or further education will be successful.

Applications: Applicants should submit a description of the proposed project; a recent statement of accounts and balance sheet; a copy of the constitution; details of tax and legal or charitable status (including the Inland Revenue Charities Division reference number); a copy of the latest annual report; a list of committee officers; information on other sources of finance; a contact address and telephone number.

It would be helpful for administration purposes if three copies of the appeal documentation were to be forwarded.

To avoid delay in considering applications the trust advisers require a copy of the most recent financial accounts and the Inland Revenue Charities Division reference number with the original application.

The Mole Charitable Trust

£57,000 (1993/94)

Jewish, Manchester, general

2 Okeover Road, Salford M7 4JX
0161-832 8721

Correspondent: M Gross, Secretary

Trustees: M Gross; D Z Lopian; Mrs L P Gross.

Beneficial area: UK, with a preference for Manchester.

Information available: Full accounts are on file at the Charity Commission.

General: In 1993/94, the trust had an income of £61,000 including a Gift Aid payment of £34,000. Grants totalled £57,000 including £21,000 to the Broom Foundation and £12,000 to Yeshivas Shaarei Torah. Most grants were to Jewish organisations, with a preference for those in Manchester.

Eight grants were for £1,100 to £3,750 including those to Manchester Jewish Grammar School (£3,750), Manchester Charitable Trust (£2,800), Charity Service Ltd (£2,000) and Beth Hamidrash and North Salford Synagogue (both £1,100). 11 grants were for under £1,000. Most of the grants are recurrent.

Applications: In writing to the correspondent.

The Willie & Mabel Morris Charitable Trust

£82,000 (1992/93)

Medical, general

Kempson House, Camomile Street, London EC3A 7AN
0171-283 2434

Correspondent: Messrs Norton Rose

Trustees: Michael Macfadyen; Joyce Tether; Peter Tether; Hugh Jackson.

Beneficial area: UK.

Information available: Full accounts are on file at the Charity Commission.

General: The trust was constituted for general charitable purposes and specifically to relieve physical ill health, particularly cancer, heart trouble, spasticity, arthritis and rheumatism.

In 1992/93, the trust had assets of £1.3 million and an income of £107,000. Grants totalled £82,000, including the trustees' own allocation of grants totalling £24,000.

The £58,000 was made up of 23 grants ranging from £2,000 to £4,000 with one grant of £750. Typical beneficiaries include Action Research (£4,000), Invalids at Home (£2,000), Mental Health Foundation (£3,000), Motor Neurone Disease Association (£3,000) and RUKBA (£2,000). Non-medical related causes supported include the Church Urban Fund (£2,000), National Trust – Sutton House Appeal (£4,000) and the Royal Commonwealth Society Library Appeal (£4,000).

The list of causes supported by the trustees' allocation was similar to the general list of grants, although more non-medical organisations were supported. Grants averaged about £500.

Applications: The trustees "formulate an independent grants policy at regular meetings so that funds are already committed".

Morrison Charitable Foundation

£23,000 (1991/92)

Jewish

Warner Bearman, 16 Wimpole Street, London W1M 8BH
0171-580 6341

Correspondent: L M Perkin

Trustees: M D Paisner; Mrs J Flanders; H Sapir.

Beneficial area: UK and Israel.

Information available: Accounts up to 1991/92 are on file at the Charity Commission.

General: In 1991/92, the trust had assets of £382,000 and an income of £59,000. Grants totalled £23,000, with a surplus of £32,000 carried forward.

16 grants were given in the year. All the main grants, some of which were recurrent, were given to charities for the benefit of the Jewish community in England and Israel. The largest were £11,000 to McGill University and £6,700 to British Friends of the Rubin Academy. The only other grants over £1,000 were to British Friends of Art Museum and Hadasseh Medical Relief Association UK. Other grants were mainly under £500.

Grants to non-Jewish organisations included £250 to Crusaid, £150 to the Society of Animal Welfare and £100 to the Kings Appeal Memorial.

Exclusions: Generally the trustees do not consider applications for individual grants.

Applications: In writing to the correspondent.

The G M Morrison Charitable Trust

£76,000 (1994/95)

General

11J Stuart Tower, 105 Maida Vale, London W9 1UH

Correspondent: G M Morrison

Trustees: G M Morrison; N W Smith.

Beneficial area: UK.

Information available: Full accounts are on file at the Charity Commission.

General: In 1993/94, the trust had assets of £3.1 million and an income of £104,000. Grants totalled £70,000. In 1994/95, grants totalled £76,000; no further information is available for this year.

"The policy of the trustees has always been to build up regular annual support for a range of charities, often at the initiative of the trustees." The trustees have effectively created an annual list of subscriptions. In 1993/94, the trust gave 114 grants, mainly £500 or under. Only six small grants had been added to the list of the previous year. Grants were given to a range of causes including education and medical research.

Exclusions: No support for individuals.

Applications: See above. The trust states: "In practice nearly every appeal is rejected; particularly as some charities are approached on the initiative of the trustees". Grants are distributed once a year in January.

The Moss Charitable Trust

£379,000 (1993/94)

Christian

7 Church Road, Parkstone, Poole, Dorset BH14 8UF

Correspondent: P D Malpas

Trustees: R L Malpas; A W Malpas; J H Simmons; A F Simmons; J L Simmons; P L Simmons.

Beneficial area: UK, with an interest in Dorset, Hampshire and Sussex.

Information available: No accounts are on file at the Charity Commission since those for 1990/91.

General: The trust receives covenanted and Gift Aid donations from companies and individuals, and redistributes them as requested by the donors, and approved by the trustees. In a sense, it acts like the Charities Aid Foundation except, in this case, giving grants specifically for Christian causes.

The trust makes grants to Christian causes and individuals in full-time Christian ministry. In 1993/94, grants were made to about 200 beneficiaries totalling £379,000.

The trust's income and distributions were substantially increased in this year as it administered funds from a legacy of £276,000. The trust has no funds available for general distribution.

Exclusions: "In view of the purpose and method of operation of the trust, unsolicited applications for any purpose are not considered."

Applications: "No funds are available by direct application" – see above.

The Mount 'A' & Mount 'B' Charitable Trusts

£70,000 (1992/93)

Mainly local projects in Bristol, Jersey and Italy

The Barbinder Trust, 9 Greyfriars Road, Reading RG1 1JG
01734-597111

Correspondent: The Director

Trustees: The Barbinder Trust.

Beneficial area: UK, but with a strong preference for Bristol, Jersey and Italy.

Information available: Full accounts are on file at the Charity Commission.

General: These two trusts seem effectively to operate as one. Their grants lists appear to more or less replicate each other, and are very similar in size. In 1991/92, both had assets of just under £250,000 generating an income of £35,000 each.

Mount 'A' gave 43 grants totalling £32,000. Mount 'B' gave 44 grants totalling £35,000. The grants lists are exactly the same with the exceptions of grants to RNLI Jersey and the National Art Collection's Fund from Mount 'A' and to Clifton College Bristol, Riding for the Disabled and SHIP from Mount 'B'.

Grants were mainly to local projects in Bristol, Jersey and Italy. The largest (with the figure being the sum of the two grants) were to the Italian Charitable Trust (£10,000), St Martin's Church, Jersey (£8,000) and Famiglia Bardigiana and Parrocchia Grezzo (both £5,000). Other grants ranged from £250 to £4,500 with beneficiaries including Associazione Sportiva Bardi, Birthright, Bristol Age Care, Bristol YMCA, Jersey Arts Council, Men of the Trees, Jersey Wildlife Preservation Trust, Royal Opera House and Variety Club Jersey.

Applications: In writing to the correspondent. Presumably a letter to either trust will be considered by both.

The Edwina Mountbatten Trust

£77,000 (1993)

Medical

1 Grosvenor Crescent, London SW1X 7EF
0171-235 5231

Correspondent: The Secretary

Trustees: Countess Mountbatten of Burma, Chairman; Marquess of Camden; Noel Cunningham-Reid; Lord Farringdon; Douglas Fairbanks; Lord Romsey; P H T Mimpriss; Mrs C Fagan.

Beneficial area: UK and overseas.

Information available: Accounts are on file at the Charity Commission for 1993, but without a full list of grants.

General: The trust was set up as a memorial to Edwina Countess Mountbatten of Burma. Its main objects are:

1. Support for the St John Ambulance Brigade (of which she was Superintendent-in-Chief);
2. Support for Save the Children (of which she was president);
3. Promotion and improvement of the art of nursing (she was patron or vice-president of a number of nursing organisations). The trust supports specific projects rather than general running costs.

In 1993, the trust had assets of £1.1 million and an income of £95,000. Grants totalled £77,000.

In 1992, grants totalled £87,000, of which £30,000 was categorised in the accounts as "discretionary grants". These were to organisations other than those listed above and included £10,000 to the Sick Children's Trust and £12,000 to St John Opthalmic Hospital, Jerusalem (the salary for a nurse). Seven other grants ranged from £400 to £5,000 including those to Leonora Children's Cancer Fund (£5,000), Anglican Church of Papua New Guinea (divided between two schools of nursing), and the Royal College of Midwives towards a Tangerian Midwives Association (both £1,500). The others grants were to enable attendance at courses, conferences or projects related to nursing.

Exclusions: No grants to individual nurses working in the UK for further professional training.

Applications: In writing to the correspondent. The trustees meet once a year, generally in May/June.

The N R Charitable Trust

£130,000 (1994)

Christian, general

246 Bishopsgate, London EC2M 4PB
0171-220 3398

Correspondent: Bryan K H Rogers

Beneficial area: UK, overseas.

Information available: Full accounts are on file at the Charity Commission.

General: In 1993, the trust had an income of £103,000, of which £101,000 came from covenants and Gift Aid donations. Grants totalled £97,000. In 1994, the grant total increased to £130,000, but no further information is available for this year.

In 1993, the largest grants of £10,000 went to the Leprosy Mission, London Bible College and St Helen's Church, Bishopsgate. Recipients of £5,000 included British Youth for Christ, Kerigma Video Trust and TEAR Fund. Other grants ranged from £500 to £2,500. Most grants went to Christian organisations, the few exceptions including the Bosnia-Herzegovina Information Centre (medical supplies), Chartered Accountants' Benevolent Association, Cockney Spirit Sailing Trust, Prader-Willi Syndrome and Crisis.

Grants are usually only given to projects or people known personally to the trustees.

Applications: In writing to the correspondent, but note above. Applications are considered annually in April.

The Kitty & Daniel Nabarro Charitable Trust

£52,000 (1992/93)

Jewish, health and welfare

930 High Road, London N12 9SA

Correspondent: D J N Nabarro

Trustees: D J N Nabarro; Mrs K Nabarro; Ms E Cohen.

Beneficial area: UK.

Information available: Full accounts are on file at the Charity Commission.

General: The trust was established in 1991, with an initial settlement of £500,000. In 1992/93, assets stood at £507,000 generating an income of £46,000. Grants totalled £52,000 and were categorised as follows:

Children	£1,200	(2%)
Education	£1,100	(2%)
Disabled	£1,700	(3%)
Medical	£19,800	(38%)
Elderly	£1,900	(4%)
Social	£25,000	(49%)
Miscellaneous	£700	(1%)

The largest grants went to BACUP (£10,000), CBF World Jewish Relief (£6,600), Jewish Care (£3,600), Shelter (£2,600), Bristol Cancer Help Centre, Norwood Child Care and the Samaritans (all £1,000). Of the 45 grants given, half were to Jewish organisations, with the rest mainly to national health and welfare charities such as Age Concern, NSPCC and Scope. The National Trust Lake District Appeal, Salvation Army and Richmond Theatre Trust were also supported.

Applications: The trust states: "The trustees have decided where to allocate funds and we recommend to charities that they do not spend money on applications".

The Willie Nagel Charitable Trust

£35,000 (1993/94)

Jewish, general

Russell Bedford House, City Forum, 250 City Road, London EC1V 2QQ
0171-490 7766

Correspondent: The Secretary

Trustees: W Nagel; A L Sober.

Beneficial area: UK and overseas, particularly Israel.

Information available: Accounts are on file at the Charity Commission, but without a list of grants since that for 1989/90.

General: In 1993/94, the trust had an income of £81,000, mostly from covenanted donations. Grants totalled £35,000, but no information is available as to their distribution.

In 1989/90, grants totalled £52,000, with 35 of the 47 grants given to Jewish organisations. The largest went to the Friends of Wiznitz (£20,000), Board of Deputies Charitable Trust (£5,300) and the Israel Music Foundation (£3,200). Grants to other organisations included £5,000 to the Victoria & Albert Museum, £2,000 to Foundation for Business Responsibility and £1,000 to Business in the Community. All the other beneficiaries were national health and welfare charities. 11 grants were for £1,000 or more, the rest for £500 or less.

Applications: In writing to the correspondent.

The Naggar Charitable Trust

£449,000 (1990-92)

Jewish, general

15 Grosvenor Gardens, London
SW1W 0BD

Correspondent: G A Naggar

Trustees: G A Naggar; M Naggar.

Beneficial area: Worldwide.

Information available: Full accounts are on file at the Charity Commission.

General: The accounts for this trust on file at the Charity Commission cover a two year period and the trust has a UK account and a US account.

In 1990-92, the trust had assets of £752,000 and an income of £681,000. This includes a deed of covenant to the trust of £250,000 a year (£500,000 in the two year accounting period) and a Gift Aid payment of £133,333 in 1991/92.

Grants totalled £449,000 with well over half this total going to the Merephdi Foundation (Soroka Cardiology Project) which received £245,000 plus $72,000 from the US account. The Society of Friends of the Torah received £68,000 and the Jerusalem Foundation £50,000. Six other grants of over £1,000 were all to Jewish organisations.

About 12 of the 45 grants were made were to non-Jewish organisations, most for £100. The exceptions were £1,000 to Barbican Arts Centre Trust and £400 to Barnardo's. The remaining grants were to arts and medical causes.

In the previous two-year period, grants totalled £76,000 plus a further $55,000 from the US account. The Society of Friends of the Torah was the main beneficiary (£15,000 plus $50,000). A further £20,000 went to the Oxford Centre for Post Graduate Studies and £10,000 to Boys Town Jerusalem. Birthright received £3,350 with smaller grants again given to arts and medical organisations.

Applications: In writing to the correspondent.

The Janet Nash Charitable Trust

£179,000 (1993)

Medical, general

Nabarro Nathanson, The Old Chapel, New Mill Eversley, Hampshire RG27 0RA
01734-730300

Correspondent: R Gulliver

Trustees: Janet M Nash; Ronald Gulliver.

Beneficial area: UK.

Information available: Full accounts are on file at the Charity Commission.

General: In 1993, the trust had an income of £219,000 of which £162,000 was given by City Electrical Factors Ltd under deed of covenant. Grants totalled £179,000.

Most of the grants and about half the grant total was given for the medical treatment of individuals. A further £12,000 in total was given as the Janet Nash Fellowship Scholarship for a UK surgeon to study advanced techniques for six months at the Universitätsspital in Zurich.

Eight grants were given to organisations. The largest was £25,000 to Kenilworth Community Care Council, a regular beneficiary. Other large grants went to Birmingham Royal Institute for the Blind (£19,000), Royal School of Medicine (£16,000), St Martin's School, Solihull (£10,000) and South Warwickshire Scanner Appeal (£5,000). Small grants went to Children in Need and All Saints Church Leamington Spa (both £250) and the Cancer Relief Macmillan Fund (£200).

Applications: In writing to the correspondent.

The National AIDS Trust

£235,000 (1993/94)

HIV/AIDS

6th Floor, Eileen House, 80 Newington Causeway, London SE1 6EF
0171-972 2845

Correspondent: Antony Light, Director of Fundraising & Finance

Trustees: Prof M Adler; J Balfour; J M Grimshaw; F S Law; Mrs M Littman; Rt Hon Sir Patrick Nairne; Ms D Platt; Sir Evelyn de Rothschild; J F Mayne; Mrs M Moore; Ms D Reid; M Mansfield; P Westland.

Beneficial area: UK.

Information available: Accounts are on file at the Charity Commission but without a list of grants for the latest year.

General: This trust not only makes grants to voluntary organisations working in the field of HIV/AIDS, but also provides them with management and fundraising training.

In 1993/94, the trust made 39 grants of £223 to £25,000 and totalling £235,000. No information was available on the grants beneficiaries.

In 1991/92, the trust made 41 grants totalling £348,000 and ranging between £1,000 and £15,000. Twenty-four grants (totalling £162,000) were given to HIV specific organisations, six to drugs agencies and other grants were awarded to non-HIV specific voluntary sector agencies towards developing projects around the issue, eg. the housing sector. Projects benefiting included FACTS (£8,000), Immunity (£11,000), Immune Development Trust (£10,000), Positively Women (£5,000), NAZ (£18,000), Mainliners (£18,684), Turning Point's Griffin Project (£8,000), St Bartholomew's House (£9,000), London Churches Resettlement Agency (£7,000) and NAM publications (£5,000).

Exclusions: No grants to individuals or for conferences or videos.

Applications: Application forms are available from the correspondent. Grants are made twice a year. Dates for funding rounds and application forms are available from Davel Patel at the above address. It is helpful to receive applications as far in advance of deadlines as possible.

The National Association of Rags

General: Rags and weeks have traditionally been the most common way for students to raise money for charity. They are organised by each individual students' union and fundraise throughout the year, although in some cases the fundraising is concentrated in to one or two weeks in the year.

Background: There are about 200 Rags nationally, which give away over £2 million annually Each Rag operates individually, and there is no central administrative body.

Records of all Rags are kept, however, by the Students' Charities' Appeal at Manchester University, and this can be used as an initial point of contact. It is generally better to contact your local universities and colleges direct.

Direct grants: Rags give grants to charities from the proceeds of their fundraising events organised throughout the year. Grants are usually between £50 and £1,000, and may occasionally be as much as £10-£20,000. Direct grants are normally only made to small charities local to the university or college.

How to Apply: There is no central way of applying to all Rags for a grant. All applications have to be made directly to the local Rag committee. They decide who the beneficiaries will be each year. You may have to complete an application form. Do not overwhelm them with brochures as many Rags receive several hundred applications each year. Some rags visit short-listed charities before making their final decision. Most Rags will have a beneficiaries or charities liaison officer, and it would be wise to contact this person for advice before an application is made.

Donations in kind: Rags are normally happy to provide volunteer help to any charity, local or otherwise, and will often be prepared to travel the length of the country to do this. Perhaps the most effective methods of fundraising with Rags are street collections, or collections at sports grounds, concerts etc.. Both Manchester and Loughborough Rags keep permit databases of cities all over the country, which both charities and Rags use for information. Including your permits on these databases does not by any means guarantee that help will be forthcoming, but may sometimes have startling results.

Who can apply: Local and regional charities take preference over national charities for direct grants. In some cases, a project of a national charity based wholly in the local area will be deemed suitable. Check the policy of each Rag you apply to. The type of grants and the priority by which they are allocated is usually included with the application form. The college Rag Mags also include a list of grants given in the previous year and give an idea of the size of grants and the type of organisations that they support.

When to Apply: It is important to send applications at the right time as it may not be passed on to the following year's committee as there is little or no continuity from one year to the next. Presentation of funds will mostly take place in May/June or in September/October. Some Rags will accept applications right up until their Presentation, but many will choose beneficiaries a year in advance. The timing of Rag Weeks is unpredictable, but many are concentrated in February. To find out when to apply, contact the rag directly, or the Student Union may be able to help.

Addresses to find contacts: Alan Clayton, General Manager, Manchester University Students' Charities' Appeal, Manchester University Students' Union, Oxford Road, Manchester M13 9PR (0161-275 2987).

The National Association of Round Tables

General: The Round Table is similar to a social club. It meets twice a month and raises money for local charities and organisations. The club consists of 1,200 individual Tables throughout the country. They all raise money in their own locality for local charities/organisations. National organisations are rarely supported, though some local branches may occasionally be helped. All Tables are run autonomously. A typical Table would consist of about 30 men, aged from 18-40 years old. A parallel organisation was set up for the female partners of the Round Table, which has since been open to other women wishing to join. Each Table raises thousands of pounds for local charities/organisations and may get involved actively in providing other sorts of help.

Charities can advertise, and maybe have features, in the Round Table magazine, *The Tabler*, which has a circulation of about 25,000 and is distributed to all the local Tables. Many charities/organisations receive support following an advert in the magazine.

Address: To contact your local Round Table send a letter, to the address below, giving brief details of your charity, project and financial situation. Your letter will be forwarded to your local Table, who will then contact you. Most Tables receive many applications and cannot support them all.

Write to: National Association of Round Tables, Marchesi House, 4 Embassy Drive, Calthorpe Road, Edgbaston, Birmingham B15 1TP (0121-456 4402).

The National Catholic Fund

£190,000 (1993)

Catholic welfare

39 Eccleston Square, London SW1V 1BX
0171-630 8279

Correspondent: Msr Philip Carroll

Trustees: Cardinal Basil Hume; Rev Michael Bowen; Rev Derek Worlock; Rev John Ward; Rev Maurice de Murville; Baron Craigmyle; Mrs Elspeth Orchard; John Gibbs.

Beneficial area: UK.

Information available: Full accounts are on file at the Charity Commission.

General: The fund, formerly the New Pentecost Fund, is concerned with "the advancement of the Roman Catholic religion in England and Wales". Grants are only given to organisations for the national work of the Catholic Church.

In 1993, it had an income of £1 million mainly from diocesan assessments. The majority of its income was spent on running the Catholic Media and the General Secretariat, but £190,000 was spent on Christian organisations. 22 grants were made, with all the beneficiaries receiving similar amounts the previous year. £64,000 went to Catholic Youth Services and £20,000 to Diocesan Vocation Services. Other grants included the Association of Catholic Deaf, Bourne Trust, Lifeline, National Board of Catholic Women and Pax Christi.

Exclusions: No grants to individuals, local projects or projects not immediately advancing the Roman Catholic religion.

Applications: To the correspondent.

The National Gardens Scheme Charitable Trust

£1,300,000 (1995)

Nursing, gardens, gardening

Hatchlands Park, East Clandon, Guildford, Surrey GU4 7RT
01483-211535

Correspondent: Lt Col T A Marsh, Director

Beneficial area: UK.

Information available: We were unable to see the file at the Charity Commission.

General: The trust exists to support charities administered by the Queens' Nursing Institute; to assist the Gardens Fund of the National Trust, to assist County Nursing Associations and other charities determined by the Council.

£1.3 million was available for distribution in 1995. No further information available.

Applications: The trust has long-standing relationships with all its beneficiaries and makes no grants for other purposes. Applications are therefore not accepted.

The National Hospital Trust

£81,000 (1991/92)

Hospitals

119 Horseley Fields, Wolverhampton WV1 3DG
01902-455633

Correspondent: R A Cummins, Administrator

Trustees: Sir Adrian Blennerhasset; John Evans; Prof Leslie Reid.

Beneficial area: UK.

Information available: Full accounts are on file at the Charity Commission.

General: The trust was set up in 1988 to distribute the income from the NHS Loto. It gives grants towards medical, surgical or other equipment, facilities or buildings for use by the National Health Service or other organisations involved in providing health care. The income varies depending on the proceeds from the NHS Loto: £64,000 in 1991/92; £114,000 in 1990/91; £109,000 in 1989/90 (when total income was £147,000).

Grants totalled £81,000 in 1991/92, given to University of Manchester – Withington Hospital (£31,000) and Southlands Hospital – Academic Practice Unit (£50,000). It appears that grants are allocated a year in advance, with the two grants given in 1991/92 being referred to in the accounts of the previous year.

In 1990/91, four grants totalled £156,000. Grants were given to the University Hospital of Wales (£50,000), Royal Devon & Exeter Hospital (£41,000), Aberdeen Royal Infirmary (£40,000) and University of Leeds – Department of Obstetrics & Gynaecology (£25,000).

Applications: In writing to the correspondent.

The Nazareth Trust Fund

£31,000 (1993/94)

Christian

Kewferry House, 10 Kewferry Road, Northwood, Middlesex HA6 2NY
01923-827923

Correspondent: R W G Hunt, Trustee

Trustees: R W G Hunt.

Beneficial area: Worldwide.

Information available: Full accounts are on file at the Charity Commission for 1993/94.

General: In 1993/94, the trust had an income of £64,000 and gave 61 grants totalling £31,000. There were nine grants of £1,000 or more and many organisations received a number of grants during the year.

Northwood Hills Evangelical Church received seven grants totalling almost £18,000, and Crusaders three grants totalling £3,500. The other larger grants were to Hamilton Baptist Church (£1,300) and Latin Link (£1,000).

Most other grants were for £100 to £500 and were generally for Christian organisations. World Vision UK received four grants totalling £500. Other beneficiaries included: Bible Society; Christians in Sport; Evangelical Alliance; Far East Broadcasting Association; London City Mission; Scripture Union; Sight Savers and Tear Fund. A number of grants were made to missionaries.

Applications: The trust supports causes already known to the trustees. Unsolicited applications are not supported.

Nesswall Ltd

£92,000 (1992/93)

Jewish

28 Overlea Road, London E5 9BG
0181-806 2965

Correspondent: Mrs R Teitelbaum

Trustees: I Teitelbaum; Mrs R Teitelbaum; I Chersky.

Beneficial area: Worldwide.

Information available: Full accounts are on file at the Charity Commission.

General: In 1992/93, the trust had an income of £92,000 of which £73,000 was from covenants. 22 grants totalled £92,000 all to Jewish organisations.

The largest grants were given to Friends of Horim Establishments (£36,000), Torah Vochesed L'Ezra Vesaad (£21,000) and Emunah Education Centre (£10,000). The other grants ranged form £18 to £3,600.

Applications: In writing to the correspondent.

The New Durlston Trust

£35,000 (1994)

Christian

c/o Herbert Pool Ltd, 95 Fleet Road, Fleet, Hants GU13 8PJ
01252-620444

Correspondent: N A H Pool

Trustees: H H Pool; N A H Pool; M L Fenton-Jones.

Beneficial area: UK; occassionally third world.

Information available: Full accounts are on file at the Charity Commission.

General: The trust tends to support about 10 to 20 main organisations each year, from the likes of Tear Fund to local churches. There has to be a clear Christian element to the project. About 75% of grants are recurrent or allocated a long time in advance to charities the trust has knowledge of. Overseas grants are usually given to Christian charities working in the third world that are known to the trust.

In 1994, the trust held almost 71,000 £1 ordinary shares in Herbert Pool Estates Ltd (26.38% of the total issued share capital of the company) and had an income of £58,000 (£77,000 in 1991). Only £34,000 (£30,000 in 1991) was given in grants. Grants are usually in the range of £100 to £5,000.

During the year, the trust's grants were: St John's Church, Woodbridge (£6,000); Fleet Bible Bookshop (£2,500); Interserve (£2,200) and Farnborough Parish Church (£2,000). There were eight grants of £1,000 to Bible Society; Crookham Baptist Church; Farnborough Christian Outreach Trust; Far Eastern Broadcasting Association; Mission Aviation Fellowship; Scripture Union; Tear Fund and Woodlands Centre Trust. 67 other charities received grants of £500 or less, totalling £12,250.

Exclusions: No grants to individuals for further education.

Applications: In writing to the correspondent.

The New Horizons Trust

£42,000 (1993/94)

See below

Paramount House, 290-292 Brighton Road, South Croydon, Surrey CR2 6AG
0181-666 0201

Correspondent: The Secretary

Trustees: A M Pilch CBE; Mrs B C Pilch; A R Neale; J R Foulds; Ms K Dibley.

Beneficial area: UK.

Information available: Full accounts are on file at the Charity Commission.

General: The trust gives grants to groups of older people carrying out projects for the benefit of the community, not vice versa. Grants are given to any group proposing a good idea that will benefit the community provided that:

- There are at least 10 people in the group;
- At least half of them are aged 60 or over;
- The project is new and makes use of the knowledge and experience of group members.

Applications may be made by new or existing groups, but in the latter case they must show that it is an innovative departure and will be managed as an entirely separate project. Grants are usually for £500 to £1,000. In 1993/94, the trust had an income of £60,000 and gave grants totalling £42,000. 44 new grants were given, totalling £33,000.

Grants may cover any costs involved in planning, organising and running a project for up to 18 months for items such as rent, heating, light, furniture, office equipment, materials and supplies.

Examples of projects supported by the trust include art groups, credit unions, embroidery, ethnic minority support, sheltered housing, luncheon clubs and tractor restoration. The programme welcomes innovative ideas.

Exclusions: No funding is given to on-going projects. Grants are not given: to repay loans or to meet any previous obligations that may already have been incurred by a group before their project has been approved by the trust; to pay salaries, although legitimate expenses may be reimbursed to volunteers provided these do not form an excessive proportion of the total; for travelling expenses, although limited expenditure on transport may be approved where it forms an integral part of the project.

Applications: On a form available from the correspondent.

Newpier Ltd

See below

Jewish, general

Halpern & Woolf, 301-305 Euston Road, London NW1 3SS

Correspondent: The Secretary

Beneficial area: UK.

Information available: No accounts are on file at the Charity Commission.

General: The following information repeats the entry from the last edition of the Guide, as the situation regarding information on this trust has not changed.

The trust was registered in 1986. No accounts are on file at the Charity Commission, although according to the Commission the trust's income was £244,000 in 1990/91. It is not known how much of this was given in grants. Support is mainly for Jewish organsiations.

Applications: In writing to the correspondent. The address given above is effectively a PO Box, from where letters are passed on to the trustees.

The Newton Settlement

£42,000 (1993/94)

Christian

26 North Quay, Abingdon Marina, Oxford OX14 5RY
01235-535377

Correspondent: Peter Clarke

Trustees: P Clarke; D M Holland; W W Leyland.

Beneficial area: UK.

Information available: Full accounts are on file at the Charity Commission.

General: This trust has the same correspondent, trustees and general policy as the Norwood Trust (*see separate entry*). The trust favours Methodist and other Free Churches, Methodist and Free Church causes generally, smaller national charities in which the settlor and her late husband had a particular interest, and other charitable causes. Where churches are concerned, the trustees take particular note of the contribution towards the project, the subject of the application, and the level of commitment of the church members to the project as indicated by their own contribution.

In 1993/94, the trust had assets of £1.1 million and an income of £76,000. After expenses of £25,000 (£23,000 in administration and legal expenses), the trust had £51,000 available for distribution. 16 grants totalled £42,000 and ranged from £750 to £8,000. Seven were to Methodist churches and five to other churches engaged in the building of new premises or in making improvements to their existing premises. The other grants went to the National Council of YMCA's (£8,000), Scripture Union – International Council (£3,000), and the Holding Hands Appeal and 11th Clacton (Jaywick) Scout Group (both £1,000).

Exclusions: No grants to individuals.

Applications: In writing to the correspondent. In normal circumstances, the trustees' decision is communicated to the applicant within 21 days (if a refusal) or, if successful, within 42 days of receipt of full information from the applicant, which may be requested after the initial application.

The Nimrod & Glaven Charitable Settlement

£72,000 (1993/94)

General

The Glebe, Letheringsett, Holt, Norfolk NR25 7YA

Correspondent: Hon Beryl Cozens-Hardy

Trustees: Hon Beryl Cozens-Hardy; Mrs Phelps; J E V Phelps.

Beneficial area: Norfolk and Merseyside.

Information available: Full accounts are on file at the Charity Commission.

General: The trust supports a few national charities in the fields of medicine, health, welfare, and general purposes through the Charities Aid Foundation. It supports some local charities in Norfolk and Merseyside.

In 1993/94, the trust had assets of £1 million and a net income of £89,000. Grants totalled £80,000. About 200 grants were made with most for a few hundred pounds.

£1,000 grants were given to each of Africa in Crisis, Gresham's School Development Appeal, Holt & Neighbourhood Housing Society, St John Council for Lancashire and St John Ophthalmic Hospital Jerusalem. The only larger amounts were £9,750 to CAF and £1,500 to Lancashire Constabulary (for Cozens-Hardy Travel Fellowship).

Applications: To the correspondent, before December. The main distribution list is prepared in January. No telephone calls.

The Noel Buxton Trust

£113,000 (1993)

Child and family welfare, penal matters, Africa, reconciliation and human rights

28 Russell Square, London WC1B 5DS

Correspondent: Margaret Beard, Secretary

Trustees: Richenda Wallace, Chairman; Joyce Morton; Simon Buxton; Paul Buxton; David Birmingham; Angelica Mitchell; Jon Snow; Jo Tunnard.

Beneficial area: UK and Africa.

Information available: Full accounts are on file at the Charity Commission.

General: Grants are made for the following (**see exclusions below**):

- Child and family welfare (EXCLUDING anything medical or relating to mental or physical handicap);
- Education and development in Africa (East, Central and Southern only);
- Penal matters and the welfare of prisoners and their families;
- Reconciliation, human rights, and international understanding;
- Youth (but not conventional youth clubs, sports clubs etc.).

In 1993, the trust had assets of £1.5 million and an income of £113,000. It gave 168 grants, but seldom gives grants of more than £2,000 each. However, applications for recurrent funding over several years and for "core" running costs are considered. While the trustees do not respond to appeals from large and well-supported national charities, they welcome appeals from small local groups (normally with charitable registration) in England, Scotland and Wales.

In 1993, 61 grants for child and family welfare totalled £29,000 (26% of grant total). The largest grants were given to Howgill Centre, Whitehaven (£2,500) and Kid's Club Network (£2,000). Other grants to local organisations ranged from £250 to £1,500 with beneficiaries including Bristol Children's Scrapstore, Edinburgh & Lothian Women's Aid, Redditch Home Start, Scunthorpe Gingerbread Advice Centre and West Glamorgan CVS (for a young families drop-in centre). 12 holiday grants of £100 were given to local groups.

12 grants for education and development in Africa totalled £16,800 (15%). Recipients included ApT Design & Development and the Harambee Educational Fund, Uganda (both £3,500), Peninsula School Feeding Association, Cape Town (£2,500) and Book Aid International for work in Namibia (£1,500).

19 grants for penal matters totalled £22,000 (19%), including £2,750 to the Prisoners' Wives & Families Society, London, £2,500 to the Prison Reform Trust and £2,000 each to the Institute for the Study & Treatment of Deliquency and Prisoners Abroad. Five grants of £500 were given to various organisations for summer projects for young people at risk of offending conducted by or with the police.

23 grants in the fields of reconciliation, human rights and international understanding totalled £18,600, divided as follows:

Reconciliation: Seven grants totalling £6,800. The largest were £2,000 each to Mediation UK and Responding to Conflict, Woodbrooke College, Birmingham. The other grants ranged from £300 to £1,000. Three were to local groups and the others to Jewish Council for Community Relations and National Family Mediation.

Human rights: Eight grants totalling £8,500. The Family Rights Group received £5,500, with the other grants ranging from £250 to £1,000. Other beneficiaries included Children's Legal Centre, Community Central Hall, Glasgow (travellers project) and Northern Refugee Centre, Leeds.

International understanding: Five grants totalled £6,500. The largest grant was £1,500 to Dudley One World. Smaller grants were given to Malvern Third World Centre and South Yorkshire Development Education Centre.

27 grants to youth projects/organisations totalled £15,500 (14%) all to local projects. Grants of £1,000 or more went to Bradford Study Support Network, Brook Advisory Centres, Consett Churches Detached Youth Project, St Basil's Centre, Birmingham and the Who Cares? Trust. The remaining grants were for £500 or less.

Other social welfare grants, of which there were 18, totalled £11,500 (10%). Most grants were to local projects or organisations including Arran Information & Advice Service, Emmaus UK and Reading Rape Crisis Line. Grants ranged from £250 to £3,000.

The trust has on-going commitments for 1994 of £18,650, and for 1995 of £3,350. Grants totalling £5,250 were offered in 1993 but were not claimed by the beneficiaries.

Exclusions: The trust does not give to academic research; animals; the arts; buildings; the elderly; expeditions, exchanges, visits, etc.; individuals for education or any other purpose; anything medical or connected with mental or physical handicap or illness; Northern Ireland (a grant is given to the Northern Ireland Voluntary Trust to be disbursed at NIVT's discretion); anywhere abroad except for East, Central, and Southern Africa; alcohol and drug projects; environmental causes.

Applications: There is no application form and applications may be submitted at any time. Applications should include the organisation's charity registration number, and the name of the organisation to which grants should be paid if different from that at the head of the appeal letter. Rising costs and the need to conserve funds for grant-making make it impossible to acknowledge receipt of applications, but every effort is made to communicate a decision on appropriate appeals as soon as possible. **No replies to inappropriate appeals.**

The Norman Family Charitable Trust

£152,000 (1993/94)

Animal welfare, social welfare and young people in the South West

5 Coastguard Road, Budleigh Salterton, Devon EX9 6NU
01395-445177

Correspondent: W K Norman

Trustees: Kenneth Norman; Philip Norman; Roger Dawe; Margaret Evans.

Beneficial area: Devon, Cornwall and Somerset only.

Information available: Full accounts are on file at the Charity Commission.

General: In 1993/94, the trust had assets of £2 million and an income of £231,000. It gave grants totalling £152,000 to over 250 organisations. The trustees' report states that the trust is receiving an "ever increasing number of requests and maintaining its policy of giving smaller amounts to an increasing number of charities".

The trust mainly funds organisations in Devon, Cornwall and Somerset, or because of a specific connection. The main project for the year was "Care for the Homeless" and several large grants were given in this field. In 1991/92, £5,000 was given to each of Centrepoint, Exmouth Community College, Lyme Regis Charitable Trust and YMCA Exeter.

28 other grants were for £1,000 or more to organisations such as Age Concern, Animal Aid, Blue Cross Animal Welfare, Devon County Association for the Blind, Exeter Women's Aid, Guide Dogs for the Blind, Marie Stopes International, Pathway to Recovery Trust and the Youth Enquiry Service.

The rest of the grants ranged from £50 to £1,000. The majority of organisations received modest amounts ranging from £100 to £250. A wide variety of causes were supported; most involved in social welfare or the care of animals. About half the grants were recurrent.

Exclusions: No grants for the maintenance or running of churches.

Applications: In writing to the correspondent. All applicants should observe the geographical interests of the trust. The correspondent stresses that "there is no point in charities outside this area sending us glossy brochures when we have no intention of looking at them".

The Northmoor Trust

£139,000 (1992/93)

General

44 Clifton Hill, London NW8 0QG
0171-372 0698

Correspondent: Mrs Hilary Edwards, Secretary to the Trustees

Trustees: Lord Runciman; Ruth Runciman; Canon E A James; Fran Bennett.

Beneficial area: UK.

Information available: Accounts are on file at the Charity Commission up to 1990/91 only.

General: The trustees note that they only consider applications from bodies or projects of which one or more trustees has a direct personal knowledge. It is useful therefore to give some background about the public life of these distinguished trustees. Garry Runciman, now Lord Runciman of Doxford, serves as chairman of Andrew Weir & Co, Runciman Investments Ltd, the Royal Commission on Criminal Justice and as treasurer of the Child Poverty Action Group. Lady Runciman is chair of the Mental Health Act Commission and a member of the Advisory Council on the Misuse of Drugs. The Reverend Canon Eric James is Chaplain to the Queen and former (now honorary) director of Christian Action. Fran Bennett is a former director of the Child Poverty Action Group.

The disbursements by the trust have varied greatly. In 1989/90, only £38,000 was given in grant-aid. The trust realised shares in Walter Runciman plc and this introduced assets worth an additional £3 million to the trust. In the following year, 1990/91, £433,000 was disbursed in 25 grants. £213,000 was disbursed in 1991/92 which apparently was its total income for the year.

The trust has reported that its income has since "fallen back and total distributions for the last financial year (1992/93) amounted to £139,000".

To quote the 1993 Edition of this guide: "Several beneficiaries have received grants over a number of years although not always in succession, including the Child Poverty Action Group and Prison Reform Trust. Other beneficiaries have included the University of Newcastle-upon-Tyne Development Trust, Urban Learning Foundation, Action Homeless Concern, Immigrants' Aid Trust, Handicapped Adventure Playground, Streetwise Youth and the Tamil Refugee Resettlement Fund."

In 1990/91, major grants were also given to the Runciman Charitable Trust (£110,000) and the Creative and Supportive Trust (CAST) which assists women prisoners (£32,000).

Exclusions: The trustees only consider applications from bodies or projects of which one or more of the trustees has direct personal knowledge.

Applications: In writing to the correspondent. Trustees meetings are held in April.

The Northumberland Village Homes Trust

£72,000 (1991/92)

Children and young people

c/o Savages, Bellwood Buildings,
36 Mosley Street, Newcastle-upon-Tyne
NE1 1DG
0191-221 2111

Correspondent: Mrs E P Savage

Trustees: D Welch; Mrs J M Paley; B Porter; Mrs L I Lawrence; Richard Baron Gisborough; Mrs E P Savage; K Hunt; J M O'Neill.

Beneficial area: UK, with a priority for North East England.

Information available: Full accounts are on file at the Charity Commission up to 1991/92.

General: The objects of the trust are the relief of poverty, distress and sickness among children and young people under the age of 18; to promote the education and training of such young people; and to attain these objectives by making regular allowances and emergency payments out of the income of the trust.

In 1991/92, the trust had assets of £910,000 and an income of £56,000. Just under 100 grants were given totalling £72,000. The largest grants were £10,500 to Children - North East and £7,500 to Catholic Care North East. The Isle of Man Children Centre and NSPCC Sunderland both received £3,000, NCH St Albany's Children's House received £2,500, and £2,000 was given to Save the Children Fund.

The other grants ranged from £100 to £1,000 mainly to charities concerned with children and young people, with a strong preference for the North East. Examples include British Ski Federation Trust, Consett YMCA, Derwentside Women's Aid, Kent Learning Centre for Disabled Children, Lincoln Toy Library, Newton Aycliffe Youth Centre, Re-Solv and Youth Clubs UK.

Exclusions: No personal applications will be considered unless supported by a letter from a registered charity, local authority, or unless the applicant is personally known to one of the trustees.

Applications: The trustees meet in May and November. Applications should be made on or before 31st March and 30th September respectively. Applications should be in writing and should state:

- Whether the applicant is an individual, private charity or registered charity;
- The objects (if a charity);
- The amount required and what it is for;
- Any other sources of funding.

The Norton Foundation

£101,000 to organisations (1993/94)

Young people under 25 years of age

PO Box 040, Kenilworth, Warwickshire
CV8 2ZR

Correspondent: Mrs J M Emms, Clerk

Trustees: H Antrobus; P S Birdi; Mrs E Corney; Mrs P Francis; Mrs S V Henderson; J R Kendrick; B W Lewis; D P J Monk; A Newland; D F Perkins; R H G Suggett.

Beneficial area: UK, but particularly Birmingham and Warwickshire.

Information available: Full accounts are on file at the Charity Commission.

General: The trust was created in 1990. Its objects are to help children and young people under 25 who are in "need of care or rehabilitation or aid of any kind, particularly as a result of delinquency, deprivation, maltreatment or neglect or who are in danger of lapsing or relapsing into delinquency". The trust is currently restricting its giving to applicants from Birmingham and Warwickshire.

In 1993/94, the trust had assets of £2.6 million and an income of £142,000. Grants to individuals totalled £96,000 and to organisations £101,000. The latter are broken down as follows (number of grants in brackets):

	1993/94	1992/93
Education	£11,000 (4)	£2,000 (1)
Homelessness	£47,000 (6)	£30,000 (2)
Training	£11,000 (4)	£19,000 (6)
Holidays	£13,000 (5)	£5,500 (2)
Leisure activities	£19,000 (6)	£9,000 (4)

No further information is available on the beneficiaries.

Grants to individuals are given for clothing, education, household expenses, leisure activities, maintenance, training and holidays, with 456 of the 588 grants for clothing and household expenses.

Applications: On a form available from the correspondent. Applications from organisations are normally processed by the trustees at their meeting in June each year.

The Norwich Town Close Estate Charity

£281,000 to organisations (1993/94)

Welfare, education in Norwich

10 Golden Dog Lane, Magdalen Street,
Norwich NR3 1BP
01603-621023

Correspondent: N A Ogilvie, Administrator

Beneficial area: Within a 20-mile radius of the Guildhall of the city of Norwich.

Information available: Accounts are on file at the Charity Commission, but without a list of grants.

General: In 1993/94, the trust had assets of £4.6 million and an income of £500,000. Grants were given as follows:

Educational grants	£81,000
Pensions	£73,000
TV licences	£10,000
Relief-in-need	£12,000
Other organisations	£281,000

The charity is primarily for Freemen of Norwich, to whom the grants in the first four categories are given.

The last category included many grants, but as we were unable to see a list of grants we cannot comment on the size of grant or give examples of the range of beneficiaries. Only charities within a 20-mile radius of Norwich are eligible and the grant must be for educational purposes.

In 1992/93, "other organisations" received a total of £134,000. This was given in just three grants: £100,000 to the Norfolk & Norwich Heritage Trust, £30,000 to

University of East Anglia and £5,000 to the Norfolk Museums Service.

Further information on grants to individuals are given in the two Guides: *The Educational Grants Directory* and *A Guide to Grants for Individuals in Need*.

Exclusions: No grants to individuals who are not Freemen of the city of Norwich; charities more than 20 miles from Norwich; charities which are not educational.

Applications: Individuals should apply on a form provided by the administrator; organisations should write a letter of application. The trustees meet quarterly for most of their business and have two meetings, in February and August, to consider applications from other bodies.

The Norwood Settlement

£93,000 (1993/94)

Christian

26 North Quay, Abingdon Marina, Abingdon, Oxford OX14 5RY
01235-535377

Correspondent: Peter Clarke

Trustees: P Clarke; D M Holland; W W Leyland.

Beneficial area: UK.

Information available: Full accounts are on file at the Charity Commission.

General: This trust has the same correspondent, trustees and general policy as the Newton Settlement (*see separate entry*). The trust favours Methodist and other Free Churches, Methodist and Free Church causes generally, smaller national charities in which the settlor and his widow had a particular interest, and other charitable causes. Where churches are concerned, the trustees take particular note of the contribution towards the project, the subject of the application, and the level of commitment of the church members to the project as indicated by their own contribution.

In 1993/94, the trust had assets of £2.1 million and an income of £144,000. Expenses totalled £33,000, including administration and legal charges of £31,000.

The trust gave 27 grants totalling £93,000 ranging from £1,000 to £11,000. Most were to Methodist churches engaged in the building of new premises or in making improvements to existing premises. Two churches supported were in Wales and one in Northern Ireland, the others being scattered throughout England. Six grants were not to churches: £11,000 to the National Council of YMCAs, and grants of £1,000 to £2,000 to Royal Sailors Rests, Hornsey YMCA, Wesley Diaconal Order (Edgbaston), the Havering branch of the Multiple Sclerosis Society and the Mudchute Association.

Exclusions: No grants to individuals and rarely to large national charities.

Applications: In writing to the correspondent. In normal circumstances, the trustees' decision is communicated to the applicant within 21 days (if a refusal), and if successful, within 42 days of receipt of full information from the applicant, which may be requested after the initial application.

The Notgrove Trust

£58,000 (1992/93)

Hospitals, general

The Manor, Notgrove, Cheltenham, Gloucestershire GL54 3BT
01451-850239

Correspondent: David Acland

Trustees: David Acland; Elizabeth Acland.

Beneficial area: UK, but with a strong interest in Cheltenham.

Information available: Full accounts on file at the Charity Commission.

General: The trust was set up in 1979 by Elizabeth Acland and her husband David. Its objects are general charitable purposes and the relief from poverty of any of the Aclands' employees. "The trustees contribute to some local Gloucestershire charities on a regular basis."

"The capital of the trust is invested in Stock Exchange securities with a general policy of trying to balance income and growth to maintain the real value of both the capital and income of the trust. The trust has no expensive administrative back-up. Therefore it is regretted that appeals will not be acknowledged. As the trustees have considerable involvement in charitable activities they usually have information about the causes they wish to support. They seek to discourage speculative appeals as these tend to wasted the resources of the appellant to no effect."

The trust had £1.2 million of assets in 1992/93 which generated an income of £69,000. £58,000 was given out to 31 organisations. The largest grants were £15,000 to Friends of Moore Cottage Hospital – which has been a regular beneficiary – and £8,000 to the Crime Concern Trust. £5,000 each was given to the Royal Botanic Gardens Kew Foundation and Spinal Injuries Association.

Other grants ranged from £25 to £4,000 and were given to a range of national charities and local organisations in the Cheltenham area, particularly in the fields of health and welfare. Beneficiaries included British Wheelchair Sports Foundation, Countryside Foundation, Iris Fund for the Prevention of Blindness, Notgrove Village Hall Trust, Spinal Injuries Association, Tewkesbury Abbey Appeal and Victim Support Cheltenham.

Applications: No applications are invited – see above.

The Oakdale Trust

£94,000 (1993/94)

General in Mid-Wales, overseas

Tan-y-Coed, Panty-dwr, Rhayader, Powys LD6 5LR

Correspondent: B Cadbury

Trustees: B Cadbury; Mrs F F Cadbury; R A Cadbury; F B Cadbury; Mrs O H Tatton-Brown; Dr R C Cadbury.

Beneficial area: Worldwide, especially Wales.

Information available: Full accounts are on file at the Charity Commission.

General: The trust states: "as we are one of the few grant-making foundations in mid-Wales, the trustees have decided that they will concentrate on making grants to charities and causes in Wales, and not respond to any new appeals from the rest of Britain. Grants are only made to registered charities and individuals should not apply. We will continue to make grants to bodies working overseas".

1993/94 was therefore a transitional period with geographical distribution of grants as follows:

Welsh charities	£22,000
English charities	£42,000
Overseas work	£30,000

In 1993/94, the trust had an income of £88,000 and 83 grants totalled £94,000. The trust summarizes its grants as follows:

Penal reform, prison aftercare etc.	£14,000
Medical and medical research	£7,600
Children, youth and social work	£18,137
Education	£9,700
Church and Quaker work	£3,850
Animal welfare	£250
Art, theatre	£5,240
International (Mexico, Bosnia, Gambia)	£30,350
Conservation	£5,350

The largest grants were £9,700 to Kings College, Cambridge, £6,000 to Personal Empowerment Programme and £5,000 each to Prisoners of Conscience, Medical Foundation for Care of Victims of Torture, Female Prisoners' Welfare Project and the Brandon Centre. Other grants ranged from £12 to the Institute of Advanced Motorists to £4,500 to the Creative and Supportive Trust. A range of Welsh charities received grants including Carmarthen Playscheme, Dyfed Wildlife Trust, Montgomery Music Festival, Prestatyn Gingerbread, Trust for Sick Children in Wales and the Welsh Chess Education Trust.

Exclusions: No grants to individuals or to appeals from charities outside Wales unless the work is international.

Applications: In writing to the correspondent but owing to the lack of secretarial help no acknowledgement can be expected. Trustees usually meet twice a year.

The Ofenheim & Cinderford Charitable Trusts

£89,000 (1993/94)

Health and welfare, environment, general

Baker Tilly, Iveco Ford House, Station Road, Watford, Hertfordshire WD1 1TG
01923-816400

Correspondent: G Wright

Trustees: R J Clark; R Fitzherbert-Brockholes; R McLeod.

Beneficial area: UK.

Information available: Full accounts are on file at the Charity Commission.

General: Since 1985, the grants given by the two trusts have been listed together. The trusts support nationally known and well-established organisations of personal interest to the trustees. Most grants are given in the fields of health, welfare and the environment, with some to arts organisations. Almost all are recurrent.

In 1993/94, the trusts had combined assets of over £3.3 million with an income of £128,000. The assets of the Cinderford Trust have increased recently to £2.6 million, owing to £1.16 million received as the value of investments from Dr Angela Ofenheim who died in 1992. Presumably the income of the trust will increase in future years.

The grants total was £89,000, £38,000 from the Ofenheim and £51,000 from the Cinderford Trust. The largest grants were to St Wilfred's Hospice, Eastbourne (£9,300) and Save the Children Fund (£7,000). The other 40 grants included 27 of £1,000 to £5,000, and 13 of under £1,000.

Other beneficiaries included the Musicians Benevolent Fund (£4,900), National Youth Orchestra (£2,800), Wildfowl Trust (£2,800), National Fund for Research into Crippling Diseases (£1,400), National Art Collections Fund (£700), Link Centre for Deafened People (£700) and the Tree Council (£700).

Applications: In writing to the correspondent. Unsuccessful applications will not be acknowledged.

The Ogle Trust

£145,000 (1993)

Evangelical Christianity

6 Chanctonbury View, Henfield, West Sussex BN5 9TW
01273-495185

Correspondent: Chris Fischbacher, Secretary

Trustees: E Fischbacher, Chairman; A I Kinnear; D J Harris; S Procter; C A Fischbacher.

Beneficial area: Worldwide.

Information available: Accounts are on file at the Charity Commission, but those for 1993 do not include a grants list.

General: In practice funds are mainly directed to new initiatives in evangelism worldwide, support of missionary enterprises, Bible student training, help to retired missionary workers and famine and other relief funds.

Grants in 1993 totalled £145,000 but no further information is available.

In 1991, when grants totalled £197,000, they were broken down as follows:

Regular beneficiaries	
Individuals	£15,000
Organisations	£86,000
Occasional beneficiaries	£96,000

The largest grants were given for famine relief in Africa (£20,000) and Operation Mobilisation (£15,000).

Exclusions: Grants are seldom made to individual applicants. Those granted require accreditation by a sponsoring organisation.

Applications: In writing to the correspondent. Trustees meet in May and November, but applications can be made at any time.

The Old Broad Street Charity Trust

£21,000 (1993/94)

General

1 Hanover Square, London W1A 4SR

Correspondent: B M Covell

Trustees: Mrs Louis Franck; P A Hetherington; A T J Stanford; Mme M Cartier-Bresson; C J Sheridan.

Beneficial area: UK and overseas.

Information available: Full accounts are on file at the Charity Commission.

General: In 1993/94, the trust had assets of £866,000, generating an income of £67,000. Only five grants were made totalling £21,000, leaving a surplus for the year of £45,000. The previous year grants totalled £16,000 from an income of £66,000. It is not known why the trust is accummulating its income in this way.

The grants were to: Berzirksfursorges, Saanen (£9,100); International Menuhin Music Academy (£4,500); Fondation de Bellerive (£2,200); Les Petits Frères des Pauvres (£2,200) and Victoria & Albert Museum (£2,500).

There is a separate Louis Franck Scholarship Trust Fund Account which in 1993/94 gave five £5,000 scholarships.

Applications: In writing to the correspondent.

The Old Possums Practical Trust

£70,000 (1992/93)

Medical, literary history

Baker Tilly, Iveco Ford House, Station Road, Watford WD1 1TG
01923-816400

Correspondent: The Secretary

Trustees: Esme Eliot; Charles Willett; Brian Stevens.

Beneficial area: UK and overseas.

Information available: Full accounts are on file at the Charity Commission.

General: This trust was established in 1990 to support medical research and education of the public in the literary history of England.

In 1992/93, the trust had assets of £50,000 and an income of £69,000, of which £68,000 was from deeds of covenant. 15 grants totalled £70,000 with the largest grants to St Stephen's 125th Anniversary (£10,000) and September Press and Lincoln Theological College (both £7,000).

Nine grants of £5,000 were given to two libraries (the British and London), three colleges (Merton, Wyndham Lewis Memorial and Wolfson), Medical Foundation, Poetry Book Society, Royal National Theatre and St Michael's East Coker. The remaining grants were given to Garsington Opera Trust and Peterborough High School (both £500) and the Opera Factory (£300).

Applications: In writing to the correspondent.

The Raymond Oppenheimer Foundation

£48,000 (1992/93)

General

17 Charterhouse Street, London EC1N 6RA
0171-430 3762

Correspondent: D Murphy

Trustees: John B Martin; Alec G Berber; David Murphy.

Beneficial area: UK.

Information available: Full accounts are on file at the Charity Commission.

General: Raymond Oppenheimer, a member of the family made famous by the De Beers diamond mining company, set up this foundation shortly before his death in 1984, with an initial endowment of investments worth over £150,000. The executors of his will appointed a further £750,000 to the foundation in ensuing years.

The accounts for 1992/93 show investments with a market value of £616,000. The proceeds of these gave the foundation most of its £38,000 income. Five grants were made totalling £48,000 and were given to: Game Conservancy Trust (£25,000); Jesus College, Cambridge (£12,500); Emmanuel School and Donmar Playhouse (£5,000 each) and Imperial Cancer Research (£500).

Applications: In writing to the correspondent.

The Orpheus Trust

£71,000 (1993)

Music, especially for people with disabilities

Trevereux Manor, Limpsfield Chart, Oxted, Surrey RH8 0TL

Correspondent: Richard Stilgoe

Trustees: Rev Donald Reeves; Dr Michael Smith; Esther Rantzen; Alex Armitage; Andrew Murison.

Beneficial area: UK.

Information available: Full accounts are on file at the Charity Commission.

General: In 1993, the trust had an income of £73,000. Grants totalled £71,000. The beneficiaries included Music and the Deaf (£14,000), Strathclyde Orchestra Production (£25,000) and Music Courses for People with Disabilities (£5,000).

Applications: In writing to the correspondent.

The Ouseley Trust

£115,000 (1994)

Choral services of the Church of England, Church in Wales and Church of Ireland

74 Sweet Briar, Welwyn Garden City, Herts AL7 3EA
01707-322132

Correspondent: K B Lyndon, Clerk to the Trustees

Trustees: H G Pitt, Chairman; Dr J A Birch; Dr L F Dakers; Prof B W Harvey; Sir John Margetson; Dr J H H Oliver; C J Robinson; R J Shephard; N E Walker; Rev A F Walters; Rev A G Wedderspoon; Sir David Willcocks.

Beneficial area: UK and Ireland.

Information available: Full accounts are on file at the Charity Commission.

General: The trust administers funds made available from trusts of the former St Michael's College, Tenbury. In 1993, the trust had assets of £1.8 million and an income of £139,000.

Grants tend to fall into six categories. Every application must have a direct bearing on promoting and maintaining a high standard of choral service.

Courses, instruction: Grants are awarded only where an already acceptable standard of choral service will be raised.

Endowment grants: To provide an immediate contribution to an endowment fund.

Fees: Individual.

Music: Grants for the replacement of old, or the purchase of new, music.

Organs: Generally grants will not be awarded unless the organ is an instrument of particular significance and an integral element in a choral service of high standard.

Other: Each application will be considered on its merits within the terms of the trust deed. Unique, imaginative ventures will receive careful consideration.

In 1994, 35 grants totalled £115,000. 12 of these were towards fees for choristers and for chorister scholarship endowments at various cathedrals. Several grants of £200 to £1,000 were given to various churches under the Music category. Other grants included £5,000 to Beverley Minster for organ restoration, £1,000 to fund a Diocesan Music Adviser in Birmingham and £10,500 towards running costs of the boys' choir at Coventry Cathedral.

The trust does not normally award further grants to successful applicants within a two-year period.

Exclusions: Under normal circumstances, grants will not be awarded for buildings, cassettes, commissions, compact discs, furniture, organ tuition, outside vocal tuition, pianos, robes, tours or visits. Grants to individuals are only made through an institution.

Applications: Applications must be submitted by an institution on a form (with guidelines) available from the correspondent. Closing dates for applications are the 31st January and 30th June. The trustees usually meet in March and September/October.

The Paget Charitable Trust
(also known as the Herbert-Stepney Charitable Settlement)

£103,000 (1994)

General

41 Priory Gardens, London N6 5QU

Correspondent: Joanna Herbert-Stepney

Trustees: Joanna Herbert-Stepney; Lesley Mary Rolling; Mrs Joy Pollard.

Beneficial area: Worldwide, and local in Loughborough.

Information available: Full accounts are on file at the Charity Commission.

General: In 1993/94, the trust had assets of £2.2 million, an income of only £92,000 and gave grants totalling £103,000. Sheer need is paramount. The main areas of work the trust supports are: deprived children; elderly people; third world; carers; organic farming and animal welfare. Grants are usually of £500 or £1,000.

Larger grants went to Oxfam (£7,000), Children's Family Trust (£4,000) and Find Your Feet (£3,000). 18 grants of £2,000 were given including those to the Cambodia Trust, Crossroads, Friends of the Earth, Humane Slaughter Society, Impact, John Storer House and Sightsavers. Grants of £1,000 or £2,000 were given to eight hospices.

Other grants of £1,000 or £500 went to a range of UK and overseas organisations, and charities in the Loughborough area such as Calcutta Rescue, Loughborough CAB, Headway, Intermediate Technology, Loughborough & District Victim Society, Marie Stopes International, Shelter, and the Tibet Relief Fund.

Exclusions: Normally registered charities only. The trust does not support individuals, projects for people with mental disabilities or medical research.

Applications: In writing to the correspondent; there is no application form. The trustees meet in spring and autumn.

The Gerald Palmer Trust

£47,000 (1993/94)

General

Eling Estate Office, Hermitage, Newbury, Berks RG16 9UF
01635-200268

Correspondent: C J Pratt

Trustees: C J Pratt; J M Clutterbuck; D R W Harrison; J N Abell.

Beneficial area: UK, especially Berkshire.

Information available: Full accounts are on file at the Charity Commission.

General: The trust's main activity is the management of its Eling Estate, but it also gives grants to organisations. In 1993/94, it had assets of £6.3 million and an income of £530,000. The net surplus available for distribution was £149,000 after expenditure on the estate. Grants totalled £47,000 leaving £101,000 transferred to the income accumulation account which now stands at £592,000.

The page in the accounts that includes the grants list was missing from the file at the Charity Commission, but was present for the previous year. In 1992/93, 31 grants were given totalling £88,000.

By far the largest was £30,000 to Hampstead Norreys Amenity Trust. £5,000 was given to each of the Mary Hare Foundation, Institute of Agricultural History & Museum of English Rural Life, Motor Neurone Disease Appeal and Ravenswood Village Appeal. The other grants ranged from £20 to £4,000, with most for £1,000 to £2,500. Beneficiaries were mainly UK medical and health-related charities together with a range of local charities in Berkshire.

Beneficiaries included the African Medical and Research Foundation, Chieveley Playground Appeal, Fight for Sight, Iris Fund (the only charity which also received support the previous year), Museum of Hunting Trust, Newbury Spring Festival and Newbury Stroke Club.

Exclusions: No grants to individuals or to small local charities geographically remote from Berkshire.

Applications: In writing to the correspondent.

The Rudolph Palumbo Charitable Foundation

£434,000 (1992/93)

Education, relief of poverty, conservation, general

37a Walbrook, London EC4N 8BS

Correspondent: T H Tharby

Trustees: Lord Mishcon; Sir Matthew Farrer; Lady Palumbo; T H Tharby; J G Underwood.

Beneficial area: Worldwide.

Information available: Full accounts are on file at the Charity Commission.

General: Peter Palumbo won the battle to replace the old Mappin & Webb listed buildings in the city of London with a more progressive building. Voluntary groups have been able to use the undeveloped site rent-free. Palumbo's City Acre Property Investment Trust signed a four year covenant to pay the Rudolph Palumbo Charitable Foundation (named after his father) £350,000 a year from 1990. It is not known whether this covenant will be renewed after 1994.

Total income in 1992/93 was £371,000 which with funds brought forward left £701,000 available for distribution. Donations totalled £434,000 leaving £266,000 in hand.

In 1990/91, grants were classified under the following headings:
Advancement of Education
Conservation of the Environment
Relief of Poverty
General Purposes.

In the 1992/93, 40 grants were given, including two very large grants to St Stephen's Church Walbrook (£123,000) and Painshill Park Trust (£100,000). £25,000 was given to each of the Anastasia Trust, Birkbeck College, Chicken Shed Theatre, LSE – Butlers Wharf Appeal, Great Ormond Street Hospital, and £20,000 to both the Natural History Museum and Royal Marsden Hospital.

11 further grants ranged from £1,000 to £12,500 with 20 under £1,000. Support was given to medical and welfare charities including Action on Addiction, Leonora Cancer Fund, NSPCC, Trinity Hospice and Turning Point. A few arts organisations also received support including the English National Ballet School and Glyndebourne Productions Ltd.

Applications: In writing to the correspondent.

The Frank Parkinson Agricultural Trust

£40,000 (1993)

Agriculture

29 Ludgate Hill, London EC4M 7JE
0171-919 9100

Correspondent: A D S Robb, Secretary

Trustees: Prof P N Wilson; Prof J D Leaver; W M Hudson; J S Sclanders.

Beneficial area: UK.

Information available: Full accounts are on file at the Charity Commission.

General: In 1993, the trust had assets of £933,000 and an income of £58,000. Two grants were given totalling £40,000. Otley College of Agriculture and Horticulture received £35,000. The second grant was to the Scottish Association of Agriculture. Other recent beneficiaries have included the Hadlow College of Agriculture and Horticulture, University of Nottingham and the Scottish Agricultural College.

Exclusions: Grants are given to corporate bodies. The trust cannot give financial help to any individuals undertaking postgraduate studies or degree courses.

Applications: In writing to the correspondent at the secretary's office (33 Prospect Lane, West Common, Harpenden, Herts AL5 2PL), or to Prof J D Leaver at the registered address above specifying "Frank Parkinson Agricultural Trust". The trustees meet annually in April.

The Arthur James & Constance Paterson Charitable Trust

£64,000 (1992/93)

Medical research, health, welfare of children and elderly people

71 Queen Victoria Street,
London EC4V 4DE
0171-489 1188

Correspondent: The Royal Bank of Canada Trust Corporation Ltd

Trustees: The Royal Bank of Canada Trust Corporation Ltd.

Beneficial area: UK.

Information available: Full accounts are on file at the Charity Commission.

General: These two trusts share the same trustees and correspondent, so we have combined them within a single entry. In 1992/93, the trusts had assets of £682,000 (Arthur James) and £584,000 (Constance). The income of the trusts was £50,000 (Arthur James) and £41,000 (Constance). Each paid nearly 20% of their income in trustees' fees. For the first time the grants were categorised by the trusts as below.

The Arthur James Paterson Trust: Grants are paid in March and August, with some beneficiaries receiving two grants. Grants totalled £27,000 as follows:

Education	£9,000	2 grants
Medical research	£9,000	8 grants
Children/adults/aged	£9,000	12 grants

The largest grants went, as usual, to the bursars of Glenalmond College and Worcester College (£4,500 each in two instalments). The largest grant in the medical research category went to the Rayne Institute (£3,000), with the other grants for £500 or £1,000 to national organisations such as Ataxia, British Epilepsy Association and the Schizophrenia Association. The largest grants in the remaining category were £1,500 to NSPCC and Age Concern. Most grants went to national charities and many received a grant the previous year.

The Constance Paterson Charitable Foundation: Grants totalled £37,000 as follows:

Children's welfare	£7,400	(8)
General welfare	£6,400	(9)
Aged	£7,400	(7)
Health and research	£7,400	(9)
Servicemen's welfare	£3,900	(5)
"Special category"	£3,900	(7)

Grants ranged from £350 to £1,600. The largest were made to Counsel & Care and the NSPCC (£1,600 each) and to the Macmillan Fund, Multiple Sclerosis Society and Shelter (£1,400 each).

Exclusions: No grants to individuals.

Applications: In writing to the correspondent.

The Patients' Aid Association Hospital & Medical Charities Trust

£51,000 (1993)

Medical in the Midlands

Paycare House, George Street,
Wolverhampton WV2 4DX
01902-713131

Correspondent: Andy Garside, Secretary

Trustees: E P Booth; D Bradley; J Dickie; T P Horan; G F Lewis; T E Ratcliffe; H Reynolds.

Beneficial area: The East and West Midlands.

Information available: Full accounts are on file at the Charity Commission.

General: The main aim of the trust is "to provide equipment and amenities to aid the treatment and recovery of patients in hospitals, to the aged, infirm or handicapped in places of care and to registered charities of a general nature, also to assist with medical research". In 1993, the trust had an income of £83,000. This included £80,000 paid under deed of covenant from the Patients' Aid Association. During 1993, 74 applications were approved and 87 rejected on the grounds that they fell outside the aims of the trust. Grants to hospitals and medical charities totalled £51,000.

71 grants were given ranging from £100 to £6,400. The largest went to Wolverhampton Foetal Monitor (£6,400), Methodist Homes for the Aged (£2,600) and the Hearing Centre Keele Trust (£2,200). Other beneficiaries in the Midlands included Abbeyfield Wolverhampton, Link - Derby, Rainbow House - Walsall, Smethwick Care Support Project and Stoke Gingerbread. Grants are given for items such as defibrillators, vehicle accessories (eg. tail-lifts for ambulances), computer equipment, physiotherapy equipment, bath aids, wheelchairs and other specialised equipment.

The accounts categorise the grants by county as follows:

West Midlands	40 grants	£30,000
Derby	3 grants	£2,700
East Midlands	2 grants	£1,000
Shropshire	2 grants	£1,700
Staffordshire	18 grants	£11,000
Rest of UK	16 grants	£4,700

The grants outside the Midlands were all under £900, with beneficiaries including Guernsey Ambulance and Rescue, Help the Aged London, Life Care Leamington Spa and Teesside Hospice Cancer Care.

Applications: Application forms are available from the secretary. Any hospital or registered charity may apply for a grant and all such applications are considered by the trustees who meet four times a year. "[The] reason for the rejection of appeals is due usually to an excessive amount involved, to the appeal being outside the trust's permitted area of donations, or a similar charity recently having received a donation."

The Late Barbara May Paul Charitable Trust

£159,000 (1994)

Elderly, young people, medical care and research, preservation of buildings

Lloyds Private Banking Ltd, South Midlands Area Office, 22-26 Ock Street, Abingdon, Oxon OX14 5SW
01235-554000

Correspondent: The Manager

Trustees: Lloyds Bank plc.

Beneficial area: UK, with a preference for East Anglia.

Information available: Full accounts are on file at the Charity Commission up to 1993. The information for this entry was supplied by the trust.

General: In 1994, the trust had assets of £702,000 and an income of £30,000. Grants totalled £159,000. Most grants are for about £1,000, but occasionally some capital projects may receive between £5,000 and £10,000. The trust supports organisations such as Age Concern – Suffolk; British Red Cross – Suffolk; Children's Haven Appeal, and hospices for children and elderly people.

Applications: In writing to the correspondent.

The Michael Peacock Charitable Foundation

£84,000 (1993)

Elderly, addiction, education

21 Woodlands Road, Barnes, London SW13 0JZ

Correspondent: I M Peacock, Chairman

Trustees: M Peacock; R Wheeler Bennett.

Beneficial area: UK.

Information available: Full accounts are on file at the Charity Commission.

General: The trust has three main areas of interest:

1. *Care of the elderly:* It supports Counsel & Care and sponsored the 1993 Counsel & Care Graham Lecture.

2. *Research into causes and treatment of addictions:* The trust has continued to fund the Peacock Foundation Research Fellowship at the National Addiction Centre. It also supports Kings College London, for work on a book on addictions and addictive substances.

3. *Peacock Foundation Scholarships:* The trust has a ten year commitment to the LSE Foundation to fund up to four annual scholarships at the LSE for post-graduate scholars from Eastern Europe and the former Soviet Union. The first will be awarded in 1994/95.

In 1993, the trust had assets of £2.1 million and an income of £88,000, Grants totalled £84,000 given in six grants: Counsel & Care (£15,000 and £2,500 for the Graham Lecture), LSE (£24,000), Action on Addiction (£33,000), Kings College and Life Anew Trust (both £5,000). The trust also had commitments of £74,000 for 1994.

Applications: In writing to the correspondent.

The Susanna Peake Charitable Trust

£52,000 (1993/94)

Disability, general

PO Box 191, 10 Fenchurch Street, London EC3M 3LB
0171-956 6600

Correspondent: Kleinwort Benson Trustees Ltd

Trustees: Susanna Peake; David Peake.

Beneficial area: UK, but an emphasis on Gloucestershire.

Information available: Full accounts are on file at the Charity Commission.

General: The trust is another of the Kleinwort family trusts, a number of which have entries in this Guide or in *A Guide to the Major Trusts Vol. 1*. It was set up by Susanna Peake in 1981 for general charitable purposes.

Assets in 1993/94 stood at £1 million and produced an income of £50,000. 47 grants totalled £52,000. The largest were £5,000 to ApT Design and Development and £4,000 to YMCA. 10 grants were of £2,000 including those to the Heythrop Hunt Charitable Trust, Iris Fund, North Cotswolds Voluntary Help Centre, Population Concern, Theatre Chipping Norton and Trinity Hospice.

Other grants ranged from £100 to £1,000, with most support going to national disability, health and welfare charities and charities in Gloucestershire. Beneficiaries included Alzheimer's Disease Society, Association for Stammerers, Gloucestershire Old People's Housing Society Ltd, Gloucestershire Society and Hearing Dogs for the Deaf.

There also appears to be an interest in environment/conservation with support for the Zoological Society of London, Cotswold Canals Trust and the International Centre for Conservation Education.

Exclusions: No grants to individuals.

Applications: To the correspondent in writing.

The Hon Charles Pearson Charity Trust

£55,000 (1993/94)

General

Pollen House, 10-12 Cork Street, London W1X 1PD
0171-439 9061

Correspondent: The Secretary

Trustees: The Cowdray Trust Ltd.

Beneficial area: UK.

Information available: Full accounts are on file at the Charity Commission.

General: In 1993/94, the trust had assets of £1.4 million and an income of £50,000. 11 grants were given totalling £55,000.

Four of the beneficiaries also received grants the previous year the Association for the Protection of Rural Scotland and Population Concern (both £10,000), Cambridge University Veterinary School Trust (£5,000) and Dreams Come True Charity Ltd (£2,000).

Other larger grants were given to the Friends of King Edward VII Hospital, Midhurst (£10,000), Gordon Highlanders Museum Campaign and the National Society for Cancer Relief (both £5,000).

The remaining four grants were for £1,000 or £2,000 and given to Battle of Britain Memorial Trust, Gordon Forum for the Arts, Leconfield Hall Management Committee and Tewkesbury Abbey Appeal Trust.

Exclusions: No grants to individuals; registered charities only.

Applications: In writing to the correspondent. No application forms are needed and there is no deadline. Acknowledgements are not sent to unsuccessful applications.

The Charles Peguy Trust

Not known

See below

Messrs Thompson Quarrell, 35 Essex Street, London WC2R 3BE
0171-353 5703

Correspondent: The Secretary

Beneficial area: UK.

Information available: No accounts are on file at the Charity Commission since those for 1979.

General: According to the Charity Commission the income of the trust was £147,000 in 1991/92. We were unable to obtain any information on the grants given by the trust.

Applications: In writing to the correspondent.

The Pennycress Trust

£45,000 (1993/94)

General

Heron Place, 3 George Street, London W1H 6AD
0171-486 9231

Correspondent: A J M Baker, Trustee

Trustees: Lady Aline Cholmondeley; A J M Baker; C G Cholmondeley.

Beneficial area: UK, with a preference for Cheshire and Norfolk.

Information available: Full accounts are on file at the Charity Commission.

General: The trust's policy is to make donations to smaller charities and especially to charities based in Cheshire and Norfolk, with some donations to national charities.

In 1993/94, the trust had assets valued at £1.1 million. The income for the year was £82,000. Grants totalled £45,000, leaving a surplus of £25,000.

140 grants were given ranging from £200 to £600 with the exception of £1,000 to Peter Greenham Scholarship Appeal at the Royal Academy Schools. Most grants went to national charities with about a quarter to local organisations in the North West (especially Cheshire), Norfolk and London. Charities in the fields of health, welfare, disability, children, young people, and animal welfare were all supported.

Beneficiaries included Arthritis Care, King's Lynn; Donkey Sanctuary; National AIDS Trust; National Music for the Blind; Notting Hill Housing Trust; Rural Youth Bus Project (north west Norfolk); Salvation Army; Stockport Canal Trust for Handicapped People; Turning Point, Chester and Victim Support, Kensington & Chelsea.

Exclusions: No support for individual applications.

Applications: In writing to the correspondent. Trustees meet twice during the year, usually in July and December.

The Reginald M Phillips Charitable Foundation

£143,000 (1992/93)

General

National Westminster Bank plc, Financial & Investment Services, 153 Preston Road, Brighton BN1 6BD
01273-545111

Correspondent: The Manager

Trustees: National Westminster Bank plc.

Beneficial area: UK.

Information available: Full accounts are on file at the Charity Commission.

General: In 1993/94, the trust had assets of £930,000 and an income of £104,000 (almost half of which was from rent).

Grants are made to a range of organisations, but mainly for research and development into diseases relating to ageing such as Alzheimer's and Parkinson's Disease. In 1993/94, 11 grants were made totalling £143,000 (spending surplus income from previous years).

By far the largest grant in this and previous years was to the Trafford Foundation (£90,000). Other grants went to Sussex University (which annually receives £10,000), Royal Marsden Hospital (£25,000), and another regular beneficiary STA Schooners (£5,000). Six grants were for £2,000 and one for £1,000. Beneficiaries included the Association for Spina Bifida & Hydrocephalus, Lubavitch Foundation, RAF Wings Appeal and St Peters Hospice.

The trust states that further funding is already committed to the Trafford Foundation which will leave little money for additional requests.

Applications: In writing to the correspondent, but note the above.

The Ruth & Michael Phillips Charitable Trust

£143,000 (1992/93)

General, Jewish

Berkeley Square House, 12 Berkeley Square, London W1
0171-491 3763

Correspondent: M L Phillips

Trustees: M L Phillips; Mrs R Phillips; M D Paisner.

Beneficial area: UK.

Information available: Full accounts are on file at the Charity Commission.

General: Up until 1991/92, the grants list attached to the accounts included all the organisations the trust had ever supported and the total amount each organisation had received. The main recipients were JPAIME, Phillips Family Charitable Trust and the Foundation for Education.

In 1992/93, the trust had assets of £1 million and an income of £139,000 including a donation of £50,000. 48 grants were given totalling £143,000. The largest were generally given to Jewish organisations. £61,000 was given to the Jewish Education Development Trust, £25,000 to the Foundation for Education and £16,000 to JPAIME. Other grants were under £8,000 and most were for £500 or less. Many of the grants are recurrent.

Non-Jewish recipients included Birthright, NSPCC and Royal Opera House Benevolent Fund.

Applications: In writing to the correspondent.

The David Pickford Charitable Foundation

£39,000 (1993/94)

Christian

Elm Tree Farm, Mersham, Ashford, Kent TN25 7HS
01233-720200

Correspondent: D M Pickford

Trustees: D M Pickford; Mrs E G Pickford.

Beneficial area: UK and overseas.

Information available: Full accounts are on file at the Charity Commission.

General: In 1993/94, the trust had assets of £752,000 and an income of £52,000. The trustees gave 41 grants totalling £39,000, 20 of which were recurrent from 1992/93. Grants ranged from £100 to £5,000; 14 were for £1,000 or more.

The correspondent states: "It is our general policy only to give to charities to whom we are personally known". The largest grants given by the trust were to: Prison Fellowship and Philo Trust (both £5,000); Luis Palau Evangelistic Assciation (£4,000); Saltmine Trust (£3,000); CARE Trust, Genesis Arts Trust and Chasah Trust (each £2,000), and Youth with a Mission (£1,700). The majority of grants are given to Christian organisations.

Exclusions: See above.

Applications: In writing to the correspondent.

The Austin & Hope Pilkington Trust

£153,000 (1992/93)

General

c/o Messrs Coopers & Lybrand,
9 Greyfriars Road, Reading RG1 1JG
01734-597111

Correspondent: The Secretary

Trustees: Dr L H A Pilkington; Mrs J M Jones; Mrs P S Shankar.

Beneficial area: UK, with a preference for Merseyside.

Information available: Full accounts are on file at the Charity Commission.

General: In 1992/93, the assets of the trust were £4.6 million generating an income of £265,000. 39 grants totalled £153,000.

£10,000 went to each of Age Concern St Helens, British Council for the Prevention of Blindness, National Trust Lake District Appeal and the Royal Academy of Music, and £7,500 to each of London Philharmonic, Royal National College for the Blind and Save the Children Fund.

Other grants ranged from £500 to £6,000 given to a range of organisations covering welfare, arts, conservation/environment, medical and churches. National and local charities in Merseyside received support including Care Trust, Groundwork Trust, Halle Endowment Trust, Intermediate Technology, Live Music Now!, Liverpool Repertory Theatre, Royal Commonwealth Society for the Blind and URC St Helens.

Exclusions: No grants to individuals. Grants for purely local organisations, except in the St Helens area, are excluded.

Applications: In writing to the correspondent.

The Cecil Pilkington Charitable Trust

£99,000 (1992/93)

Conservation, third world development, general on Merseyside

c/o Coopers & Lybrand, 9 Greyfriars Road, Reading RG1 1JG
01734-597111

Correspondent: The Secretary

Trustees: A R Pilkington; Dr L H A Pilkington; Mrs E Bankes; R F Carter-Jones.

Beneficial area: Worldwide, with a preference for Liverpool and St Helens.

Information available: Full accounts are on file at the Charity Commission.

General: In 1992/93, the trust had assets of £2 million an increase from £1.4 million in 1991/92, due to the sale of some freehold property. The income was £101,000, and grants were given to 16 organisations totalling £99,000.

Grants have traditionally been mainly to conservation projects, together with support for third world development and Merseyside charities. In 1992/93, the largest grants went to the Forestry Commission (£21,700), St Helens Hospice (£20,000) and Intermediate Technology (£10,000). Seven grants were for £5,000 including those to Action Aid, BTCV, Royal Liverpool Philharmonic Society and the Jersey Wildlife Preservation Trust. The remaining six grants were for £3,000 or less, mainly to conservation charities. A few of the beneficiaries receive a regular grant, though most appear to be one-off.

Applications: In writing to the correspondent.

The Pilkington Charities Fund

£1,000,000 (1993/94)

General

Coppice End, Colborne Road, St Peter Port, Guernsey, Channel Islands GY1 1EP
01481-725078

Correspondent: Dr L H A Pilkington, Trustee

Trustees: Dr L H A Pilkington; Hon. Mrs J M Jones; A P Pilkington; D D Mason.

Beneficial area: Worldwide with a preference for Merseyside.

Information available: Full accounts are on file at the Charity Commission.

General: The trust was established in 1966 originally for the benefit of employees, ex-employees and their dependants, of Pilkingtons plc. In 1975 the objects of the trust were widened to cover relief-in-need generally. In 1993/94, the assets of the trust were £8.7 million including investments still held in Pilkingtons plc.

The income fell from £528,000 in 1992/93 to £378,000 in 1993/94. The grant total also fell from £1.26 million to £1 million. In the last two years the fund has supported the same four organisations with substantial grants as follows:

	1993/94	1992/93
St Helens Meals on Wheels	£25,000	£25,000
SOS Sahel	£7,000	£25,000
Age Concern Project	£690,000	£511,000
C & A Pilkington Trust Fund	£327,000	£294,000

Of the above commitments, the Age Concern project has now finished and St Helens Meals on Wheels receives regular support, presumably of about the same amount each year. Before 1992/93, except for a large grant to the C & A Pilkington Trust Fund (for the benefit of employees and ex-employees of Pilkingtons), grants were given to a wide range of charities especially medical and welfare, with a preference for Merseyside.

Applications: In writing to the correspondent.

The Platinum Trust

About £175,000

Disability

19 Victoria Street, St Albans, Herts AL1 3JJ
01727-52244 (voice and minicom)

Correspondent: Miss P Panayiotou, Secretary

Trustees: G K Panayiotou; A D Russell; C D Organ.

Beneficial area: UK.

Information available: Full reports and accounts.

General: The trust has the following object: "Relief of children with special needs and for mentally or physically handicapped adults requiring special attention". It was funded up until March 1993 by a four year covenant. During the year ended March 1994, two donations were made to the fund by the settlor under Gift Aid totalling £370,000.

This, together with investment income meant the trust had an income of £390,000 in 1993/94. It gave grants totalling £721,000 spending a large part of the trust's capital. Following discussions with the settlor, a further donation of £175,000 is expected in March 1995. In future the amount to be given to the trust will be decided by the settlor on a yearly basis. It is therefore anticipated that grant-making by the trust will be at a much more modest level (about £175,000) in future years. In any case 1993/94 was an exceptional year.

The lower level of funding in future years will be used to support a small number of the many organisations which have been funded by the trust so far; unsolicited applications from new applicants will not be considered. If the trust wishes to continue funding a particular organisation, it will make the approach.

To indicate the type of beneficiary of the trust the following received grants of £10,000 or more in 1993/94: Gateshead Voluntary Organisations Council, Muscle Power, SHIFT, British Council of Organisations of Disabled People, London Deaf Visual Arts Forum, National Schizophrenia Fellowship, Southwark Disablement Forum, Supportive Parents for Special Children and Learning Together Magazine.

Exclusions: The trust cannot consider applications from services run by statutory or public bodies, or from mental health organisations. No grants for: medical research/treatment/equipment; mobility aids/wheelchairs; community transport/disabled transport schemes; holidays/exchanges/holiday playschemes; special needs playgroups; toy and leisure libraries; special olympic and paralympics groups; sports/recreation clubs for disabled people; residential care/sheltered housing/respite care; carers; conservation schemes/city farms/horticultural therapy; sheltered or supported employment/community business/"social firms"; purchase/construction/repair of buildings; conductive education/other special educational programmes.

Applications: The trust no longer accepts unsolicited applications; all future grants will be allocated by the trustees to groups they have already made links with.

The George & Esme Pollitzer Charitable Settlement

£124,000 (1992/93)

Health, social welfare, Jewish welfare

Saffery Champness, Fairfax House, Fulwood Place, London WC1B 6UB
0171-405 2828

Correspondent: The Secretary

Trustees: M J Harrison; B G Levy; R F C Pollitzer.

Beneficial area: UK.

Information available: Full accounts are on file at the Charity Commission.

General: In 1992/93, the trust had assets of £403,000 and an income of £181,000. Most of this income was received from the George Pollitzer First Personal Settlement with smaller amounts from the George Pollitzer Second Personal Settlement and the E M Pollitzer 1969 Settlement.

£124,000 was distributed in grants. Five grants accounted for about half the total: Norwood Child Care (£20,000), Nightingale House (£11,000), and Abbeyfield Camden Society Ltd, Royal Hospital & Home for Incurables and Sundridge Court (£10,000 each). The other 49 grants ranging from £500 to £5,000, went to UK charities in the fields of health and social welfare and to Jewish charities. Beneficiaries included the Aidis Trust, Child Psychotherapy Trust, Gingerbread, National Listening Library, Ravenswood Foundation, Shaftesbury Society and Youth Clubs UK.

Exclusions: Only registered charities are supported.

Applications: In writing to the correspondent.

The E & F Porjes Charitable Trust

£335,000 (1992/93)

Jewish, general

c/o Warner Bearman, 16 Wimpole Street, London W1M 8BH
0171-580 6341

Correspondent: The Secretary

Trustees: B Davis; M D Paisner.

Beneficial area: Worldwide.

Information available: Full accounts are on file at the charity Commission.

General: In 1992/93, the trust had assets of £1.7 million and an income of £134,000. Grants totalled £335,000 including an exceptional grant of £100,000 to the Endowment Fund for the British Friends of the Art Museums of Israel. The trust tends to give a small number of large grants.

17 grants were given in total with other large grants going to Royal Marsden Hospital (£57,000), Oxford Centre for Post-graduate Hebrew Studies (£50,000), Friends of the Neurim House for the Mentally Handicapped (£37,500) and the British Friends of the Council for a Beautiful Israel (£28,000). Other grants ranged from £750 to £17,000 mainly to Jewish causes but also including £2,500 to Whitchurch Silk Mill and £4,000 to Queen Mary and Westfield College.

The correspondent did point out that the trustees are bound by the wills of the two settlors who had specified a list of those organisations who should receive money from the charity, and that few, if any, grants were given to groups not on the list.

Applications: To the correspondent, but see above.

The John Porter Charitable Trust

£208,000 (1992/93)

Jewish, education

Personal Financial Management Ltd, 22 Mount Sion, Tunbridge Wells, Kent TN1 1NN
01892-510510

Trustees: Sir Leslie Porter; John Porter; Steven Porter; Peter Green.

Beneficial area: Worldwide.

Information available: Full accounts are on file at the Charity Commission.

General: Up until 1992/93, this trust had a regular surplus of income over expenditure, presumably to build up its assets. By 1992/93, the assets stood at £3.9 million which generated an income of £174,000. Grants totalled £208,000.

Only seven grants were given, with by far the largest going to the Tel Aviv University Trust (£169,000). The other six grants were to: Stamford University (£27,000), Anne Frank Centre (£7,000), British Museum and Israel Diaspora Trust (both £2,000), Weiner Library Endowment Fund (£900) and City of Westminster Charity Fund (£100).

The previous year the trust gave £75,000, all to Templeton College, Oxford.

Applications: In writing to the correspondent.

The PPP Medical Trust Ltd

£411,000 (1993)

Medical research, care of the elderly and disabled people

PPP House, Vale Road, Tunbridge Wells, Kent TN1 1BJ
01892-512345

Correspondent: M E Kirkham, Appeals Secretary

Trustees: P H Lord; Sir Richard Bayliss; Dr R H McNeilly; Prof B L Pentecost.

Beneficial area: UK.

Information available: Accounts are on file at the Charity Commission, but without the usual details of donations.

General: Donations by this trust, closely associated with the Private Patients Plan provident association, fluctuate according to the timing of individual donations.

In 1993, the trust had an income of £266,000. Grants totalled £411,000. Donations were categorised as follows (1992 figures in brackets):

Medical research	£325,000	(£142,000)
Care of the elderly	£35,000	(£3,000)
Care of the disabled	£48,000	(£32,000)
Miscellaneous	£2,500	(£6,500)

No further details of grants are given.

Exclusions: No grants to other grant-making trusts, fee-charging charities, for running costs, students' fees and expenses.

Applications: In writing to the correspondent, with supporting documents and the latest report and accounts, where appropriate. Grant applications for medical research projects should include the following: research protocol; summary; costings; cv's of personnel; relationship with other research in the same field; outcome of other funding applications; anticipated methods of promulgating and applying results. Meetings are usually held in February, June and October each year.

The W L Pratt Charitable Trust

£37,000 (1992/93)

General

Messrs Grays, Duncombe Place, York YO1 2DY
01904-634771

Correspondent: C C Goodway

Trustees: J L C Pratt; R E Kitching; C C Goodway.

Beneficial area: UK, particularly York, and overseas.

Information available: Full accounts are on file at the Charity Commission.

General: In 1992/93, the trust had assets of £999,000 and an income of £47,000. Grants totalled £37,000 with a further £5,800 given as fees to the correspondent. 37 grants were given ranging from £200 to £3,600. Only five new grants were given, all in the local charities list. The trust categorises its grant-giving as follows:

Overseas charities: Four grants totalling £6,700 all to regular beneficiaries (Oxfam, Christian Aid, Royal Commonwealth Society for the Blind, Commonwealth Society for the Deaf). No additions have been made to the regular beneficiaries in recent years.

Local charities in the York area: 20 grants totalling £20,600. New grants were: £200 to Camphill Village Trust (Botton Village); £1,000 to Critical Care Unit; £100 to Salvation Army, York; £100 to an After School Club; £500 to Selby Abbey Appeal. Regular grants include those to the York Diocesan Board of Finance (£3,600), York Minster Fund (£3,200), Wilberforce Home for the Multiple Handicapped (£2,400) and York CVS (£1,700). The other beneficiaries were mainly local branches of national welfare charities.

UK national charities: 13 grants totalling £9,900 all to charities who received a grant the previous year. The beneficiaries tend to be the larger well known charities including the Salvation Army (£2,200); Marie Curie Memorial Fund (£1,700); ASBAH, Guide Dogs for the Blind, RNLI and St John Ambulance (£900 each).

Applications: In writing to the correspondent.

The Sir John Priestman Charity Trust

£193,000 (1993)

Social welfare, churches in County Durham

Messrs McKenzie Bell & Sons, 19 John Street, Sunderland SR1 1JQ
0191-567 4857

Correspondent: R W Farr

Trustees: J R Kayll, Chairman; J R Heslop; R W Farr; T R P S Norton.

Beneficial area: UK, but with a strong preference for County Durham, with particular emphasis on the County Borough of Sunderland.

Information available: Full accounts on file at the Charity Commission.

General: The trust was set up by Sir John Priestman, then of Sunderland, with an endowment made up of shares in several railway companies including the Great Western, the London & North Eastern, the London Midland and Scottish, and the Southern. He set aside £100,000 to be known as "the Clothing Fund" which would provide for the clothing of poor children in the Borough of Sunderland, and £150,000 ("the General Fund") for the following purposes:

- To provide assistance to local organisations for the feeding of poor people resident in Sunderland;
- To pay annuities to old, aged, blind, deaf, dumb, infirm or invalid poor persons resident in County Durham;
- To assist the education at any English university of young men as candidates for Holy Orders in the Church of England who will undertake to remain and work after ordination in the County of Durham for a period of not less than six years;
- The establishment of hospitals or homes for the benefit of the poor of County Durham;
- To provide for the employment of nurses for the sick and infirm;
- To improve and maintain churches in County Durham.

The main activity of the trust continues to be the support of other charities in the County of Durham and in particular the town of Sunderland. Help has been given to the aged and needy in the form of grants, to needy clergymen, to support young people in the area, and for the maintenance of church buildings and organs.

In 1993, the trust had assets of £1.4 million and an income of £221,000. The vast majority of grants went to organisations in County Durham, and are broken down thus:

Charitable organisations	£109,000
Maintenance of churches and church buildings	£35,000
Relief & maintenance of clergy, church officials & their families	£20,000
School fees (five grants)	£7,000
Other charitable purposes	£16,000
Grants for the elderly (mainly individuals)	£6,000

14 "charitable organisations" received grants in the £2,000 to £5,000 range and 39 received £1,000 to £1,900. Beneficiaries included Blackhill Playgroup, Consett; Northumberland Sea Cadets Corp; NSPCC Durham; PDSA Sunderland, Red Feather Appeal; Samaritans Sunderland; SHAW Cramlington; Three C's; Wildfowl Trust; WRVS; YMCA Weardale House.

24 churches, mainly in the North East, received grants of £1,000 or £2,000, with one grant for £500.

Eight grants were given for relief and maintenance ranging from £1,000 to £5,000. Except for the Church of England Pensions Board, all beneficiaries were in Durham and included three schools and three diocesan level organisations.

"Other charitable purposes" included 16 grants of £200 to £4,400. Most of the beneficiaries were organisations for young people including St Nicholas Sea Scout Group and Doxford Park Handicapped Youth Project. Other charities supported included the Advice & Resource Centre in Hartlepool and Aquila Housing Association Appeal.

Applications: To the correspondent in writing. The trustees meet quarterly in January, April, July and October.

The Prince Foundation

£88,000 (1992/93)

Medicine

c/o Messr Rothman Pantall & Co, 10 Romsey Road, Eastleigh, Hants SO50 9AL
0170-361 4555

Correspondent: D L Morgan

Trustees: A C Prince; Mrs S J Prince; D L Morgan.

Beneficial area: Southern England.

Information available: Full accounts are on file at the Charity Commission.

General: The trust was established in 1988 and receives £10,000 a year under deed of covenant. In addition, in 1992/93 further donations of £39,000 were received from Mr & Mrs Prince. The income in 1992/93 was £71,000 with £70,000 from donations.

Grants totalled £88,000. Two major gifts were made to local medical research organisations in Hampshire: £50,000 to the Wessex Cardiac Appeal and £36,000 to the Wessex Neurological Centre Charitable Trust. No grants had been made by the foundation in the previous year.

Applications: In writing to the correspondent.

Princess Anne's Charities

£104,000 (1993/94)

Children, medical, welfare, general

Buckingham Palace, London SW1

Correspondent: Lt Col P E W Gibbs

Trustees: Lt Col P E W Gibbs; Sir Matthew Farrer; Commander T J H Laurence.

Beneficial area: UK.

Information available: Accounts are on file at the Charity Commission, but without a list of grants.

General: In 1993/94, the trust had assets of £2 million and an income of £116,000. Grants totalled £104,000. Grants were given to the following areas:

Social welfare & benevolent charities	£42,000
Medical charities	£24,000
Armed service & public utility charities	£19,000
Youth, school, sports and institutional charities	£16,000
Miscellaneous	£3,000

The trustees have built up an accumulated cash surplus of £412,000 which is being used to increase the assets base.

Exclusions: No grants to individuals. "The trustees are not anxious to receive unsolicited general applications as these are unlikely to be successful and only increase the cost of administration."

Applications: In writing to the correspondent.

The Princess of Wales' Charities Trust

£147,000 (1993/94)

Areas in which the Princess of Wales has a particular interest

St James's Palace, London SW1A 1BS

Correspondent: P D C Jephson.

Trustees: P D C Jephson; Sir Matthew Farrer.

Beneficial area: UK.

Information available: Full accounts are on file at the Charity Commission.

General: In 1993/94, the trust had assets of £986,000 and an income of £164,000 including £114,000 from donations. Grants totalled £147,000 to:

Medical charities	£75,600
Schools	£1,300
Social, benevolent and welfare charities	£12,000
Miscellaneous	£55,000
Churches	£1,000
Youth and sports	£1,600

The trust had a surplus of £17,500 which is being used to build up its assets. The accounts include a list of about 140 beneficiaries, with a further £50,000 given in anonymous donations and "gifts in specie to charities for auction to the value of £2,250".

Presumably most of the grants are small, under £1,000. Beneficiaries include national charities such as the British Red Cross, Church Army, Schizophrenia Association of Great Britain and the Sports Aid Foundation, as well as numerous local charities including Brecon & District Disabled Club, Doorstep of Hull, Leamington Boys' Club, Sale, Altrincham & District Spastics Society, Wessex Cancer Trust and Women's Aid Newry.

Exclusions: No grants to individuals. "The trustees are not anxious to receive unsolicited general applications as these are unlikely to be successful and only increase the cost of administration of the Charity."

Applications: In writing to the correspondent.

The Priory Foundation

£90,000 (1993/94)

Health and social welfare, especially children

The Priory, 54 Totteridge Village, London N20 8PS

Correspondent: M Kelly

Trustees: N W Wray; L E Wray; T W Bunyard.

Beneficial area: UK.

Information available: Full accounts are on file at the Charity Commission.

General: The trust was established in 1987 to make donations to charities and appeals which directly benefit children. In 1993/94, the trust's assets were £1.7 million.

200 grants were given totalling £90,000. The largest grants were to the London Borough of Barnet – social needs cases (£8,600), and ABCD, Birthright and MEP (all £5,000).

Most of the remaining grants were under £1,000 with beneficiaries including: Action for Sick Children, Childline, Disability Aid Fund, East Belfast Mission, Sandy Gall's Afghanistan Appeal, Teenage Trust Cancer Appeal and the Training Ship Broadsword. Most were one-off and given to national organisations.

Applications: In writing to the correspondent.

The Privy Purse Charitable Trust
(formerly The January 1987 Charitable Trust)

£208,000 (1993/94)

General

Buckingham Palace, London SW1A 1AA
0171-930 4832

Correspondent: John Parsons

Trustees: Sir Matthew Farrer; Major Sir Shane Blewitt; J C Parsons.

Beneficial area: UK.

Information available: Full accounts are on file at the Charity Commission, but without a list of grants.

General: In 1993/94, the trust had net assets of £1.1 million and an income of £340,000, of which £262,000 was received in donations (it is not known if this was directly from The Queen or from other sources), £30,000 in sundry income and £48,000 was from dividends and interest.

After grants of £208,000 were given, the trust had a surplus of income over expenditure of £128,000. The trustees state in their report "that a reserve is being established to guard against a future decline in the level of donations received".

There is no grants list with the accounts, but the trust does break down charitable donations as follows:

Ecclesiastical	£103,000
Youth, school, sports and institutional charities	£67,000
Social benevolent and welfare charities	£17,000
Armed service and public utility charities	£5,000
Medical charities	£11,000
Animal charities	£2,000
Miscellaneous	£3,000

Applications: The trust makes donations to a wide variety of charities, but does not respond to appeals.

The Puebla Charitable Trust

£203,000 (1993/94)

Education, religion, relief of poverty, general

Ensors, Cardinal House, 46 St Nicholas Street, Ipswich IP1 1TT
01473-233332

Correspondent: Mrs Ranson

Trustees: Lord Justin Phipps; M A Strutt.

Beneficial area: Worldwide.

Information available: Accounts are on file at the Charity Commission, but without a list of grants.

General: The trust states: "At present, the council limits its support to charities which assist the poorest sections of the population and community development work – either of these may be in urban or rural areas, both in the UK and overseas."

Grants are normally in the region of £5,000 to £20,000, with support given over a number of years where possible. Most of the trust's income is therefore already committed, and the trust rarely supports new organisations.

During 1992/93, the trust received a special donation of £138,000 to add to its funds. The ordinary income was £114,000 from assets of £1.8 million. The grant total, £15,000, was down on previous years, but £173,000 was distributed early in the next year. No list of grants was available.

Exclusions: No grants for capital projects, religious institutions, institutions for disabled people or research. Individuals are not sponsored and no scholarships are given.

Applications: In writing to the correspondent. The trust is unable to acknowledge applications.

The Pyke Charity Trust

£133,000 (1992/93)

Social welfare

Barlocco Farm, Auchencairn, Castle Douglas, Dumfries & Galloway DG7 1RQ

Correspondent: N van Zwanenberg

Trustees: J M van Zwanenberg; Mrs R van Zwanenberg; N J van Zwanenberg; Mrs J Macpherson.

Beneficial area: UK.

Information available: Full accounts are on file at the Charity Commission.

General: The foundation supports four general areas:

  Education and training;
  Disabled welfare;
  Social and community needs;
  Medical welfare but not research.

Only registered charities are supported. The overall policy of the trustees is to support underfunded voluntary organisations to enable the disabled and those who are disadvantaged through social or economic circumstances to make a contribution to the community. In general consideration is not given to appeals on a national or general scale, but to activities at a local level. Usually the trust can only provide "top-up" finance, rather than help with a complete project. Most grants are one-off, with very few commitments made over two or more years. Applications for salaries and wages are not supported per se.

The following guidelines were provided by the trust.

Education and training:
Projects for disabled people which offer employment training, life skills and independent living.

Projects which enhance educational opportunities for children up to secondary school level. (No adult or tertiary educational projects considered.)

Projects which will enhance the wider education and understanding and promotion of life skills for young people.

In very few, very exceptional cases help may be given to stabilize the education and home life of children. Only the most exceptional cases of need are investigated. Full disclosure of all the circumstances leading to the application is required and a home visit will be necessary.

Social and community needs:
Projects which assist the disabled and disadvantaged to play a part in the community.

Community centres for all ages – family centres, youth clubs, elderly people's clubs, child care provision and drop-in clubs.

Disabled people – any project that will enhance the quality of life for disabled people.

Promotion of health – home nursing schemes, day care centres for the disabled and elderly.

Civic responsibility – the trustees support projects which encourage respect for the local community and environment, crime prevention.

Medical:
Due to the lack of resources available to the trust, it was decided that no more funds would be allocated to medical research.

The trustees support projects where equipment can enhance the lives of individual disabled people or families.

In 1992/93, the trust had assets of £1.34 million and an income of £120,000. Grants totalled £133,000 and were allocated as follows:

Research	£360
Children and young people	£11,000
Elderly people	£2,500
Disabled people	£37,000
Medical	£13,000
Education	£1,500
General	£25,000
School fees	£42,000

No further information on the grants was available for 1992/93, the following details refer to 1991/92.

Research: Three grants totalling £5,000, to three past beneficiaries including the Development Trust for the Young Disabled.

Children and young people: 11 grants totalling £6,800. There are four regular beneficiaries which receive grants of £1,000: Barnardo's, the Children's Society, National Children's Home and the NSPCC.

Elderly people: Six grants totalling £3,000, with £1,000 each to the Distressed Gentlefolk's Aid Association and Mary Tates Almshouses.

Disabled people: 29 grants totalling £17,000. Seven beneficiaries received £1,000, including the Crossroads Care Scheme; Royal Hospital Home – Putney; Searchlight 1990; Workshop Appeal and MacIntyre. Most of the other grants were for £500 or less.

Medical: 10 grants totalling £4,400, including a recurrent grant of £1,000 to the Arthritis and Rheumatism Council.

Education: 11 grants totalling £7,000, including £2,800 to St Martin's School and £1,000 to the Royal Grammar School.

General: 19 grants totalling £9,000. The major grant was £4,000 to another grant-making organisation which regularly receives support, the Royal Masonic Grand Charity. Eight grants of £500 included those to Rape Helpline – Cornwall, Red Cross – Wiltshire, World Wide Fund for Nature and Stadium Youth.

School fees: 19 grants to 13 schools for fees totalling £41,400.

Exclusions: "The trustees regret that, as the funds available are limited, they do not support all fields of voluntary and charitable activity. In order to concentrate our grant giving programme within the four areas of concern, the following are deemed to lie outside the guidelines and are therefore not eligible:

All medical research

All postgraduate studies

All arts projects (dance, theatre, music, painting etc.)

All individual sponsorship

Drug or alcohol related charities

Headquarters of national charities

All holiday groups

National and local government responsibilities

Organisations which are not registered charities

Activities which collect funds for subsequent re-distribution to other charities

Expeditions or overseas travel

Animal charities

Promotion of religion

Fabric appeals for places of worship

Loans and business finance."

Applications: Applications must be in writing to the correspondent, in good time for meetings in April, August and December. All applications should include:

(i) Charity title, address, telephone number and correspondents name;
(ii) Registered charity number (if not registered the name of a registered charity who will take responsibility for any grant);
(iii) Brief description of the activities of the charity, its size and any other special features;
(iv) Details of the specific project for which the grant is sought;
(v) Details of how much needs to be raised, how much has been raised at the time of writing, a budget and a time-scale. Also where the bulk of the money required will come from;
(vi) Audited balance sheet and statement of accounts. These should be to a year ending no more than 15 months before the date of the letter (even if only in draft form).

Applications should be as concise as possible. In general, they should not cover more than two sides of A4. Make it long enough to properly describe your project, but short enough to be easy to take in at first reading.

The trustees regret that the demands made on the trusts funds always outstrip the funds available and this means that many good applications whilst meeting the criteria still have to be refused. At present the trust can only help about 1 in every 10 applications.

Please do not ask for a particular sum. We will give as much as we can towards your cause.

Please apply at least two months before the next meeting to be considered for that meeting. The trustees meet three times a year in April, August and December.

Successful applicants should leave at least a year before applying for further support and should note that they must submit up to date accounts when they re-apply.

Unsuccessful applicants are advised to leave at least one year before re-applying and to consider the advice in this section carefully when doing so.

The average grant is rarely in excess of £2,000, and applicants should bear this in mind when submitting their appeal.

The R T Trust

£123,000 (1991/92)

Health and welfare in Shropshire

The Postings, Pant Glas, Oswestry, Shropshire SY10 7HS

Correspondent: Erica Wyn Moss

Trustees: Erica Wyn Moss; Griffith M Humphreys.

Beneficial area: UK, but with a strong preference for Shropshire, especially Oswestry.

Information available: Full accounts are on file at the Charity Commission.

General: According to the Charity Commission database the trust had an income of £92,000 in 1993/94, but no further information was available for this year.

In 1991/92, the trust had an income of £80,000 most of which came from covenants and Gift Aid. Grants totalled £123,000.

The trust supports health and welfare charites and some children's and youth organisations, mostly in the Oswestry area. 48 grants were given ranging from £30 to £35,000. Over half the grant total went to five causes: the Macmillan Nurses (£35,000); MRI Orthopaedic & Victoria Centre Residential Care Unit (£20,000); Shropshire & Mid Wales Hospice (£10,000); Kingswell Centre, Oswestry (£6,000) and SACRED (£5,000).

Most grants were between £100 and £500, including grants to the National Childbirth Trust, Oswestry Special Arts for Handicapped, Oswestry Rugby Club and Salop Rural Development. Only about a quarter of the grants were recurrent from the previous year.

Applications: The trust receives more local applications than it can currently support. It is very unlikely that appeals from outside Shropshire will be supported.

The Radcliffe Trust

£194,000 (1992/93)

Music, crafts, conservation, academic fellowships

5 Lincoln's Inn Fields, London
WC2A 3BT
0171-242 9231

Correspondent: Ivor F Guest

Trustees: Sir Ralph Verney; Lord Wilberforce; Sir Edgar Williams; Lord Quinton; Lord Balfour of Burleigh; Lord Cottesloe.

Beneficial area: UK.

Information available: Full report and accounts are on file at the Charity Commission. An annual report is available from the trust.

General: The trust was founded in 1714 by the Will of Dr John Radcliffe. The trustees' present grant-making policy is concentrated in two main areas: music and the crafts, but they may consider applications outside those two categories provided they do not fall within the exclusions below. The following is taken from the trustees report 1992/93:

"In the area of music they operate a scheme under which the Allegri Quartet make regular visits to a selected number of universities and other centres, giving concerts, masterclasses and teaching sessions. The trustees also sponsor a Radcliffe Composer-in-Residence with the City of Birmingham Symphony Orchestra, and have initiated specialist seminars in double-reed playing and on the technology of pianos. In addition the trustees make grants for classical music education.

"In the area of crafts, the main thrust is the support of apprentices, mostly, but not exclusively, in cathedral workshops. For other grants, the trustees' main concern is to achieve a standard of excellence in crafts related particularly to conservation. The trustees monitor the progress of projects for which grants are made, particularly those which are spread over a period of more than one year, in which cases satisfactory progress reports are required as a condition of later instalments being paid.

"The trustees make small grants for the repair and conservation of church furniture, including bells and monuments. Such grants are made only through the Council for the Care of Churches; direct applications are not accepted. Grants are not made for structural repairs to church buildings, nor for organs."

Miscellaneous applications which do not fall within the above categories may be considered subject to availability of surplus income and with the exclusions listed below. The trustees also support fellowships in history and philosophy which are serviced by specialised committees in Oxford.

The trust's assets have been valued at about £7.7 million. The income in 1992/93 was £330,000. Of this £194,000 was given in grants, £76,000 was spent on administration, legal and audit expenses, with the balance being carried forward for distribution in future years. Grants were distributed as follows:

Music: 16 grants totalling £43,000 with a further £14,000 towards the Allegri scheme. Larger grants included £6,000 over two years to the British Federation of Young Choirs for the regional choral scheme; £5,000 to the National Youth Orchestra of Great Britain for bursaries for string students and £4,000 to the Philharmonia for musical workshops. Other beneficiaries included the Handbell Ringers of Great Britain (£700), London Sinfonietta (£2,500 for an education project for visually impaired people) and Nettleford Festival Trust (£500 for workshops).

Crafts: 15 grants totalling £59,000 with a further £14,000 spread over three years for the Apprentice Scheme. The largest grant went to Fitzwilliam Museum for conservation of the Founder's Library (£15,000 over three years). Other beneficiaries included Hertfordshire Building Preservation Trust (£4,500 over three years for an apprentice blacksmith), Scottish Maritime Museum (£3,000 over two years for training in boat building) and the Embroiderers Guild (£1,000 to the Young Textile Group).

Miscellaneous: 13 grants totalling £40,000. The largest grants went to Buckinghamshire County Museum (£10,000), Roehampton Institute (£10,000 over two years), Forestry Trust (£6,000 over three years) and Buildings of Scotland Trust (£5,000).

Exclusions: No grants for construction, conversion, repair or maintenance of buildings; individuals for education fees or maintenance; sponsorship of musical and theatrical performances; medical research; social welfare; expeditions. Grants are not given to clear deficits.

Applications: In writing to the correspondent before the end of March and September each year. Applications for music grants are shortlisted for consideration by a panel of musicians who make recommendations where appropriate; recommended applications are then placed before the trustees for decision. The music panel usually meets in March and October in advance of the trustees' meetings in June and December.

Radio Tay – Caring for Kids (Radio Tay Listeners Charity)

£96,000 (1993/94)

Children and youth

PO Box 123, Dundee DD1 9UF
01382-200800

Correspondent: Lorraine Stevenson, Co-ordinator

Trustees: Lord J Elphinstone, Chairman; A Wilke; K Codognato; A Ballingall; M Naulty; M Laird.

Beneficial area: Tayside and North East Fife.

Information available: The information for this entry was supplied by the trust.

General: The fundraising appeal starts in August and continues until after Christmas. The main event is the station's charity auction, for which donated gifts usually include a new caravan. All the money raised is distributed within the community covered by the radio service. £96,000 was raised in 1993/94.

Allocations to individuals benefitted 292 children and allocations to organisations benefitted over 5,000 children either directly or indirectly. The largest grant of £7,000 went to Tayside Conductive Education Group to enable them to bring four conductors over from the Peto Institute. Other beneficiaries included Auchtergaven Nursery (£100), Perth Action on Autism (£600), Peter Pan Playgroup Carnoustie (£100), 2nd Montrose Scout Group (£1,000) and Tayside & Western Isles Association for the Deaf (£1,000).

Applications: In writing to the correspondent. Grants are awarded in February and March.

The Rainford Trust

£51,000 (1993/94)

Social welfare, general

c/o Pilkington plc, Prescot Road, St Helens WA10 3TT
01744-20574

Correspondent: George Gaskell, Secretary

Trustees: Mrs J Graham; A L Hopkins; Lady Pilkington; R E Pilkington; R G Pilkington; Mrs R M Potter; I S Ratiu; Mrs I Ratiu.

Beneficial area: Worldwide, with a preference for areas in which Pilkington plc have works and offices, especially St Helens and Merseyside.

Information available: Full accounts are on file at the Charity Commission.

General: This is a Pilkington family trust. In 1993/94, the trust had assets of £3.8 million but only an income of £119,000. Grants totalled £51,000. In addition, included in the analysis by charitable classification below was £2,000 on the Rainford Trust Music Awards and £750 to the Citadel Arts Centre.

Geographical distribution of grants

St Helens	£18,000	(33.3%)
Merseyside	£5,000	(9.6%)
Rest of UK and national charities	£26,000	(48.1%)
Overseas	£5,000	(9%)

Analysis of expenditure by charitable classification

Medical	£11,250	(21.1%)
Welfare including:	£34,570	(64.7%)
general	£23,375	
old	£1,700	
young	£9,495	
Education	£1,800	(3.4%)
Humanities	£3,064	(5.7%)
Religion	£1,300	(2.4%)
Environment	£1,450	(2.7%)

1,113 applications were received and 135 grants given. The previous year, 1,235 applications were received and 146 grants given.

Most of the grants are necessarily small with many for as little as £50 or £100. Larger grants were to Industrial Experience Projects Ltd and St Matthew's Church Building Fund (both £2,500) and Apex Trust (£1,500). Grants of £1,000 went to British Red Cross – International Relief Work, Broadgreen Medical Centre Appeal, Portland College, Quest and St Helens Cancer Counselling Centre Ltd. All other grants were under £1,000. Some grants were given to organisations outside Merseyside, such as the Scottish Wildlife Trust (£200), Inverclyde Child Support Volunteers (£400) or the Bristol Cancer Help Centre (£750), but these are very much in the minority. More typical are Relate St Helens (£300), Garston Adventure Playground (£220) and Wirral Christian Drugs Action (£250). Few grants are recurrent from year to year.

Exclusions: No grants to individuals for educational purposes will be considered unless the individual is normally resident in St Helens.

Applications: At any time. Only successful applications will be acknowledged.

The Joseph & Lena Randall Charitable Trust

£140,000 (1993/94)

Jewish, general

Europa Residence, Place des Moulins, Monte-Carlo, MC 98000, Monaco
010-33-93 50 03 82

Correspondent: D A Randall

Trustees: D A Randall; B Y Randall.

Beneficial area: Worldwide.

Information available: The information for this entry was supplied by the trust.

General: In 1993/94, the trust had assets of £1.6 million and an income of £163,000. Grants totalling £140,000 were given to a wide range of charities, mostly regular donations over many years for the resettlement of refugees. Grants are also given to infrastructure projects, medical relief and research, old people's homes, educational facilities and the arts.

The largest donations were to Jewish charities but the trust is non-denominational.

Exclusions: No grants to individuals.

Applications: The trust states that all income is allocated or promised so it regrets that it cannot extend its list of charities at present.

The Rank Prize Funds

£441,000 (1993)

Nutrition, opto-electronics

12 Warwick Square, London SW1V 2AA
0171-834 7731

Correspondent: John A Wheeler

Trustees: The Earl of Selborne, Chairman; Robin Cowen; Dr Jack Edelman; Prof Cyril Hilsum; Sir Alex Jarratt; Joseph Newton; Prof Sir Richard Southwood.

Beneficial area: UK and overseas.

Information available: Full accounts are on file at the Charity Commission.

General: In 1993, the trust gave grants totalling £441,000 (including prizes). The trust is run as two separate funds.

The objects of the trust are the advancement of education and learning in crop husbandry, human and animal nutrition and in the science of opto-electronics. The trustees aim to "support those projects which are likely to make a significant contribution to the furtherance of the two sciences, either by acknowledging past achievements in the hope of encouraging others, or in stimulating interest in a subject which is considered will be developed for the benefit of mankind". The main work of the funds is now the awarding of prizes in recognition of significant developments in the two areas of science and the organisation and funding of symposia for invited participants. In each case the objects of support are identified by advisory committees of eminent scientists and academics.

In 1993, the nutrition fund had an income of £194,000 and the opto-electronics fund £216,000. Expenditure from the funds included:

Nutrition Fund

Symposia	£47,000
Prizes	£25,000
Grants	£78,000

Three grants were given to Glasgow University, Southampton University and St Bartholomew's Hospital Medical School.

Opto-electronics Fund

Symposia	£64,000
Prizes	£80,000
Grants	£84,000

Two grants were given to King's College London – Thermal Biology Research Unit and to Southampton University to provide funding for a Rank Chair over five years.

Commitments over the next five years amount to £392,000 (nutrition) and £373,000 (opto-electronics).

Exclusions: No grants outside the two scientific fields above. No grants to individuals for education or research.

Applications: In general the trustees do not support unsolicited applications.

The Eleanor Rathbone Charitable Trust

£172,000 (1992/93)

General, especially Merseyside

Rathbone Bros & Co, 4th Floor, Port of Liverpool Building, Pier Head, Liverpool L3 1NW
0151-236 8674

Correspondent: Barbara Pedersen

Trustees: Dr B L Rathbone; W Rathbone; Ms Jenny Rathbone; P W Rathbone.

Beneficial area: UK, with the major allocation for Merseyside.

Information available: Increasingly brief accounts are on file at the Charity Commission, occasionally – but not latterly – with a list of grants attached.

General: In 1992/93, the trust's income was £200,000 (no information on assets) and grants totalled £172,000. No further information was available. The following information is repeated from the last edition of this Guide.

The trust has a special interest in women's projects, improving race relations and public arts. 60% of grants ranged from £100 to £10,000. Major donations went to the Royal Liverpool Philharmonic Appeal, Women's Education Training Trust, Womankind Worldwide and Abbeyfield North Mersey Society.

Exclusions: No grants to individuals, major national appeals, church buildings or to appeals from areas not in the trust's stated geographical areas of interest.

Applications: In writing to the correspondent.

The Elizabeth Rathbone Charity

£68,000 (1992/93)

Social welfare, general in Merseyside

Rathbone Brothers & Co, 4th Floor, Port of Liverpool Building, Pier Head, Liverpool L3 1NW
0151-236 8674

Correspondent: Barbara Pedersen

Trustees: S A Cotton; S D Rathbone; Mrs V P Rathbone; R S Rathbone.

Beneficial area: UK, with a strong preference for Merseyside.

Information available: Full accounts are on file on the Charity Commission.

General: Preference is given to charities in Merseyside and social work charities in which the trust has a special interest.

In 1992/93, the trust's income was £48,000. 66 grants were given totalling £68,000. The largest were £5,000 to the Women's Technology Group and Merseyside Haig Homes, and £3,000 to Liverpool Cathedral Committee and the Henshaw Society for the Blind. 24 other grants were for over £1,000, with beneficiaries including Childline, Clatterbridge Cancer Research Trust, Liverpool Playhouse, Merseyside CVS, Merseyside Youth Association, Shelter and Skill Share Africa.

Applications: In writing to the correspondent.

The Ravensdale Trust

£41,000 (1993)

General

Messrs Alsop Wilkinson, India Buildings, Liverpool L2 0NH
0151-227 3060

Correspondent: The Secretary

Trustees: Dr L H A Pilkington; Mrs E Bankes; D D Mason.

Beneficial area: UK, with a preference for Merseyside.

Information available: Full accounts are on file at the Charity Commission.

General: In 1993, the trust had assets of £1.6 million and an income of £61,000. Grants totalled £41,000 to 95 beneficiaries. Over 75% were recurrent from the previous year. Over a third of the grants were to Merseyside, especially Liverpool and St Helens.

Support was given to charities in the fields of health, welfare, children, young people, conservation, heritage and Christian causes. The largest grants were £3,000 each to Lancashire Youth Clubs

Association and St Helens United Reform Church. Other grants ranged from £100 to £2,500. Beneficiaries included Age Concern (both national and the St Helens branch), British and Foreign Bible Society, British Red Cross, Crisis, Friends of the Lake District, Girl Guides Heritage, Imperial Cancer Research Fund and Youth Clubs UK.

Exclusions: No grants to individuals.

Applications: In writing to the correspondent. Grants are paid in March and October.

The Roger Raymond Charitable Trust

£91,000 (1992/93)

General

Roddis House, 4-12 Old Christchurch Road, Bournemouth, Dorset BH1 1LG

Correspondent: The Secretary

Trustees: R W Pullen; P F Raymond; M G Raymond.

Beneficial area: UK.

Information available: Full accounts are on file at the Charity Commission.

General: In 1992/93, the trust had assets of £2.8 million and an income of £143,000. This is divided between two funds: the main fund gave grants totalling £91,000 (from an income of £106,000); the number 2 fund gave £40,000 to fund Bloxham School Scholarships (from an income of £40,000).

Of the 48 grants made by the main fund by far the largest was £15,000 to the Isle of Purbeck Arts Club. Other larger grants were £5,000 to the Royal Commonwealth Society for the Blind; £4,000 each to ITGD and Salvation Army, and £3,000 each to the Multiple Sclerosis Society and Leonard Cheshire Foundation. Most of these received the same size grant the previous year.

The other grants included 18 of £2,000, 19 of £1,000 and 5 of £500. Over half were made to national medical and welfare charities including the Brain Research Trust, Help the Aged, National Asthma Campaign and the Royal British Legion.

Other beneficiaries included both the Girl Guides Association and Scout Association, British Wheelchair Sports Foundation, Salisbury and Winchester Cathedrals, Woodland Trust and World Wide Fund for Nature. Three grants were to charities working overseas Save the Children Fund, UNICEF and WaterAid.

Applications: The trust states, "No applications are considered".

The Rayne Trust

£165,000 (1992/93)

Jewish, general

33 Robert Adam Street, London W1M 5AH
0171-935 3555

Correspondent: R D Lindsay Rea

Trustees: Lord Rayne; Lady Jane Rayne; R A Rayne.

Beneficial area: UK.

Information available: Full accounts are on file at the Charity Commission.

General: This trust is administered from the same office as the much larger Rayne Foundation (see *A Guide to the Major Trusts Vol. 1*), and shares with that foundation the practice of giving a large number of relatively small grants. In 1992/93, the trust had assets of £460,000, an income of £160,000 (including a donation of £100,000) and gave grants totalling £165,000. It also has future commitments totalling £171,000.

Most 1992/93 beneficiaries (over 90%) were specifically Jewish organisations, led by the West London Synagogue (£50,000), Jewish Care (£17,000 in four grants), Chicken Shed Theatre Company (£17,000 in four grants), Group Relations Educational Trust (£10,000) and the Manor House Trust and Jews College (both £5,000). Of the 160 plus grants given, 35 were for more than £1,000.

Grants to non-Jewish organisations included those to the Abbeyfield Camden Society (£5,000), Open University (£3,000), Royal Opera House Trust (£2,400) and Handicapped Children's Aid Committee (£2,000).

Exclusions: No grants to individuals.

Applications: In writing to the correspondent.

The Albert Reckitt Charitable Trust

£81,000 (1993/94)

General

Southwark Towers, 32 London Bridge Street, London SE1 9SY
0171-939 2360

Correspondent: J Barrett, Secretary

Trustees: Sir Michael Colman; B N Reckitt; Mrs M Reckitt; Mrs G M Atherton; Mrs S C Bradley; D F Reckitt; J Hughes-Reckitt; P C Knee.

Beneficial area: UK.

Information available: Accounts are on file at the Charity Commission, but without a list of grants.

General: In 1993/94, the trust had assets of £1.4 million and an income of £62,000. Grants are separated between subscriptions (annual grants) totalling £35,000 and donations (one-off) totalling £46,000.

The trust has a preference for national organisations rather than local. No further information available.

Exclusions: No grants for political or sectarian charities, except for Quaker organisations.

Applications: In writing to the correspondent.

The C A Redfern Charitable Foundation

£154,000 (1992/93)

General

9 Greyfriars Road, Reading, Berks RG1 1JG
01734-597111

Correspondent: Coopers & Lybrand

Trustees: C A G Redfern; T P Thornton; S R Ward.

Beneficial area: UK.

Information available: Full accounts are on file at the Charity Commission.

General: In 1992/93, the trust had assets of £2.3 million and an income of £173,000. The trustees gave 42 grants, ranging from

£500 to £20,000, totalling £154,000. The largest grants were to the Saints and Sinners Club (£20,000), South Bucks Riding for the Disabled (£12,000), and BEN (£10,000). The latter two are regular beneficiaries of the trust.

13 grants of £5,000 or £6,000 were paid to a variety of charities including Children in Cities, East Grinstead Medical Research Trust, London Lighthouse, PMS Help, St Joseph's Hospice, Victim Support Kensington and Chelsea and the Winged Fellowship Trust. Of the remaining grants, 20 were for £1,000 to £4,000, and five for £500. Most beneficiaries are health/welfare charities with others ranging from BTCV to the Rainbow Theatre via the Boys Clubs of Scotland.

The trust also provided a list of grants to be paid in December 1993/January 1994, as requested by the three trustees. The lists included 38 grants totalling £133,000 of which 26 were to charities supported in the previous year. Most of the 12 new recipients were welfare charities including CRUSE, Cansearch Clinic Campaign, John Groom's Working with Disabled People, Relate and Kensington Day Centre.

Applications: In writing to the correspondent.

Cliff Richard Charitable Trust

£185,000 (1993/94)

Spiritual and social welfare

Harley House, 94 Hare Lane, Claygate, Esher, Surrey KT10 0RB
01372-467752

Correspondent: Bill Latham

Trustees: Philip Parker; Peter Gormley; William Latham; Malcolm Smith.

Beneficial area: UK.

Information available: Accounts on file at the Charity Commission, but without a detailed breakdown of all donations.

General: In 1994, the trust had assets of £263,000 and an income of £185,000. Grants totalled £185,000. This included £80,000 to TEAR Fund, £10,000 to the Evangelical Alliance Arts Centre Group, £6,000 to the Genesis Art Trust, £5,000 to the Shaftesbury Society, £2,500 each to the Timothy Trust and Eurovangelism, and £2,000 to the Crusaders Union. The remaining £73,000 is listed in the accounts as sundry donations.

In 1992/93, grants totalled £120,000 including £52,000 in sundry donations. The Evangelical Alliance Arts Centre Group received a similar size grant to 1993/94. The largest grant was £50,000 to the NSPCC. ACET received a grant of £2,000.

Exclusions: Capital building projects, church repairs and renovations are all excluded.

Applications: Applications should be from registered charities only, in writing, and for one-off needs. All applications are acknowledged. Grants are made quarterly in January, April, July and October.

The Clive Richards Charity Ltd

£124,000 (1993/94)

General

Avalon House, 57-63 Scrutton Street, London EC2A 4PJ

Correspondent: C Richards

Trustees: W S C Richards; Mrs S A Richards.

Beneficial area: UK, preference for Herefordshire.

Information available: Full accounts are on file at the Charity Commission.

General: In 1993/94, the trust had assets of £729,000 and an income of £90,000, including £14,000 from donations. Grants totalled £124,000. The previous year grants totalled £227,000 from an income of £99,000. The assets have therefore decreased in the last two years, after rising steadily up to 1992, to over £900,000.

In 1993/94, the largest grants were to the SAS Benevolent Fund (£27,000, and £70,000 the previous year for its Golden Jubilee), Bishop Vesey's Grammar School (£14,500) and Herefordshire Federation of Young Farmers (£12,500). Six other grants were for £5,000 to £10,000 the beneficiaries being Christ College Brecon, Conquest Theatre Bromyard, Macmillan Appeal, Royal Opera House Trust and both Hereford and Winchester Cathedral schools. A number of these appear to receive regular grants.

13 other grants are listed, all over £600 with a further £8,841 given in various grants of £600 or less. Most grants are to local organisations in Herefordshire, one notable exception being a grant of £2,500 to the Friends of St Mary the Angel Church, New Zealand. Other recipients included the British Diabetic Association, Bromyard Sports Foundation, Hereford Herd Book Society, National Gardens Scheme, Ullingswick Parish Church and Victim Support - Hereford.

Applications: In writing to the correspondent.

The Violet M Richards Charity

£71,000 (1992/93)

Medical research, health and social welfare for the elderly

c/o Wedlake Bell (ref CAH), 16 Bedford Street, London WC2E 9HF
0171-379 7266

Trustees: Mrs E H Hill; G R Andersen; C A Hicks; Mrs M Davies.

Beneficial area: UK.

Information available: Full accounts are on file at the Charity Commission.

General: The trust supports charities all concerned with medical research, health or social welfare for the elderly. In 1992/93, it had assets of £947,000 and an income of £68,000. Six grants totalled £71,000.

In previous years the trust has given regular support to a number of charities. This year only one organisation had received a grant the previous year, the Royal Free Hospital School of Medicine, which received £17,600 in 1993/94 and £33,000 in 1992/93.

The largest grant was £31,000 to the Royal Post-graduate Medical School. The other grants went to Hammersmith Hospital Medical School (£15,000), Royal College of Nursing and Schizophrenia Research Appeal (£2,500 each) and the Miscarriage Association (£2,000).

The trust also has commitments of £104,000 over the next three years, presumably to several of its current beneficiaries.

Exclusions: No support for individuals.

Applications: In writing to the correspondent. Trustees meetings usually take place half-yearly.

The Ripple Effect Foundation

£55,000 (1993/94)

Environment, third world development, deprived young people in the UK

No. 1 Epsom Square, Trowbridge, Wiltshire BA14 0XG
01225-776677

Correspondent: J G Gilbertson

Trustees: Miss Caroline Marks; Ian Marks; Miss Mary Falk; Ian Wesley.

Beneficial area: UK and the developing world.

Information available: Full accounts are on file at the Charity Commission including a very detailed trustees report.

General: In 1993/94, grants totalled £55,000 from an income of £53,000 and assets of £967,000. The trust has continued its policy of making grants to "effective charities" working in the broad fields of environmental work, third world development and empowering deprived young people in the UK.

Environmental work

The Gaia Foundation received a one-off grant of £32,000 and the first part of a three-year commitment of £5,000.

Third world development

New commitments, but as yet no grants, were made to the Ashoka (UK) Trust of £6,000. The second year of a three year commitment of £5,000 was given to the Opportunity Trust, through the Network Foundation. £2,294 was given to the Debt Crisis Network in order to joint fund a senior lobbyist.

Empowering deprived young people

The trust made a commitment of £33,000 at the end of the financial year to the Network Foundation. This was mainly allocated to nine projects, including St Basil's Centre, Kidscape, Crime Concern, SEAD and research and writing about a street children project in Brazil.

The trust also started a new three year commitment to support Newpin for £10,000, £5,000 and £5,000 over respective years.

Exclusions: Unsolicited applications from individuals and charities will not be considered nor acknowledged.

Applications: The trust is proactive in seeking applications from projects that meet their funding criteria and areas of interest. Full assessments are made of each application, and evaluated before a further year's funding is released.

The River Trust

£114,000 (1992/93)

Christian

c/o Kleinwort Benson Trustees Ltd, PO Box 191, 10 Fenchurch Street, London EC3M 3LB
0171-956 6600

Correspondent: The Secretary

Trustees: Kleinwort Benson Trustees Ltd.

Beneficial area: UK, with a preference for Sussex.

Information available: Full accounts are on file at the Charity Commission.

General: Gillian Warren formed the trust in 1977 with an endowment mainly of shares in the merchant bank Kleinwort Benson (85,000). It is one of the many Kleinwort trusts, several of which are included in A Guide to the Major Trusts Volume 1 as well as this Guide.

The River Trust is one of the smaller of the family trusts. In 1992/93, the trust had assets of £365,000 and an income of £116,000 including a donation of £30,000 from the Ernest Kleinwort Charitable Trust. The trust supports Christian causes.

54 grants were made totalling £114,000. Most of them are recurrent, and about half for under £1,000. The largest awards went to the following organisations, all of whom have received money from the trust in the past: Youth with a Mission (four grants totalling £23,600); Scripture Union (£13,500); Care Trust (£13,000); Ashburnham Christian Trust (£8,000) and Genesis Arts Trust (£5,500). Other beneficiaries included the Association of Christian Counsellors, God on Monday Project, Prison Christian Fellowship, Riding Lights Theatre Company, Romanian Missionary Society and the Timothy Trust.

Exclusions: Only appeals for Christian causes will be considered. No grants to individuals.

Applications: In writing to the correspondent.

The Helen Roll Charitable Trust

£88,000 (1992/93)

General

Morrell Peel & Gamlen, 1 St Giles, Oxford OX1 3JR

Correspondent: F R Williamson

Trustees: Jennifer Williamson; Dick Williamson; Paul Strang; Christine Chapman; Terry Jones.

Beneficial area: UK.

Information available: Full accounts are on file at the Charity Commission.

General: The trust was set up in 1988 and now has assets of £1.27 million. In 1992/93, the income was £93,000 and 30 grants were given totalling £88,000.

The largest grants were to Radcliffe Memorial Foundation (£10,000) and Purcell School (£9,000). Oxford University received a total of £19,500 divided between Pembroke College (£7,500), Bodleian Library (£7,000) and Ashmolean Museum (£5,000). Further grants of £4,500 to £5,500 went to Nuffield Orthotics Appeal, Friends of Home Farm Trust, Mid Counties Autistic Society, St Luke's Home and the Sick Children's Trust. Most beneficiaries of these larger grants also receive regular support.

Grants of £2,000 to £3,000 were given to the Children's Family Trust (£3,000), Berkshire, Buckinghamshire & Oxfordshire Naturalists Trust (£2,850), Playhouse Theatre Trust (£2,500) and Victim Support (£2,500). Seven grants were for £1,000 to £1,500 and seven for £250 to £500. A range of charities received these smaller grants including medical, welfare and animal causes.

Applications: In writing to the correspondent.

The Cecil Rosen Foundation

£173,000 (1992/93)

Not known

118 Seymour Place, London W1H 5DJ
0171-262 2003

Correspondent: M J Ozin

Trustees: Mrs L F Voice; M J Ozin.

Beneficial area: UK.

Information available: Accounts are on file at the Charity Commission without a list of grants.

General: In 1992/93, the trust had assets of £1.8 million and an income of £240,000 including £210,000 from rents.

Grants totalled £173,000, leaving a surplus of unspent income of £67,000. No further information was available on the type of beneficiary or size of grants.

The trust's assets are steadily increasing as the trust has a regular surplus of income over expenditure: £88,000 in 1991/92; £177,000 in 1990/91; £150,000 in 1989/90; £96,000 in 1988/89.

The trust stated that "we are presently providing for a project which it is hoped will be established in the near future to use up all of the surplus income of the foundation".

Applications: The correspondent stated that "no new applications can be considered".

The Teresa Rosenbaum Golden Charitable Trust

£78,000 (1993/94)

Jewish, general

140 High Street, Edgware, Middlesex HA8 7LW
0181-951 1996

Correspondent: R Ross

Trustees: T Rosenbaum; R Ross; R M Abbey.

Beneficial area: UK.

Information available: Full accounts are on file at the Charity Commission.

General: In 1993/94, the trust had an income of £70,000 from covenants and donations and made grants totalling £78,000. About 100 grants were made, with the largest to Jewish Care (£10,000), JPAIME (£7,000), Royal Free Hospital School of Medicine and Nightingale House (both £5,000) and Alzheimers Disease Society (£4,500).

The other grants ranged from £100 to £4,000 to Jewish organisations and medical and welfare charities. Other beneficiaries included SANE (£3,000), Child Resettlement Fund and Royal College of Anaesthetists (both £1,000) and SENSE (£750).

Applications: In writing to the correspondent.

The Rotary Foundation

About £1,166,000 in Great Britain and Ireland

Rotary scholarships and exchanges; third world development

Kinwarton Road, Alcester, Warwickshire B49 6BP
01789-765411

Correspondent: Sharon Davis

Beneficial area: Worldwide.

Information available: Annual report and detailed guidance notes available from the correspondent.

General: The foundation is Rotary International's own charity with headquarters in the USA operating as a non-profit corporation supported solely by contributions from Rotarians and others. It exists to supplement the well known charitable activities of local Rotary clubs and districts around the world in support of its objective of achieving world understanding and peace through international charitable and educational programmes. The foundation spent over $20 million on its programmes in 1991-92.

The foundation has two main areas of work. First there is an extensive programme of international scholarships and exchanges, instigated through local Rotary groups rather than on any centralised basis. These are described in detail in the Directory of Social Change's companion book, *The Educational Grants Directory.*

Secondly the foundation has become a major supporter of help for the developing countries of the world. For example, in the Polio Plus campaign, the foundation is supplying the vaccine for the massive polio eradication campaign which is part of the immunisation programme against the six vaccine-preventable diseases affecting children being carried out under the auspices of the Save the Children Fund. This is a development of an existing programme for Health, Hunger and Humanity. Under this scheme the foundation gives grants for large scale, one to five year projects, international in scope, that emphasise self-help and improve health, alleviate hunger and enhance human and social development.

Exclusions: "Scholarships may only be taken outside the British Isles."

Applications: In all cases, projects arise from individual Rotary clubs or Rotarians. The foundation cannot respond to appeals arising in any other way.

The Rothermere Foundation

£136,000 (1991/92)

Education, general

Swepstone Walsh, Ref: GBWW,
9 Lincoln's Inn Fields, London WC2A 3BP
0171-404 1499

Correspondent: G B W Walsh

Trustees: Rt Hon Viscount Rothermere; G B W Walsh; V P W Harmsworth; J Harmsworth; J G Hemingway.

Beneficial area: Worldwide.

Information available: Full accounts are on file at the Charity Commission.

General: This trust was set up in 1956, initially endowed with £50,000-worth of ordinary stock in Daily Mail & General Trust, which was then a private company. Its purpose was to support general charitable causes, but also to establish and maintain "Rothermere Scholarships" to be awarded to graduates of the Memorial University of Newfoundland to enable then to undertake further periods of study in Britain.

In 1991/92, the foundation had assets with a market value of £9.6 million, still mainly consisting of ordinary shares in Daily Mail & General Trust. These generated an income of only £296,000 which supported charitable expenditure of £136,000 in the year.

The bulk of this went in fellowship grants (£46,000), scholarships (£10,000), and other awards (£17,000 including £2,800 to the Oxford School of Drama). Other grants totalling £63,000 were also made, including £47,000 to set up a fund to support the studies of students from Duke University (USA) attending programmes at Oxford University. The trust intends to make this a regular commitment. The remaining four grants were given to Willaim Ellis School (£10,000), Mayfield & Five Ashes Play Area (£3,000), Atlee Foundation (£2,000) and London Library Anniversary Appeal (£700).

The surplus of income over expenditure was £142,000 in 1991/92 and £201,000 the previous year. It is not known whether funds are being accummulated for future major projects or due to insufficient appropriate applications.

Applications: In writing to the correspondent.

The Rothley Trust

£99,000 to organisations (1993/94)

Social welfare, general in the North East

Mea House, Ellison Place,
Newcastle-upon-Tyne NE1 8XS
0191-232 7783

Correspondent: Peter L Tennant, Secretary

Trustees: R P Gordon, Chairman; Dr H A Armstrong; Mrs R Barkes; C J Davies; Mrs A Galbraith; R R V Nicholson; C J Pumphrey.

Beneficial area: There is a strong preference for charities based in the North East of England, or with a strong North East connection (the North East is taken to mean Northumberland, Durham, Cleveland, Tyne and Wear and North Yorkshire).

Information available: Full accounts are on file at the Charity Commission.

General: In 1993/94, the trust had assets of £1.6 million generating an income of £142,000. £17,000 was spent on administration, £17,000 as a contribution to the MEA Trust (administration and secretarial expenses), £23,000 in educational grants (mainly school fees for individuals), and £99,000 in grants to organisations.

This trust is unusual in the large number of small grants it makes. In 1993/94, it made 281 grants, only 15 of which were £1,000 or over and well over half were £250 or less. Subscriptions to charities, subject to annual review, amount to about £44,000 a year. Many of the larger grants appear to be regular donations; few of the smaller ones are.

The trust gives almost all its grants in the North East of England, with the exceptions of the Northern Ireland Voluntary Trust and the Corrymeela Community (with which the trust has had links stretching back over 20 years), Voluntary Service, Belfast and three grants in Africa to Afar Aid (Addis Ababa), Harambee Edcuational Fund, Uganda and Institute of Cultural Affairs, Zambia.

The largest grants continue to be to Newcastle CVS (£6,000) and the Tyne and Wear Foundation (£4,000). The rest of the grants over £1,000 went to Age Concern Newcastle; Community Council for Northumberland; Marie Curie Memorial Foundation; Newcastle CAB; NSPCC Newcastle; Relate in Northumberland and Tyneside; SSAFA in Tyne and Wear; St Oswald's Hospice Ltd and Westfield School Appeal.

Exclusions: Organisations for the elderly, ex-services, the arts and wildlife will not be considered (although some of these categories are supported under "subscriptions"). Applications for help with capital items are preferred to those for running costs.

Applications: By letter to the secretary explaining the charitable status and the constitution of the applicant body and enclosing a budget of proposed expenditure. Trustees meet quarterly. All applications from the preferred area (the North East of England) will be acknowledged.

The Roughley Charitable Trust

£107,000 (1993/94)

General, with a preference for the West Midlands

2B Bracebridge Road, Sutton Coldfield, West Midlands B74 2SB

Correspondent: Mrs M K Smith

Trustees: Mrs M K Smith; G W L Smith; Mrs D M Newton; M C G Smith; J R L Smith.

Beneficial area: Worldwide, especially West Midlands.

Information available: Full accounts are on file at the Charity Commission.

General: In 1993/94, the trust had assets of £822,000 generating an income of £78,000. Grants totalled £107,000.

32 grants were given, over three quarters of which were £500 or less. Alongside the preference for groups in the West Midlands, there also seems to be an emphasis on Christian and social welfare projects. The largest grants were to the Birmingham Settlement, Emmaus UK, Midlands Arts Centre and St James Church Building Appeal.

Other grants of £30 to £1,000 went to a range of organisations including Amnesty International, Handsworth Day Care Centre, Intermediate Technology Development Group, Relate and Sutton Coldfield Handicapped Children's Association.

The trust tends to concentrate its giving on a few projects and then spread a range of annual subscriptions across a wider field.

Applications: "The funds are fully committed to charities known to the trustees; no further applications wanted."

The RVW Trust

£254,000 (1993)

Music, especially British, both contemporary and neglected music of the past

7th Floor, Mansfield House,
376-379 Strand, London WC2R 0LR

Correspondent: Bernard Benoliel, Secretary/Administrator

Trustees: Michael Kennedy, Chairman; John Alldis; Lord Armstrong of Ilminster; Lord Chelmer; Eric Downing; Eva Hornstein; Bruce Roberts; Jeremy Dale Roberts; Mrs Ralph Vaughan Williams; Miss Muriel Williams.

Beneficial area: UK.

Information available: Full accounts are on file at the Charity Commission.

General: The objects of the trust include the support of public performance of musical works (including operas and concerts), copying/publication of music and music festivals – all of a standard calculated to promote the aesthetic education or improve the artistic taste of the public; advancement of public education in music; publication of books on music; relief of poverty among musicians and their dependants and support for music students.

In 1993, the trust had assets of £529,000 and an income of £309,000. Grants totalled £254,000, including £37,500 set aside for electro-acoustic music scholarships of up to £7,500 each for young composers to study in Europe. The trust believes that it is "clearly important that the level of electro-acoustic knowledge available to British composers did not fall substantially below the level available on the continent".

The Royal College of Music received £25,000. No further information available.

Applications: In writing to the correspondent.

The Audrey Sacher Charitable Trust

£69,000 (1993/94)

Arts, medical, care

c/o Marks & Spencer plc, Michael House, 47 Baker Street, London W1A 1DN
0171-935 4422

Correspondent: Mrs I Bailey

Trustees: S J Sacher; J M Sacher; M H Sacher.

Beneficial area: UK.

Information available: Full accounts are on file at the Charity Commission.

General: The trust states its main areas of work as arts, medical and care. Grants are only made to charities known personally to the trustees.

In 1993/94, the trust had assets of £606,000 and an income of £51,000. 43 grants totalled £69,000, with the largest given to the Royal Opera House Trust (£24,000), Anna Freud Centre (£12,000), Contemporary Dance Trust and Glyndebourne Productions Ltd (both £10,000).

Five other grants were for £1,000 to £2,000, given to the Discovery Factory, Marie Curie Cancer Care, National Gallery, NSPCC and Save Britain's Heritage. The remaining grants were for £500 or less, mainly given to arts, medical and welfare charities. Beneficiaries included Action for Dysphasic Adults, Crusaid, Help the Aged, Help Tibet, Rainbow Family Trust and the Turtle Key Arts Centre. A few of the grants are recurrent.

Exclusions: No grants to individuals or organisations which are not registered charities.

Applications: In writing to the correspondent.

The Michael Sacher Charitable Trust

£124,000 (1993/94)

Jewish, general

H W Fisher & Co, Acre House,
11-15 William Road, London NW1 3ER
0171-388 7000

Trustees: Simon John Sacher; Jeremy Michael Sacher; Michael Harry Sacher.

Beneficial area: UK and Israel.

Information available: Accounts are on file at the Charity Commission but without a recent list of grants.

General: In 1993/94, the trust had an income of £99,000 and gave grants totalling £124,000. Unfortunately there have been no grants lists included since that for 1984/85 when the trust gave £131,000 in grants. Grants given to non-Jewish organisations totalled less than £500 and were given to NSPCC, Leukaemia Research Fund and Kids.

The main grants were: JPAIME (£101,000); Friends of the Hebrew University of Jerusalem (£11,750); Central British Fund (£5,000); Hebrew University (£2,000). There were seven grants of £1,000 to £1,500, one for £750 to the Anglo Israel Association and all other grants were for £10 to £500.

Applications: In writing to the correspondent.

Dr Mortimer and Theresa Sackler Foundation

£214,000 (1992)

Arts, hospitals

66 Chester Square, London SW1W 9DU

Correspondent: Mrs Helen Bonneau

Trustees: Mortimer Sackler; Theresa Sackler; Christopher Mitchell; Robin Stormonth-Darling; Raymond Smith.

Beneficial area: UK.

Information available: Accounts on file at the Charity Commission up to the end of December 1992 only.

General: The foundation was set up in 1985 by Mortimer Sackler of Rooksnest, Berkshire for general charitable purposes and "the advancement of the public in the UK and elsewhere in the fields of art, science and medical research generally." Under a four year deed of covenant (ending 1991) the foundation received (unspecified) donations from Bard Pharmaceuticals Ltd, and the company in 1990/91 also made a special donation of £667,000.

The assets of the foundation have been built up by these donations, and in December 1992 stood at £1.58 million. With no more money coming in from the company, it seems likely that donations generally will fall, particularly as the foundation has a number of significant commitments. These, amounting to £990,000, were to the Tate Gallery (£125,000), the National Gallery (£160,000), King's College (£100,000), the National Maritime Museum (£100,000), St Thomas' Hospital and Royal Marsden Hospital (both £215,000); and the Ashmoleum Museum, Oxford (£75,000). Several of these organisations also received awards in 1991/92 – the Tate Gallery

(£125,000), King's College (£40,000) and the National Maritime Museum (£37,500).

Only 10 other grants were given in 1991/92, ranging between £100 and £2,400. Beneficiaries included Birthright, International Council for Bird Preservation, London Library Appeal, Project Trust, Royal Opera House Trust and West Berkshire Macmillan Appeal.

Bearing in mind the very large commitments the foundation has entered into and the probability of a lower income, it seems unlikely that new applicants to this foundation will be successful.

Applications: To the correspondent in writing, but see the reservations made above.

The Raymond & Beverley Sackler Foundation

£461,000 (1992)

Art, science, medical research

15 North Audley Street, London W1Y 1WE

Correspondent: C B Mitchell, Solicitor

Trustees: Dr R R Sackler; Dr R S Sackler; J D Sackler; C B Mitchell; Dr R B Miller; Paul Manners; R M Smith.

Beneficial area: UK.

Information available: Full accounts are on file at the Charity Commission.

General: The trust supports the "advancement of education in the fields of art, science and medical research". The trust tends to give major support to a few organisations over a number of years.

In 1992, the trust had assets of £1.3 million and an income of £142,000. Grants totalled £461,000 given to just four organisations. Two new commitments were entered into: funding the refurbishment of galleries at the British Museum (£156,000) and establishment of a visiting fellowship fund for the Institute of Astronomy at the University of Cambridge (£100,000). The trust also continued to fulfil its five-year commitment to fund an Institute of Medical Sciences at the University of Cambridge (£200,000). The only other grant was £5,000 to the British Museum Press.

The trust has further commitments totalling £1 million.

Applications: In writing to the correspondent.

Saddlers' Company Charitable Fund

£252,000 (1993/94)

General

Saddlers' Hall, 40 Gutter Lane, London EC2V 6BR
0171-726 8661

Correspondent: Group Captain W S Brereton-Martin CBE

Trustees: The Saddlers' Company.

Beneficial area: UK, with a preference for the City of London.

Information available: Accounts are on file at the Charity Commission, but without a list of grants for the last few years.

General: The objectives of the fund are to support the City of London, the saddlery trade, the equestrian world, education and general charities. The 1992/93 trustees report states: "The trustees' commitment to support a number of organisations with the above aims, reviewed annually, accounts for the greater part of the annual income. Twice a year, in January and July, the company's charity committee makes grants for general charitable purposes as a result of letters of appeal".

Grants totalled £252,000 in 1993/94, and £307,000 in 1992/93. No further information is available on these grants. The following information refers to the grants given in 1991/92.

Of the total income distributed, £200,000 was committed in advance, the largest grants being £125,000 to Alleyn's School, £25,000 to the Riding for the Disabled Association, £15,000 to the British Horse Society for equestrian training, £10,000 to the Lord Mayor's Appeal, £4,000 to the Leather Conservation Centre, £3,000 to the Combined Services Equitation Association and £2,000 to the Museum of Leathercraft.

In 1994/95, £80,000 is available for distribution in response to appeals received from charities. The trustees have decided to focus their support on charities for disabled people.

Exclusions: Appeals by individuals for educational grants cannot be considered.

Applications: By letter, with supporting background information.

The Leonard Sainer Charitable Trust

£71,000 (1993/94)

Jewish, arts, welfare

2 Serjeants' Inn, London EC4Y 1LT
0171-583 5353

Correspondent: Titmuss Sainer Dechert

Trustees: S Krendel; E R Footring; C L Corman; A P Sainer.

Beneficial area: UK.

Information available: Full accounts are on file at the Charity Commission.

General: In 1993/94, the trust had assets of £498,000 and an income of £37,000. Grants totalled £71,000.

Nightingale House received £20,000 and Jewish Care £5,250. The other 25 grants ranged from £100 to £5,000. Most were to Jewish causes, arts organisations (including £2,900 to the Royal Opera House Trust) and national welfare charities (including the Leonard Cheshire Foundation and Entertainment Artistes' Benevolent Fund).

Exclusions: No grants to individuals (students, project workers etc.).

Applications: In writing to the correspondent, but please note: the annual income is already fully committed.

The Jean Sainsbury Animal Welfare Trust (formerly The Jean Sainsbury Charitable Trust)

£184,000 (1993)

Animal welfare

PO Box 469, London W14 8PJ

Correspondent: Miss Ann Dietrich, Administrator

Trustees: Jean Sainsbury; Cyril Sainsbury; Colin Russell; Gillian Tarlington; James Keliher; Mark Spurdens; Jane Winship.

Beneficial area: Worldwide.

Information available: Full accounts are on file at the Charity Commission.

General: Almost all grants are given to animal welfare charities. In 1993, the trust had assets of £4.5 million and an income of £254,000. Expenses totalled £64,000 including management fees of £22,000. Grants totalled £184,000.

All of the 110 grants were given to animal welfare charities except £250 given to the Charities Tax Reform Group. Grants ranged from £250 to £10,000, with most for £500 or £1,000. Grants of £6,000 to £10,000 went to Brent Lodge Bird & Wildlife Trust, Cramar Cat Rescue, Freshfields Animal Rescue Centre, Horse Rescue Fund, National Petwatch, North Clwyd Animal Rescue, Three Owls Bird Sanctuary and the Wildlife Hospital Trust.

To give an indication of the range of charities supported the following are those beginning with the letter 's': Sandbach Animal Rescue Society, Sheffield Trust for Orphaned and Abandoned Puppies, Society for Abandoned Animals (Harrogate branch), Society for the Welfare of Horses and Ponies, Spaywatch, Staffordshire Badger Conservation Group, Stour Valley Cat Rescue, Swan Lifeline and the Swan Sanctuary.

Exclusions: No grants/loans to individuals.

Applications: In writing to the correspondent. The trustees meet three times a year, usually in March, July and November.

The Saint Edmund, King & Martyr Trust

£56,000 (1993/94)

Church of England in London

c/o 2 Amen Court, Warwick Lane, London EC4M 7BU
0171-248 3312

Correspondent: J F Kennedy

Trustees: Rt Rev & Rt Hon the Lord Bishop of London; Archdeacon of London; Andrew Buxton; James Barclay; Rector of St Edmunds the King & St Mary's Woolnoth.

Beneficial area: UK, especially London.

Information available: Full accounts are on file at the Charity Commission.

General: The trust was set up through the accumulated funds of the church of St Edmund King and Martyr, Lombard Street, London. It now has nearly £1 million in assets generating an income of over £50,000 a year. In 1993/94, 32 grants were made totalling £56,000. All were connected to the Church of England in some way and with a special emphasis on the City of London.

Grants were to: the Lord Bishop of London float account (£4,750); the Archdeacon of London float account (£3,500); Mildmay Mission Hospital Appeal (£2,500); Nine O'Clock Trust (£2,500) Mayflower Family Centre (£2,000); St Mary's & Convent Nursing Home (£1,500), Globe Centre (£1,000) and CARA (£500).

The trust also helped out a number of vicars across the country with payments totalling £6,000.

Applications: In writing to the correspondent.

St James' Trust Settlement

£191,000 (1992)

General

44a New Cavendish Street, London W1M 7LG

Correspondent: Richard Stone

Trustees: Jane Wells; Richard Stone; Cathy Ingram.

Beneficial area: Worldwide.

Information available: Full accounts are on file at the Charity Commission up to 1992.

General: The trustees state that they "have committed all their income for a group of major projects". The trust has a preference for organisations unlikely to raise significant income from other sources.

The grant total in 1992 was £191,000 distributed between nine organisations. The Age Exchange Theatre Trust received £100,000 and the Noah Trust £30,000. £10,000 was given to each of Bayswater Hotel Homelessness Project, British Friends of Yeshiva Hamvitar, Exploring Parenthood, Jewish Child's Day, Park Lane Group and Prisoners Abroad. The remaining £1,000 went to London Council for the Welfare of Women & Girls.

Applications: "As funds are not available for new grants, the trustees do not feel justified in allocating administrative costs to responding to applications."

The St Katharine and Shadwell Trust

£158,000 (1993)

Education, training, general, in and around Wapping

PO Box 1779, London E1 8NL
0171-782 6962; Fax: 0171-782 6963

Correspondent: Jenny Dawson, Director

Trustees: The trust is run by a board of governors: Sir David Hancock, Chairman; Margaret Clark; Sir David Hardy; Gus Fischer; Sylvia McAtee; Mary Nepstad; Sir Edward Pickering; Jane Reed; Richard Roberts; Charles Sainty; Cllr Shiraz; Eric Sorensen; Peter Stehrenberger; Cllr Mrs Pola Manzila Uddin.

Beneficial area: The St Katharine and Shadwell wards in the borough of Tower Hamlets.

Information available: Full accounts are on file at the Charity Commission, and available from the correspondent.

General: The trust was created in 1990 by Wapping Neighhourhood and News International. News International made a £3.5 million endowment to the trust, covenanted over four years. It is designed to offer a framework for partnership between business, residents and the local authority, to enable the community to develop the self-confidence needed to overcome the social and economic disadvantages the area faces.

The trust is run by a board of governors, currently fourteen in all, and chaired by Sir David Hancock who is a director of Hambros, the merchant bank "whose headquarters overlook the Tower and Wapping". The board includes local residents, councillors from the local authority, the chief executive of London Docklands Development Corporation and "local" businesses – Gus Fischer, Jane

Reed, Peter Stehrenberger and Sir Edward Pickering are all from News International. Although News International provides an office for the trust free of charge and has four members on the board, the trust is independent. Investments are managed by Cazenove Fund Management and the trust is not linked to the fortunes of the company as there are no holdings in News International.

The objectives of the trust are "deliberately wide ranging to allow it to meet the changing needs of future generations", but are primarily:

- The advancement of education and learning (including training) – this is the main priority of the trust;
- The provision of recreation and leisure facilities;
- The relief of poverty and sickness;
- The arts;
- The provision of housing and accommodation.

The final News International payment was made in December 1993, leaving the total endowment at £5.2 million. Grants for the year totalled £158,000.

48 grants were given plus four special project grants. The latter were to Fairbridge (£20,000 for outreach work with young people at risk), Summer Holiday Programme (£6,700 for eleven youth clubs' summer programme at Shadwell Basin Project), ARC Tower Hamlets (£6,000 for training and consultancy work for voluntary organisations) and the Mother Tongue Project (£25,000 to pay for a full-time co-ordinator for mother tongue classes and to provide learning materials).

The trust gives some grants over several years, for example to the Association for Prevention of Addiction (£5,000 a year for three years towards the costs of a drug education programme), Chinese Association of Tower Hamlets (£4,000 a year for two years towards the salary of a worker to run an open access course for Chinese women) and Tower Hamlets Community Transport (£9,300 in year one and £9,690 in year two to provide a shopping bus service for elderly or disabled residents on one and a half days a week).

Other beneficiaries included Children Education Group (£500 to pay for equipment and provide safe storage); Kids Club Networks (£5,000 towards the cost of a training course for local people wanting to start after school care clubs); St Patrick's Social Club (£500 towards the cost of a Christmas party for elderly members); Steel's Lane Toy Library (£2,200 towards the salary of a bi-lingual worker); Tower Hamlets Advanced Technology Training (£10,000 towards establishing practice firms at Shadwell Institute), and Tower Hamlets Wheelers (£1,000 for building materials to be used by volunteer workers).

Exclusions: No support for: individuals; school journeys or residential courses; expeditions, exchanges or study tours; publicly funded institutions which ought to be funded by government; carnivals; religious organisations unless providing a non-religious service to the wider community; any organisation whose aims and objectives are of a political nature; pure research (although exploratory studies and action research projects may be considered); fundraising events for charity; retrospective grants; mortgages, deficits or loans. No payments for work to buildings.

Applications: No application forms. "Applicants are invited to write a letter explaining who they are and what they want." Applicants are usually visited by the Director, and grant decisions are made by the full board which meets four times a year. Applicants are advised to observe the trust's preference for work concerned with education and training.

The Saints & Sinners Trust

£87,000 (1992/93)

General

Lewis Golden & Co, 40 Queen Anne Street, London W1M 0EL
0171-580 7313

Correspondent: N W Benson

Trustees: The Council of Management: N W Benson; Sir Donald Gosling; P Moloney; N C Royds.

Beneficial area: Worldwide.

Information available: Full accounts are on file at the Charity Commission.

General: The Saints & Sinners Club has 100 members, who raise funds by holding golf tournaments and other events. Members nominate causes/organisations to support and grants generally range from £1,000 to £5,000.

In 1992/93, the trust had assets of £167,000. The income was £72,000 and 35 grants totalled £87,000. An exceptionally large grant of £20,000 was given to Shaftesbury Homes & Aruthusa. Other grants ranged from £500 to £3,500 and were given to a range of causes including the Albanian Relief Appeal, Charterhouse in Southwark, Crusaid, Marine Conservation Society, Relate, Research Institute for International Law and John Grooms Association for Disabled People. Over half the recipients received a grant the previous year.

The correspondent told us that applications from organisations with no contacts with the club would not be supported.

Applications: Applications are not considered unless nominated by members of the club.

The Salamander Charitable Trust

£116,000 (1992/93)

Christian, general

8 Market Street, Poole, Dorset BH15 1NF

Correspondent: John R T Douglas

Trustees: John R T Douglas; Mrs Sheila M Douglas.

Beneficial area: Worldwide.

Information available: Full accounts are on file at the Charity Commission.

General: This trust has grown quickly in size in a relatively short time. In 1992/93, its assets stood at £1.3 million. This generated an income of £117,000 with £116,000 given in a large number of small grants. The grant total decreased to about £92,000 in 1993/94.

Only the five largest grants are listed in the 1992/93 accounts: Christian Discovery Trust (£5,500); Middle East Media (£2,000); Parish Church of St Mary Dunstall (£5,000); St Paul's Building Project (£5,000) and South American Missionary Society (£2,000). The trust gave a further 283 grants of up to £1,000. Most of the grants are recurrent and to Christian organisations.

Exclusions: No grants to individuals. Only registered charities are supported.

Applications: The trust's income is fully allocated each year, mainly to regular beneficiaries. The trustees would prefer to have no new requests.

Salters' Charities

£68,000 (1992/93)

General

The Salters' Company, Salters' Hall, 4 Fore Street, London EC2Y 5DE
0171-588 5216; Fax 0171-638 3679

Correspondent: The Education & Charities Manager

Trustees: The Salters' Company.

Beneficial area: Greater London or UK.

Information available: Full accounts are on file at the Charity Commission.

General: In 1992/93, the charities had an income of £78,000. £68,000 was given in 92 grants to other charities. Grants ranged from under £100 to £2,000. The largest grants, £2,000 each, went to St Luke's Development Trust, the Lord Mayor's Appeal and TEAR Fund. £1,600 went to St Giles' Church, Cripplegate.

Most grants were for £500 to £1,000 with 12 for under £500. Medical and welfare charities were well supported, with some grants to Christian organisations and churches, children and youth charities and arts organisations. Most organisations supported were national, with some local charities in London. Beneficiaries included Action Aid, Centre for Combatting Child Abuse, Church Urban Fund, International Organ Festival Society, National Association of Boys' Clubs, National Asthma Campaign, Prison Fellowship, Romanian Orphanage Trust and the World Wide Fund for Nature.

Applications: In writing to the correspondent.

The Peter Samuel Charitable Trust

£141,000 (1993/94)

Health and welfare, conservation, Jewish care

Farley Farms, Bridge Farm, Reading Road, Arborfield, Berkshire RG2 9HT
01734-760280

Correspondent: Mrs Wendy Lucken, Secretary

Trustees: Viscount Bearsted; Nicholas Samuel; Michael Samuel.

Beneficial area: UK, and local organisations in Berkshire and Hampshire.

Information available: Accounts are on file at the Charity Commission, but without a list of grants since 1991/92.

General: The 1993/94 trustees report states: "The trust seeks to perpetuate the family's interest in the medical sciences, the quality of life in the local areas, heritage and land/forestry restoration".

The trust's assets were £2.7 million and income £160,000. Grants totalled £141,000, but no list of grants was included with the accounts.

In 1991/92, the trust's income was £176,000; grants totalled £125,000. 42 grants were given with about half to regular beneficiaries. Two major beneficiaries received the same grant the previous year; the RFHSM Investment in Health Fund (£60,000) and Campaign for Oxford Trust Fund (£10,000). The Jewish Philanthropic Association received £5,000 (£20,000 in 1990/91).

The largest one-off grants were £5,000 each to Jewish Care and the Anna Freud Centre. Remaining grants ranged from £150 to £3,000 and were generally given to health and social welfare organisations. Recipients included the RNID, RNLI, NSPCC, Age Concern England, National Trust, National Association for Gifted Children and Game Conservancy (Grouse Research).

Exclusions: No grants to individuals. No local charities other than those in Berkshire and Hampshire.

Applications: In writing to the correspondent. Trustees meet twice yearly.

The Sandra Charitable Trust

£86,000 (1993/94)

Not known

St Paul's House, Warwick Lane, London EC4P 4BN
0171-248 4499

Correspondent: R Moore

Trustees: R Moore; M Macfayden.

Beneficial area: UK.

Information available: Accounts are on file at the Charity Commission for 1986/87 and 1992/93, but the latter did not include a grants list. The following information was provided by the trust.

General: In 1993/94, the trusts assets were £792,000 including an interest free loan of £800,000 from ITCO Ltd. The income was £63,000 and grants totalled £86,000. Unfortunately no information is available on the beneficiaries.

In 1990/91, the trust gave two grants totalling £6,000 from an income of £19,000. The beneficiaries were Leigh on Sea Scout Group (£5,500) and St Paul's Cathedral Choir School Foundation (£500).

Applications: In writing to the correspondent.

The Sarum St Michael Educational Charity

£175,000 (1993)

Christian education in Salisbury diocese

2nd Floor, 13 New Canal, Salisbury, Wiltshire SP1 2AA
01722-422296

Correspondent: The Clerk to the Governors

Trustees: Lt Col C C G Ross; J Jarvis; M Marriott; R Martin; Mrs J Smith; Rt Rev Dr D S Stancliffe; Very Rev H G Dickinson; Brig C C Owen; H Head.

Beneficial area: The diocese of Salisbury.

Information available: Accounts are on file at the Charity Commission, but without a list of grants.

General: The trust's objects are "the advancement of education in accordance with the principles and doctrines of the Church of England". It has a preference for applications from within, or of likely benefit to, the Salisbury diocese; after these it will consider applications from neighbouring dioceses.

In 1993, the trust had assets of £2.75 million and an income of £140,000. Grants totalled £175,000, and were given to schools, colleges, parishes and individuals (in further and higher education only).

Applications: On a form available from the correspondent.

The Scarfe Charitable Trust

£41,000 (1993/94)

Research, social welfare, churches

1 Gainsborough Road, Felixstowe, Suffolk IP11 7HT
01394-285537

Correspondent: E E Maule

Trustees: N Scarfe; E E Maule.

Beneficial area: UK, with an emphasis on Suffolk.

Information available: Full accounts are on file at the Charity Commission.

General: In 1993/94, the trust had assets of £640,000 and an income of £51,000. Grants totalled £41,000.

The main grants were £22,000 to the Institute of Neurology and £5,800 to the Suffolk Wildlife Trust. These two beneficiaries also received grants the previous year, but most of the other grants were one-off. Grants of £1,000 or more went to Magdalen College, Norfolk Museums Service and Bury St Edmunds Theatre Royal.

Other grants, ranging from £25 to £750, were given to national and local organisations, especially for social welfare and to churches.

Applications: In writing to the correspondent.

The Annie Schiff Charitable Trust

£114,000 (1994)

Orthodox Jewish

8 Highfield Gardens, London NW11 9HB
0181-458 9266

Correspondent: J Pearlman

Beneficial area: UK, overseas.

Information available: Full accounts are on file at the Charity Commission.

General: In 1994, the trust had an income of £194,000. 21 grants totalled £114,000, of which 18 were for £1,000 or more. The largest grants were to Menorah Grammar School Trust (£50,000) and Agudas Israel Housing Assoication (£10,000).

Grants are given exclusively to orthodox Jewish religious and educational institutions.

Applications: In writing to the correspondent.

The Schreib Trust

£80,000 (1993/94)

General

3rd Floor, 5-13 Hatton Wall, London EC1N 8HX
0171-430 2552

Correspondent: Irene Schreiber

Trustees: Irene Schreiber; Jacob Schreiber; David Schreiber.

Beneficial area: UK.

Information available: Accounts are on file at the Charity Commission, but without a list of grants.

General: It is impossible to glean an enormous amount of information about this trust's grant-giving policies as only a single brief set of accounts are on file at the Charity Commission. Although the trust's objects are general, it lists its particular priorities as relief of poverty, advancement of religious education.

The trust has a modest asset base of £16,000, although a healthy income for the year of £95,000 made up almost exclusively of donations. This enabled the trust to distribute a large amount of money (£80,000), although it is not known who received the money or what size the grants were.

Applications: In writing to the correspondent.

The Schreiber Charitable Trust

£89,000 (1992/93)

Jewish

9 West Heath Road, London NW3 7VX
0171-433 3434

Correspondent: G S Morris

Trustees: Graham S Morris; David A Schreiber; Sara Schreiber.

Beneficial area: UK.

Information available: Accounts are on file at the Charity Commission, but without a list of grants for 1992/93.

General: In 1992/93, the trust had assets of £944,000 about half of which were unlisted investments in Schreiber Holdings Ltd. The income was £147,000 and grants totalled £89,000. Unfortunately no list of grants was available for this year, or for the previous year when the income was £87,000 and grants totalled £95,000.

In 1990/91, the trust gave grants totalling £92,000 from an income of £99,000. About 90 grants were made including £22,000 to JPAIME, £16,000 to Classics Charitable Trust and £5,000 to Menorah Grammar School. According to the Charity Commission database, the Classics Charitable Trust has general charitable purposes. All the other grants made appear to be to Jewish organisations, with the exception of £100 to Guide Dogs for the Blind.

Applications: In writing to the correspondent.

The Frieda Scott Charitable Trust

£181,000 (1993/94)

Lakeland charities

Sand Aire House, Kendal, Cumbria LA9 4BE
01539-723415

Correspondent: Donald J Harding, Secretary

Trustees: Mrs C Brockbank, Chair; Mrs O Clarke; Mrs C R Scott; O Turnbull; R A Hunter; P R Hensman; D Y Mitchell.

Beneficial area: The Westmoreland and Lonsdale parliamentary constituency area as well as the area covered by the South Lakeland District Council.

Information available: Full accounts are on file at the Charity Commission.

General: The trust shares the same correspondent and address (though not trustees) as the Francis Scott Trust (*see A Guide to the Major Trusts Volume 1*).

In 1993/94, the trust had investments with a market value of £4.2 million. These produced an income of £133,000 out of which donations totalling £181,000 were made. In 1993 the income was £182,000. This decline in income is partly due to a decline in the dividend paid by Provincial Insurance (which holds 20% of the trust's investments) and partly due to the fall in interest rates. The Provincial Insurance Company has now returned to profitability and the trust's income should be restored to some extent to former levels.

There were 65 awards, 19 going to organisations that received grants the year before, mainly for a few hundred pounds. The trust gives particular support to the Brewery Arts Centre in Kendal which it helped to found in 1970 (it received £74,000 in 1993/94). It also gives an annual donation of £10,000 to the Gateway Trust in Edinburgh in accordance with the wishes of the settlor.

Other large grants went to Armitt Trust, Ambleside and Stricklandgate House Trust (both £15,000), South Lakeland Council for Voluntary Action (£6,500) and Cancer Relief Macmillan Fund and National Trust Lake District Appeal (both £5,000). Several arts organisations received funding, including Westmoreland Orchestra (£1,000), Renaissance Theatre in Ulverston (£800) and Kendal Mid-day Concert Society (£750).

Other local causes supported include a parish hall and church restoration, youth organisations, holidays for children with special needs, and local training establishments offering facilities for disabled people.

Exclusions: Applications outside the beneficial area.

Applications: By letter to the correspondent. Applications are considered three times a year. All applicants will be notified of the trustees' action. Intending applicants are welcome to telephone the correspondent for an informal discussion prior to making a formal application.

The Sir Samuel Scott of Yews Trust

£238,000 (1992/93)

Medical research

c/o Currey & Co, 21 Buckingham Gate, London SW1E 6LS

Correspondent: The Secretary

Trustees: P A Scott; D G Bosanquet; Oliver Scott.

Beneficial area: UK.

Information available: Full accounts are on file at the Charity Commission.

General: Similarly to the Francis C Scott Charitable Trust (see *A Guide to the Major Trusts Vol. 1*) and the Frieda Scott Charitable Trust (see *separate entry*), this trust has most of its investments in Sand Aire Investments plc. In 1992/93, the trust had assets of £1.8 million and an income of £225,000. Grants totalled £238,000.

The trust "concentrates on medical research and will reject all other appeals. The trustees favour new ventures or emergency funding of established programmes of medical research, but only for limited periods, since they do not undertake core funding. Most grants are non-recurrent. Grants are only made to registered charities."

67 grants were made in 1992/93, with all but five for £1,000 or more. Especially large amounts went to the Cancer Research Campaign (£30,000), Preclinical Cancer Research Fund (£20,000) and Mental Health Foundation (£12,000). £10,000 was given to each of Jefferiss Research Wing Trust (St Mary's Hospital), Brain Research Trust, British Neurological Research Trust and the Cassel Hospital – research into mental illness. Other beneficiaries included the Allergy Inflammation Research Trust, Cystic Fibrosis Trust, Medical Aid for Poland Fund, Research into Ageing and the Sylvan Trust – music therapy.

Exclusions: No core funding. No support for purely clinical work. No grants to individuals (although research by an individual may be funded if sponsored by a registered charity through which the application is made). No support for research leading to higher degrees (unless the departmental head concerned certifies that the work is of real scientific importance). No grants for medical students' elective periods. No grants for expeditions (unless involving an element of genuine medical research).

Applications: Should be made in writing through the correspondent. Trustees hold their half-yearly meetings in March and October; the appeal lists are closed on 31st January and 31st August. There are no special forms, but applicants should give the following information:

1. The nature and purpose of the research project or programme.
2. The names, qualifications and present posts of the scientists involved.
3. Reference to any published results of their previous research.
4. Details of present funding.
5. If possible, the budget for the next twelve months or other convenient period.

All applications are acknowledged and both successful and unsuccessful applicants are notified after each meeting of the trustees. No telephone calls.

The Scottish Churches Architectural Heritage Trust

£79,000 (1993)

Scottish church buildings

15 North Bank Street, The Mound, Edinburgh EH1 2LP
0131-225 8644

Correspondent: Mrs Florence Mackenzie, Director

Trustees: Lord Ross, Chairman; Donald Erskine; Magnus Magnusson; Rev Robin Barbour; Sir Jamie Stormonth Darling; Lady Fraser; Mrs Mary Millican; George Russell.

Beneficial area: Scotland.

Information available: The trust is registered in Scotland.

General: The trust was established "to care for Scottish church buildings in use for public worship, principally by raising funds for their repair and restoration and by acting as a source of technical advice and assistance on maintenance and repair".

In 1993, the assets of the trust were £460,000 and it had an income of £102,000 including £63,000 in donations. Grants totalled £79,000.

Geographically churches benefitting ranged from Scarista, Isle of Lewis to Aberdeen and from Gatehouse of Fleet to Papa Westray. Churches of all denominations were supported: 26 Church of Scotland; 7 Scottish Episcopal Churches, and one each of Roman Catholic, Methodist, Free, Evangelical and Baptist. Grants ranged from £500 to £5,000. Specific projects included steeple repair, rot and damp eradication, windows and leadwork repairs, and roof repairs.

Applications: In writing to the correspondent, after which an application form will be sent. The grants committee meets four times a year.

The Scottish Housing Associations Charitable Trust (SHACT)

£48,000 (committed in 1993/94)

Housing associations or housing related projects in Scotland

38 York Place, Edinburgh EH1 3HU
0131-556 5777

Correspondent: Alison Campbell, Trust Administrator

Trustees: Andrew Robertson; Ronald Ironside; David Harley; Gordon Woods; Harry Mulligan; Gavin McCrone; Anne Yanetta; Susan Torrence; Paul Farrell; Robert McDowall; Margaret Richards; David Chalmers.

Beneficial area: Scotland.

Information available: The charity is registered in Scotland. It produces an application form and guidance notes for applicants.

General: SHACT was set up in 1979. It exists to support the voluntary housing movement in Scotland. It gives grants and loans to housing associations and other voluntary organisations in the following general categories:
- Homelessness with emphasis on young homeless people.
- People with special needs including those with physical, mental health or learning difficulties.
- Older people.
- Care and repair charitable funds – for small repairs and to top up grant-aided work.
- Projects in rural areas.
- Projects to benefit people of ethnic minorities.
- Community regeneration projects run by housing associations or co-operatives.
- Research into Scotland's housing problems and solutions.
- Training for voluntary committee members.

Most grants will be for under £5,000.

In 1993/94 committed grants were broken down as follows:

Homelessness £12,600 (26%) including support for Aberdeen Cyrenians, the Big Issue and the Scottish Youth Housing Network.

Elderly people £9,600 (19%) including support for Lorne Social Centre (Leith), Partick Housing Association and Central Buchan Care & Repair.

Special needs £3,700 (8%) including support for Moncrieff Terrace Neighbourhood Support Association and Special Needs Housing Conference.

Training £800 (2%) to two housing associations.

Rural projects £11,500 (24%) including support for Nithsdale Housing Advice Service, Orkney H A Low Energy Project and Western Isles Women's Aid.

Ethnic minorities £2,000 (4%) to Dundee Asian Housing Forum.

Community regeneration £8,300 (17%) including grants to Community Self-Build Scotland, Glasgow North Employment Initiative and Portree Self-Build Initiative.

SHACT works closely with, and receives a substantial grant from HACT (an entry for HACT can be found in *A Guide to the Major Trusts Vol. 1*). Scottish applications can be made to either trust but the trusts discuss these with each other.

Exclusions: Grants or loans will not be made to individuals, large national organisations except for specific projects or large general appeals.

Applications: The trustees meet four times a year and all applications will be acknowledged. Applicants are encouraged to telephone the Administrator beforehand for a general discussion.

The Scouloudi Foundation

£150,000 (1993/94)

Historical awards, social welfare, environment

c/o Hays Allan, Southampton House,
317 High Holborn, London WC1V 7NL
0171-831 6233

Correspondent: The Administrators

Trustees: J M Carr; A J Parr; M E Demetriadi; Miss B R Masters; J D Marnham; Miss S E Stowell.

Beneficial area: UK, "but not for activities of a purely local nature".

Information available: Full accounts are on file at the Charity Commission. Guidance notes available from the correspondent.

General: The trust splits its donations into three categories, "regular" and "special" donations, and historical awards. Historical awards generally make up around one half of total grants, and are for individuals, primarily to fund research in the historical field. These awards totalled £60,000 in 1993/94.

"Regular" donations are made annually to a basic list of some 110 national charitable organisations, a list which is very unlikely to be extended by the trustees. The amounts are distributed by the Charities Aid Foundation, and are for £1,000 or less, and totalled £60,000 in 1993/94. A few "regular" recipients occasionally get "special" donations.

"Special" donations are made to organisations working in the fields of: disasters; education; environment; overseas aid and refugees; handicapped and disabled; humanities; medicine and health. These are the ones to apply for, and are usually for £1,000 or under. Most are not recurrent, and are for special appeals.

In 1992/93, 27 organisations received £30,000 between them. The largest grants went to the Royal Academy Trust (£6,000), National Deaf Children's Society and Reed's School Foundation (£3,000 each for anniversary appeals), Guy's Hospital Evelina Children's Appeal (£2,500) and Staffordshire University (£1,500). Other recipients included British School of Osteopathy, Mudchute Association Ltd, Norfolk Autistic Society, Wigan Hospice and Y Care International - India

Earthquake Appeal. Four grants of £400 were given towards expeditions by colleges/schools.

Exclusions: Except for historical awards, grants are only made to registered charities and no grants are made to individuals. No grants for activities of a purely local nature.

Applications: Only about 22% of grants are uncommitted. Applications giving full but concise details should be sent to the correspondent. These applications are considered once a year in March.

The Searchlight Electric Charitable Trust

£47,000 (1992/93)

General

Searchlight Electric Ltd, Water Street, Manchester M3 4JU
0161-834 5452

Correspondent: H E Hamburger, Trustee

Trustees: H E Hamburger; D M Hamburger; M E Hamburger; J S Fidler.

Beneficial area: UK.

Information available: Accounts are on file at the charity Commission, but without a list of grants.

General: In 1992/93, the trust had assets of £485,000 and an income of £85,000. Grants totalled £47,000 but no further information is available on the grant beneficiaries.

The trust received a loan from Searchlight Electric Ltd to help set up the trust, this appears to have been mostly repaid.

Applications: In writing to the correspondent.

The Searle Charitable Trust

£329,000 (1993/94)

Medical, elderly

Windyridge, The Close, Totteridge, London N20 8PT
0181-446 7281

Correspondent: A C Southon

Trustees: Arthur C Southon; Noel A V Lister; Ian R D Andrews; Brendan J C Hall.

Beneficial area: UK, overseas.

Information available: Full accounts are on file at the Charity Commission.

General: In 1993/94, the trust's assets were valued at £3 million and the income was £159,000. Grants were paid to 32 organisations totalling £329,000, utilising some of the undistributed income brought forward.

The grants list is dominated by grants of £250,000 to Donald Searle Outdoor Activities Charitable Company and £40,000 to RONA Trust, both regular beneficiaries of large grants.

Other larger grants went to Amyloid Research (£15,000), Body Scanner Appeal Mount Vernon Hospital (£5,000), Scout Association (£2,000), Sense Barnet Appeal (£5,000), VSO (£1,000) and the Wooden Spoon Society (£7,000). Except for the latter two, all these were new beneficiaries.

Of the other 24 grants, all £500 or less, 14 were recurrent from the previous year. Most were the larger well-known health and welfare charities including Age Concern, BLISS and the NSPCC. Other grants went to BTCV and the Council for the Protection of Rural England.

Exclusions: No grants for individuals.

Applications: In writing to the correspondent.

The Seedfield Trust

£65,000 (1993)

Christian, relief of poverty

Folly Bank Farm, Goodshaw Lane, Rossendale, Lancs BB4 8DW
01706-228627

Correspondent: Keith Buckler

Trustees: John Atkins; Keith Buckler; David Ryan; Lionel Osborn; Janet Buckler.

Beneficial area: Worldwide.

Information available: Full accounts are on file at the Charity Commission.

General: The trust's assets trebled to £717,000 during 1991. Following the settlor's death in 1992, further assets were transferred from his estate into the trust. The assets in 1993 stood at £1.1 million and income for the year was £71,000. Grants totalled £65,000.

The following refers to 1991, when grants totalled £62,000. Nine grants were given, all but one to organisations which had received equivalent funding the year before. The largest grants were £14,000 to the Overseas Missionary Fellowship, £12,000 to European Christian Mission, and £10,000 each to the Restorer Trust and the Dorothea Trust.

Other beneficiaries included the Muller Homes (£6,000), Gideon's International (£5,000), Pentecostal Childcare Alliance (£3,000) and the National Children's Home (£1,000).

Applications: In writing to the correspondent.

The Leslie Sell Charitable Trust

£63,000 (1993/94)

Scouts and guides

8 Upper Marlborough Road, St Albans, Herts AL1 3UR
01727-843603

Correspondent: D Watts

Trustees: Mrs M R Wiltshire; P S Sell; D Watts.

Beneficial area: UK.

Information available: Full accounts are on file at the Charity Commission.

General: In 1993/94, the trust had assets of £1.2 million and an income of £116,000. Grants totalled £63,000 including £5,500 to Cottesloe School Adventure Fund.

Grants went mainly to scout and guide groups throughout the UK and Northern Ireland. 85 grants were given ranging from £50 to £1,500. 16 grants went to individuals connected with scout or guide groups.

Applications: In writing to the correspondent. Applications are considered fortnightly.

The Sharon Trust

£27,000 (1993)

Christian

3 Mount Pleasant, Lowestoft, Suffolk NR32 4JB
01502-560602

Correspondent: Mrs H G Taylor

Trustees: J F Warnes; F W Warnes; Mrs H G Taylor; Miss M H Warnes; W R Warnes.

Beneficial area: Worldwide.

Information available: Full accounts are on file at the Charity Commission.

General: In 1993, the trust had assets of £388,000 and an income of £95,000, £74,000 under Gift Aid. Grants totalled £27,000. The surplus of £67,000, added to the accumulated surplus of previous years, will increase the assets of the trust and allow more money to be distributed at a later date.

Of the 70 grants given, all except three — which totalled less than £200 — were given to Christian organisations. The largest grants were to the North Kasia Mission (£4,900); Lord's Work Trust (£1,700); Foreign Labourers' Fund (£2,150) and Tonning Street Hall (£3,100). All but the latter appear to be regular beneficiaries of larger grants.

Most grants are under £500 and are given to a wide range of Christian organisations working in the UK and overseas eg. British Youth for Christ (£100), European Christian Mission (£440), London City Mission (£80), Operation Mobilization (£420), Slavic Gospel Association (£120) and Transworld Radio (£45).

Exclusions: Only Christian causes are supported.

Applications: In writing to the correspondent. The trust points out that while it can receive up to five appeals a day, it tends to support the same interests each year. Only applications enclosing an sae will receive a reply.

The Sheffield Town Trust

£249,000 (1993)

General in Sheffield

Old Cathedral Vicarage, St James' Row, Sheffield S1 1XA
0114-272 2061

Correspondent: G Connell, Law Clerk

Beneficial area: Sheffield only.

Information available: Full accounts are on file at the Charity Commission.

General: In 1993, the trust had assets of £3.5 million and an income of £256,000. This was distributed as follows:

Annually recurring grants	£60,000
Scholarships	£6,000
Non-recurring	£188,000

Annual grants are given to mainly health and welfare charities in Sheffield and range from £450 to £4,500. Beneficiaries include Age Concern, Sheffield CVS, St Mary's Community Centre, Sheffield Dial-a-Ride, Northern Refuge Centre and a number of youth organisations. Scholarships are restricted to students in the Department of History and Department of Geology at the University of Sheffield.

112 non-recurring grants were given with a wide range of organisations supported. The largest grants went to St Luke's Hospice (£25,000), Lodge Moor Spinal Unit Sports Club (£10,000), Voluntary Action Sheffield (£8,000) and Lifetrain (£7,500). £5,000 each went to Hillsborough Community Development Trust, St Margaret's Church Brightside, St Mary's Co-operative Children's Centre, Stannington PCC, Steel Valley Forum, Taptonholme, Church of St Leonard Norwood and Wadsley Parish Church.

Other grants ranged from £150 to £3,000. Beneficiaries included Castle & Manor Credit Union Ltd, Hallam Community Physiotherapy Project, Norfolk Park Community Carnival, Opportunities for People with Disabilities, Sheffield Gypsy & Traveller Support Group, Yemeni Language Training Project and Yorkshire Youth Music.

Exclusions: No grants to individuals except through a very small associated scholarship fund.

Applications: In writing to the correspondent. Applications are considered quarterly. A note of the trust's requirements is available from the correspondent.

The Sheldon Trust

£102,000 (1993/94)

General

Box S, White Horse Court, 25c North Street, Bishop's Stortford, Herts CM23 2LD

Correspondent: The Trust Administrator

Trustees: Rev R S Bidnell; J K R England; R V Wiglesworth; J C Barratt; R M Bagshaw.

Beneficial area: UK, especially Warwickshire and the Midlands.

Information available: Full accounts are on file at the Charity Commission, with a very informative trustees report, much of which is summarised below.

General: Support is concentrated on the Midlands and on deprived areas, aiming to relieve poverty and distress, by supporting community projects or projects directed to special needs groups.

The original trustees had a great interest in the Methodist Church and its work in the community, and this interest still continues. "These community projects in turn provide help for young and old alike through counselling, meetings, playgroups, advice, youth clubs and elderly clubs." There is also a continuing interest in the Methodist Homes for the Aged.

In the 1980's, the trustees invited one or two charities to which they had made smallish grants to put forward proposals for major funding over three years. This resulted in the trust being involved in the funding of the first advanced training course in Family Therapy in England.

More recently, two major projects were funded. The first was a grant of £15,000 a year for three years to the Asthma Society Training Centre to improve the care of childhood asthma by providing training courses for professionals including nurses, doctors and teachers as well as parents. Due to the success of this programme funding was given for a further three years. The second project was the Institute of Family Therapy (London), where £15,000 a year for three years was given for the salary of a training administrator.

The trustees have decided to continue with larger awards, focusing on the mental health field. "It seemed this was a low priority area for funding, both from government and public. A further area of concern were problems encountered by people being discharged from hospital into the community, with no proper back-up services."

Support was given to the National Schizophrenia Fellowship Midlands (£10,000 for two years towards the cost of employing a training officer), and to the Alzheimer's Disease Society in Cambridge (£5,000 for two years and £2,500 for a further year towards the cost of employing a co-ordinator).

An annual grant is given to Personal Services in Birmingham which gives grants to individuals in need and provides a debt counselling service. About £4,000 a year is also given to holiday projects which in 1992/93 included Breakout Children's Holidays, Bethany Christian Fellowship and Hockley Playscheme Association.

In 1992/93, the trust had assets of £1 million and an income of £122,000. Grants totalled £144,000. Except the commitments referred to above (to the National Schizophrenia Midlands, Alzheiners Disease Society and Asthma Society Training Centre), grants ranged from £500 to £6,000 with the exception of £10,000 to Warwickshire Family Health Services.

In the field of mental health and mental handicap, grants in 1992/93 were given for equipment and general expenses to Bowthorpe Community Trust, Camphill Community, CCHA Extra Care, Cherry Orchards, Guideposts Trust, McIntyres, Rowan Foundation, West Midlands Autistic Society and Wilshire Challenge.

Support for community work was given to Birmingham Settlement, Centre for Black & White Christian Partnership, Coventry Citizen Advocacy, Coventry Society for the Blind, Halow, HARP, Kingsbury Child & Family Centre, Sandwell Day Care Centre, Sheldon Community Centre and West Worcester Live at Home Scheme.

"The trustees play a very active role in the trust and review policy and criteria regularly and, although having a central policy, ensure that this is open minded so that they can react to changes in the environment and the community alike. The trustees will, for the present, be committing a good proportion of their income to continuing grants, which means that they will have less income to distribute to other organisations."

Applications: In writing to the correspondent. Applications are considered in March, July and November.

The David Shepherd Conservation Foundation

£156,000 (1994)

Conservation of endangered mammals

PO Box 123, Godalming, Surrey GU8 4JS
01483-208576

Correspondent: Melanie Shepherd, Co-ordinator

Trustees: Anthony Athaide; Sir Robert Clark; Peter Giblin; David Gower OBE; Avril Shepherd; David Shepherd OBE.

Beneficial area: Worldwide.

Information available: Full information has been supplied by the foundation for this entry.

General: The foundation has written the following about its work: "The foundation supports and complements other wildlife and conservation charities associated with:

- The conservation and management of endangered mammals.
- Anti-poaching activities in Africa and elsewhere and the abolition of the illegal trade in endangered species.
- Education of young people in matters relating to the conservation of the world's wildlife, natural resources and wild places, but with an emphasis on endangered mammals.

"The foundation generates funds from membership, auctions, sponsorship, gifts and donations, fundraising events and sales of products derived from David Shepherd's work for the foundation.

"The income is used to respond quickly and directly to the needs of organisations in the UK and overseas, with whose objectives it is in sympathy, where it believes its contribution will have a significant effect on the achievement of specific project aims, and when it has been satisfied that its funds will be effectively applied."

Grants given in 1994 totalled £156,000 distributed as follows:

£63,500 to Zambia for elephant conservation;
£29,500 to the Dian Fossey Gorilla Fund;
£18,000 to Rhino Campaign;
£10,000 to Tiger Trust for anti-poaching work in Siberia;
£10,000 to RADAR;
£9,800 to the Humane Society of the US;
£5,000 to support elephant and rhino work in Namibia;
£3,200 to research baby elephant translocation in South Africa;
£2,500 for the Regional Enforcement Conference;
£1,900 for monitoring rhino in Assam;
£2,400 to support 12 young people's expeditions.

Exclusions: Applications for grants must be related to the conservation of the world's major endangered mammals.

Applications: In writing, in detail, to the administrator.

The Archie Sherman Cardiff Charitable Foundation

£119,000 (1993/94)

Jewish

c/o Rothschild Trust Guernsey Ltd,
St Julian's Court, St Peter Port, Guernsey,
Channel Islands
01481-713713

Correspondent: Mrs Lorna Hubert

Trustees: Rothschild Trust Co Ltd.

Beneficial area: UK and overseas.

Information available: Full accounts are on file at the Charity Commission.

General: In 1993/94, the trust had assets of £332,000 and an income of £118,000 of which £104,000 was from rents. Three grants were made totalling £119,000. The Tel Aviv Foundation received £65,000, the Shaare Zedek Hospital £41,000 and the Foundation for Education £14,000.

Details of the much larger Archie Sherman Charitable Trust appear in Volume 1 of this Guide.

Applications: In writing to the correspondent.

The Barnett & Sylvia Shine No 1 & No 2 Charitable Trusts

£30,000 (1993/94)

General

Bouverie House, 154 Fleet Street, London EC4A 2DG
0171-353 0299

Correspondent: M D Paisner

Trustees: No 1: M D Paisner; S S Shine. No 2: M D Paisner; B J Grahame; R Grahame.

Beneficial area: Worldwide.

Information available: Accounts are on file at the Charity Commission, but without a list of grants for 1992/93 or 1993/94.

General: The No 1 Charitable Trust was established in 1975 by Sylvia Shine. In 1980, half the assets of the trust were transferred to the No 2 Charitable Trust. In 1981, the executors of the estate of the late Sylvia Shine transferred several paintings, jewellery and cash to the trusts. Two paintings have subsequently been sold.

In 1993/94, the trusts had assets totalling over £1.8 million generating a combined income of £102,000. Grants totalled only £30,000; £20,000 from the No 1 Trust and £10,000 from No 2. No information is available on the grants since 1991/92.

In 1991/92, the No 1 Charitable Trust gave grants totalling £12,000 from an income of £61,000. The nine grants included £5,000 to Soweto Black Women's Charitable Trust. Six grants were for £1,000 including those to Childline, Greenpeace, Samaritans and two hospices.

The No 2 trust gave grants totalling £3,000 including £500 to Church Poverty Action Group, Airey Neave Trust and Oxfam.

Both trusts appear to have a consistently large surplus of income over expenditure. It is not clear if the income is being retained for a particular purpose, to build up its assets or due to insufficient appropriate applications.

Applications: In writing to the correspondent.

The Shiyich Charitable Trust

£50,000 (1991/92)

Jewish

12 Courtleigh Gardens, London NW11 9JX
0171-278 9395

Correspondent: J Waller

Trustees: Jeremy Waller; Sarah Waller.

Beneficial area: UK, overseas.

Information available: Full accounts are on file at the Charity Commission up to 1991/92.

General: In 1991/92, the trust had an income of £53,000 and gave six grants totalling £50,000, all to Jewish organisations. The major beneficiary was the Ravenswood Foundation which received £30,000.

The other five recipients were the Chesed Charitable Trust (£14,000) Woodstock Sinclair Charitable Trust (£4,000), London Academy of Jewish Studies (£1,500), Project Seed Europe (£1,000), and the Torah Teminah Primary School (£200).

Applications: In writing to the correspondent.

The Shuttlewood Clarke Foundation

£59,000 (1992/93)

Health and welfare

Ulverscroft Grange, Ulverscroft, Leicester LE67 9QB
01530-244914

Correspondent: D A Clarke

Trustees: D A Clarke; M Freckelton; D N Murphy; K P Byass.

Beneficial area: 10-mile radius of Ulverscroft.

Information available: Accounts are on file at the Charity Commission, but without a list of grants.

General: In 1992/93, the trust had assets of £5.3 million and an income of £350,000. After running costs for the houses it runs (see below) the trust gave £59,000 to other charities.

The foundation is particularly keen to give grants for the relief of need, hardship, suffering or distress of elderly and young people. In 1992/93, 23 grants were given ranging from £18,750 to Loughborough University to £500 to Relate. Other larger grants were given to Peter Le Marchant Trust (£4,000), Ryder Cheshire Mission (£3,500) and Charnwood Community Council (£3,000). The remaining grants included six for £2,000 and 12 for £1,000 given to organisations local to Ulverscroft, including the CAB, Victim Support Scheme, scouts and the community college.

The trust also owns two houses in the country. In the last two years, over 500 groups (8,000 people) have spent a day at the houses. Visiting groups are given a free dinner (donations are accepted towards the costs). The houses cost about £100,000 each a year to run, including visitors meals.

Applications: In writing to the correspondent.

The Huntly & Margery Sinclair Charitable Trust

£45,000 (1992/93)

Medical, general

c/o Trowers & Hamlins, Trustees Solicitor, 6 New Square, Lincoln's Inn, London WC2A 3RP
0171-831 6292

Correspondent: Eric Payne

Trustees: Mrs A M H Gibb; Mrs M A H Stainton; Mrs J Floyd.

Beneficial area: UK.

Information available: Full accounts are on file at the Charity Commission.

General: In 1992/93, the trust had assets of £702,000 and an income of £62,000. 24 grants were given totalling £45,000.

Rendcomb College has been the major beneficiary for the last two years, receiving £30,000 in 1992/93, and £31,000 in 1991/92. Seven organisations received £1,000, of which six were national medical charities (including Alzheimers Disease Society, Imperial Cancer Research Fund and National Asthma Campaign), the other being the Gloucestershire Old Peoples Housing Society.

The other 16 grants were for £500 each and given to a range of charities covering medical, conservation, animal welfare and disability, most of which did not receive a grant the previous year. Grants also went to a church and two parochial church councils which receive regular support.
Beneficiaries included British Red Cross, Finchale Training College for the Disabled, International League for the Protection of Horses, Scottish Wildlife Trust, Sculpture Workshop and University of Edinburgh Development Trust Fund.

Applications: In writing to the correspondent.

The Charles Skey Charitable Trust

£36,000 (1992/93)

Health and social welfare

Flint House, Park Homer Road, Colehill, Wimborne, Dorset BH21 2SP
01202-882180

Correspondent: J M Leggett

Trustees: M K Holloway; B Blamey; J M Leggett; C B Berkeley.

Beneficial area: UK.

Information available: Full accounts are on file at the Charity Commission.

General: In 1992/93, the trust had assets of £960,000 generating an income of £59,000. Grants totalled £36,000 with a further £5,400 transferred to the Educational Trust.

39 grants were given, mainly to health and social welfare organisations. Both national and local grants were given. About a quarter were recurrent from the previous year. The largest grant was £5,000 to the Good Shepherd Hospice. Grants of £1,000 to £2,500 were given to Botton Village Trust, Careforce, Child Resettlement Fund, Friends of Victoria Hospital, Home Farm Trust, Joint Education Trust, National Aural Group, National Society for Epilepsy, Netherley Youth Trust, One Hundred Hours, John Passmore Trust, St Christopher's Hospice, St Oswald's Hospice and the Stepping Stones Trust.

Beneficiaries of smaller grants included the Animal Welfare Fund, Birmingham Rathbone Society, Habitat Scotland, South Cerney Village Hall Appeal and the Wheelchair Sports Foundation

Applications: "There is no application form and written applications are not acknowledged."

The Skinners' Company Lady Neville Charity

£162,000 (1993/94)

General

The Skinners' Company, Skinners' Hall, 8 Dowgate Hill, London EC4R 2SP
0171-236 5629

Correspondent: The Clerk

Trustees: The Master and Wardens of the Worshipful Company of Skinners.

Beneficial area: UK.

Information available: Full accounts are on file at the Charity Commission.

General: The charity was created in November 1978 to administer the bequest of Mr Ralph Neville JP, who died in 1923 leaving property and monies to the Skinners' Company. Subsequently, the charity has become the vehicle for the Company's general charitable giving to registered charities.

In 1993/94, £126,500 was given to the Company's schools, namely the Judd School in Tonbridge, Skinners' School in Tunbridge Wells, and the Skinners' Company's School for Girls in Hackney. This left about £35,000 to be distributed among 120 charities. Most of these received grants of £100 to £300, although Lincoln College, Oxford received £5,000 and the Treloar Trust £1,000.

Organisations concerned with young people feature strongly in the grants list, as do charities caring for ex-members of the services, the arts, people with disabilities, and conservation. Grants are normally one-off, although the accounts list eight recurrent donations, some annual, some for six years and one, the Treloar Trust, for ten. Beneficiaries included Army Benevolent Fund, Atlantic College, Live Music Now!, Ranfurly Library Service, Signed Performances in Theatres, Royal School for the Blind and Winged Fellowship.

Exclusions: Registered charities only. No grants to: schools other than the Skinners' Company's own schools; medical or other research; purely local charities outside London; almshouses or old people's homes other than those run by the Skinners' Company. An charity that has received a grant will not normally be considered again until more than a year has elapsed.

Applications: By letter to the clerk by 31st March or 30th September, enclosing a copy of the latest audited accounts. Applications are not normally acknowledged.

The John Slater Foundation

£91,000 (1991/92)

General

Midland Private Banking, 3rd Floor, 4 Dale Street, Liverpool L69 2BZ
0151-801 2188

Correspondent: Julian Bishop

Trustees: Mrs J Hume; T Hume; A Taylor; C Band.

Beneficial area: UK, with a preference for the north of England especially West Lancashire.

Information available: Full accounts are on file at the Charity Commission up to 1991/92.

General: In 1991/92, the trust had assets of £736,000 and an income of £170,000. Grants totalled £91,000.

There were about 63 beneficiaries of which about half received two grants during the year, presumably they are regular beneficiaries. The largest grants were to Blackpool Ladies Sick Poor Fund (£8,000 in total), Abbeyfield Lytham St Annes and Brian Wyers Memorial Fund Trinity Hospice (both £7,000).

25 further grants were for £2,000 to £3,000, and 58 for £1,000. Beneficiaries were mainly medical and welfare charities, but also included a wide range of other organisations. Examples included the Adlington Scout Group, Animal Welfare Trust, Barnardo's Horsforth, Bingley Little Theatre, British Polio Foundation, Cheshire Homes Garstang, Grand Theatre Blackpool, Hoylake Cottage Hospital, Liverpool School of Tropical Medicine, Manorlands Home Oxenhope, Redwing Horse Sanctuary, St Gemma's Hospice Leeds and Save the Children.

Applications: Applications are considered twice a year on 1st May and 1st November.

The SMB Trust

£64,000 (1992/93)

Christian, general

Grosvenor Lodge, 72 Grosvenor Road, Tunbridge Wells, Kent TN1 2AQ

Correspondent: E D Anstead, Trustee

Trustees: Miss K Wood; B H Mitchell; E D Anstead.

Beneficial area: UK.

Information available: Full accounts are on file at the Charity Commission.

General: In 1992/93, the trust had assets of £1.5 million (including freehold properties which are rented out) and an income of £128,000. 80 grants totalled £64,000 leaving a surplus for the year of £55,000.

The trust has had a regular surplus in recent years: £52,000 in 1991/92; £61,000 in 1990/91; £50,000 in 1989/90.

The chairman's report in 1992/93 stated: "The trustees have continued to give regular support to a number of core charities covering a wide spectrum of needs".

Grants ranged from £500 to £4,000, but were mainly £500. Those receiving £1,000 and over were generally Christian organisations including the Baptist Missionary Society, Boys Brigade, Cause for Concern, Liverpool City Mission, Mid-Africa Ministry, Shaftesbury Society and TEAR Fund. The London City Mission (£4,000 in 1992/93) is always the largest recipient.

Other grants were also to Christian causes and to health and social welfare organisations including the British Red Cross, Marie Curie Foundation, Re-Solv, VSO and the YMCA. Probably fewer than half were recurrent from the previous year.

Applications: In writing to the correspondent.

The Albert and Florence Smith Memorial Trust

£194,000 (1992/93)

Social welfare

Messrs Tolhurst & Fisher, Trafalgar House, 870 Nelson Street, Southend-on-Sea SS1 1EF
01702-352511

Correspondent: The Secretary

Trustees: J E Tolhurst; W J Tolhurst; P J Tolhurst.

Beneficial area: UK, with an emphasis on Essex.

Information available: Full accounts are on file at the Charity Commission.

General: The trust supports nominated charities on an annual basis, with the balance given to local charities in Essex.

In 1992/93, the trust had assets of £1.47 million, including eight properties valued at £1.2 million. The income was £335,000 (£311,000 in rent). Grants totalled £194,000 and other expenditure totalled £58,000 (including property costs), leaving a surplus of £83,000.

Fifteen grants were given, with £150,000 given to the Fowler Memorial Trust (*see separate entry*). Grants of £10,000 went to Bournemouth Park URC, Princes Trust and the Norman Garon Trust. The other grants went to SOS Guild of Help (£5,000), Thomas Philip Price Trust (£3,000), St Cuthbert's Church (£2,000) and Rainbow Club for the Blind, Adventure Unlimited, Tommy Appeal, Caring Hand, Lennox Children's Cancer Fund, 15th Southend Scout Group and British Brain and Spine Foundation (all £25 to £500).

In previous years more grants were given, about 60 in 1990/91 and about 40 in 1988/89. In 1990/91, there were six grants for more than £1,000. They went to Adventure Unlimited (£30,000), Scouts Offshore (£30,000), the trustees of Brentwood RC Diocese (£25,000), Hockley Old People's Home and the NSPCC (£6,000), and Help the Aged (£4,000).

It may be that the trust has decided to give fewer larger grants.

Applications: To the correspondent, but see above.

The E H Smith Charitable Trust

£121,000 (1992/93)

General

1 Sherbourne Road, Acocks Green, Birmingham B27 6AB
0121-706 6100

Correspondent: K H A Smith

Trustees: K H A Smith; Mrs B M Hodgskin-Brown; D P Ensell.

Beneficial area: UK, some preference for the Midlands.

Information available: Full accounts are on file at the Charity Commission.

General: The trust has assets of only £166,000, but usually receives covenanted donations from several related companies. In 1992/93, no such donations were received and the income for the year was only £17,000. Charitable donations totalled £121,000 using unspent income from previous years. In 1991/92, the income was £75,000 with covenanted donations received from four companies: E H Smith (Westhaven) Ltd, Avery Estates Ltd, E H Smith (Millers) Ltd, E H Smith (London) Ltd. Grants in 1991/92 totalled £45,000.

The trust has given substantial grants to Christadelphian rest homes: the Bethany Guild received £100,000 in 1992/93, £7,000 in 1991/92, and £100,000 in 1990/91; the Winterdyne Trust received £25,000 in 1991/92. This substantial support for Christadelphian causes is unlikely to be repeated to any extent in future years.

The only other grants of £1,000 or more in 1992/93 were to the National Federation of Roofing Contractors (£5,000) and Alder Hey Family House Trust (£1,000). £1,242 was paid to Northcot Brick for bricks given to the Princes Trust. About 120 grants were given in all, most for £100. National and local charities were supported, with some preference for the Midlands. A range of causes were supported including medical, welfare, arts, disability, children/youth and environment/conservation.

Applications: In writing to the correspondent.

The Leslie Smith Foundation

£69,000 (1992/93)

General

Eversheds (Solicitors), Paston House, Princes Street, Norwich NR3 1BD
01603-272727

Correspondent: P R Norton

Trustees: M D Wilcox; Mrs E A Hayles.

Beneficial area: UK, with a preference for Berkshire.

Information available: Full accounts are on file at the Charity Commission.

General: In 1992/93, the trust had assets of £323,000 (with a market value of over £1 million) and an income of £106,000. Grants were given mainly to small local charities in Berkshire and are usually one-off for specific projects.

The trust prefers to support charities of which it has special knowledge or interest, with emphasis on research and treatment of addiction, arthritis/rheumatism and asthma; child care treatment; care of the elderly and bereaved, and children and youth charities, including schools.

In 1992/93, 17 grants were given totalling £69,000. Eight of the beneficiaries received a grant the previous year, including £10,000 to the College of St Barnabas (£10,000 in 1991/92) and £8,700 to Castle School Newbury (£50,000 in 1991/92).

The largest grant was £25,000 to St Francis School. Other beneficiaries of over £2,000 were Centre 33 and the Paul Strickland Scanner Centre (both £5,000) and Relate (£3,000). The remaining grants ranged from £250 to £2,000. Three grants went to animal welfare charities, RSPCA, British Wildlife Appeal and FRAME, all of which got grants the previous year. Grants were also given to the RNLI, another school and two churches.

Exclusions: Registered charities only; no grants to individuals.

Applications: In writing to the correspondent. Only successful appeals are acknowledged.

The N Smith Charitable Trust

£82,000 (1992/93)

General

1 Booth Street, Manchester M2 2HA
0161-833 9771

Correspondent: Bullock Worthington & Jackson

Trustees: J S Cochrane; T R Kendal; P R Green; J H Williams-Rigby.

Beneficial area: Worldwide.

Information available: Full accounts are on file at the Charity Commission.

General: Following an inheritance from the estate of Miss N Smith in 1992, there was a large increase in the assets of this trust which in 1992/93 stood at £1.5 million. There has been a corresponding rise in the income to £94,000 and in the grants total to £82,000. The grants were categorised in the accounts for the first time as follows (number of grants in brackets):

Health & medical research	£25,500	(17)
Poverty & social work	£21,700	(35)
Education	£8,400	(10)
Environmental work & animals	£7,300	(10)
Arts	£1,800	(3)
Overseas aid	£17,500	(10)

The grants are distributed in October and March, with most beneficiaries within one category in the same month, receiving the same size grant. Examples and size of grants given within the different categories were as follows:

Health & medical research: £700 or £1,080 to Alzheimers Disease Society, Crohns in Childhood Research Association, Haemophilia Society and Schizophrenia Association.

Poverty & social work: £500 or £750 to Age Concern, Boys & Girls Welfare Society, Church Army, Shelter and Telephones for the Blind.

Education: £800 or £900 mainly to activity based groups such as Duke of Edinburgh Awards and Outward Bound Trust, but also to British Blind Sport and Cities in Schools.

Environmental work & animals: £900 or £1,000 to UK charities such CPRE, PDSA, RSPB and the Woodland Trust. The only local beneficiary was Knutsford & District Trust for Animals.

Arts: £800 or £500 to Clonter Music Farm, Opera North and the Royal Shakespeare Company.

Overseas aid: £1,000 or £2,000 with one grant for £5,000. Beneficiaries included Oxfam, Prisoners Abroad, TEAR Fund and Tools for Self Reliance.

Exclusions: Grants are only made to registered charities and not to individuals.

Applications: In writing to the correspondent.

The Stanley Smith General Charitable Trust

£21,000 (1993/94)

General

BDO Binder Hamlyn, 20 Old Bailey, London EC4M 7BH
0181-688 4422

Correspondent: J Norton

Trustees: J L Norton; J J Dilger.

Beneficial area: UK.

Information available: Full accounts are on file at the Charity Commission.

General: In 1993/94, the trust had assets of £1 million, a rise from £560,000 in the previous year after sale of investments. The income was only £43,000, but would be expected to rise in future years. Grants totalled only £21,000 (down from £31,000 in 1992/93, from an income of £51,000).

Nine grants were given, with £10,000 going to the NSPCC. Four grants of £2,000 went to Fane Hall, Hearing Research Trust, Hornsby Centre (Wandsworth) and Reza Ali Khazeni Memorial Foundation. Brecon Cathedral 900th Anniversary Appeal received £1,000 and the remaining grants of £500 were given to Church Action on Disability, Millfield School's Diamond Jubilee Appeal and Wessex Cancer Trust.

Three of the beneficiaries also received a grant the previous year, when grants of £10,000 were given to both Shelter and the Pestalozzi Children's Village.

Applications: In writing to the correspondent.

The Stanley Smith UK Horticultural Trust

£50,000 (1992/93)

Horticulture

BDO Binder Hamlyn, 44 Exeter Road, Newmarket, Suffolk CB8 8LR
01638-665718

Correspondent: Sophie Peters

Trustees: Christopher Brickell; John Norton; John Dilger.

Beneficial area: UK.

Information available: Full accounts are on file at the Charity Commission.

General: The trust's objects are the "advancement of horticulture". This remit is broadly interpreted, but excludes assistance to students for courses (although bodies providing such courses have been supported).

In 1992/93, the trust had assets of £851,000 and an income of £109,000. Expenses totalled £58,000 (including £14,000 for a former director's pension and £22,000 "professional charges").

Grants are made to identified projects and totalled £50,000 ranging from £500 to £11,000. The largest went to the Historic Houses Association (£11,000 for continuation of the gardener's training programme); National Trust (£10,000 to cover the cost of a mature student to take part in the gardener's training scheme); Thomas Phillips Price Trust (£5,000, second of two grants to pay for the training of a horticultural technician); Chelsea Physic Garden (£5,000, second of three to employ an education officer). Other grants included help with the improvement of the international Clematis Society's journal and production of its yearbook, and a collection of threatened orchids.

Exclusions: No support for commercial horticulture projects (crop production etc.).

Applications: In writing to the correspondent. There is no application form as such. Guidelines are available from the correspondent. Applications can be presented in the manner best suited to the applicant and the project for which assistance is sought. They are considered twice a year (April and October); closing dates are March 15th and September 15th respectively.

The Solo Charitable Settlement

£42,000 (1992/93)

Jewish, general

Touche Ross & Co, Hill House, 1 Little New Street, London EC4A 3TR
0171-936 3000

Correspondent: S Midwinter

Trustees: P D Goldstein; Edna Goldstein; R Goldstein; H Goldstein.

Beneficial area: UK and Israel.

Information available: Full accounts are on file at the Charity Commission.

General: The assets of the trust have been steadily increasing and in 1992/93 were £1.6 million. These generated an income of £121,000. 18 grants were given totalling £42,000. About half the grants went to Jewish causes and most were recurrent from the previous year.

The main beneficiaries which appear to receive regular grants were the Jewish Philanthropic Association (£22,500) and the Ashten Trust (£12,500). Three other grants of over £1,000 went to Jewish Care, Ravenswood Foundation and the Weizmann Institute. The other grants ranged from £60 to £1,000, with a few to non-Jewish organisations including the Cystic Fibrosis Research Trust and the Sportsman's Aid Charity.

Applications: In writing to the correspondent.

The Solomon Family Charitable Trust

£106,000 (1992/93)

Education, religion and welfare

Hillsdown House, 32 Hampstead High Street, London NW3 1QD
0171-794 0677

Correspondent: Sir Harry Solomon

Trustees: Sir Harry Solomon; Lady Judith Solomon; J I Goldring.

Beneficial area: UK.

Information available: Accounts are on file at the Charity Commission, but without a list of grants.

General: Unfortunately very little information is available on this trust. In 1993/94, the trusts assets were £151,000. During the year the company Faithwood Investments went into liquidation, and the investments held in the company by the trust had to be written off.

The trust received gifts of £200,000 in 1992/93 and gave grants totalling £106,000. No information is available on the beneficiaries.

Applications: In writing to the correspondent.

The E C Sosnow Charitable Trust

£33,000 (1992/93)

General

25-31 Moorgate, London EC2R 6AR

Correspondent: E S Birk

Trustees: Elias Birk; E R Fattal; Mrs F J M Fattal.

Beneficial area: UK, overseas.

Information available: Full accounts are on file at the Charity Commission.

General: In 1992/93 the trust had assets of £1 million and an income of £70,000. 32 grants were given totalling £33,000.

The largest grants were given to the London School of Economics (£10,000), Jewish Care (£3,700), Weizman Institute – Hebrew University (£2,500) and Redbridge Youth Centre (£2,200). Other grants included three for £1,500 (two of which were to Birthright), and four for £1,000.

Beneficiaries of smaller grants included British Red Cross Somalia, Medical Foundation for the Victims of Torture and Riding for the Disabled.

Applications: In writing to the correspondent.

The South Square Trust

£147,000 (1993/94)

Social welfare, medical, disability, education

8-10 New Fetter Lane, London EC4A 1RS
0171-203 5000

Correspondent: W Paul Harriman

Trustees: C R Ponter; A E Woodall; W P Harriman; C P Grimwade.

Beneficial area: UK.

Information available: Full accounts are on file at the Charity Commission.

General: In 1993/94, the trust had assets of £2.4 million and an income of £162,000. After administration expenses of £41,000, the trust made grants totalling £147,000. The donations are divided between:

- **Annual donations** totalling £35,000 (35 grants of £1,000 each). All except two of the beneficiaries also received a grant the previous year. Most were national charities in the fields of medical and social welfare such as Action Research, Cruse Bereavement Care, MIND and the Royal Star & Garter Home, with grants also given to charities such as the Woodland Trust and Suffolk Historic Churches Trust.
- **General donations** totalling £45,000 (71 grants mainly for £1,000 or £500, with a few for £250). Six of the beneficiaries also received a grant the previous year. As with annual donations, most grants were to social welfare, medical and disability organisations, with grants also given in the fields of conservation, animal welfare and the arts. The largest grants of £1,500 went to Childlink and the F M Alexander Trust. Other beneficiaries included Alone in London Service, Association of Wheelchair Children, Blue Cross, Community Action Trust, Drug & Alcohol Foundation, Foundation for Conductive Education, Intermediate Technology, Richmond Theatre Trust, Suffolk Wildlife Trust and the Sue Ryder Foundation.
- **Bursaries and sabbaticals** totalling £47,000. Grants were given to five organisations, four of which received grants the previous year: Byam Shaw School of Art, St Paul's School, Textile Conservation Centre and West Dean College. The other grant went to the Slade School of Art.
- **Directly aided and single award payments** totalling £20,000. These are grants to individual students.

Applications: In writing to the correspondent. Individuals should apply by letter with a CV, a photograph, budget and references at least three months before funds are required.

The W F Southall Trust

£170,000 (1993/94)

Quaker, general

c/o Rutters Solicitors, 2 Bimport, Shaftesbury, Dorset SP7 8AY
01747-852377

Correspondent: S Rutter, Secretary

Trustees: Mrs D Maw; C M Southall; D H D Southall; Mrs A Wallis; M Holtom.

Beneficial area: UK.

Information available: Full accounts are on file at the Charity Commission.

General: In 1993/94, the trust had an income of £171,000 and gave grants totalling £170,000. Grants are divided into the following categories (number of grants in brackets):

Central Committees of the Society of Friends	£66,000	(5)
Birmingham District charities	£2,200	(6)
Meeting House appeals	£7,500	(9)
Other Quaker charities	£24,000	(23)
Other charities	£70,000	(117)

The six grants given to charities in the Birmingham district ranged from £300 to £600. Beneficiaries included Birmingham YMCA and Birmingham Royal Institute for the Blind.

Meeting houses from St Andrews to Bath benefitted from grants in that category.

The grants in the "other charities" category were given to a vast array of local and national organisations working variously for human rights, ecology and conservation, overseas aid and development work, health, social welfare and a number of other innovative projects with which Quakers have traditionally been associated with. Grants in this category ranged from £100 to £5,500, with the majority £500 or under.

Grants of £1,000 or more were given to the Bedford Institute Association, Dudley One World, Harmony Community Trust, Intermediate Technology, Money for Madagascar, Northern Refugee Centre, Open Door, Oxfam, Responding to Conflict, Tools for Self Reliance, UNA Trust and the Woodland Trust.

Exclusions: No grants to individuals.

Applications: In writing to the correspondent.

The Jessie Spencer Trust

£107,000 (1993/94)

General

Evershed Solicitors, 14 Fletcher Gate, Nottingham NG1 2FX
0115-936 6000

Correspondent: The Trustees

Trustees: V W Semmens; C W H Morton; Mrs P C Hanmer; Mrs E K M Brackenbury.

Beneficial area: UK, with a preference for Nottinghamshire.

Information available: Accounts are on file at the Charity Commission, but without a list of grants for 1993/94.

General: In 1993/94, the trust had assets of £1 million and an income of £99,000. Grants totalled £112,000. No grants list was available for this year.

In 1992/93, 92 grants totalled £60,000. Eight grants were for £2,000 to £5,000 including those to Crest Appeal, Home Farm Trust, Macmillan Fund – Haywood House Appeal, Peter Le Marchant Trust, Nottingham YWCA, Southwell Minster Appeal and two churches.

Other grants ranged from £100 to £1,000. The trust gave to a very wide range of organisations in Nottinghamshire, whilst outside Nottinghamshire grants were awarded to the Alone in London Service, Boys Brigade Belfast, British Red Cross, Centrepoint Soho, Childline and DEBRA.

Applications: In writing to the correspondent including the latest set of audited accounts. Unsuccessful applications will not be acknowledged.

Spitalfields Market Training Initiative

£209,000 (1993/94)

Education, training in Bethnal Green

St Margaret's House, 21 Old Ford Road, London E2 6LX
0181-980 2092

Correspondent: Jim Smith

Trustees: Nuno Guerreiro; John Jordan; William Kelly; Mark Kiddle; Peter Metcalfe; Peter Woof; Cllr. Kofi Appiah; Cllr. Abdul Rohim; Karen Goldman.

Beneficial area: London Borough of Tower Hamlets, specifically Bethnal Green.

Information available: Full information was supplied for this entry by the correspondent. Full accounts are on file at the Charity Commission.

General: The initiative was "founded in 1990 by the Bethnal Green Economic Development Unit to oversee the distribution of planning gain monies resulting from the relocation of Spitalfields Market which were specifically allocated to training local people for employment or re-employment", especially those living in the London borough of Tower Hamlets. It has been covenanted £150,000 a year for the next five years by the Spitalfields Development Agency and could grow to become quite a strong local force. The trustees were nominated by local bodies and selected for their knowledge of training and employment issues in Bethnal Green.

To date funding has been "mainly in the field of information technology although woodworking and horticultural projects have been funded. The majority of grant awards have been further complemented by Government and European funding initiatives available to inner urban areas and LETEC.

"The first award was made to secure the establishment of a quality training centre which would meet the future accommodation needs of training organisations within Bethnal Green. The major subsequent awards have served to establish a series of 21 week computer aided graphic and design courses run by Tower Hamlets Advanced Technology Training and customised training projects tailored to meet the specific demands of local employers undertaken by Community Job Link East, mainly in the administrative field. Trustees have expressed the wish to consider proposals for artisan training in the practical fields of plumbing, electricians etc.."

In 1993/94, the trust had an income of £159,000 including the £150,000 covenant. Grants totalled £209,000 given in 12 large grants: TH Advance Technology Training (£56,000); Community Job Link East (£28,000); Poetry in Wood (£23,000); LCT (£21,000); Action Resource Centre and BG Training Centre (£15,000 each); Davenant Centre and Toynbee (£14,000 each); Spitalfields Farm (£9,000); Avenues Unlimited (£6,500); Legal Ease (£5,000) and TH Health Strategy Group (£2,000).

Exclusions: No grants to individuals and no grants to organisations based outside Bethnal Green.

Applications: Applications are invited from accredited training organisations serving Bethnal Green residents to provide training matched to local employers' needs (trainees must be 18 years or over). The main criteria is that it should be aimed at existing job opportunities. Applications are considered for awards twice yearly. The Initiative regrets that it cannot send replies to applications outside the areas of interest described above.

The Stanley Charitable Trust

£65,000 (1990/91)

Jewish religious charities

8 Stanley Road, Salford M7 4EG
0161-205 7055

Correspondent: A M Adler

Trustees: A M Adler; I Adler; J Adler.

Beneficial area: UK, with a preference for Greater Manchester.

Information available: Brief accounts for 1990/91 are on file at the Charity Commission.

General: We have not been able to obtain more recent finanicial information on this trust, although the trust did clarify its policy for this entry.

In 1990/91, this trust owned 30% of the Nailsea Estate Co and also had £204,000 in property. Its income of £113,000 included £36,000 from rent, £33,000 loan interest and £41,000 "share of surplus joint venture". Expenditure totalled £39,000, including £31,000 on a bank overdraft. This left a net income of £74,000 out of which £65,000 was given in unspecified donations.

The trust supports Jewish religious charities, with a preference for those in Greater Manchester and for projects and people known to the trustees.

Exclusions: Only registered charities are supported.

Applications: In writing to the correspondent, but the trust states funds are fully allocated for the near future.

The Stanley Foundation Ltd

£73,000 (1986/87)

Elderly, medical, education, social welfare

19 Holland Park, London W11 3TD

Correspondent: The Secretary

Trustees: The Council of Management: Nicholas Stanley (Chairman); D J Aries; M D A Stanley; S R Stanley; Albert Rose; P T Stanley.

Beneficial area: UK.

Information available: The only accounts on file at the Charity Commission since those for 1976/77 are those for 1986/87. This situation has not changed since the last edition of this Guide.

General: In 1986/87, the trust gave 59 grants totalling £73,000. The five largest grants of £5,000 were given to: Thomas Heatherley Educational Trust; University College London; Chest Heart & Stroke Association; Ludgrove School and the School of Pharmacy. A further 31 grants of £1,000 or over were given to wide ranging and mainly national charities involved with elderly people, children and youth, sickness and disability and education. The remaining 19 grants were for £500 or under, including one for £5.

We have not been able to update this information, other than obtain an income figure for 1992/93 from the Charity Commission database – £148,000.

The trust has stated that most of its funds are committed for the near future.

Applications: In writing to the correspondent.

The Peter Stebbings Memorial Trust

£73,000 (1992/93)

Welfare, general

2 Langland Gardens, Hampstead,
London NW3 6PY
0171-435 4416

Correspondent: The Clerk to the Trustees

Trustees: Mrs Pamela Mary Cosin; Nicholas Frank Cosin; Mrs Jennifer Mary Clifford; Andrew John F Stebbings.

Beneficial area: Worldwide.

Information available: Full accounts are on file at the Charity Commission.

General: The trust was set up in 1977 by Dr Cyril Frank Cosin. It supports charities generally but has a preference for:
1. Medical research and education;
2. The welfare of people who are sick, poor or elderly.

In 1992/93, the trust had assets of £680,000 and an income of £59,000, £10,000 of which was received from donations. It gave 41 grants totalling £73,000, the largest of which were to Crossroads and Westminster Pastoral (£10,000 each); North London Hospice, MIND, Royal Marsden Hospital and Field Lane Homeless Centre (£5,000 each); Family Service Units (£3,000); St John's Hospice (£2,500) and CAS (£2,000).

There were 24 grants of £750 to £1,200 to mainly national organisations such as Songmakers Almanac; Intermediate Technology Development; Royal Surgical Aid Society; Help the Aged; Oxfam; NSPCC; Amnesty International; ARMS; Ravenswood Foundation and a number of benevolent funds (eg. police, medical, musicians). Eight smaller grants of £50 to £500 were given to organisations such as: RNLI; Royal Academy of Music; Royal Free Hospital and St Helens Hospice.

Applications: The trust only supports charities known to the trustees. Further applications are not required.

The Sir Sigmund Sternberg Charitable Foundation

£49,000 (1992/93)

Jewish, Catholic and interfaith causes, general

18 St George Street, Hanover Square,
London W1R 0LL
0171-493 1205

Correspondent: D Clayton

Trustees: Sir S Sternberg; M Sternberg; Lady Hazel Sternberg.

Beneficial area: Worldwide.

Information available: Full accounts are on file at the Charity Commission.

General: In 1992/93, the trust had assets of £1.8 million and an income available for distribution of £122,000. Grants totalled only £49,000.

142 grants were made, mostly under £1,000. Larger grants were given to the Institute of Archaeo-Metalurgical Studies (£13,000 in several grants), Council of Christians and Jews (£3,500), St John Ambulance (£2,000) and the Weizman Institute (£1,300).

Many of the grants appear to be recurrent, and about half were to Jewish organisations. Smaller grants were given to a range of organisations including the Airey Neave Trust, Apex Trust, Cancer Relief Macmillan Fund, Royal College of Music, Simon Community and the Turkish Earthquake Fund.

Applications: The foundation has stated in the past that its funds are fully committed.

The Stevenson Family's Charitable Trust

£58,000 (1993/94)

General

33 King William Street, London
EC4R 9AS
0171-280 2840

Correspondent: H A Stevenson

Trustees: H A Stevenson; Mrs C M Stevenson; J F Lever.

Beneficial area: Worldwide.

Information available: Full accounts are on file at the Charity Commission.

General: The trust had assets of only £169,000 in 1993/94 and up to this year was accumulating income. In 1990/91, grants totalled £18,000 from an income of £26,000 and in 1992/93 grants totalled £49,000 from an exceptionally high income of £173,000 (which included £158,000 Gift Aid payment). In 1993/94, the trust had an income of only £13,000 and gave grants totalling £58,000.

23 grants were made with the largest to the Institute of Child Health (£16,500), Shakespeare Globe Trust (£16,000), St Michael & All Angels, Sunninghill (£10,000) and St Hilda's College, Oxford (£5,250).

The remaining grants ranged from £50 to £1,350 and were mainly to medical and welfare causes, with arts and heritage organisations also benefiting. Beneficiaries included Ethiopaid (£1,350), the Salvation Army and British Museum Society (both £1,000), ACET (£600) and the Sick Children's Trust (£350). About nine of the grants were recurrent.

The previous year almost half the grant total was given to Glyndebourne Productions Ltd (£24,000 to the building fund) and £10,000 went to St Mary's Hospital Medical School Development Trust.

Applications: In writing to the correspondent.

The Stoll Moss Theatres Foundation

£81,000 (1993)

Theatre, general

21 Soho Square, London W1V 5FD

Correspondent: Richard Johnston

Trustees: Mrs Janet Holmes à Court; Sir Michael Clapham; R A Johnston; Derek Williams.

Beneficial area: UK.

Information available: Full accounts are on file at the Charity Commission.

General: The trust currently maintains a limited programme of support for projects it has initiated and does not provide funding in response to applications. This policy will be reviewed in July 1997. The primary focus of the trust has been the advancement of development of the theatrical arts, with the major beneficiary in previous years being the Almeida Theatre.

The foundation is mainly funded by a covenanted donation from Heytesbury (UK) Ltd.

In 1993 (over an 18 month accounting period), the trust had an income of £83,000, and gave 17 grants totalling £81,000. The largest grants were to Merton College (£55,000), Black Swan Theatre Co (£9,000) and New Musicals Alliance (£5,000).

In 1994, grants of £1,000 to £2,500 were made to Fin De Siecle Theatre Company, Mercury Workshop, NSPCC, RADA, Sarah Esdaile Productions, Shape London, Soho Theatre Company, Talawa Theatre Company and Zanana Theatre Company.

Applications: Rather than responding to applications, the foundation prefers to initiate its own projects.

The Stoller Charitable Trust

£103,000 (1993/94)

General

c/o Seton Healthcare Group plc, Tubiton House, Oldham, Lancs OL1 3HS
0161-652 2222

Correspondent: Roger Gould

Trustees: Norman Stoller; Diane Stoller; Roger Gould; Fred Fowler.

Beneficial area: UK, with some preference for the North West.

Information available: Accounts are on file at the Charity Commission.

General: The trust owns about one million shares in Seton Healthcare Group plc, which went public for £23 million in 1990. It gave grants totalling £103,000 in 1993/94. The size of grants varies and a wide range of causes is supported. There is a bias towards charities in the north west of England, where the trust is based.

Previous recipients have included established charities such as Help the Aged, Oxfam, RNIB, RNLI, St John's Ambulance, Salvation Army and Save the Children, and local causes such as Oldham Museum, Royal Northern College of Music and Salford University.

Applications: In writing to the correspondent.

The Stone Foundation

£60,000 (1992/93)

Research into addiction, medical research

20 Wilton Row, London SW1X 7NS
0171-235 4871

Correspondent: Lady Gosling, Chair of the Trustees

Trustees: Lady Shauna Gosling; Dr R I Wolman; Lady Treacher; Dr B Wells.

Beneficial area: UK.

Information available: Full accounts are on file at the Charity Commission.

General: The foundation exists to fund the research, education and treatment of chemical dependency, eating disorders and other addictions, as well as supporting organisations working to combat poverty. Initially the foundation funded a research project into the availability and quality of all treatment facilities in the UK (private and NHS). Further research was carried out into services and treatment methods in the USA and to a limited extent in Europe.

Grants have hitherto been made to the Self Help Addiction Recovery Programme, Action on Addiction, Addiction Recovery Foundation, Centre for Research on Drugs & Health Behaviour and the Liver Foundation. The trust continues to research developments in treatment methods in the US and elsewhere and the possibility of their adaptation for use in the UK.

In 1992/93, the trust had assets of £2.2 million and an income of £110,000. Two grants of £30,000 each were given to: Self Help Addiction Recovery Programme (the final payment of a three-year commitment) and the British Liver Trust for a research fellowship on alcoholic liver disease.

Applications: In writing to the correspondent.

The M J C Stone Charitable Trust

£175,000 (1989/90)

Medicine, education, animals and children

Estate Office, Ozleworth Park, Wotton under Edge, Gloucestershire GL12 7QA
01435-845591

Correspondent: M J C Stone

Trustees: M J C Stone; Louisa Stone; C R H Stone; N J Stone; A J Stone.

Beneficial area: UK.

Information available: Full accounts are on file at the Charity Commission up to 1989/90.

General: The most recent information available is for 1989/90, when the trust had assets of £503,000 and an income of £214,000 of which £94,000 came from covenants.

Grants totalled £175,000, of which the most significant were £100,000 given to St Catherine's Hospice and £25,000 to the Game Conservancy Trust. Other sizable grants included £10,000 to the European Business School Development Foundation and Friends of Killhope, and £5,000 to each of the Peter Scott Memorial Appeal, BBC Children in Need Appeal, and Tower Hamlets Environment Trust.

Ten other grants were for £1,000 with beneficiaries including St Johns' Ambulance, Surrey Farming & Wildlife Advisory Group, Mental Health Foundation and Royal Agricultural Benevolent Institution. The remaining grants ranged from £100 to £500.

Applications: In writing to the correspondent.

The Janatha Stubbs Foundation

£54,000 (1993/94)

General

Messrs Roberts Legge & Co, PO Box 4, Liverpool L37 1YJ

Correspondent: J H Roberts

Trustees: J H Roberts; Mrs J L Walker; D W Stubbs; J H Roberts.

Beneficial area: Worldwide.

Information available: Full accounts are on file at the Charity Commission.

General: In 1993/94, the trust had assets of £119,000 and an income of £55,000, of which £48,000 was given by the Moores Family Charitable Foundation.

The trustees state: "Donations made during the year reflect the foundation's continuing support for education in the fine arts and the provision of facilities for recreation and leisure time occupation. A new development in the latter field was begun in February 1989 with the Foundation of Ir Razzett Tal Hbiberija, a leisure park of four acres in a fishing port in Malta. It is especially designed for the needs and relaxation of handicapped people of all denominations. At present the park is held on a 10-year lease with an option to purchase by November 1994 at a cost of £150,000".

12 grants were given totalling £54,000 of which by far the largest was £39,000 to Razzett Tal Hbiberija. A further £8,000 was given towards ballet fees and costs. No other grant was for more than £1,600 with beneficiaries including Lyons Music Conservatoire (£1,600), Playing Fields Association (£1,200) and Mount Carmel Hospital (£885). Tarxien Parish Church and Tarxien Youth Club both received grants (£300 and £950 respectively) as did two youth centres (Sirens and Zabbar).

Applications: Unsolicited applications are not considered.

Sueberry Ltd

£118,000 (1991/92)

Jewish

11 Clapton Common, London E5 9AA
0181-806 5142

Correspondent: Mrs M Davis

Trustees: J Davis; Mrs M Davis; Mrs H Davis.

Beneficial area: UK and overseas.

Information available: Full accounts are on file at the Charity Commission.

General: The trust had an income of £124,000 in 1991/92, mostly derived from covenants. Over 150 grants were given totalling £118,000. All the grants went to Jewish organisations, the largest being £33,000 to the Society of the Friends of the Torah (£39,000 in 1990/91). Grants of between £5,000 and £11,000 went to Friends of Lanaido Hospital, Hachnosas Kalah and Shallix Co Ltd. Most of the grants were for under £500 (nearly half were under £100) and recurrent from previous years.

Four non-Jewish organisations received support in 1990/91: the Friends of Incurables, Great Ormond Street Hospital, National Association for Mental Health and the Spastics Society (now SCOPE), all receiving grants of less than £100.

Applications: In writing to the correspondent.

The Alan Sugar Foundation

£223,000 (1993/94)

Jewish, general

Smallfields, 53 Broad Street, Green Road, Great Totham, Maldon, Essex CM9 8NW

Correspondent: Colin Sandy

Trustees: A M Sugar; C T Sandy.

Beneficial area: UK, overseas.

Information available: Full accounts are on file at the Charity Commission.

General: In 1993/94, the trust's assets were valued at £217,000. The trustees gave grants totalling £223,000, mainly to Jewish organisations. The seven beneficiaries were Jewish Care (£50,000); United Synogogue Educational Trust (£150,000), Redbridge Jewish Youth & Community Centre (£11,000), GRET (£5,000), Metropolitan Police Benevolent Fund (£5,000), Helen Harris Memorial Trust (£1,000) and Macmillan Cancer Research Fund (£500).

In 1992/93, seven grants totalled £538,000. The three major beneficiaries were the same, with Jewish Care and United Synagogue Educational Trust receiving the same amounts both years, and Redbridge Jewish Youth & Community Centre received an exceptional £298,000. The other recipients were the Ravenswood Foundation (£25,000), Jew's College, London (£10,000), National Youth Theatre (£5,000) and Babes in Arms (£500).

Exclusions: No grants for individuals.

Applications: In writing to the correspondent.

The Sutasoma Trust

£42,000 (1992/93)

Education, general

Palmer Wheeldon, Daedalus House, Station Road, Cambridge CB1 2RE

Correspondent: J M Lichtenstein

Trustees: J H R Carver; M K Hobart; Dr A R Hobart; M A Burgauer; J M Lichtenstein.

Beneficial area: Worldwide.

Information available: Full accounts are on file at the Charity Commission.

General: The trust's object is "to advance education in particular by providing grants to graduate students in the social sciences and humanities".

The trustees report in 1992/93 stated: "The trustees have committed themselves to regular donations totalling approximately £21,000 per annum. The trustees have also morally committed themselves to providing a maximum of £6,000 per annum for donations to applicants under 'the hardship fund'. This provides assistance by way of small single payments (maximum £350) to full-time students for one-off projects related to their studies".

In 1992/93, there were 14 annual donations, some continuing to 1994, others to 1996, three until further notice and one indefinitely. Recipients include Dr Carey of the Cambodia Trust, Emslie Horniman Anthropological Scholarship Fund, Health Unlimited, Universitas Udayana and the Womens Council.

£6,000 was given to the hardship fund with the remaining £25,000 given in grants of £1,000 or £2,000. Beneficiaries included Medical Aid to Bosnia and the Victoria & Albert Museum, with a further grant given to Health Unlimited. A number of annual and other grants were given to named individuals at research institutions.

Applications: In writing to the correspondent.

● Swire Charitable/John Swire/Sykes/Sylvanus

The Swire Charitable Trust

£78,000 (1992)

General

John Swire & Sons Ltd, Swire House,
59 Buckingham Gate, London SW1E 6AJ
0171-834 7717

Correspondent: G D W Swire

Trustees: Sir J Swire CBE; Sir Adrian Swire; G D W Swire; M J B Todhunter; P Baring; Sir Kerry St Johnston.

Beneficial area: Worldwide.

Information available: Accounts are on file at the Charity Commission up to 1992, but without a grants list since that for 1991.

General: In 1992, the trust had assets of over £2.2 million, the bulk of it held in Swire companies' shares. The income was £104,000 with grants totalling £78,000. The accounts do not specify the beneficiaries in that year, but in 1991 the Glyndebourne Building Fund received £25,000, Ashmolean Museum £20,000, Cystic Fibrosis Research Trust £8,000 and the Ranfurly Library Service £4,500.

The other grants ranged from £20 to £4,000 to a range of organisations including Marrow Environment Fund (£4,000), British Dyslexia Association (£1,500), Understanding Industry (£1,000), Pathfinder Association 50th Anniversary and Ungweni Orphanage Trust – Romania (both £500), Jubilee Sailing Trust, Reeds School and Suffolk Wildlife Trust (each £250).

Applications: In writing to the correspondent.

The John Swire (1989) Charitable Trust

£81,000 (1993)

General

John Swire & Sons Ltd, Swire House,
59 Buckingham Gate, London SW1E 6AJ
0171-834 7717

Correspondent: G D W Swire

Trustees: Sir John Swire CBE; G D W Swire; J S Swire; B N Swire; M C Robinson; Lady Swire.

Beneficial area: Worldwide.

Information available: Accounts are on file at the Charity Commission, but without a list of grants.

General: The trust was established in 1989 by Sir John Swire. In 1993, it had assets of £1.3 million and an income of £167,000. Grants totalled £81,000 leaving a surplus of £86,000. The previous year there was a surplus of £40,000. It is not known whether the trust is still building up its assets or accumulating funds for some future large project.

No details of the grants made was available for 1993. In 1991, the trust gave grants to the Cancer Relief Macmillan Fund (£10,000), Kent Gardens Trust (£2,500), and King's School Canterbury, National Autistic Care & Training Appeal, and University College and Middlesex Hospitals (all £1,000).

18 other grants were for £500 or less to a range of causes including the British Trust for Ornithology, Hornsey Trust for Handicapped Children, Kurdish Disaster Fund, Pilgrims Hospice Canterbury, River Derwent Appeal and the Royal Academy Trust.

Applications: In writing to the correspondent.

The Hugh & Ruby Sykes Charitable Trust

£188,000 (1993/94)

General, medical, local

Bamford Hall Holdings Ltd, Bamford,
Sheffield S30 2AU
01433-651190

Correspondent: Hugh Sykes

Trustees: Hugh Sykes; Ruby Sykes.

Beneficial area: Principally South Yorkshire and Derbyshire.

Information available: Accounts for 1993/94 are on file at the Charity Commission. They do not have a list of grants. Information for this entry was supplied by the trust.

General: Set up in 1987 for general charitable purposes by Hugh Sykes and his wife Ruby Sykes, the trust had assets of £1.6 million by 1994, comprised largely from capital and revenue donated by the founders.

The trust made interest-free loans of about £6,000 in 1993/94. Total expenditure was £189,000 including £188,000 given in grants.

The trust has noted that "it is the policy of the trust to distribute income and preserve capital". Existing commitments are expected to absorb income until 1996 when the trustees plan to review their grant-making policy.

Recent commitments have included those to the South Yorkshire Foundation, Peak Park Trust, a number of medical charities including St Luke's Hospice and Westcare, and national charities including Westminster Abbey Trust and Prince's Youth Business Trust.

Applications: To the correspondent in writing. In order to save administration costs, replies are not sent to unsuccessful applicants. If the trustees are able to consider a request for support, it is intended to express interest within one month. "It would be appreciated if applicants could enclose an sae."

The Sylvanus Charitable Trust

£165,000 (1992)

Animal welfare

5 Raymond Buildings, Grays Inn, London
WC1R 5DD

Correspondent: J C Vernor Miles

Trustees: J C Vernor Miles; A D Gemmill.

Beneficial area: Worldwide.

Information available: Full accounts are on file at the Charity Commission.

General: The trust was founded by Claude, Countess of Kinnoull, of California, USA, who was primarily interested in animal welfare and religion. Most of the trust's money goes to animal welfare causes.

In 1992, the trust had assets of £1.1 million and an income of £172,000, including £119,000 from the sale of investments. Ten grants totalling £165,000 were given.

The largest were to RSPCA (£65,000), Society for St Pius X – England (£50,000 towards the cost of property for a new school in Highclere, Berkshire); Fraternity of Saint Pius X – Switzerland (£25,000). The RSPCA receives a regular grant, the other two did not receive a grant the previous year; but have in the past.

All the other beneficiaries received a grant the previous year. In the UK grants were given to the Donkey Sanctuary, FRAME, National Canine Defence League and PDSA. Grants ouside the UK were given to the Instituto Zoofilo Quinta Carbone (Portugal), Mauritius Wildlife Appeal and Stiftung Lumen Gentium (Switzerland).

A further grant of $9,000 was paid from the US$ account to the Department of National Parks & Wildlife Management (Zimbabwe). This account had an income of $42,000.

Applications: In writing to the correspondent, but note that the income of the trust is usually fully committed.

The Stella Symons Charitable Trust

£34,000 (1993/94)

General

20 Mill Street, Shipston-On-Stour, Warwickshire CV36 4AW

Correspondent: J S S Bosley

Trustees: Mrs M E Mitchell; J S S Bosley; Mrs K A Willis.

Beneficial area: UK, with preference for Warwickshire.

Information available: Full accounts are on file at the Charity Commission.

General: In 1993/94, the trust had assets of £670,000 and an income of £56,000. Grants totalled £34,000 leaving £21,000 surplus for the year. The trust also had a surplus of £50,000 in the previous year and still appears to be building up its assets.

The trustees gave grants to 118 organisations all but two of which were for £500 or less. The exceptions were £1,250 to Stratford Ambulance and £1,000 to Chobe Wildlife Trust. Most grants were to health and welfare organisations such as RUKBA, Hearing Research Trust, Dreams Come True, Samaritans and Shaftesbury Homes.

A number of local organisations received grants, with some preference for Warwickshire, although charities throughout England are supported. Local beneficiaries included Birmingham Rathbone Society, Bolton Mountain Rescue Team, Boys' Brigade (Somerset), Daventry Contact, Lancaster Homeless Action Service and Link-up (Nuneaton) Association. A number of international organisations also received support eg. TAFTA South Africa, Leprosy Mission and African Medical & Research, as did a number of animal welfare/conservation organisations eg. Animal Welfare Trust, Environment Africa Trust and Scottish Wildlife Trust.

Applications: In writing to the correspondent.

The Talbot Trusts

£105,000 (1993/94)

Convalescent and disablement services in Sheffield

Sheffield Health Authority,
Westbrook House, Sharrow Vale Road,
Sheffield S11 8EH
0114-267 0333

Correspondent: Ronald Jones, Clerk

Trustees: C S Barker; R P Harper; Miss B P Jackson; Dr L C Kershaw; Sir John Osborn; Mrs A J Riddle.

Beneficial area: Sheffield.

Information available: Full accounts are on file at the Charity Commission.

General: In 1993/94, the trust had assets of £1.1 million and an income of £112,000. The trust supports convalescent and disablement services not readily available from other sources. Grants totalled £105,000 including £32,000 to Sheffield Area Health Authority specifically for medical social workers' use and £15,000 to St Luke's Nursing Home. Both of these appear to receive a large annual grant.

The remaining 23 grants ranged from £200 to £7,500. 17 received a grant the previous year including Dial-a-Ride (£2,000), Hallam Community Physiotherapy Project (£3,000), North Sheffield Federation for the Disabled (£6,500), Sheffield Family Health Services Authority (£7,500) and Sheffield MIND (£3,000). The other recipients were all medical/health charities in Sheffield, with new beneficiaries in the year including Mencap Homes Foundation (£1,000), Sheffield Childhood Asthma Campaign (£750) and the Sheffield branch of National Schizophrenia Fellowship (£2,000).

Exclusions: No grants for non-registered charities or those that do not directly benefit the residents of Sheffield and surrounding districts.

Applications: Application forms are available from the correspondent, and should be submitted by 31st May and 31st October for the trustees meetings held in July and December.

Talteg Ltd

£92,000 (1992)

Jewish, welfare

90 Mitchell Street, Glasgow G1 3NQ
0141-221 3353

Correspondent: F S Berkeley

Trustees: F S Berkeley; M Berkeley; A Berkeley; A N Berkeley; M Berkeley; Miss D L Berkeley.

Beneficial area: UK, with a preference for Scotland.

Information available: Full accounts are on file at the Charity Commission.

General: In 1992, the trust had an income of £175,000 including £134,000 in covenants and Gift Aid payments. Grants totalled only £92,000. The trust is building up its assets which stood at £514,000.

48 grants were made of which 34, including the larger grants, were to Jewish organisations. The British Friends of Laniado Hospital received £30,000 and £20,000 was given to both the Centre for Jewish Studies and the Society of Friends of the Torah. The other grants over £1,000 were to JPAIME (£6,000), Glasgow Jewish Community Trust (£5,000), National Trust for Scotland (£2,250) and the Friends of Hebrew University of Jerusalem (£1,000).

The remaining grants were all under £1,000 with several to Scottish charities including Ayrshire Hospice (£530), Earl Haig Fund – Scotland (3200) and RSSPCC (£150). Other small grants went to welfare organisations, with an unusual grant of £775 to Golf Fanatics International.

Applications: In writing to the correspondent.

The A R Taylor Charitable Trust

£57,000 (1993/94)

Health, social welfare, independent schools, military charities, general

c/o Birkett Westhorp & Long, Solicitors, 20-32 Museum Street, Ipswich IP1 1HZ
01473-232300

Correspondent: J Bristol

Trustees: A R Taylor; E J Taylor.

Beneficial area: UK, but with some emphasis on Hampshire.

Information available: Full accounts are on file at the Charity Commission.

General: In 1993/94, £57,000 was given in grants. Half the income is committed to annual gifts; most of the balance is given in one-off grants. In 1993/94, £10,000 went to military charities. Independent schools, churches, hospices and the elderly figured prominently.

Exclusions: No grants to individuals are considered.

Applications: In writing to the correspondent. The trust points out that virtually all the funds available are fully committed and that very few external applicants for grants are ever successful. All applications are submitted to the trustees on a monthly basis. Replies are not sent to unsuccessful applicants.

The Thames Wharf Charity

£50,000 (1991/92)

General

Lee Associates, 6 Great Queen Street, London WC2B 5DG
0171-831 3609

Correspondent: K Hawkins

Trustees: P H Burgess; G H Camamile; J M Young; A Lotay.

Beneficial area: Worldwide.

Information available: Accounts are on file at the Charity Commission up to 1991/92, but without a list of grants.

General: In 1991/92, the trust had assets of £107,000 and an income of £85,000. Part of these assets are a 100% share-holding in Thames Wharf Management Services Ltd.

The grant total of £50,000 is not strictly accurate as it also includes all other expenses incurred by the charity in this its first year of grant-making. As there is no information available about the grants made it is not possible to do more than give this total figure.

Applications: In writing to the correspondent.

The Loke Wan Tho Memorial Foundation

£102,000 (1991/92)

Environment, medical

Coopers & Lybrand, 9 Greyfriars Road, Reading RG1 1JG
01734-597111

Correspondent: The Trustees

Trustees: Lady McNeice; Mrs T S Tonkyn; A Tonkyn.

Beneficial area: Worldwide.

Information available: Full accounts are on file at the Charity Commission.

General: In 1991/92, the trust had assets of £901,000 and an income of £51,000. 12 grants were given ranging from £500 to £20,000, totalling £51,000. The trust appears to make a small number of large grants sometimes for a number of years and a number of smaller one-off grants. Half the grants and most of the grant total went to environment/conservation organisations.

The largest grants were given to the Wildfowl & Wetlands Trust (£20,000), Asian Wetland Bureau (£11,000) and Jersey Wildlife Preservation Trust (£5,000). All three of these charities received the same size grant the previous year, although none of the other beneficiaries did. £2,000 grants went to the the British Ornithologist's Union, Churches Commission on Overseas Students, Liverpool School of Tropical Medicine, Pesticides Trust, St Bede's School and the Natural History Museum. £1,000 each went to Leprosy Mission and Dhammamaat Foundation and £500 to Oxford University Medical School.

Applications: In writing to the correspondent.

The Thompson Charitable Trust

£63,000 (1994)

Social welfare

13A Pond Road, Blackheath, London SE3 0SL
0181-852 8893; Fax: 0181-318 9091

Correspondent: A P Thompson

Trustees: Mrs A R Way; J Way; Mrs P J Leslie.

Beneficial area: UK.

Information available: Full accounts are on file at the Charity Commission.

General: In 1994, the trust had assets of £180,000 and an income of £35,000. Grants in 1993 and 1994 were around £60,000 and will remain at around that level. Its main area of activity is social welfare and, in 1994, it introduced new guidelines. These are:

1. It intends supporting a limited number of ventures for short, often start-up periods and will generally cease after that period is ended; it is interested in self-help projects in areas such as parenting and homelessness, but is fairly fully committed for the next two years.

2. Other commitments will only be made to charities in which members of the settlor's family have some personal interest.

3. The trust does not support major national charities.

4. The trust does not support unsolicited appeals from medical charities.

In 1994, its largest grants were: Deptford Newpin (£10,000, first of three years); Churches Community Care (£6,000, second of three years); Brixwork, Christ Church, North Brixton (£5,000); Opportunity Trust (£5,000, second of three years); Ashoka (£2,500); Church of the Ascension Blackheath (£3,900); Blackheath Concert Halls (£2,000); Debt Crisis Network (£2,000); Amici di Verdi (£1,500); Southwark Homeless Information

Project (£1,500); Breakthrough Breast Cancer (£1,500); Compass (£2,000).

Applications: In writing to the correspondent.

The Thompson Family Charitable Trust

£34,000 (1992/93)

General

1 Dover Street, London W1X 3PJ
0171-491 8839

Correspondent: R B Copus, Secretary

Trustees: D B Thompson; Mrs P Thompson.

Beneficial area: UK.

Information available: Full accounts are on file at the Charity Commission.

General: This trust seems to be consistently underspending its income by a considerable amount. In 1992/93, assets of £12 million generated an income of £1.4 million. Donations for the year totalled £34,000 leaving a surplus of over £1.3 million.

1985/86 was the first year of accounts on file at the Charity Commission. In that year assets were £3.6 million. Since then the trust has never given more than £85,000 in any one year (apart from 1986/87 when it gave £153,000, £84,000 of which was given to the National Horse Racing Museum and £20,000 to the Equine Virology Research Fund).

We understand that the trust is accumulating the majority of its income because certain specific charitable projects that are being considered will require support greater than the current capacity of the trust.

The trust appears to give grants for a wide range of activities. The large grants to equine organisations in 1986/87 appear exceptional. In more recent grant-giving, there may be a preference for health and disability organisations and local grants tend to be given in the South East.

In 1992/93, 12 grants were given including £14,000 to the Ascot Charity Appeal. £5,000 was given to both the National Theatre Endowment Fund and the Racing & Breeding Fine Arts Fund. Other grants were given to Cancer Relief Macmillan Fund (£4,000), Medjugorje Bosnia Appeal (£2,000), League of Friends of Chailey Heritage and British Wheelchair Sports Foundation (both £1,000). Other beneficiaries (of £200 or £500) were the Handicapped Girls' Holiday Group, Imperial Cancer Research Fund, International Agricultural Training Programme and Riding for the Disabled.

In 1991/92, 24 grants were given totalling £85,000. £25,000 was given to the Whitefield Development Trust (Home for Blind Children); £25,000 in two grants to Macmillan Nurses Cancer Fund; £10,000 to St Andrew's Church, Totteridge, and £5,000 each to Cancer Research and the National Theatre. The remainder ranged from £250 to £2,500. Beneficiaries included Help the Hospices, Pembury Hospital Baby Unit, Racing Welfare Trust and British Blind Sport.

Applications: In writing to the correspondent. The trustees meet to consider applications at least once a month (or more often if necessary).

The Thornton Foundation

£143,000 (1989/90)

General

Saffrey Champness, Fairfax House, Fulwood Place, Gray's Inn, London WC1V 6UB
0171-405 2828

Correspondent: G J Holbourn

Trustees: A H Isaacs; G Powell; H D C Thornton; R C Thornton; S J Thornton.

Beneficial area: UK.

Information available: Accounts for 1989/90 are on file at the Charity Commission.

General: No more up-to-date information was on file at the Charity Commission since that contained in the last Edition of this Guide. The information in this entry therefore repeats that of the previous Edition.

In 1989/90, the trust had assets of £2.6 million generating an income of just £87,000. Grants totalled £143,000, the shortfall in income being made up from capital.

The largest grants were £50,000 to the Astrid Trust; £37,000 to Keble College, Oxford; £10,000 each to the Sackpole Trust and the RNLI Special Appeal; £9,000 to Cheltenham Young People's Orchestra and £5,000 each to Helen House and Piper Harrow Foundation. All of these main beneficiaries also received similar size grants the previous year, except the RNLI.

Grants were given for a wide range of charitable purposes and to both national and local organisations. Over half of the 18 grants were recurrent from the previous year.

Applications: In writing to the correspondent.

The Thornton Trust

£112,000 (1993/94)

Evangelical Christian, education, relief of sickness and poverty

Hunters Cottage, Hunters Yard, Saffron Walden, Essex CB11 4AA

Correspondent: D H Thornton

Trustees: D H Thornton; Mrs B Y Thornton; H R Webber; J D Thornton.

Beneficial area: UK and overseas, with a preference for the South East.

Information available: Full accounts are on file at the Charity Commission.

General: In 1993/94, the trust had assets of £1.2 million, generating an income of £101,000. Grants totalling £112,000 were given to 67 organisations. 56 of these had also received a grant the previous year.

The trust supports mainly, but not exclusively, Christian causes including churches, missionary societies and colleges/bible schools.

Applications: The trust states: "Our funds are fully committed to charities which the trustees have supported for many years and we regret that we are unable to respond to the many calls for assistance we are now receiving".

The Tikva Trust

£173,000 (1992)

Christian

Christmas Cottage, 81 Wycombe Road, Marlow, Bucks SL7 3HZ
01628-476988

Correspondent: R A Jameson

Trustees: R A Jameson; R J Flenley.

Beneficial area: Worldwide.

Information available: Accounts are on file at the Charity Commission.

General: In 1991, the trust had an income of £162,000 and gave grants totalling £173,000. No information was available on the beneficiaries, but the trust supports evangelical Christian causes.

Applications: In writing to the correspondent.

The Tolkien Trust

£93,000 (1993/94)

General

1 St Giles, Oxford OX1 3JR
01865-242468

Correspondent: Cathleen Blackburn

Trustees: John Tolkien; Christopher Tolkien; Priscilla Tolkien; Frank Williamson.

Beneficial area: UK.

Information available: Full accounts are on file at the Charity Commission.

General: The residuary estate of J R R Tolkien provides the trust with its income, and although there is no permanent endowment, there should always be an income from book royalties.

In 1993/94, the trust's income was £47,000 of which £44,000 was in royalties. This is down from an income of £89,000 in 1992/93, when £79,000 came in royalties. Grants totalled £93,000 (£108,000 in 1992/93).

46 grants were given to both national and local organisations, most of which had received a grant in the previous year. The largest were £14,000 to Find Your Feet Ltd, £6,000 to the City of Oxford Orchestra and £5,000 each to CAFOD and the Social Care Unit St Martin in the Field, all regular recipients of larger grants.

Other grants ranged from £200 to £4,500. The seven new beneficiaries included the Inter Faith Network (£500), Redwing Horse Sanctuary (£300), RNIB (£500), Sense (£500) and Friends of the Earth (£200). Other recipients of grants included Catholic Housing Aid Society, Chester Aid to the Homeless, CPRE, De Paul Trust, Marie Curie Cancer Care, Medical Foundation for the Victims of Torture, NACRO and Shelter.

Applications: In writing to the correspondent.

The Tory Family Foundation

£51,000 (1992/93)

General in Kent

Five Badgers, Ridgehill Farm, Etchinghill, Folkestone, Kent CT18 8NR

Correspondent: P N Tory

Trustees: P N Tory; J N Tory; Mrs S A Rice.

Beneficial area: International and Kent.

Information available: Full accounts are on file at the Charity Commission.

General: In 1992/93, the trust had an income of £138,000. Expenses totalled £7,000 leaving £131,000 for distribution. Grants totalled £51,000 leaving a surplus of £79,000 for the year. The trust classifies its grants as follows:

Education – 10 grants totalling £17,000 including two to individuals. The largest grants in this category were £3,500 to Metropole Arts Centre, Folkestone and the Folkestone Menuhin Violin Competition (sponsorship of winners). Other beneficiaries included the Newlife Foundation for Handicapped Children, Teachers of Tomorrow and the YMCA.

Local – 4 grants totalling £6,500. Grants were £2,500 to Kent Trust for Nature Conservation to buy Lydden Down, £2,000 to Stowting Community Council for repair of the village hall, £1,500 to Relate Folkestone and £500 to Ashford Samaritans.

Church – 4 grants totalling £3,500 to four churches in Kent.

Health – 8 grants totalling £21,000. The largest grant was £7,000 to the F Matthias Alexander Trust for the publication of research material. The other grants were given to organisations in Kent including a hospital and a hospice, with the exception being a grant of £1,500 to St Benedicts Hospital in the West Indies.

Overseas – 4 grants totalling £3,000 given to Prisoners Abroad, Project Trust, Salvation Army West Indies and VSO.

Exclusions: Applications outside Kent are unlikely to be considered. Only selected correspondence/appeals are acknowledged to keep expenses to a minimum.

Applications: In writing to the correspondent.

The Tower Hill Improvement Trust

£51,000 (1993/94)

General

Atlee House, 28 Commercial Street, London E1 6LR
0171-377 6614

Correspondent: James Connelly, Secretary

Trustees: C G A Parker; Maj Gen C Taylor; David Palmer; Captain D J Cloke; Mrs Davina Walter.

Beneficial area: The East End of London.

Information available: Full accounts are on file at the Charity Commission.

General: Grants can be given to organisations working for the relief of need or sickness; to provide leisure and recreation facilities for social welfare and in support of education; and to provide and maintain gardens and open spaces. The beneficial area covers Great Tower Hill, Tower Hill and St Katherine's Ward in the London borough of Tower Hamlets.

The assets of the trust appear to be steadily rising, with the trust having a regular surplus of income over expenditure. In 1993/94, the trust had assets of £1.3 million and an income of £145,000. Grants totalled £51,000. No further information available.

In 1992/93, £27,000 was given in two grants to Turks Head Co (£25,000) and the Environment Trust (£2,000). The income was £98,000.

In 1991/92, the trust gave five grants totalling £58,000 from an income of £99,000. These were given to St George in the East (£25,000); London Music Hall Trust (£20,000); Ensign Youth Club (£10,000); London Pageant - litter bins (£2,675), and Trinity Square Gardens (£269).

In 1990/91, the trust only gave two grants: £25,000 to the All Hallow Church and £10,000 to St George in the East.

Applications: In writing to the correspondent. The trustees meet every three months to consider applications.

The Jonathan Towler Foundation

£39,000 (1992/93)

General

Hill Farm, Halse, Brackley, Northamptonshire NN13 6DY

Correspondent: Mrs M M Towler

Trustees: Mrs M M Towler; J E Robinson.

Beneficial area: UK.

Information available: Accounts are on file at the Charity Commission, but without a list of grants since those for 1990/91.

General: In 1992/93, the trust had assets of £576,000 and an income of £56,000. Grants totalled £39,000. No further information was available on the grants given, but the trust has a list of regularly supported charities which is unlikely to be added to.

In 1990/91, grants totalled £21,000. The largest were to World Vision (£2,000), Save the Children Fund (£1,250), WWF (£600) and Brackly PCC (£625). About 58 grants were given, most for £500 or £250. A range of causes were supported including health and welfare, overseas aid/development, animal welfare and Christian.

Applications: The trust does not respond to unsolicited applications.

The Tramman Trust

£64,000 (1992)

General

Rufus House, 41 Edgar Road, Winchester SO23 9TN
01962-865393

Correspondent: D A Quayle

Trustees: D A Quayle; S A Quayle; T V Simmonds; J D Quayle.

Beneficial area: UK.

Information available: Full accounts are on file at the Charity Commission up to 1992.

General: In 1992, the trust had assets of £666,000 and an income of £56,000. Grants totalled £64,000, categorised as follows (1991 figures in brackets):

Health & welfare	£16,000	(£19,000)
Children's welfare	£8,000	(£7,000)
Education	£26,000	(£13,000)
Arts & cultural	£2,000	(£6,000)
Other	£12,000	(£4,000)

Health and welfare: 19 grants, the largest being £3,000 to NACRO and £2,000 each to Wessex Nuffield Hospital and Reynaud's & Scleroderma Association. The other grants ranged from £200 to £1,400 including those to Oxfam, Victim Support and Action Research.

Children's welfare: 6 grants including £4,200 to the Children's County Holiday Camp Fund and two grants to the Romanian Orphanage Trust totalling £1,500.

Education: 3 grants including £15,000 to Brighton College and a further £11,000 to support a student at the same college.

Arts & culture: 3 grants including £1,000 to Leith School of Art and a Polish choir tour.

Other: 7 grants including £5,000 to Winchester Cathedral Appeal and £2,000 to Colden Common Community Association. Most of the grants were not recurrent.

The trust states that from 1994 it has committed all its resources to the Beatrice Royal Galleries project in support of contemporary art.

Applications: In writing to the correspondent.

The Constance Travis Charitable Trust

£88,000 (1991/92)

Not known

Quinton Rising, Quinton, Northants NN7 2EF

Correspondent: E R A Travis, Trustee

Trustees: Mrs C M Travis; E R A Travis.

Beneficial area: UK.

Information available: Accounts are on file at the Charity Commission up to 1991/92, but without a list of grants.

General: The trust, originally set up with shares in Travis & Arnold plc, now has assets of £1.9 million mainly in the form of shares in Travis Perkins plc (formed by the merger of Travis & Arnold with Sandell-Perkins in 1988).

These shares generated £87,000 in dividends in 1991/92, and the total trust income was £152,000. Grants totalled £88,000, a drop from £149,000 the previous year, when the total income was £170,000. Unfortunately the accounts do not include any details on the grants given.

Applications: In writing to the correspondent.

The Triangle Trust 1949 Fund

£103,000 to organisations (1993/94)

General

Glaxo House, Berkeley Avenue, Greenford, Middlesex UB6 0NN
0181-966 8285

Correspondent: Mrs S Mehew, Secretary

Trustees: J C Maisey, Chairman; M Pearce; J Seres; Rev D Urquhart; Dr Marjorie Walker; Mrs D Ware; Miss L Wilson.

Beneficial area: UK.

Information available: Accounts are on file at the Charity Commission without a list of grants.

General: In 1993/94, grants totalled £312,000, broken down as follows:

Poverty & hardship relief	£153,000
Education	£56,000
Registered charities	£103,000

No further information was available on the beneficiaries of grants.

Exclusions: No grants for private medicine or education, holidays or overseas educational trips, nursing home fees, loans or research grants.

Applications: The trust's funds are fully allocated. The trustees initiate their own projects and do not respond to unsolicited applications.

The Truemark Trust

£93,000 (1993/94)

General

PO Box 2, Liss, Hampshire GU33 7YW

Correspondent: Mrs W A Collett

Trustees: Mrs Dione Smith; Alan Thompson; Sir William Wood; Michael Collishaw; Michael Meakin; Richard Wolfe.

Beneficial area: UK.

Information available: Full accounts are on file at the Charity Commission.

General: In 1993/94, the trust had assets of £1.4 million and an income of £140,000. Grants totalled £93,000. In 1992/93, income was £113,000 and grants £73,000.

In 1993/94, the trust made 80 grants, ranging from £250 to £8,000, the majority being of £500 or £1,000.

The largest were to the College of Physic Studies (£8,000) and Law for All (£4,000). £2,000 was given to each of the Addictive Diseases Trust, Bristol Cancer Help Centre, Christ Church North Brixton Appeal, Hoxton Health Group, Leap Theatre Workshop, Southwark Playgrounds Trust and Walsall Cancer Centre Appeal.

Almost all were one-off grants to small local charities.

Exclusions: No grants to individuals, or for scientific or medical research or for church buildings.

Applications: In writing to the correspondent, including the most recent set of accounts. Trustees meet four times a year and only applications from eligible bodies are acknowledged.

The Tufton Charitable Trust
(formerly the Wates Charitable Trust)

£21,000 (1993/94)

Christian

16a St James's Street, London SW1A 1ER
0171-930 7621

Correspondent: The Secretary

Trustees: Sir Christopher Wates; Lady Georgina Wates.

Beneficial area: UK.

Information available: Full accounts are on file at the Charity Commission.

General: The trust was registered in May 1989. It appears to have no connection with the Wates Foundation (see *A Guide to the Major Trusts Vol. 1*). It appears to be still building up its assets, regularly having a surplus of income over expenditure:

Year	income	grants
1993/94	£309,000	£21,000
1992/93	£183,000	£8,000
1991/92	£133,000	£37,000

The assets had risen to £617,000 by 1993/94, with £300,000 of the £309,000 income from a Gift Aid payment. Of the £21,000 given in grants £17,500 was given to various churches.

The other ten grants went to Christian, health and welfare causes including £1,700 to the Action Institute for the Study of Religion & Liberty. The remaining grants were all for £500 or less with beneficiaries including the Mary Hare Foundation, Romania Orphanage Trust and Scottish Spina Bifida Association.

Applications: In writing to the correspondent.

The Florence Turner Trust

£115,000 (1993/94)

General

c/o Harvey Ingram, 20 New Walk, Leicester LE1 6TX
0116-254 5454

Correspondent: The Secretary

Trustees: Roger Bowder; Allan A Veasey; Caroline A Macpherson.

Beneficial area: UK, but with a strong preference for Leicestershire.

Information available: Full accounts are on file at the Charity Commission.

General: Florence Turner, then living in 'Sandfield', Leicester, founded the trust in 1973 with an endowment of 106,383 shares in W E Turner Ltd. By 1993/94, there was a wide portfolio of investments with a market value of £2.7 million. The income was £137,000 and grants totalled £115,000.

Of the 120 grants made, the vast majority of recipients were Leicestershire organisations. Many awards were recurrent, about one third for £1,000 or more. The largest grants were given to Leicester Grammar School for bursaries (£14,700) and Braunstone Hall School Minibus Appeal (£10,000).

A wide range of causes were supported including local charities and local (in Leicestershire) branches of national charities. Beneficiaries included Age Concern, Leicester; East Midlands Choir Festival; Hinckley & District Scout Council; Leicester Sea Cadets Corps; Melton Mowbray & District Mencap; PDSA; South Charnwood Summer Playscheme and St Gabriel's Community Centre – Luncheon Club.

Applications: In writing to the correspondent.

The Ultach Trust

£105,000 (1992/93)

Irish language activities

Room 202, Fountain House, 19 Donegall Place, Belfast BT1 5AB
01232-230749

Correspondent: Aodan Mac Poilin, Rosie Ni Bhaoill

Trustees: Ian Adamson; Ruairi O Bleine; Leslie Burnett; Sean O Coinn; Barry Kinghan; Ferdia Mac an Fhaili; Risteard Mac Gabhann; Sue MacGeown; Christopher McGimpsey; Seamus de Napier; Peter Quinn; Maolcholaim Scott.

Beneficial area: Northern Ireland.

Information available: The trust is registered in Northern Ireland.

General: The main aim of the trust is to increase appreciation of the Irish language and culture throughout the Northern Ireland community. The trust funds new and established groups in Northern Ireland. Grants are usually for specific projects and schemes rather than for on-going costs. Particular consideration will be given to groups developing cross-community Irish language activities.

In 1992/93, the trust had assets of £870,000 and an income of £105,000. 67 grants were given totalling £105,000. The largest grants were £10,000 to Bunscoil an Iuir, Newry and Meanscoil Feirste, Belfast. Other grants ranged from £200 to £7,000 including Beechmount Mother & Toddler Group (Belfast), Belcoo & District Historical Society, Downtown Women's Centre (Belfast), Save the Cavehill Campaign (Belfast) and the Linen Hall Library (Belfast).

Exclusions: The trust will not normally fund individuals, support on-going running costs, fund major capital programmes, respond to cutbacks in statutory funding, or support travel expenses, publications or videos.

Applications: On a form available from the correspondent. Monthly meetings are held from September to June and applications can be accepted up to two weeks before each meeting.

The Ulting Overseas Trust

£110,000 (1993/94)

Christian

41 Rectory Park, South Croydon, Surrey CR2 9JR
0181-657 6767

Correspondent: C Harland, Secretary

Trustees: Dr J B A Kessler; Mrs M K Kessler; J S Payne; N W H Sylvester; P D Warren; A J Bale; C Harland; Dr D G Osborne.

Beneficial area: Overseas only.

Information available: Full accounts are on file at the Charity Commission.

General: In 1993/94, the trust had assets of £1.58 million and an income of £106,000. 19 grants totalled £110,000, of which 13 were recurrent.

The three main beneficiaries, who also received similar grants the previous year, were International Fellowship of Evangelical Students (£17,000), Scripture Union (£16,000) and the Langham Trust (£10,000). All the beneficiaries were Christian causes including a number of Bible colleges throughout the world.

Applications: The funds of the trust are already committed. Unsolicited applications cannot be supported.

The Ulverscroft Foundation

£500,000 (1994)

Sick, especially visually impaired people, ophthalmic research

1 The Green, Bradgate Road, Anstey, Leicester LE7 7FU
0116-236 4325

Correspondent: Joann Snookes

Trustees: David Thorpe, Chairman; Dr Frederick Thorpe; Barbara Bassett; Michael Rich; Allan Leach; Michael Down.

Beneficial area: UK plus other English speaking countries, particularly Australia, New Zealand, Canada and the USA.

Information available: Full accounts are on file at the Charity Commission.

General: The foundation was set up in 1974 by Frederick Thorpe, then living in Ulverscroft in Leicestershire, to help sick people or particularly those suffering from defective eyesight and to promote ophthalmic research. Its assets comprise the entire share capital of the Ulverscroft Group Ltd (publishers of large print books) as well as cash and property. The Ulverscroft Group Ltd is a major provider of funds, and the assets of the foundation have risen from £2.7 million in 1986 to £10 million in 1993.

A brochure has been produced by the trust listing projects supported by the foundation to February 1993. These are categorised under the following headings:

- Research and education;
- Ophthalmic and medical equipment and facilities;
- Libraries and associated services;
- Organisations concerned with blind and partially sighted people;
- Recreational.

In the research and education category, major initiatives have been the creation and funding of the Chair of Ophthalmology and the Director of Medical Education at the University of Leicester, and the establishment of a Chair of Ophthalmology at the Royal Australian College of Ophthalmologists, New South Wales, Australia. Other beneficiaries have included "Books on Whee",ls a film to promote the services of the WRVS; Brixham Community College for their Access to Community Education Programme; the publishing of the books Eye Diseases in Hot Climates and Eye Surgery in Hot Climates to be used by field hospitals in third world countries; the Genetic Interest Group and various universities for relevant research.

Grants for equipment and facilities have been given to hospitals, research centres and national charities such as the British Diabetic Association for two mobile Retinopathy Screening services and the British Red Cross Society for a minibus and toy library equipment.

A number of libraries have received support, for example towards computerised reading machines, large print books and specially built mobile libraries for disabled and partially sighted people.

Various local and a few national organisations concerned with blind and partially sighted people have been supported including Aberdeen Old People's Welfare, Blind Centre for Northern Ireland, Brecon & District Disabled Club, British Heart Foundation, Gateshead Dispensary and Leicestershire Association. Grants have been given towards large print books, specialist equipment, specially adapted vehicles and recording equipment. Organisations working overseas have also been supported including Oxfam (for the Shandhani National Eye Donation Society in

Ulverscroft/Underwood/United

Bangladesh), Romanian Orphans' Eye Appeal and St Lucy's School for the Blind in Meru, Kenya.

Grants in the recreational category have been given to organisations to enable blind or partially sighted people to have holidays or take part in various activities.

In addition grants have been given to individuals through the Disability Aid Foundation and Electronic Aids for the Blind.

Applications: In writing to the correspondent. The trustees meet about three times a year to consider applications.

The Underwood Trust

£334,000 (1993/94)

General

32 Haymarket, London SW1Y 4TP

Correspondent: Antony P Cox, Manager

Trustees: C Clark; R Clark; Mrs P A H Clark.

Beneficial area: UK.

Information available: Accounts for 1993/94 are on file at the Charity Commission, but without a schedule of grants.

General: The trust was set up in 1973 by Robert Clark and Mrs M B Clark. It has stated: "Donations are only made to registered charities engaged in the activities covered by the following broad classifications: medicine and health; general welfare; education, sciences, humanities and religion; environmental resources."

The trust's income is committed to long term projects, therefore new applications are very unlikely to be considered. "Apart from a restricted list of annual donations, recurring donations are seldom made."

In 1993/94, the trust had £2.4 million of assets, an increase from £1.6 million in 1992/93, owing to shares worth £620,000 bequeathed under the will of the late Mrs M B L Clark.

Income for the year 1993/94 was £544,000, with grants totalling £334,000. The accounts for the last two years were skeletal, with no narrative report or list of grants, which compares unfavourably with 1991/92 which had a complete list of grants and showed investments in gilts and Taylor Clark plc.

Grants were allocated as shown in the table below.

The following information is taken from the last Edition of this Guide as no more up-to-date information is available.

In 1991/92, the total grant-aid was £306,000. 52 donations were made, many of them recurrent, and six for £10,000 or more. Most grants were for £1,000 or £5,000.

21 donations were made in the field of medicine and health (which also includes disability), the largest award (£15,000) being to the Association of Stammerers. Hospitals and hospices are featured on the list with £5,000 going to the Friends of Eastbourne Hospitals, the Association of Friends of Westminster Hospital, and King Edward VII's Hospital for Officers. Other awards went to the Royal National Institute for Deaf People, Talking Books for the Handicapped and Invalids at Home.

Education, sciences, humanities and religion received nine donations and the largest grants are featured here. Most went to the Robert Clark Centre for Technical Education (£79,000) and to the National Association of Young Farmers Clubs (£25,000). Arts and heritage seem to fall under this category too. Grants for £10,000 and under were made to an International Musicians Seminar, the London Library, Paisley Abbey Restoration Fund, the organ appeal of the United Reform Church at St Andrew's Frognal and Scottish Opera.

The Chartered Accountants' Benevolent Association are recognised in the field of welfare (a £5,000 donation) and the Royal Association for Disability and Rehabilitation received £3,000 to play Deaf Tennis at The Ball Park. £5,000 went to the RNLI, the Police Dependants' Trust, and advice organisations, including the Samaritans and Childline.

Under environmental resources, £10,000 went to the Crime Concern Trust, whilst £5,000 grants went to the Blue Cross, the Council for the Protection of Rural England, the National Trust, Friends of the Earth, Game Conservancy and the National Trust for Scotland.

Exclusions: No grants to individuals. The trust states that approaches are still received from individuals despite the foundation's absolute exclusion of such applications under any circumstances. Grants are not made for expeditions, nor to overseas projects.

Applications: All applicants should note the statement above that new applications are very unlikely to be considered. There is no application form. Applications are not normally acknowledged.

The United Trusts

£343,000 (1993/94)

General

PO Box 14, 8 Nelson Road, Edge Hill, Liverpool L69 7AA
0151-709 8252

Correspondent: Fred Freeman, Chairman, or John Pritchard, Administrator

Trustees: Up to 20 people elected by members.

Beneficial area: UK, but at present mainly north west England.

Information available: Literature available from United Trusts.

General: The trusts promote tax-free charitable giving (mainly but not exclusively payroll giving) through the formation and development of Local United Trust Funds. These consist of

Category	1993/94 £	%	1992/93 £	%	1991/92 £	%
Medicine and health	77,000	23	69,000	33	83,000	26
Education, sciences, humanities and religion	140,000	42	64,000	31	145,000	45
Welfare	84,000	25	42,000	20	54,000	17
Environmental resources	33,000	10	31,000	15	41,000	13

workplace controlled charitable funds (workplace trusts), local citizen controlled charitable funds (community trusts) and "local trust funds" for distribution by United Trusts within the donor-designated local area.

Grants are given to benefit charities serving within the local communities concerned. Potentially all charities are eligible, including in some areas grants for the relief of individual cases of poverty and hardship (these are routed through "umbrella charities"). United Trusts is not in itself a payroll-giving agency charity. Services are supplied in association with United Way, Charities Aid Foundation and all payroll-giving agency charities.

A breakdown of distributions by local United Trust Funds (including community trusts) for 1993/94 (and 1992/93) was as follows:

Merseyside and Cheshire	£127,000	(£182,000)
Greater Manchester	£4,000	(£6,000)
Cumbria	£1,000	(£7,000)
Lancashire	£10,000	(£7,000)
Total	**£142,000**	**(£202,000)**

The breakdown of distributions by United Trusts Workplace Trusts in 1993/94 (and 1992/93) was:

Merseyside and Cheshire	£151,000	(£166,000)
Cumbria	£41,000	(£41,000)
Lancashire	£8,000	(£4,000)
Total	**£201,000**	**(£211,000)**

Exclusions: No grants to individuals directly. "Grants to individuals are made through 'umbrella charities' in cases where the government does not feel it has a responsibility."

Applications: Application should be made to the secretary of the local United Trust Fund concerned.

The David Uri Memorial Trust

£16,000 (1993/94)

Jewish, general

48 Avenue Close, Avenue Road, London NW8 6DA
0171-722 3922

Correspondent: Mrs Z S Blackman, Trustee

Trustees: Mrs Z S Blackman.

Beneficial area: Worldwide.

Information available: Accounts are on file at the Charity Commission, but without a list of grants since that for 1991/92.

General: In 1993/94, the trust had assets of £871,000 and an income of £132,000 mostly from rents. Grants totalled £16,000 leaving a surplus of £61,000. The previous year grants totalled £17,000 from an income of £83,000, leaving a surplus of £45,000. It is not known whether the trust is still seeking to build up its assets or accumulating funds for a major project in the future.

No information is available on the beneficiaries of the trust since 1991/92. In that year grants totalled £28,000, with most grants to Jewish organisations. The largest were £15,000 to Yakar Education Foundation and £2,500 to the National Jewish Chaplaincy Board. All the other grants to Jewish organisations were under £500.

Grants to non-Jewish organisations included £5,000 to the Jefferies Research Wing Trust, with all the others receiving under £500, including Age Concern, Crisis at Christmas and NSPCC.

Applications: In writing to the correspondent.

The Albert Van Den Bergh Charitable Trust

£54,000 (1993/94)

Jewish, general

2 Bloomsbury Street, London WC1B 3ST

Correspondent: M R Nathan

Trustees: P A Van Den Bergh; M R Nathan.

Beneficial area: UK and overseas.

Information available: Full accounts are on file at the Charity Commission.

General: The trust was established in 1987, and has now built up assets of £1.1 million. In 1993/94, the income was £76,000 and grants totalled £53,000.

72 grants were given to institutions totalling £44,000, and 18 grants to individuals for degree level studies totalling £9,000. The largest grants went to charities which also received large grants the previous year: United Charities Fund – Liberal Jewish Synagogue (£4,500); Association for Jewish Youth and Stepney Jewish Clubs & Settlement (both £4,000); Council and Care for the Elderly (£2,800) and Bishop of Guildford's Foundation (£2,500).

Eight grants were for £1,000 and the rest for £100 to £500. Most grants went to national charities in the fields of health, welfare and disability. About 10 grants went to Jewish organisations and 10 to Surrey-based charities. A few grants went to local charities elsewhere, mainly in the London area.

Applications: In writing to the correspondent, including accounts and budgets.

The Van Neste Foundation

£177,000 (1992/93)

Social welfare, third world

15 Alexandra Road, Bristol BS8 2DD
0117-929 7151

Correspondent: Fergus Lyons, Secretary

Trustees: M T M Appleby (Chairman); F J F Lyons (Secretary); G J Walker MBE.

Beneficial area: UK, especially Avon, and overseas.

Information available: Full accounts are on file at the Charity Commission.

General: The trustees currently give priority to the following:
1. Third world;
2. Disabled and elderly people;
3. Advancement of religion;
4. Community and Christian family life;
5. Respect for the sanctity and dignity of life.

In 1992/93, the trust had assets of £3.7 million and an income of £218,000. 51 grants were given totalling £177,000.

The largest grants went to Mill Hill African Missionaries (£21,000), Catholic Students Trust (£15,000), South Cotswold Benevolent Polish Project (£13,000), and £10,000 each to Avon District Boys' Club, Gordonstoun Thailand Appeal & Water Project, Movement for Faith & Justice and the Citizens' Organising Foundation. 11 further grants were for £5,000 and the rest ranged from £250 to £4,000.

About one third of the grants went to organisations in the Avon area such as Abbeyfield Bristol Homes for the Elderly, Avon Youth Service, Bristol Cyrenians and Victim Support Service Bristol.

Other beneficiaries included the Rainbow Centre, International Conference of Priests Africa, Disabled Living Services, Medical Education Trust, Samaritans and the Serbian Orthodox Church St Saviours.

Exclusions: No grants to individuals.

Applications: No particular form is required to make an application. It should be in the form of a concise letter setting out the clear objectives to be obtained which must be charitable. Information must be supplied concerning agreed funding from other sources and also a timetable for achieving the objectives of the appeal.

The foundation does not normally make grants on a continuing basis. Grants are only considered from registered charities. Applications must be made in writing only.

To keep overheads to a minimum not all applications are acknowledged unless they have been successful. Even then it may be a matter of months before any decision can be expected depending on the dates of trustees' meetings.

The Vardy Foundation

£140,000 (1992/93)

Education in the North East

c/o Reg Vardy plc, Houghton House, Wessington Way, Sunderland SR5 3RJ
0191-549 4949

Correspondent: Mrs Fiona Laughlin, Secretary to the Trustees

Trustees: P Vardy; Margaret Vardy; R Dickinson.

Beneficial area: UK.

Information available: Full accounts are on file at the Charity Commission.

General: The trust was set up in 1989 with general charitable objectives. In 1992/93, it had assets of £777,000, mostly in the form of shares in Reg Vardy plc.

As part of a four-year covenant, a sum of £125,000 gross has been paid to the foundation each year since 1990, and a grant for the same amount has been given to the Emmanuel College CTC (City Technology College) in Gateshead.

In 1992/93, for the first time grants were also given to other organisations: £12,000 to St Michaels, Houghton-le-Spring and £2,000 to Felling Male Voice Choir.

Applications: In writing to the correspondent.

Vendquot Ltd

£11,000 (1991/92)

Jewish education

7 St Andrew's Grove, London N16 5NF

Correspondent: Mrs J Davis, Secretary

Trustees: D Davis; J Davis; Mrs S Davis.

Beneficial area: Worldwide.

Information available: Full accounts are on file at the Charity Commission up to 1991/92.

General: The trust had a large increase in its income in 1991/92 to £134,000 including £60,000 in dividends (possibly from a subsidiary company) and £40,000 in donations. The income was only £28,000 in 1990/91, and £14,000 in 1989/90.

Grants totalled £11,000 in 1991/92, with no grants given the previous year and £14,000 in 1989/90. No grant was for more than £1,250, and most were to Jewish educational organisations.

Applications: In writing to the correspondent.

The Vestey Foundation

£78,000 (1992)

General

c/o Union International plc, 29 Cloth Fair, London EC1A 7JX
0171-710 1212

Correspondent: J R Cuthbert

Trustees: E H Vestey; Rt Hon S G Armstrong; Baron Vestey; Hon M W Vestey; T R G Vestey.

Beneficial area: UK.

Information available: Full accounts are on file at the Charity Commission.

General: The foundation is solely funded from the Western United Investment Company Ltd, the holding company for the Vestey Group of companies. In 1992, the income was £109,000 and grants (in the form of covenants) totalled £78,000. The previous year the income was £99,000 and grants (covenants) totalled £78,000, with a further £11,000 in donations.

The 11 beneficiaries of covenants were the same in both years, with the largest grant, £60,000, to the Royal Veterinary College. Other large grants went to the Royal Opera House (£5,000), Prince's Youth Business Trust (£3,000) and Dunn Nutrition Centre (£2,500). The remaining grants, from £267 to £2,000, included support for three cathedrals, St Paul's, Ely and Liverpool.

All the covenants are for four years except a nine-year commitment to the Royal Veterinary College.

In 1991, other grants were made ranging from £250 to £1,500. The largest were to British Wheelchair Sports Foundation, Care Holidays, Prince's Trust and Rural Youth Trust.

Applications: In writing to the correspondent.

The Vincent Wildlife Trust

£131,000 (1993)

Wildlife, environmental conservation

10 Lovat Lane, London EC3R 8DT
0171-283 2089

Correspondent: Terence O'Connor

Trustees: Vincent Weir, Chairman; Ronald Yarham; Michael Macfadyen.

Beneficial area: UK.

Information available: Full accounts are on file at the Charity Commission.

General: The detailed trustees report included in the 1993 accounts states: "During 1993, most of the trust's resources were directed towards mammal research and conservation, either through grant aiding other organisations and individuals or financing our own projects. 18 staff were employed and all of them, except the two administrative officers at head office, were engaged in mammal work. Nine were working on bats, four on otters, one on polecats, one on dormice and one on mink/water vole interaction".

In 1993, the assets of the trust were £8.6 million and the income £1.4 million. Expenditure on the trusts own projects, reserves and administration totalled £623,00, grants totalled £131,000 and the surplus for the year was £625,000.

42 grants were made with the largest to: University of Bristol (£41,000 for five projects); Herpetological Conservation Trust and Plantlife – Gloucestershire Hedgerow Project (both £20,000); Lady Margaret Hall Oxford (£15,000); Royal Holloway & Bedford College – Red Data Book (£5,000).

The other grants were up to £4,600, with most under £500. 13 bat groups received grants with at least 16 other grants to groups or individuals for bat-related work. Other beneficiaries included the Otter Project Wales, Red Squirrel Trust, Suffolk Wildlife Trust and two schools.

Applications: In writing to the correspondent.

The Nigel Vinson Charitable Trust

£31,000 (1993/94)

General

Messrs Hoare Trustees, 37 Fleet Street, London EC4P 4DQ
0171-353 4522

Correspondent: The Secretary

Trustees: Rt Hon Lord Vinson of Roddam Dene; M F Jodrell; P R Fyson.

Beneficial area: UK.

Information available: Full accounts are on file at the Charity Commission.

General: In 1993/94, the trust had assets of £688,000 and an income of over £58,000. Grants totalled £31,000 and there was a surplus of £16,000 after a transfer of £8,000 to capital and £4,750 to the Lord Vinson Charitable Trust.

26 grants were given, mostly for £500 or £1,000. Larger grants were £3,000 to Horris Hill School Trust, Foundation for Industry, Tyne & Wear Foundation and the Foundation for Manufacturing & Industry; £2,000 to Student Exploration Appeal; £1,500 to Job Ownership Trust and St Oswalds School. Other beneficiaries included Northumberland Wildlife Trust, National Federation of City Farms, Salvation Army, Northern Sinfonia Trust, Prisoners Abroad and Young Enterprise. There appears to be some preference for the North East.

Applications: In writing to the correspondent.

The Viznitz Foundation

£14,000 (1991/92)

Not known

23 Overlea Road, London E5
0181-557 9557

Correspondent: H Feldman

Trustees: H Feldman; E Kahan; E S Margulies.

Beneficial area: UK.

Information available: Accounts are on file at the Charity Commission up to 1991/92, but without a list of grants.

General: In 1991/92, the trust had an income of £163,000 and made grants totalling only £14,000. It appears to be still building up its assets which stood at £776,000. The previous year grants totalled only £27,000 from an income of £139,000.

Unfortunately no information is available on the number or type of beneficiaries.

Applications: In writing to the correspondent.

The Charity of Thomas Wade & Others

£168,000 (1994)

General in Leeds

Dibb Lupton Broomhead,
117 The Headrow, Leeds LS1 5JX
0113-243 9301

Correspondent: W M Wrigley

Trustees: Lord Mayor; Rector of Leeds; J Roberts; E M Arnold; S C Thompson; R T P Peacock; J Horrocks; P J D Marshall; I A Ziff; Dr A Cooke; Cllr J L Carter; Cllr N Mackie; M J Dodgson; J M Barr; Cllr D Atkinson; J Tinker; M S Wainwright.

Beneficial area: Leeds, within the pre-1974 boundary of the city.

Information available: Full accounts are on file at the Charity Commission.

General: In 1994, the trust had a net income of £139,000. 59 grants were given totalling £168,000. The trust supports a range of charities in Leeds covering largely community/youth organisations.

The three major beneficiaries appear to receive large grants each year, these being Hunslet Boys Club (£30,000), YMCA Leeds (£30,000) and Voluntary Action Leeds (£15,000 general grant and £3,000 for various projects).

Other large grants went to Leeds Parish Church Restoration Appeal (£10,000 plus a further £2,000 for a market place project and £1,200 for the choir), YWCA Middleton (£7,500 for the Upstone Centre and £2,000 for Trevor Stubbs House), Age Concern Leeds (£6,500) and Central Yorkshire Scout Council (£6,000).

The remaining grants ranged from £200 to £5,000. 27 of the grants were recurrent. Beneficiaries included Chapeltown Nursery (£500), East Leeds Family Service Unit (£2,000), Harehills Community Centre Irish Music Project (£500), LGI Kidney Patients Association (£2,000), South Leeds Groundwork Trust (£1,000) and the South Sudanese Welfare Association (£750).

Exclusions: No grants to individuals or to schools (unless special needs). The trustees tend not to support medical/health orientated bodies.

Applications: In writing to the correspondent. The trust also has a grants applications advisor: Ken Jones, 26 Kingsley Drive, Adel, Leeds LS16 7PB (0113-261 0141).

Applicants must submit accounts and a contact telephone number with the application. They should be submitted not later than one month before the trustees' meeting. All suitable applicants will be visited by the applications advisor, and further reports are required in the event of a grant being made. Trustees consider applications in April, July and November.

The Wakefield Trust

£78,000 (1992/93)

General

Martineau Johnson, St Philips House, St Philips Place, Birmingham B3 2PP
0121-200 3300

Correspondent: D Turfrey

Trustees: Mrs M P Mitchell; Dr A N Brain; C D Torlesse; M B Shaw.

Beneficial area: UK, with a preference for Devon.

Information available: Full accounts are on file at the Charity Commission.

General: In 1992/93, the trust had assets of £859,000 and an income of £88,000. Ten grants were given totalling £78,000. In addition the trust completed commission of the sculpture of Thomas Attwood MP "Birmingham Man", now sited in Chamberlain Square, Birmingham.

By far the largest grant was £50,000 to Cambridge University Department of Criminology and a further £10,000 was given to other projects at Cambridge University.

Four grants were given in Devon: £5,000 to both Totnes Parish Church and Devonshire Historic Churches Trust, and £1,000 to both the Devonshire Collection of Period Costume and Dartington Summer Arts Foundation. Other grants were given to Birmingham Cathedral (£3,000), Royal Opera House Trust and Lincoln Cathedral Fabric Appeal (both £1,000) and British-Australia Society (£500).

Applications: In writing to the correspondent.

The Walker Trust

£133,000 (1993/94)

Health, education in Shropshire only

The Shirehall, Abbey Foregate, Shrewsbury SY2 6ND
01743-252725

Correspondent: Mr Hewitt, Administrator

Trustees: Viscount Boyne; A E Heber-Percy; G Raxster; P F Phillips (the chairman and vice-chairman of Shropshire County Council always fill these last two positions).

Beneficial area: Shropshire.

Information available: Full accounts are on file at the Charity Commission.

General: In 1993/94, the trust had assets of £2.5 million and an income of £147,000. Grants totalled £133,000 given mainly to health-related charities in Shropshire and to individuals for educational purposes.

The accounts list all grants of £1,000 or more, of which there were 16 to organisations (totalling £75,000) and 7 to individuals (totalling £7,300). The remaining £51,000 was given in grants of under £1,000.

The largest grants went to the Pines Trust (£14,000 with a further £14,000 to be paid over two years), Hope House Children's Respite Hospice (£12,500) and St John Ambulance in Shropshire (£10,000). Grants of £5,000 went to each of Condover Hall School for the Blind, Shropshire Nuffield Hospital, Girl Guides Lyneal Activity Centre and Shropshire Regimental Museum.

The trust pays some larger grants over a number of years and has a list of five organisations which receive an annual grant, including £2,500 to Victoria County History of Shropshire, £2,000 to British Schools Exploring Society and £1,600 to VSO.

Exclusions: Appeals from outside Shropshire will not be considered or replied to.

Applications: Applications should be addressed to the administrator at the above address. Details of other assistance applied for must be given and, in the case of organisations, the latest annual report and accounts. The trustees meet in January, April, July and September each year, but arrangements can be made for urgent applications to receive consideration between meetings. Applications must reach the clerk not less than one month before a decision is required.

The Wall Charitable Trust

£102,000 (1993/94)

General

Meade-King, 24 Orchard Street, Bristol BS1 5DF
0117-926 4121

Correspondent: P G B Letts

Trustees: P G B Letts; Orchard Executor & Trustee Company.

Beneficial area: UK with a preference for Bristol.

Information available: Full accounts are on file at the Charity Commission.

General: The trust supports a range of charities with a preference for the Bristol area. The trustees have stated that they are inundated with requests for support, possibly receiving over 2,000 a year while giving 100 grants. The volume is such that they are unable to consider more than a fraction and they have no difficulty in distributing the money available.

In 1993/94, the trust had assets of £1.6 million, an income available for distribution of £100,000 and gave 128 grants totalling £102,000. The trustees have retained the balance of income as a fund out of which to give emergency grants.

The trustees report for 1993/94 states: "Primary points considered by the trustees in assessing applications are whether the applicants are local, young, disabled or deprived. The opportunity was also taken to support longer term projects such as the new premises of the Avon & Bristol Boys Clubs, BRACE, local cultural appeals and the Museum of the Empire & Commonwealth Trust. A one-off donation was made to Oxfam for aid to Bosnia."

Although the trust supports a number of charities on an annual basis, the greater part of the income is spent on one-off payments in response to appeals, particularly local charities. Grants ranged from £100 to £8,000 and were generally for £500. About one-third went to children and youth charities, one-third to medical charities and charities for the disabled, and one-third for social welfare organisations. Beneficiaries included Avon Wildlife Trust, Bristol Age Care, Bristol Home Start, Gingerbread, National Osteoporosis

Society, Prisoners Abroad, Streetwise Youth and Windmill Hill City Farm.

Exclusions: Only in exceptional circumstances will the trustees give grants to animal charities and never to individuals.

Applications: In writing to the correspondent. Applications are dealt with on a monthly basis, but requests will not normally be acknowledged in view of the additional administrative cost.

The Ward Blenkinsop Trust

£159,000 (1992/93)

Medicine, social welfare, general

Broxbury, Codmore Hill, Pulborough, West Sussex RH20 2HY

Correspondent: J H Awdry, Trustee

Trustees: A M Blenkinsop; J H Awdry; T R Tilling.

Beneficial area: UK, with a special interest in the Merseyside area.

Information available: Full accounts are on file at the Charity Commission.

General: The trust had investments with a market value of £3.1 million in April 1993 (an increase of over 200% from its book value of £900,000). The trust income was £146,000 and £40,000 was transferred from the capital account to cover expenditure for the year.

Grants to organisations totalled £159,000, with a further £19,000 given to ex-employees of Ward Blenkinsop & Co and £6,000 spent on Christmas boxes for pensioners.

The two largest grants were £24,000 to the Stephen Park Trust and £16,000 to the Royal Academy of Dancing. Six other grants were over £5,000, ie. those to Royal Opera House Education Department (£8,400); Manchester Youth Theatre (£7,500); Cheshire County Council (two grants of £6,250 – one for the Youth Arts Institution and one for the Year of Culture for special needs groups, Seaside Venture Group); Riding for the Disabled (£5,900), and the Bristol Old Victoria Theatre School (£5,700).

70 other grants were given ranging from £100 to £3,000. Most were to medical and social welfare charities, with a number of children/youth organisations also supported. There is a preference for the Merseyside area. Beneficiaries included Action Research, British Polio Fellowship, Diabetes Foundation, NSPCC Warrington, Hillside Youth Club, Southport & District Samaritans, Shetland Rescue and Speke Environmental Projects.

Exclusions: No grants to individuals. Charitable organisations only.

Applications: In writing to the correspondent.

Mrs Waterhouse's Charitable Trust

£195,000 (1992/93)

Health and social welfare

92 Whalley Road, Wilpshire, Blackburn BB1 9LJ

Correspondent: D H Dunn, Trustee

Trustees: D H Dunn; Mrs E Dunn.

Beneficial area: UK, with an interest in Lancashire.

Information available: Full accounts are on file at the Charity Commission.

General: The trust channels its donations mainly, but not exclusively, to charities based in, or with branches in, the Lancashire area. It aims to provide funds on a regular basis so most grants are recurrent. It may also make a limited number of more substantial grants to finance capital projects.

In 1992/93, the trust had assets of £2.6 million and an income of £257,000. 42 grants were given totalling £195,000. By far the largest grant was £70,000 to the BHRVHA Endowment Fund (£67,000 in 1991/92). The only other grant over £3,000 was £25,000 to Derian House (£10,000 in 1991/92).

All the other grants were for £2,000 to £5,000 and almost all were to health and social welfare organisations. Over half were given in Lancashire. All but nine were recurrent from the previous year. Beneficiaries included Blackburn & Darwen Society for the Blind, East Lancashire Hospice Fund, East Lancashire Scout Council, National Trust (Lake District Appeal), Royal Society for Mentally Handicapped Children and St Omer Handicapped Children's Trust.

Applications: In writing to the correspondent. There is no set time for consideration of applications, but donations are normally made in March each year.

The Roger Waters 1989 Charity Trust

£50,000 (1992/93)

General

Forsyte Kerman, 79 New Cavendish Street, London W1M 8AQ
0171-637 8566

Correspondent: M Lewis

Trustees: G R Waters; A Russell.

Beneficial area: UK.

Information available: Full accounts are on file at the Charity Commission.

General: The trust was registered in March 1990 and is still building up its assets which stood at £544,000 in 1992/93. In the same year it had an income of £156,000 consisting of £100,000 covenant, £23,000 share of Pink Floyd income and £33,000 bank interest.

Only one grant was given, £50,000 to Eureka!. In 1991/92, three grants were given: £30,000 to the Hospital for Sick Children, £5,000 to the Ibstock Place Appeal and £1,000 to the Salvation Army.

Two grants were given in 1990/91 totalling £9,100; one to Victor Edelstein Shelter (£4,100) and one to the International League for the Protection of Horses for (£5,000).

Applications: The trust states: "the trustees follow their own selection criteria and do not respond to unsolicited requests for support".

Watside Charities

£75,000 (1991/92)

Not known

Messrs Frere Chomley Bischoff, 4 John Carpenter Street, London EC4Y 0NH
0171-615 8000

Correspondent: C F Eadie

Trustees: J Reid; C F Eadie.

Information available: Accounts are on file at the Charity Commission, but without a list of grants.

General: Watside Charities own two companies, Happenstance and J Bondi Ltd, which are "engaged in the exploitation of entertainers outside the UK and Ireland".

In 1992/93, the income was £151,000 including £150,000 from shares in group undertakings. Grants totalled only £10,000 leaving a large surplus. There has also been a surplus in the two previous years, but the grant total was higher: £75,000 in 1991/92 from an income of £103,000 and £41,000 in 1990/91 from an income of £101,000.

No information was available on the grants given.

Applications: In writing to the correspondent.

John Watson's Trust

£140,000 (1993)

Educational needs of children and young people

Signet Library, Parliament Square, Edinburgh EH1 1RF
0131-220 1640

Correspondent: J Penney, Administrator

Trustees: Six representatives of the Society of Writers to Her Majesty's Signet; two from Lothian Regional Council; one from the Merchant Company Education Board; one from the Lothian Association of Youth Clubs; and one additional member.

Beneficial area: Scotland, with a preference for Lothian.

Information available: Background notes are available from the trust.

General: Grants to children and young people under 21 who are physically or mentally disabled or socially disadvantaged, for education and training, equipment, travel, recreational and cultural activities. Grants are given both to individuals and charitable organisations. There is provision for a limited number of boarding school grants.

The trust's assets in 1993, were valued at £2.9 million, generating an income of £164,000. After expenses, donations totalled £140,000.

The grants committee met six times during 1993 and gave 179 grants to disabled or disadvantaged children and young people under 21. Grants to individuals included equipment for disabled people, in-school special expenses, living expenses for children forced to leave home, special school fees, post-school education for disadvantaged people, apprentice tools and equipment. Grants ranged from £34 to £3,000.

There were 72 grants to organisations, most of which were based in the Lothian area. Grants included general funding for some important local organisations, funding of school projects, playschemes, after-school clubs, the new University of Edinburgh Special Entry Summer School, and research into improved special teaching of severely deprived children and other aspects of child educational welfare. Grants ranged from £50 to £4,500.

Awards to individuals and organisations totalling £51,000 were committed for 1994.

Exclusions: No grants to: people over 21, overseas causes or for medical purposes.

Applications: On a form available from the correspondent for individual applicants. By letter for organisations.

The Weavers' Company Benevolent Fund

£128,000 (1993)

Young people at risk from criminal involvement, young offenders' and prisoners' organisations

Saddlers' House, Gutter Lane,
London EC2V 6BR
0171-606 1155

Correspondent: J G Ouvry

Trustees: The Worshipful Company of Weavers.

Beneficial area: UK.

Information available: The fund places accounts on file at the Charity Commission each year with a schedule of the twenty largest grants.

General: In 1993, the trust had assets of £3.95 million and an income of £177,000. Grants totalled £128,000.

The income of the trust may be used for any charitable purpose, but the company has selected three particular areas of support:

- Projects concerned with helping young people who for any reason are at risk from criminal involvement;
- Projects concerned with helping young offenders;
- Projects concerned with helping prisoners and ex-prisoners.

Applications may be considered from projects anywhere in the UK, but priority is given to those within the London area (where the company is based).

The committee will pay particular attention to the following:

1. The company does not provide long-term funding to projects and it would wish to be assured that all possible sources of finance had been explored and that efforts were being made to obtain long-term funding from other voluntary and statutory sources.
2. It prefers to support small or new organisations where the company's grant would form a substantial part of the funds required.
3. It does not often support central administrative or umbrella bodies, but prefers projects working directly in its chosen fields.
4. It is particularly interested in innovatory projects which are trying to get off the ground and which could act as a catalyst for other similar projects elsewhere.
5. It is willing to consider applications for grants for equipment and capital projects and also salaries and running costs, subject to its overall policy not to provide long-term funding. Deficit funding is not provided for established projects.

A list of the twenty largest grants is given in the annual accounts. In 1993, this included Charterhouse-in-Southwark, Devon Care Trust, Howard League, NACRO, New Bridge, Newham Motorcycle Project, Sobriety Project, Spitalfields Farm and Tower Hamlets Youth Counselling Service. Most grants are in the range of £2,000 to £5,000 and rarely exceed £10,000.

Exclusions: No grants to individuals.

Applications: Registered charities only should write in the first instance to the correspondent with details of their requirements and include a set of their most recent accounts. The trustees meet three times a year in January, June and October, but applications may be submitted at any time.

The Webber Trust

£244,000 (1992/93)

Evangelical Christian, welfare

66 Hillway, Highgate, London N6 6DP

Correspondent: Horace R Webber, Trustee

Trustees: D H Thornton; H R Webber; V M Webber.

Beneficial area: UK and overseas.

Information available: Full accounts are on file at the Charity Commission.

General: The trustees report from 1992/93 states: "The policy of the trustees continues to be to support those charities in which they have developed a personal interest or concern and unsolicited applications for grants are not welcomed, nor has the trust the facilities to respond to such".

The trust supports evangelical Christian causes and charities involved in the relief of sickness, suffering and poverty.

"The list of recipients was largely the same as the previous year and included amongst special grants made were donations towards hostels for London's homeless and for the re-habilitation of released prisoners; accommodation for mentally handicapped adults and for the physically handicapped; improvement of facilities at a sailing school and at a mountain school for the training of young people."

In 1992/93, the trust had assets of £319,000 and an income of £240,000 including £162,000 from donations. Grants totalled £244,000; the larger ones are listed in the accounts. Most of the grants made by the trust were recurrent, and nearly all went to Christian causes. Six grants were for £10,000 or more, the beneficiaries being: AIM International, Christian Concern for the Mentally Handicapped, Christian Home for the Physically Handicapped, Crusaders, Scripture Union and UCCF. 17 grants ranged from £2,500 to £9,999, all to Christian organisations.

Applications: "The trustees are unable to accept or respond to unsolicited applications."

The William Webster Charitable Trust

£99,000 (1993/94)

Social welfare in the North East

Barclays Bank Trust Co Ltd, Executorship & Trustee Service, Osborne Court, Gadbrook Park, Northwich, Cheshire CW9 7RE
01606-313173

Correspondent: The Trust Administrator

Trustees: Barclays Bank Trust Co Ltd.

Beneficial area: The North East of England.

Information available: Full accounts are on file at the Charity Commission.

General: The trust only gives grants in the North East. In 1993/94, the income of the trust was £104,000. Grants totalled £99,000 and the management costs of Barclays were £21,000, "calculated as a percentage of capital value".

105 grants were given ranging from £100 to £7,000. The largest of £7,000 went to the Children's Foundation. The Tyne & Wear Foundation and Dame Allen's School both received £5,000. The Newcastle High School Centenary Appeal received £3,500 and £2,000 went to each of Boys' Brigade (North of England District), Carrville Methodist Church, Corbridge Scout & Guide Building Fund, High Sheriff of Northumberland Awards, Key Project, Lanchester Emergency Appeal Fund, Northern Counties School for the Deaf and Westfield School.

Over 20 grants went to churches or church-related projects. Other major beneficiaries appear to be youth organisations (including schools).

Exclusions: No grants to individuals or to non-charitable organisations.

Applications: Applications should be submitted by the end of May for consideration in July; by the end of September for consideration in November; and by January for consideration in March. They should include details of the costings of capital projects, of funding already raised, a set of the latest annual accounts and details of the current charity registration.

The Weinberg Foundation

£103,000 (1992/93)

Jewish, general

Spencer House, 27 St James Street, London SW1A 1NR
0171-493 8111

Correspondent: Maria Torok

Trustees: Neville Ablitt; Freddie Mauwer.

Beneficial area: UK.

Information available: Full accounts are on file at the Charity Commission.

General: The assets of this trust are decreasing as it continues to give out more in grants than it receives in income. It has pledges which it intends to honour, but this will leave little money for general appeals.

In 1992/93, it made grants totalling £103,000 from an income of £38,000, leaving assets of £191,000. The previous year, grants totalled £140,000 from an income of £85,000.

The largest grants in 1992/93 were given to JPAIME and the NSPCC (both £25,000), Foundation for Communication (£15,000), and Richmond Fellowship, Leonora Fund and Royal National Theatre Endowment Fund (all £5,000). 34 other grants were given ranging from £100 to £3,400, mainly to Jewish organisations and medical and welfare charities.

Applications: To the correspondent in writing, but note the above.

The Weinstein Foundation

£98,000 (1992/93)

Medical, Jewish

13 Dorset Square, London NW1 6QB
0171-262 5163

Correspondent: M L Weinstein

Trustees: E Weinstein; Mrs S R Weinstein; M L Weinstein; P D Weinstein; Mrs L A F Newman.

Beneficial area: Worldwide.

Information available: The only accounts on file at the Charity Commission since those for 1986/87 are those for 1992/93, but these do not include a grants list.

General: In 1992/93, the trust had assets of £1.2 million and an income of £104,000. Grants totalled £98,000 but no further information is available for this year.

In 1986/87, 33 grants were made to medical organisations and Jewish causes.

Applications: In writing to the correspondent.

The James Weir Foundation

£153,000 (1993)

Health, social welfare, heritage, research

84 Cicada Road, London SW18 2NZ
0181-870 6233

Correspondent: Mrs L Lawson, Secretary

Trustees: Dr George Weir; Simon Bonham; William Ducas.

Beneficial area: UK, with a special interest in Scotland.

Information available: Full accounts are on file at the Charity Commission.

General: In 1993, the trust had assets of £3 million (up from £1.9 million in 1991) and an income of £176,000. Grants totalled £153,000.

The trust deed lists seven specific beneficiaries to be supported. In 1993, six of these received a grant: the Royal Society – Edinburgh and London (£28,000 and £2,000 respectively); University of Strathclyde Engineering Foundation (£2,500); RAF Benevolent Fund (£2,000) and Royal College of Physicians and Royal College of Surgeons (both £1,000). The British Association for the Advancement of Science did not receive a grant.

About 120 other grants were given of which 93 were for £1,000 and 14 for £500. The largest grant was £4,000 to South Ayrshire Hospitals NHS Trust, with £2,000 to each of the British American Education Foundation, Leonard Cheshire Foundation, National Galleries of Scotland, National Trust for Scotland and the Prospect Foundation Appeal.

Most charities supported were in the fields of health, welfare and disability such as British Blind Sport, Childline, Disability Aid Fund, MIND, NACRO and Samaritans. A number of conservation and animal welfare organisations also received support including International Fund for Animal Welfare, Scottish Wildlife Trust and World Wide Fund for Nature.

The trust also has a special interest in Scotland, with beneficiaries in addition to those already mentioned including Age Concern Scotland, Association of Youth Clubs in Strathclyde, Buildings of Scotland Trust, Prison Fellowship Scotland and Riding for the Disabled Glasgow. About half the grants were recurrent.

Exclusions: Recognised charities only. No grants to individuals.

Applications: In writing to the correspondent. Distributions are made twice yearly in June and November.

The Welsh Church Funds

£660,000 (1993/94)

General in Wales

Clwyd: The Chief Executive, Clwyd County Council, Shire Hall, Mold, Clwyd CH7 6NR (01352-702406)

Dyfed: The County Secretary, Dyfed County Council, County Hall, Carmarthen, Dyfed SA31 1JP (01267-233333: Fax; 01267-221904)

Gwent: M J Perry, Secretary to the Trustees, Gwent County Council, County Hall, Cwmbran, Gwent NP44 2XH (01633-832841)

Gwynedd: The County Secretary, County Offices, Caernarfon, Gwynedd LL5 1SH (01286-672255)

Mid Glamorgan: The Treasurer's Department, Mid Glamorgan County Council, County Hall, Cardiff CF1 3NE (01222-820820)

Powys: The Chief Executive, Powys County Council, Powys County Hall, Llandrindod Wells, Powys LD1 5LG (01597-826000)

South Glamorgan: Barbara Lees, South Glamorgan County Council, County Hall, Atlantic Wharf, Cardiff CF1 5UW (01222-872423)

West Glamorgan: The County Clerk, West Glamorgan County Council, The Guildhall, Swansea, West Glamorgan SA1 4PA (01792-471111)

Beneficial area: Wales.

General: There are eight county Welsh Church Funds. All the information below refers to 1993/94 financial year.

County	assets £m	income £	grants £
Clwyd	n/a	34,000	26,000
Dyfed	1.4	123,000	£193,000
Gwent	1.69	433,000	£108,000
Gwynedd	0.9	67,000	58,000
Mid Glamorgan	2.6	327,000	190,000
Powys	1.18	75,000	57,000
South Glamorgan	0.52	40,000	28,000
West Glamorgan	2.0	174,000	0

Each fund restricts its support to organisations in its county although some national (ie. Welsh) charities may be supported where this will benefit people in the county.

Clwyd: The fund gives grants for listed buildings including churches, community groups, scouts, halls, Eisteddfodau, and other charities. Grants may also be given to individuals, for example those with outstanding sporting ability.

The trust gave 50 grants ranging from £100 to £5,000 (but usually for £250 or £500). The largest grants were given to Royal National Eisteddfod Wales (£5,000) and Urdd Gobaith Cymru Bro Maelor (£2,000). There were also five grants of £1,000 each to the Clwyd Deaf Society, Cambrian Educational Foundation for Deaf Children, Trust for Sick Children in Wales, Clwyd Historic Buildings Preservation Trust and Clwyd Fine Arts Trust.

Dyfed: The fund gives grants to a wide range of charities and organisations in Wales. After a successful application, an organisation cannot re-apply for another three years.

Almost half the number of grants (68), and more than half the grant total (£104,000), was given to churches and chapels. The largest grants in this category were to: Llanbadarn Fawr Church Aberystwyth (£10,000); St Martin's Church, Haverfordwest and Angle Parish Church (£3,000 each). Most other grants in this category were for about £200 to £2,600.

Village/church/memorial halls received £30,000 in 19 grants of £100 to £3,000.

Local appeals accounted for 42 grants totalling £35,000. The largest grants were to Rhoserchan Project £5,150 and Ein Stiwdio NI £5,000. 27 of the grants were for less than £1,000; many were for £100. The remaining grants in this category were for between £1,000 and £2,000.

National appeals received 25 grants totalling £22,000. By far the largest grants were to Welsh Heart Research Unit (£15,000) and Llanelli YMCA (£3,000); all other grants were for £100 to £330. Individuals (all of whom must live in the county) received grants totalling £2,500.

Gwent: The trust is for the benefit of education, for relief in need, public\historic buildings, libraries, museums, art galleries and for medical and social research, treatment and probation. Grants were broken down as follows:

Music and the arts	£9,300
Chapels and churches	£41,500
OAP and village halls	£40,500
Education and miscellaneous (organisations and individuals)	£13,000

Unfortunately this list is not broken down any further.

About half the grant total is given for the support of places of worship, including churches, chapels, mosques, etc. and also to other buildings such as community halls. The maximum grant is £500 for such buildings. Other grants are given to local charities in Gwent.

Gwynedd: Grants were categorised in the accounts of the fund as follows:

Eisteddfod/musical/cultural	35%	£19,300
Opera/theatres/art galleries	13%	£7,300
Youth	5%	£3,000
Village halls/community centres	10%	£5,250
Disabled/social services/nursery	24%	£13,052
Religious establishments	7%	£3,950
Others	6%	£3,169

In all, 110 grants were given ranging from £64 to £5,000. Most were for £500 or less to local charities in Gwynedd, with a few to national (Welsh) charities. The sum currently granted to the local Eisteddfodau is £125. If an application is for a substantial sum, the fund may consider funding over a number of years. When giving a grant for work on fire precautions in village halls/community centres, this will be up to a maximum of one third of the total cost.

Mid Glamorgan: The fund can award grants for the following: education, relief of sickness or need; libraries, museums, art galleries; social and recreational purposes; historic buildings; medical and social research treatment; probation; blind people; the elderly; places of worship and burial grounds; emergencies and disasters. No further information available.

Powys: Grants totalled £57,000, but no information was available on the beneficiaries.

Grants are given for the following purposes:

- Restoration of churches, chapels etc: repair and restoration work of the main fabric of places of worship will be considered, but running costs or maintenance are excluded. Interior work is usually not supported.
- Encouraging the arts, social and recreational activities.
- Protection of historic buildings.
- Medical and social research.
- Relief in need of sick or disabled people.
- Other charities.

South Glamorgan: 16 grants were made ranging from £150 to £6,000. The largest were to South Glamorgan Historic Buildings (Ecclesiastical) Fund Committee and Cardiff City Farm Trust (both £6,000), and the Schools Museum Trust (£5,000). Other beneficiaries included Rumney War Memorial Fund (£1,500), Cambrian Educational Foundation (£500), Roose & District Community Association and seven churches.

West Glamorgan: This is the only fund that does not appear to be giving grants at present. From its income of £174,000 expenses were incurred of £3,000 towards work on the Old Guildhall, Swansea.

The objects of the fund remain as they were in 1946, with the trust able to give grants for the following: education; relief in sickness; relief in need; libraries, museums and art galleries; social and recreational; historic buildings; medical and social research; probation; blind people; elderly people; places of public worship and burial grounds; emergencies and disasters and other charitable purposes.

Exclusions: Clwyd: Non-listed buildings including churches are not supported.

Dyfed: No grants to organisations with licensed premises on their land.

Gwent: No support for individuals for education or training where funding has not been offered by the education authority.

Gwynedd: Only registered charities are supported. The following guidelines should be noted:

- With regard to foreign tours, applications from choirs, bands or orchestras will not be considered if they have already received a grant in the last five years.
- Grants will not be given towards building work on churches and chapels which are used regularly for worship or for denominational purposes.
- Grants will not be given towards capital work on community centres/village halls where a 50% grant by the education committee has already been made.
- Community newspapers are not supported.
- The fund is unlikely to give a grant where this will benefit only one group or organisation.

Mid Glamorgan: No grants to students, individuals in need or projects of other local authorities.

Powys: Grants are very rarely given to organisations which are not registered charities.

West Glamorgan: Individual or personal applications are not normally considered. The fund will not give support where this would normally be dealt with out of the annual budgets of the Council's Service Committees or other public agencies and will not commit itself to regular payments or to provide recurring annual running expenses. A grant from the fund will not usually cover the whole cost of a project.

Applications: On a form available from the correspondent for all the funds except Gwynedd, where applications should be in writing.

The finance sub committee for Clwyd meets in June and December, for Dyfed applications are considered quarterly and for Mid Glamorgan the closing date is July each year.

The Westcroft Trust

£61,000 (1993/94)

International understanding, overseas aid, Quaker, Shropshire

32 Hampton Road, Oswestry, Shropshire SY11 1SJ

Correspondent: Dr Edward P Cadbury

Trustees: Dr Edward P Cadbury; Mary C Cadbury; Richard G Cadbury; James E Cadbury; Erica R Cadbury.

Beneficial area: Unrestricted, but with a special interest in Shropshire – causes of local interest outside Shropshire are rarely supported.

Information available: Full accounts are on file at the Charity Commission.

General: In 1993/94, the trust had asssets of £1.32 million and an income of £75,000. Grants totalled £61,000. Currently the trustees have five main areas of interest:

- International understanding, including conflict resolution and the material needs of the third world;
- Religious causes, particularly for social outreach, usually for the Society of Friends (Quakers) but also for those originating in Shropshire;
- Development of the voluntary sector in Shropshire;
- Special needs for those with disabilities, primarily in Shropshire;
- Development of community groups and reconciliation between different cultures in Northern Ireland.

The trustees favour charities with low administrative overheads and which pursue clear policies of equal opportunity in meeting need. Printed letters signed by the great and good are wasted on them. Few grants are for capital or endowment. The only support for medical education is for expeditions abroad for pre-clinical students. Medical aid, education and relief work in developing countries is supported, but only through UK agencies. The core of the trust's programme is regular support for a wide variety of work towards international peace and understanding, social welfare and those with disabilities.

The trustees are keen to develop partnerships with the voluntary sector particularly in Shropshire. They are now moving towards making fewer, but larger grants without reducing the overall fields of interest.

In 1993/94, the categories which received the largest allocation from the trust were international understanding and overseas aid, accounting for 46% (£28,000) of the trust's donations. 16 grants were given for international understanding totalling £13,000 with £7,900 given to the Quaker Peace Studies Trust. Other beneficiaries of larger grants were the Research School, PAC, Australian National University (£1,500) and the Medical Education Trust (£1,100).

Overseas aid grants were subdivided into:

Medical – beneficiaries included Action in International Medicine (Uganda), Calcutta Rescue Fund and Nicaragua Health Fund;

Education – beneficiaries included Budiriro Trust (£1,100), Canon Collins Trust for Southern Africa (£510) and Mobile Outreach Ministry Manzini Swaziland (£1,500);

Relief work – beneficiaries included Action on Disability and Development (£650), Oxfam (£1,400) and Tools for Self Reliance (£160).

Social services, health and education continue to be well favoured at nearly 32% of allocations, divided into projects in Shropshire at 14.7% and elsewhere in the UK and Northern Ireland at 16.9%. Beneficiaries included Homeless in Oswestry Action Project, Shropshire County Council Prison Book Fund, North Shropshire Macmillan Nurse Appeal, Shropshire Sharks, Re-Solv, RNID, Liverpool One-Parent Families, Welsh Women's Aid and Voluntary Service Belfast.

Quaker activities around the country received 17.1% of donations. The balance of under 5% of allocations were made to the fields of medical and surgical research and education on projects favoured on a personal basis by trustees.

Exclusions: Grants to charities only. No grants to individuals or for medical electives, sport, the arts, repairs to church buildings or armed forces charities. Requests for sponsorship are not supported. Annual grants are withheld if recent accounts are not available or do not satisfy the trustees as to continuing need.

Applications: No application forms. A statement of financial needs and resources, charitable status, and a copy of the most recent annual accounts should be sent to the correspondent. Applications should be restricted to a maximum of three sheets of paper. No acknowledgements are given.

Replies to relevant but unsuccessful applicants will be sent only if a self-addressed envelope is enclosed. As some annual grants are made by Bank Giro, details of bank name, branch, sort code, and account name and number should be sent in order to save time and correspondence.

The Westminster Amalgamated Charity

£146,000 to organisations (1993)

Welfare in Westminster

4-5 Gough Square, London EC4A 3DE
0171-353 9991; Fax: 0171-583 5331

Correspondent: J A Turner, Clerk to the Trustees

Trustees: N P M Elles; P J M Prain; Mrs J Bianco; B C Burrough; K Gardner; Miss J M Jacob; Dr C Nemeth; G B Parkin; D A Shirley; Ms M Sykes; D E Weeks.

Beneficial area: London borough of Westminster.

Information available: Accounts are on file at the Charity Commission, but without a grants list for 1993.

General: In 1993, the trust had assets of £2.8 million and an income of £243,000. Grants totalled £185,000 including £146,000 to organisations and £39,000 to individuals. No grants list was included with the accounts for this year.

In 1992, £34,000 was given to Age Concern, Westminster. Other recipients included St Martin-in-the-Field Social Care Unit (£6,000) and the Westminster Children's Society (£7,500). Other grants ranged from £1,000 to £5,000 and were given to a range of organisations including the Bayswater Family Centre, Ebury Bridge Youth Club, Marylebone Bangladesh Society, shared Experience Theatre Company, Turning Point and Westminster Women's Aid.

Grants to individuals were mostly for heating, in cash or in kind, or for holidays and holiday fares. Further information in *A Guide to Grants for Individuals in Need*.

Applications: In writing to the correspondent (or by application form for individual grants).

The Westward Trust

£116,000 (1993/94)

Quaker, general

4 The Chestnuts, Winscombe,
Avon BS25 1LD
01934-842154

Correspondent: Donald Ironside

Trustees: Donald Ironside; Jean Ironside; John Ironside; Ruth Dodd.

Beneficial area: UK, with a preference for the South West.

Information available: Full accounts are on file at the Charity Commission.

General: The trust has a special interest in the Religious Society of Friends and the South West of England. The trustees allocate most of the funds to organisations whose work is already known to them.

In 1993/94, the trust had assets of £427,000 and an income of £36,000 and made grants totalling £116,000. This was distributed as follows:

Society of Friends (Quakers)	£19,000
Sidcot School	£48,000
Mediation UK	£40,000
Research into Ageing	£1,500
23 grants under £1,000	£7,500

Applications: In writing to the correspondent. Unsolicited appeals are not welcomed and are not acknowledged, unless accompanied by a stamped or pre-paid addressed envelope.

The Whitaker Charitable Trust

£96,000 (1993/94)

Education, general

c/o Currey & Co, 21 Buckingham Gate,
London SW1E 6LS
0171-828 4091

Correspondent: Theresa Skelton

Trustees: D W Price; Mrs E J R Whitaker; E R H Perks.

Beneficial area: Worldwide.

Information available: Full accounts are on file at the Charity Commission.

General: In 1993/94, the trust had assets of £3.5 million but an income of only £116,000. Grants totalled £96,000 including £80,000 to the United World College of Atlantic. This college is regularly the main beneficiary of the trust.

20 other grants were given, ranging from £250 to £4,000. Recipients included a range of charities in the fields of education, conservation and medicine. Grants went to both national and local organisations throughout the UK including the Harambee Educational Trust, Intermediate Technology, Bassetlaw Mencap, Retford and District Scouts Association, Soil Association, National Medicine Research Trust and Retford Theatre Trust. About three quarters of the grants were recurrent from the previous year.

In previous years a number of grants have been given to Northern Ireland charities, including Belfast Housing Aid, Omagh Integrated School Project and Castlereagh Community Association, but no grants appear to have been given there in 1993/94.

Exclusions: No grants are given to individuals or for the repair or maintenance of individual churches.

Applications: From registered charities only, to the correspondent in writing.

The Simon Whitbread Charitable Trust

£34,000 (1993/94)

Medicine, churches, general in Bedfordshire

Dawson & Co, 2 New Square, Lincoln's Inn, London WC2A 3RZ
0171-404 5941

Correspondent: E C A Martineau, Administrator

Trustees: Mrs H Whitbread; S C Whitbread; E C A Martineau.

Beneficial area: UK, with a preference for Bedfordshire.

Information available: Full accounts are on file at the Charity Commission.

General: Set up by Major Simon Whitbread in the early 1960s, in 1993/94 the trust had assets valued at £2.1 million. The income was £58,000 and 69 grants were made totalling £34,000.

The largest grants were to Southill PCC (£3,000), Bushey Place (£2,200 for an individual), St Mark's Church Centre Community Project (£1,500) and Marie Curie Cancer Care (£1,000). The other grants were generally for £200 to £500. A number of individuals in higher education and Raleigh International were supported, as were general organisations including Brickhill Youth Club, British Horse Foundation, CPRE, Haemophilia Society, Pearson's Holiday Fund, Research into Ageing and Volunteer Reading Help.

Applications: In writing to the correspondent.

Humphrey Whitbread's First Charitable Trust

£60,000 (1993/94)

Churches, general

34 Bryanston Square, London W1H 7LQ
0171-402 0052

Correspondent: Mary Scallan, Secretary

Trustees: H Whitbread; S C Whitbread; H C Whitbread; C R Skottowe.

Beneficial area: UK.

Information available: Full accounts are on file at the Charity Commission.

General: In 1993/94, the trust had assets with a market value of £2.16 million generating an income of £61,000. £60,000 was given in about 360 grants, most of which were clearly very small.

15 grants were for £1,000 or more with the largest to Cambridge Arts TT and Cardington PCC (both £3,000) and £2,000 to Southill PCC. Recipients of £1,000 included Alzheimers Disease Society, Family Welfare Association, Furniture History Society, Notting Hill Housing Trust, Trevor Jones Tetraplegic Trust and two churches.

A wide range of charities were supported in the fields of welfare, medical, disability, animal welfare, heritage, arts and churches.

Applications: In writing to the correspondent.

The Norman Whiteley Trust

£65,000 (1993/94)

Evangelical Christianity

Fallbarrow Park, Rayrigg Road, Windermere, Cumbria LA23 3DL

Correspondent: D Foster

Trustees: Mrs B M Whiteley; P Whiteley; W Thomas; D Dickson; J Ratcliff.

Beneficial area: Cumbria only.

Information available: Full accounts are on file at the Charity Commission.

General: The trust supports Christian charities in Cumbria. In 1993/94, it had assets of £1.9 million and gave grants totalling £64,000. No further information for this year is available.

In 1992/93, the assets were £1.4 million and the income £165,000. Grants totalled £46,000 leaving a surplus for the year of £77,000 (£86,000 in 1991/92).

The largest grant was £10,000 to the Potteries Trust. Most of the grants are recurrent, with beneficiaries including Wessex Christian Centre and the Overseas Missionary Fellowship.

Applications: In writing to the correspondent. Trustees meet to consider applications two or three times a year.

The Whitley Animal Protection Trust

Generally about £130,000

Animal care and protection, conservation

Edgbaston House, Walker Street, Wellington, Telford, Shropshire TF1 1HF
01952-641651

Correspondent: M T Gwynne, Secretary

Trustees: E Whitley; Mrs P A Whitley; Mrs V Thompson; E J Whitley; J Whitley.

Beneficial area: UK.

Information available: No accounts are on file at the Charity Commission since those for 1987.

General: The trust gave grants totalling £1.9 million in 1990. This figure should be regarded as exceptional as it had accumulated income in previous years which it decided to distribute during 1990. A more accurate annual figure would be about £130,000, although according to the Charity Commission database the income for 1992 was £444,000.

The trust supports animal care and protection and other related conservation projects. In 1990, it gave a small number of very considerable grants together with some smaller awards. These included: £1 million to the Jersey Wildlife Preservation Trust; £300,000 to Dee District Salmon Fishing Board; £250,000 to the Flora and Fauna Preservation Society; £100,000 to the Wildfowl and Wetlands Trust and £36,000 to World Wide Fund for Nature UK. It has also earmarked £50,000 for the Atlantic Salmon Trust, £25,000 for Gaia Quest Trust and £10,000 for the WWF-UK Shropshire Appeal.

Grants also went to animal welfare and protection organisations (eg. RSPCA, RSPB, Swan Rescue and the Rare Breeds Survival Trust); research at Liverpool University (£44,000), and international expeditions (£11,000).

Liverpool and Shropshire appear to be areas of particular interest to the trustees. The secretary comments that the present trustees are tending to concentrate on preservation of animals rather than protection against cruelty.

Applications: In writing to the correspondent.

The Wilkinson Charitable Foundation

£160,000 (1992/93)

Scientific research

Messrs Alsop Wilkinson, 6 Dowgate Hill, London EC4R 2SS
0171-248 4141

Trustees: B D S Lock; Prof G Wilkinson; Dr Anne M Hardy.

Beneficial area: UK.

Information available: Full accounts are on file at the Charity Commission.

General: The trust was set up for the advancement of scientific knowledge and education at Imperial College, University of London and for general purposes.

In 1992/93, the trust had assets of £671,000, an income of £141,000, of which £64,000 was from Patent Royalties and £17,000 from gains on the disposal of investments. Only five grants were given totalling £160,000.

The grants were made to: Imperial College of Science & Technology, London for research in the Department of Chemistry (£110,500, and £76,000 in 1991/92); Wolfson College, Oxford (£50,000 over the last two years) to supplement a Wolfson Foundation grant; Royal Postgraduate Medical School, Hammersmith (£16,200 in 1992/93 and £29,000 in 1991/92) for research in the Department of Virology; University of Wales, College of Cardiff (£6,000, following £13,500 in 1991/92) for support of new x-ray facilities, and a grant of £2,000 to Professor Carlo Redi at University of Pavia, Italy.

Applications: In writing to the correspondent.

The Williams Family Charitable Trust

£87,000 (1993/94)

Jewish

8 Holne Chase, London N2 0QN

Correspondent: Harry Landy, Trustee

Trustees: Harry Landy; Shimon Benison; Arnon Levy.

Beneficial area: Worldwide.

Information available: Full accounts are on file at the Charity Commission.

General: This trust was set up in 1959 by Walter Nathan Williams. In 1993/94, the trust had assets of £1.7 million, an income of £154,000 and gave 45 grants totalling £87,000.

The only grant which may have not been Jewish was to Hand in Hand Association (£180). The largest grants were: Yeshivat Kiryat Arba (£9,000); Jewish Philanthropic Trust (£6,000) and Shmarya Rabinowitz Gemilut Head (£4,000). There were 14 grants of £1,000 to £3,500 and 28 of £50 to

£500. All grants were to Jewish organisations involved mainly with welfare, education or medical.

Applications: In writing to the correspondent.

The Dame Violet Wills Charitable Trust

£87,000 (1993)

Evangelical Christianity

Ricketts Cooper & Co, Thornton House, Richmond Hill, Bristol BS8 1AT
0117-973 8441

Correspondent: H E Cooper

Trustees: Dr D M Cunningham, Chairman; H E Cooper; S Burton; Mrs J G Caine; A J G Cooper; Miss J R Guy; G J T Landreth; Prof A H Linton; Rev J A Motyer; R D Spear.

Beneficial area: UK and overseas.

Information available: Full accounts are on file at the Charity Commission.

General: The trust supports evangelical Christian activities both within the UK and overseas. It is not the practice of the trustees to guarantee long-term support to any work, however worthy. The typical categories of Christian work supported are:
- Building
- Missions – UK
- Missions – other countries
- Literature
- Radio Broadcasts
- Sundries

The trustees report states: "Whilst a vast number of appeals are received each year grants are more likely to be made to those which are personally known to one or more of the trustees".

In 1993, the trust had assets of £1 million and an income of £95,000. 104 grants totalled £87,000. The largest were £6,800 to the Western Counties & South Wales Evangelisation Trust (a regular beneficiary), £4,200 to Echoes of Service – Bristol and £3,000 to the Bristol International Students Centre. Other grants of £1,000 or more were given to Arab World Ministries, Church Pastoral Aid Society, Disabled Christian Fellowship, European Christian Mission and the Mission Aviation Fellowship. Some were recurrent from previous years.

Exclusions: No grants to individuals.

Applications: In writing to the correspondent.

The Wiltshire Community Foundation

£65,000 (1993/94)

Community welfare in Wiltshire

Wyndhams, St Josephs Place, Devizes, Wilts SN10 1DD
01380-729284; Fax: 01380-729772

Correspondent: The Grants Manager (to be appointed March 1995); Anna Marsden is the Director

Trustees: David Newbigging OBE, Chairman; Jack Ainslie; Charles Bartholomew; Joan Blackledge; John Emmerson; Moyra James; Maj Gen Tony Jeapes; Jane Mactaggart; Gill Prior; Zandria Pauncefort; Ann Poole; Col David Rogers; Sir John Sykes; Steve Willcox.

Beneficial area: Wiltshire only.

Information available: Full report and accounts are on file at the Charity Commission. Information and guidelines (which we would advise all potential applicants to obtain) are available from the foundation.

General: The foundation (WCF) was set up in 1991. It incorporates the former Wiltshire Community Trust and the Thamesdown Community Trust. The grants committees have representation from the public, private, and voluntary sectors.

The foundation is keen to play a pro-active role. It supports voluntary and community groups in Wiltshire whose primary aim is to improve the quality of people's lives through social and community care provision. WCF's recently commissioned report – *Communities at risk in Wiltshire* – has highlighted problems and needs in the county and led WCF to refocus its grant policy as follows:

- **Main project fund:** About 50% of the budget will be used to seek out and support projects meeting the following criteria:
Supporting community care – working especially with users eg. the frail elderly, disabled people, and with carers eg. those caring at home for elderly or disabled relatives.
Tackling isolation – working in particular to improve access to services and information; improve transport in rural areas; support minority groups.
Investing in young people – concentrating on homelessness and education, training and self-development.

- **Community development fund:** About 35% of the budget will be used to concentrate on one major project each year, either to tackle a special need such as rural transport or to meet the needs of a specific geographical area of Wiltshire. In 1993/94, it was decided to support SCOPE - A Strategy for the Care of Older People in Eastern Wiltshire (£20,000 for two years).

- **Initiatives fund:** About 15% of the budget will be used for one-off grants for innovative applications outside the main priority areas such as a response to an emerging need, local research and feasibility studies and response to local emergencies.

The foundation wishes to promote equal opportunities through its grant-making programme. This involves questions of access and community involvement and representation within the project, as well as gender and race.

Over 50 grants were allocated in 1993/94 totalling £65,000. Beneficiaries in the *Supporting Community Care* category include Trowbridge Lifestyles (£5,000 over 3 years), Wessex MS Therapy Centre (£4,500 over 3 years), Carers Network West Wiltshire (£1,500 over 3 years) and Penhill Furniture Cabin (£1,500).

Under the *Investing in Young People* category the foundation supported HAY – Housing Action for the Young (£6,000 over 3 years to employ advice/support worker), Grub Club (£1,980 over 2 years for creche expenses for a young single parent project) and Wiltshire Wildlife Trust (£6,000 over 3 years for a countywide education officer encouraging the interest of young people).

Tackling Isolation grants were given to the Hostel Workers Group (£1,200 for an information directory), Wootton Bassett Advice Point (£6,000 over 3 years), CRUSE Bereavement Care (£4,500 over 2 years) and Swindon Family Mediation Service (£6,000 over 3 years).

Grants may be for a maximum of three years. Groups who have previously received three years' funding from the WCF can apply for support for new developments. One-off grants are also considered, as are applications for running costs. Grants not taken up after 12 months will be reviewed.

Exclusions: Applications will not be considered for projects operating outside the county of Wiltshire, individuals, sponsored events, general/large appeals, promotion of religion, party political activities. "The foundation does not intend to substitute monies and support normally provided by the statutory sector. However it is conscious that the boundaries are becoming increasingly blurred. By working closely with the local authorities WCF is able to become involved in complementary and partnership funding with the statutory sector."

Applications: A grants policy booklet is available on application to the foundation and groups are encouraged to make early contact with the Grants Manager to discuss the project before to completing an application form. All applications will be followed up with an on-site visit. Decisions are made at quarterly meetings and applicants should contact the office to obtain closing dates for applications.

Monitoring and evaluation: WCF encourages organisations applying for funds to develop methods for evaluating their work. Contact is made with groups six months into the grant period and groups in receipt of more than one year's funding will be subject to a yearly review, prior to handover of subsequent monies. A written report will be required on completion of the project/funding period, and groups should plan ways of measuring their progress against the development plan and objectives.

Grant aid is viewed as part of an on-going relationship. Organisations in receipt of a grant are asked to provide reports, updates, newsletters, to include mention of the foundation's grant in their annual report and accounts and to invite WCF to their AGM. The foundation is also prepared to be involved in discussions on future developments.

The Harold Hyam Wingate Foundation

£195,000 (1993/94)

Medical aid & disability, medical research, the arts, general

38 Curzon Street, London W1Y 7AF
0171-465 0565

Correspondent: Karen Cohen

Trustees: Mrs M Wingate; R C Wingate; A J Wingate.

Beneficial area: UK and occasionally overseas (mainly Israel).

Information available: Full accounts are on file at the Charity Commission.

General: This foundation was set up in 1960 for the general advancement of Jewish and other charitable organisations. A schedule of 21 Jewish organisations was given with the founding deed along with provisions to verify as necessary the Jewish credentials of other organisations with the Chief Rabbi. Whilst the foundation continues to support many Jewish causes it also supports a wide range of other charities.

In 1993/94, the trust had assets of £5.1 million giving an income of £645,000. General donations have continued to drop steeply, to £195,000 from £277,000 in 1992/93 and £710,000 in 1990/91. In its report the trustees commented that the 30% decrease in the level of grants was to "build up reserves as a future safeguard". The foundation increased by 7% its Wingate Scholarship Fund totalling £331,000 in 1993/94. £103,000 was transferred to the accumulated fund.

The foundation also runs a separate tied Whitechapel Fund and gave a donation of £158,000 in 1993/94 – with similar grants in the two previous years – to the Whitechapel Society which funds the gastro-intestinal unit at the London Hospital.

Apart from this major commitment the foundation gave 77 grants totalling £195,000 in 1993/94. The majority (45) were between £1,000 and £10,000 with 30 lower than £1,000. At least 21 grants totalling £74,000 were given to Jewish organisations. The schedule of grants showed a particular interest in medical research and health care, in education (particularly Jewish studies) and the arts particularly opera.

The largest of the general donations were to Birkbeck College, London University (£33,200), followed by the Oxford Centre for Postgraduate Hebrew Studies (£15,500). Both these appear to be regular beneficiaries of substantial grants. Other major beneficiaries included Appel Unifie Juif de France (£6,900); B'nai B'rith Hillel Foundation (£8,500); English Touring Opera (£7,500); Institute of Jewish Studies (£7,500); School of Oriental & African Studies (£7,500), and the Variety Club Children's Charity Ltd (£10,000).

The foundation also operates a scholarship scheme for students over the age of 24. Details may be obtained from Jane Reid at the above address or from *The Educational Grants Directory*.

Exclusions: No grants to individuals.

Applications: In writing to the correspondent. Applications are considered about every three months. The scholarship scheme has an annual closing date of 1st February.

The Maurice Wohl Charitable Trust

£114,000 (1992/93)

Jewish

9 Cavendish Square, London W1M 0JT
0171-580 3777

Correspondent: D Davis, Executive Director

Trustees: D Davis; Mrs E Latchman; E Latchman; M Wohl; Mrs V Wohl; Prof D Latchman; M Paisner.

Beneficial area: Worldwide.

Information available: Full accounts are on file at the Charity Commission.

General: The activities of this trust have been cut back sharply since the late 1980s when it was giving grants totalling over £350,000 a year. In 1992/93, income was £192,000, similar to previous years, but grants totalled only £114,000. The trust has had a surplus of income over expenditure for a few years and its assets now stand at £1.7 million.

About three quarters of the grants were to Jewish organisations, including all the larger grants. The largest were to Pardes House School Ltd, London (£25,000), Hatzola (£15,000) and the Communaute Israelite de Geneve (£7,400). A further 13 grants were for £1,000 or more, all to Jewish organisations.

Other beneficiaries included medical, health and welfare charities such as Age Concern, Child Psychotherapy Trust, Haemophilia Society, Motability, National Listening Library and Schizophrenia Association of Great Britain.

Exclusions: No grants to individuals.

Applications: To the correspondent in writing.

The Women Caring Trust

£111,000 (1993)

Children and families in Northern Ireland

38 Ebury Street, London SW1W 0LU
0171-730 8883; Fax: 0171-130 8885

Correspondent: Mrs Elizabeth Kennedy, General Secretary

Trustees: Mrs G Darling; Lady Fisher; Mrs M Garland; Lady Hayhoe; Mrs J Herdman; D J R Ker; Mrs D Lindsay; Mrs B Lushington; M MacLoughlin; Mrs L McGown; Lady Quinlan.

Beneficial area: Northern Ireland.

Information available: Full accounts are on file at the Charity Commission.

General: The trust supports a wide range of small local groups concerned with women, children and young people, especially those working on a cross-community basis, eg. self-help groups in need of pump-priming, integrated schools, playgroups, community holidays, music groups etc.. Grants for under £500 can be processed quickly.

In 1993, the trust gave 152 grants totalling £111,000. Grants ranged from £100 to £2,000, with a special grant to Voluntary Service Belfast towards the cost of a new minibus. Annual grants are given to well-established youth organisations and many smaller grants under £500 are made to medium or small groups. Typical recipients include Shantallow Controlled Youth Club/Ballyarnett Church Youth for a year-long cross-community scheme; Oakgrove Integrated Primary School for a nursery unit, and Dee Street Busters in Belfast for their summer scheme.

All projects are visited and monitored by Northern Ireland trustees or their advisers.

Exclusions: No grants for individuals, large capital expenditure or salaries, organisations solely for the welfare of physically or mentally disabled people or drug or alcohol related projects. No grants for holidays outside the island of Ireland.

Applications: Apply in writing giving full details of the project, with copies of accounts showing simple details of income and expenditure. A bank statement is not sufficient. Telephone queries are welcomed from Monday to Thursday. Please give a daytime telephone number where you can be contacted if necessary. Trustees meet quarterly. The trust states that many more applications are received than can be accepted.

Woodlands Green Ltd

£160,000 (1992/93)

Jewish

5 Park Way, Golders Green, London NW11 0EX
0181-905 5432

Correspondent: A J Braceiner

Trustees: A Ost; E Ost; D J A Ost; J A Ost.

Beneficial area: Worldwide.

Information available: Accounts are on file at the Charity Commission, but without a list of grants.

General: In 1992/93, the trust had assets of £844,000 and an income of £242,000. Grants totalled £160,000, but unfortunately no information is available on the beneficiaries.

Applications: In writing to the correspondent.

The Woodroffe Benton Foundation

£89,000 (1993)

General

11 Park Avenue, Keymer, Hassocks, West Sussex BN6 8LT
01273-843244

Correspondent: K P W Stoneley

Trustees: James Hope; Kenneth Stoneley; Colin Russell; Gordon Bartlett; Miss Celia Clout.

Beneficial area: UK.

Information available: Accounts are on file at the Charity Commission, but without a list of grants.

General: In 1994, the trust had assets of £3.8 million, a gross income of £182,000 and an income after expenses of £124,000. £10,000 was given in "Trustees' Personal Donations". The remainder was split equally (£16,400 each) to the following five funds:

Disasters (which distributed £14,500)
Care for the elderly (nil)
Environmental (£25,000)
Educational (£17,700)
General (£22,200)

The amount remaining in each fund varies from £13,000 to £29,000. This is primarily to build and run a nursing home on the campus of a residential home already supported by the trust.

A note to the accounts states: "At a trustees meeting on 16th January 1990 it was resolved that as from 3rd December 1989 proceeds of sales and rent received, less outgoings, from all freehold property owned by the foundation be directed towards sheltered accommodation". Property to the value of £525,000 was allocated. It is the intention of the trustees to provide sufficient funds from the eventual sale of these properties to set up a small nursing home for elderly people in need of sheltered accommodation.

Exclusions: Grants are not made outside the UK and are only made to registered charities. No grants to individuals. Branches of national charities should not apply as grants - if made - would go to the national charity headquarters.

Applications: In writing to the correspondent. Trustees meet quarterly.

The main grants are made at the end of the financial year in December. If applications have to be hand written, and type written is preferred, then black ink should be used as applications are photocopied for the trustees. Audited accounts are invariably required. All applications are acknowledged but further letters are only sent to successful applicants.

The Geoffrey Woods Charitable Foundation

£223,000 (1993/94)

Education, medical and welfare

The Girdlers Company, Girdlers Hall,
Basinghall Avenue, London EC2V 5DD
0171-638 0488

Correspondent: The Clerk

Trustees: The Girdlers Company;
N K Maitland; A J R Fairclough.

Beneficial area: UK.

Information available: Accounts are on file at the Charity Commission, but without a list of grants.

General: The trust has general charitable objects, but in particular the "advancement of education, relief of poverty, and the advancement of religion".

The trust's expenditure is accounted for within three funds of which the largest is the Benefactions Fund. This fund had an income of £182,000 in 1993/94 and grants totalled £173,000. These were divided as follows:

Other benefactions	£157,600
Christmas benefactions	£7,200
General Court Charity	£8,200

Educational grants are given to institutions rather than individuals. Grants to medical and welfare projects are primarily to UK organisations. The trust supports specific projects rather than providing general funding. Grants to overseas charities are only considered on the personal knowledge and recommendation of members of the Girdler's Company. No further information is available on how the fund actually distributes its money.

The other funds are: the New Zealand Fund, which gave grants of £29,000 from an income of £35,000, purely for students from New Zealand to attend Corpus Christi College, Cambridge; the General Court Charity which gave grants totalling £21,000 from an income of £20,000. No further information was available.

Exclusions: No grants to individuals for education.

Applications: In writing to the correspondent. Deadlines for applications are the end of September and end of February.

The A & R Woolf Charitable Trust

£43,000 (1993/94)

General

38 Main Avenue, Moor Park,
Nr Northwood, Middlesex HA6 2LQ
01923-821385

Correspondent: Mrs J D H Rose

Beneficial area: Worldwide, local in Hertfordshire.

Information available: Full accounts are on file at the Charity Commission.

General: In 1993/94, the trust had an income of £67,000 and gave 91 grants totalling £43,000. The largest grants were given to the British Diabetic Association, Lace Market Heritage Trust, UK Committee for UNICEF and the University of Hertfordshire (all £5,000); Queen Charlottes Hospital and the Magistrates Association both received £4,000.

The other grants ranged from £50 to £2,000. About 20 grants were to Jewish organisations with the rest to animal welfare and conservation causes, health and welfare charities. Both UK and overseas charities (through a British-based office) received support, together with local charities in Hertfordshire. Up to half the grants were recurrent from the previous year.

Applications: Support is only given to causes known to the trustees. The trust does not respond to unsolicited applications.

The World in Need

£106,000 (1993/94)

Charities compatible with Christian objectives

103 High Street, Oxford OX1 4BW
01865-794411

Correspondent: Nicholas Colloff, Director

Trustees: M O Feilden, Chair; J A Bridgland; J C Cole; H B Faulkner; Sir John Ford; J R O'N Martin; N F Maynard; Mrs P V Maynard; M Robson; R Stanley; Mrs S Webster; N K Wright, Chair Finance Committee.
Consultant Trustees: M Graham-Jones; Felix Appelbe.

Beneficial area: Worldwide.

Information available: Full accounts are on file at the Charity Commission. The trust also publishes a leaflet called "WIN: A brief account of activities".

General: This trust, previously known as the Phyllis Trust, supports seed-corn projects, compatible with Christian objectives, which are seen to be initiating innovative work or developing the scale of an existing charity's activities. The trust aims to support projects which are potentially self-financing and self-managing after WIN's support has expired (usually after two or three years).

As the major AIDS initiatives supported by the trust progressed towards becoming self-sufficient in 1991, the emphasis changed to finding new areas of need. In 1992, the trust's focus moved to setting up a fund-raising trust in the UK (the Opportunity Trust) to support programmes in microenterprise development amongst the poor in developing countries. After research, the trustees authorised a budget of £60,000 in 1991 to cover the cost of establishing the trust and it has continued to receive substantial support.

World in Need annually derives income from Helping Hands Charity Shops Limited and Andrews & Partners Limited. After a relatively poor year in 1991/92, the income from these sources has increased again with £109,000 from the Partners and £91,000 from the Shops in 1993/94. The total income was £210,000, and the trust has assets of £363,000.

The Opportunity Trust received £99,000 of the £106,000 given in grants. This trust in turn gave £420,000 to overseas projects in 1993/94, from an income of £480,000.

The two smaller grants given by World in Need were £3,500 to Bath Cancer Research Unit and £3,000 to Common Land Trust. The trustees also sanctioned grants, not yet spent, amounting to £173,000.

Exclusions: No grants to individuals or for the construction, restoration or alteration of buildings, nor for the general subsidy of on-going work. "We tend to focus on one or two major projects at any one time which the trustees are involved in. We do not want to exclude the possibility of smaller grants to innovative projects that might not otherwise come into being without our support." Registered charities only.

Applications: To the correspondent, but see above.

The World Memorial Fund for Disaster Relief

£100,000 (1993)

Disaster relief

Europa House, 13-17 Ironmonger Row, London EC1V 3QN
0171-250 1700

Correspondent: David Childs, Director

Trustees: David Puttnam; Sir Peter Ramsbotham; Lady Ryder of Warsaw.

Beneficial area: Worldwide.

Information available: Accounts are on file at the Charity Commission.

General: The fund aims to raise money in memory of each of the victims of war this century (£5 for each of 100 million lives) to provide a permanent global fund.

Initially, while the trust was raising the endowment, a special fundraising appeal called 1st AID was set up to give grants. These grants were for British charities involved with emergency disaster relief. The United Nations (among others) informed and updated the trust of disasters around the world and grants were usually given in the first three to four days of the disaster. Disaster relief does not include on-going third world development projects. Grants were given to the most effective organisations, large or small, working in the area.

In the first couple of months of operation, 1st AID supported Feed the Children (for food lorries to Bosnia for Christmas); British Red Cross (for flood victims in Iran), and Woman Kind (for cyclone victims in the Soloman Islands). This fund has now ceased to function separately.

In 1993/94, the fund had assets of £534,000 and income of £287,000 with grants totalling £51,000. No information on the grant beneficiaries was available.

Exclusions: No grants for individuals; development aid; organisational, administrative or office overheads; and disaster prevention or amelioration.

Applications: In writing to the correspondent in writing, or by telephone or fax (for emergency disaster appeals).

The Fred & Della Worms Charitable Trust

£169,000 (1992/93)

Jewish, education, arts

Frederick House, 58a Crewyf Road, London NW2 2AD
0181-458 1181

Correspondent: F S Worms

Trustees: Mrs D Worms; M Paisner; F S Worms.

Beneficial area: UK.

Information available: Full accounts are on file at the Charity Commission.

General: In 1992/93, the trust had assets of £1.46 million. Grant-making dropped by £34,000 from the previous year to £169,000. About 100 grants were given. 20 of these were small subscriptions, 62 grants were between £100 and £1,000, and 19 grants were £1,000 and higher.

All but eight of the grants were to Jewish organisations, with other grants particularly to major arts organisations — the Royal Academy, the National Theatre and the London Philharmonic Orchestra. Many grants are recurrent.

By far the largest grant in 1992/93 was given to the Jewish Education Development Trust (£56,500). Other larger grants were given to: the Jerusalem Foundation (£25,000, also given in the previous year); the Child Settlement Fund,

Emunah (£15,100, with £5,080 in the previous year); Society of Friends of Jewish Refugees (£8,000 with £10,000 in the previous year).

Applications: In writing to the correspondent.

Worshipful Company of Chartered Accountants General Charitable Trust

£38,000 (1992/93)

General

Abbotswood, Stelling Minnis, Canterbury, Kent CT4 6BJ

Correspondent: J E Maxwell

Trustees: D B Shaw; J A Ferguson; R W J Foster; K A Jeffries; J J Macnamara; F E Worsley.

Beneficial area: Worldwide.

Information available: Full accounts are on file at the Charity Commission.

General: In 1992/93, the trust had assets of £562,000 and an income of £82,000. Grants totalled £38,000 leaving a surplus of £29,000.

The trust selects a project theme for each year and gives a single large grant to one project from the suitable applications it receives. Small grants may be given to other suitable applicants. In 1993, the project theme was "People with disabilities", with a grant of £25,000 going to "Cherry Trees" a respite care home for children in East Clandon. Small donations totalling £6,000 were given to about 30 other applicants.

In 1993/94, the project theme was "Hospices and other support for the terminally ill."

The trust also continues to support the Lord Mayor's Appeal (£2,500) and the development of the profession in certain Commonwealth countries (£100). 10 general grants totalling £3,100 were also given, but the beneficiaries are not listed.

Applications: In writing to the correspondent.

The Worshipful Company of Shipwrights

£48,000 (1994)

Maritime charities, youth and heritage, general

Ironmongers Hall, Barbican,
London EC2Y 8AA
0171-606 2376

Correspondent: The Clerk

Trustees: Michael Robinson; Richard Moore; Captain Channon.

Beneficial area: UK, with a preference for the London area.

Information available: Accounts are on file at the Charity Commission, but without a list of grants.

General: In 1994, the trust had assets of £488,000 and an income of £74,000, of which £30,000 was received from the Sir John Fisher Foundation. Grants totalled £48,000 and were categorised as follows:

Annual donations	£20,000;
General donations	£6,000;
Outdoor Activity Bursaries	£22,000.

21 annual donations were given, the largest being £3,000 to the Royal Merchant Navy School Foundation and £2,000 each to City of London Sea Cadets, City of London Outward Bound Association and George Green's School in the Isle of Dogs (a school founded by a famous shipbuilder and shipowner). Other annual grants went mainly to national charities associated with seafaring eg. British Sailors Society, King George's Fund for Sailors, Missions to Seamen and the Sail Training Association.

12 general donations were made mainly for £500, with beneficiaries including six local sea cadet groups (mainly for repairs to headquarters), Hendon Unit Sea Training Corps, Jubilee Sailing Trust and the "Not Forgotten" Association.

Bursaries were awarded to five organisations including the Ocean Youth Club, Outward Bound Trust and the Sail Training Association.

Exclusions: Any application without a clear maritime/waterborne connection. Outdoor activities bursaries are awarded only to young people sponsored by liverymen in response to an annual invitation.

Applications: In writing to the correspondent. Applications are considered in February, June and November.

The Matthews Wrightson Charity Trust

£58,000 (1994)

Caring and Christian charities

The Farm, Northington, Alresford,
Hants SO24 9TH

Correspondent: Adam Lee, Secretary & Administrator

Trustees: Miss Priscilla W Wrightson; Anthony H Isaacs; Guy D G Wrightson.

Beneficial area: UK and some overseas.

Information available: Full accounts are on file at the Charity Commission.

General: The trust has net capital of £1.3 million and gave 142 grants totalling £58,300 in 1994. The trustees like to support smaller charities seeking to raise under £250,000 (and particularly under £25,000), with an emphasis on care. Areas of concern are youth and education, recovery from addiction, disabled and elderly people, homelessness or other caring charities including a few international organisations.

The largest grant is to the Royal College of Art for student bursaries. Donations are occasionally made to individuals, students or participants in expeditions under charitable auspices.

Gifts are made in units of £250/£300, with a few larger gifts deriving from long-standing or special connections, from a list reviewed annually. No commitments are made beyond one year. The trust categorised its grants as follows:

Arts and arts welfare	19%
Christian	9%
Homeless and disabled	10%
Individuals	10%
International	4%
Medical	7%
Old	2%
Rehabilitation	9%
Youth	16%
Unclassified	3%

Charities receiving £1,000 to £1,500 included several organisations with a Christian slant: CARE Trust, Life for the World and the Genesis Arts Trust. Other beneficiaries of £1,000 grants included the Camphill Village Trust (Botton Village), Disabled Housing Trust, Prince's Youth Business Trust and St Mungo Association Charitable Trust.

Most of the remaining grants were for £250, and were given to a variety of causes as outlined above, including Afghan Aid, Centrepoint Soho, Home Farm Trust, Pro Corda and Voluntary Service Belfast.

Exclusions: No support for unconnected local churches, village halls, schools etc.. No animal charities. Non-qualifying applications are not reported to the trustees.

Applications: In writing to the correspondent. No special forms, although latest financial accounts are desirable. 1-2 sheets (usually the covering letter) are circulated monthly to the trustees, who meet six-monthly only for policy and administrative decisions. Replies are only sent to successful applicants; allow up to two months for answer. No need for an sae, unless an answer is required if unsuccessful.

The correspondent receives about 1,000 applications a year; "winners have to make the covering letter more attractive than the 80 others each month".

The Yapp Education & Research Trust

£91,000 (1991)

Schools, universities, colleges of higher education and hospitals

Kidd Rapinet, Solicitors, 14-15 Craven Street, London WC2N 5AD

Correspondent: L V Waumsley

Trustees: D C Hutchison; Rev T C Brooke; Miss A J Norman; M W Rapinet.

Beneficial area: UK.

Information available: Guidance notes for applicants, reprinted below. Full accounts are on file at the Charity Commission up to 1991.

General: In 1990/91, the trust had assets of £1.44 million with an income of £104,000. Grants are only given to applicants who have charitable status under the law of any part of the United Kingdom.

Grants are given to schools, universities, colleges of higher education and hospitals, for the advancement of education and learning, and of scientific and medical research.

In 1990/91, grants totalled £91,000 with £10,000 each given to the Hearing Research Trust and Keratec – St George's Medical School. Other beneficiaries included Cystic Fibrosis Research Trust, Earthwatch Europe, Friends of the Earth, Joint Educational Trust, Liverpool Drug Dependency Clinic, Maxilla Nursing Centre, Postgraduate Medical Centre – South Tyneside District Hospital and Stepping Stones Farm.

Exclusions: The trustees do NOT make grants within the following categories:

- Applications made by, or on behalf of, individuals;
- Applications made by non-charities in the name, or under the auspices, of a third party with charitable status;
- University expeditions;
- School building or development funds;
- Applications where the total amount of the appeal exceeds £100,000 (unless the balance of the appeal at the date of application is less than this figure);
- Applications from any applicant who has already received a grant from either the trust or the Yapp Welfare Trust (*see following entry*) within the preceding THREE YEARS.

Applications: In writing to the correspondent. Applicants are invited to complete and return a short standard application form. The trustees also expect to receive a copy of the applicant's latest accounts. Annual reports, newsletters or brochures should also be included with any application, but such supporting documentation should be kept reasonably brief. Applicants must include five copies of any supporting documents, and "applications submitted without the necessary supporting documents will be rejected automatically".

The trustees meet three times a year (usually in the middle of March, July and November) to consider grant applications. The list of applications is closed six weeks before the date of each meeting, and any application received after the closing date for one meeting is automatically carried forward to the next. All applicants will be notified of the outcome of their appeal.

The Yapp Welfare Trust

£163,000 (1990/91)

Social welfare

Kidd Rapinet, Solicitors, 14-15 Craven Street, London WC2N 5AD

Correspondent: L V Waumsley

Trustees: D C Hutchinson; R St J Pitts-Tucker; A J Norman; M W Rapinet; T Brooke.

Beneficial area: UK.

Information available: Full accounts are on file at the Charity Commission for 1990/91.

General: The trust was set up in 1968 by the will of William Yapp, who died in 1946. This was only just in time to fulfil the wishes of Mr Yapp, who directed that a scheme for the distribution of his residuary trust fund among charitable institutions should be settled within 21 years of his death (the scheme was made in 1967). Its objects are:

- To assist with the care and housing of older people;
- To assist youth clubs, youth hostels and student hostels concerned with the welfare of young people;
- To assist with the care and education of mentally or physically disabled people;
- The advancement of moral welfare.

The trust still pursues these objects, with these category headings in the accounts. Total grants made by the trust to date are £1.7 million, with about £425,000 given in each of the four categories.

In 1990/91 the trust had £1.7 million of assets, an income of £196,000 and gave grants totalling £163,000. These were distributed as follows:

Care of older people – £42,000 (23 grants). Both national and local organisations were supported including Age Concern Gloucestershire, Asian Elderly Project, PSS and Scarborough District CVS Dial A Ride.

Youth clubs and similar institutions – £44,000 (39 grants). Grants were mainly to local organisations including Christchurch District Scouts, Dudley Caribbean Friends Association, North Hull Adventure Playground Association, Northern Ireland Association of Boys' Clubs and Welsh Association of Youth Clubs.

Physical and mental disability – £40,000 (34 grants). National and local charities were supported including the Association for Brain Damaged Children, Kent Learning Centre for Disabled Children, Leicester & County Mission for the Deaf, Mobility Trust, Polka Theatre for Children and Vale of Llangollen Canal Boat Trust.

Moral welfare – £41,000 (25 grants). Beneficiaries included the Bridge Project, Portsmouth Housing Trust, Prestatyn Gingerbread and West Lothian Drugs & Alcohol Concern.

Most grants were for £1,000 or less, in contrast to the previous year, when fewer grants were given with only two under £1,000 and most for £3,000 or more.

Applications: To the correspondent in writing, including the most recent accounts. Trustees meet three times a year. The correspondent pointed out that less than 10% of income a year is spent on all administration by the charity, and that applicants spending more than this would stand less chance of success.

The John Young Charitable Settlement

£40,000 (1992/93)

General

Messrs Lee Associates, 6 Great Queen Street, London WC2B 5DG
0171-831 3609

Correspondent: K A Hawkins

Trustees: J M Young; G H Camamile.

Beneficial area: UK.

Information available: Full accounts are on file at the Charity Commission.

General: The trust has seen a large increase in its income in the last two years through donations received. In 1992/93, it received £53,000 in donations and had a total income of £58,000. In 1990/91, the income was £44,000 having risen from only £5,000 in 1990/91. It is not known whether or not the trust will continue to receive donations to maintain its grant giving at its current level.

Grants totalled £40,000 in 1992/93. 12 grants were made ranging from £100 to £6,000. The RSPB received £6,000, having also received £12,600 the previous year, one of only three charities to receive a grant in both years. Six charities received £5,000: Age Concern, Breakfast Club, International Cancer Relief Fund, One World Action, Riverside Studios and Sightsavers. Most recipients were health or welfare charities.

Applications: In writing to the correspondent.

The William Allen Young Charitable Trust

£129,000 (1992/93)

General

The Ram Brewery, Wandsworth, London SW18 4JD
0181-870 0141

Correspondent: J A Young

Trustees: J A Young; T F B Young; J G A Young.

Beneficial area: UK.

Information available: Full accounts are on file at the Charity Commission.

General: The trust has been left shares in Young & Co's Brewery plc in various bequests. Their market value, at one stage over £2 million, has now fallen to £1.6 million. These assets generated an income in 1992/93 of £102,000. Grants totalled £129,000 atrust spent surplus income from previous years.

77 grants were given ranging from £200 to £10,000, with most for £1,000. The largest grants were given to the British Benevolent Fund, Madrid (£10,000) and St Ann's Church, Wandsworth (£8,000) both of which also received large grants in the previous year. Only 14 of the other grants were recurrent, including £5,000 to Aldenham School.

Other large grants went to ADT College Orchestra (£8,000), Corpus Christi College Cambridge (£6,000), and Alexander Kennedy Fund, Jubilee Sailing Trust, King's School Bruton, Manic Depression Fellowship and St Peter's Church Wisborough Green (all £5,000). Most grants were given to national or south London organisations. There was a preference for health and social welfare organisations, but support was also given to a number of churches and education related organisations.

Applications: In writing to the correspondent.

The I A Ziff Charitable Foundation

£109,000 (1992/93)

Education, Yorkshire, arts, youth, medicine

Town Centre House, The Merrion Centre, Leeds LS2 8LY
0113-245 9172

Correspondent: K N Riley, Secretary to the Trustees

Trustees: I Arnold Ziff; Marjorie E Ziff; Michael A Ziff; Edward M Ziff; Ann L Manning.

Beneficial area: UK, preference for Yorkshire.

Information available: Full accounts are on file at the Charity Commission.

General: In 1992/93, the foundation had assets of of £941,000. From an income of £187,000 donations of £109,000 were made. The trust has a preference for Yorkshire.

The University of Leeds received three grants totalling £51,500, whilst £10,000 was given to each of the Ashten Trust, Jewish Philanthropic Association and Prince's Youth Business Trust. Other beneficiaries included Birthright (£1,200), British Heart Foundation (£1,000), Israel Philharmonic Orchestra (£3,000), Leeds City Council (£1,700), Leeds Jewish Welfare Board (£1,000) and Leeds Lord Mayor's Appeal (£1,000 towards the Lineham Farm Challenge).

About 90 grants were made of less than £500 and were given to a wide range of organisations.

Applications: In writing to the correspondent.

Subject index

The following is a subject index for both *A Guide to the Major Trusts Volume 1* and *A Guide to the Major Trusts Volume 2*. It begins with a list of categories used. The categories are fairly wide-ranging to keep the index as simple as possible. These are followed by the index itself. Before using the index, please note the following:

How the index was compiled

1. The index aims to reflect **the most recently recorded grant-making practice**. It is therefore based on our interpretation of what each trust has actually given to, rather than what its policy statement says or charitable objects allow it to do in principle.

2. We have tried to ensure that each trust has given significantly in the areas mentioned (usually at least £10,000), therefore **small, apparently untypical grants have been ignored for this classification**.

3. To be placed in a specific category (eg. Women) there must be a **declared specific interest** rather than a more general inclusion of the subject in the trust's overall grant-making.

4. The index has been **compiled from the latest hard information available to us**. We have cross-checked the index with FunderFinder (for Volume 1) and with our own specialist Guides (eg. *The Arts Funding Guide, Environmental Grants* and *HIV and AIDS*).

Limitations

1. We have **not been able to categorise every grant for every trust**. Even with some large grants it is effectively impossible to decipher precisely what the grant was given for. We have tried to guess intelligently, but sometimes we have been forced either to ignore grants given or simply include the trust in a more general category than it may actually warrant.

2. **Some classifications may simply be incorrect**. For example, a grant may have been given not because the trust supports a particular area of activity but rather because it liked an individual project, or because of a personal contact between the grant-making trust and the applying charity. Obviously such factors would not show up in the grants lists.

3. It has not been possible to contact all 1,000 trusts specifically with regard to this index so **policies may have changed** or an apparent trust interest was in fact merely a passing fancy.

4. Sometimes there will be a **geographical restriction** on the trust's grant which is not shown up in this index, or it doesn't give for the **specific purposes you require within that general heading**. Therefore please check:

(a) The trust gives in your geographical area of operation.
(b) The trust gives for the specific purposes you require.
(c) There is no other reason to prevent you making a decent application to this trust.

5. We have **omitted** the **General** category as the number of trusts included made it unusable. We have only included the top 100 trusts in the **Welfare general** category for the same reason.

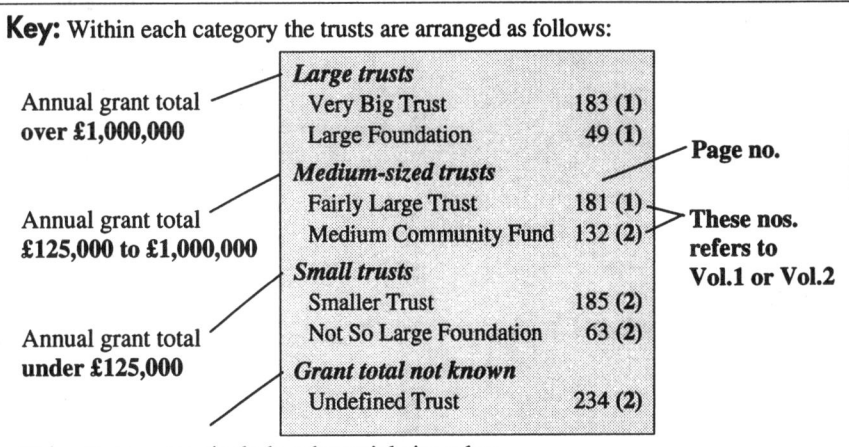

Key: Within each category the trusts are arranged as follows:

Annual grant total over £1,000,000
Large trusts
Very Big Trust   183 (1)
Large Foundation   49 (1)

Annual grant total £125,000 to £1,000,000
Medium-sized trusts
Fairly Large Trust   181 (1)
Medium Community Fund   132 (2)

Annual grant total under £125,000
Small trusts
Smaller Trust   185 (2)
Not So Large Foundation   63 (2)

Grant total not known
Undefined Trust   234 (2)

— Page no.
— These nos. refers to Vol.1 or Vol.2

This category may include substantial givers but we have been unable to obtain up-to-date figures. Their entries should be scrutinised carefully.

Each section is ordered by the **trust's annual grant total, NOT by the amount given in each category**. The largest trusts come first. The reasons for this are:
(a) It is impossible to give an accurate figure for each trust under each heading.
(b) We are trying to point our readers to the largest trusts first as they have by far the most money and generally (though not always) give larger grants.

Under no circumstances should the index be used as a simple mailing list. Remember that each trust is different and that often the policies or interests of a particular trust do not fit easily into the given categories. **Each entry must be read individually and carefully before you send off an application. Indiscriminate applications are usually unsuccessful. They waste time and money and greatly annoy trusts.**

Subject index

The categories are as follows:

Arts *page 257*

A very wide category including performing, written and visual arts, theatres, museums, and galleries.

Civil & social rights

Civil rights/social justice *page 258*
This heading is interpreted very widely to include economic, political, social and legal rights, the democratic process and abuse of power, and equal opportunities.

Ethnic minorities/race relations *page 258*
Equal opportunities is mainly covered under civil rights/social justice, but there is some overlap between these two categories.

Community development and sport/recreation

Local/community development *page 258*
A very wide-ranging category including community associations, local economic regeneration and business start-up and employment initiatives.

Sport/recreation *page 259*
This includes leisure.

Conservation, environment & buildings

Building restoration/preservation *page 259*
Includes secular and religious buildings.

Conservation/environment *page 259*
This includes urban environment as well as global issues.

Animals/wildlife *page 260*
Wildlife and animal conservation. There will be some cross-over with conservation/environment above.

Disaster *page 260*

Both UK and overseas. Includes emergencies.

Overseas development *page 260*

Includes overseas aid and development, not disaster aid.

Education & training *page 261*

A very wide category including support for schools, colleges and universities, training schemes.

Health & welfare

Welfare generally *page 263*
A very general category for social welfare work which does not fit easily into the following categories. Only the largest 100 trusts that give within this category are listed.

Children/youth *page 263*
Mainly for welfare and welfare-related activities.

Elderly *page 265*
Mainly for welfare and welfare-related activities, other than support for hospices.

Women *page 265*
Projects which help redress disadvantage suffered by women.

Homelessness/housing *page 266*
This covers both the provision of housing, shelter and support services for homeless people.

Advice *page 266*
General and welfare rights advice. See also specific categories elsewhere in the health and welfare section (eg. health/medical, disability, HIV/AIDS).

Medical/health generally *page 266*
A wide category which centres on support for people with a medical condition rather than research. It also includes mental health and addictions.

Disability *page 268*

This has been used when the trust has distinguished between disability work and other health-related activities. Again, it centres on support work rather than research. Mental health is largely covered in Medical/health generally.

HIV/AIDS *page 269*
Generally support work for people with AIDS/HIV and their carers.

Hospitals/hospices *page 269*
Generally capital and equipment costs, but will also include some medical research in hospitals.

Marine *page 270*

Seafaring organisations, history of seafaring, seamen's missions and welfare of seafarers.

Non-charitable work *page 270*

Almost all the trusts in the guides can only support charitable work. Two can give grants to non-charitable activity.

Peace & international relations *page 270*

This includes cultural relations.

Penal & crime prevention *page 270*

Includes crime prevention and rehabilitation of offenders.

Religion

Religion general *page 270*
Mainly ecumenical or inter-faith work and where the trust gives grants to more than one faith.

Jewish *page 270*
Welfare, educational and religious work both in the UK and overseas.

The number in brackets after the page reference refers to Vol. 1 or Vol.2 of A Guide to the Major Trusts – **Subject index**

Christian
page 271

Missionary/evangelistic work both in the UK and overseas as well as churches, cathedrals and other Christian building projects. Church-based welfare projects are included in Welfare generally or a more specific heading in the Health & welfare section.

Quaker
page 272

This has been kept separate from Christianity to reflect the specific interests of Quaker foundations.

Islam
page 272

Promoting the Islamic faith rather than work within the community.

Research

Medical research
page 272

Generally clinical research.

Scientific research
page 273

Non-medical scientific research, including the natural sciences.

Research into social issues and the humanities
page 273

Includes social and economic research and some academic research.

Arts

Large trusts

Foundation for Sport and the Arts	221 (1)
Tudor Trust	238 (1)
Baring Foundation	35 (1)
Garfield Weston Foundation	255 (1)
Esmée Fairbairn Charitable Trust	91 (1)
Wolfson Family Charitable Trust	260 (1)
City Parochial Foundation	67 (1)
Monument Trust	164 (1)
John Ellerman Foundation	88 (1)
Robertson Trust	196 (1)
Clothworkers' Foundation	71 (1)
Paul Hamlyn Foundation	109 (1)
Linbury Trust	155 (1)
Peter Moores Foundation	169 (1)
Gannochy Trust	96 (1)
Gulbenkian Foundation	106 (1)
Jerusalem Trust	132 (1)
Mercers' Charitable Foundation	164 (1)
King's Fund	134 (1)
National Art Collections Fund	170 (1)
Headley Trust	116 (1)
Lord Ashdown Charitable Trust	33 (1)
Rayne Foundation	193 (1)
Vivien Duffield Foundation	83 (1)
Goldsmiths' Company's Charities	102 (1)
Save & Prosper Educational Trust	210 (1)
Pilgrim Trust	182 (1)
Mackintosh Foundation	158 (1)
Clore Foundation	70 (1)
J Paul Getty Trust	100 (1)
Kirby Laing Foundation	142 (1)

Medium-sized trusts

Sir James Knott 1990 Trust	139 (1)
Henry Moore Foundation	166 (1)
Djanogly Foundation	82 (1)
P F Charitable Trust	180 (1)
Spitalfields Market Community Trust	221 (1)
Porter Foundation	184 (1)
Welton Foundation	253 (1)
Carnegie United Kingdom Trust	52 (1)
Warbeck Fund Limited	248 (1)
MacRobert Trusts	159 (1)
Maurice Wohl Charitable Foundation	259 (1)
Eranda Foundation	90 (1)
Francis C Scott Charitable Trust	212 (1)
Northern Ireland Voluntary Trust	173 (1)
Daiwa Anglo-Japanese Foundation	81 (1)
Raymond & Beverley Sackler Foundation	206 (2)
Rudolph Palumbo Charitable Foundation	186 (2)
J A Clark Charitable Foundation	70 (1)
Sir John Fisher Foundation	94 (1)
Ernest Cook Trust	75 (1)
John Coates Charitable Trust	73 (1)
John S Cohen Foundation	74 (1)
Chippenham Borough Lands Charity	65 (1)
P H Holt Charitable Trust	124 (1)
Weinstock Fund	251 (1)
Summerfield Charitable Trust	228 (1)
TSB Foundation for Scotland	237 (1)
Raymond Montague Burton Charitable Trust	55 (2)
Great Britain Sasakawa Foundation	104 (1)
Robert Gavron Charitable Trust	104 (2)
Catherine, Lady Grace James and John & Rhys Thomas James Foundation	130 (1)
Kreitman Foundation	139 (1)
Stanley Kalms Foundation	144 (2)
Network Foundation	171 (1)
RVW Trust	204 (2)
Coral Samuel Charitable Trust	210 (1)
Inverforth Charitable Trust	129 (1)
Michael Marks Charitable Trust	161 (1)
Simon Gibson Charitable Trust	101 (1)
Dr Mortimer and Theresa Sackler Foundation	205 (2)
Chase Charity	63 (1)
Harold Hyam Wingate Foundation	248 (2)
Radcliffe Trust	197 (2)
St James' Trust Settlement	207 (2)
Bernerd Foundation	41 (2)
Gilbert & Eileen Edgar Foundation	87 (2)
Britten-Pears Foundation	49 (2)
Eleanor Rathbone Charitable Trust	199 (2)
Fred & Della Worms Charitable Trust	251 (2)
Nancie Massey Charitable Trust	164 (2)
Ward Blenkinsop Trust	239 (2)
Millichope Foundation	170 (2)
Austin & Hope Pilkington Trust	190 (2)
John Jarrold Trust	139 (2)
Sir Jack Lyons Charitable Trust	160 (2)
Roy Fletcher Charitable Trust	98 (2)
Scouloudi Foundation	212 (2)
Bryant Trust	52 (2)
Margaret Davies Charity	80 (2)
Sue Hammerson's Charitable Trust	119 (2)
Hobson Charity Ltd	129 (2)
Michael & Ilse Katz Foundation	144 (2)
Godinton Charitable Trust	107 (2)
Golden Bottle Trust	108 (2)
D'Oyly Carte Charitable Trust	77 (2)
Leche Trust	153 (2)
Idlewild Trust	134 (2)
Equity Trust Fund	92 (2)
Marsh Christian Trust	163 (2)
Granada Foundation	111 (2)

Small trusts

Ouseley Trust	185 (2)
Rosemary Bugden Charitable Trust	52 (2)
Michael Bishop Foundation	43 (2)
Milton Keynes Community Trust	170 (2)
I A Ziff Charitable Foundation	254 (2)
Morris Leigh Foundation	154 (2)
Elmgrant Trust	89 (2)
Gordon Fraser Charitable Trust	101 (2)

● **Subject index** – The number in brackets after the page reference refers to Vol. 1 or Vol.2 of A Guide to the Major Trusts

INTACH (UK) Trust	136 (2)
Grand Order of Water Rats Charities Fund	111 (2)
Stoll Moss Theatres Foundation	223 (2)
Edward & Dorothy Cadbury Charitable Trust	56 (2)
Elm Trust II	89 (2)
Swire Charitable Trust	226 (2)
Baltic Charitable Fund	37 (2)
J G Graves Charitable Trust	112 (2)
Ashden Charitable Trust	33 (2)
Gibbs Charitable Trusts	106 (2)
Orpheus Trust	185 (2)
Leonard Sainer Charitable Trust	206 (2)
Old Possums Practical Trust	185 (2)
Holst Foundation	129 (2)
Audrey Sacher Charitable Trust	205 (2)
Jack Goldhill Charitable Trust	108 (2)
Esme Mitchell Trust	173 (2)
Ironmongers' Quincentenary Fund	138 (2)
Stevenson Family's Charitable Trust	223 (2)
Clifton Charitable Trust	67 (2)
Anthony & Elizabeth Mellows Charitable Settlement	168 (2)
Janatha Stubbs Foundation	224 (2)
Charlotte Bonham-Carter Charitable Trust	46 (2)
Jack & Ruth Lunzer Charitable Trust	158 (2)
Robert Kiln Charitable Trust	146 (2)
Worshipful Company of Shipwrights	252 (2)
David Cohen Family Charitable Trust	68 (2)
Mayfield Valley Arts Trust	165 (2)

Grant total not known

Dandelion Trust	78 (2)
National Lottery	171 (1)
Ireland Funds	136 (2)

Civil rights/social justice

Large trusts

Tudor Trust	238 (1)
Baring Foundation	35 (1)
Joseph Rowntree Charitable Trust	199 (1)
Westminster Foundation for Democracy	255 (1)
Barrow Cadbury Trust	45 (1)
Lord Ashdown Charitable Trust	33 (1)
Mackintosh Foundation	158 (1)

Medium-sized trusts

Trust for London	234 (1)
Methodist Relief & Development Fund	168 (2)
Northern Ireland Voluntary Trust	173 (1)
Hilden Charitable Fund	121 (1)
Alan and Babette Sainsbury Charitable Fund	208 (1)
Barrow Cadbury Fund Ltd	45 (1)

Network Foundation	171 (1)
Polden-Puckham Charitable Foundation	183 (1)
St James' Trust Settlement	207 (2)
W F Southall Trust	221 (2)
Lyndhurst Settlement	159 (2)
Batchworth Trust	38 (2)

Small trusts

Ajahma Charitable Trust	30 (2)
Chownes Foundation	64 (2)
Noel Buxton Trust	180 (2)
Bromley Trust	50 (2)

Ethnic minorities/race relations

Large trusts

Tudor Trust	238 (1)
Baring Foundation	35 (1)
Joseph Rowntree Charitable Trust	199 (1)
Lankelly Foundation	146 (1)
Barrow Cadbury Trust	45 (1)
Housing Associations Charitable Trust (HACT)	125 (1)
J Paul Getty Trust	100 (1)

Medium-sized trusts

Trust for London	234 (1)
Spitalfields Market Community Trust	221 (1)
Hilden Charitable Fund	121 (1)
Alan and Babette Sainsbury Charitable Fund	208 (1)
John Moores Foundation	168 (1)
Allen Lane Foundation	145 (1)
Barrow Cadbury Fund Ltd	45 (1)
Laura Ashley Foundation	33 (2)
Eleanor Rathbone Charitable Trust	199 (2)
St Katharine and Shadwell Trust	207 (2)
Bryant Trust	52 (2)
Lyndhurst Settlement	159 (2)
Irish Youth Foundation (UK) Ltd	137 (2)

Small trusts

Ultach Trust	232 (2)
Liverpool & Merseyside Charitable Fund	156 (2)
Ireland Funds	136 (2)

Local/community development

Large trusts

Tudor Trust	238 (1)
Henry Smith's (Kensington Estate) Charity	214 (1)
Baring Foundation	35 (1)
Shetland Islands Council Charitable Trust	214 (1)
City Parochial Foundation	67 (1)
Rank Foundation	190 (1)

Joseph Rowntree Charitable Trust	199 (1)
Clothworkers' Foundation	71 (1)
Dulverton Trust	84 (1)
Lankelly Foundation	146 (1)
Gulbenkian Foundation	106 (1)
Barrow Cadbury Trust	45 (1)
Alchemy Foundation	27 (1)
Headley Trust	116 (1)
Lord Ashdown Charitable Trust	33 (1)
Goldsmiths' Company's Charities	102 (1)
J Paul Getty Trust	100 (1)
Wates Foundation	249 (1)

Medium-sized trusts

Sir James Knott 1990 Trust	139 (1)
Trust for London	234 (1)
Tyne & Wear Foundation	245 (1)
Gosling Foundation Ltd	103 (1)
TSB Foundation for England and Wales	235 (1)
MacRobert Trusts	159 (1)
Charles Hayward Trust	115 (1)
Northern Ireland Voluntary Trust	173 (1)
Richmond Parish Lands Charity	195 (1)
Hilden Charitable Fund	121 (1)
Laing's Charitable Trust	140 (1)
William Leech Charity	150 (1)
John Moores Foundation	168 (1)
AIM Foundation	27 (1)
Chippenham Borough Lands Charity	65 (1)
United Trusts	234 (2)
P H Holt Charitable Trust	124 (1)
Barrow Cadbury Fund Ltd	45 (1)
Mrs Smith and Mount Trust	219 (1)
Hull & East Riding Charitable Trust	128 (1)
Spitalfields Market Training Initiative	222 (2)
Puebla Charitable Trust	195 (2)
Divert Trust	83 (2)
Van Neste Foundation	235 (2)
Charles S French Charitable Trust	102 (2)
St Katharine and Shadwell Trust	207 (2)
Roy Fletcher Charitable Trust	98 (2)
Alfred Haines Charitable Trust	118 (2)
Pyke Charity Trust	195 (2)
Irish Youth Foundation (UK) Ltd	137 (2)

Small trusts

Enkalon Foundation	91 (2)
Barbour Trust	37 (2)
Greatham Hospital of God	114 (2)
Greater Bristol Foundation	112 (2)
Earl Cadogan's Charity Trust	57 (2)
Women Caring Trust	249 (2)
Milton Keynes Community Trust	170 (2)
GWR Community Trust	116 (2)
Amelia Chadwick Trust	61 (2)
Carnegie Dunfermline Trust	58 (2)
Sheldon Trust	214 (2)
Liverpool & Merseyside Charitable Fund	156 (2)
Cleveland Community Foundation	66 (2)
Ireland Fund of Great Britain	136 (2)
Billmeir Charitable Trust	42 (2)

The number in brackets after the page reference refers to Vol. 1 or Vol.2 of A Guide to the Major Trusts – Subject index

Belvedere Trust	39 (2)
Millfield House Foundation	169 (2)
Wiltshire Community Foundation	247 (2)
Thompson Charitable Trust	228 (2)
Ironmongers' Quincentenary Fund	138 (2)
Westcroft Trust	244 (2)
Girling (Cwmbran) Trust	107 (2)
Gay & Peter Hartley's Hillards Charitable Trust	123 (2)
New Horizons Trust	179 (2)

Grant total not known

Dandelion Trust	78 (2)
Community Trusts	72 (2)
Ireland Funds	136 (2)

Sport/recreation

Large trusts

Foundation for Sport and the Arts	221 (1)
Tudor Trust	238 (1)
Shetland Islands Council Charitable Trust	214 (1)
Bernard Sunley Charitable Foundation	229 (1)
Childwick Trust	65 (1)
Gannochy Trust	96 (1)

Medium-sized trusts

Sir James Knott 1990 Trust	139 (1)
Lord's Taverners	157 (1)
Welsh Church Funds	242 (2)
Ulverscroft Foundation	233 (2)
Daiwa Anglo-Japanese Foundation	81 (1)
Searle Charitable Trust	213 (2)
Prince of Wales' Charities Trust	185 (1)
Great Britain Sasakawa Foundation	104 (1)
Lister Charitable Trust	156 (2)
Bedford Charity	39 (2)
Privy Purse Charitable Trust	195 (2)
Divert Trust	83 (2)
Christopher Laing Foundation	149 (2)
Gilbert & Eileen Edgar Foundation	87 (2)
Football Association Youth Trust	98 (2)
Football Association National Sports Centre Trust	98 (2)
John Watson's Trust	240 (2)

Small trusts

Norton Foundation	182 (2)
Sir Jeremiah Colman Gift Trust	70 (2)
A M Fenton Trust	95 (2)
J G Graves Charitable Trust	112 (2)
Friarsgate Trust	103 (2)
Chetwode Samworth Charitable Trust	63 (2)
Alan & Rosemary Burrough Charitable Trust	54 (2)
Chris Brasher Trust	48 (2)
Janatha Stubbs Foundation	224 (2)
Tower Hill Improvement Trust	230 (2)
Worshipful Company of Shipwrights	252 (2)

Grant total not known

National Lottery	171 (1)

Building restoration/preservation

Large trusts

Wolfson Foundation	261 (1)
Garfield Weston Foundation	255 (1)
Esmée Fairbairn Charitable Trust	91 (1)
Monument Trust	164 (1)
Robertson Trust	196 (1)
Lankelly Foundation	146 (1)
Architectural Heritage Fund	31 (1)
Mercers' Charitable Foundation	164 (1)
Headley Trust	116 (1)
Goldsmiths' Company's Charities	102 (1)
Pilgrim Trust	182 (1)
J Paul Getty Trust	100 (1)

Medium-sized trusts

Sir James Knott 1990 Trust	139 (1)
Rufford Foundation	207 (1)
Manifold Trust	161 (1)
Historic Churches Preservation Trust	122 (1)
P F Charitable Trust	180 (1)
Marshall's Charity	161 (1)
Carnegie United Kingdom Trust	52 (1)
Laing's Charitable Trust	140 (1)
John Coates Charitable Trust	73 (1)
G C Gibson Charitable Trust	101 (1)
Beaverbrook Foundation	42 (1)
Sir James Colyer-Fergusson's Charitable Trust	75 (1)
Catherine, Lady Grace James and John & Rhys Thomas James Foundation	130 (1)
Simon Gibson Charitable Trust	101 (1)
Iliffe Family Charitable Trust	135 (2)
Chase Charity	63 (1)
Sir John Priestman Charity Trust	193 (2)
Christopher Laing Foundation	149 (2)
Charity of Thomas Wade & Others	237 (2)
Chapman Charitable Trust	62 (2)
Late Barbara May Paul Charitable Trust	188 (2)
Francis Coales Charitable Foundation	67 (2)
Hobson Charity Ltd	129 (2)
Heritage of London Trust Ltd	126 (2)
Idlewild Trust	134 (2)
Edward Cecil Jones Settlement	142 (2)

Small trusts

Alan Evans Memorial Trust	92 (2)
Inland Waterways Association	135 (2)
Doris Field Charitable Trust	96 (2)
Lasletts (Hinton) Charity	150 (2)
C L Loyd Charitable Trust	158 (2)
Scottish Churches Architectural Heritage Trust	211 (2)
Fairway Trust	93 (2)
Wakefield Trust	238 (2)
Swire Charitable Trust	226 (2)
Arbib Foundation	31 (2)
John & Ruth Howard Charitable Trust	132 (2)
Anthony & Elizabeth Mellows Charitable Settlement	168 (2)
Stanley Smith UK Horticultural Trust	220 (2)
Robert Kiln Charitable Trust	146 (2)
Judge Charitable Foundation	143 (2)

Grant total not known

Dandelion Trust	78 (2)
National Lottery	171 (1)

Conservation/environment

Large trusts

Tudor Trust	238 (1)
Baring Foundation	35 (1)
Garfield Weston Foundation	255 (1)
Esmée Fairbairn Charitable Trust	91 (1)
Shetland Islands Council Charitable Trust	214 (1)
Monument Trust	164 (1)
John Ellerman Foundation	88 (1)
Robertson Trust	196 (1)
Bernard Sunley Charitable Foundation	229 (1)
WWF UK	263 (1)
Dulverton Trust	84 (1)
Lankelly Foundation	146 (1)
Linbury Trust	155 (1)
Gannochy Trust	96 (1)
Whitley Animal Protection Trust	246 (2)
Mercers' Charitable Foundation	164 (1)
National Gardens Scheme Charitable Trust	178 (2)
J Paul Getty Trust	100 (1)
Kirby Laing Foundation	142 (1)
Maurice Laing Foundation	143 (1)
Ernest Kleinwort Charitable Trust	138 (1)
Westminster Foundation	254 (1)

Medium-sized trusts

Sir James Knott 1990 Trust	139 (1)
Manifold Trust	161 (1)
P F Charitable Trust	180 (1)
Spitalfields Market Community Trust	221 (1)
Steel Charitable Trust	226 (1)
Porter Foundation	184 (1)
Mr and Mrs J A Pye's Charitable Settlement	188 (1)
Kulika Charitable Trust	140 (1)
Rudolph Palumbo Charitable Foundation	186 (2)
Ernest Cook Trust	75 (1)
John Coates Charitable Trust	73 (1)
Sir James Reckitt Charity	194 (1)
Prince of Wales' Charities Trust	185 (1)
Sir James Colyer-Fergusson's Charitable Trust	75 (1)
Norwich Town Close Estate Charity	182 (2)

259

● **Subject index** – The number in brackets after the page reference refers to Vol. 1 or Vol.2 of A Guide to the Major Trusts

Joseph Strong Frazer Trust	96 (1)
Network Foundation	171 (1)
Mary Snow Trusts	220 (1)
Rowan Trust	199 (1)
Michael Marks Charitable Trust	161 (1)
Simon Gibson Charitable Trust	101 (1)
Iliffe Family Charitable Trust	135 (2)
Polden-Puckham Charitable Foundation	183 (1)
Greggs Charitable Trust	115 (2)
M J C Stone Charitable Trust	224 (2)
Nancie Massey Charitable Trust	164 (2)
W F Southall Trust	221 (2)
Chapman Charitable Trust	62 (2)
Skinners' Company Lady Neville Charity	217 (2)
David Shepherd Conservation Foundation	215 (2)
Hadrian Trust	117 (2)
Millichope Foundation	170 (2)
Austin & Hope Pilkington Trust	190 (2)
John Jarrold Trust	139 (2)
Scouloudi Foundation	212 (2)
Delves Charitable Trust	81 (2)
Peter Samuel Charitable Trust	209 (2)
Golden Bottle Trust	108 (2)
Lyndhurst Settlement	159 (2)
George W Cadbury Charitable Trust	56 (2)
D'Oyly Carte Charitable Trust	77 (2)
Benham Charitable Settlement	40 (2)
Vincent Wildlife Trust	236 (2)
Idlewild Trust	134 (2)
Lord Faringdon First & Second Charitable Trusts	94 (2)
Marsh Christian Trust	163 (2)

Small trusts

Jephcott Charitable Trust	140 (2)
Macdonald-Buchanan Charitable Trust	160 (2)
Leach Fourteenth Trust	153 (2)
Alan Evans Memorial Trust	92 (2)
Christopher Cadbury Charitable Trust	55 (2)
Paget Charitable Trust	186 (2)
Loke Wan Tho Memorial Foundation	228 (2)
Inland Waterways Association	135 (2)
Cecil Pilkington Charitable Trust	190 (2)
Whitaker Charitable Trust	245 (2)
Ecological Foundation	87 (2)
Woodroffe Benton Foundation	249 (2)
Ofenheim & Cinderford Charitable Trusts	184 (2)
Gordon Fraser Charitable Trust	101 (2)
CLA Charitable Trust	65 (2)
Bromley Trust	50 (2)
INTACH (UK) Trust	136 (2)
Dennis Curry Charitable Trust	77 (2)
Frognal Trust	103 (2)
Hamamelis Trust	118 (2)
Ashden Charitable Trust	33 (2)
Dr & Mrs A Darlington Charitable Trust	79 (2)
Gwendoline Davies Charity	79 (2)
Wilfrid & Constance Cave Foundation	61 (2)
Lance Coates Charitable Trust 1969	67 (2)
Chris Brasher Trust	48 (2)
Hon Charles Pearson Charity Trust	189 (2)
Ripple Effect Foundation	202 (2)
Clifton Charitable Trust	67 (2)
Jill Franklin Trust	100 (2)
Norman Franklin Trust	100 (2)
Susanna Peake Charitable Trust	188 (2)
Tower Hill Improvement Trust	230 (2)
Gough Charitable Trust	110 (2)
Stanley Smith UK Horticultural Trust	220 (2)
Gunter Charitable Trust	116 (2)
Raymond Oppenheimer Foundation	185 (2)
Robert Kiln Charitable Trust	146 (2)
Geoffrey Burton Charitable Trust	54 (2)
Ravensdale Trust	199 (2)
Ellis Campbell Charitable Foundation	57 (2)
Countryside Trust	74 (2)

Grant total not known

National Lottery	171 (1)

Animals/wildlife

Large trusts

Rank Foundation	190 (1)
John Ellerman Foundation	88 (1)
Beit Trust	39 (2)

Medium-sized trusts

Rufford Foundation	207 (1)
Steel Charitable Trust	226 (1)
Jones 1986 Charitable Trust	142 (2)
Martin Laing Foundation	149 (2)
Saddlers' Company Charitable Fund	206 (2)
Mary Webb Trust	251 (1)
Iliffe Family Charitable Trust	135 (2)
Jean Sainsbury Animal Welfare Trust	206 (2)
Sylvanus Charitable Trust	226 (2)
David Shepherd Conservation Foundation	215 (2)
Lennox Hannay Charitable Trust	120 (2)
Millichope Foundation	170 (2)
Norman Family Charitable Trust	181 (2)
Duke of Cornwall's Benevolent Fund	74 (2)
R J Harris Charitable Settlement	122 (2)
Benham Charitable Settlement	40 (2)
Vincent Wildlife Trust	236 (2)
Marsh Christian Trust	163 (2)

Small trusts

Harebell Centenary Fund	121 (2)
Marjorie Coote Animal Charity Fund	73 (2)
Whitley Animal Protection Trust	246 (2)
Macdonald-Buchanan Charitable Trust	160 (2)
Dinam Charity	83 (2)
Alan Evans Memorial Trust	92 (2)
Christopher Cadbury Charitable Trust	55 (2)
Barry Green Memorial Fund	114 (2)
Dumbreck Charity	85 (2)
Eleanor Hamilton Educational Trust	119 (2)
Combined Charities Trust	71 (2)
Wilfred & Elsie Elkes Charity Fund	88 (2)
Hamamelis Trust	118 (2)
Astor of Hever Trust	34 (2)
Dr & Mrs A Darlington Charitable Trust	79 (2)
Ambika Paul Foundation	31 (2)
Gwendoline Davies Charity	79 (2)
Beryl Evetts & Robert Luff Animal Welfare Trust	93 (2)
Kennel Club Charitable Trust	146 (2)
Wilfrid & Constance Cave Foundation	61 (2)
Geoffrey Burton Charitable Trust	54 (2)
Pennycress Trust	189 (2)
Higgs Charitable Trust	128 (2)
Marchig Animal Welfare Trust	162 (2)
Countryside Trust	74 (2)

Disaster

Large trusts

Tudor Trust	238 (1)
Charity Projects	59 (1)
Clothworkers' Foundation	71 (1)

Medium-sized trusts

Bulldog Trust	52 (2)
Golden Bottle Trust	108 (2)

Small trusts

Peter Birse Charitable Trust	42 (2)
World Memorial Fund for Disaster Relief	250 (2)
Oakdale Trust	183 (2)
Woodroffe Benton Foundation	249 (2)
Bacta Charitable Trust	36 (2)

Overseas development

Large trusts

Tudor Trust	238 (1)
Charity Projects	59 (1)
Gatsby Charitable Foundation	97 (1)
Baring Foundation	35 (1)
Clothworkers' Foundation	71 (1)
Bernard Sunley Charitable Foundation	229 (1)
Paul Hamlyn Foundation	109 (1)
Westminster Foundation for Democracy	255 (1)
Beit Trust	39 (2)

The number in brackets after the page reference refers to Vol. 1 or Vol. 2 of A Guide to the Major Trusts – Subject index

Aga Khan Foundation	26 (1)
Kirby Laing Foundation	142 (1)
Maurice Laing Foundation	143 (1)
Rotary Foundation	203 (2)
Ernest Kleinwort Charitable Trust	138 (1)
Concern Universal	72 (2)

Medium-sized trusts

Methodist Relief & Development Fund	168 (2)
Christmas Cracker Trust	64 (2)
Steel Charitable Trust	226 (1)
Sir Halley Stewart Trust	227 (1)
Beatrice Laing Trust	141 (1)
Mrs L D Rope Third Charitable Settlement	198 (1)
J A Clark Charitable Foundation	70 (1)
J G Joffe Charitable Trust	132 (1)
AIM Foundation	27 (1)
Douglas Turner Trust	244 (1)
Charles and Elsie Sykes Trust	231 (1)
William Adlington Cadbury Charitable Trust	48 (1)
Network Foundation	171 (1)
Rowan Trust	199 (1)
Burdens Charitable Foundation	53 (2)
Puebla Charitable Trust	195 (2)
Miriam K Dean Refugee Trust Fund	81 (2)
Cleopatra Trust	66 (2)
Van Neste Foundation	235 (2)
Christopher Laing Foundation	149 (2)
British Council for Prevention of Blindness	49 (2)
W F Southall Trust	221 (2)
John Jarrold Trust	139 (2)
Roy Fletcher Charitable Trust	98 (2)
Dorus Trust	84 (2)
Ajahma Charitable Trust	30 (2)
Cross Trust	75 (2)
Benham Charitable Settlement	40 (2)
Batchworth Trust	38 (2)
Marsh Christian Trust	163 (2)

Small trusts

Mansfield Cooke Trust	72 (2)
Jephcott Charitable Trust	140 (2)
Peter Birse Charitable Trust	42 (2)
Noel Buxton Trust	180 (2)
Dinam Charity	83 (2)
Paget Charitable Trust	186 (2)
Langdale Trust	149 (2)
Fawcett Charitable Trust	94 (2)
Cecil Pilkington Charitable Trust	190 (2)
Oakdale Trust	183 (2)
Ecological Foundation	87 (2)
Mrs C S Heber Percy Charitable Trust	125 (2)
Ashden Charitable Trust	33 (2)
M A Hawe Settlement	124 (2)
Westcroft Trust	244 (2)
Cumber Family Charitable Trust	76 (2)
Ripple Effect Foundation	202 (2)
Clifton Charitable Trust	67 (2)
Jill Franklin Trust	100 (2)
Norman Franklin Trust	100 (2)
Bacta Charitable Trust	36 (2)
Millhouses Charitable Trust	170 (2)
Besom Foundation	41 (2)
Gunter Charitable Trust	116 (2)
Thomas Sivewright Catto Charitable Settlement	60 (2)
Walter Guinness Charitable Trust	116 (2)
Vernon N Ely Charitable Trust	89 (2)
New Durlston Trust	178 (2)
Beacon Trust	38 (2)

Education/training

Large trusts

Tudor Trust	238 (1)
Wolfson Foundation	261 (1)
Leverhulme Trust	153 (1)
Gatsby Charitable Foundation	97 (1)
Baring Foundation	35 (1)
Garfield Weston Foundation	255 (1)
Esmée Fairbairn Charitable Trust	91 (1)
Wolfson Family Charitable Trust	260 (1)
Nuffield Foundation	176 (1)
City Parochial Foundation	67 (1)
Rank Foundation	190 (1)
Robertson Trust	196 (1)
Clothworkers' Foundation	71 (1)
Bernard Sunley Charitable Foundation	229 (1)
Church Urban Fund	66 (1)
Dulverton Trust	84 (1)
Childwick Trust	65 (1)
Charles Wolfson Trust	260 (1)
29th May 1961 Charitable Trust	244 (1)
Paul Hamlyn Foundation	109 (1)
Linbury Trust	155 (1)
Gannochy Trust	96 (1)
Bible Lands Society	43 (1)
Gulbenkian Foundation	106 (1)
Jerusalem Trust	132 (1)
Mercers' Charitable Foundation	164 (1)
Beit Trust	39 (2)
Headley Trust	116 (1)
Lord Ashdown Charitable Trust	33 (1)
Aga Khan Foundation	26 (1)
Rayne Foundation	193 (1)
Allchurches Trust Ltd	29 (1)
Save & Prosper Educational Trust	210 (1)
Carnegie Trust for the Universities of Scotland	51 (1)
Sutton Coldfield Municipal Charities	231 (1)
Clore Foundation	70 (1)
Leathersellers' Company Charitable Fund	149 (1)
Kirby Laing Foundation	142 (1)
Archie Sherman Charitable Trust	213 (1)
Rhodes Trust Public Purposes Fund	195 (1)
Wates Foundation	249 (1)
Dawn James (No 2) Charitable Foundation	131 (1)
Fishmongers' Company's Charitable Trust	95 (1)
Hayward Foundation	115 (1)
Westminster Foundation	254 (1)
Hampton Fuel Allotment Charity	112 (1)

Medium-sized trusts

Sir James Knott 1990 Trust	139 (1)
Sir John Cass's Foundation	56 (1)
Jane Hodge Foundation	123 (1)
Trust for London	234 (1)
Cripplegate Foundation	78 (1)
Djanogly Foundation	82 (1)
Cripps Foundation	79 (1)
Hedley Foundation Ltd	118 (1)
Equitable Charitable Trust	90 (1)
TSB Foundation for England and Wales	235 (1)
Christmas Cracker Trust	64 (2)
Philip and Pauline Harris Charitable Trust	114 (1)
P F Charitable Trust	180 (1)
Spitalfields Market Community Trust	221 (1)
Porter Foundation	184 (1)
Lambeth Endowed Charities	144 (1)
Carnegie United Kingdom Trust	52 (1)
Rose Foundation	198 (1)
Zochonis Charitable Trust	264 (1)
Jones 1986 Charitable Trust	142 (2)
Campden Charities	49 (1)
Oxfam	179 (1)
Eranda Foundation	90 (1)
Sir Cyril Kleinwort Charitable Settlement	137 (1)
Jewish Continuity	141 (2)
Edward Cadbury Trust	48 (1)
Mr and Mrs J A Pye's Charitable Settlement	188 (1)
Leverhulme Trade Charities Trust	152 (1)
William Harding's Charity	114 (1)
Carlton Television Trust	50 (1)
Ulverscroft Foundation	233 (2)
Mrs L D Rope Third Charitable Settlement	198 (1)
W O Street Charitable Foundation	228 (1)
Richmond Parish Lands Charity	195 (1)
Daiwa Anglo-Japanese Foundation	81 (1)
Neil Kreitman Foundation	139 (1)
Lord Leverhulme's Charitable Trust	152 (1)
Sir Siegmund Warburg's Voluntary Settlement	249 (1)
Rudolph Palumbo Charitable Foundation	186 (2)
Sir John Fisher Foundation	94 (1)
Ernest Cook Trust	75 (1)
John Moores Foundation	168 (1)
John Coates Charitable Trust	73 (1)
John S Cohen Foundation	74 (1)
Sir James Reckitt Charity	194 (1)
Horne Foundation	124 (1)
Chippenham Borough Lands Charity	65 (1)
Underwood Trust	234 (2)
P H Holt Charitable Trust	124 (1)

Subject index – The number in brackets after the page reference refers to Vol. 1 or Vol. 2 of A Guide to the Major Trusts

Trades House of Glasgow	233 (1)
Beaverbrook Foundation	42 (1)
Martin Laing Foundation	149 (2)
Prince of Wales' Charities Trust	185 (1)
Sidney & Elizabeth Corob Charitable Trust	77 (1)
H D H Wills 1965 Charitable Trust	258 (1)
Summerfield Charitable Trust	228 (1)
TSB Foundation for Scotland	237 (1)
Raymond Montague Burton Charitable Trust	55 (2)
Great Britain Sasakawa Foundation	104 (1)
Sir George Martin Trust	162 (1)
Rees Jeffreys Road Fund	131 (1)
Robert Gavron Charitable Trust	104 (2)
Norwich Town Close Estate Charity	182 (2)
Catherine, Lady Grace James and John & Rhys Thomas James Foundation	130 (1)
Joseph Strong Frazer Trust	96 (1)
Alice Ellen Cooper-Dean Charitable Foundation	77 (1)
GRP Charitable Trust	106 (1)
All Saints Educational Trust	28 (1)
Mary Snow Trusts	220 (1)
Bedford Charity	39 (2)
Laura Ashley Foundation	33 (2)
Newby Trust Limited	172 (1)
Grocers' Charity	105 (1)
Geoffrey Woods Charitable Foundation	250 (2)
Viscount Amory's Charitable Trust	29 (1)
Spitalfields Market Training Initiative	222 (2)
Needham Cooper Charitable Trust	171 (1)
Privy Purse Charitable Trust	195 (2)
John Porter Charitable Trust	192 (2)
Harry Crook Foundation	80 (1)
Inman Charity	135 (2)
Peter Kershaw Trust	146 (2)
Bulldog Trust	52 (2)
Harold Hyam Wingate Foundation	248 (2)
Burden Trust	53 (2)
Comino Foundation	71 (2)
M J C Stone Charitable Trust	224 (2)
Sarum St Michael Educational Charity	209 (2)
Gilbert & Eileen Edgar Foundation	87 (2)
Roald Dahl Foundation	78 (2)
Lawlor Foundation	151 (2)
Nancie Massey Charitable Trust	164 (2)
A S Hornby Educational Trust	130 (2)
Lord Austin Trust	36 (2)
Skinners' Company Lady Neville Charity	217 (2)
Wilkinson Charitable Foundation	246 (2)
St Katharine and Shadwell Trust	207 (2)
Forte Charitable Trust	99 (2)
Boltons Trust	46 (2)
James Weir Foundation	242 (2)
Roy Fletcher Charitable Trust	98 (2)
Alfred Haines Charitable Trust	118 (2)
Catherine Lewis Foundation	155 (2)
South Square Trust	221 (2)
Margaret Davies Charity	80 (2)
John Watson's Trust	240 (2)
Acacia Charitable Trust	28 (2)
Hobson Charity Ltd	129 (2)
British Schools and Universities Foundation (Inc.)	49 (2)
10th Duke of Devonshire's Trust (1949)	82 (2)
Thornton Foundation	229 (2)
Vardy Foundation	236 (2)
R J Harris Charitable Settlement	122 (2)
Rothermere Foundation	203 (2)
Pyke Charity Trust	195 (2)
Walker Trust	238 (2)
Benham Charitable Settlement	40 (2)
Church Burgesses Educational Foundation	65 (2)
Vincent Wildlife Trust	236 (2)
Hoover Foundation	130 (2)
Irish Youth Foundation (UK) Ltd	137 (2)
William Allen Young Charitable Trust	254 (2)
Astor Foundation	34 (2)
Equity Trust Fund	92 (2)
Marsh Christian Trust	163 (2)
City Educational Trust Fund	65 (2)

Small trusts

Clive Richards Charity Ltd	201 (2)
Thomas Freke & Lady Norton Charity	102 (2)
Harebell Centenary Fund	121 (2)
Charles Littlewood Hill Trust	128 (2)
Westward Trust	245 (2)
Atlantic Foundation	35 (2)
Chownes Foundation	64 (2)
Florence Turner Trust	232 (2)
Peter Birse Charitable Trust	42 (2)
Victor Mishcon Charitable Trust	172 (2)
Thornton Trust	229 (2)
Everard & Mina Goodman Charitable Foundation	109 (2)
Roger & Sarah Bancroft Clark Charitable Trust	65 (2)
I A Ziff Charitable Foundation	254 (2)
Solomon Family Charitable Trust	220 (2)
Christopher Cadbury Charitable Trust	55 (2)
GWR Community Trust	116 (2)
Amelia Chadwick Trust	61 (2)
Marjorie Coote Old People's Charity	73 (2)
Triangle Trust 1949 Fund	231 (2)
Carnegie Dunfermline Trust	58 (2)
Norton Foundation	182 (2)
Elmgrant Trust	89 (2)
Fawcett Charitable Trust	94 (2)
William Webster Charitable Trust	241 (2)
Neville & Elaine Blond Charitable Trust	45 (2)
Whitaker Charitable Trust	245 (2)
Sir Jeremiah Colman Gift Trust	70 (2)
Yapp Education & Research Trust	252 (2)
John Martin's Charity	164 (2)
Ecological Foundation	87 (2)
Woodroffe Benton Foundation	249 (2)
Helen Roll Charitable Trust	202 (2)
London Law Trust	157 (2)
CLA Charitable Trust	65 (2)
Edgar E Lawley Foundation	151 (2)
Mr Thomas Betton's Charity (Educational)	41 (2)
Michael Peacock Charitable Foundation	188 (2)
INTACH (UK) Trust	136 (2)
Mrs C S Heber Percy Charitable Trust	125 (2)
Eleanor Hamilton Educational Trust	119 (2)
Edward & Dorothy Cadbury Charitable Trust	56 (2)
Vivienne & Samuel Cohen Charitable Trust	68 (2)
Dennis Curry Charitable Trust	77 (2)
A M Fenton Trust	95 (2)
Fairway Trust	93 (2)
Vestey Foundation	236 (2)
G M Morrison Charitable Trust	174 (2)
Isabel Blackman Foundation	44 (2)
Armourers & Brasiers Gauntlet Trust	32 (2)
Baltic Charitable Fund	37 (2)
Charles Brotherton Trust	51 (2)
J G Graves Charitable Trust	112 (2)
Harry Bottom Charitable Trust	47 (2)
Stanley Foundation Ltd	222 (2)
Peter Stebbings Memorial Trust	223 (2)
Astor of Hever Trust	34 (2)
Leslie Smith Foundation	219 (2)
Friarsgate Trust	103 (2)
Ambika Paul Foundation	31 (2)
Chetwode Samworth Charitable Trust	63 (2)
Beaufort House Trust	38 (2)
Gem Charitable Trust	104 (2)
M B Foundation	160 (2)
Fowler Memorial Trust	100 (2)
Ian Karten Charitable Trust	144 (2)
Tramman Trust	231 (2)
Wilfrid & Constance Cave Foundation	61 (2)
Cumber Family Charitable Trust	76 (2)
Shuttlewood Clarke Foundation	216 (2)
A R Taylor Charitable Trust	228 (2)
John & Freda Coleman Charitable Trust	69 (2)
Girling (Cwmbran) Trust	107 (2)
D J W Jackson Charitable Trust	139 (2)
Bowland Charitable Trust	48 (2)
Linda Marcus Charitable Trust	162 (2)
Anthony & Elizabeth Mellows Charitable Settlement	168 (2)
Gay & Peter Hartley's Hillards Charitable Trust	123 (2)
Charlotte Bonham-Carter Charitable Trust	46 (2)
John & Celia Bonham Christie Charitable Trust	64 (2)
Haymills Charitable Trust	124 (2)
Tory Family Foundation	230 (2)

The number in brackets after the page reference refers to Vol. 1 or Vol.2 of A Guide to the Major Trusts – **Subject index**

Tower Hill Improvement Trust	230 (2)
Col-Reno Ltd	68 (2)
Dove-Bowerman Trust	85 (2)
Raymond Oppenheimer Foundation	185 (2)
Robert Kiln Charitable Trust	146 (2)
Humanitarian Trust	133 (2)
Walter Guinness Charitable Trust	116 (2)
Judge Charitable Foundation	143 (2)
Reginald Graham Charitable Trust	110 (2)
Huntly & Margery Sinclair Charitable Trust	216 (2)
Sutasoma Trust	225 (2)
Airflow Community Ltd	29 (2)
Frank Parkinson Agricultural Trust	187 (2)
Ellis Campbell Charitable Foundation	57 (2)
Beacon Trust	38 (2)
Girdlers' Company Charitable Trust	106 (2)
Abell Trust	28 (2)
Lanvern Foundation	150 (2)
Hinrichsen Foundation	128 (2)
Hobart Charitable Trust	129 (2)

Grant total not known

Dandelion Trust	78 (2)

Welfare generally

Large trusts

Tudor Trust	238 (1)
Henry Smith's (Kensington Estate) Charity	214 (1)
Baring Foundation	35 (1)
Garfield Weston Foundation	255 (1)
Esmée Fairbairn Charitable Trust	91 (1)
Shetland Islands Council Charitable Trust	214 (1)
Joseph Rowntree Foundation	203 (1)
John Ellerman Foundation	88 (1)
Joseph Rowntree Charitable Trust	203 (1)
Robertson Trust	196 (1)
Clothworkers' Foundation	71 (1)
Church Urban Fund	66 (1)
Dulverton Trust	84 (1)
Lankelly Foundation	146 (1)
29th May 1961 Charitable Trust	244 (1)
Linbury Trust	155 (1)
Peter Moores Foundation	169 (1)
Joseph Rank Benevolent Trust	192 (1)
Gannochy Trust	96 (1)
Bible Lands Society	43 (1)
Gulbenkian Foundation	106 (1)
Alchemy Foundation	27 (1)
Lord Ashdown Charitable Trust	33 (1)
Rayne Foundation	193 (1)
Vivien Duffield Foundation	83 (1)
Goldsmiths' Company's Charities	102 (1)
Allchurches Trust Ltd	29 (1)
Peacock Charitable Trust	181 (1)
Pilgrim Trust	182 (1)

Sutton Coldfield Municipal Charities	231 (1)
Clore Foundation	70 (1)
J Paul Getty Trust	100 (1)
Kirby Laing Foundation	142 (1)
Archie Sherman Charitable Trust	213 (1)
Wates Foundation	249 (1)
David and Frederick Barclay Foundation	35 (1)
Fishmongers' Company's Charitable Trust	95 (1)
Hayward Foundation	115 (1)
Westminster Foundation	254 (1)
Hampton Fuel Allotment Charity	112 (1)

Medium-sized trusts

Pilkington Charities Fund	191 (2)
Rufford Foundation	207 (1)
Cripplegate Foundation	78 (1)
John and Lucille van Geest Foundation	245 (1)
Tyne & Wear Foundation	245 (1)
Hedley Foundation Ltd	118 (1)
Grand Charity of Freemasons	103 (1)
Leeds Hospital Fund Charitable Trust	154 (2)
TSB Foundation for England and Wales	235 (1)
Christmas Cracker Trust	64 (2)
Steel Charitable Trust	226 (1)
Porter Foundation	184 (1)
Welton Foundation	253 (1)
Lambeth Endowed Charities	144 (1)
Joseph Levy Charitable Foundation	154 (1)
Campden Charities	49 (1)
MacRobert Trusts	159 (1)
Maurice Wohl Charitable Foundation	259 (1)
Charles Hayward Trust	115 (1)
Eranda Foundation	90 (1)
Beatrice Laing Trust	141 (1)
Francis C Scott Charitable Trust	212 (1)
William Harding's Charity	114 (1)
Peabody Community Fund	181 (1)
Mrs L D Rope Third Charitable Settlement	198 (1)
Northern Ireland Voluntary Trust	173 (1)
W O Street Charitable Foundation	228 (1)
Richmond Parish Lands Charity	195 (1)
William Leech Charity	150 (1)
Rudolph Palumbo Charitable Foundation	186 (2)
J A Clark Charitable Foundation	70 (1)
Alan Edward Higgs Charity	120 (1)
Sir James Reckitt Charity	194 (1)
Sir John Eastwood Foundation	88 (1)
Horne Foundation	124 (1)
Allen Lane Foundation	145 (1)
Lloyd's Charities Trust	156 (1)
Chippenham Borough Lands Charity	65 (1)
Alexandra Rose Day	30 (2)
Underwood Trust	234 (2)
United Trusts	234 (2)
P H Holt Charitable Trust	124 (1)

Trades House of Glasgow	233 (1)
Christopher Reeves Charitable Trust	194 (1)
Normanby Charitable Trust	173 (1)
Weinstock Fund	251 (1)
Beaverbrook Foundation	42 (1)
Charles and Elsie Sykes Trust	231 (1)
Searle Charitable Trust	213 (2)
Prince of Wales' Charities Trust	185 (1)
William Adlington Cadbury Charitable Trust	48 (1)
Haberdashers' Eleemosynary Charity	109 (1)
Anton Jurgens Charitable Trust	133 (1)
Sidney & Elizabeth Corob Charitable Trust	77 (1)
Hampstead Wells and Campden Trust	112 (1)
Summerfield Charitable Trust	228 (1)
TSB Foundation for Scotland	237 (1)
Raymond Montague Burton Charitable Trust	55 (2)
Sir George Martin Trust	162 (1)
George A Moore Foundation	166 (1)

Children/youth

Large trusts

Tudor Trust	238 (1)
BBC Children in Need Appeal	40 (1)
Henry Smith's (Kensington Estate) Charity	214 (1)
Charity Projects	59 (1)
Gatsby Charitable Foundation	97 (1)
Baring Foundation	35 (1)
Prince's Youth Business Trust	187 (1)
Garfield Weston Foundation	255 (1)
Esmée Fairbairn Charitable Trust	91 (1)
Prince's Trust and the Royal Jubilee Trusts	186 (1)
City Parochial Foundation	67 (1)
Rank Foundation	190 (1)
Variety Club Children's Charity Limited	247 (1)
Clothworkers' Foundation	71 (1)
Bernard Sunley Charitable Foundation	229 (1)
Church Urban Fund	66 (1)
Dulverton Trust	84 (1)
Lankelly Foundation	146 (1)
Linbury Trust	155 (1)
Joseph Rank Benevolent Trust	192 (1)
Gulbenkian Foundation	106 (1)
Alchemy Foundation	27 (1)
Headley Trust	116 (1)
Aga Khan Foundation	26 (1)
Vivien Duffield Foundation	83 (1)
Eveson Charitable Trust	91 (1)
Save & Prosper Educational Trust	210 (1)
Mackintosh Foundation	158 (1)
Clore Foundation	70 (1)
J Paul Getty Trust	100 (1)

● **Subject index** – The number in brackets after the page reference refers to Vol. 1 or Vol.2 of A Guide to the Major Trusts

Kirby Laing Foundation	142 (1)
Maurice Laing Foundation	143 (1)
Ernest Kleinwort Charitable Trust	138 (1)
Wates Foundation	249 (1)
Children Nationwide Medical Research Fund	64 (1)
Westminster Foundation	254 (1)
Hampton Fuel Allotment Charity	112 (1)

Medium-sized trusts

Pilkington Charities Fund	191 (2)
Sir James Knott 1990 Trust	139 (1)
Rufford Foundation	207 (1)
Trust for London	234 (1)
Cripplegate Foundation	78 (1)
John Lyon's Charity	158 (1)
Tyne & Wear Foundation	245 (1)
Hedley Foundation Ltd	118 (1)
P F Charitable Trust	180 (1)
Capital Radio – Help A London Child	49 (1)
Carnegie United Kingdom Trust	52 (1)
Warbeck Fund Limited	248 (1)
Joseph Levy Charitable Foundation	154 (1)
Percy Bilton Charity Ltd	43 (1)
Rose Foundation	198 (1)
Oxfam	179 (1)
MacRobert Trusts	159 (1)
Sir Halley Stewart Trust	227 (1)
Radio Clyde – Cash for Kids at Christmas	189 (1)
Beatrice Laing Trust	141 (1)
Sir Cyril Kleinwort Charitable Settlement	137 (1)
Mr and Mrs J A Pye's Charitable Settlement	188 (1)
Francis C Scott Charitable Trust	212 (1)
Kulika Charitable Trust	140 (1)
Northern Ireland Voluntary Trust	173 (1)
Baron Davenport's Charity Trust	82 (1)
Tompkins Foundation	233 (1)
Alan Edward Higgs Charity	120 (1)
Sir James Reckitt Charity	194 (1)
Clover Trust	73 (1)
Horne Foundation	124 (1)
Allen Lane Foundation	145 (1)
AIM Foundation	27 (1)
Chippenham Borough Lands Charity	65 (1)
Alexandra Rose Day	30 (2)
Christopher Reeves Charitable Trust	194 (1)
Weinstock Fund	251 (1)
Beaverbrook Foundation	42 (1)
Herbert & Peter Blagrave Charitable Trust	45 (1)
Bernard van Leer Foundation	246 (1)
Prince of Wales' Charities Trust	185 (1)
Adint Charitable Trust	25 (1)
Summerfield Charitable Trust	228 (1)
Great Britain Sasakawa Foundation	104 (1)
George A Moore Foundation	166 (1)
Jill Kreitman Foundation	148 (2)
Cash for Kids	59 (2)

Joseph Strong Frazer Trust	96 (1)
Cotton Trust	77 (1)
Sheffield Town Trust	214 (2)
Bedford Charity	39 (2)
Burdens Charitable Foundation	53 (2)
Hull & East Riding Charitable Trust	128 (1)
Patrick Charitable Trust	180 (1)
W A Handley Charity Trust	113 (1)
Viscount Amory's Charitable Trust	29 (1)
Privy Purse Charitable Trust	195 (2)
Harry Crook Foundation	80 (1)
Chase Charity	63 (1)
Divert Trust	83 (2)
Greggs Charitable Trust	115 (2)
Sir John Priestman Charity Trust	193 (2)
Homelands Charitable Trust	129 (2)
Burden Trust	53 (2)
Emmandjay Charitable Trust	90 (2)
Gilbert & Eileen Edgar Foundation	87 (2)
Charity of Thomas Wade & Others	237 (2)
Nancie Massey Charitable Trust	164 (2)
Yapp Welfare Trust	253 (2)
Lord Austin Trust	36 (2)
Skinners' Company Lady Neville Charity	217 (2)
Charles S French Charitable Trust	102 (2)
St Katharine and Shadwell Trust	207 (2)
Hadrian Trust	117 (2)
Prince's Scottish Youth Business Trust	186 (1)
Norman Family Charitable Trust	181 (2)
Roy Fletcher Charitable Trust	98 (2)
Alfred Haines Charitable Trust	118 (2)
Man of the People Fund	160 (2)
Westminster Amalgamated Charity	244 (2)
Dorus Trust	84 (2)
10th Duke of Devonshire's Trust (1949)	82 (2)
Northmoor Trust	181 (2)
Black Charitable Trusts	43 (2)
Benham Charitable Settlement	40 (2)
Irish Youth Foundation (UK) Ltd	137 (2)
Lord Barnby's Foundation	37 (2)
Castle Educational Trust	60 (2)
Weavers' Company Benevolent Fund	240 (2)
Edward Cecil Jones Settlement	142 (2)

Small trusts

Thomas Freke & Lady Norton Charity	102 (2)
Barbour Trust	37 (2)
Peter Minet Trust	171 (2)
Access 4 Trust	29 (2)
Bill Butlin Charity Trust	55 (2)
Charles Littlewood Hill Trust	128 (2)
Greater Bristol Foundation	112 (2)
Noel Buxton Trust	180 (2)
Earl Cadogan's Charity Trust	57 (2)
Everard & Mina Goodman Charitable Foundation	109 (2)
Women Caring Trust	249 (2)
J N Derbyshire Trust	81 (2)
Dinam Charity	83 (2)

I A Ziff Charitable Foundation	254 (2)
Norman Collinson Charitable Trust	70 (2)
Princess Anne's Charities	194 (2)
Paget Charitable Trust	186 (2)
Carnegie Dunfermline Trust	58 (2)
Handicapped Children's Aid Committee	119 (2)
Sheldon Trust	214 (2)
Wall Charitable Trust	238 (2)
Norton Foundation	182 (2)
Fawcett Charitable Trust	94 (2)
Whitaker Charitable Trust	245 (2)
Radio Tay – Caring for Kids	197 (2)
Cleveland Community Foundation	66 (2)
Sir Jeremiah Colman Gift Trust	70 (2)
Harris Charity	122 (2)
Oakdale Trust	183 (2)
Priory Foundation	194 (2)
Harold Bridges' Charitable Foundation	48 (2)
Hallam FM - Help a Hallam Child Appeal (Money Mountain Trust)	118 (2)
London Law Trust	157 (2)
Gordon Fraser Charitable Trust	101 (2)
Dumbreck Charity	85 (2)
Eleanor Hamilton Educational Trust	119 (2)
Wilfrid Bruce Davis Charitable Trust	80 (2)
Frognal Trust	103 (2)
Fairway Trust	93 (2)
Isabel Blackman Foundation	44 (2)
Baltic Charitable Fund	37 (2)
Charles Brotherton Trust	51 (2)
Augustine Courtauld Trust	75 (2)
Arnopa Trust	32 (2)
Wilfred & Elsie Elkes Charity Fund	88 (2)
De Haan Charitable Trust	80 (2)
Northumberland Village Homes Trust	182 (2)
Leslie Smith Foundation	219 (2)
Salters' Charities	209 (2)
Friarsgate Trust	103 (2)
Ambika Paul Foundation	31 (2)
M A Hawe Settlement	124 (2)
Gwendoline Davies Charity	79 (2)
Tramman Trust	231 (2)
Emerton Charitable Settlement	90 (2)
Leslie Sell Charitable Trust	213 (2)
Jim Marshall Products Charitable Trust	164 (2)
David Brooke Charity	51 (2)
Bill Brown's Charitable Settlement	51 (2)
Shuttlewood Clarke Foundation	216 (2)
Bowland Charitable Trust	48 (2)
Ripple Effect Foundation	202 (2)
Clifton Charitable Trust	67 (2)
Anthony & Elizabeth Mellows Charitable Settlement	168 (2)
Arthur James & Constance Paterson Charitable Trust	187 (2)
Haymills Charitable Trust	124 (2)
Besom Foundation	41 (2)
General Charity Fund	105 (2)

The number in brackets after the page reference refers to Vol 1 or Vol 2 of A Guide to the Major Trusts - **Geog. index**

North East

Baring Foundation	35 **(1)**
Sir James Knott 1990 Trust	139 **(1)**
Tyne & Wear Foundation	245 **(1)**
William Leech Charity	150 **(1)**
Charles and Elsie Sykes Trust	231 **(1)**
Mendal Kaufman Charitable Trust	133 **(1)**
Greggs Charitable Trust	115 **(2)**
W A Handley Charity Trust	113 **(1)**
Greatham Hospital of God	114 **(2)**
Hadrian Trust	117 **(2)**
Joicey Trust	142 **(2)**
Rothley Trust	204 **(2)**
William Webster Charitable Trust	241 **(2)**
Ruth & Lionel Jacobson Trust (Second Fund) No 2	139 **(2)**
Northumberland Village Homes Trust	182 **(2)**
Benfield Motors Charitable Trust	40 **(2)**
Raymond Montague Burton Charitable Trust	55 **(2)**

Cleveland
Cleveland Community Foundation	66 **(2)**

Durham
Sir John Priestman Charity Trust	193 **(2)**

Humberside
Hull & East Riding Charitable Trust	128 **(1)**
Castle Educational Trust	60 **(2)**
Joseph & Annie Cattle Trust	60 **(2)**
Peter Birse Charitable Trust	42 **(2)**

Hull
Sir James Reckitt Charity	194 **(1)**

North Yorkshire
Norman Collinson Charitable Trust	70 **(2)**
A M Fenton Trust	95 **(2)**
W L Pratt Charitable Trust	193 **(2)**

York
Charles Brotherton Trust	51 **(2)**

South Yorkshire
Hugh & Ruby Sykes Charitable Trust	226 **(2)**
Hallam FM	118 **(2)**
Mayfield Valley Arts Trust	165 **(2)**

Sheffield
Sheffield Church Burgesses Trust	213 **(1)**
Sheffield Town Trust	214 **(2)**
Church Burgesses Educational Foundation	65 **(2)**
Talbot Trusts	227 **(2)**
J G Graves Charitable Trust	112 **(2)**

Tyne & Wear
Wates Foundation	249 **(1)**
R W Mann Trustees Limited	161 **(2)**
Barbour Trust	37 **(2)**
Millfield House Foundation	169 **(2)**

Sunderland
Sir John Priestman Charity Trust	193 **(2)**

West Yorkshire

Emmandjay Charitable Trust	90 **(2)**
Charity of Thomas Wade & Others	237 **(2)**
Charities Fund	62 **(2)**
Charles Brotherton Trust	51 **(2)**
A M Fenton Trust	95 **(2)**

Yorkshire generally

Leeds Hospital Fund Charitable Trust	154 **(2)**
Sir George Martin Trust	162 **(1)**
Normanby Charitable Trust	173 **(1)**
George A Moore Foundation	166 **(1)**
Constance Green Foundation	105 **(1)**
Manny Cussins Foundation	77 **(2)**
I A Ziff Charitable Foundation	254 **(2)**
Barry Green Memorial Fund	114 **(2)**
Harry Bottom Charitable Trust	47 **(2)**
Gay & Peter Hartley's Hillards Charitable Trust	123 **(2)**
N & P Hartley Memorial Trust	123 **(2)**

North West

Westminster Foundation	254 **(1)**
Francis C Scott Charitable Trust	212 **(1)**
Lord Leverhulme's Charitable Trust	152 **(1)**
United Trusts	234 **(2)**
Charles and Elsie Sykes Trust	231 **(1)**
Granada Foundation	111 **(2)**
Stoller Charitable Trust	224 **(2)**
Liverpool & Merseyside Charitable Fund	156 **(2)**
Harold Bridges' Charitable Foundation	48 **(2)**
A M Fenton Trust	95 **(2)**
Charles Brotherton Trust	51 **(2)**
Bowland Charitable Trust	48 **(2)**
Gay & Peter Hartley's Hillards Charitable Trust	123 **(2)**

Cheshire
Pennycress Trust	189 **(2)**

Cumbria
Francis C Scott Charitable Trust	212 **(1)**
Sir John Fisher Foundation	94 **(1)**
Frieda Scott Charitable Trust	210 **(2)**
Norman Whiteley Trust	246 **(2)**

Greater Manchester
Zochonis Charitable Trust	264 **(1)**
Peter Kershaw Trust	146 **(2)**
Alliance Family Foundation	31 **(2)**
J E Joseph Charitable Fund	143 **(2)**
Stanley Charitable Trust	222 **(2)**

Manchester
Mole Charitable Trust	173 **(2)**

Salford
Booth Charities	46 **(2)**

Lancashire
Mrs Waterhouse's Charitable Trust	239 **(2)**
Harris Charity	122 **(2)**
John Slater Foundation	217 **(2)**
M A Hawe Settlement	124 **(2)**
Barry Green Memorial Fund	114 **(2)**

Merseyside
Baring Foundation	35 **(1)**
Wates Foundation	249 **(1)**
Pilkington Charities Fund	191 **(2)**
Moores Family Charity Foundation	167 **(1)**
John Moores Foundation	168 **(1)**
P H Holt Charitable Trust	124 **(1)**
Eleanor Rathbone Charitable Trust	199 **(2)**
Ward Blenkinsop Trust	239 **(2)**
Austin & Hope Pilkington Trust	190 **(2)**
Johnson Group Cleaners Charity	141 **(2)**
Amelia Chadwick Trust	61 **(2)**
Fairway Trust	93 **(2)**
Nimrod & Glaven Charitable Settlement	180 **(2)**
Elizabeth Rathbone Charity	199 **(2)**
Mason Bibby 1981 Trust	41 **(2)**
General Charity Fund	105 **(2)**
Ravensdale Trust	199 **(2)**
Cecil Pilkington Charitable Trust	190 **(2)**
Rainford Trust	198 **(2)**

Midlands

Ratcliff Foundation	193 **(1)**
Maud Elkington Charitable Trust	88 **(1)**
Millichope Foundation	170 **(2)**
W E Dunn Trust	86 **(2)**
E H Smith Charitable Trust	218 **(2)**
Michael Bishop Foundation	43 **(2)**
Christopher Cadbury Charitable Trust	55 **(2)**
Sheldon Trust	214 **(2)**
Dumbreck Charity	85 **(2)**
Hornton Charity	131 **(2)**
Hallam FM	118 **(2)**
Chetwode Samworth Charitable Trust	63 **(2)**
Patients' Aid Association Hospital & Medical Charities Trust	187 **(2)**
GNC Trust	107 **(2)**

Derbyshire
Hugh & Ruby Sykes Charitable Trust	226 **(2)**
10th Duke of Devonshire's Trust (1949)	82 **(2)**
Harry Bottom Charitable Trust	47 **(2)**

● **Geog. index** - The number in brackets after the page reference refers to Vol 1 or Vol 2 of A Guide to the Major Trusts

Hereford & Worcester

Eveson Charitable Trust	91 (1)
Lasletts (Hinton) Charity	150 (2)
Judge Charitable Foundation	143 (2)

Evesham

John Martin's Charity	164 (2)

Leicestershire

Henry Smith's (Kensington Estate) Charity	214 (1)
Cotton Trust	77 (1)
Florence Turner Trust	232 (2)
P & C Hickinbotham Charitable Trust	127 (2)
Everard Foundation	93 (2)

Lincolnshire

John and Lucille van Geest Foundation	245 (1)

Loughborough

Paget Charitable Trust	186 (2)

Ulverscroft

Shuttlewood Clarke Foundation	216 (2)

Northamptonshire

Cripps Foundation	79 (1)
Horne Foundation	124 (1)
Benham Charitable Settlement	40 (2)

Nottinghamshire

Jones 1986 Charitable Trust	142 (2)
A H and B C Whiteley Charitable Trust	258 (1)
Sir John Eastwood Foundation	88 (1)
Lady Hind Trust	122 (1)
J N Derbyshire Trust	81 (2)
Thomas Farr Charitable Trust	94 (2)
Jessie Spencer Trust	221 (2)

Nottingham

Djanogly Foundation	82 (1)
Charles Littlewood Hill Trust	128 (2)

Shropshire

Roy Fletcher Charitable Trust	98 (2)
Walker Trust	238 (2)
Westcroft Trust	244 (2)

Oswestry

R T Trust	196 (2)

Staffordshire

Wilfred & Elsie Elkes Charity Fund	88 (2)
R M Douglas Charitable Trust	84 (2)

Warwickshire

Norton Foundation	182 (2)
Stella Symons Charitable Trust	227 (2)

Stratford-upon-Avon

College Estate Charity	69 (2)

Warwick

Warwick Municipal Charities – King Henry VIII Charity	249 (1)

West Midlands

Edward Cadbury Trust	48 (1)
Cash for Kids (formerly BRMB—Birmingham Walkathon)	59 (2)
Lord Austin Trust	36 (2)
Alfred Haines Charitable Trust	118 (2)
Bryant Trust	52 (2)
Lillie Johnson Charitable Trust	141 (2)
Roughley Charitable Trust	204 (2)
Edward & Dorothy Cadbury Charitable Trust	56 (2)

Birmingham

Baron Davenport's Charity Trust	82 (1)
Douglas Turner Trust	244 (1)
Norton Foundation	182 (2)
Langdale Trust	149 (2)
Charles Brotherton Trust	51 (2)
Grantham Yorke Trust	112 (2)

Coventry

29th May 1961 Charitable Trust	244 (1)
Alan Edward Higgs Charity	120 (1)

Sutton Coldfield

Sutton Coldfield Municipal Charities	231 (1)

South West

Dulverton Trust	84 (1)
Duke of Cornwall's Benevolent Fund	74 (2)
Norman Family Charitable Trust	181 (2)
R J Harris Charitable Settlement	122 (2)
Westward Trust	245 (2)
GWR Community Trust	116 (2)
Good Neighbours Trust	109 (2)
Prince Foundation	194 (2)
Clifton Charitable Trust	67 (2)
GNC Trust	107 (2)
Elmgrant Trust	89 (2)

Avon

Van Neste Foundation	235 (2)
Rosemary Bugden Charitable Trust	52 (2)
Higgs Charitable Trust	128 (2)
A M McGreevy No 5 Charitable Settlement	166 (2)

Bristol

Dawn James (No 2) Charitable Foundation	131 (1)
Pontin Charitable Trust	184 (1)
Needham Cooper Charitable Trust	171 (1)
Harry Crook Foundation	80 (1)
Greater Bristol Foundation	112 (2)
Wall Charitable Trust	238 (2)
Mount 'A' & Mount 'B' Charitable Trusts	174 (2)

Devon

Heathcoat Trust	118 (1)
Viscount Amory's Charitable Trust	29 (1)
Wakefield Trust	238 (2)
Dr & Mrs A Darlington Charitable Trust	79 (2)
L & R Gilley Charitable Trust	106 (2)

Barnstaple

Bridge Trust	48 (2)

Dorset

Moss Charitable Trust	174 (2)
Clover Trust	73 (1)
Alice Ellen Cooper-Dean Charitable Foundation	77 (1)

Gloucestershire

Barnwood House Trust	39 (1)
Sir Cyril Kleinwort Charitable Settlement	137 (1)
Ernest Cook Trust	75 (1)
Susanna Peake Charitable Trust	188 (2)

Cheltenham

Summerfield Charitable Trust	228 (1)
Notgrove Trust	183 (2)

Wiltshire

Herbert & Peter Blagrave Charitable Trust	45 (1)
Thomas Freke & Lady Norton Charity	102 (2)
Wiltshire Community Foundation	247 (2)
Wilfrid & Constance Cave Foundation	61 (2)
Walter Guinness Charitable Trust	116 (2)

Chippenham

Chippenham Borough Lands Charity	65 (1)

Salisbury

Sarum St Michael Educational Charity	209 (2)

South East

Henry Smith's (Kensington Estate) Charity	214 (1)
Herbert & Peter Blagrave Charitable Trust	45 (1)
Carlton Television Trust	50 (1)
Moss Charitable Trust	174 (2)
Lawlor Foundation	151 (2)
Late Barbara May Paul Charitable Trust	188 (2)
Francis Coales Charitable Foundation	67 (2)
John Jarrold Trust	139 (2)
Peter Samuel Charitable Trust	209 (2)
Thornton Trust	229 (2)
Fawcett Charitable Trust	94 (2)
Prince Foundation	194 (2)

The number in brackets after the page reference refers to Vol 1 or Vol 2 of A Guide to the Major Trusts - **Geog. index**

C L Loyd Charitable Trust	158 (2)
Cumber Family Charitable Trust	76 (2)
John & Freda Coleman Charitable Trust	69 (2)
Marchday Charitable Fund	161 (2)
Walter Guinness Charitable Trust	116 (2)
Robert Kiln Charitable Trust	146 (2)
Abel Charitable Trust	27 (2)

Bedfordshire
Steel Charitable Trust	226 (1)
Simon Whitbread Charitable Trust	245 (2)

Bedford
Bedford Charity	39 (2)

Berkshire
Earley Charity	86 (2)
Englefield Charitable Trust	90 (2)
Leslie Smith Foundation	219 (2)
Gerald Palmer Trust	186 (2)

Buckinghamshire
Aylesbury
William Harding's Charity	114 (1)

Milton Keynes
Milton Keynes Community Trust	170 (2)

Cambridgeshire
Hereward FM CNFM & KLFM Appeal	126 (2)

East Sussex
Brighton
Dunhill Medical Trust	87 (1)

Hastings
Isabel Blackman Foundation	44 (2)

Essex
Colchester Catalyst Charity	68 (2)
Albert and Florence Smith Memorial Trust	218 (2)
Charles S French Charitable Trust	102 (2)
Edward Cecil Jones Settlement	142 (2)
Augustine Courtauld Trust	75 (2)
Fowler Memorial Trust	100 (2)

Hampshire
A R Taylor Charitable Trust	228 (2)
Charlotte Bonham-Carter Charitable Trust	46 (2)
GNC Trust	107 (2)
Ellis Campbell Charitable Foundation	57 (2)

Basingstoke
Sir Jeremiah Colman Gift Trust	70 (2)

Hythe & Dibden
Hythe and Dibden Allotments for the Labouring Poor	128 (1)

Hertfordshire
Clive Richards Charity Ltd	201 (2)
A & R Woolf Charitable Trust	250 (2)

Kent
Sir James Colyer-Fergusson's Charitable Trust	75 (1)
Astor of Hever Trust	34 (2)
Tory Family Foundation	230 (2)

Norfolk
Lady Hind Trust	122 (1)
Charles Littlewood Hill Trust	128 (2)
Nimrod & Glaven Charitable Settlement	180 (2)
Pennycress Trust	189 (2)

Norwich
Norwich Town Close Estate Charity	182 (2)

Oxfordshire
P F Charitable Trust	180 (1)
Mr and Mrs J A Pye's Charitable Settlement	188 (1)
Doris Field Charitable Trust	96 (2)

Henley
Arbib Foundation	31 (2)

Oxford
DLM Charitable Trust	84 (2)

Suffolk
Scarfe Charitable Trust	213 (2)
Britten-Pears Foundation	49 (2)

Ipswich
Mrs L D Rope Third Charitable Settlement	198 (1)

Needham Market
Simon Gibson Charitable Trust	101 (1)
Geoffrey Burton Charitable Trust	54 (2)

Newmarket
G C Gibson Charitable Trust	101 (1)

Surrey
Billmeir Charitable Trust	42 (2)
Sir Edward Lewis Foundation	155 (2)

Godalming
Hamamelis Trust	118 (2)

Sussex generally
Ernest Kleinwort Charitable Trust	138 (1)
River Trust	202 (2)
Gibbins Trust	105 (2)
Ian Askew Charitable Trust	34 (2)

London

Henry Smith's (Kensington Estate) Charity	214 (1)
Bridge House Estate Fund Charity	45 (1)
Baring Foundation	35 (1)
City Parochial Foundation	67 (1)
King's Fund	134 (1)
Goldsmiths' Company's Charities	102 (1)
Wates Foundation	249 (1)
Westminster Foundation	254 (1)
Hampton Fuel Allotment Charity	112 (1)
Sir John Cass's Foundation	56 (1)
Trust for London	234 (1)
Milly Apthorp Charitable Trust	31 (1)
John Lyon's Charity	158 (1)
Grand Charity of Freemasons	103 (1)
Capital Radio – Help A London Child	49 (1)
Peabody Community Fund	181 (1)
Carlton Television Trust	50 (1)
Sir Siegmund Warburg's Voluntary Settlement	249 (1)
Metropolitan Hospital – Sunday Fund	164 (1)
Wakefield Tower Hill Trinity Square Trust	248 (1)
Mulberry Trust	170 (1)
All Saints Educational Trust	28 (1)
City Educational Trust Fund	65 (2)
Heritage of London Trust Ltd	126 (2)
J E Joseph Charitable Fund	143 (2)
Salters' Charities	209 (2)
Belvedere Trust	39 (2)
Mitchell Charitable Trust	172 (2)
Saint Edmund, King & Martyr Trust	207 (2)
Tower Hill Improvement Trust	230 (2)
Worshipful Company of Shipwrights	252 (2)
Abel Charitable Trust	27 (2)

Camden
Hampstead Wells and Campden Trust	112 (1)

City of London
Fishmongers' Company's Charitable Trust	95 (1)
Cripplegate Foundation	78 (1)
Drapers' Charitable Fund	83 (1)
Haberdashers' Eleemosynary Charity	109 (1)
Saddlers' Company Charitable Fund	206 (2)

Islington
Cripplegate Foundation	78 (1)
Richard Cloudesley's Charity	73 (1)

Kensington
Campden Charities	49 (1)

Lambeth
Lambeth Endowed Charities	144 (1)
Peter Minet Trust	171 (2)

Richmond-upon-Thames
Richmond Parish Lands Charity	195 (1)

Tower Hamlets
Spitalfields Market Community Trust	221 (1)
Spitalfields Market Training Initiative	222 (2)

● **Geog. index** - The number in brackets after the page reference refers to Vol 1 or Vol 2 of A Guide to the Major Trusts

St Katharine and Shadwell Trust	207 (2)

Westminster

Hyde Park Place Estate Charity – Civil Trustees	134 (2)
Westminster Amalgamated Charity	244 (2)

Channel Islands

Welton Foundation	253 (1)
Mount 'A' & Mount 'B' Charitable Trusts	174 (2)
Clarkson Jersey Charitable Trust	66 (2)

Wales

Prince's Youth Business Trust	187 (1)
Jane Hodge Foundation	123 (1)
Historic Churches Preservation Trust	122 (1)
TSB Foundation for England and Wales	235 (1)
Marshall's Charity	161 (1)
Welsh Church Funds	242 (2)
G C Gibson Charitable Trust	101 (1)
Catherine, Lady Grace James and John & Rhys Thomas James Foundation	130 (1)
Joseph Strong Frazer Trust	96 (1)
Simon Gibson Charitable Trust	101 (1)2
Dinam Charity	83 (2)
Oakdale Trust	183 (2)
Gwendoline Davies Charity	79 (2)
Jenour Foundation	140 (2)

North Wales

Ratcliff Foundation	193 (1)

South Wales

Margaret Davies Charity	80 (2)
Hoover Foundation	130 (2)

Gwent

Cwmbran

Girling (Cwmbran) Trust	107 (2)

Newport

Elaine Lloyd Charitable Trust	156 (2)

Gwynedd

Anglesey

Isle of Anglesey Charitable Trust	129 (1)

Scotland

Baring Foundation	35 (1)
Robertson Trust	196 (1)
Gannochy Trust	96 (1)
Carnegie Trust for the Universities of Scotland	51 (1)
P F Charitable Trust	180 (1)
MacRobert Trusts	159 (1)
TSB Foundation for Scotland	237 (1)
Nancie Massey Charitable Trust	164 (2)
Prince's Scottish Youth Business Trust	186 (1)
James Weir Foundation	242 (2)
Talteg Ltd	227 (2)
Scottish Churches Architectural Heritage Trust	211 (2)
Gough Charitable Trust	110 (2)
Scottish Housing Associations Charitable Trust (SHACT)	212 (2)

Fife

Dunfermline

Carnegie Dunfermline Trust	58 (2)

Lothian

John Watson's Trust	240 (2)

Strathclyde

Glasgow

Radio Clyde – Cash for Kids at Christmas	189 (1)
Trades House of Glasgow	233 (1)
Hoover Foundation	130 (2)

Tayside

Radio Tay – Caring for Kids (Radio Tay Listeners Charity)	197 (2)
Ellis Campbell Charitable Foundation	57 (2)

Perth

Gannochy Trust	96 (1)

Northern Ireland

Prince's Youth Business Trust	187 (1)
Joseph Rowntree Charitable Trust	199 (1)
Barrow Cadbury Trust	45 (1)
Wates Foundation	249 (1)
Charles Hayward Trust	115 (1)
Northern Ireland Voluntary Trust	173 (1)
Ernest Cook Trust	75 (1)
John Moores Foundation	168 (1)
William Adlington Cadbury Charitable Trust	48 (1)
Barrow Cadbury Fund Ltd	45 (1)
Enkalon Foundation	91 (2)
Women Caring Trust	249 (2)
Ultach Trust	232 (2)
Esme Mitchell Trust	173 (2)

Overseas

Baring Foundation	35 (1)
J W Laing Trust	142 (1)
Aga Khan Foundation	26 (1)
Aid to the Church in Need	26 (1)
Kirby Laing Foundation	142 (1)
Concern Universal	72 (2)
Christmas Cracker Trust	64 (2)
William Adlington Cadbury Charitable Trust	48 (1)
Feed the Minds	95 (2)
Sylvanus Charitable Trust	226 (2)
David Shepherd Conservation Foundation	215 (2)
Ajahma Charitable Trust	30 (2)
Cross Trust	75 (2)
Jephcott Charitable Trust	140 (2)
Access 4 Trust	29 (2)
Salamander Charitable Trust	208 (2)
Thornton Trust	229 (2)
Dinam Charity	83 (2)
Loke Wan Tho Memorial Foundation	228 (2)
World Memorial Fund for Disaster Relief	250 (2)
Bromley Trust	50 (2)
N Smith Charitable Trust	219 (2)
Dumbreck Charity	85 (2)
Cumber Family Charitable Trust	76 (2)
Clifton Charitable Trust	67 (2)
Jill Franklin Trust	100 (2)
Besom Foundation	41 (2)
Sutasoma Trust	225 (2)
Airflow Community Ltd	29 (2)
A S Charitable Trust	27 (2)

Commonwealth

Nuffield Foundation	176 (1)
Prince's Trust and the Royal Jubilee Trusts	186 (1)
British Schools and Universities Foundation (Inc.)	49 (2)
Robert McAlpine Foundation	166 (2)

Third World/ Developing World

Paul Hamlyn Foundation	109 (1)
Alchemy Foundation	27 (1)
Headley Trust	116 (1)
Aga Khan Foundation	26 (1)
Methodist Relief & Development Fund	168 (2)
Hilden Charitable Fund	121 (1)
J G Joffe Charitable Trust	132 (1)
Burdens Charitable Foundation	53 (2)
Ogle Trust	184 (2)
Ashden Charitable Trust	33 (2)
Lyndhurst Trust	159 (2)
Ripple Effect Foundation	202 (2)
New Durlston Trust	178 (2)

The number in brackets after the page reference refers to Vol 1 or Vol 2 of A Guide to the Major Trusts - **Geog. index**

Africa

Charity Projects	59 (1)
Gatsby Charitable Foundation	97 (1)
John Ellerman Foundation	88 (1)
Joseph Rowntree Charitable Trust	199 (1)
Childwick Trust	65 (1)
Aga Khan Foundation	26 (1)
Concern Universal	72 (2)
Burdens Charitable Foundation	53 (2)
Noel Buxton Trust	180 (2)

East Africa

Dulverton Trust	84 (1)
Beit Trust	39 (2)
Kulika Charitable Trust	140 (1)

Tanzania

Miriam K Dean Refugee Trust	81 (2)

Asia

Aga Khan Foundation	26 (1)

Far East

J E Joseph Charitable Fund	143 (2)

China

Keswick Foundation Ltd	146 (2)

Hong Kong

Keswick Foundation Ltd	146 (2)

Japan

Daiwa Anglo-Japanese Foundation	81 (1)
Great Britain Sasakawa Foundation	104 (1)

India

Paul Hamlyn Foundation	109 (1)
Miriam K Dean Refugee Trust Fund	81 (2)
INTACH (UK) Trust	136 (2)
Ambika Paul Foundation	31 (2)

Europe

Lyndhurst Trust	159 (2)

Eastern Europe

Charity Know How	58 (1)
Feed the Minds	95 (2)

Germany

Anglo-German Foundation for the Study of Industrial Society	30 (1)

Ireland

Gulbenkian Foundation	106 (1)
Lawlor Foundation	151 (2)
Irish Youth Foundation (UK) Ltd	137 (2)
Ouseley Trust	185 (2)
Ireland Fund of Great Britain	136 (2)
Ireland Funds	136 (2)

Italy

Mount 'A' & Mount 'B' Charitable Trusts	174 (2)

Portugal

Aga Khan Foundation	26 (1)

Middle East

Holy Lands

Wolfson Foundation	261 (1)

Israel

Wolfson Family Charitable Trust	260 (1)
Bible Lands Society	43 (1)
Archie Sherman Charitable Trust	213 (1)
George Balint Charitable Trust	34 (1)
Samuel Sebba Charitable Trust	212 (1)
Porter Foundation	184 (1)
Paul Balint Charitable Trust	34 (1)
Charity Association Manchester Ltd	58 (1)
Dellal Foundation	82 (1)
Maurice Wohl Charitable Foundation	259 (1)
Andrew Balint Charitable Trust	34 (1)
Neil Kreitman Foundation	140 (1)
J B Rubens Charitable Foundation	207 (1)
Itzchok Meyer Cymerman Trust Ltd	81 (1)
Barnard Kahn Charitable Trust	133 (1)
Harry and Abe Sherman Foundation	213 (1)
Jill Kreitman Foundation	148 (2)
Kreitman Foundation	139 (1)
Kennedy Leigh Charitable Trust	151 (1)
Cyril and Betty Stein Charitable Trust	226 (1)
Harold Hyam Wingate Foundation	248 (2)
E Alec Colman Charitable Fund Ltd	70 (2)
A Hubert 1971 Charitable Trust	133 (2)
Acacia Charitable Trust	28 (2)
Michael Sacher Charitable Trust	205 (2)
Craps Charitable Trust	75 (2)
Caritas	57 (2)
Everard & Mina Goodman Charitable Foundation	109 (2)
W I Hubert 1974 Charitable Trust	133 (2)
Bornstein Charitable Settlements	47 (2)
Vivienne & Samuel Cohen Charitable Trust	68 (2)
Bertie Black Foundation	43 (2)
Richard & Frances Harris Charitable Trust	123 (2)
Katzauer Charitable Settlement	144 (2)
Abrams Charitable Trusts	28 (2)
Col-Reno Ltd	68 (2)
Humanitarian Trust	133 (2)
George Elias Charitable Trust	88 (2)
Solo Charitable Settlement	220 (2)
Willie Nagel Charitable Trust	175 (2)
Morrison Charitable Foundation	173 (2)
Raymond Montague Burton Charitable Trust	55 (2)

Palestine

J E Joseph Charitable Fund	143 (2)

North America

Ulverscroft	233 (2)
Beaverbrook	42 (1)
George C Cadbury	56 (2)

South America

Concern Universal	72 (2)

A list of trusts in A Guide to the Major Trusts Volume 1

Action Research
Adint Charitable Trust
Aga Khan Foundation
Aid to the Church in Need
AIM Foundation
Al-Fayed Charitable
Alchemy Foundation
All Saints Educational Trust
Allchurches Trust Ltd
H B Allen Charitable Trust
Viscount Amory's Charitable Trust
Andrew Anderson Trust
Anglo-German Foundation for the Study of Industrial Society
Milly Apthorp Charitable Trust
Architectural Heritage Fund
Artemis Charitable Trust
Lord Ashdown Charitable Trust

Andrew Balint Charitable Trust
George Balint Charitable Trust
Paul Balint Charitable Trust
David and Frederick Barclay Foundation
Baring Foundation
Barnabas Trust
Barnwood House Trust
BBC Children in Need Appeal
Beaverbrook Foundation
Benesco Charity Limited
Bible Lands Society
Percy Bilton Charity Ltd
Herbert & Peter Blagrave Charitable Trust
Bridge House Estate Fund Charity

Barrow Cadbury Fund Ltd
Barrow Cadbury Trust
Edward Cadbury Trust
William Adlington Cadbury Charitable Trust
Campden Charities
Capital Radio - Help A London Child
Carlton Television Trust
Carnegie Trust for the Universities of Scotland
Carnegie United Kingdom Trust
Sir John Cass's Foundation
Charities Aid Foundation
Charity Association Manchester Ltd
Charity Know How
Charity Projects
Chase Charity
Children Nationwide Medical Research Fund
Childwick Trust
Chippenham Borough Lands Charity

Church Urban Fund
City Parochial Foundation
Elizabeth Clark Charitable Trust
J A Clark Charitable Foundation
Clore Foundation
Clothworkers' Foundation
Richard Cloudesley's Charity
Clover Trust
John Coates Charitable Trust
John S Cohen Foundation
Colt Foundation
Sir James Colyer-Fergusson's Charitable Trust
Ernest Cook Trust
Alice Ellen Cooper-Dean Charitable Foundation
Coppings Trust
Sidney & Elizabeth Corob Charitable Trust
Cotton Trust
Cripplegate Foundation
Cripps Foundation
Crisis
Harry Crook Foundation
Itzchok Meyer Cymerman Trust Ltd

Daiwa Anglo-Japanese Foundation
Baron Davenport's Charity Trust
Dellal Foundation
Djanogly Foundation
Drapers' Charitable Fund
Vivien Duffield Foundation
Dulverton Trust
Dunhill Medical Trust

Sir John Eastwood Foundation
Maud Elkington Charitable Trust
John Ellerman Foundation
Equitable Charitable Trust
Eranda Foundation
Eveson Charitable Trust

Esmée Fairbairn Charitable Trust
FBT Charitable Fund
Sir John Fisher Foundation
Fishmongers' Company's Charitable Trust
Donald Forrester Trust
Joseph Strong Frazer Trust

Gannochy Trust
Gatsby Charitable Foundation
J Paul Getty Trust
G C Gibson Charitable Trust
Simon Gibson Charitable Trust
Goldsmiths' Company's Charities

Gosling Foundation Ltd
Grand Charity of Freemasons
Great Britain Sasakawa Foundation
Constance Green Foundation
Grocers' Charity
GRP Charitable Trust
Gulbenkian Foundation

Haberdashers' Eleemosynary Charity
Paul Hamlyn Foundation
Hampstead Wells and Campden Trust
Hampton Fuel Allotment Charity
W A Handley Charity Trust
William Harding's Charity
Philip and Pauline Harris Charitable Trust
Charles Hayward Trust
Hayward Foundation
Headley Trust
Heathcoat Trust
Hedley Foundation Ltd
Help the Aged
Alan Edward Higgs Charity
Hilden Charitable Fund
Lady Hind Trust
Historic Churches Preservation Trust
Jane Hodge Foundation
P H Holt Charitable Trust
Horne Foundation
Housing Associations Charitable Trust (HACT)
Hull & East Riding Charitable Trust
Hythe and Dibden Allotments for the Labouring Poor

Inverforth Charitable Trust
Isle of Anglesey Charitable Trust

Catherine, Lady Grace James and John & Rhys Thomas James Foundation
Dawn James (No 2) Charitable Foundation
Rees Jeffreys Road Fund
Jerusalem Trust
Jewish Community Allocations Board
J G Joffe Charitable Trust
Anton Jurgens Charitable Trust

Barnard Kahn Charitable Trust
Mendal Kaufman Charitable Trust
Kay Kendall Leukaemia Fund
King's Fund
King George's Fund for Sailors
Graham Kirkham Foundation Ltd
Sir Cyril Kleinwort Charitable Settlement
Ernest Kleinwort Charitable Trust
Sir James Knott 1990 Trust

A list of trusts in A Guide to the Major Trusts Volume 1

Kreitman Foundation
Neil Kreitman Foundation
Kulika Charitable Trust

Laing's Charitable Trust
Beatrice Laing Trust
J W Laing Biblical Scholarship Trust
J W Laing Trust
Kirby Laing Foundation
Maurice Laing Foundation
Lambeth Endowed Charities
Allen Lane Foundation
Lankelly Foundation
Largsmount Ltd
Leathersellers' Company Charitable Fund
William Leech Charity
Kennedy Leigh Charitable Trust
Leigh Trust
Lord Leverhulme's Charitable Trust
Leverhulme Trade Charities Trust
Leverhulme Trust
Joseph Levy Charitable Foundation
Linbury Trust
Enid Linder Foundation
Lloyd's Charities Trust
Lord's Taverners
Robert Luff Foundation Ltd
John Lyon's Charity

Mackintosh Foundation
MacRobert Trusts
Manifold Trust
Michael Marks Charitable Trust
Marshall's Charity
Sir George Martin Trust
Mayfair Charities Ltd
Mental Health Foundation
Mercers' Charitable Foundation
Metropolitan Hospital-Sunday Fund
Monument Trust
George A Moore Foundation
Henry Moore Foundation
Moores Family Charity Foundation
John Moores Foundation
Peter Moores Foundation
Mulberry Trust

National Art Collections Fund
National Lottery
Needham Cooper Charitable Trust
Network Foundation
Newby Trust Limited
Frances and Augustus Newman Foundation
Normanby Charitable Trust
Northern Ireland Voluntary Trust
Nuffield Foundation
Nuffield Provincial Hospitals Trust

Orbcrest Ltd
Oxfam

P F Charitable Trust
Patrick Charitable Trust
Peabody Community Fund
Peacock Charitable Trust
Dowager Countess Eleanor Peel Trust
Pilgrim Trust
Polden-Puckham Charitable Foundation
Pontin Charitable Trust
Porter Foundation
J E Posnansky Charitable Trust
Prince of Wales' Charities Trust
Prince's Scottish Youth Business Trust
Prince's Trust and the Royal Jubilee Trusts
Prince's Youth Business Trust
Mr and Mrs J A Pye's Charitable Settlement

Queen Mary's Roehampton Trust

Radio Clyde - Cash for Kids at Christmas
Rank Foundation
Joseph Rank Benevolent Trust
Ratcliff Foundation
Rayne Foundation
Sir James Reckitt Charity
Christopher Reeves Charitable Trust
Rhodes Trust Public Purposes Fund
Richmond Parish Lands Charity
Robertson Trust
Ronson Foundation
Mrs L D Rope Third Charitable Settlement
Rose Foundation
Rowan Trust
Rowanville Ltd
Joseph Rowntree Charitable Trust
Joseph Rowntree Foundation
Joseph Rowntree Reform Trust Limited
J B Rubens Charitable Foundation
Rubin Foundation
Rufford Foundation

Alan and Babette Sainsbury Charitable Fund
Sainsbury Family Charitable Trust
Robert & Lisa Sainsbury Art Trust
Saint Sarkis Charity Trust
Basil Samuel Charitable Trust
Coral Samuel Charitable Trust
Save & Prosper Educational Trust
Francis C Scott Charitable Trust
Samuel Sebba Charitable Trust
Sheffield Church Burgesses Trust
Archie Sherman Charitable Trust
Harry and Abe Sherman Foundation
Shetland Islands Council Charitable Trust

Henry Smith's (Kensington Estate) Charity
Mrs Smith and Mount Trust
Mary Snow Trusts
Sobell Foundation
Spitalfields Market Community Trust
Foundation for Sport and the Arts
Steel Charitable Trust
Cyril and Betty Stein Charitable Trust
Sir Halley Stewart Trust
W O Street Charitable Foundation
Summerfield Charitable Trust
Bernard Sunley Charitable Foundation
Sutton Coldfield Municipal Charities
Charles and Elsie Sykes Trust

Sir Jules Thorn Charitable Trust
Tompkins Foundation
Trades House of Glasgow
Trust for London
TSB Foundation for England and Wales
TSB Foundation for Scotland
Tudor Trust
Douglas Turner Trust
29th May 1961 Charitable Trust
Tyne & Wear Foundation

John and Lucille van Geest Foundation
Bernard van Leer Foundation
Variety Club Children's Charity Limited

Wakefield Tower Hill Trinity Square Trust
Wallington Missionary Mart and Auctions
Warbeck Fund Limited
Sir Siegmund Warburg's Voluntary Settlement
Warwick Municipal Charities - King Henry V111 Charity
Wates Foundation
Mary Webb Trust
Weinstock Fund
Wellcome Trust
Welton Foundation
Westminster Foundation
Westminster Foundation for Democracy
Garfield Weston Foundation
A H and B C Whiteley CharitableTrust
Will Charitable Trust
H D H Wills 1965 Charitable Trust
Francis Winham Foundation
Maurice Wohl Charitable Foundation
Charles Wolfson Trust
Wolfson Family Charitable Trust
Wolfson Foundation
WWF UK (World Wide Fund for Nature)

Zochonis Charitable Trust

Sources of advice on applying to trusts

Charities new to the business of applying to trusts for money, and those seeking information about local trusts too small for inclusion in these Guides, may find help from their local Charities Information Bureau (if there is one). Alternatively, try your local Council for Voluntary Service (bodies seeking to promote development of voluntary action of all kinds in their areas) or the county Rural Community Council.

These are listed below but readers should be aware that they vary greatly in the assistance which they can give. The Charities Information Bureaux usually have the assistance of grant-seekers as one of their specific aims. Some Councils for Voluntary Service and Rural Community Councils have their own internal information bureaux with substantial resources, but others are completely without means of helping in this way.

*There is also a computerised database of all the trusts in "A Guide to the Major Trusts Volumes 1 & 2" and the "Directory of Grant-Making Trusts" published by the Charities Aid Foundation. The database is called **FunderFinder**. You can either subscribe to **FunderFinder** for in-house use or the umbrella bodies above may have a copy which you can use (sometimes a fee is chargeable). Further information is available from the West Yorkshire Charities Information Bureau (01924-382120).*

Charities Information Bureaux

The following are all members of the Federation of Charity Advice Services (Fcas).

Cleveland Council for Voluntary Service
47 Princes Road,
Middlesborough TS1 4BG
01642-240651/2

Coventry Voluntary Service Council
58-64 Corporation Street,
Coventry CV1 1GF
01203-220381

Derbyshire Rural Community Council
Church Street, Wirksworth,
Matlock DE4 4EY
01629-824797

Dorset Charities Information Bureau
Dorchester Library, Colliston Park, Dorchester DT1 1XT
01305-205059

Charities Advice Service, Hampshire Council of Community Service
Beaconsfield House, Andover Road, Winchester SO22 6AT
01962-854971

Community Council of Hereford & Worcester
Great Malvern Station, Station Approach, Malvern
WR14 3AU
01684-573334

Hounslow Voluntary Action
The Voluntary Action Centre,
12 School Road, Hounslow
TW3 1QZ
0181-577 3226

Charities Information Service, Community Council for Lancashire
15 Victoria Road, Fulwood,
Preston PR2 8PS
01772-718710/717461

Inner City Forum, Newcastle Council for Voluntary Service
Mea House, Ellison Place,
Newcastle upon Tyne
NE1 8XS
0191-232 7445

Charity Funds Advisor, Norfolk Rural Community Council
20 Market Place, Hingham,
Norfolk NR9 4AF
01953-851408

Funding Information North East
John Haswell House, 8-9 Gladstone Terrace, Gateshead NE8 4GY
0191-477 1253

Charities Advice Service, Northern Ireland Council for Voluntary Action
127 Ormeau Road, Belfast
BT7 1SH
01232-321224

Nottingham Council for Voluntary Service
33 Mansfield Road,
Nottingham NG1 3FF
01159-476614

Nottinghamshire Rural Community Council
Minster Chambers, Church Street, Southwell, Notts
NG25 0HD

South Yorkshire Funding Advice Bureau
47 Wilkinson Street, Sheffield
S10 2GB
0114-2765460

Community Council of Staffordshire
Castle House, Newport Road,
Stafford ST16 1DX
01785-42525

Suffolk ACRE
Alexandra House, Rope Walk,
Ipswich IP4 1LR
01473-230000

Charities Information Bureau (Sussex)
c/o The Chapel Royal, North Street, Brighton BN1 1EA
01273-21398

Wales Council for Voluntary Action
Llys Ifor, Crescent Road,
Caerffili, Mid Glamorgan
CF8 1XL
01222-869224

West Midlands Charities Information Bureau
138 Digbeth, Birmingham
B5 6DR
0121-643 8477

West Yorkshire Charities Information Bureau
11 Upper York Street,
Wakefield WF1 3LQ
01924-382120

Wiltshire Charities Information Bureau
Wyndham's St Joseph's Place,
Devizes, Wiltshire SN10 1DD
01380-729279

British Trust for Conservation Volunteers
5 Garnet Street, Reading
RG1 6BA
01491-39766 ext 29

Charity Help
12 Ashley Road, Taunton,
Somerset TA1 5HP
01823-217353

Councils for Voluntary Service

A Directory of Councils for Voluntary Service (plus updates) is available from NACVS, 3rd Floor, Arundel Court, 177 Arundel Street, Sheffield S1 2NU (0114-278 6636).
The CVSs are listed in alphabetical order of town or city.

Adur District Association of Voluntary Service
Office 1, Harbour House, 27 High Street, Shoreham by Sea BN43 5DD
01273-441662

Amber Valley Council for Voluntary Service
33 Market Place, Ripley, Derbyshire DE5 3HY
01773-512076

Arun Council for Voluntary Service
The Tamarisk Centre, 42 Beach Road, Littlehampton, West Sussex BN17 5HT
01903-726228

Banbury & District Council for Voluntary Service
Suite 3, Borough House, Marlborough Road, Banbury, Oxon OX16 8TH
01295-255863

Barking & Dagenham Voluntary Services Association
Faircross Community Complex, Hulse Avenue, Barking, Essex IG11 9UP
0181-591 5275

Barnet Borough Voluntary Service Council
Hertford Lodge, East End Road, London N3 3QE
0181-346 9723

Barnsley Voluntary Action
35 Queens Road, Barnsley, South Yorkshire S71 1AN
01226-242726

Barrow & District Council for Voluntary Service
Nelson St Centre, Nelson Street, Barrow-in-Furness LA14 1NF
01229-823144

Basildon, Billericay & Wickford Council for Voluntary Service
CVS Office, Basildon Centre, Pagel Mead, Basildon, Essex SS14 1DL
01268-288870

Basingstoke Voluntary Services
Chute House, Church Street, Basingstoke RG21 7QT
01256-21611

Bassetlaw Community & Voluntary Service
The Dukeries Centre, The Old St Mary's School, Park Street, Worksop, Notts S80 1HH
01909-476118

Bath Centre for Voluntary Service
3 Abbey Green, Bath BA1 1NW
01225-464015

Bebington Council for Voluntary Service
65 The Village, Bebington, Wirral, Merseyside L63 7PL
0151-643 7275

Bedfordshire Rural Communities Charity
The Old School, Cardington, Bedford MK44 3SX
01234-838771

Berkshire Community Council
Epping House, 55 Russell Street, Reading RG1 7XG
01734-566556

Beverley Borough Council for Voluntary Service
Morley's House, Morley's Yard, Walkergate, Beverley, Humberside HU17 9BY
01482-871077

Bexley Voluntary Service Council
8 Brampton Road, Bexleyheath, Kent DA7 4EY
0181-304 0911

Birmingham Voluntary Service Council
138 Digbeth, Birmingham B5 6DR
0121-643 4343

Blackburn, Hyndburn & Ribble Valley Council for Voluntary Service
St John's Centre, Victoria Street, Blackburn BB1 6DW
01254-583957

Blackpool, Wyre & Fylde Council for Voluntary Service
Rear All Saints Church Hall, 98a Park Road, Blackpool, Lancashire FY1 4ES
01253-24505

Blyth Valley Council for Voluntary Service
22 Beaconsfield Street, Blyth, Northumberland NE24 2DP
01670-353623

Bognor Regis & District Council for Voluntary Service
The Town Hall, Clarence Road, Bognor Regis, West Sussex PO21 1LD
01243-827821

Bolton District Council for Voluntary Service
Bridge House, Pool Street South, Bolton, Lancashire BL1 2BA
01204-396011

Boothferry Council for Voluntary Service
21 Pasture Road, Goole, North Humberside DN14 6BP
01405-766237

Bournemouth Helping Services Council
Flat A, 29 Alma Road, Winton, Bournemouth, Dorset BH9 1AB
01202-536336

Bracknell Council for Voluntary Service
Coopers Hill Centre, Bagshot Road, Bracknell, Berkshire RG12 3QS
01344-52424

Bradford Area Association of Councils for Voluntary Service
19/25 Sunbridge Road, Bradford, West Yorkshire BD1 2AY
01274-722772

Brentwood Council for Voluntary Services
1/2 Seven Arches Road, Brentwood. Essex CM14 4JG
01277-222299

Brighton Council for Voluntary Service
17-19 Ditchling Rise, Brighton, East Sussex BN1 4QL
01273-571560

Bristol Council for Voluntary Service
The St Paul's Settlement, 1st floor, City Road, Bristol BS2 8UH
0117-942 3300

Buckinghamshire Council for Voluntary Service
Walton House, Walton Street, Aylesbury, Buckinghamshire HP21 7QQ
01296-21036

Burnley, Pendle & Rossendale Council for Voluntary Service
83 Hammerton Street, Burnley, Lancashire BB11 1LE
01282-33740

Bury Metropolitan Council for Voluntary Service
6 Tenterden Street, Bury, Lancashire BL9 0BG
0161-764 2161

Calderdale Council for Voluntary Service
32 Clare Road, Halifax, West Yorkshire HX1 2HX
01422-363341

Cambridge Council for Voluntary Service
Llandaff Chambers, 2 Regent Street, Cambridge CB2 1AX
01223-464696

Cambridgeshire Community Council
218 High Street, Cottenham, Cambridge CB4 4RZ
01954-50144

Sources of advice on applying to trusts

Camden Voluntary Action
1st floor, Instrument House,
207/215 King's Cross Road,
London WC1X 9DB
0171-837 5544

Canterbury & Thanet Council for Voluntary Service
CVS - Community Support Centre, Beach House, Beach Street, Herne Bay CT6 5PT
01227-373293

Carlisle Council for Voluntary Service
27 Spencer Street, Carlisle, Cumbria CA1 1BE
01228-512513

Charnwood Community Council
John Storer House, Wards End, Loughborough LE11 3HA
01509-230131

Chelsea Social Council
The Crypt, St Luke's Church, Sydney Street, London SW3 6NH
0171-351 3210

Chester Council for Voluntary Service
Folliott House, 53 Northgate Street, Chester CH1 2HQ
01244-323527

Chesterfield & N E Derbyshire Council for Voluntary Service and Action (LINKS)
Office 1, The Market Hall, Chesterfield S40 1AR
01246-274844

Chichester & District Council for Voluntary Service
173b Broyle Road, Chichester PO19 4AA
01243-532765

Chorley & South Ribble Council for Voluntary Service
213 Eaves Lane, Chorley, Lancashire PR6 0AG
01257-263254

Cleveland Council for Voluntary Service
47 Princes Road, Middlesborough TS1 4BG
01642-240651

Colchester Council of Voluntary Service
Winsley's House, High Street, Colchester, Essex CO1 1UG
01206-45283

Coventry Voluntary Service Council
58-64 Corporation Street, Coventry CV1 1GF
01203-220381

Craven Voluntary Action
St Andrew's Church Hall, Skipton, North Yorkshire BD23 2EJ
01756-701056

Crawley Council for Voluntary Service
The Tree, 103 High Street, Crawley, West Sussex RH10 1DD
01293-526248

Crewe & Nantwich Council for Voluntary Service
Ashton House, 1a Gatefield Street, Crewe CW1 3AU
01270-211545

Croydon Voluntary Action
Eldon House, 78 Thornton Road, Thornton Heath, Surrey CR7 6BA
0181-684 3862

Cumbria Voluntary Action
The Old Stables, Redhills, Penrith, Cumbria CA11 0DT
01768-868086

Dacorum Council for Voluntary Service
48 High Street, Hemel Hempstead HP1 3AF
01442-253935

Darlington Council for Voluntary Service
Bennet House, 14 Horse Market, Darlington, County Durham DL1 5PT
01325-468055

Dartford, Swanley & Gravesham Council for Voluntary Service
Enterprise House, 8 Essex Road, Dartford DA1 2AU
01322-291060

Derby Council for Voluntary Service
4 Charnwood Street, Derby DE1 2GT
01332-46266

Derbyshire Rural Community Council
Rural Community House, Church Street, Wirksworth, Derbyshire DE4 4EY
01629-824797

Doncaster Council for Voluntary Service
Community House, 7 Nether Hall Road, Doncaster, South Yorkshire DN1 2PH
01302-341010

Droitwich Council for Voluntary Service
The Old Library Centre, 65 Ombersley Street East, Droitwich Spa, Hereford & Worcester WR9 8RA
01905-779115

Dudley Council for Voluntary Service
7 Albion Street, Brierley Hill, West Midlands DY5 3EE
01384-73381

Dunstable & District Council for Voluntary Organisations
Beacon House, 5 Regents Street, Dunstable, Bedfordshire LU6 1LR
01582-477727

Durham Rural Community Council
Park House, Station Road, Lanchester, Durham DH7 0EX
0191-384 9266

Ealing Voluntary Service Council
84 Uxbridge Road, West Ealing, London W13 8RA
0181-579 6273

Easington District Council for Voluntary Service
25 Yoden Way, Peterlee, Durham SR8 1BP
0191-586 5427

East Grinstead Council for Voluntary Service
Old Court House, College Lane, East Grinstead, West Sussex RH19 3LB
01342-328080

East Staffordshire Council for Voluntary Service
Voluntary Services Centre, Union Street Car Park, Burton on Trent, Staffs DE14 1AA
01283-543414

East Yorkshire Council for Voluntary Service
26 Marton Road, Bridlington, Humberside YO16 5AL
01262-677555

Eastbourne Association of Voluntary Service
8 Saffrons Road, Eastbourne, East Sussex BN21 1DG
01323-639373

Eastleigh Council of Community Service
Town Hall Centre, Leigh Road, Eastleigh Hampshire SO50 9DE
01703-629448

Ellesmere Port & Neston Council for Voluntary Service & Volunteer Bureau
4 Shrewsbury Road, Ellesmere Port, South Wirral L65 8AP
0151-357 2931

Enfield Voluntary Service Council
341a Baker Street, Enfield, Middlesex EN1 3LF
0181-342 1898

Epping Forest Voluntary Services Committee
Civic Offices, High Street, Epping, Essex CM16 4BZ

Exeter Council for Voluntary Service
1 Wynards, Magdalen Street, Exeter EX2 4HX
01392-58223

Farnham Voluntary Service Council
Vernon House, West Street, Farnham, Surrey GU9 7DR
01252-725961

Gateshead Voluntary Organisations Council
John Haswell House, 8/9 Gladstone Terrace, Gateshead NE8 4GY
0191-478 4103

Sources of advice on applying to trusts

Gedling Council for Voluntary Service
Park View Offices, Arnot Hill Park, Nottingham Road, Arnold, Notts NG5 6LU
0115-926 6750

Glanford Council for Voluntary Service
Assembly Rooms, Queen Street, Barton-on-Humber, South Humberside DN18 5QP
01652-633297

Greater Manchester Centre for Voluntary Organisations
The St Thomas Centre, Ardwick Green North, Manchester M12 6FZ
0161-273 7451

Grimsby & Cleethorpes Council for Voluntary Service
14 Town Hall Street, Grimsby DN31 1HN
01472-353446

Halton Voluntary Action
Brook Chambers, High Street, Runcorn, Cheshire WA7 1JH
01928-577626

Hammersmith & Fulham Association of Community Organisations
Palingswick House, 241 King Street, London W6 9LP
0181-741 5875

Hampshire Council of Community Service
Beaconsfield House, Andover Road, Winchester SO22 6AT
01962-854971

Harlow Council for Voluntary Service
Bentham House, Hamstel Road, Harlow CM20 1EP
01279-432146

Harrogate and Area Council for Voluntary Service
6 Victoria Avenue, Harrogate, North Yorkshire HG1 1ED
01423-504074

Harrow Association of Voluntary Service
The Lodge, 64 Pinner Road, Harrow HA1 4HZ
0181-863 6707

Hartlepool Voluntary Development Agency
36 Victoria Road, Hartlepool, Cleveland TS26 8DD
01429-262641

Hastings Voluntary Action
31a Priory Street, Hastings TN34 1EA
01424-444010

Havant Council for Voluntary Service
21 East Street, Havant, Hampshire PO9 1AA
01705-645777

Hertfordshire Community Council
2 Townsend Avenue, St Albans, Herts AL1 3SG
01727-852298

Heswall & District Council for Voluntary Service
Hillcroft, Rocky Lane, Heswall, Wirral L60 0BY
0151-342 6115

Hillingdon Association of Voluntary Services
Christ Church, Redford Way, Uxbridge, Middlesex UB8 1SZ
01895-239830

Hinckley and Bosworth Area Council for Voluntary Service
16A Rugby Road, Hinckley, Leicester LE10 0QD
01455-633002

Hove & Portslade Voluntary Care Services
38a Station Road, Portslade, East Sussex BN41 1AG
01273-886800

Hoylake & District Council for Voluntary Service
c/o Hilbre High School, Frankby Road, West Kirby, Wirral L48 6EQ
0151-625 6078

Hull Council for Voluntary Service
Voluntary Organisations Centre, 29 Anlaby Road, Hull HU1 2PG
01482-324474

Community Council of Humberside
14 Market Place, Howden, Goole, North Humberside DN14 7BJ
01430-430904

Ipswich & District CVS
19 Tower Street, Ipswich, Suffolk IP1 3BE

Isle of Wight Rural Community Council
Reed Posting House, 24 Holyrood Street, Newport, Isle of Wight PO30 5AZ
01983-524058

Islington Voluntary Action Council
322 Upper Street, London N1 2XQ
0171-226 4862

Kent Rural Community Council
15 Manor Road, Folkestone, Kent CT20 2AH
01303-850816

Kingston Council for Voluntary Service
36a Fife Road, Kingston upon Thames, Surrey KT1 1SY
0181-546 0184

Kingswood Centre for Voluntary Service Ltd
Kingswood Foundation Estate, Wesley Studios, Britania Road, Kingwood, Bristol BS15 2DB
0117-947 6406

Kirklees Council for Voluntary Service
28 Alfreds' Way, Batley, West Yorkshire WF17 5DR
01924-472702

Knowsley Council for Voluntary Service
Community Services Centre, Lathom Road, Huyton, Merseyside L36 9XS
0151-489 1222

Lancashire Community Council
15 Victoria Road, Fulwood, Preston PR2 4PS
01772-718710

Lancaster District Council for Voluntary Service
Trinity Community Centre, Middle Street, Lancaster LA1 1JZ
01524-63760

Ledbury & District Council for Voluntary Service
Council Office, Church Street, Ledbury HR8 1DL
01531-636006

Leeds Voluntary Action
34 Lupton Street, Hunslet, Leeds LS10 2QW
0113-270 0777

Leicester Voluntary Action
4th Floor, Market Centre Offices, 11 Market Street, Leicester LE1 5GG
0116-251 3999

Leicestershire Association of Voluntary Agencies
Beaumont Enterprise Centre, Boston Road, Leicester LE4 1HB
0116-234 1577

Leighton Linslade Council of Voluntary Organisations
Crombie House, 36 Hockliffe Street, Leighton Buzzard, Bedfordshire LU7 8JW
01525-850559

Lewisham Voluntary Action
120 Rushey Green, Catford, London SE6 4HQ
0181-695 6000

Lichfield & District Council for Voluntary Service
1st Floor, Former Nurses Home, St Michael's Hospital, Trent Valley Road, Lichfield, Staffordshire WS13 6EF
01543-254341

Lincoln Area Council for Voluntary Service
22 West Parade, Lincoln LN1 1JT
01522-513564

Liverpool Council for Voluntary Service
14 Castle Street, Liverpool L2 0NJ
0151-236 7728

London Voluntary Service Council
London Voluntary Sector Resource Centre, 356 Holloway Road, London N7 6PA
0171-700 8107

Luton & District Council for Voluntary Service
Ground Floor, Redcliffe House, Mill Street, Luton LU1 2NA
01582-33418

Sources of advice on applying to trusts

Macclesfield District Council for Voluntary Service
81 Park Lane, Macclesfield, Cheshire SK11 6TX
01625-619101

Voluntary Action Manchester
Fourways House, 57 Hilton Street, Piccadilly, Manchester M1 2EJ
0161-236 3206

Mansfield Council for Voluntary Service
Community House, 36 Wood Street, Mansfield NG18 1QA
01623-651177

Medway Council for Voluntary Service
15a New Road Avenue, Chatham, Kent ME4 6BA
01634-812850

Melton Borough Council for Voluntary Service
16 Thorpe Road, Melton Mowbray LE13 1SG
01664-410007

Mendip Council for Voluntary Service
The Bread Room, Church Lane, Shepton Mallet, Somerset BA4 5LE
01749-344403

Merseyside Council for Voluntary Service
Mount Vernon Green, Hall Lane, Liverpool L7 8TF
0151-709 0990

Merton Voluntary Service Council
The Vestry Hall, London Road, Mitcham, Surrey CR4 3UD
0181-685 1771

Milton Keynes Council of Voluntary Organisations
Acorn House, 351 Midsummer Boulevard, Milton Keynes MK9 3HP
01908-661623

New Forest Council of Community Service and Volunteer Bureau
76a Brookley Road, Brockenhurst, Hampshire SO42 7RA
01590-624141/2

Newark & Sherwood Council for Voluntary Service
85 Millgate, Newark, Nottinghamshire NG24 4UA
01636-79539

Newcastle-upon-Tyne Council for Voluntary Service
Mea House, Ellison Place, Newcastle-upon-Tyne NE1 8XS
0191-232 7445

Newham Voluntary Agencies Council
St Marks Church Centre, Tollgate Road, Beckton, London E6 4YA
0171-511 3553

North Bedfordshire Council for Voluntary Service
7 Union Street, Bedford MK40 2SF
01234-354366

North Herefordshire Council for Voluntary Service
Chapel Yard, Burgess Street, Leominster, Hereford & Worcester HR6 8DE
01568-611099

North Hertfordshire Council for Voluntary Service
Free Church Hall, Gernon Road, Letchworth, Hertfordshire SG6 3HS
01462-683577

North Tyneside Voluntary Organisations Development Association
Room B1 Linkskill Terrace, North Shields, Tyne & Wear NE30 2AY
0191-296 0929

North Warwickshire Council for Voluntary Service
Community House, Coleshill Road, Atherstone CV9 1BN
01827-718080

North West Leicestershire Council for Voluntary Service
Marlene Reid Centre, 85 Belvoir Road, Coalville, Leicestershire LE67 3PH
01530-510515

North Wiltshire Council for Voluntary Service
3-4 New Road, Chippenham SN15 1EJ
01249-654089

North Yorkshire Forum for Voluntary Organisations
William House, Shipton Road, Skelton YO3 6WZ
01904-644520

Northallerton & District Voluntary Service Association
Community House, 10 South Parade, Northallerton, North Yorkshire DL7 8SE
01609-780458

Northampton & County Council for Voluntary Service
13 Hazelwood Road, Northampton NN1 1LG
01604-24121

Northern Devon Council for Voluntary Service
The Castle Centre/Court Yard, 25 Castle Street, Barnstaple EX31 1DR
01271-72811

Northumberland Community Council
Tower Buildings, 9 Oldgate, Morpeth NE61 1PY
01670-517178

Norwich & District Voluntary Services
Charing Cross Centre, St John Maddermarket, Norwich NR2 1DN
01603-614474

Notting Hill Social Council
7 Thorpe Close, London W10 5XL
0181-969 9897

Nottingham Council for Voluntary Service
33 Mansfield Road, Nottingham NG1 3FB
0115-947 6714

Nottinghamshire Rural Community Council
Minster Chambers, Church Street, Southwell, Nottingham NG25 0HD
01636-815267

Nuneaton & Bedworth Council for Voluntary Service
72 High Street, Nuneaton, Warwickshire CV11 5DA
01203-385765

Oldham Council for Voluntary Service
22 Clegg Street, New Road, Oldham OL1 1PL
0161-652 8096

Oxfordshire Council for Voluntary Action
Pratten Building, Prison Yard, New Road, Oxford OX1 1ND
01865-251946

Peterborough Council for Voluntary Service
51 Broadway, Peterborough PE1 1SQ
01733-342683

Plymouth Guild of Community Service
Ernest English House, Buckwell Street, Plymouth PL1 2DA
01752-665084

Poole Council for Voluntary Service
Dial House, 54 Lagland Street, Poole, Dorset BH15 1QG
01202-682046

Potters Bar Council for Voluntary Service
Limerick House, 114 Mutton Lane, Potters Bar, Hertfordshire EN6 2HG
01707-649561

Preston Council for Voluntary Service
95 Fishergate, Preston, Lancashire PR1 2NJ
01772-251108

Reading Voluntary Action
8 Cross Street, Reading RG1 1SN
01734-574123

Redbridge Council for Voluntary Service
1st floor, North Broadway Chambers, 1 Cranbrook Road, Ilford, Essex IG1 4DU
0181-554 5049

Sources of advice on applying to trusts

Redditch Council for Voluntary Service
Ecumenical Centre, 6 Evesham Walk, Redditch B97 4EX
01527-68403

Richmond-upon-Thames Council for Voluntary Service
51 Sheen Road, Richmond-upon-Thames, Surrey TW9 1YQ
081-940 6235

Richmondshire Voluntary Council
6 Flints Terrace, Richmond, North Yorkshire DL10 7AH
01748-822537

Rochdale Voluntary Action
158 Drake Street, Rochdale OL16 1PX
01706-31291

Rotherham District Council for Voluntary Service
Durlston House, 5 Moorgate Road, Rotherham S60 2EN
01709-829821

Rugby Council for Voluntary Service
19 & 20 North Street, Rugby CV21 2AG
01788-574258

Rushcliffe Council for Voluntary Service
Park Lodge, Bridgford Road, West Bridgford, Nottingham NG2 6AT
0115-981 6988

Salford Council for Voluntary Service
12 Irwell Place, off Church Street, Eccles, Salford M30 0FN
0161-787 7795

Salisbury & District Council for Voluntary Service
Greencroft House, 42/46 Salt Lane, Salisbury SP1 1EG
01722-421747

Scarborough District Council for Voluntary Service
Allatt House, 5/6 West Parade Road, Scarborough YO12 5ED
01723-362205

Scunthorpe & District Council for Voluntary Service
41 Frances Street, Scunthorpe, South Humberside DN15 6NS
01724-845155

Sefton Council for Voluntary Service
The Old Museum, Church Road, Waterloo, Liverpool L22 5NB
0151-920 0726

Selby Association of Voluntary Service
The Bungalow, Sherburn in Elmet, Leeds LS25 6AS
01977-684941

Voluntary Action Sheffield
69 Division Street, Sheffield, South Yorkshire S1 4GE
0114-249 3360

Community Council of Shropshire
1 College Hill, Shrewsbury SY1 1LT
01743-360641

Slough Council for Voluntary Service
William Street, Slough SL1 1XX
01753-524176

Solihull Council for Voluntary Service
Alice House, 10 Homer Road, Solihull, West Midlands B91 3QQ
0121-704 1619

South Downs Council for Voluntary Service
143 High Street, Lewes, East Sussex BN7 1XT
01273-483832

South Kent Council for Voluntary Action
Main Office, 25 Bank Street, Ashford, Kent TN23 1DG
01233-610171

South Lakeland Council for Voluntary Action
Stricklandgate House, 92 Stricklandgate, Kendal LA9 4PU
01539-729168

South Staffs CVS
Church House, 7 Church Road, Brewood, Staffordshire ST19 9BT
01902-851472

South Tyneside Voluntary Project
Victoria Hall, 119 Fowler Street, South Shields NE33 1NU
0191-456 9551

Southampton Council of Community Service
18 Oxford Street, Southampton SO14 1DJ
01703-228291

Southend Association of Voluntary Services
Friendship House, 484 Southchurch Road, Southend-on-Sea, Essex SS1 2QA
01702-619489

St Albans District Council for Voluntary Services
1a Spicer Street, St Albans, Hertfordshire AL3 4PH
01727-852657

St Helens District Council for Voluntary Service
1st floor, Corporation Buildings, 10 Corporation Street, St Helens, Merseyside WA10 1DZ
01744-21755

Staffordshire District Voluntary Services
131-141 North Walls, Stafford ST16 3AD
01785-45466

Staffordshire Moorlands Voluntary Service Council
Bank House, 20 St Edward Street, Leek, Staffordshire ST13 5DS
01538-371544

Stevenage Council for Voluntary Service
Stevenage Voluntary Centre, Swingate, Stevenage, Hertfordshire SG1 1RU
01438-353951

Stockport Council for Voluntary Service
Russell Morley House, 8-16 Lower Hillgate, Stockport SK1 1JE
0161-477 0246

Stoke-on-Trent Council for Voluntary Service
Trent Centre, 645 Leek Road, Hanley, Stoke-on-Trent ST1 3NF
01782-274898

Stratford-on-Avon District Council for Voluntary Service
The Hospital, Arden House, Arden Street, Stratford-upon-Avon CV37 6NW
01789-298115

Suffolk ACRE
Alexandra House, Rope Walk, Ipswich, Suffolk IP4 1LR
01473-264595

Sunderland Council for Voluntary Service
53 Frederick Street, Sunderland SR1 1NF
0191-565 1566

Surrey Heath Council for Voluntary Service
The Resource Centre, Rossmore House, 26-42 Park Street, Camberley, Surrey GU15 3PL
01276-684979

Surrey Voluntary Service Council
"Astolat", Coniers Way, New Inn Lane, Burpham, Guildford GU4 7HL
01483-66072

Sutton Centre for Voluntary Service
31 West Street, Sutton, Surrey SM1 1SJ
0181-643 3277

Tamworth Community Service Council
Carnegie Centre, Corporation Street, Tamworth B79 7DN
01827-69000

Taunton Deane Council for Voluntary Service
Old Municipal Buildings, Corporation Street, Taunton TA1 4AQ
01823-284470

Action in Teignbridge: Council for Voluntary Service
Bank House, 5b Bank Street, Newton Abbot, Devon TQ12 2JL
01626-331125

Sources of advice on applying to trusts

Telford Community Council
Meeting Point House, South Water Square, Off St Quentin Gate, Telford TF3 4HA
01952-291350

Tendring Council for Voluntary Service
Volunteer Centre, 92 Pier Avenue, Clacton-on-Sea, Essex CO15 1NJ
01255-425692

Thamesdown Voluntary Service Centre
1 John Street, Swindon SN1 1RT
01793-538398

Thirsk, Sowerby & District Community Care Association
21 Chapel Street, Thirsk, North Yorkshire YO7 1LU
01845-523115

Thurrock Council for Voluntary Service
Grays Adult Centre Complex, Richmond Road, Grays, Essex RM17 6DN
01375-374093

Torbay Voluntary Service
The Castleton, 11 Castle Road, Torquay, Devon TQ1 3BB
01803-212638

Trafford Council for Voluntary Service
Ashfield House, 30 Ashfield Road, Sale M33 1FF
0161-976 2448

Tunbridge Wells & District Council for Voluntary Service
19 Monson Road, Tunbridge Wells, Kent TN1 1LS
01892-530330

Vale Royal Council for Voluntary Service
The Council House, Church Road, Northwich CW9 5PD
01606-46485

Wallasey Council for Voluntary Service
222 Liscard Road, Wallasey, Merseyside L44 5TN
0151-630 4164

Walsall Guild for Voluntary Service
50 Lower Hall Lane, Walsall, West Midlands WS1 1RJ
01922-38825

Voluntary Action Waltham Forest
Unit 37, Alpha Business Centre, South Grove Road, Walthamstow, London E17 7NX
0181-521 0377

Wansbeck Council for Voluntary Service
Station Villa, Kenilworth Road, Ashington, Northumberland NE63 8AA
01670-816751

Warrington Council for Voluntary Service
5 Hanover Street, Warrington WA1 1LZ
01925-630239

Warwick District Council for Voluntary Service
109 Warwick Street, Leamington Spa CV32 4QZ
01926-881151

Watford Council for Voluntary Service
149 The Parade, Watford WD1 1NA
01923-254400

Welwyn/Hatfield Council for Voluntary Service
23 St Albans Road East, Hatfield AL10 0ER
01707-274861

VOLDA (formerly Copeland Voluntary Action)
Border House, Coach Road, Whitehaven, Cumbria CA28 9DF
01946-693023

West Lancashire Council for Voluntary Service
Sandy Lane Centre, 79 Westgate, Skelmersdale, Lancashire WN8 8LA
01695-733737

West Somerset Council for Voluntary Service
The Old Post Office, Parkhouse Road, Minehead, Somerset TA24 5AA
01643-707484

West Wiltshire Council for Voluntary Service
Bridge House, Stallard Street, Trowbridge BA14 9AE
01225-767993

Westminster Voluntary Action
1 Elgin Avenue, London W9 3PR
0171-286 3451

Weston-Super-Mare Council for Voluntary Service
Room 6, Roselawn, 28 Walliscote Road, Weston-Super-Mare BS23 1UH
01934-631169

Wigan & Leigh Council for Voluntary Service
6 Rodney Street, Wigan, Lancashire WN1 1DC
01942-514234

Wiltshire Community Council
Wyndhams, St Joseph's Place, Bath Road, Devizes, Wiltshire SN10 1DD
01380-722475

Winchester District Council of Community Service
The Winchester Centre, Parchment Street, Winchester SO23 8AZ
01962-842293

Wirral Council for Voluntary Service
46 Hamilton Square, Birkenhead L41 5AR
0151-647 5432

Woking Association of Voluntary Service
Gloucester Chambers, Town Square, Woking GU21 1GA
01483-751456

Wolverhampton Voluntary Service Council
2-3 Bell Street, Wolverhampton WV1 3PR
01902-773761

Worthing Area Guild for Voluntary Service
Methold House, North Street, Worthing BN11 1DU
01903-528629

Yeovil & District Council for Voluntary Service
Petters House, Petters Way, Yeovil BA20 1SH
01935-75914

York Council for Voluntary Service
Community House, 10 Priory Street, York YO1 1EZ
01904-621133

Yorkshire Rural Community Council
William House, Shipton Road, Skelton YO3 6WZ
01904-645271

Northern Ireland

Northern Ireland Council for Voluntary Action
127 Ormeau Road, Belfast BT7 1SH
0232-321224

Scotland

Scottish Council for Voluntary Organisations
18/19 Claremont Crescent, Edinburgh EH7 4QD
031-556 3882

Wales

Wales Council for Voluntary Action
Llys Ifor, Crescent Road, Caerphilly, Mid Glamorgan CF8 1XL
0222-869224/869111

Rural Community Councils

We were unable to obtain an up-to-date list of Rural Community Councils. You may well be able to get information from: **Action with Communities in Rural England (ACRE),** *Somerford Court, Somerford Road, Cirencester, Gloucestershire GL7 1TW (01285-653477). Your local Council for Voluntary Service may also help.*

Applying to charitable trusts – how to be successful

In these notes I want to give some broad hints on how best to approach trusts and what you can do to improve your chances of success. But before doing this, there are some general points which I believe are important:

(a) Trusts vary greatly and there is no single formula that will guarantee success.
(b) Common sense and perseverance are essential qualities in approaching trusts.
(c) At all times you should be thinking of developing a partnership with trusts rather than begging for help.
(d) Believe in what you are doing. If you don't, why should anyone else? Just as trusts vary a lot, so do projects. Different projects and people will find different ways of selling themselves. So adapt any points I make to suit yourself and your organisation.

Preparation and planning

The development of a successful organisation depends on good preparation and planning. This applies equally to successful fundraising. If you spend time on proper planning, the other aspects of fundraising will follow logically.

Trusts are only one source of funds. There are many others such as industry, events, legacies etc. Thus you should have an overall strategy for raising funds for your organisation, and fundraising from trusts should be seen as one element in that strategy.

A fundraising strategy should be an integral part of the strategy for the development of your organisation as a whole. Planning this involves a series of logical steps:

1. Clarify the **problem** or the **need** that is to be met.
2. Define the **aims** and **objectives** of the project.
3. Decide on the **methods** to achieve the aims.
4. Draw up short-term and long-term **plans**.
5. Prepare a financial **budget** (cost the plans).
6. Identify possible sources of **funds**.

It is a good idea to involve your whole organisation in this process as far as possible.

A useful preliminary exercise is to write down succinctly:

1. The problem or the need your organisation is concerned with.
2. The goals of your organisation.
3. How your organisation is trying to achieve these goals.

If you cannot do this succinctly it probably means there is some confusion in your thinking. And if you yourself are confused about what you are doing, it will not be very easy to persuade others to support you.

Raising money, especially from trusts, can be a slow process, so start your efforts in good time. Good planning will help to ensure you raise money when you need it. Do not make the mistake of waiting until you are in a crisis and then trying to raise money. This is all too common.

Decide what you are going to do and then raise money for that. Do not work the other way around. Too often I have found organisations doing projects because there is money available rather than doing the project they really want to do. This distorts the organisation's purpose and can lead to internal disagreements.

Defining your project

It is important to have a good project to take to trusts. You should be clear about the need you are meeting and be able to state this clearly. Do not assume others will understand what the need is. Spell it out.

In my experience most trusts prefer to support a specific project and they tend not to like contributing to on-going running costs or to topping up government grants. If you are a large organisation, it can pay to break your work into convenient projects so that trusts have something to latch on to.

Applying to charitable trusts – how to be successful

Many trusts like projects which are new, imaginative and innovative. However, this is not always the case, especially with trusts with a very specific remit which may support the same organisation over a long period.

Often trusts like projects that will be monitored and which will produce reports. In this way others can benefit from the experience, or the success of the project might influence government policies. This process is an integral part of trusts being interested in new and pioneering work. In defining your project remember that the project is the product you are selling. However well this product is packaged, you are only likely to be successful if it is a good project.

Selecting your targets

There are many trusts (some 2,500 are listed in the *Directory of Grant Making Trusts*), and it is important to recognise that they do not form a homogeneous group. Some are large, some are small; some are public, some are private; some creative, some are conservative; some take risks, some play safe; some employ staff, some do not. Only a few of them are likely to be interested in your work. Thus it is important to research carefully into their policies, their size, and how they like to deal with applicants (where such information is available). This is vital if you are not going to waste a lot of time/money/paper in making pointless applications.

Your researches will lead you to discard most trusts. Of those remaining there will be two main categories. The first will comprise of a few large trusts with clear policies. The second will be a larger list of those that are worth a try but not worth spending too much time on. Your type of approach is likely to vary with each category.

Critical information to find out before approaching trusts includes the following: their policies and priorities (where these are stated); size of their grants; who they have supported in your geographic area and area of interest; if they are accessible and who to contact; when they make decisions; if you know their staff or trustees.

Finding out the above information will enable you to identify that aspect of your work which might appeal to each trust. You should then try and tailor your application as far as possible to meet the requirements of each trust. However, do not distort what you are actually planning to do.

For those trusts that are just 'worth a try' it will not be worth while spending too much time on your application to them. Here you will have to resort to what is in effect a circular mailing. But you will improve your chances very substantially if you personalise the letters by at least 'topping and tailing' the letter, that is, addressing each individually, having a personal salutation rather than a 'Dear Sir/Madam' and signing each letter personally.

Building your credibility

As well as convincing the trust that your project is worthwhile and a priority, you must also convince them that your organisation is well equipped to carry it out.

The process of establishing credibility involves publicising the work of your organisation and its track record. If you have a positive public image it is more likely that your organisation will have been heard of and that you will receive sympathetic consideration.

One of the first questions trustees will ask is: *Do I know or know of this group or the people involved?* If they have not themselves heard of a project they may ask an adviser in the same area of the country as the project for their comments. Thus it is important to ensure as far as you can that trusts and their advisers have a favourable impression of your work.

For new and small organisations, particularly those operating in very run-down areas or undertaking some unappealing area of work, it is often difficult to establish credibility. One way to tackle this problem is to provide evidence of support or references from reputable establishment figures such as the local clergy or the director of the local council for voluntary service, which say how important your efforts are.

Most trusts will want evidence that your organisation has been properly set up with a constitution and that it is a charity. In addition, it is a good idea to supply a list of those who are on the management committee and the range and expertise of its members.

Written documents also provide evidence of the merits of your organisation. It is worth taking some trouble over producing your annual report and accounts, as well as any other reports your produce. Also, make a point of collecting favourable comments about your organisation written by independent outsiders. Keep a file of articles and press-cuttings about your organisation and its work; these can then be produced or quoted from when you are trying to build your credibility.

Working out your budget

Trusts want to know what you need and for how long you need it. Too often, groups fail to spell this out. This is often a symptom of poor planning. So prepare a budget, and remember that the preparation of this is an integral part of your planning process.

In preparing a budget remember the following points:

(a) Allow for all your costs. If you forget a particular item, you will not have the money to pay for it.

(b) Break your costs down into capital costs (equipment, premises, vehicles) and running costs like rent, telephone, salaries.

(c) Estimate your costs realistically. Do research where necessary.

(d) For long-term projects estimate your needs over time. Budget for how much you will need not just in the first year, but also in subsequent years. This will enable you to establish long-term plans for getting support for the project.

(e) Allow for inflation. Remember that you will be applying for next year's costs and you should not use current costs but allow for the current rate of inflation. For future years you will need to make an estimate of how inflation will continue and it is best to state your assumptions.

(f) Allow for a reasonable proportion of the overheads of the organisation when costing a project (such as rent, rates, phone, heat, stationery) except where you are applying for a specific item of equipment. Most trusts will accept this and be happy to contribute what seems a reasonable amount.

Quite often, people under-cost their projects. If you apply for too little, you will have a continuing fundraising problem. However, do not inflate your costs; you must put realistic figures into your budget.

Don't forget to look at all the possible sources of finance and then decide what proportion of a particular item or which items are appropriate for each particular trust. Different trusts can then be approached for different items.

Make sure that you ask each trust for an amount that is possible for them. However, a mistake that groups often make is to ask for a sum that is much too large for a particular trust, say £10,000, when a request for a smaller amount for some item in the budget, say costing £2,000, might have been successful.

Trusts will want to know where else you expect to get or have got funds from. They will often be prepared to co-fund with other trusts, and it is important to recognise that many trusts share information about projects. So it is essential to state who has already agreed to support the project, who else you are approaching and what other plans you have to achieve your fundraising target. You can also get advice from any trust which is prepared to fund you about which other trusts might be interested or worth approaching.

Trusts will want to know that you have thought about your future. This is especially true for trusts interested in supporting new projects. So make it clear that you have thought ahead and that you have some ideas on where funds might come from once the trust funding comes to an end.

It often helps to be able to demonstrate an element of self-help in funding as trustees may feel this is evidence of the commitment of the people involved to manage project work. So support from your local community and through your own fundraising efforts and the amount of income you can generate as earned income (where this is possible) are all important points to highlight.

Presenting your application

Raising money from trusts is a very competitive business. Trusts receive thousands of applications and the situation is getting worse. The majority of applications they receive are turned down. Thus presentation is very important.

When writing your application, be concise. You must get your basic message over in as short a space as possible. Trustees will not have time to read detailed documents about every project. However, where the trust has a full-time secretary or director, he/she may be able to look at more detailed documentation. Thus a one- or two-page letter plus supporting documents is my favoured formula. In this you should convey clearly, without using jargon, exactly what you want to do and why. Don't forget to provide evidence of the need for your project.

In the case of the small group of trusts you have selected as likely to be most interested in your work, try to relate your application to the interests of each trust you are approaching. Try and make them feel that you share a common purpose with them, that you share their priorities, and that you wish to foster a partnership with them.

When you are writing an application, convey your sense of enthusiasm and excitement. The more you can create a feeling of personal commitment to the project the better. Try to avoid being too remote, too dry and too impersonal.

Trustees will want to know that they will get value for their money, so spell out who and how many people will be affected by your project.

Your letter should state clearly how much you want and how urgently help is required.

Supply a budget and some evidence of your organisational credibility such as your annual report and accounts, press cuttings, and references or quotes which support your case.

Personal contact and a developing relationship

In all types of fundraising a personal approach is normally the best. However, this is not always possible. For instance, some trusts will not meet applicants. The more you can make personal contact the better the chance of establishing a sense of partnership and common purpose.

There are different ways of developing contact. Only the larger trusts employ full-time (or part-time) staff to deal with applicants. For smaller trusts a personal contact with a trustee can be important. For the larger trusts, most do not like phone calls out of the blue from new applicants. They prefer to deal on the basis of a written application. You can choose to send a full application, or just an outline of your project and what is involved. In either case you can then suggest that they come and see your project or request a meeting with the trust when you can present your case. If they think they might be interested, many will be happy to do this. You can follow up your written communication with a phone call to enquire whether they have received and read your application and whether a meeting is possible (but do leave a reasonable period before doing this).

If you have had previous contact with a trust, then it is much easier. You can even arrange a meeting to discuss an idea or ask for advice. If you do not know the trust, you may be able to get a personal introduction from an intermediary who knows your work and is respected by the trust.

Wherever it is possible, it can pay dividends to involve a trust's secretary or director in discussions about a project before you make a formal application. This will help to cultivate a sense of partnership and may affect what that particular trust might be happy to support. Be careful to listen to the advice they give. It is very irritating for a trust to spend time talking about a project to people who then make a formal application for something that they have been told is outside the trust's priorities.

Applying to charitable trusts – how to be successful

The first trust I ever applied to for a grant taught me the lesson that trusts will often back people as much as ideas or organisations. They had been going to turn down the application on the basis of the written material because it failed to convey a sense of personal commitment and belief in the project. Happily, when I met them, my own enthusiasm for what I was doing persuaded them to think again.

Most people will need to go back to trusts on many further occasions, so develop your relationship with them over time. Trusts are on the whole most likely to support people or organisations they know and trust.

So send regular reports on your project including a statement of how the trust's money was spent. Keep trusts aware of your work even when you are not asking them for money. This last point is extremely important.

It is important to keep very careful records of all your contact with trusts so that you can refer to previous contacts when you next apply to the trust. Failure to acknowledge previous contacts can be a cause of irritation.

At all times aim to reinforce the good feelings of those who have given you support. Trustees like to feel enlightened, imaginative and reassured that their judgement was right in backing your project instead of other projects. Acknowledge a trust's support at every opportunity.

Hugh Frazer, formerly Director, the Northern Ireland Voluntary Trust

Some do's and don'ts

The following are a summary of some of the key points mentioned above:

Do

1. Plan a strategy
2. Plan ahead
3. Select a good project
4. Believe in what you are doing
5. Select a target
6. Write an application tailored to the needs of the trust you are approaching
7. Use personal contact
8. Prepare a realistic and accurate budget for the project
9. Be concise
10. Be specific
11. Establish your credibility
12. Keep records of everything you do
13. Send reports and keep trusts informed
14. Try to develop a partnership or long-term relationship
15. Say thank you

Don't

1. Send a duplicated mail shot
2. Ask for unrealistic amounts
3. Assume trusts will immediately understand the need you are meeting
4. Make general appeals for running costs
5. Use jargon
6. Beg

Index

A B: A B Charitable Trust	27
A S: The A S Charitable Trust	27
Abel: The Abel Charitable Trust	27
Abell: The Abell Trust	28
Abrahams: The Henry & Grete Abrahams Charitable Foundation	28
Abrams: The Abrams Charitable Trusts	28
Acacia: The Acacia Charitable Trust	28
Access: Access 4 Trust	29
Achiezer: Achiezer Association Ltd	29
Adenfirst: Adenfirst Ltd	29
Airflow: Airflow Community Ltd	29
Ajahma: The Ajahma Charitable Trust	30
Alexandra: Alexandra Rose Day	30
Alglen: Alglen Ltd	30
Alliance: The Alliance Family Foundation	31
Altajir: The Altajir Trust	31
Ambika: The Ambika Paul Foundation	31
Arbib: The Arbib Foundation	31
Archbishop: The Archbishop of Canterbury's Charitable Trust	32
Armourers: The Armourers & Brasiers Gauntlet Trust	32
Arnopa: The Arnopa Trust	32
Arup: The Ove Arup Foundation	32
Ashden: The Ashden Charitable Trust	33
Ashley: The Laura Ashley Foundation	33
Askew: The Ian Askew Charitable Trust	34
Astor: The Astor Foundation	34
The Astor of Hever Trust	34
Atlantic: The Atlantic Foundation	35
ATP: The ATP Charitable Trust	35
Aurelius: The Aurelius Charitable Trust	35
Austin: The Lord Austin Trust	36
Bacta: The Bacta Charitable Trust	36
Baker: The Baker Charitable Trust	36
Baltic: The Baltic Charitable Fund	37
Barbour: The Barbour Trust	37
Barnby's: Lord Barnby's Foundation	37
Batchworth: The Batchworth Trust	38
Beacon: The Beacon Trust	38
Beaufort: The Beaufort House Trust	38
Beauland: Beauland Ltd	38
Bedford: The Bedford Charity (also known as the Harpur Trust)	39
Beit: The Beit Trust	39
Belvedere: The Belvedere Trust	39
Benfield: Benfield Motors Charitable Trust	40
Benham: The Benham Charitable Settlement	40
Bernerd: The Bernerd Foundation	41
Besom: Besom Foundation	41
Betton's: Mr Thomas Betton's Charity (Educational)	41
Bibby: The Mason Bibby 1981 Trust	41
Billmeir: The Billmeir Charitable Trust	42
Birse: The Peter Birse Charitable Trust	42
Bishop: Michael Bishop Foundation	43
Black: The Black Charitable Trusts	43
The Bertie Black Foundation	43
The Harry & Esther Black Foundation	44
Black's: Sir Alec Black's Charity	44
Blackman: The Isabel Blackman Foundation	44
Blair: The Blair Foundation	44
Blond: The Neville & Elaine Blond Charitable Trust	45
Bluston: The Bluston Charitable Settlement	45
Bohm: The Bohm Foundation	45
Boltons: The Boltons Trust	46
Bonham-Carter: The Charlotte Bonham-Carter Charitable Trust	46
Booth: The Booth Charities	46
Bornstein: The Bornstein Charitable Settlements	47
Bottom: The Harry Bottom Charitable Trust	47
Boulton: The A H & M A Boulton Trust	47
The P G & N J Boulton Trust	47
Bowland: The Bowland Charitable Trust	48
Brasher: The Chris Brasher Trust	48
Bridge: The Bridge Trust	48
Bridges': The Harold Bridges' Charitable Foundation	48
British: The British Council for Prevention of Blindness (also known as SEE – Save Eyes Everywhere)	49
British Schools and Universities Foundation (Inc.)	49
Britten-Pears: The Britten-Pears Foundation	49
Bromley: The Bromley Trust	50
Brooke: The David Brooke Charity	51
Brotherton: The Charles Brotherton Trust	51
Brown's: Bill Brown's Charitable Settlement	51
Brushmill: Brushmill Ltd	52
Bryant: The Bryant Trust	52
Bugden: The Rosemary Bugden Charitable Trust	52
Bulldog: The Bulldog Trust	52
Burden: The Burden Trust	53
Burdens: Burdens Charitable Foundation	53
Burrough: The Alan & Rosemary Burrough Charitable Trust	54
Burton: The Arnold James Burton Charitable Trust	54
The Audrey & Stanley Howard Burton 1960 Charitable Trust	54
The Geoffrey Burton Charitable Trust	54
The Raymond Montague Burton Charitable Trust	55
Butlin: The Bill Butlin Charity Trust	55
Cadbury: The Christopher Cadbury Charitable Trust	55
The Edward & Dorothy Cadbury Charitable Trust	56
The George W Cadbury Charitable Trust	56
Cadogan's: The Earl Cadogan's Charity Trust	57
Campbell: The Ellis Campbell Charitable Foundation	57
Caritas: Caritas	57
Carlee: Carlee Ltd	58
Carlton: The Carlton House Charitable Trust	58
Carmichael-Montgomery: The Carmichael-Montgomery Charitable Trust	58
Carnegie: The Carnegie Dunfermline Trust	58
Cash: Cash for Kids (formerly BRMB – Birmingham Walkathon)	59
Castle: The Castle Educational Trust	60
Cattle: The Joseph & Annie Cattle Trust	60
Catto: The Thomas Sivewright Catto Charitable Settlement	60
Cave: The Wilfrid & Constance Cave Foundation	61
Cayzer: The B G S Cayzer Charitable Trust	61
Chadwick: The Amelia Chadwick Trust	61
Chamberlain: The Chamberlain Foundation	62

Index

Chapman: The Chapman Charitable Trust — 62
Charities: The Charities Fund — 62
Chetwode: The Chetwode Samworth Charitable Trust — 63
Children's: The Children's Research Fund — 63
Childs: The Childs Charitable Trust — 63
Chiron: The Chiron Trust — 63
Chownes: Chownes Foundation — 64
Christie: The John & Celia Bonham Christie Charitable Trust — 64
Christmas: The Christmas Cracker Trust — 64
Church: The Church Burgesses Educational Foundation — 65
City: The City Educational Trust Fund — 65
CLA: The CLA Charitable Trust — 65
Clark: The Roger & Sarah Bancroft Clark Charitable Trust — 65
Clarkson: The Clarkson Jersey Charitable Trust — 66
Cleopatra: The Cleopatra Trust — 66
Cleveland: The Cleveland Community Foundation — 66
Clifton: The Clifton Charitable Trust — 67
Coales: The Francis Coales Charitable Foundation — 67
Coates: The Lance Coates Charitable Trust 1969 — 67
Cohen: The David Cohen Family Charitable Trust — 68
The Vivienne & Samuel Cohen Charitable Trust (also known as the Charitable Trust of 1965) — 68
Col-Reno: Col-Reno Ltd — 68
Colchester: The Colchester Catalyst Charity — 68
Coleman: The John & Freda Coleman Charitable Trust — 69
College: The College Estate Charity — 69
Collinson: The Norman Collinson Charitable Trust — 70
Colman: The E Alec Colman Charitable Fund Ltd — 70
The Sir Jeremiah Colman Gift Trust — 70
Combined: The Combined Charities Trust — 71
Comino: The Comino Foundation — 71
Community: Community Trusts — 72
Concern: Concern Universal — 72
Cooke: The Mansfield Cooke Trust — 72
Cooper: The Cooper Charitable Trust — 73
Coote: The Marjorie Coote Animal Charity Fund — 73
The Marjorie Coote Old People's Charity — 73
The Nicholas Coote Charitable Trust — 74
Coren: The Gershon Coren Charitable Foundation — 74
Cornwall's: The Duke of Cornwall's Benevolent Fund — 74
Countryside: The Countryside Trust — 74
Courtauld: The Augustine Courtauld Trust — 75
Craps: The Craps Charitable Trust — 75
Cross: The Cross Trust — 75
CRUSAID: CRUSAID — 76
Cumber: The Cumber Family Charitable Trust — 76
Curry: The Dennis Curry Charitable Trust — 77
Cussins: The Manny Cussins Foundation — 77

D'Oyly: The D'Oyly Carte Charitable Trust — 77
Dahl: The Roald Dahl Foundation — 78
Daily: The Daily Prayers Union Trust Ltd — 78
Dandelion: The Dandelion Trust — 78
Darlington: The Dr & Mrs A Darlington Charitable Trust — 79
Datnow: Datnow Limited — 79
Davies: The Gwendoline Davies Charity — 79
The J Davies Charities Ltd — 79
The Margaret Davies Charity — 80
Davis: The Wilfrid Bruce Davis Charitable Trust — 80
De: The De Haan Charitable Trust — 80
Dean: The Miriam K Dean Refugee Trust Fund — 81
Delves: The Delves Charitable Trust — 81
Dent: The Dent Charitable Trust — 81
Derbyshire: The J N Derbyshire Trust — 81
Devonshire's: The 10th Duke of Devonshire's Trust (1949) — 82
Dibdin: The Thomas Peter Dibdin Foundation — 82
Dinam: The Dinam Charity — 83
Divert: The Divert Trust (formerly the Intermediate Treatment Fund) — 83
DLM: The DLM Charitable Trust — 84
Dollond: The Dollond Charitable Trust — 84
Dorus: The Dorus Trust — 84
Douglas: The R M Douglas Charitable Trust — 84

Dove-Bowerman: The Dove-Bowerman Trust — 85
Dumbreck: The Dumbreck Charity — 85
Dunn: The W E Dunn Trust — 86
Dyers': The Dyers' Company Charitable Trust — 86

Earley: The Earley Charity — 86
Ebenezer: The Ebenezer Trust — 87
Ecological: The Ecological Foundation — 87
Edgar: The Gilbert & Eileen Edgar Foundation — 87
The Gilbert Edgar Trust Fund — 87
Edwards: The W G Edwards Charitable Foundation — 88
Elias: The George Elias Charitable Trust — 88
Elkes: The Wilfred & Elsie Elkes Charity Fund — 88
Ellador: Ellador Ltd — 88
Ellinson: The Ellinson Foundation — 89
Elm: The Elm Trust II — 89
Elmgrant: The Elmgrant Trust — 89
Ely: The Vernon N Ely Charitable Trust — 89
Emerton: The Emerton Charitable Settlement — 90
Emmandjay: The Emmandjay Charitable Trust — 90
Englefield: The Englefield Charitable Trust — 90
Enkalon: The Enkalon Foundation — 91
Entindale: Entindale Ltd — 91
Entwood: Entwood Charities Ltd — 91
Epigoni: The Epigoni Trust — 91
Equity: The Equity Trust Fund — 92
Evans: The Alan Evans Memorial Trust — 92
Everard: The Everard Foundation — 93
Evetts: The Beryl Evetts & Robert Luff Animal Welfare Trust — 93
Exilarch's: Exilarch's Foundation — 93

Fairway: The Fairway Trust — 93
Faringdon: The Lord Faringdon First & Second Charitable Trusts — 94
Farr: The Thomas Farr Charitable Trust — 94
Fawcett: The Fawcett Charitable Trust — 94
Feed: Feed the Minds — 95
Fenton: The A M Fenton Trust — 95
Ferguson: Ferguson Benevolent Fund Ltd — 96

Index

Field: The Doris Field Charitable Trust — 96
Finnart: The Finnart House School Trust — 96
Finnie: The David Finnie & Alan Emery Charitable Trust — 97
Fitton: The Fitton Trust — 97
Fitzwilliam: The Earl Fitzwilliam Charitable Trust — 97
Flatau: The Rose Flatau Charitable Trust — 97
Fletcher: The Roy Fletcher Charitable Trust — 98
Football: The Football Association National Sports Centre Trust — 98
The Football Association Youth Trust — 98
Ford: The Oliver Ford Charitable Trust — 99
Forte: The Forte Charitable Trust — 99
Foundation: The Foundation for Education — 99
Fowler: The Fowler Memorial Trust — 100
Franklin: The Jill Franklin Trust — 100
The Norman Franklin Trust — 100
Fraser: The Gordon Fraser Charitable Trust — 101
Freedman: The Louis Freedman Charitable Settlement — 102
Freke: The Thomas Freke & Lady Norton Charity — 102
French: The Charles S French Charitable Trust — 102
Freshfield: The Freshfield Foundation — 103
Friarsgate: The Friarsgate Trust — 103
Frognal: The Frognal Trust — 103
Frost: The Patrick Frost Foundation — 103

Gableholt: Gableholt Limited — 104
Gavron: The Robert Gavron Charitable Trust — 104
Gem: The Gem Charitable Trust — 104
General: The General Charity Fund — 105
Gertner: The Gertner Charitable Trust — 105
Gibbins: The Gibbins Trust — 105
Gibbs: The Gibbs Charitable Trusts — 106
Gilley: The L & R Gilley Charitable Trust — 106
Girdlers': The Girdlers' Company Charitable Trust — 106
Girling: The Girling (Cwmbran) Trust — 107
Glasser: The B & P Glasser Charitable Trust — 107
GNC: The GNC Trust — 107
Godinton: The Godinton Charitable Trust — 107
Goldberg: The Sydney & Phyllis Goldberg Memorial Trust — 108
Golden: The Golden Bottle Trust — 108
Goldhill: The Jack Goldhill Charitable Trust — 108
Good: The Good Neighbours Trust — 109
Goodman: The Everard & Mina Goodman Charitable Foundation — 109
Gough: The Gough Charitable Trust — 110
Grace: The Grace Charitable Trust — 110
Graham: The Reginald Graham Charitable Trust — 110
Grahame: The Grahame Charitable Foundation — 111
Granada: The Granada Foundation — 111
Grand: The Grand Order of Water Rats Charities Fund — 111
Grantham: The Grantham Yorke Trust — 112
Graves: The J G Graves Charitable Trust — 112
Greater: The Greater Bristol Foundation — 112
Greatham: The Greatham Hospital of God — 114
Green: The Barry Green Memorial Fund — 114
The Green Foundation — 114
Greggs: The Greggs Charitable Trust — 115
Gresham: The Gresham Charitable Trust — 115
Grove: The Grove Charitable Trust — 115
Grundy: The Stanley Grundy Trust — 116
Guinness: The Walter Guinness Charitable Trust — 116
Gunter: The Gunter Charitable Trust — 116
GWR: The GWR Community Trust — 116

Hadrian: The Hadrian Trust — 117
Haines: The Alfred Haines Charitable Trust — 118
Hallam: Hallam FM – Help a Hallam Child Appeal (Money Mountain Trust) — 118
Hamamelis: The Hamamelis Trust — 118
Hamilton: The Eleanor Hamilton Educational Trust — 119
Hammer: The B Hammer Charitable Trust — 119
Hammerson's: Sue Hammerson's Charitable Trust — 119
Handicapped: The Handicapped Children's Aid Committee — 119
Hannay: The Lennox Hannay Charitable Trust — 120
Hannington: The James Hannington Memorial Trust — 120
Hanover: The Hanover Charitable Trust — 120
Harbour: The Harbour Charitable Trust — 121
The Harbour Foundation — 121
Hare: The Hare of Steep Charitable Trust — 121
Harebell: The Harebell Centenary Fund — 121
Harris: The Harris Charity — 122
The Richard & Frances Harris Charitable Trust — 122
The R J Harris Charitable Settlement — 122
Hartley: The N & P Hartley Memorial Trust — 123
Hartley's: Gay & Peter Hartley's Hillards Charitable Trust — 123
Hatter: The Hatter (IMO) Foundation — 124
Hawe: The M A Hawe Settlement — 124
Hawthorne: The Hawthorne Charitable Trust — 124
Haymills: The Haymills Charitable Trust — 124
Hearnshaw's: May Hearnshaw's Charity — 125
Heber: The Mrs C S Heber Percy Charitable Trust — 125
Help: Help the Homeless — 125
Help the Hospices — 126
Herbert: The G D Herbert Charitable Trust — 126
Hereward: Hereward FM CNFM & KLFM Appeal (previously known as the Hereward Radio Appeal) — 126
Heritage: The Heritage of London Trust Ltd — 126
Hesed: The Hesed Trust — 127
Heuberger: The Bernhard Heuberger Charitable Trust — 127
Hickinbotham: The P & C Hickinbotham Charitable Trust — 127
Higgs: The Higgs Charitable Trust — 128
Hill: The Charles Littlewood Hill Trust — 128
Hinrichsen: The Hinrichsen Foundation — 128
Hobart: The Hobart Charitable Trust — 129
Hobson: Hobson Charity Ltd — 129
Holst: The Holst Foundation — 129
Homelands: The Homelands Charitable Trust — 129

Index

Homestead: The Homestead Charitable Trust — 130
Hood's: Sir Harold Hood's Charitable Trust — 130
Hoover: The Hoover Foundation — 130
Hornby: The A S Hornby Educational Trust — 130
Hornby's: Mrs E G Hornby's Charitable Settlement — 131
Hornton: The Hornton Charity — 131
Hospital: The Hospital Saturday Fund Charitable Trust — 131
Howard: The John & Ruth Howard Charitable Trust — 132
HSA: The HSA Charitable Trust — 132
Hubert: The A Hubert 1971 Charitable Trust — 133
The W I Hubert 1974 Charitable Trust — 133
Humanitarian: The Humanitarian Trust (also known as the Michael Polak Foundation) — 133
Hunt: The Albert Hunt Trust — 133
Huntingdon: The Huntingdon Foundation Limited — 134
Hyams: The P Y N & B Hyams Trust — 134
Hyde: The Hyde Park Place Estate Charity – Civil Trustees — 134

Idlewild: The Idlewild Trust — 134
Iliffe: The Iliffe Family Charitable Trust — 135
Inland: The Inland Waterways Association — 135
Inman: The Inman Charity — 135
INTACH: INTACH (UK) Trust — 136
Ireland: The Ireland Fund of Great Britain — 136
The Ireland Funds — 136
Irish: The Irish Youth Foundation (UK) Ltd — 137
Ironmongers': The Ironmongers' Quincentenary Fund — 138
ISA: The ISA Charity — 138
ITF: The ITF Seafarers Trust — 138

Jackson: The D J W Jackson Charitable Trust — 139
Jacobs: The Dorothy Jacobs Charity — 139
Jacobson: The Ruth & Lionel Jacobson Trust (Second Fund) No 2 — 139
Jarrold: The John Jarrold Trust — 139
Jenour: The Jenour Foundation — 140
Jephcott: The Jephcott Charitable Trust — 140
Jewish: Jewish Child's Day — 140
Jewish Continuity (amalgamated with the Jewish Educational Development Trust) — 141
Joels: The Joels Charitable Trust — 141
Johnson: The Johnson Group Cleaners Charity — 141
The Lillie Johnson Charitable Trust — 141
Joicey: The Joicey Trust — 142
Jones: The Jones 1986 Charitable Trust — 142
The Edward Cecil Jones Settlement — 142
Joseph: The J E Joseph Charitable Fund — 143
The Lady Eileen Joseph Foundation — 143
Judge: The Judge Charitable Foundation — 143

Kalms: The Stanley Kalms Foundation (formerly the Kalms Family Charitable Trust) — 144
Karten: The Ian Karten Charitable Trust — 144
Katz: The Michael & Ilse Katz Foundation — 144
Katzauer: The Katzauer Charitable Settlement — 144
Kaufman: The C S Kaufman Charitable Trust — 144
Kaye: The Emmanuel Kaye Foundation — 145
The Geoffrey John Kaye Charitable Foundation — 145
Kennedy: The Patrick Joseph Kennedy Charitable Trust — 145
Kennel: The Kennel Club Charitable Trust — 146
Kershaw: The Peter Kershaw Trust — 146
Keswick: Keswick Foundation Ltd — 146
Kiln: The Robert Kiln Charitable Trust — 146
Kinross: The Mary Kinross Charitable Trust — 147
Kobler: The Kobler Trust — 147
Kreditor: The Kreditor Charitable Trust — 148
Kreitman: The Jill Kreitman Foundation — 148
Kroch: The Heinz & Anna Kroch Foundation — 148

Laing: The Christopher Laing Foundation — 149
The David Laing Foundation — 149
The Martin Laing Foundation — 149
Langdale: The Langdale Trust — 149
Lanvern: The Lanvern Foundation — 150
Lark: The Lark Trust — 150
Lasletts: Lasletts (Hinton) Charity — 150
Lass: Rachel & Jack Lass Charities Ltd — 150
Lauffer: The R & D Lauffer Charitable Foundation — 150
Laurence: The Kathleen Laurence Trust — 151
Lawley: The Edgar E Lawley Foundation — 151
Lawlor: The Lawlor Foundation — 151
Lawrence: The Mrs F B Lawrence 1976 Charitable Settlement — 152
Lawson: The Carole & Geoffrey Lawson Foundation — 152
Lawson-Beckman: The Lawson-Beckman Charitable Trust — 153
Leach: The Leach Fourteenth Trust — 153
Leche: The Leche Trust — 153
Lee: The Arnold Lee Charitable Trust — 153
Leeds: The Leeds Hospital Fund Charitable Trust — 154
Leigh: The Morris Leigh Foundation — 154
Lewis: Lewis Family Charitable Trust — 154
The Sir Edward Lewis Foundation — 155
The Catherine Lewis Foundation (formerly The David Lewis Charitable Foundation Ltd) — 155
Lions: Lions Clubs International — 155
Lister: The Lister Charitable Trust — 156
Liverpool: The Liverpool & Merseyside Charitable Fund — 156
Lloyd: The Elaine Lloyd Charitable Trust — 156
Localtrent: Localtrent Ltd — 157
Locker: The Locker Foundation — 157
Loftus: The Loftus Charitable Trust — 157
London: The London Law Trust — 157
Longman: The William & Katherine Longman Trust — 158
Loseley: The Loseley Christian Trust — 158
Loyd: The C L Loyd Charitable Trust — 158
Lunzer: The Jack & Ruth Lunzer Charitable Trust — 158
Lyndhurst: The Lyndhurst Settlement — 159
The Lyndhurst Trust — 159
Lyons: The Sir Jack Lyons Charitable Trust — 160

M B: The M B Foundation (also known as Mossad Horav Moshe Aryeh Halevy) — 160
Macdonald-Buchanan: Macdonald-Buchanan Charitable Trust — 160

Index

Man: The Man of the People Fund	160
Mann: R W Mann Trustees Limited	161
March's: The Earl of March's Trust Company Ltd	161
Marchday: The Marchday Charitable Fund	161
Marchig: The Marchig Animal Welfare Trust	162
Marcus: The Linda Marcus Charitable Trust	162
Marks: The Hilda & Samuel Marks Foundation	162
Markus: The Erich Markus Charitable Foundation	163
Marsh: The Marsh Christian Trust	163
Marshall: The Charlotte Marshall Charitable Trust	164
The Jim Marshall Products Charitable Trust	164
Martin's: John Martin's Charity	164
Massey: The Nancie Massey Charitable Trust	164
Matchan: The Leonard Matchan Fund Ltd	165
Maxwell: The Maxwell Family Foundation	165
Mayfield: The Mayfield Valley Arts Trust	165
McAlpine: The Robert McAlpine Foundation	166
McCarthy: The McCarthy Foundation	166
McGreevy: The A M McGreevy No 5 Charitable Settlement	166
Mckenna: The Mckenna & Co Foundation	167
Mclaren: The Mclaren Foundation	167
Melchett: The Julian Melchett Trust	167
Mellows: The Anthony & Elizabeth Mellows Charitable Settlement	168
Melodor: Melodor Ltd	168
Menuchar: Menuchar Ltd	168
Methodist: The Methodist Relief & Development Fund	168
Millfield: The Millfield House Foundation	169
Millhouses: Millhouses Charitable Trust	170
Millichope: The Millichope Foundation	170
Milton: The Milton Keynes Community Trust Ltd	170
Minet: The Peter Minet Trust	171
Misener: The Laurence Misener Charitable Trust	172
Mishcon: The Victor Mishcon Charitable Trust	172
Mitchell: The Mitchell Charitable Trust	172
The Esme Mitchell Trust	173
Mole: The Mole Charitable Trust	173
Morris: The Willie & Mabel Morris Charitable Trust	173
Morrison: Morrison Charitable Foundation	173
The G M Morrison Charitable Trust	174
Moss: The Moss Charitable Trust	174
Mount: The Mount 'A' & Mount 'B' Charitable Trusts	174
Mountbatten: The Edwina Mountbatten Trust	174
N R: The N R Charitable Trust	175
Nabarro: The Kitty & Daniel Nabarro Charitable Trust	175
Nagel: The Willie Nagel Charitable Trust	175
Naggar: The Naggar Charitable Trust	176
Nash: The Janet Nash Charitable Trust	176
National: The National AIDS Trust	176
The National Association of Rags	176
The National Association of Round Tables	177
The National Catholic Fund	177
The National Gardens Scheme Charitable Trust	178
The National Hospital Trust	178
Nazareth: The Nazareth Trust Fund	178
Nesswall: Nesswall Ltd	178
New: The New Durlston Trust	178
The New Horizons Trust	179
Newpier: Newpier Ltd	179
Newton: The Newton Settlement	179
Nimrod: The Nimrod & Glaven Charitable Settlement	180
Noel: The Noel Buxton Trust	180
Norman: The Norman Family Charitable Trust	181
Northmoor: The Northmoor Trust	181
Northumberland: The Northumberland Village Homes Trust	182
Norton: The Norton Foundation	182
Norwich: The Norwich Town Close Estate Charity	182
Norwood: The Norwood Settlement	183
Notgrove: The Notgrove Trust	183
Oakdale: The Oakdale Trust	183
Ofenheim: The Ofenheim & Cinderford Charitable Trusts	184
Ogle: The Ogle Trust	184
Old: The Old Broad Street Charity Trust	184
The Old Possums Practical Trust	185
Oppenheimer: The Raymond Oppenheimer Foundation	185
Orpheus: The Orpheus Trust	185
Ouseley: The Ouseley Trust	185
Paget: The Paget Charitable Trust (also known as the Herbert-Stepney Charitable Settlement)	186
Palmer: The Gerald Palmer Trust	186
Palumbo: The Rudolph Palumbo Charitable Foundation	186
Parkinson: The Frank Parkinson Agricultural Trust	187
Paterson: The Arthur James & Constance Paterson Charitable Trust	187
Patients': The Patients' Aid Association Hospital & Medical Charities Trust	187
Paul: The Late Barbara May Paul Charitable Trust	188
Peacock: The Michael Peacock Charitable Foundation	188
Peake: The Susanna Peake Charitable Trust	188
Pearson: The Hon Charles Pearson Charity Trust	189
Peguy: The Charles Peguy Trust	189
Pennycress: The Pennycress Trust	189
Phillips: The Reginald M Phillips Charitable Foundation	189
The Ruth & Michael Phillips Charitable Trust	190
Pickford: The David Pickford Charitable Foundation	190
Pilkington: The Austin & Hope Pilkington Trust	190
The Cecil Pilkington Charitable Trust	190
The Pilkington Charities Fund	191
Platinum: The Platinum Trust	191
Pollitzer: The George & Esme Pollitzer Charitable Settlement	192
Porjes: The E & F Porjes Charitable Trust	192
Porter: The John Porter Charitable Trust	192
PPP: The PPP Medical Trust Ltd	192
Pratt: The W L Pratt Charitable Trust	193
Priestman: The Sir John Priestman Charity Trust	193
Prince: The Prince Foundation	194
Princess: Princess Anne's Charities	194

Index

The Princess of Wales' Charities Trust — 194
Priory: The Priory Foundation — 194
Privy: The Privy Purse Charitable Trust (formerly The January 1987 Charitable Trust) — 195
Puebla: The Puebla Charitable Trust — 195
Pyke: The Pyke Charity Trust — 195

R T: The R T Trust — 196
Radcliffe: The Radcliffe Trust — 197
Radio: Radio Tay – Caring for Kids (Radio Tay Listeners Charity) — 197
Rainford: The Rainford Trust — 198
Randall: The Joseph & Lena Randall Charitable Trust — 198
Rank: The Rank Prize Funds — 198
Rathbone: The Eleanor Rathbone Charitable Trust — 199
The Elizabeth Rathbone Charity — 199
Ravensdale: The Ravensdale Trust — 199
Raymond: The Roger Raymond Charitable Trust — 200
Rayne: The Rayne Trust — 200
Reckitt: The Albert Reckitt Charitable Trust — 200
Redfern: The C A Redfern Charitable Foundation — 200
Richard: Cliff Richard Charitable Trust — 201
Richards: The Clive Richards Charity Ltd — 201
The Violet M Richards Charity — 201
Ripple: The Ripple Effect Foundation — 202
River: The River Trust — 202
Roll: The Helen Roll Charitable Trust — 202
Rosen: The Cecil Rosen Foundation — 203
Rosenbaum: The Teresa Rosenbaum Golden Charitable Trust — 203
Rotary: The Rotary Foundation — 203
Rothermere: The Rothermere Foundation — 203
Rothley: The Rothley Trust — 204
Roughley: The Roughley Charitable Trust — 204
RVW: The RVW Trust — 204

Sacher: The Audrey Sacher Charitable Trust — 205
The Michael Sacher Charitable Trust — 205
Sackler: Dr Mortimer and Theresa Sackler Foundation — 205

The Raymond & Beverley Sackler Foundation — 206
Saddlers: Saddlers' Company Charitable Fund — 206
Sainer: The Leonard Sainer Charitable Trust — 206
Sainsbury: The Jean Sainsbury Animal Welfare Trust (formerly The Jean Sainsbury Charitable Trust) — 206
St Edmund: The Saint Edmund, King & Martyr Trust — 207
St James: St James' Trust Settlement — 207
St Katharine: The St Katharine and Shadwell Trust — 207
Saints: The Saints & Sinners Trust — 208
Salamander: The Salamander Charitable Trust — 208
Salters: Salters' Charities — 209
Samuel: The Peter Samuel Charitable Trust — 209
Sandra: The Sandra Charitable Trust — 209
Sarum: The Sarum St Michael Educational Charity — 209
Scarfe: The Scarfe Charitable Trust — 210
Schiff: The Annie Schiff Charitable Trust — 210
Schreib: The Schreib Trust — 210
Schreiber: The Schreiber Charitable Trust — 210
Scott: The Frieda Scott Charitable Trust — 210
The Sir Samuel Scott of Yews Trust — 211
Scottish: The Scottish Churches Architectural Heritage Trust — 211
The Scottish Housing Associations Charitable Trust (SHACT) — 212
Scouloudi: The Scouloudi Foundation — 212
Searchlight: The Searchlight Electric Charitable Trust — 213
Searle: The Searle Charitable Trust — 213
Seedfield: The Seedfield Trust — 213
Sell: The Leslie Sell Charitable Trust — 213
Sharon: The Sharon Trust — 214
Sheffield: The Sheffield Town Trust — 214
Sheldon: The Sheldon Trust — 214
Shepherd: The David Shepherd Conservation Foundation — 215
Sherman: The Archie Sherman Cardiff Charitable Foundation — 215
Shine: The Barnett & Sylvia Shine No 1 & No 2 Charitable Trusts — 216
Shiyich: The Shiyich Charitable Trust — 216

Shuttlewood: The Shuttlewood Clarke Foundation — 216
Sinclair: The Huntly & Margery Sinclair Charitable Trust — 216
Skey: The Charles Skey Charitable Trust — 217
Skinners: The Skinners' Company Lady Neville Charity — 217
Slater: The John Slater Foundation — 217
SMB: The SMB Trust — 218
Smith: The Albert and Florence Smith Memorial Trust — 218
The E H Smith Charitable Trust — 218
The Leslie Smith Foundation — 219
The N Smith Charitable Trust — 219
The Stanley Smith General Charitable Trust — 219
The Stanley Smith UK Horticultural Trust — 220
Solo: The Solo Charitable Settlement — 220
Solomon: The Solomon Family Charitable Trust — 220
Sosnow: The E C Sosnow Charitable Trust — 220
South: The South Square Trust — 221
Southall: The W F Southall Trust — 221
Spencer: The Jessie Spencer Trust — 221
Spitalfields: Spitalfields Market Training Initiative — 222
Stanley: The Stanley Charitable Trust — 222
The Stanley Foundation Ltd — 222
Stebbings: The Peter Stebbings Memorial Trust — 223
Sternberg: The Sir Sigmund Sternberg Charitable Foundation — 223
Stevenson: The Stevenson Family's Charitable Trust — 223
Stoll: The Stoll Moss Theatres Foundation — 223
Stoller: The Stoller Charitable Trust — 224
Stone: The Stone Foundation — 224
The M J C Stone Charitable Trust — 224
Stubbs: The Janatha Stubbs Foundation — 224
Sueberry: Sueberry Ltd — 225
Sugar: The Alan Sugar Foundation — 225
Sutasoma: The Sutasoma Trust — 225
Swire: The Swire Charitable Trust — 226
The John Swire (1989) Charitable Trust — 226
Sykes: The Hugh & Ruby Sykes Charitable Trust — 226
Sylvanus: The Sylvanus Charitable Trust — 226
Symons: The Stella Symons Charitable Trust — 227

Index

Talbot: The Talbot Trusts — 227
Talteg: Talteg Ltd — 227
Taylor: The A R Taylor Charitable Trust — 228
Thames: The Thames Wharf Charity — 228
Tho: The Loke Wan Tho Memorial Foundation — 228
Thompson: The Thompson Charitable Trust — 228
 The Thompson Family Charitable Trust — 229
Thornton: The Thornton Foundation — 229
 The Thornton Trust — 229
Tikva: The Tikva Trust — 230
Tolkien: The Tolkien Trust — 230
Tory: The Tory Family Foundation — 230
Tower: The Tower Hill Improvement Trust — 230
Towler: The Jonathan Towler Foundation — 231
Tramman: The Tramman Trust — 231
Travis: The Constance Travis Charitable Trust — 231
Triangle: The Triangle Trust 1949 Fund — 231
Truemark: The Truemark Trust — 232
Tufton: The Tufton Charitable Trust (formerly the Wates Charitable Trust) — 232
Turner: The Florence Turner Trust — 232

Ultach: The Ultach Trust — 232
Ulting: The Ulting Overseas Trust — 233
Ulverscroft: The Ulverscroft Foundation — 233
Underwood: The Underwood Trust — 234
United: The United Trusts — 234
Uri: The David Uri Memorial Trust — 235

Van den Bergh: The Albert Van Den Bergh Charitable Trust — 235
Van Neste: The Van Neste Foundation — 235

Vardy: The Vardy Foundation — 236
Vendquot: Vendquot Ltd — 236
Vestey: The Vestey Foundation — 236
Vincent: The Vincent Wildlife Trust — 236
Vinson: The Nigel Vinson Charitable Trust — 237
Viznitz: The Viznitz Foundation — 237

Wade: The Charity of Thomas Wade & Others — 237
Wakefield: The Wakefield Trust — 238
Walker: The Walker Trust — 238
Wall: The Wall Charitable Trust — 238
Ward: The Ward Blenkinsop Trust — 239
Waterhouse: Mrs Waterhouse's Charitable Trust — 239
Waters: The Roger Waters 1989 Charity Trust — 239
Watside: Watside Charities — 239
Watson: John Watson's Trust — 240
Weavers: The Weavers' Company Benevolent Fund — 240
Webber: The Webber Trust — 241
Webster: The William Webster Charitable Trust — 241
Weinberg: The Weinberg Foundation — 241
Weinstein: The Weinstein Foundation — 241
Weir: The James Weir Foundation — 242
Welsh: The Welsh Church Funds — 242
Westcroft: The Westcroft Trust — 244
Westminster: The Westminster Amalgamated Charity — 244
Westward: The Westward Trust — 245
Whitaker: The Whitaker Charitable Trust — 245
Whitbread: Humphrey Whitbread's First Charitable Trust — 245
 The Simon Whitbread Charitable Trust — 245
Whiteley: The Norman Whiteley Trust — 246

Whitley: The Whitley Animal Protection Trust — 246
Wilkinson: The Wilkinson Charitable Foundation — 246
Williams: The Williams Family Charitable Trust — 246
Wills: The Dame Violet Wills Charitable Trust — 247
Wiltshire: The Wiltshire Community Foundation — 247
Wingate: The Harold Hyam Wingate Foundation — 248
Wohl: The Maurice Wohl Charitable Trust — 248
Women: The Women Caring Trust — 249
Woodlands: Woodlands Green Ltd — 249
Woodroffe: The Woodroffe Benton Foundation — 249
Woods: The Geoffrey Woods Charitable Foundation — 250
Woolf: The A & R Woolf Charitable Trust — 250
World: The World Memorial Fund for Disaster Relief — 250
 The World in Need — 251
Worms: The Fred & Della Worms Charitable Trust — 251
Worshipful: The Worshipful Company of Chartered Accountants General Charitable Trust — 251
 The Worshipful Company of Shipwrights — 252
Wrightson: The Matthews Wrightson Charity Trust — 252

Yapp: The Yapp Education & Research Trust — 252
 The Yapp Welfare Trust — 253
Young: The John Young Charitable Settlement — 253
 The William Allen Young Charitable Trust — 254

Ziff: The I A Ziff Charitable Foundation — 254